THE ALBANIAN FILES

THE ALBANIAN FILES
Freedom and Architecture

Edited by Anneke Abhelakh
Published by Lars Müller Publishers

THE ALBANIAN FILES

In Albania, the word *file* carries a long and painful memory. Files were instruments of fear. They were made of people followed into their lives, their homes, their friendships, their whispers. Even their silences.

They cataloged gestures, doubts and intimacies, turning private life into evidence, imagination into suspicion and difference into guilt.

Files were not meant for understanding. They were meant to control. They were written about people, without them.

The files in this book are the exact opposite. They are instruments for foreseeing possible futures. They are made of traces from encounters between architects and Albania – its body, its posture, its openings, its depths. Its lights and its darkness. Even its soul.

They do not follow people. They follow a story. They do not judge. They record. They track how the idea of building changes when it meets a place. How it bends when it encounters history. How it resists, adapts or deepens under the pressure of reality.

If the old files reduced life to evidence, these new ones restore evidence to life. They are not archives of obedience, but of becoming. This book exists to ensure that what is unfolding on the path toward new realities of stone and steel does not disappear, but remains as a precious behind-the-scenes record of a gathering of minds that is lifting Albania in a way that nobody saw coming.

Albania is not a country that draws the world's most visionary architects with money, glitter or promises. It draws them with something far more difficult to define and impossible to counterfeit: a shared belief in the realness of a dream and in the trust that it can be carried. Not despite being here, but precisely here.

Something alive.

Something unrepeatable.

Something still free from the suffocating comfort of overregulation and prepackaged certainty. Or, as one of the members of the mighty ArchArmy put it, a freedom from "no" in all its forms.

This book is not simply about distinguished architects, young and seasoned alike, who have come from both hemispheres to a place that until only a few decades ago was the most closed space on Earth. It is first and foremost about the distinctiveness of a beautiful moment in history, created by a simple conviction: Architecture can transform not only spaces, but minds. Not only locations, but the imagination of a community, its sense of place, its vision of the future and its self-confidence.

The *Albanian Files* documents a democratic wager made of new places to live, fueled by the conviction that space is never neutral, that form carries values, and that communities must constantly renegotiate their relationships, territorial and spiritual alike, by reflecting on the past with humility and daring to face the future with fearlessness. Yes, this book gathers renowned architects. But these files are not about them. They are about what happens between them and Albania. They capture what attracts, provokes, unsettles and inspires in an adventure where nothing is fully resolved, and therefore everything remains possible. That is why it matters that some of the most visionary architects of our time, from Europe, the Americas, Japan, South Korea and China, have chosen to embrace Albania in this moment of renewal. Not as distant observers. Not as solitary stars. But as participants in a shared experiment, building not just in a place, but with it.

And something special emerges from such an embrace, where they are not only received, but hosted. Not only hosted, but integrated. In that integration, Albania has also become the largest open-air architecture school. A school without walls, where young Albanian architects work as local partners to the great studios of the world. They learn by doing – in the company of masters, inside real projects and facing real risks. Knowledge is not delivered through lectures, but forged on-site, through debate, results, correction and responsibility. What emerges is a conversation not only in concrete, texture and light, but in time and memory. Not a collage of styles, but a communion of intentions. Perhaps the most precious part of these files is this: Architects do not simply leave a mark. They carry something forward. They help us see not one path, but many, sometimes straight, sometimes circular, tracing a geometry of belonging.

There is real energy in what architecture can generate, an energy sparked by Albania's questions and by a shared ambition to answer them, not only about how to make buildings, but about how to build a future worth fighting for. Albania today is no longer merely a stage. It is a catalyst. Not just a location, but a collaborator. And in a world obsessed with icons, authorship and ownership, what is quietly unfolding here feels almost subversive: the making of something truly common, and yet like nothing else.

Opening the files may tell you far more. And who knows, perhaps it will even be a different story from the one I have just written.

Enjoy.

Edi Rama

INTRODUCTION

Anneke Abhelakh

Albania is a place of many layers, where history is visible in the streets, the hills and the buildings. Three million people live in this Central European country between the Adriatic and Ionian Seas, bordered by Greece, North Macedonia, Kosovo and Montenegro. Walking through Tirana, you feel the traces of what has passed and what is still being made: Ottoman mosques, Italian governmental buildings, communist housing blocks, post-socialist interventions. Every corner tells a story, and every building carries memory, ambition, power. Architecture here is never neutral. It is alive. It shapes how people move, gather and imagine themselves as a collective.

After the dictatorship fell in 1992, space itself became a political act. Streets, homes and public buildings – once instruments of control – were reclaimed by people who had lived under decades of surveillance. As Prime Minister Edi Rama has put it, "Returning to individualism was very traumatic." For the first ten years, private space had to be reclaimed. Public space remained, in many ways, abandoned. Thirty years on, Albania is still in transition – culturally, socially and architecturally. This ongoing renewal has placed architecture at the center of national discourse and created a specific opportunity for architects.

Tempting as it may be to focus on this opportunity, I can't separate architecture from power. Not in an abstract way, but in the sense of who gets to make decisions, how these decisions are made, and what becomes visible in the world as a result of them. Architecture is never just about form or function; it is entangled in systems that give some voices weight and others less so. What gets built, who commissions it, how it is received – all of this is shaped by forces that are often uneven, sometimes fragile and always in motion. I think of Christian Kerez's parking structures in Bahrain, built as part of the Pearling Path, intended to support everyday life, and then partially dismantled soon after completion. It's a striking reminder that even the most solid structures can be contingent. What appears to be fixed can shift quickly when priorities change. Architecture doesn't simply endure; it records the conditions under which it was allowed to exist.

In *The Edifice Complex: The Architecture of Power*, Deyan Sudjic reminds us that architecture is a way in which power makes itself visible. Walking through a city, I see it: buildings that impress, anchor identity, signal ambition. But power is not only imposed – it is lived, negotiated, resisted, imagined. Architecture is also about care, reflection and attention. It reminds us that the world we inhabit is made, and that it can be made differently.

I keep returning to Jodi Dean and her idea of the "comrade." She traces the word back to *camera* – the room. A shared space. A comrade, then, is not a label or an identity, but a condition: being in a room together, present with others, engaged in something that is held in common. There is something simple and at the same time demanding about that. It asks for proximity, for attention, for a willingness to stay with others even when things are unresolved. When I look at architecture in Albania through that lens, it feels less like the work of isolated authors and more like a shared undertaking.

That is how architecture works at its best: relationally. Professionals, communities, clients and institutions, all participating, shaping and being shaped by what is built. Buildings become traces of collaboration, compromise, conflict, negotiation and care. They hold the memory of those relations.

In Albania, these entanglements between architecture, power and everyday life are not abstract – they are deeply felt, and they unfold over time through people, decisions and relationships. I often find myself thinking about how consistently space has been used here as a way of shaping life. Under the long political trajectory of Edi Rama – from minister of culture to mayor of Tirana and now prime minister – the transformation of the city has not been separate from governance. Urban projects, public spaces and architectural commissions are not just interventions in the built environment; they are ways of imagining how people live together, how a country presents itself, and how and by whom it wants to be seen.

Since the early 2000s, international competitions have brought many foreign architects into this landscape. But this flow of movement is not neutral. It raises questions about exchange, about influence, about who speaks and who is heard. Figures like Elia Zenghelis entered Albania not only as architects, but as part of a broader conversation about the future of the city. For Zenghelis, architecture has always been inseparable from politics – not as ideology, but as a way of engaging with the conditions of shared life. His work suggests that architecture can propose futures, but also that it must remain attentive to the realities it enters. In Albania, this becomes particularly visible: different cultural positions, different ways of working, different assumptions about authorship and responsibility meet, overlap and sometimes collide.

Being part of such a shared "room" is never simple. It asks for more than participation; it asks for awareness. What does it mean to contribute to a place that is not your own, but that you are helping to shape? How do you remain attentive without becoming extractive? How do you engage with power without dissolving into it? These questions are not theoretical. They appear in everyday decisions about how projects are developed, negotiated and realized. In a context where political and economic conditions can shift quickly, the position of the architect, or more broadly the professional, is never fixed. It is always relational, always contingent, always in need of reflection.

What becomes visible over time is the fact that buildings do not simply occupy space. They sit within a web of relations – social, political, economic – and they make these relations tangible. What seems stable can shift, and what was meant to endure can instead reveal the fragility of the moment in which it was produced.

I recognize how architecture is often used to project power – to give form to ambition, to make authority visible, to stabilize identity. But what I see in Albania is that this projection is never complete. Buildings are inhabited, reinterpreted, sometimes resisted. They do not simply communicate power; they also expose its limits, its dependencies and its need to be constantly renegotiated.

This brings me back to Jodi Dean's understanding of the comrade – the shared room, the shared project. In Albania, architecture feels like such a room: a space where many actors are present at once, where decisions are made at the same time, unevenly, sometimes in tension, but somehow always in relation. It is not a closed system, but an open, shifting field of participation. To work here is to be part of something that exceeds individual authorship – a longer, collective process of shaping space, meaning and life.

And perhaps this is what becomes most visible in Albania: that architecture is not only about building, but about being in relation. About understanding that every intervention enters an existing fabric of histories, desires and inequalities. About recognizing that what is being built is never just form, but a way of living together – complex, interwoven and always unfinished.

—

This book brings together sixty international offices currently working in Albania, some of which have been active in the country since as early as 2003. Each office submitted a contribution with reflections on their experiences in Albania and on architecture in progress – ingredients to bring to the kitchen table rather than only finished projects. The degree of autonomy with which these contributions were written – and the way in which this autonomy has been retained by design – makes this collection like no other and allows the joy of diversity to shine through, with individual interpretations and different ways of handling similar concepts. Different design cultures, attitudes and positions are expressed without hierarchy.

Most of the contributions are eight pages long, but offices that have been working in Albania since the early 2000s have double that amount since they have more to show and to tell about the changes the country has undergone in the last twenty years, as seen through their projects.

In addition to the contributions, I added elements one might find in files: an administrative page with factual data about each office, including local collaborations and when the engagement with Albania started; a one-page interview; and a list of projects with details on location, whether the project is public or private, which phase it is in, and in some cases the envisioned size, as well as developers and engineers that are involved. Although these elements add structure, they still allow room for autonomy, with the various offices interpreting the questions differently and deciding individually which details to provide.

The interconnections between the interviews, contributions and project lists show a kaleidoscopic range of approaches, perspectives and ways to deal with the beauty and complexity of Albania's character and landscape.

The work described and discussed in the pages that follow – ranging from built projects to unbuilt proposals and paper architectures – was produced in a context where development moved quickly, where land was reimagined as opportunity and where architecture was frequently asked to give form to ambition before its terms were fully negotiated.

Looking at Tirana, the figure of the developer becomes central. Not as a singular actor, but as a composite: investor, initiator, negotiator, sometimes speculator. The brief was seldom just a program. It was a set of wishes – for density, visibility, return, speed – often clear in intent and flexible in method. Architecture entered this space in short order, translating wishes into proposals, images and, ultimately, built form.

Within this proximity, tensions accumulated – between quality and quantity, between long-term value and immediate return, between authorship and execution, and between engagement and extraction.

Freedom was present – real, immediate and operational. But it did not arrive alone. It was accompanied by pressure, urgency and the possibility of acting quickly and, at times, opportunistically. Some moved through this moment accordingly, aligning with its speed, taking what it offered, and leaving little trace beyond the project itself. Others remained longer, working within the same conditions but at a different pace – absorbing, negotiating, insisting, occasionally resisting.

What emerged was less a unified architectural position than a field of attitudes. The interviews that are included as part of each file are situated within this field. Although the questions asked do not always name the tensions directly, they were shaped by them.

In the years to come, these questions will likely be read less as neutral prompts and more as coordinates within a particular alignment between architects, developers and a form of capital that arrived with urgency and expectation, often ahead of the structures meant to frame it.

The interview questions have been compressed in the files, and in many cases the answers have been shortened as well. Here are the full questions, along with my reasons for asking them.

How were you introduced to Albania? Introductions often determine alignment. Whether through a competition, by invitation or via personal networks or chance, the manner of becoming acquainted establishes proximity and may determine with whom one works, and under what expectations. The answer to this question was often similar – with many of the architects being introduced to Albania through the PM or through the many public competitions held – that it was taken out in cases, leaving space for more relations and other stories.

What is the context you mainly work in, and can you describe the biggest differences/similarities in (the) building (process)? Difference is not only procedural and cultural. It is embedded in how decisions are made, how quickly they must be made and under whose influence they unfold.

How do you organize yourself in the Albanian context? What is your goal and what partnerships are you setting up to achieve it? Organization reflects position and intention. Partnerships indicate alignment. Over time, these structures reveal whether one integrates, negotiates or simply operates through the context.

Do you share the design work with the local office or do they strictly execute your proposal? Why did you choose this setup? This question relates to the distribution of work, of knowledge, of responsibility. It also signals whether architecture is treated as collaboration, delegation or control.

What are the opportunities/challenges for an architect in Albania? (> 10 years: And has this changed over time?) Opportunity is often tied to access, while challenge is tied to what that access requires in return. Both tend to become more visible over time.

What would be a way to integrate greater responsibility for quality in projects? Where speed dominates, quality must be asserted. The question is by whom, and at what cost.

How can the role of the architect in balancing quality and density be enhanced, and how can this responsibility be communicated as a guiding principle? Could this process be expanded to involve more stakeholders in maintaining design integrity? Balancing implies tension. Expanding implies redistribution. Both depend on whether architecture is permitted to hold a position, or expected to adapt continuously.

Is there a project in Albania that is an example or is inspiring for you? Inspiration may lie not only in form, but in how a project negotiates its conditions – what it accepts, what it transforms and what it leaves unresolved.

What is the toolbox Albania gives you as an architect as you engage in developing for the future? A toolbox includes methods, but also thresholds: what one is willing to do, how far one is willing to go, when one decides not to proceed.

Three decades after the fall of dictatorship, Albania remains in transition culturally, socially and architecturally. High capitalism did not arrive gradually; it appeared with intensity, resetting the field while leaving many of its structures incomplete. Practice advanced rapidly, often in direct dialogue with development. Academia continues to reposition itself, still recovering its capacity to critique and guide. Society engages unevenly, with few platforms for reflection or debate.

Architecture, in this context, occupies a central yet exposed role.

From the perspective of the future what becomes legible is a series of decisions made over time. Some of these decisions are driven by ambition. Some by necessity. Some by conviction. Some, undeniably, by opportunism.

The questions remain. They do not resolve the tensions. They situate them.

March 2026

NAME OFFICE

51N4E

DATE
January 2026

PLACE
Brussels, Belgium

WORKING IN ALBANIA SINCE
2004

PROJECT TEAM
Johan Anrys
Freek Persyn
Peter Swinnen
Ulrike Franzel
Bob De Wispelaere
Jeroen Beerten
Joost Körver
Aglaia De Mulder
Chris Blackbee
Astrit Vranovci
Joram Van Den Brande
Tom Baelus
Konstantinos Pantazis
Aline Neirynck
Karol Wawrzyniak
Andreas Amodio
Jan Das
Valbona Koçi
Marian Beschoner
Sotiria Kornaropoulou
Samuel Jaubert de Beaujeu
Galaad Van Daele
Olivier Cavens
Marta Petrov
Guillaume Boulanger
Emmanuel Debroise
Maddalena Treccani
Philippe Nathan
Griet Kuppens
Marc-Achille Fillot
Jolein Bergers
Charlotte Schmidt
Guust Selhorst
Ajmona Hoxha
Gent Agolli
Ardian Rapo
Enri Leka
Annaïk Deceuninck
Francesca Zanella
Louis Bordenave
Matthieu Moreau
Ani Tafilica
Paul Steinbrück
Guillem Pons
Oscar Broeckhoven
Alice Babini
Jan Opdekamp
Arya Arabshahi
Matteo Frangi
Benoit Lanon
Yann Gueguen
Sebastian Roy
Ruben Janssens
Matthias Salaets
Laura Villeret
Maxim Le Droupéet
Jakob Hainich
Jonathan Cludts
Hunter Doyle
Victor Angelard
Baptist Chauvin
Olga Kostantinovic
Mäel Duclovel
Willem Hubrechts
Ludovica De Gaudenzi
Stefano dell'Oro
Matteo Novarino
Oana Crainic
Gianni Villa
Michele Maritano
Math-ide Vandervorst
Isra Cekaj
Kristal Virgilio
Sara Dragomir
Maria Turco

COLLABORATORS
Anri Sala
Plant en Houtgoed
Chevalier Masson
Doorzon
iRI shpk
Piovenefabi
CENTRAL ofaau
Plan Común

NICKNAME
51N4E = 51
Johan Anrys = Jehani

MAIN CONTEXT VS. ALBANIA

Based in Belgium, 51N4E has always focused on adaptive reuse. This approach is still largely absent in Albania, where projects often start from a sketch. With Skanderbeg Square, however, we were able to apply our reuse experience, creating a project that responds to what exists while embracing the potential of new interventions.

Belgium and Albania share an affinity for improvisation, flexibility and mutual trust. This continues today in our work on the Palace of Culture, building on long-term relationships established at Skanderbeg Square.

ORGANIZATION/GOAL/SETUP

For the TID Tower, we initially collaborated with a local office, bringing an Albanian architect to Brussels while also hiring an expat Albanian to join our Brussels team. Despite early difficulties, Albanian and Belgian voices continuously exchanged ideas, learning through practice. We traveled frequently, adapting to the rhythm of private commissions. Over time, Johan Anrys became central to our work in Albania.

After being selected for Skanderbeg Square, we opened a Tirana branch staffed by Albanian and international architects, with Guust Selhorst settling there. Gradually, we built a strong network of architects and engineers and later established the joint venture iRI with Gent Agolli, supporting design development and construction for us and other international practices in Albania.

SETUP IN RELATION TO LOCAL OFFICE

The collaboration with iRI succeeded thanks to the quality of the people involved – such as site engineer Ardian Rapo – and a critical mass of projects that helped absorb the unpredictability of the design process. Today, we are no longer part of iRI, as it has gained its own stability and credibility.

Now, our main design team is based in Milan, led by Matteo Frangi, in close collaboration with Brussels and the iRI team in Tirana. iRI remains deeply involved in the design process, enabling strong alignment and genuine knowledge exchange. Key design decisions often happen on-site, with frequent travel by Johan Anrys and Matteo Frangi and the design team. This sustained presence – heightened by working from Milan – allows projects to truly take shape in Albania.

OPPORTUNITIES/CHALLENGES

Starting work in Albania at thirty years old, we entered a context open to risk. This enabled an architecture that could create a local construction culture through close collaboration and material engagement, while also embracing a Mediterranean collective life largely lived outdoors. The opportunity lies in mutual trust and shared learning; the challenge is ongoing instability. As projects grow in scale, managing complexity becomes harder within a still-evolving architectural culture – for all involved.

HOW TO INTEGRATE GREATER RESPONSIBILITY FOR QUALITY IN PROJECTS

Today, projects are still very much judged on their formal quality and their promise to be new. There is a need to enhance the understanding of what quality actually is, and according to us, the development of this understanding is foremost a question of developing the culture and education.

BALANCING QUALITY AND DENSITY/INVOLVING STAKEHOLDERS

Balancing quality and density in Albania is a shared responsibility between policymakers, clients and designers. In a volatile context where both projects and policies are evolving, continuous debate is essential to avoid exploitation or rigid outcomes. As international architects, we must acknowledge that our role is often used to justify increased density. We should be mindful of securing the qualities that meaningful density needs.

This position is not easy. Housing programs are typically highly standardized, and our attempts to argue for alternatives often go unheard. This is where policymakers should take responsibility, by recognizing and promoting existing ways of life, such as the extended family model still prevalent in Albania.

EXAMPLE/INSPIRATION

Two projects stood out during our first visits and remain inspiring. The Palace of Culture, with its monumental arcade that operates as an interface between urban clarity and architectural and programmatic flexibility. We are also inspired by the open staircases of socialist housing, which mediate between the domestic and the urban, making buildings porous and lively.

STARTING FULLY UNPREPARED

Our first encounter with Albania in 2004 confronted us with the realization that we didn't really know how to situate the country. We read about isolation and grimness, with the image of the Eastern bloc in mind. Instead, we landed in a sunny place with a pleasant Mediterranean climate, and were suddenly surrounded by warm and hospitable people with a thirst for capitalism and its kind of progress and, of course, chaos. The contrast between the developer's black, tinted-window Mercedes and the crumbling, sometimes even unpaved, roads sums up the situation well (figs. 1, 2).

Tirana was a bold capital, a boulevard without a city, Albanians were joking. Its history diverse – a sequence of different political regimes, of story of revolutions, riots, dictatorships and economic pyramids. Daily life radiated a roughness that seemed intimidating at first but became endearing and sincere over time. One thing was clear: Established ways of working would not hold. Tirana made heavy demands on (Western European) stamina while offering the opportunity to conceive and build in an environment found nowhere else in Europe.

The combination of ambition and dedication – accompanied by the necessary humor – set the tone for the first project, the TID Tower (fig. 3). Its core idea emerged as an intuitive response to the tensions experienced on-site: the unspoken demand for a workable building within urban planning regulations that did not provide for it. In the end, the project took seven years to realize due to many factors, above all because of Tirana's brutally idiosyncratic reality, unlike any other urban conditions 51N4E had worked in before. It was a difficult challenge to face fully unprepared!

What saved us was another intuition: We went to Tirana to learn, and not to teach. Developing a high-rise in Tirana meant putting aside all preconceived ideas about the task and embracing the place wholeheartedly, internalizing its logic before even imagining how to contribute to or transform it. We saw this first project, and all others following it, as an encounter and a collaboration. Being on equal terms, we focused on what all parties involved had to offer, and how the sum could become more than its parts. What we have learned: Architecture can become a vehicle for more than itself. In the process of inventing and making it, it can become a catalyst for change in multiple dimensions. While deciding on shapes and forms, it has the capacity to trigger transformations on many fronts. In an old country that is also a young democracy, the process of architecture can help create the stability for meaningful change.

We have made these projects together with different clients, while keeping the real client – the city and its citizens – always in mind. We focused on offering solutions, while also understanding our capacity to inspire and influence what the brief asks for. This has been the real opportunity Tirana offered. To go beyond the initial brief of clients and use design to expand what one can dream of. A dream beyond the cliché desires of an individualistic lifestyle, towards a future much more rooted in the collective and welcoming culture of Albania as we have come to see it. This is the underlying drive that connects all of these projects, realized and ongoing.

1.

2.

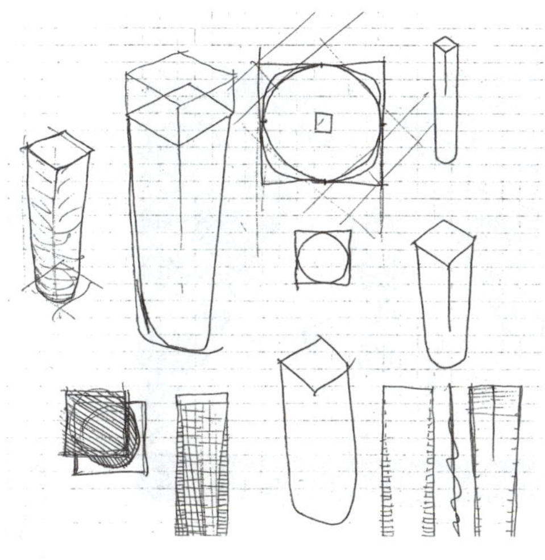

3.

4.

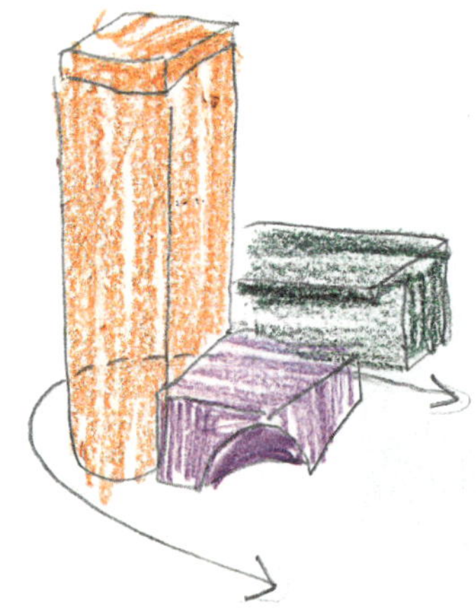

5.

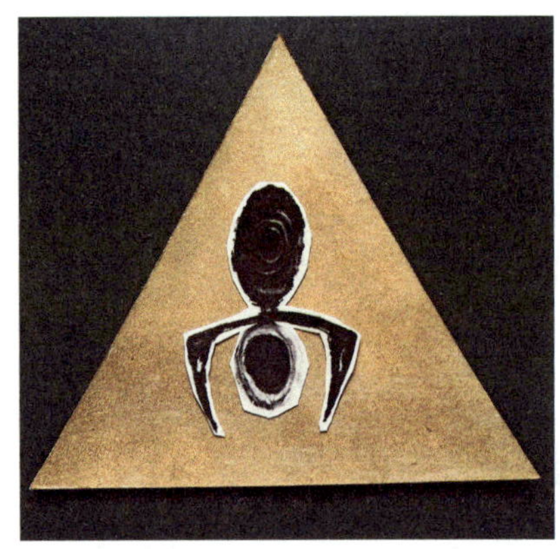

6.

7.

8.

9.

DISCOVERING THE POWER OF SHAPE

From the initial proposal we learned that architecture setting boundaries facilitates dialogue and negotiation. A design offers a framework for a shared vision. In a country that is in the process of daring to dream again, architecture offers form and openness to embark on a joint quest to discover what these dreams can be, and how they can become reality.

The proposal to let the tower evolve from an ellipse to a rectangle (fig. 11) is a formal response, an elegant, intriguing design that offers space where needed and captures - through shadow - the particular and almost surreal presence of Mediterranean light (fig. 12). Seen from the square, the tower adds an element to the historical lineup of mosque and clock tower, proposing a stable form in response to the vital urban dynamics of a country in full transformation (fig. 4). In response to the whirlwind of people, dreams and interventions, the tower stubbornly remains itself and becomes part of a greater whole. On the ground floor, the project provides continuity with the public spaces of the city (fig. 5). Its open-air galleria, with low thresholds on the ground floor, can be crossed daily by passersby, linking the tower to Skanderbeg Square and anchoring it in the city.

During the development of the project, the essence of the form remained unquestioned, by us and by the client: on the one hand, the shape of the tower, mathematically defined, and on the other, the shape of the quarter dome over the memorial to Suleiman Pasha (fig. 7). That gesture, bold and generous, was an example of a new pact that our architecture could make in this place - treating history as a raw material, blending old and new, generating something timeless. It worked as new start, quite literally a canvas, for which Maks Velo proposed murals on his own initiative (fig. 6). Unfortunately, they were never realized.

A similar fusion occurred in the memorial on the main boulevard for four victims of a political demonstration against corruption in 2011. A contour was drawn on the spots of their deaths, and an impression of the existing pavement was cast in bronze (fig. 9). Its outline on the floor recalls a fallen body. An intense moment was made sustainable in a tangible material, embedding memory into a public space filled with everyday life. Edi Hila's painting (fig. 8) further inscribed this gesture into society's collective memory.

These projects show how architecture can reinterpret cultural heritage and traditions; through material and form it anchors the feelings and values a society wishes to preserve for a long time.

Architecture as a counterform to life, made sustainable in a materiality that is tangible and remains. It acts like a witness in a place where everything seems fluid and negotiable. This is reflected in the contrast between the smooth and precise paper model (fig. 12) and the rough, oversized façade (fig. 13). Throughout the process, much was tested (fig. 10) and knowledge was shared and built up on both sides. The result is something that arose from that encounter and collaboration.

10.

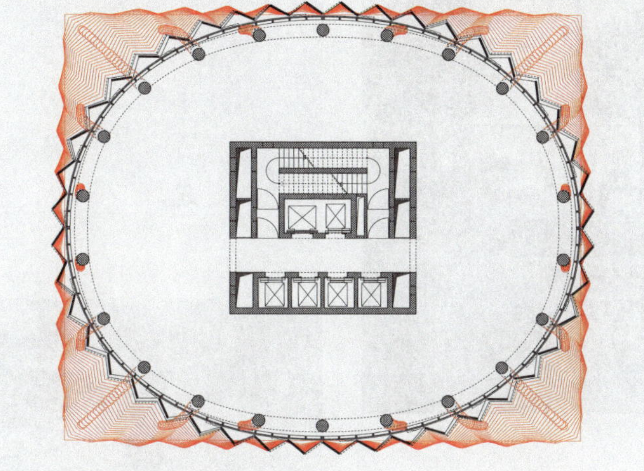

11.

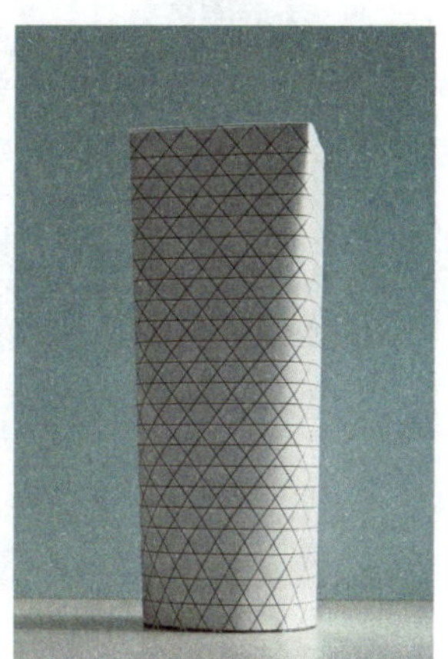

12.

13.

14.

15.

16.

17.

18.

19.

SETTING THE CONDITIONS FOR NEGOTIATION

Skanderbeg Square in the city center builds on the approach we gradually learned with the TID Tower, this time with greater precision and conviction. With the initial design, we have set a frame that combines stability and openness, with a clarity that embraces the inevitable fluidity and informality. At the start of the competition in 2008, Skanderbeg Square already contained a lot of qualities. It was a space that inspired a sense of awe, and that had a lack of definition that created a feeling of openness. In this sense, the task at hand was to look closely at the void that was already there, and to do so with the eyes of the foreigner, who can look beyond what things have ended up meaning.

As powerful as it may be, this void was charged with an uncanny overdose of ideological representation emanating from the buildings that surround it (fig. 15). Together these form a kind of three-dimensional catalog of the various political regimes that shaped Albania's history during the last century. Designing in such a space, laden with history and aspirations, is to reframe and reveal, like creating a new image that still contains the previous one. And it is also about seeing the current intervention as simply one of many which have come, and which are still to come. Inscribing the project in this long history is considering context as resource, something to build upon.

The proposal, consisting of creating a void in the middle of an urban forest (fig. 17), was a spatial layout as well as a blueprint for how we could develop and negotiate the project. The center is an imperceptibly shallow pyramid (fig. 18) made of natural stone. The top of the shallow pyramid is at the same height as the ground floor of the historic buildings surrounding the square (fig. 21). This square as an obstacle in the middle is a clear gesture. It says that claiming space for the residents and visitors of the city center is non-negotiable. This space is claimed as openness (fig. 16, 19)!

In addition to the empty, stone center, the square is surrounded by a green belt, an urban forest (fig. 14), and a collection of old and new small public spaces and gardens (fig. 20) linking the institutions lining the square. This ring around the square can change: It is a space that is both responsive and negotiable. In contrast to the square, it is not light but shaded (fig. 14), not prominent but informal, not uniform but ambiguous, not only for people, but also for plants and animals. Together, the square and the belt create a frame that is also both a spatial sequence and a decision on how things relate to each other. The choice to see the center as empty is also to see it as a civic space, allowing all remnants of history to be equally present, together creating a pantheon of beliefs and ideologies (fig. 15). This allows Albania's past to open up to new ways of reading and embracing as history on which to build.

The project derives its character from the contrast between a timeless frame and the chaos and proliferation of life. The goal of the frame is not to give a definite order. The durability of the project is not in the form but rather in the tension it creates. The goal is to just give enough structure for freedom to cling onto.

20.

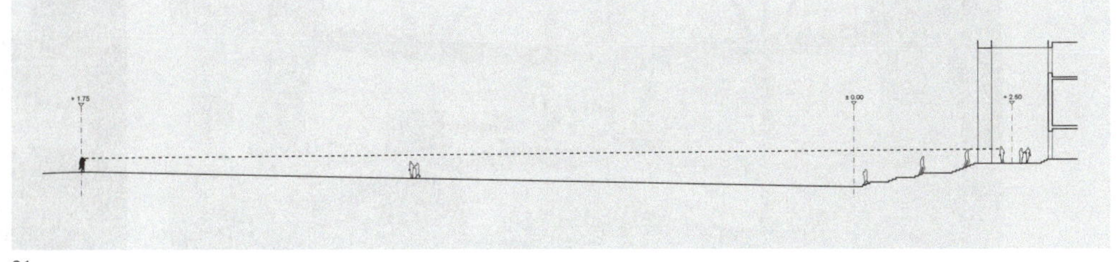

21.

22.

23.

24.

25.

26.

MAKING PUBLIC QUALITIES THROUGH A PRIVATE INITIATIVE

The image of a city densely packed with buildings, with generous public space and with biodiversity has been well received with Skanderbeg Square. The city's public space - eagerly used by residents and visitors - is a huge asset. With the TID Tower, this was capitalized on by making an open-air central gallery, protected by a roof but not shielded by a façade. It makes the city porous and accessible to many, creating an accumulation of different atmospheres and degrees of accessibility. In line with these intentions, the proposal for the Book Building was taken to the next step, creating a fusion between private and public, between park and building (fig. 23).

The Book Building is a set of buildings of different sizes and designs standing loosely next to each other alongside the emptiness of the square (fig. 26). Like a collection of objects (fig. 27), each with its own porosity, making the public space on the site continuous. Passages make the project traversable (fig. 28), and on the ground floor of the buildings, spaces are created that exceed the usual scale of cafés and shops, with the agora as the culmination point (figs. 25, 26). Various roof terraces become accessible gardens, with a monumental staircase connecting the roof to the green belt of Skanderbeg Square (figs. 22, 24). In that manner, the public space surrounding the square extends between its architectures, protecting it below its roofs and elevating it above its volumes. Suddenly the private development is activated by a set of public devices, as urban moments triggered by a private initiative: a gallery, a courtyard, a covered square, or a monumental staircase leading to a panoramic terrace.

The entire complex is an infrastructure: an open, public structure with various possibilities and gradations from public to private. Here, it is a private investment that creates a public part of the city, a neighborhood in three dimensions. The architecture is robust and allows for changeability without compromising the grand public gestures. The materiality becomes tactile when people come close. The design language is accessible, even disarming. In every way, the building aims to offer space to be appropriated and uses to be invented. It becomes a place where you can see and feel the city and thus become part of the growing dynamism of the center (fig. 29).

The volatile socioeconomic context of Albania and its speed of change required imagining a project capable of absorbing every request, leading to a building complex with multiple entrances, ground floors and circulations, creating a hybrid system capable of adapting to changing needs and programs. From this perspective, Book Building is a possible example of how density can contribute to a more porous and active city.

For us, gradually, this became a cherished attitude. We developed mainly private projects while always considering what they can offer to the public good in the space they create, the image they project and the values they bring forward. This is how, mentally, a double client emerged for every project: the one with financial interests on the one hand and the people that will live with the architecture on the other.

27.

28.

29.

30.

31.

Green Coast Hotel
Projekt Zbatim
Klient. Green Coast
51N4E
Central
Layout ID
A
A.01.1
Drawing Name
Plani Teknik i katit përdhe
LN
Korrik 2024
Drawing Scale
1:200
A0
N

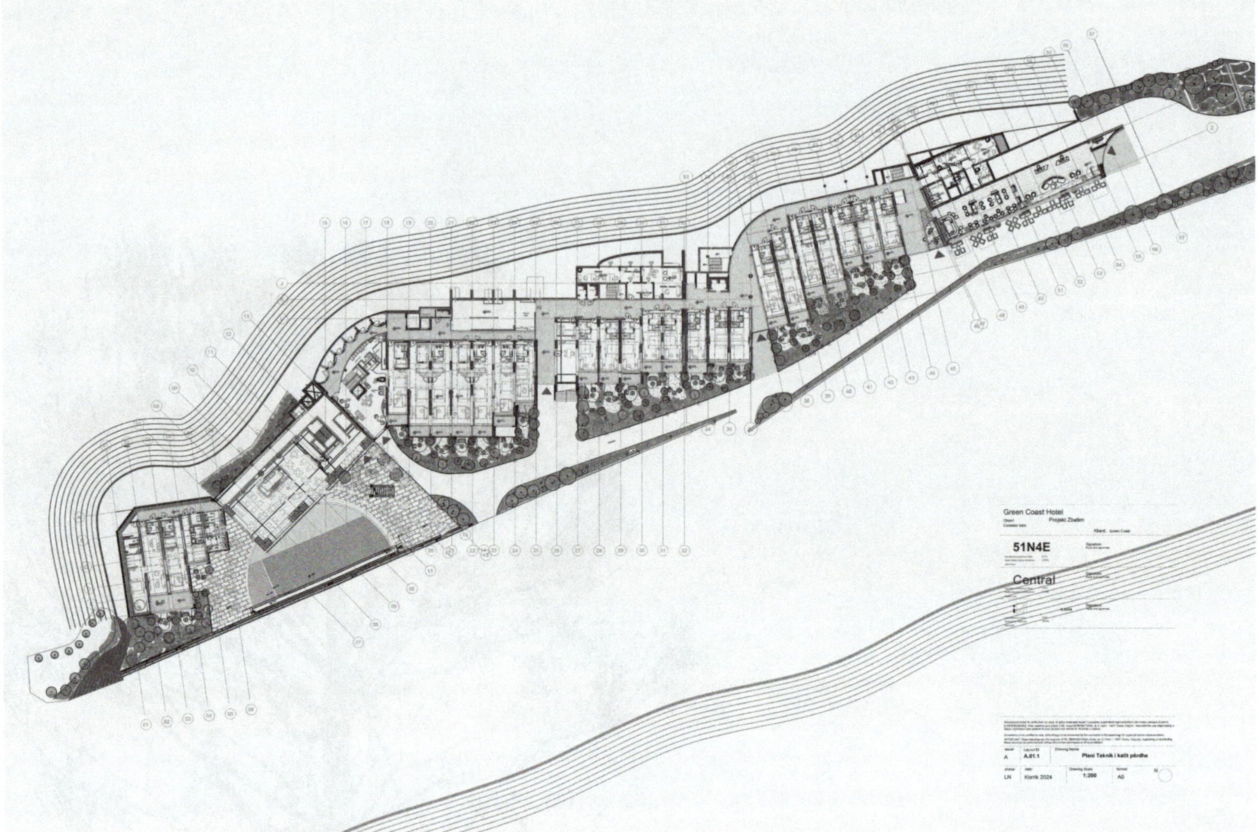

32.

33.

34.

35.

DESIGNING FOR ADAPTABILITY

With the exponential increase of tourism in recent years, many local and international investors have turned their attention to the Albanian coastline. There, planners are faced with questions raised by new developments located in untouched natural landscapes on the country's south coast, where high mountains plunge steeply into the sea, creating dramatic locations with breathtaking views. Places that were once difficult to reach and inhabit have become accessible - often through public investment - and thus the subject of new possibilities, interests and building speculation. The expansion is happening rapidly, and attention to infrastructure, landscape and public space is often uncoordinated or not happening at all, creating tensions in the area.

The Green Coast Hotel project - made in collaboration with Brussels-based office CENTRAL - is the response we decided to give within such a charged development context. Initially, the hotel was conceived as part of a housing development built on artificially raised land, retained by a reinforced terra-mesh wall constructed on the beach (fig. 34). Our reaction to the brutality of that intervention also sparked our proposal; rather than building the hotel in the middle of the development, we proposed to move its location and take the monumental retaining wall on the beach as its backdrop (fig. 32), fitting it into a place that was already compromised, densifying rather than expanding. An opportunity to transform a scar in the landscape into an exceptional location, imagining the hotel as if built in a quarry, turning it into an infrastructure connecting different atmospheres and landscapes (fig. 33).

As much infrastructure as landscape, the hotel was conceived as a collection of houses connected by open-air streets and squares rather than dormitory rooms bound by corridors and halls. Instead of a generic repetition of units extending endlessly without hierarchy, these buildings of various scales and functions define public spaces, generating a complex with greater porosity and a sense of community. The project is conceived as a Mediterranean village, a space that welcomes diversity, that grows in layers and could transform over time. This attitude allows us to create an adaptable infrastructure with the potential to evolve and maybe to become one day a school, a holiday camp or an actual village.

From an inhospitable residual zone (albeit on the beach), it has become a multifaceted place that derives its quality both from the expansive view of the horizon (fig. 36) and from the intimacy of the garden (fig. 37) between the building complex and the artificial retaining wall (fig. 35). The building itself is designed as an artificial rock formation, with a materiality that fits with the geological imagination of Albania, also literally built with locally quarried materials (figs. 38, 39).

At the coast, in relation to the touristic development, it makes sense to look at architecture from the lens of adaptive reuse, and to consider the new constructions as pieces of open-ended infrastructure whose function and program will inevitably change.

36.

37.

38.

39.

40.

41.

42.

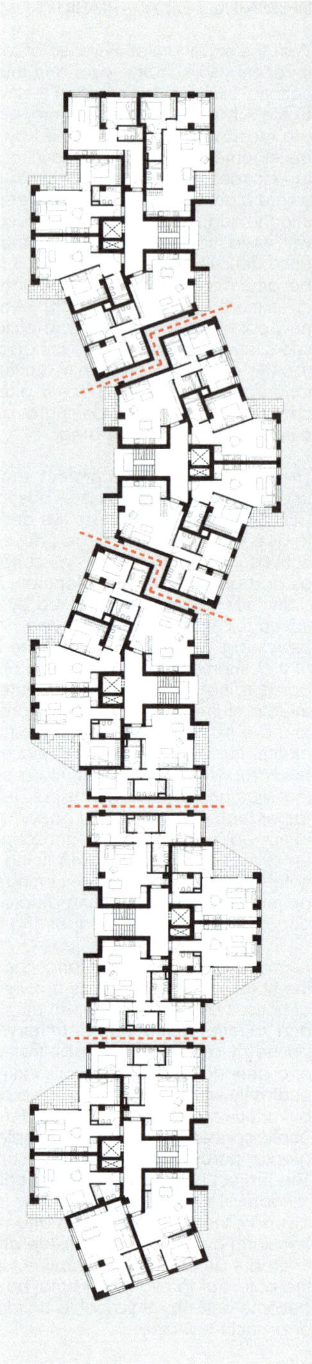

43.

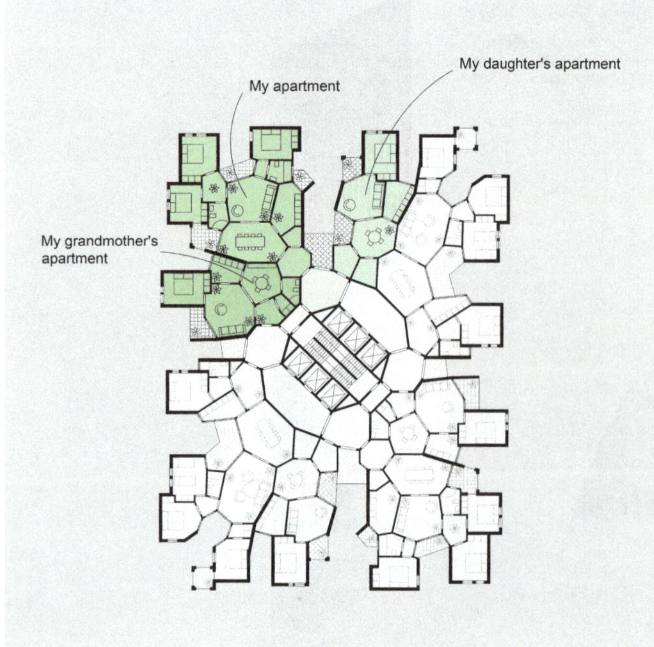

44.

45.

IMAGINING AFFORDABLE HOMES

Today, a large number of new building projects still fuels into an oversupply of high-end market offerings, and the construction of affordable housing remains grossly neglected. At the same time, traditional forms of living are slowly replaced by models that favor a more independent and individualistic lifestyle catering for the nuclear family or for the wealthy few that seek controlled climates and easier comforts. We believe however that design and creativity can help to tackle these questions by conceiving smart typologies, repeating them in an intelligent way and within economically feasible parameters.

Cornerstone, an affordable housing neighborhood located on the outskirts of Tirana, between the motorway and the Lana River, aims to offer an alternative answer to the strong price growth in the city center. For this project, a simple urban planning principle is applied to the site. Conceived as a system, it organizes around infrastructure and open space (fig. 40). Creating a clear distinction between streets (fig. 41) and gardens (fig. 42) connecting to a large park on one side and the central urban boulevard on the other. In this way, each house is linked to a larger scale that anchors it in the landscape and in the city.

The plans of the different buildings are assembled based on a limited set of typical plans (fig. 43), allowing a certain standardization without resulting in obvious repetition. This simple and affordable design produces a large amount of diverse residential spaces. To achieve this, a set of nonnegotiable qualities was defined for each dwelling to benefit from, such as multiple orientations to give sight, light and ventilation as well as a private balcony.

The Cornerstone project deals at once with architecture and urban design, offering the unusual opportunity to develop the transition from the city to the home in a slow gradient, producing meaningful transitions and liminal spaces where encounter and interaction can become a key aspect of urban life. Access via circulation cores with open staircases (fig. 46), with a generosity that we also find in old socialist buildings (fig. 47). Community life takes shape by literally giving light and air to the central infrastructure. An old quality that is still relevant and meaningful today.

A similar observation can be made about the type of family that serves as a model for the numerous developments that are taking place. Today, people often take the nuclear family as their model of cohabitation, which makes the power of life in the extended family physically impossible. Without wishing to indulge in romanticism, we do believe in the potential of devising floor plans that establish flexible relationships. In the Matrix project (figs. 44, 45), rather than making a plan that always falls back on the same pattern, we invested our creativity in imagining different ways of living together. Imagine a city made up of such variety!

With design we can advocate for a more communal way of experiencing the contemporary city. Boundaries between shared and private can increasingly be layered and fluid, to the point that it is not clear where one's home exactly begins. An important question is how to preserve these models and translate them into today's socioeconomic context.

46.

47.

TECHRIPPERS
Coca-Cola
TECHRIPPERS
Standard Chartered
Ribena
Coca-Cola
bwin
Coca-Cola
adidas

48.

SETTING UP NEW ALLIANCES

Cities in Albania are growing rapidly, and older, often oversized infrastructures are suddenly embedded in an urban fabric where they can take on new meaning. Following the successful experience of the football stadium in the center of Tirana, the Albanian government took the initiative to redevelop these in several cities.

Stadiums are often conceived as large shopping malls or sculptural objects, spaceships embedded in the urban context. As such, they have an entirely inward-oriented logic. In the proposal made for the new stadium in Durrës (fig. 48), developed in collaboration with Paris-based architecture office Plan Común, we took the opportunity to rethink the monolithic, grand approach in favor of a much more ordinary scale, where a set of buildings and permeable green spaces extends the urban fabric rather than interrupting it (fig. 52).

The stadium is an opportunity to add not only program, but also public space, thus suddenly providing a densely built-up urban area with open space that also begins to play a role in the daily life of a neighborhood (figs. 50, 51). Rather than a building or an infrastructure, the stadium becomes a kind of city center, with various facilities and an active ground floor (fig. 49), alive throughout the week.

This approach is as much about designing the architecture as about setting up the life in it. After winning the competition, a master plan was defined based on a financial strategy with a public-private alliance. The government as guarantor of the public's needs and the private sector as bearers of interests and entrepreneurial skills: all coordinated in a vision that is now ready to take shape. A clear vision, a light master plan and flexible urban regulations are producing a free collection of joyful architectures made by different actors, designed by different minds, in different times, from different countries, for different users. Yet, nonetheless, all together they create one Festival, as we called the project.

A similar question for a new alliance between actors drives the project for the renovation of the Palace of Culture in Tirana. Currently this complex building has three different owners: the government, the municipality and a set of private individuals. Already during the competition for Skanderbeg Square, we brought up the idea of opening the façade of the palace (fig. 53) and activating its courtyard, which is currently used as a car park (fig. 56). Thus, the grandeur of the arcade is matched by that of a covered hall, as a multifunctional space for art and events (fig. 57). Following this intervention, the old National Library, destined to be moved to a new location, can be extended and transformed into a library museum, reusing the current entrance while enjoying a whole new set of spaces. Once again, a joint venture between public and private that produces a fruitful complementarity of interests through a participatory process. An alliance that reframes the current fragmentation, making the different spaces parts of a new whole, accessible from all sides. Out of the old, a public centrality of a new scale emerges, intensifying a district that will be marked by many high-rises (fig. 55).

49.

50.

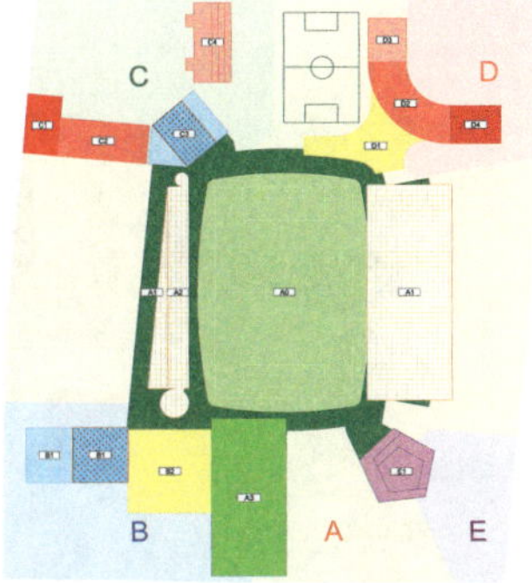

51.

52.

53.

54.

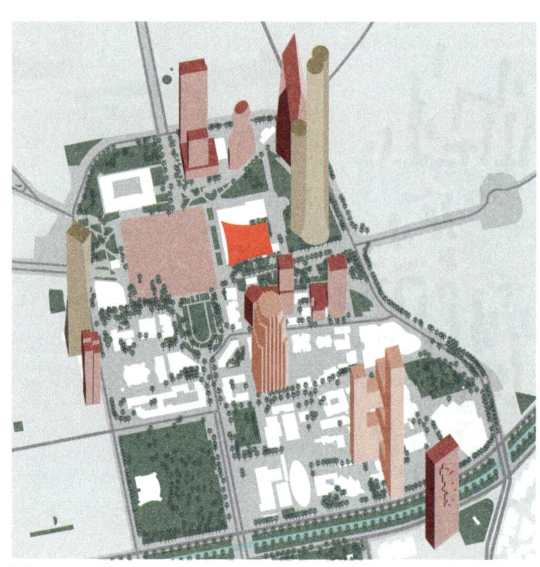
55.

56.

57.

In our 20 years of work in Albania, we have engaged with 78 collaborators on 51 projects. Of these, 12 are executed projects, 3 are publications, 2 are exhibitions, 4 are under construction, and 7 are in the active design phase. The remaining 23 are still visions on paper.

START	NAME PROJECT	LOCATION	DEVELOPER	PUBLIC/PRIVATE	PHASE
2004	TID Tower	Tirana	Tirana International Development	Private	Executed
2005	Painted façade	Tirana	Municipality of Tirana	Public	Executed
2005	Noka Bllok	Tirana	Koka	Private	Sketch
2005	Euro Petrol gas station	Tirana	Euro Petrol	Private	Executed
2008	Lana Bridge	Tirana	Municipality of Tirana	Public	Executed
2008	House for a Lawyer	Tirana		Private	Sketch
2008	Piazza	Tirana		Private	Sketch
2008	Skanderbeg Square	Tirana	Municipality of Tirana (phase 1), ADF (phase 2)	Public	Executed
2008	Mountain Collection	Tirana		Private	Executed
2008	Sports Tower	Tirana		Private	Sketch
2008	Tirana 2	Tirana		Public	Feasibility study
2008	For D.H.	Tirana		Private	Executed
2008	Zogu-i-Zi	Tirana		Private	Feasibility study
2008	River Retreat	Tirana		Private	Sketch
2009	Kastrati gas station	Tirana	Kastrati	Private	Executed
2009	Twin Villas	Tirana		Private	Sketch
2010	Italy Square	Tirana		Private	Sketch
2010	Gate of Tirana	Tirana		Private	Feasibility study
2012	Event Gate	Tirana		Private	Feasibility study
2012	Austria Bar	Tirana		Private	Partially executed
2012	Bronze Monument	Tirana	Albanian government	Public	Executed
2013	Bank of Dreams	Albania	51N4E		Survey
2013	100 Lakes	Tirana-Durrës region	KU Leuven	Public	Education
2013	Shared Infrastructure	Tirana-Durrës region	KU Leuven	Public	Education
2014	Atelier Albania	Albania	Albanian government	Public	Policy initiative
2014	Center for Openness and Dialogue (COD)	Tirana	Albanian government	Public	Executed
2015	Sauk Parkway	Tirana	ADF	Public	Partially executed
2015	The Metabolism of Albania	Albania / Netherlands	Albanian government / IABR / Dutch Embassy	Public	Study, exhibition and publication
2015	Rrogozhinë	Tirana		Private	Feasibility study
2015	Qafeshtame Socialist Resort	Qafeshtame		Private	Feasibility study
2016	How Things Meet (Art Paper Editions)				Publication
2017	Book Building	Tirana	TDT	Private	Under construction

START	NAME PROJECT	LOCATION	DEVELOPER	PUBLIC/PRIVATE	PHASE
2017	Skanderbeg Square, Tirana, Chapter #1 (Ruby Press)				Publication
2020	Art Park	Tirana	Minister of Culture	Public	Preliminary design
2020	Wall Hotel	Palasë	Green Coast	Private	Under construction
2020	Juvenilja	Tirana	TDT	Private	Feasibility study
2020	Gas station	Tirana	Fusha Group	Private	Under construction
2021	Kalaja	Tirana	TDT	Private	Feasibility study
2022	National Gallery façade	Tirana		Public	Sketch
2022	Office Hub	Tirana	BALFIN Group – Fusha Group	Private	Detail design
2022	Iceberg Villas	Palasë	Green Coast	Private	Detail design
2022	Matrix Tower	Tirana	Matrix Konstruksion	Private	Sketch
2023	Festival Stadium	Durrës	ADF	Public	Sketch
2023	Rebus master plan	Tirana	M.C. Inerte	Private	Final design
2024	Palace of Culture	Tirana	Qendra Tregtare e Zhvillimit Kulturor	Private/public	Preliminary design
2024	Cornerstone master plan	Tirana	Cornerstone	Private	Preliminary design
2024	Ksamil Village	Ksamil	AnimaCon	Private	Feasibility study
2024	Budi	Tirana	Conarc	Private	Under construction
2025	The tablecloth (model of Tirana)	Tirana	Bread & Heart	Public	Exhibition
2025	Bako	Tirana	Atrio	Private	Preliminary design
2026	Spaces in Dialogue	Tirana	Albanian government	Public	Exhibition

NAME OFFICE

AIRES MATEUS E ASSOCIADOS

DATE
February 6, 2026

PLACE
Lisbon, Portugal

WORKING IN ALBANIA SINCE
2024

PROJECT TEAM
Manuel Aires Mateus
Jorge P Silva (coordinator)
Marco Branquinho
Catarina Salgado Braz
André Xavier
Adriana Esmein
Vasco Matos

ALBANIAN PARTNERS
GI2-Albania
SINGULAR ARCH
NID
Home Planner Architects
UDV
SINGULAR ARCH
ARKEYtecture studio
SON Architects
DISPACED
Fondi shqiptar i zhvillimit

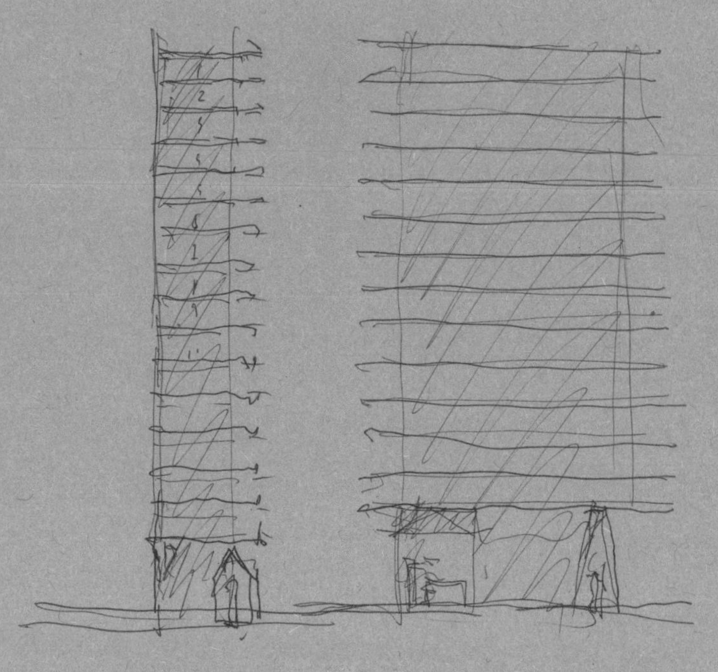

INTRODUCTION TO ALBANIA

Albania has always been a mysterious country for me. It was an Iron Curtain country in a strange location. A kind of inaccessible paradise. In fact, I visited Albania for the first time in the context of these projects.

MAIN CONTEXT VS. ALBANIA

The context in which I work in Albania is mainly residential flat blocks. Compared to the context in which I work in Portugal, there is a greater sense of freedom in Albania that allows us to experiment to an interesting degree. This is an advantage. The disadvantage is the guarantee of construction quality, which we'll have to find out how to achieve throughout the process.

ORGANIZATION/GOAL/SETUP

We always work with a local studio and naturally architecture is a participatory process, so we evolve the process with this local studio. It's obvious that we coordinate the project and decide on it, but we like to imagine that we're integrating the contributions of the whole team and therefore the local architects. My aim is always to build well and to use architecture as a tool to enhance any problem. Strategies vary from project to project and we build with this goal in mind.

SETUP IN RELATION TO ALBANIAN PARTNER

The architectural process has this idea of evolution. Projects evolve through dialogue with the team. This seems to us the most logical configuration.

OPPORTUNITIES/CHALLENGES

Albania is all under construction and if it joins the European community it will have to build all its infrastructure, so a lot is going to be built. Intelligent management of the architectural process can change Albania's outlook. The only thing it can't do is de-characterize it, and so this idea of looking for an architecture for Albania and trying to understand everything that could be tradition, everything that could be traces of an Albanian identity, is very important.

HOW TO INTEGRATE GREATER RESPONSIBILITY FOR QUALITY IN PROJECTS

There are times when things have to be top-down, so this quality has to be forced in order to create that need that doesn't exist at the moment.

BALANCING QUALITY AND DENSITY/INVOLVING STAKEHOLDERS

The only way to strengthen the role of the architect is by demonstration. It's up to architects to make projects in which you can feel the difference. A difference in every sense: a difference in use, in life, in contribution to society, and one that is completely clear to everyone.

The project must integrate everyone, which means it must integrate developers, authorities, planners and even users. Good architecture invites this convergence of everyone's interests.

EXAMPLE/INSPIRATION

The greatest inspiration for me has to do with an ancient natural environment of enormous richness. Starting here, I'm discovering projects in history and then moving on to more contemporary buildings. It's clear that there are some marked periods, such as the time of the Italian presence, which is very interesting in Albania, and there are obviously some very impressive historic buildings. From this idea of realizing a place in the geography, in nature, a trace of history, we can build these buildings that will become a reference point in Albania.

TOOLBOX ALBANIA FUTURE

In Albania, what is most suggestive is a certain idea of ambition and freedom. With these we will try to propose an investigation into Albania.

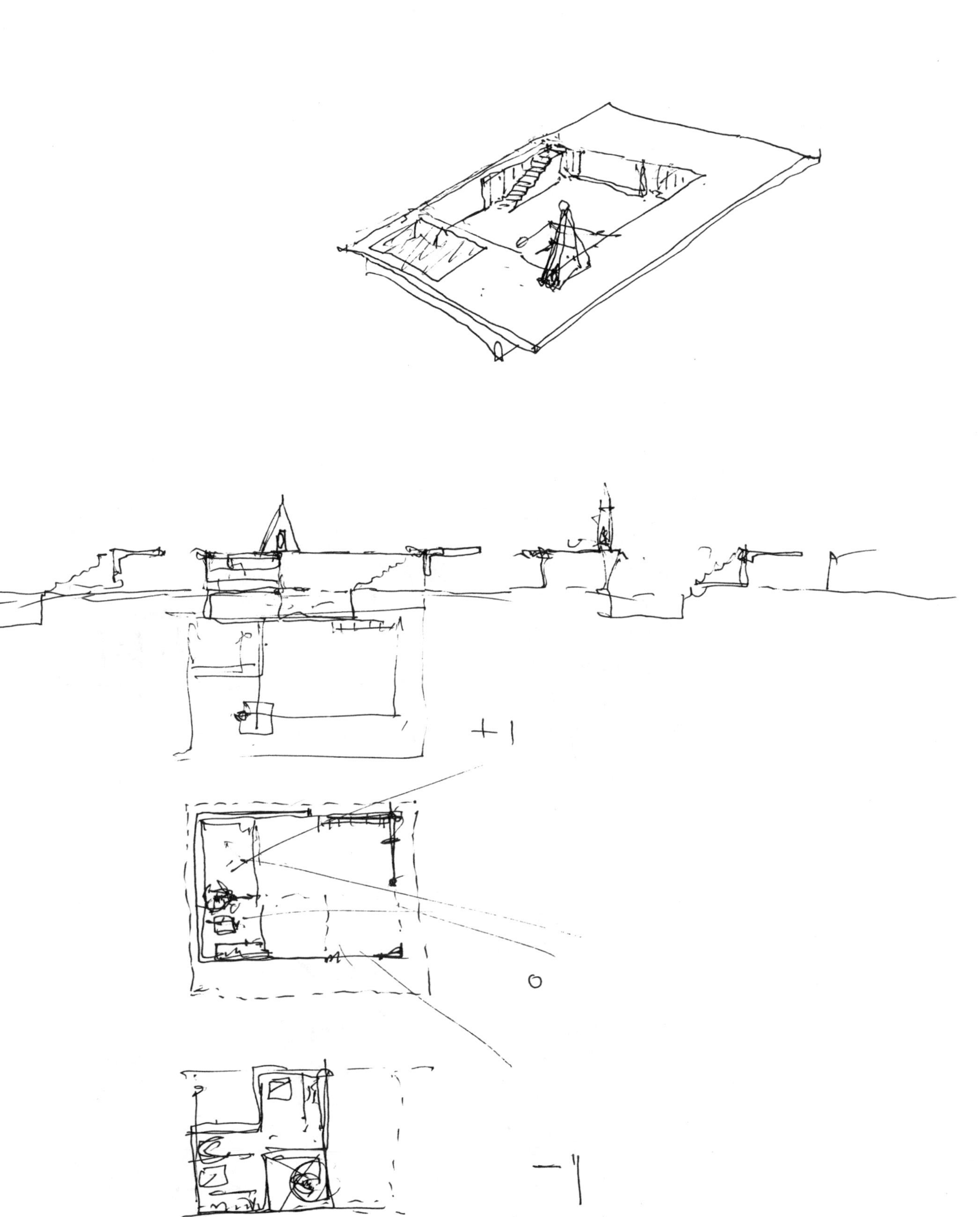

be site specific
ser específico

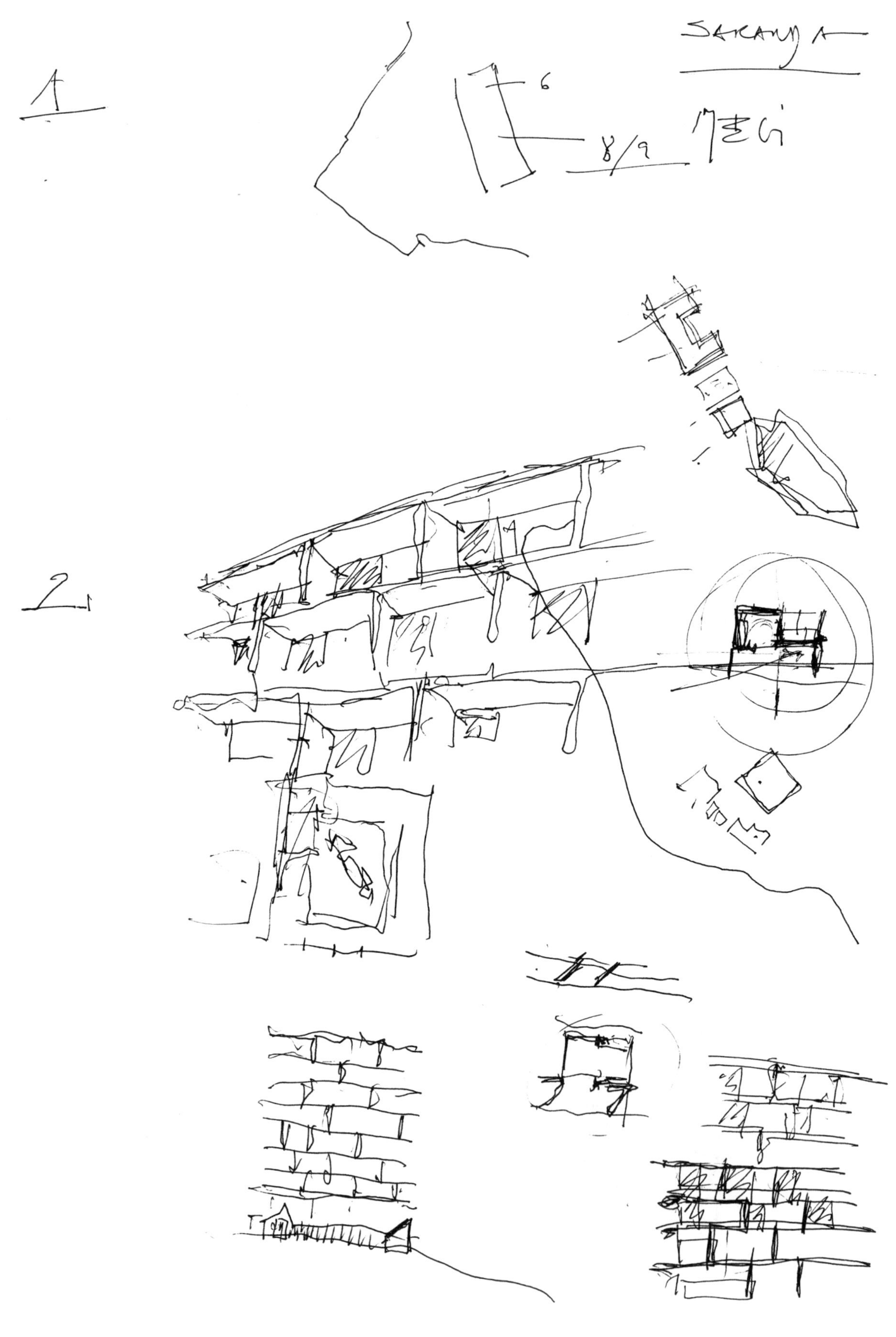

anchor an approach in history

ancorar na história uma aproximação

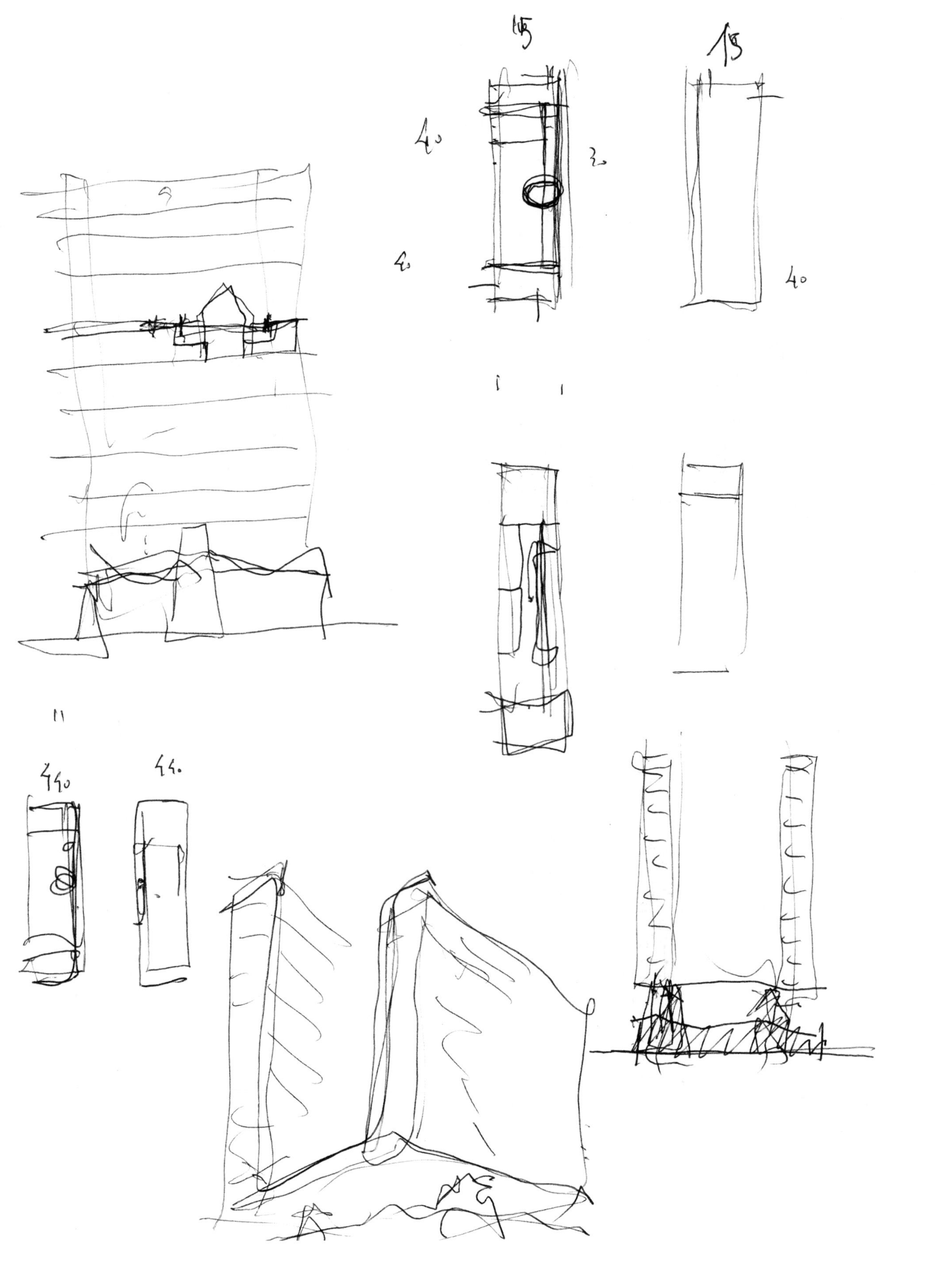

a scale for the territory
uma escala para o território

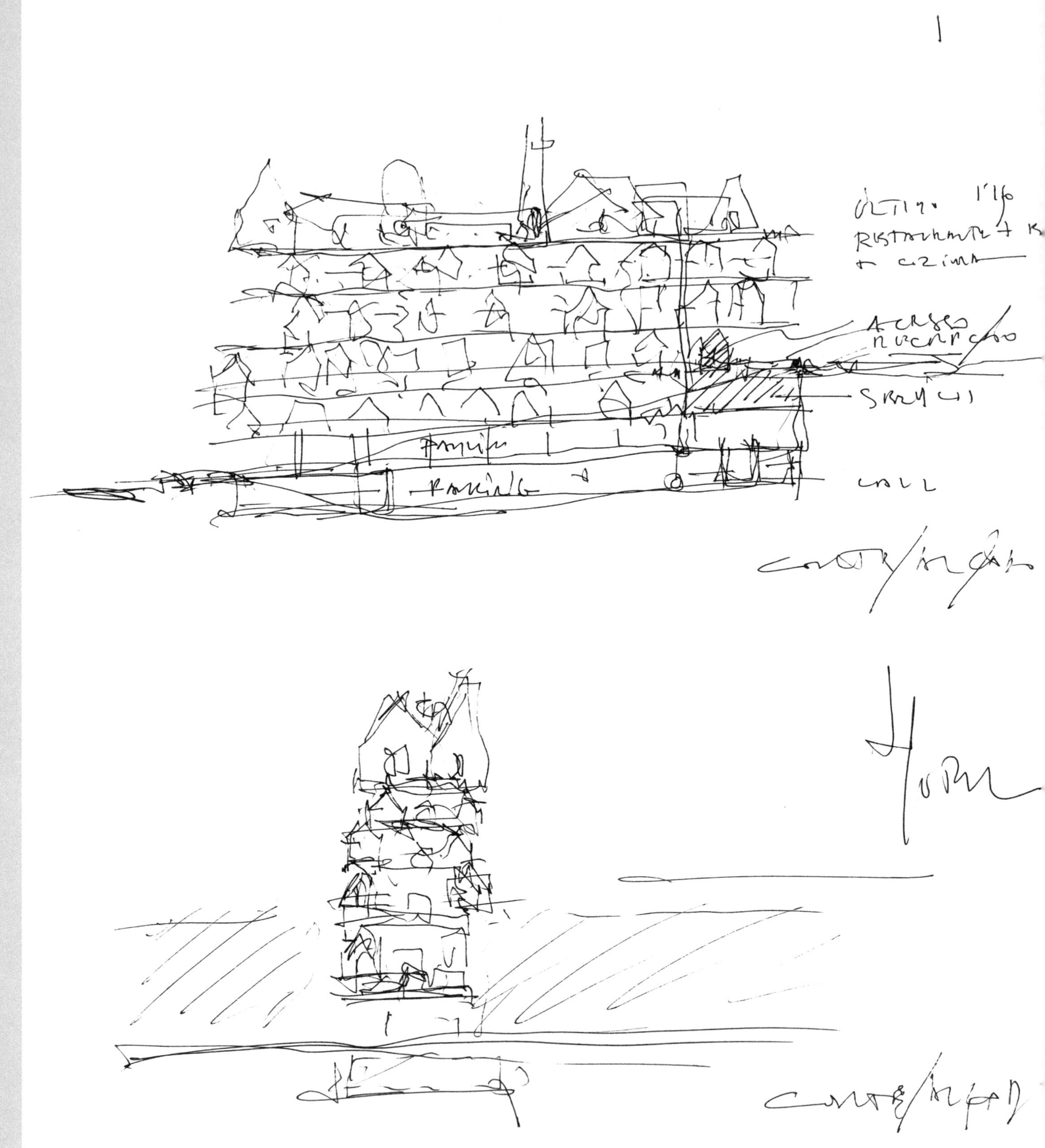

use the shape to scroll through memory

recorrer à forma para percorrer a memória

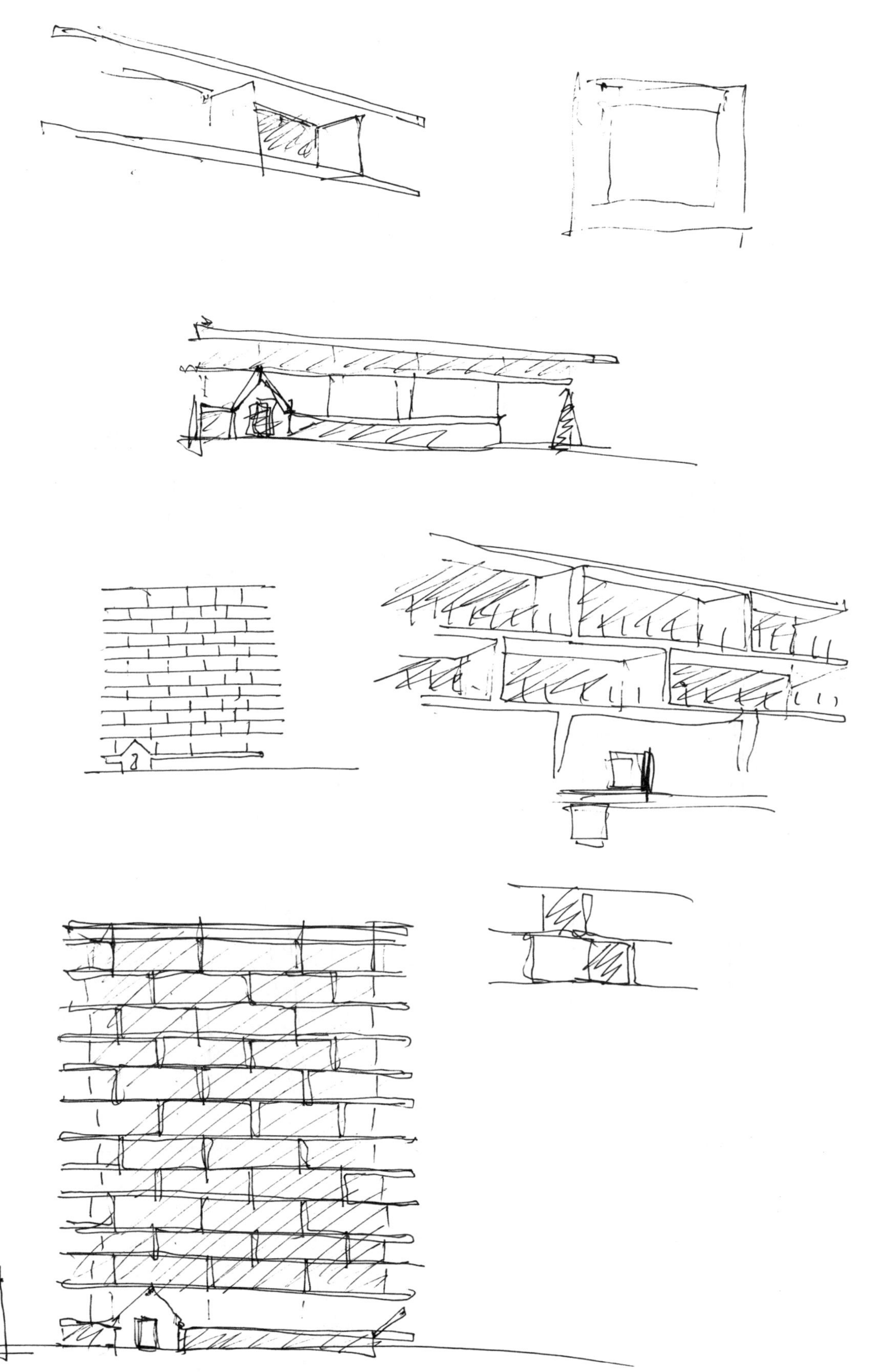

build structures as platforms to unfold life
construir estruturas como plataformas para desenrolar a vida

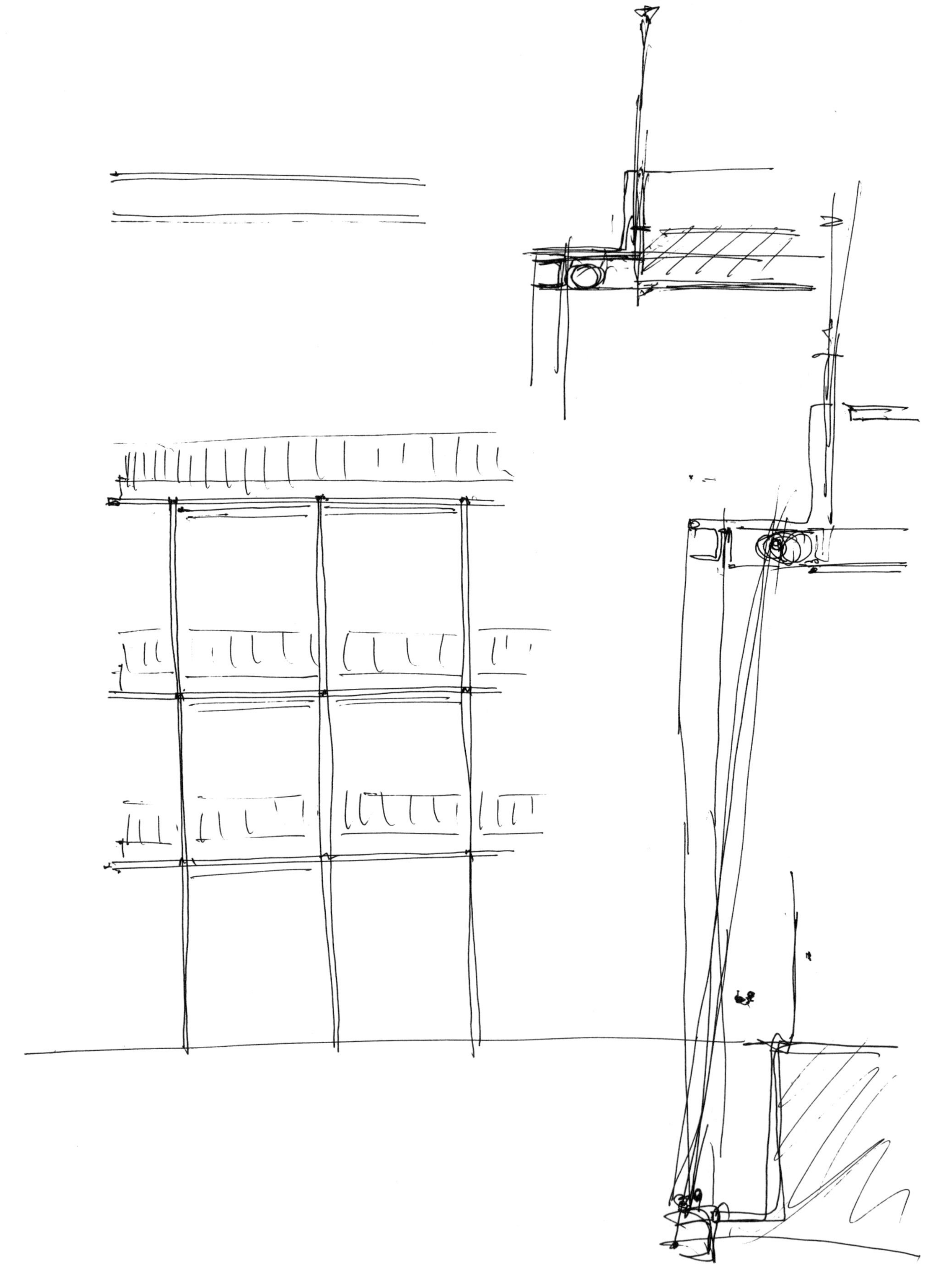

build to allow freedom in evolution

construir para permitir liberdade na evolução

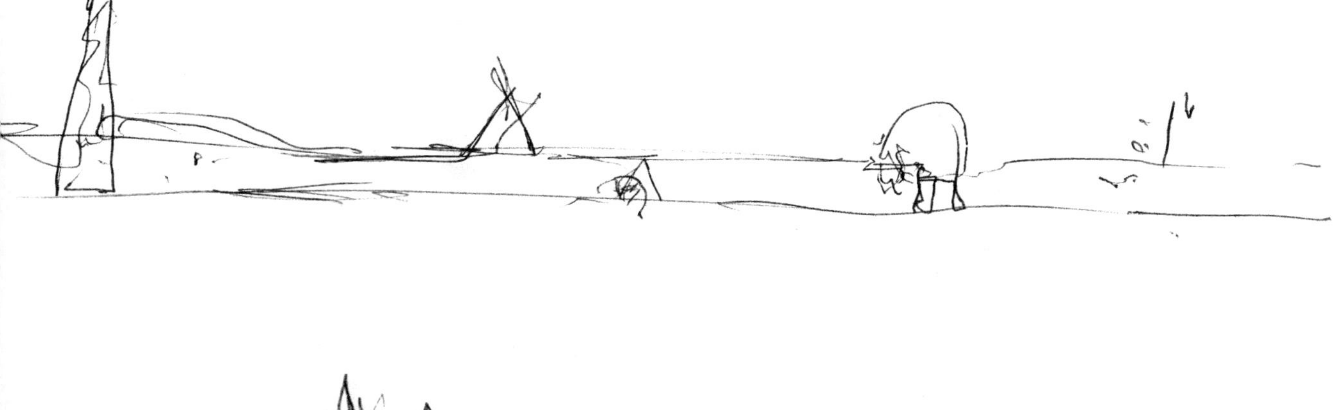

idea of belonging and identity
ideia de pertença e identidade

take advantage of the historical moment for a cultural evolution
aproveitar o momento histórico de evolução cultural

LIST OF PROJECTS

START	NAME PROJECT	LOCATION	DEVELOPER	ALBANIAN PARTNER	M²	PUBLIC/PRIVATE	PHASE
2024	Karpen Marina	Karpen	Millennium Group	GL2-Albania	120,000 m²	Private	Concept
2024	Dispanceria	Tirana	Ober shpk	SINGULAR ARCH	12,500 m²	Private	Permit phase
2024	Shëngjin	Shëngjin		NID	13,000 m²	Private	Permit phase
2024	Saranda Residences	Saranda		Home Planner Architects	15,000 m²	Private	Permit phase
2024	Ksamil	Ksamil		UDV	3,500 m²	Private	Permit phase
2024	Vlora	Vlora		SINGULAR ARCH	20,000 m²	Private	Permit phase
2024	Durrës	Durrës	Autokton Konstruksion	ARKEYtecture studio	13,000 m²	Private	Permit phase
2025	Valona	Radhimë		SON Architects	10,000 m²	Private	Permit phase
2025	Tabi	Tirana	TABI CONSTRUCTION shpk	DISPACED	13,000 m²	Private	Permit phase
2025	Mother Teresa Square	Tirana		Fondi Shqiptar i Zhvillimit	35,000 m²	Public	Concept
2025	Durrës Beach Promenade	Durrës			75,000 m²	Private	Concept

NAME OFFICE

ÁLVARO SIZA

DATE	PLACE	WORKING IN ALBANIA SINCE
July 25, 2025	Porto, Portugal	2023

PRINCIPALS
Álvaro Siza
Camilo Rebelo

PROJECT TEAM
Henrique Siza

INTRODUCTION TO ALBANIA

Following a recommendation by Camilo Rebelo, who was already doing a project for a tower in Tirana, I was introduced to the prime minister, Edi Rama. I was later invited to study the master plan for a section of Albania's beautiful Adriatic coastline, which I accepted subject to Camilo Rebelo agreeing to be associated with the execution of this plan.

SETUP IN RELATION TO ALBANIAN PARTNER

Due to my back problem, I can't travel for my international commitments. In Asia I have a partnership with Carlos Castanheira, and for Albania I made a partnership with Camilo Rebelo because I knew his works and friendship. After the first project invitation to work in Albania it continued for other projects/works. In the international project we always have support from local architects' offices. All partnerships have ongoing dialogues with points of view from all of us.

OPPORTUNITIES/CHALLENGES

First thing is the Love for Architecture, difficult to find in many contexts. The second aspect is the consciousness to Call for Architects.

HOW TO INTEGRATE GREATER RESPONSIBILITY FOR QUALITY IN PROJECTS

Since the main contemporary problem is housing and social housing, we have to learn from the history of architecture, and observe the twenties and thirties in modern architecture. We have to fight for quality for everybody, "not only for the Pope and the King." There shall be an awareness that for a town to be beautiful there shall not be a lack of quality in each unit independent of its programs.

When tourists go to Paris they visit the city center, not the peripheries . . . quality is apparently not considered necessary in the new parts of a town.

BALANCING QUALITY AND DENSITY/INVOLVING STAKEHOLDERS

It depends on the project teams – architects and engineers with commitment and support from the owners, citizens and politics.

EXAMPLE/INSPIRATION

The project for Albania with the vision and support of Prime Minister Edi Rama is unique.

DUNE

Year 2023
Architecture Álvaro Siza + Camilo Rebelo
Principals in charge Álvaro Siza + Camilo Rebelo with Susana Martins
Collaborators Leonardo Barros, Patrícia Fernandes and Pedro Pinto Ferreira
Consultant Mina Ghorbanbakhsh
Structural engineering G.O.P Lda. – Jorge Nunes da Silva
Collaborators José Pedro Martins and Francisco Valente
Visualizations Fusão
Promoter Gruppo IDA
Engineers Ilir Trebicka and Klodiana Kucuku

VLORA

Year 2023
Architecture Álvaro Siza + Camilo Rebelo
Principals in charge Álvaro Siza + Camilo Rebelo with Susana Martins
Collaborators Henrique Siza + Leonardo Barros, Patrícia Fernandes and Pedro Pinto Ferreira
Local partner ATELIER 4
Consultant Mina Ghorbanbakhsh
Structural engineering G.O.P Lda. – Jorge Nunes da Silva + aei progetti + K&K Engineering
Collaborators José Pedro Martins and Francisco Valente
Promoter Texas Development, Hel-Pet, Alb Edil

Álvaro Siza's sketches

DUNE

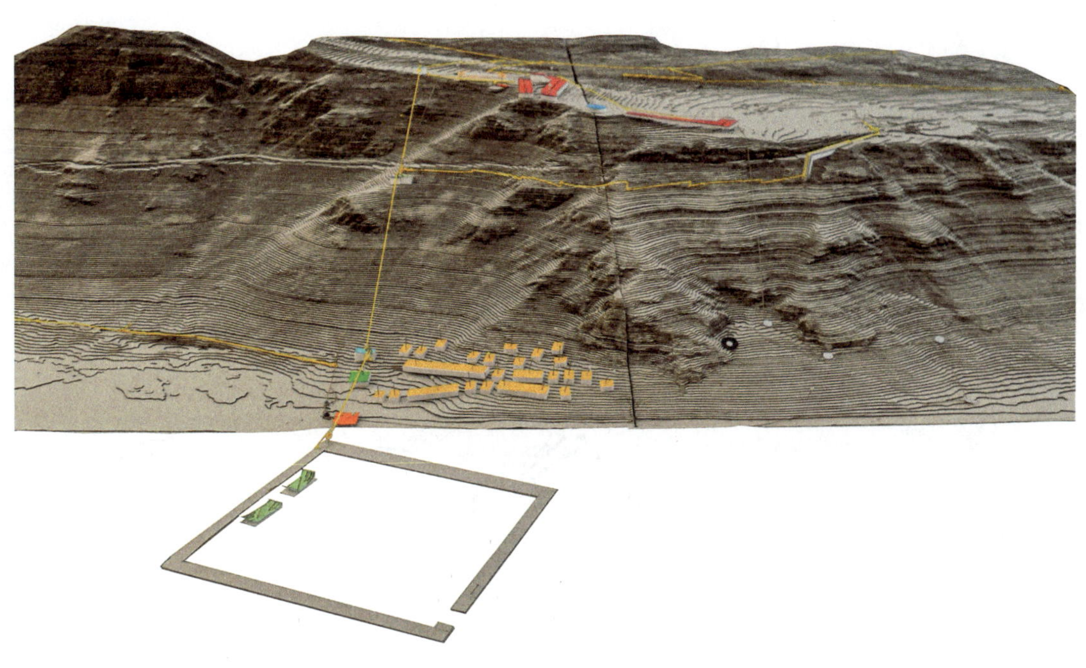

Model

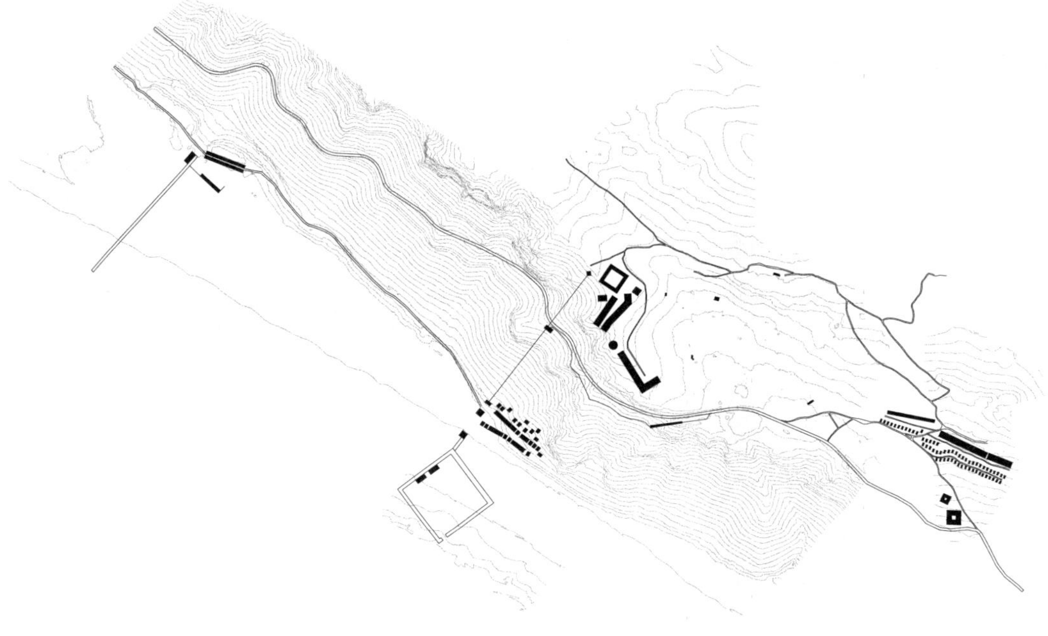

Site plan

DUNE

Render

Álvaro Siza's sketches

VLORA

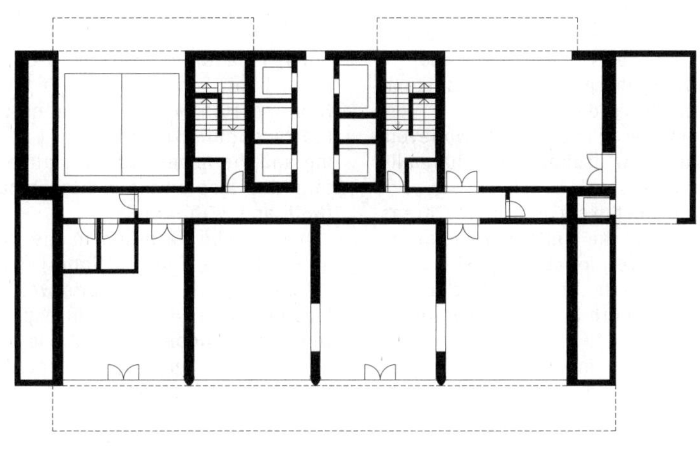

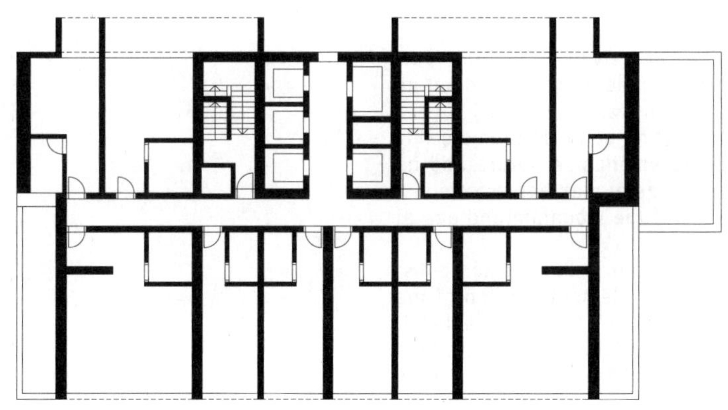

Ground floor and 3rd-floor hotel

DUNE

On the southwestern slope above the Adriatic between Montenegro and Shëngjin, the Rana e Hedhun plan is designed to define and organize the territory and its buildings.

The aim is to maintain the integrity of the beautiful landscape, concentrating construction in areas where the topography and the road system, under construction, make it advisable.

These areas are distributed on two levels of the hillside (high and low), running longitudinally from northwest to southeast.

Between the northwest end of the areas described at high level and the southeast end of the areas described at low level, a cable car with three stops connects the two levels. There is also a stop at an intermediate level where the tracks and roads cross the hillside lengthwise.

The landscape remains a continuous mass of green from which the buildings peek out, concentrated and distributed as described.

Álvaro Siza

On the Albanian coast of the Adriatic Sea, we find probably the most unique and charismatic mountain and its 110-meter-high natural dune. This natural richness shall be perceived as a natural patrimony and therefore preserved, honored and left as a legacy for future generations.

This is our starting point: to promote this beautiful landscape and emphasize nature and its qualities. Therefore, the master plan has two distinct settlements, one on top of the mountain and one at sea level.

This first settlement is like an acropolis, a composition with multiple elements on top of the mountain, situated 330 meters above sea level, that aims for a distant and open horizon, thus contemplating the Adriatic Sea with views of Italy and Montenegro.

The second settlement, located at sea level, consists of two interlocking moments: the first, at the western end, defines the arrival of the main road with the design of a tower and a pier that juts out into the sea, thus creating both a vertical and a horizontal landmark. The second, at the eastern end, is located at the base of the mountain, next to the large dune, with the design of a fragmented village and its dock.

Camilo Rebelo

VLORA

The image of the Vlora Tower results mainly from the allowed building height and the construction limits of the available plot.

The drawing repetition on the floors of the west (facing the sea) and east (facing the mountains) façades is interrupted on the technical floor (11th floor), on the floors of the spa and the gym (9th and 10th floors), on the ground and first floors (corresponding to the main entrance of the building and the access to the staircases and the elevators) and also on the two technical floors on the top (36th and 37th floors).

The variation in the north façade of the hotel (on the first ten floors) derives from a minor asymmetry of the tower's volume. On the north façade, this asymmetry corresponds to the greatest width of the floor plan, and it is a result of the intention to allow some rooms located at the back of the hotel to have views of the sea.

In each room, the balconies, with their beautiful views of the coast and the mountain, also assure the needed sunlight protection.

Álvaro Siza

LIST OF PROJECTS

START	NAME PROJECT	LOCATION	DEVELOPER	ENGINEER	PUBLIC/PRIVATE
2023	Vlora Tower	Vlora	Texas Development, Hel-Pet, Alb-Edil		Private
2023	Dune master plan	Rana e Hedhun	Gruppo IDA	Ilir Trebicka and Klodiana Kucuku	Private
2025	Borsh master plan	Borsh	Millennium Group		Private

All projects in co-authorship with Camilo Rebelo.

NAME OFFICE

ANDREA CAPUTO

DATE	PLACE	WORKING IN ALBANIA SINCE
December 19, 2025	Milan, Italy	2024

PRINCIPALS

Andrea Caputo

PROJECT TEAM

Alberto Caddeo
Berfin Bukan
Joy Lin
Manmeet Obhan
Ruzgar Bozaci
Giovanni Cesaretti
Alessandro Magnotta
Tommaso Tugnoli
Alban Kalaj
Fatlind Collaku
Marcello Stabile

ORGANIZATION/GOAL/SETUP

I wish for our private projects to always include the greatest amount of public services to local communities, generating the most stimulating conditions for people's interaction.

SETUP IN RELATION TO ALBANIAN PARTNER

Always sharing.

OPPORTUNITIES/CHALLENGES

To develop a new anti-academic and multifaceted local style.

HOW TO INTEGRATE GREATER RESPONSIBILITY FOR QUALITY IN PROJECTS

Constant exchange between foreign/local architects and developers.

BALANCING QUALITY AND DENSITY/INVOLVING STAKEHOLDERS

A local urban planning agency formed by a selection of international/local architects, along with members of the public administration, could help establish suitable density criteria for each specific site. The development of the Albanian territory, with its typographical, urban and landscape diversity, cannot be resolved solely through predetermined building indices. Especially when collaborating with international designers, a local urban planning agency would help when it comes to identifying the best urban density proposals for each site.

The agency could be established by gathering the best typologies - residential, hospitality, etc. - already realized or under development and arranging them by location and territorial conditions. This would generate an observatory of exemplary models, providing an initial body of scientific and intellectual resources for those aiming to develop or design within specific contexts. The ideal output of this agency would be a periodically published magazine. A tool for investigation and reporting, aiming to crystallize the best - and worst - developments while monitoring the intense evolution of a territory in transition.

EXAMPLE/INSPIRATION

In Tirana, along the road connecting the city to the airport, is a cubic residential building. It is an urban object made up of various technologies and materials: concrete, perforated bricks, solid bricks and plastic, arranged in what seems to be a possibly random manner, likely built at different times. A seemingly chaotic building, yet one of great visual power, emblematic of the country's development.

TOOLBOX ALBANIA FUTURE

In Albania, it is possible to undertake a design process that allows for implementation of architectural research and experimentation that is difficult to apply elsewhere. This is not due to the lack of a preexisting urban fabric or regulations, but rather because of a strong political will to enhance the quality and value of the built environment in line with the contemporary language of international architecture.

Land in Transition

The speed at which the Albanian territory is transforming is evident to anyone who observes its landscapes today. In many ways, this acceleration recalls moments of intense urban development that have also marked the history of our own country, Italy. In the decades following the Second World War, vast portions of land – particularly coastal areas connected to tourism and hospitality – underwent rapid and often radical change. Entire geographies were redefined within a relatively short span of time, reshaping not only settlements but also the cultural and environmental identity of those places.

Yet an essential question remains: what survives of the original territory? What traces persist of earlier landscapes, of pre-existing morphologies, of the delicate relationships between land, sea, and settlement that once structured these environments?

It is around these questions that this photographic inquiry and documentation has taken shape. We invited photographer Marco Cappelletti to produce a series of aerial images capable of capturing the territory from a detached yet revealing vantage point. Seen from above, patterns of transformation become legible: the layering of infrastructures, the expansion of built fabric, the tensions between continuity and rupture. These images operate almost as contemporary cartographies, offering a critical reading of an evolving landscape.

The project ultimately proposes a double reflection. On the one hand, it seeks to document the condition of the landscape as it appears today – suspended between memory and projection. On the other, it positions our own design work within this broader process of change. While the architectural proposal discussed in these pages is still in the process of becoming, its intention is not simply to occupy the site but to engage with its ongoing transformation, acknowledging both the urgency of development and the responsibility to interpret what remains.

In this sense, this contribution is not limited to presenting a project. It is an attempt to frame design as a form of territorial consciousness – a way of reading, measuring, and ultimately imagining futures that remain in dialogue with the landscapes from which they emerge.

Andrea Caputo

Tirana

Tirana

Tirana

Durrës

Tirana

Farkë e Madhe

Himara

Kune

Tirana

Vlora

Tirana

Kune Lezha

Dhërmi

Dhërmi

NAME OFFICE

ANUPAMA KUNDOO ARCHITECTS

DATE	PLACE	WORKING IN ALBANIA SINCE
February 2, 2026	Berlin, Germany	July 2024

PRINCIPLES	COLLABORATORS
Holistic development based on coexistence principles	Yet unappointed

MAIN CONTEXT VS. ALBANIA

I work and live from two bases: Mumbai and Pondicherry in India and Berlin in Germany. I believe that as humans, we are more common than different. Natural laws such as gravity and climate are universal laws, which we need to understand and adapt to. Man-made regulations and approaches, on the other hand, are different from place to place, but these need to evolve over time through visionary practices to steer society forward.

ORGANIZATION/GOAL/SETUP

We are an agile office that adapts to the project's circumstances and site-specific requirements. Our goal is to build knowledge and to build community while building buildings/environments.

SETUP IN RELATION TO ALBANIAN PARTNER

This is too premature to answer.

OPPORTUNITIES/CHALLENGES

The main opportunity is to create best practices and prototypes that are free from the baggage of habitual postindustrial practice that we see in Europe and the "developed countries," one that has led to high resource consumption and overstandardization, often leaving behind human engagement. Albania is a fertile ground to develop new and holistic strategies for the built environment in coexistence with the unbuilt, setting new standards for conscious development not just for Albania, but for Europe and the rest of the world.

HOW TO INTEGRATE GREATER RESPONSIBILITY FOR QUALITY IN PROJECTS

The best way is to showcase some exemplary prototype projects, particularly for housing. When people see what is possible, they will aspire to higher goals.

BALANCING QUALITY AND DENSITY/INVOLVING STAKEHOLDERS

There are no easy formulae. Success depends on the collective goodwill, aspirations and collaboration beyond architects.

EXAMPLE/INSPIRATION

More than projects, which I am still learning about, what is inspiring is the beauty and fertility of the region itself on the one hand, and the culture of the people and their values on the other hand.

TOOLBOX ALBANIA FUTURE

There is the sense that here one can dream big. There seems to be freedom to allow the imagination to unfold. Imagination is the critical tool for transcending past burdens and limitations in order to build new scenarios. But with great freedom comes great responsibility. So Albania is giving us the opportunity to take more responsibility while imagining new futures.

Coexistence in wetlands – where water and land meet

A biodiverse urban ecosystem – where nature, innovation and collective consciousness converge. Positioned as a global laboratory for impact, this city pioneers transformative climate solutions while achieving true harmony with the natural world.

By driving cutting-edge research, fostering global collaboration and scaling impactful strategies to meet the world's sustainability challenges, this city embeds regenerative practices, nurtures year-round ecotourism and lights the path to a more sustainable, enlightened future for all.

Set in the area of the Divjakë National Park (around 35 km long) and the large Karavasta lagoon, home to the curly pelican, a brownfield of reclaimed land (about 8 km long and 4 km wide) will be partly given back to the sea, creating canals and waterways for mobility.

Divjakë wetlands: *a vision for coexistence*

Reclaimed land

Comparing land and sea, humans have managed to divide and own land whereas the waters of the sea are beyond ownership, and the topography below determines how the edges are going to be formed.

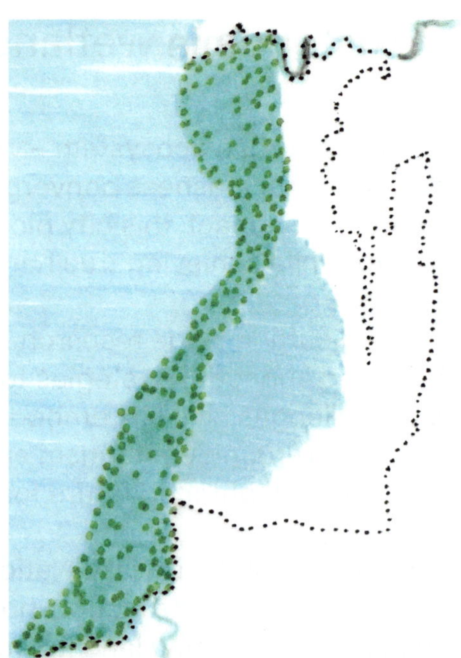

Concentrated vs. dispersing

The current planning approach focuses diverse social, economic and cultural activities within the reclaimed land, rather than spreading them across the entire national park area.

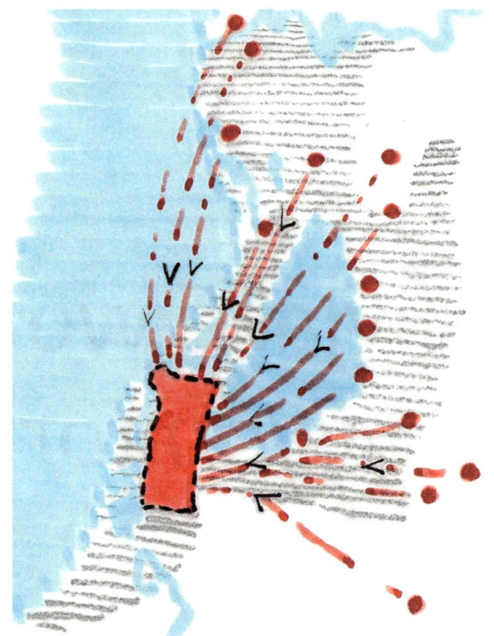

Treading lightly

At the edges of the park, four mobility hubs stand as gateways to a slower, gentler world. Here, the noise of polluting vehicles fades, replaced by electric vehicles and mass transit, as the landscape invites a deeper harmony between human and nature.

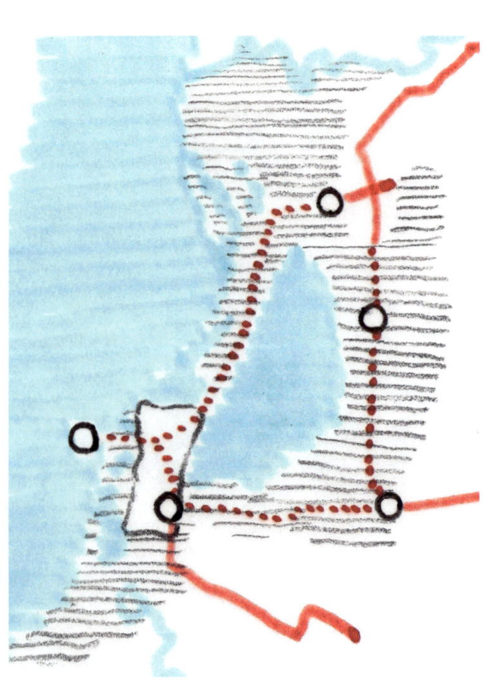

City as organism – an assemblage of landscapes

Skyscape

Elevated walkway rises mean that beneath, the ground remains free for nature, while above, humans find their path along the boardwalks. Connection flows upwards, leaving the earth untouched.

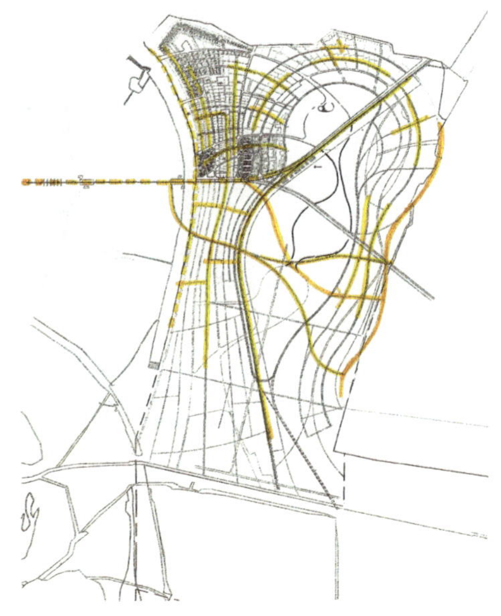

Landscape

Connected by corridors and pathways, scattered green pockets weave a continuous flow through the city, ensuring movement remains within nature.

Waterscape

A network of canals, linked to a central freshwater lake, is proposed to regulate saltwater intrusion while preserving natural hydrological and ecological balance. Simultaneously, it serves as a sustainable transit route, enabling movement by boat and enhancing connectivity.

Water and energy strategies – abundance, not shortage

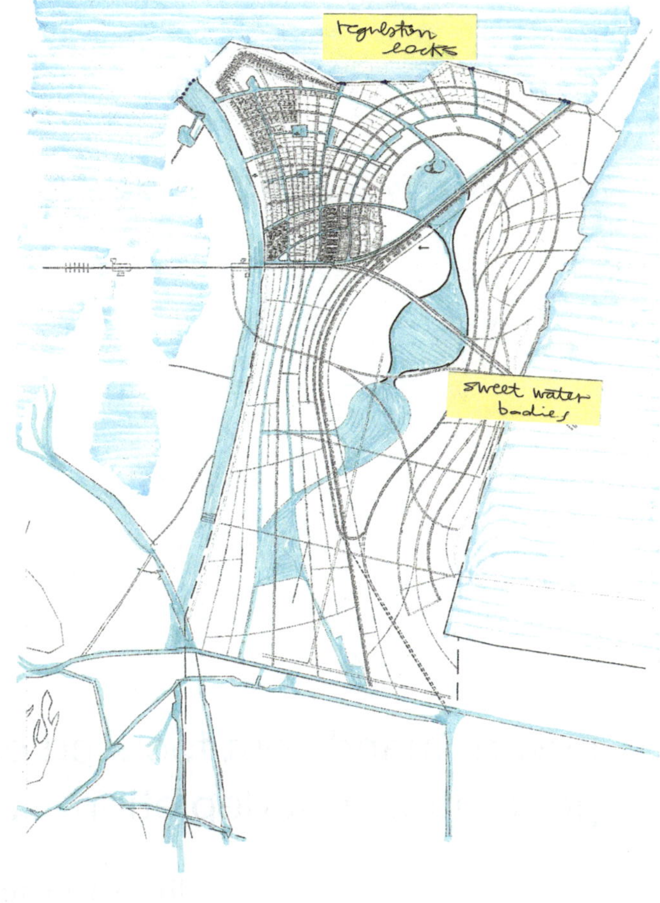

. . . sweet into salt, sea into the land,
all takes place in this continuous land . . .

A new waterbody will enable the creation of a freshwater ecology amid the saltwater one, to nurture life including human life. This waterbody will gather rainwater seasonally and hold treated wastewater on daily cycles, thereby creating a generative base for the urban ecosystem that does not suck out the rapidly depleting groundwater and counters salt-water intrusion due to overextraction for agriculture and conventional tourism. Renewable energy will support the energy demands, creating enough surplus for the region beyond this development.

Slow and silent is the future – pedestrian-centric mobility

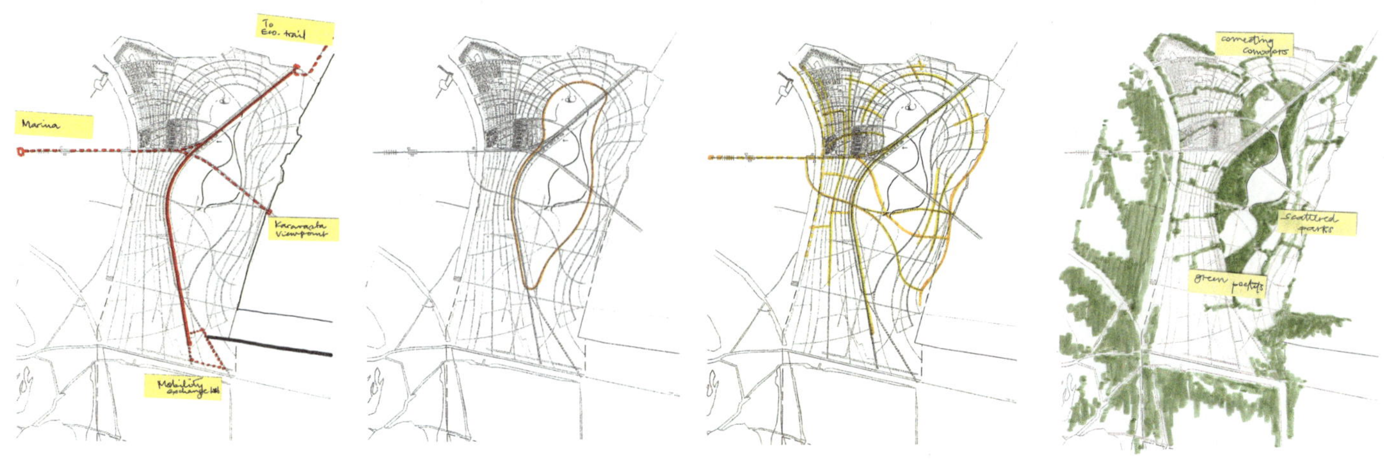

. . . new demands but focused on generation, not depletion . . .

To be pedestrian-centric and biodiversity friendly, conventional transportation will be left behind at the mobility exchange hubs at the peripheries of Divjakë Park, while nonpolluting and silent modes of transport will help navigate the waters, lands and skywalks. A central park, which will enable the urban center to remain peaceful and non-congested, will be connected to the peripheral waterfront promenades on either side through a continuous green network that will allow for uninterrupted mobility for pedestrians and animals alike.

Conscious living – celebrating diversity

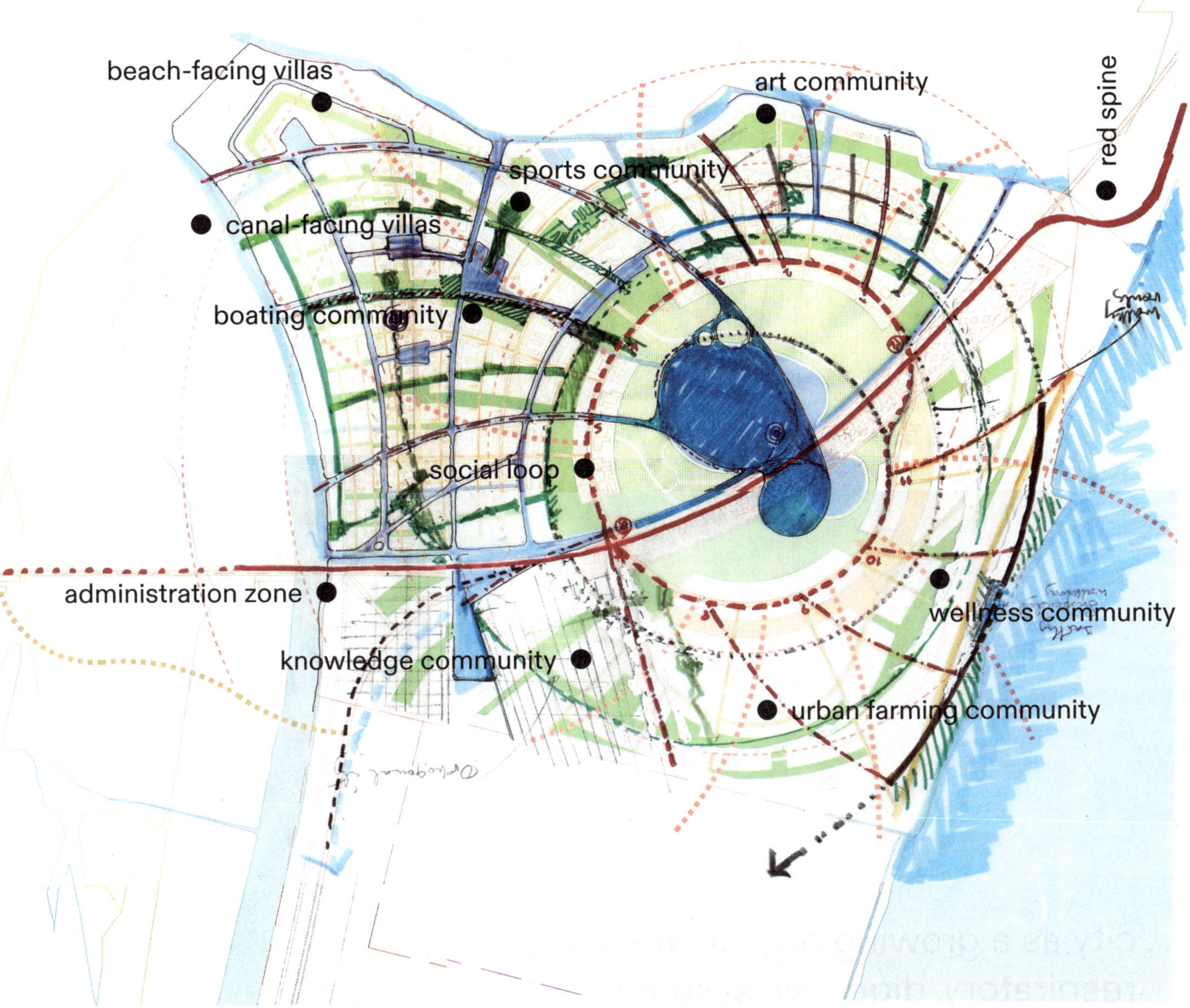

The project is based on the idea of engaging human consciousness as a driver that goes beyond intelligence and extends to collective wisdom and consciousness, ethics and collaboration, instead of competition and war.

A population of 50,000 inhabitants will be the critical mass for this laboratory settlement, which will welcome diverse inhabitants (sports community, art community, research campus and farming community) from across the globe to collaborate on all diverse issues in a synthetic, holistic approach.

A growing organism – phasing

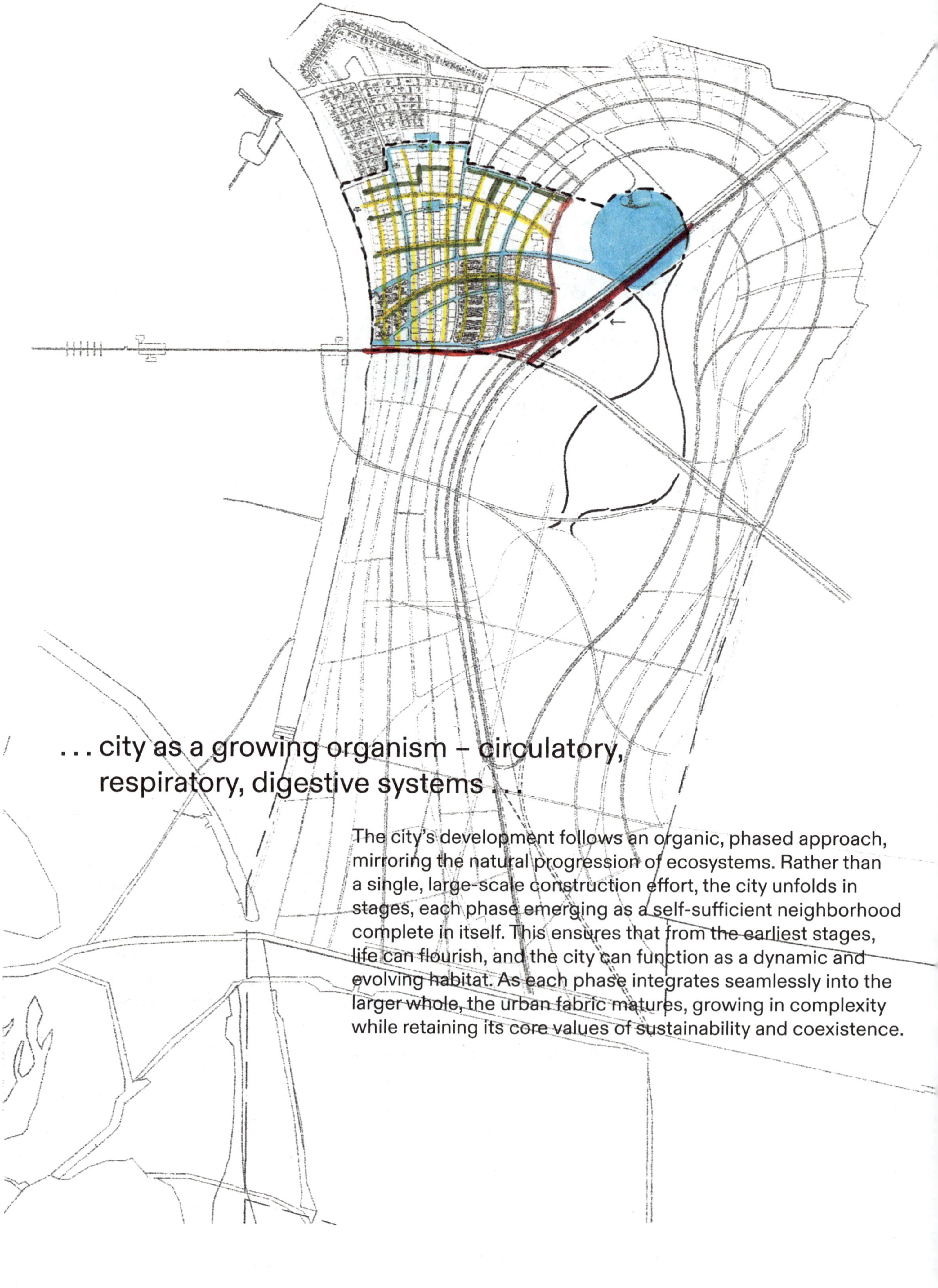

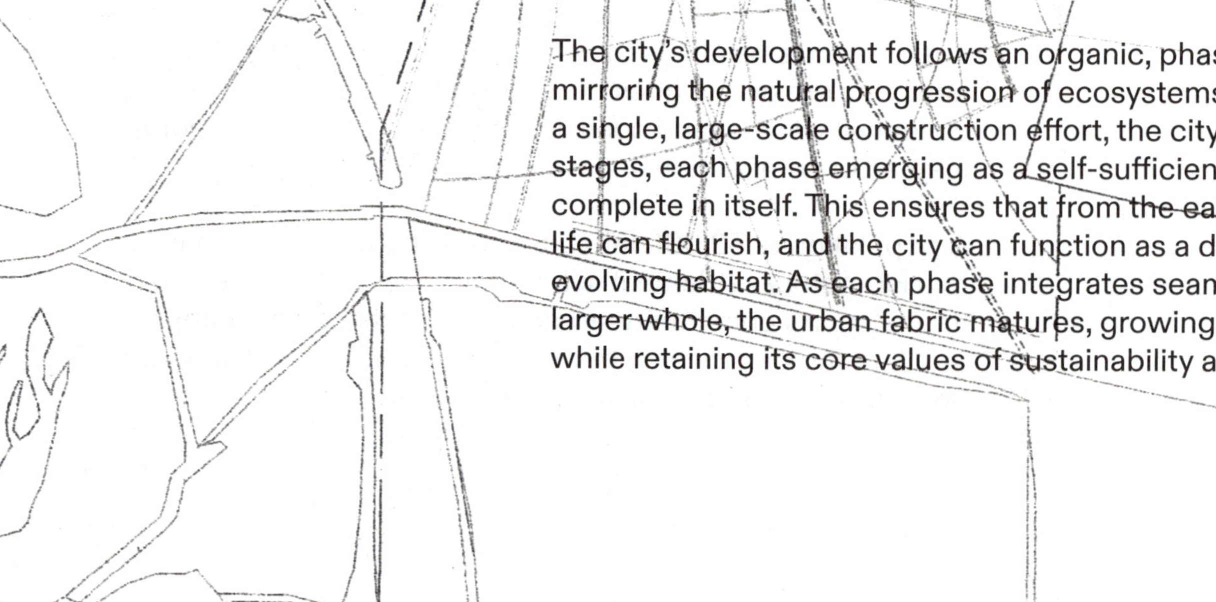

. . . city as a growing organism – circulatory, respiratory, digestive systems . . .

The city's development follows an organic, phased approach, mirroring the natural progression of ecosystems. Rather than a single, large-scale construction effort, the city unfolds in stages, each phase emerging as a self-sufficient neighborhood complete in itself. This ensures that from the earliest stages, life can flourish, and the city can function as a dynamic and evolving habitat. As each phase integrates seamlessly into the larger whole, the urban fabric matures, growing in complexity while retaining its core values of sustainability and coexistence.

START	NAME PROJECT	LOCATION	DEVELOPER	PHASE
2024	Kingscoast development	Divjakë	NIU Invest	Master planning

NAME OFFICE

ARCHEA ASSOCIATI

DATE	PLACE	WORKING IN ALBANIA SINCE
Founded 1988	Florence, Italy	2004

PRINCIPALS

Laura Andreini
Marco Casamonti
Silvia Fabi
Giovanni Polazzi

PROJECT TEAM

Alisa Bakiu
Mattia Borrione
Giovanni Cinquini
Francesco Dall'O'
Marco Gamberi
Francesco Montani
Elis Korneliu Nova
Alessandro Riccomi

INTRODUCTION TO ALBANIA

I began working in Albania in 2004 when the city council invited me to take part in a competition to design one of the ten tower buildings for the new city master plan designed by the French firm Architecture Studio, which had won a competition to design the new layout and image for the center of Tirana. Edi Rama was the mayor at the time, and following the season of change created by the famous facade "painting" interventions and the demolition of illegal construction along the Lana River, he launched competitions for the main architectural interventions in public spaces as well as buildings for the private sector. Winning the competition led to my collaboration with the country.

MAIN CONTEXT VS. ALBANIA

In reference to Italy and Europe it is obvious that there are still technological differences. However, these are diminishing rapidly over time. With regards to basic technology, where manpower is an important factor, the country offers even better performance levels. However, as far as the most advanced methods of construction and systems engineering are concerned, there are still considerable differences in capacity and experience.

ORGANIZATION/GOAL/SETUP

The best way to work consistently and to produce quality in any country is to live and work there, becoming deeply familiar with it in order to propose adequate and coherent projects and proposals. After our experience with the construction of the Albanian National Stadium, we decided to open a branch in Tirana and to give our Albanian architects the possibility of completing their training in Italy. At the same time, architects from thirty different countries are able to come to Albania, creating the cultural exchange necessary to contribute towards the technological and cultural growth of a country.

SETUP IN RELATION TO ALBANIAN PARTNER

We work all over the world: in Vietnam, China, Kazakhstan, and more generally in Asia, the Middle East or South America. In each country we always try to create a dialogue with local firms, which helps us develop the project correctly, especially in understanding the cultural contexts and identity of the region, because its unique nature constitutes the essence of our work. The reason we travel so much is to gain a deep understanding of the places where we are asked to intervene. This exchange enables us to create the dialogue of diversity that makes every architect's work so wonderful and unique. For example, the bas-reliefs on the Tirana stadium columns are not simply a form of decoration, but through a reinterpretation of elements of Albanian culture, they represent the sense of identity that transforms every city into a place that is unique.

OPPORTUNITIES/CHALLENGES

Today, the most important urban transformation example on a European level is almost certainly Tirana. For coastal development, considerable thought has been given to the type of model to be applied in answer to the demands of tourism, which has discovered the beauty and extraordinary value of the natural landscape and coastline. However, if urban density in Tirana is linked with vertical construction, building on the coast must be focused on horizontal construction, generally linked with low density planning. Furthermore, I feel it is important to understand the aims and proposals expressed by the main figures who are involved in international architectural issues and are invited to work in Albania. They must be able to integrate contemporary design with the unique character of Albanian culture.

HOW TO INTEGRATE GREATER RESPONSIBILITY FOR QUALITY IN PROJECTS

In 2014 we were asked by an Albanian company to participate in a competition to design and construct the new national Albanian sports stadium. The project defined a new football infrastructure model because it was one of the first stadiums in Europe designed as an open urban environment for everyday use, and not exclusively for sports activities inside the stadium. In a country that is undergoing such rapid and energetic change, the only way to ensure quality construction is to be on-site every day to follow the project, controlling every detail, the materials, their implementation, and being constantly involved.

BALANCING QUALITY AND DENSITY/INVOLVING STAKEHOLDERS

In this period of very rapid growth, the construction industry is one of the main driving forces of the local economy, and the role of local architects is restricted or completely stifled by the powerful interests in play. So the strategy of organizing a large number of project competitions, and inviting the best international firms to take part, not only helps expand the situation and the design culture by creating strongly expressive and artistic works, but also helps develop a new class of architects able to contrast or at least counterbalance economic interests with valid architectural results. In addition, increasing the focus on the result and the value of the project, at least for the more important works, has borne fruit, contributing towards building a new national image and identity able to provide a sense of affirmation and, naturally, a better quality of life.

EXAMPLE/INSPIRATION

The most important and significant architectural work is the project designed by Gherardo Bosio, a work of exceptional value and quality, constructed in only a few years and with an energy hard to replicate.

TOOLBOX ALBANIA FUTURE

Albania has enabled me to understand the value of Italian rationalism, which, at the beginning of the twentieth century, was able to create an original synthesis of classical and modern design in a kind of alternating style between tradition and innovation, past and future. This concept has always been present in our design procedure, and we try to apply it each time we approach a project in a new country.

Vertical and Horizontal

Project to develop a new identity for Albania between the vertical densification of the cities and the horizontal dimension of the coast

The great challenge facing Albania at this time consists of finding ways to achieve recognition of the cultural and environmental models that inspire its residential construction and urban design, reflecting the country's response to the impulse of transformation with an energy that has seen no equal in Europe. Fulfilling the powerful desire of the people to inhabit their homes and live freely in every portion of a country that was totally cloistered for decades requires clear vision and wisdom, to avoid the risks connected with madly rushing off in all directions, with the obvious probability of clashing.

The direction that we imagine does not permit half measures: Construction will have to be totally VERTICAL in the main cities of Tirana and Vlora, where the densification of the urban fabric makes the limitation of outward sprawl particularly urgent.
The answer to the lack of infrastructures will be to render the central portions pedestrian. In contrast, it will have to be completely HORIZONTAL along the coast and in the smaller towns, where the exceptions will perform the function of watchtowers, marking specific places and environments.
The landscapes currently under construction do not allow for any ambiguity and require the limitation of the "urban jam" which has destroyed entire portions of Europe.
The Albanians are in time to avoid the errors and environmental crimes committed by others.
In addition to the watchwords horizontal/vertical we would add another, which penetrates and underscores them like a steady base melody: CULTURAL IDENTITY. By this we mean the cultural identity of a country that is the acknowledged gateway to a strategic area for Europe: the Balkans. Every new project, every new transformation has to be interpreted as the opportunity for an explicit narrative of the genius loci, profoundly rooted and endowed with distinctive features in terms of images, colors, sounds, etc. On the basis of these peculiarities, to be defended and flaunted with pride, Albania can transform itself, interpreting construction as "art," as narrative, as a means of communication that says, loud and clear: "This is who we are, uniquely ourselves!"

The new national stadium of Albania in Tirana is more than just an architectural work made with a complex and uncommon (at least for Albania) engineering technology, and more than an example of the restoration and transformation of the previous stadium into a new, larger sports complex. It is also an opportunity to redevelop a strategic part of the city. In fact, for this project we planned and built a succession of areas around the new monument that respect it and enhance the image and role of a historically important district in Tirana's urban landscape. The area was conceived like a modern-day agora, the ancient Greek marketplace.

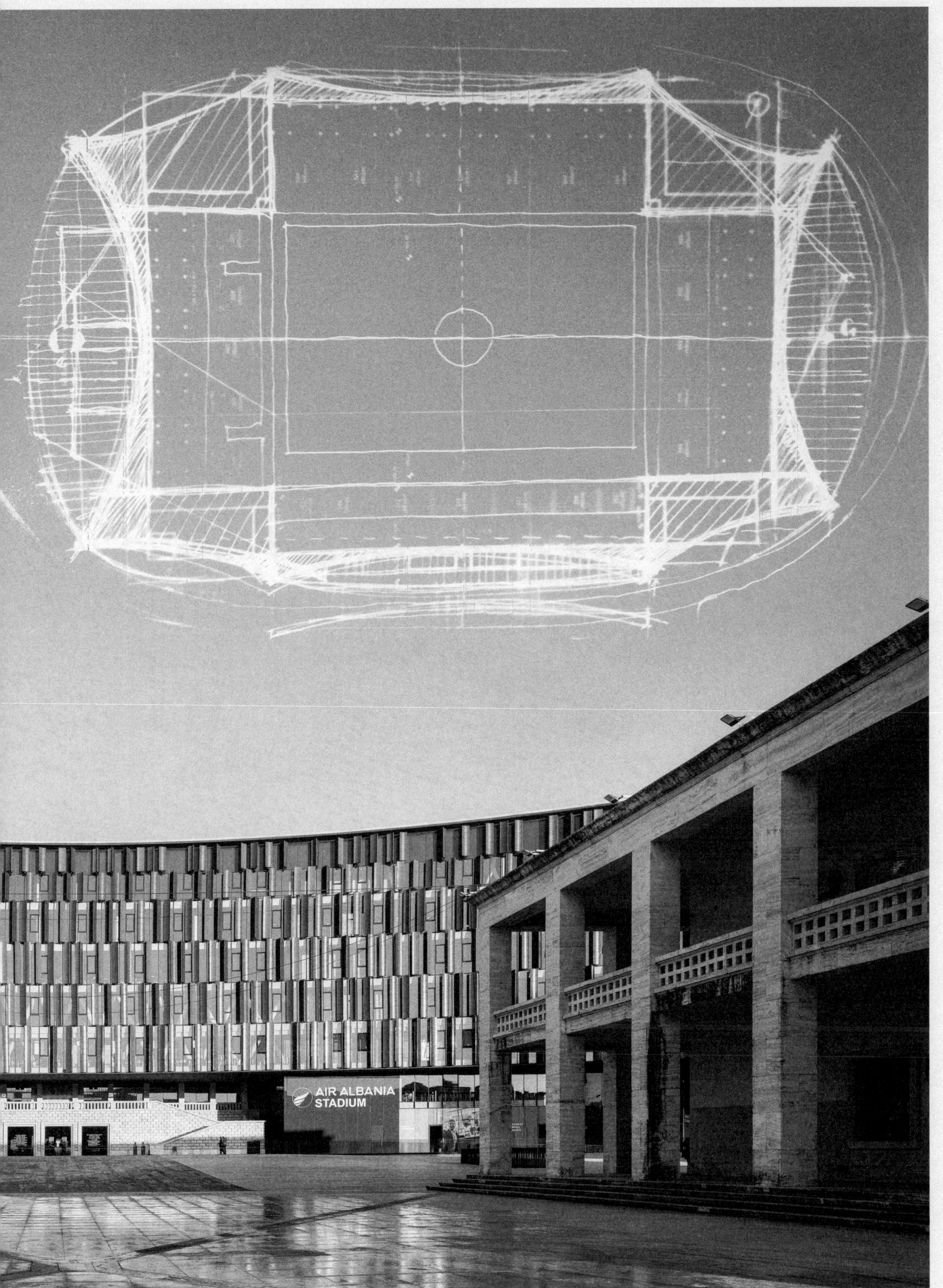
AIR ALBANIA
STADIUM

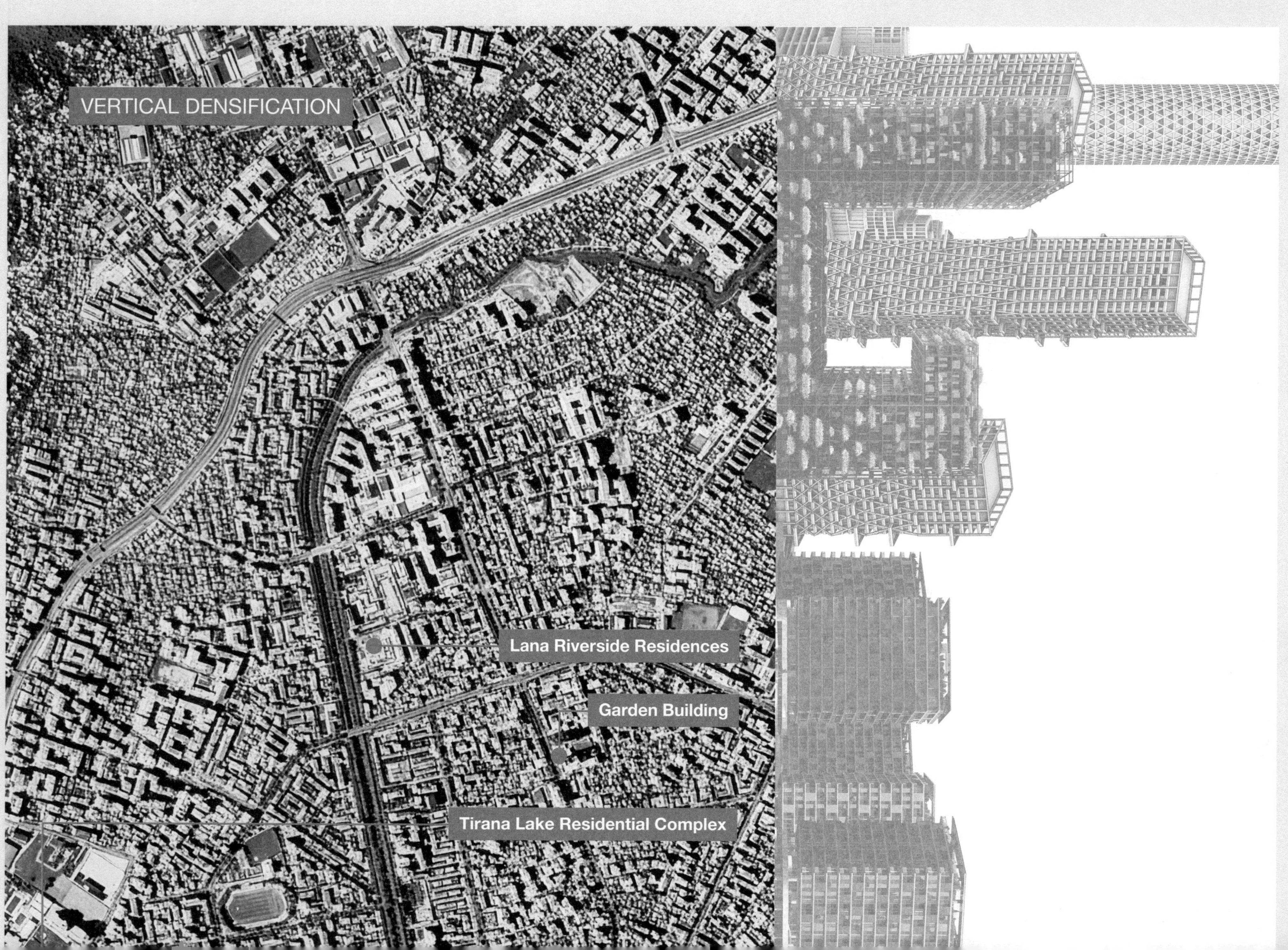
VERTICAL DENSIFICATION
Lana Riverside Residences
Garden Building
Tirana Lake Residential Complex

Rruga Brigada VIII
Stone Cube
Alban Tower
MAK Albania Hotel and Residences
Arena Kombëtare

Poro Valona, Albania

HORIZONTAL DIMENSION

ALBANIA'S IDENTITY

TIA – Tirana International Airport, Tirana

START	NAME PROJECT	LOCATION	DEVELOPER	PUBLIC/PRIVATE	PHASE
2004	Forever Green Tower (Alban Tower)	Tirana	AL & GI shpk	Private	Executed
2016	National Stadium of Albania	Tirana	AlbStar shpk	Public/private	Executed
2016	La Veliera, Covered public square	Durrës	Everest shpk & Inerti shpk	Public	Executed
2017	Garden Building, Residential complex	Tirana	Nova Construction Group	Private	Executed
2017	Stone Cube	Tirana	Nova Construction Group	Private	Under construction
2018	Park View Residence (Altana Luxury Residence)	Tirana	AlbStar shpk	Private	Executed
2019	University of Arts Tirana	Tirana	Albanian government	Public	Concept design
2019	MAK Albania Hotel and Residences	Tirana	Kastrati Group shpk	Private	Under construction
2020	Lana Riverside Residences	Tirana	Forever Construction shpk	Private	Under construction
2020	Tirana Lake Residential Complex	Tirana	Building Construction Invest	Private	Design development
2020	Dhërmi waterfront master plan	Dhërmi	Kumi Konstruksion shpk	Private	Schematic design
2022	Zvërnec master plan	Vlora	Kastrati Group shpk	Private	Concept design
2022	Poro Valona	Vlora	Natura Resort shpk	Private	Concept design
2022	Rruga Brigada VIII	Tirana	Forever Construction shpk	Private	Under construction
2022	Manhattan 1	Tirana	Forever Construction shpk	Private	Under construction
2022	Diamond Building	Tirana		Private	Schematic design
2023	Tirana Wind Tower	Tirana	Bregu shpk	Private	Design development
2023	Tirana New Boulevard	Tirana	Progeen shpk	Private	Design development
2023	Lago Secco	Tirana	Kumi Konstruksion shpk	Private	Design development
2023	Tres Hotel	Tirana	IBN shpk	Private	Design development
2023	Besa Museum	Tirana	Albanian government		Concept design
2023	Top Seven Tower	Tirana	Top Seven Construction shpk	Private	Design development
2024	West Hill Villas	Dhërmi	IMMO Invest shpk	Private	Design development
2024	Manchester City Football Academy	Durrës	Dyrrah City Football Academy	Public/private	Under construction
2024	Tirana International Airport	Tirana	Tirana International Airport shpk	Private	Under construction

NAME OFFICE

ARCHI-TECTONICS

DATE
March 7, 2025

PLACE
New York City, USA

WORKING IN ALBANIA SINCE
2024

PRINCIPALS
Winka Dubbeldam (Founder & Partner)
Justin Korhammer (Partner)

PROJECT TEAM

FESTIVAL CITY
Winka Dubbeldam
Justin Korhammer
Merrick Castillo
Stan Zhang
Santiago Herrera

MANGULL VILLAS
Winka Dubbeldam
Justin Korhammer
Stan Zhang
Santiago Herrera
Merrick Castillo
Telmen Bayasgalan

COLLABORATIONS

FESTIVAL CITY
Edil architects (Local Architect)
Burak Ogut (Structural Engineer)
Dirtworks NYC (Landscape Architect)

MANGULL VILLAS
SON Architects (Local Architect)
Dirtworks NYC (Landscape Architect)

INTRODUCTION TO ALBANIA

We were invited by the AIC (the Albanian Investment Corporation) to participate in the Invited Dual Property Competition in July 2024. We came to present the two projects in Tirana in September 2024.

MAIN CONTEXT VS. ALBANIA

We work all over Europe, the USA and China. We find that processes in general are very similar. The biggest difference is the requested speed of delivery and level of involvement in the overall design & development process. Which then results in a quality difference in the end results.

ORGANIZATION/GOAL/SETUP

We work intensively with the clients & local architects, who initially provide context, codes and regulations. Our goal is to create an architecture deeply inspired by the local (shapes, material, solidity) to design innovative projects for the future. We also are deeply invested in a climate-responsive way of building and optimizing and allowing nature to take over.

SETUP IN RELATION TO ALBANIAN PARTNER

We work completely integrated with the local offices from the start and are always in dialogue with them and the client. We see this as the most productive teamwork that can accelerate knowledge and creativity in an optimized manner.

OPPORTUNITIES/CHALLENGES

Albania has a great leader interested in culture, art and architecture, which leads to visionary, forward-looking projects. This is nowadays sadly very rare. It is a great honor to work with the prime minister's team and be included in a group of great colleagues to help build Albania as it develops over the years. For us as an office it is inspiring to see the Albanians so excited about their future, and to be able to share that with them is amazing.

HOW TO INTEGRATE GREATER RESPONSIBILITY FOR QUALITY IN PROJECTS

We hope that we are not only the "designers" of the projects but also remain involved in the construction document phase and site administration phase, as this is when the concept gets developed, and it is critical to see the concept evolve into the building details and façade development. As both master plans are quite large, our focus is to optimize the plan to its surroundings.

For example, in Festival City the height requirement was 12 stories for a 140,000-square-meter program. That meant we could only "carpet" the site with these blocks. We instead proposed to build higher along the road to the airport as a gate to the city and drastically taper down to the much smaller-scale residential neighborhood behind. That densification freed up a lot of land, which allowed for extensive green courtyards and a feeling of "living in the forest" in the middle of the city. The courtyards are also buffered from noise and provide playgrounds and terraces.

BALANCING QUALITY AND DENSITY/INVOLVING STAKEHOLDERS

This can only be stipulated in zoning rules. Or, as in Albania, by a visionary leader. We as architects assist in achieving that balance by analyzing the site conditions – like Festival City, as described above – and proposing solutions that can optimize both the urban and the inhabitant experience.

Similarly, for the Mangull master plan, the developer originally requested a very densely packed area of villas, which we managed to differentiate and open up by proposing a denser strip of town houses that freed up the site for more spacious layouts for the villas while also providing more public common green areas.

EXAMPLE/INSPIRATION

We were very inspired by the traditional Kula tower houses, with their solidity and angular features. The mountain settlements also have a great stacked density that is very inspiring for future thinking about reduction of natural resource use and a denser urban living model.

TOOLBOX ALBANIA FUTURE

Albania provides a rich history of urban and architectural examples, beautiful, often untouched natural landscapes and a palette of great natural materials. The challenge is to keep nature untouched while densifying and optimizing urban areas. Being part of the Albanian teams has been a great experience that we value and cherish. We learn as much from them as we hopefully give to them.

SYNTHETIC NATURE

Sponge City

Albania has a subtropical Mediterranean climate. Tirana, for example, has average temperatures ranging from 33°F to 90°F over the course of the year, and is rarely below 23°F or above 97°F. It is ranked among the wettest cities in Europe.

The absorption of rainwater is crucial for mitigating Albania's high risk of flooding and can make a big impact on the building's users and its surroundings.

LAPRAKË, TIRANA

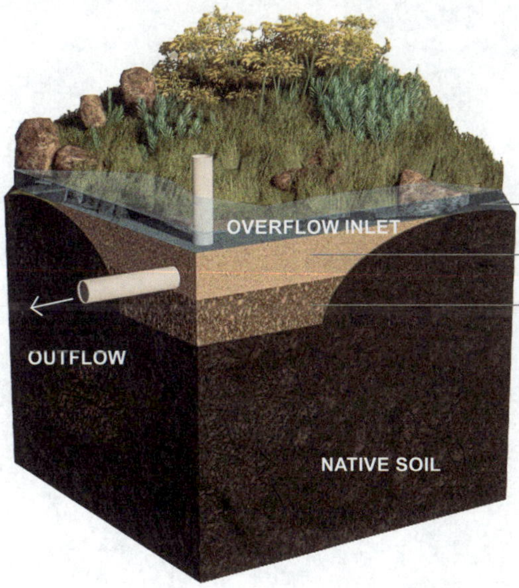

BIODIVERSITY
POND
OVERFLOW INLET
BIORETENTION SOIL
GRAVEL BED
OUTFLOW
NATIVE SOIL

BIOSWALE

NATURAL RESOURCES

Influenced by local architecture

Using local & natural materials

GREEN ROOFS

NATURE & ARCHITECTURE

LOCAL ARCHITECTURE

START	NAME PROJECT	LOCATION	DEVELOPER	M²	PROGRAM	PUBLIC/PRIVATE	PHASE
2024	Festival City	Tirana	Concord Development	180,000 m²	Mixed-use master plan with 3 towers, retail and residential with green courtyards	Public/private	Received zoning approval
2024	Mangull Villas	Mangull		28,000 m²	Residential master plan, with 54 villas, 36 duplex townhouses and a recreation building with common pool	Private	Permit phase
2025	Ali Visha Tower			19,500 m²	Residential & commercial on ground floor	Private	
2025	Alba Tower		Concord Group	21,190 m²	Residential & commercial on ground floor		

NAME OFFICE

ARQUITECTURA-G

DATE
June 2025

PLACE
Barcelona, Spain

WORKING IN ALBANIA SINCE
2022

PRINCIPALS
Jonathan Arnabat
Jordi Ayala-Bril
Aitor Fuentes
Igor Urdampilleta

PROJECT TEAM
Matteo Bassi
Maximo Bertoia
Jesús Jimenez
Andrea Muccioli
Siddartha Rodrigo
Martín Rojas
Elena Tarilonte
Almudena Tenorio

ALBANIAN PARTNERS

THE CORAL BUILDING
AB VIZION shpk and Darsi Construction shpk (Investors)
Ermir Hazizi (Local Architect)
2XKE-Studio (Structural Engineer)
Ing. Arjan Shyti (PF) (Electrical Engineer)
Meka-Pro shpk, Ing. Marsel Pylla, and
Ing. Shpresim Neçi (Hydromechanical Engineer)
Marsel Pylla (Private Fire Safety Expert)

RED CANYON
Arkitekti IM (Local Architect)

INTRODUCTION TO ALBANIA

We first got involved in Albania by partnering with BTA. After two years working in this modality, we received our first private commission in 2024.

MAIN CONTEXT VS. ALBANIA

We have extensive experience with small- and medium-scale projects across Europe and Asia, but in recent years, we've transitioned to larger-scale developments. Currently, approximately half of our projects are in Spain, with the rest distributed globally.

But more or less in every context we have worked in, we have had a relatable experience in terms of regulations and timings. While in Albania, the permissions process, for instance, is notably faster and less constrained by complex regulatory frameworks. Elsewhere, local regulations often make the journey from design to construction a long one – sometimes taking years. In Albania, it's far more fluid, with shorter timelines and fewer restrictions, which allows for a more intuitive and straightforward process.

On the construction side, we've noticed significant improvements. Not long ago, architects from abroad faced challenges due to limited local specialization in building techniques and materials. But this is changing quickly – construction companies are not only more reliable but also eager to learn and adapt. This shift has allowed us to maintain the integrity of our designs while adapting to the context.

ORGANIZATION/GOAL/SETUP

For now, most of our work is conducted from Spain, in partnership with local architects with whom we have permanent communication. Our team also makes regular site visits to ensure that we maintain oversight of the projects.

I guess our aim is to establish our participation in the Albanian context and to diversify the scope of our work to include a wider range of projects across the country. There's also a vibrant community of talented architects working in Albania right now, and we see exciting opportunities for collaboration, particularly on larger-scale projects and competitions.

SETUP IN RELATION TO ALBANIAN PARTNER

We retain full control over the design process, as this is central to our approach across all our projects, not only in Albania. The local office focuses on coordinating the permitting process and acting as the main contact with contractors during the construction phase.

We've been fortunate to work with a consistent team of local architects in Albania. Over time, we've developed a good rhythm and mutual understanding, which makes the process more efficient and aligned with our goals.

OPPORTUNITIES/CHALLENGES

Albania is in a moment of rapid development which presents unique opportunities, particularly in terms of scale and creative freedom. Promoters are very open to new approaches, and this creates a rich environment for exploration and experimentation. However, this freedom also brings significant responsibility. Architects play a pivotal role in shaping Albania's urban landscape.

HOW TO INTEGRATE GREATER RESPONSIBILITY FOR QUALITY IN PROJECTS

Even with the flexibility in regulations, there's a clear vision, coming from the prime minister, for Albania's architectural and urban development. This is reflected in the group of architects invited to work here, which has definitely had a positive impact on design standards.

The trust placed in architects by promoters, combined with the flexibility of the regulatory framework, has created an environment where high-quality design is not only encouraged but expected, and this has proven to be a very effective way of ensuring high quality across the different projects.

BALANCING QUALITY AND DENSITY/INVOLVING STAKEHOLDERS

We see this in line with what we mentioned earlier. There's been a sort of natural chain reaction in Albania, driven by the many examples of good architecture completed in recent years. These projects set a standard and, in a way, help educate both public institutions and the general population about what to expect from architecture.

While formal measures, like regulations, play a role in ensuring quality, they apply only to a specific and limited group. In contrast, when the public develops a shared awareness and appreciation of the qualities that make buildings and public spaces work, it influences everyone, which is ultimately a stronger driver for maintaining integrity and quality. In the first years of working here, it was common to encounter restrictions on projects that went too far from what people would normally expect. However, this has started to change.

EXAMPLE/INSPIRATION

The renovation of Skanderbeg Square done by 51N4E is a great and inaugural example of what is going on in Albania. A simple yet effective and interesting design. We think the role it has had in shaping Tirana's new face is clear, so in multiple ways it influences every new contribution to the city's urban landscape.

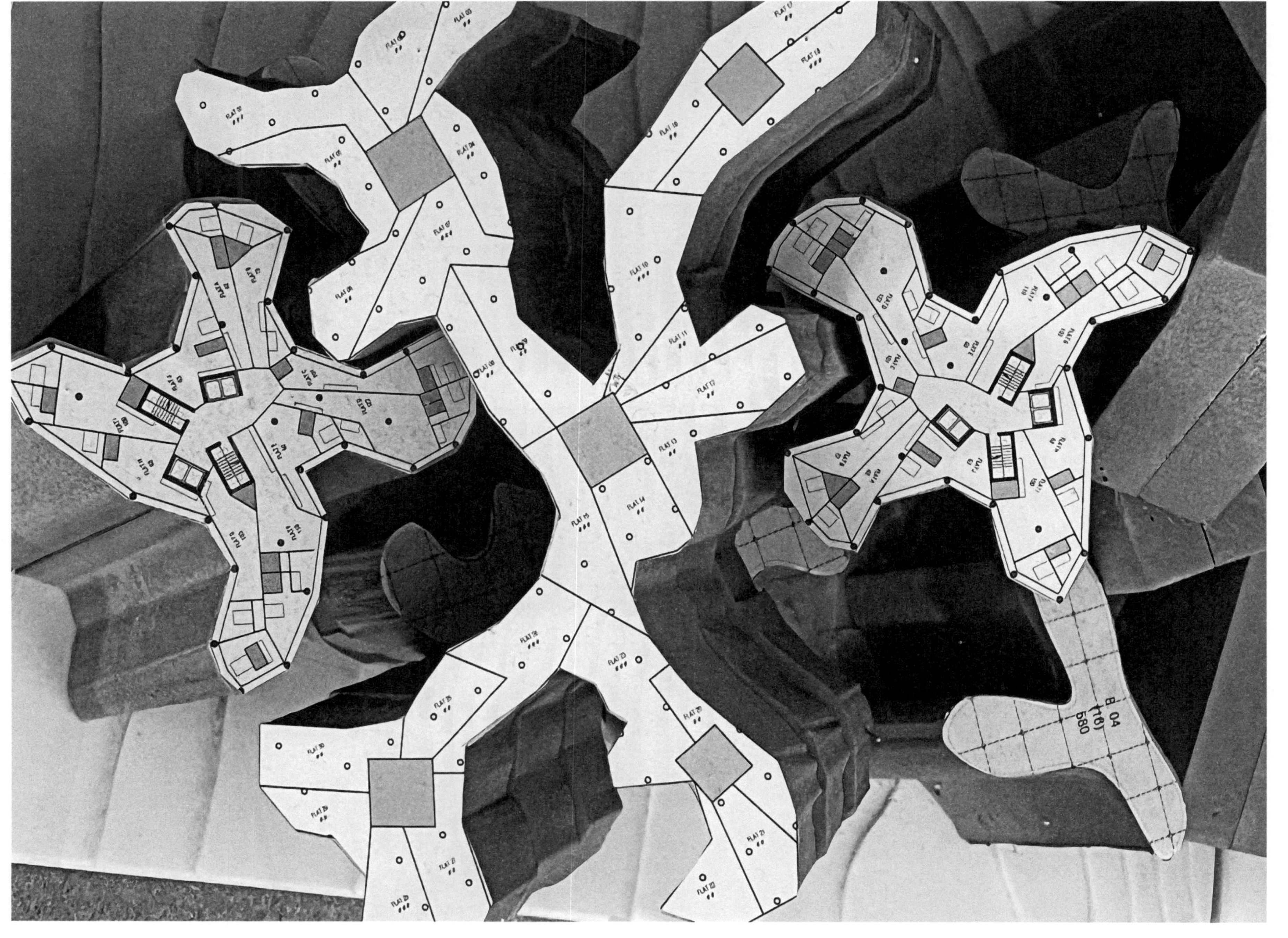
B 04
(16)
580

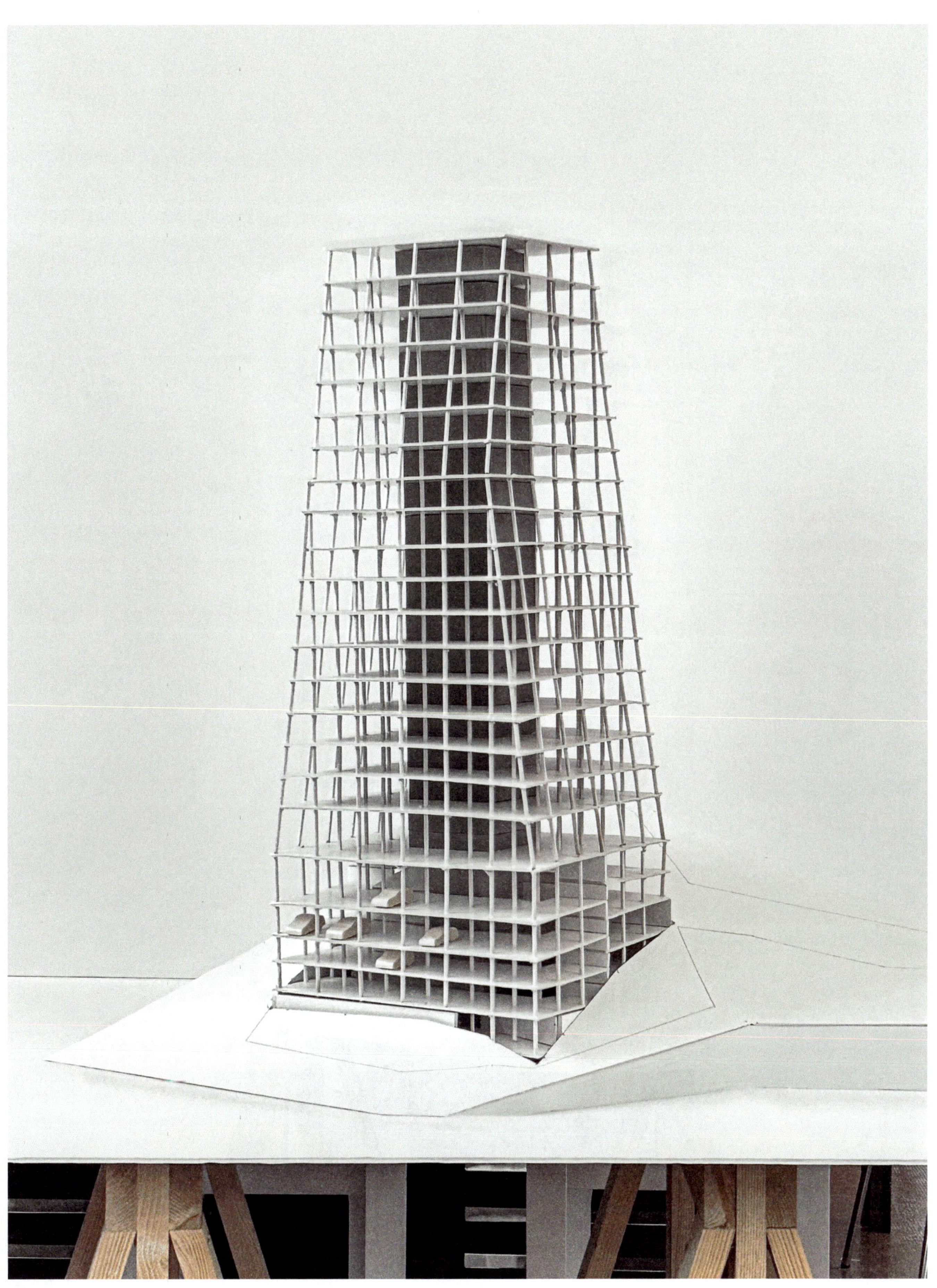

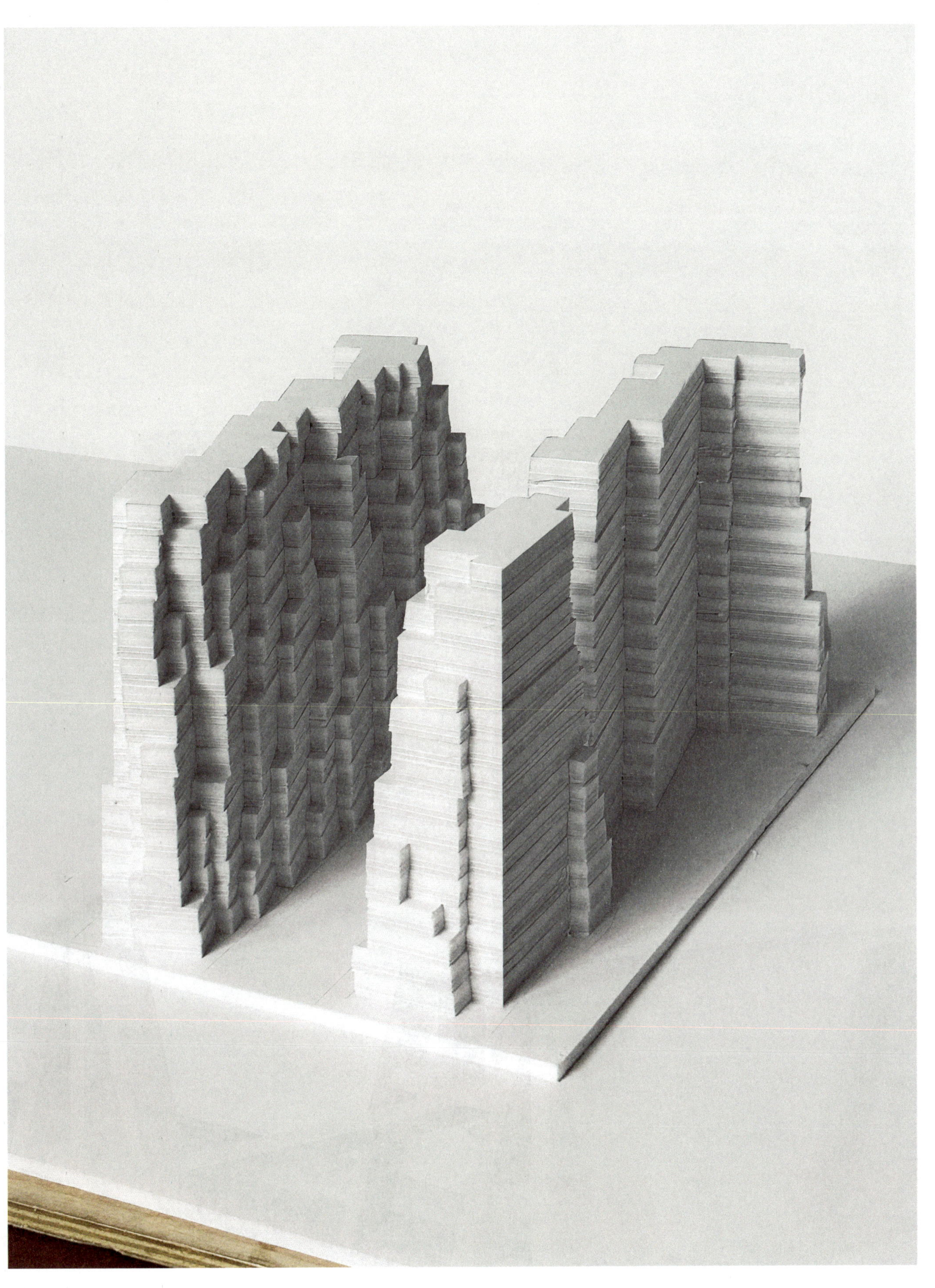

LIST OF PROJECTS

START	NAME PROJECT	LOCATION	DEVELOPER	ALBANIAN PARTNER	M²	PUBLIC/PRIVATE	PHASE
2022	Long Hill Residence*	Tirana		Ne Arkitektët	107,900 m²	Private	Under construction
2022	UET Campus*	Tirana	European University of Tirana	Ne Arkitektët	15,900 m²	Public	Under construction
2024	Liqeni i Thatë Building	Tirana	AS Investment		14,800 m²	Private	Permit phase
2024	The Coral Building	Tirana	AB Vizion, Darsi Construction	Studio Ev.	40,000 m²	Private	Under construction
2025	Red Canyon		Rokli Construction	Arkitekti IM	37,400 m²	Private	Permit phase

* Project in partnership with Bofill Taller de Arquitectura.

NAME OFFICE

AVNER YASHAR ARCHITECTS

DATE
September 2025

PLACE
Tel Aviv, Israel

WORKING IN ALBANIA SINCE
2024

PRINCIPALS
Avner Yashar (Owner)
Yoni Groswasser (Senior Partner)
Adi Iny Yashar (Partner)
Thai Yashar (Partner)
Assaf Ruder (Associate)

PROJECT TEAM
Assaf Ruder (Associate)
Adi Zanzuri (Team Leader)
Aviya Sondhelm (Team Leader)
Yotam Bekowitz (Team Leader)
Mor Avitan (Architect)
Yanir Schneiderman (Architect)
Allan Chor (Architect)
Galit Turgeman (Architect)
Noa Barda (Architect)
Hadar Batito (Architect)
Rotem Cohen (Architect)

ALBANIAN PARTNERS

THE WALL, ASTIR, MEDIA CITY
Anchor Investments (Developer)
CAD – CreativA Architectural Design,
Stela Lako, Gentian Stratoberdha, Atena Gjoka, Enirjada Rizaj, Leonida Duka, Kid Kongjoni, Aleksandra Beqiri, Rea Hiso, Enkelejda Prifti, Marsela Elezi, Nensi Hila, Arba Rrushi, Laura Ibrahimaj (Architect)

TEG
INDRIT shpk (Developer)
SON Architects,
Enkela Salku, Ilir Bejleri, Klodi Demaj (Architect)

SELIT
ANK Architecture,
Albana Koçollari, Arnest Qafa, Albjona Elezi, Orges Malaj (Architect)
ANK Architecture,
Dhimitri Papa, Armeta Gramos (Engineer)
Pajtoni Group (Developer)
Korrekt Konstruksion (Developer)
Kron Construction shpk (Developer/Contractor)
Alson Braho (Consulting Architect)
Mirjan Malaj (Administrator)

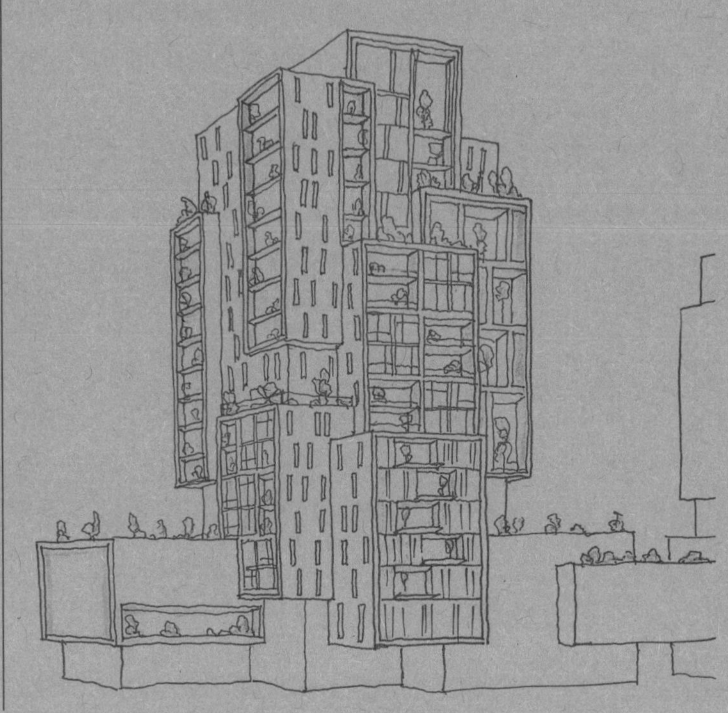

INTRODUCTION TO ALBANIA

Our love story with Albania began in 2023, when we participated in a competition to design a Marina City in the south of the country.

We had an intuition that Albania was a place that encouraged old ideas to be rethought and reinvented, so we approached this project in a way that broke from our usual design process. We brought together thirty architects from different teams across our firm and held a three-day research and design workshop, exploring Albanian culture and design ideas that could meaningfully connect with it.

What began with one proposal has expanded into multiple projects in various stages of development, and we're excited to continue contributing to Albania's architectural landscape.

MAIN CONTEXT VS. ALBANIA

Our work is mainly based in Tel Aviv and across Israel, where high density and a small territory place most projects in compact urban settings. We are known for mixed-use high-rise developments.

Our first project in Tirana confronted a radically different context. Located on the hills outside the city, it required a sensitive response to landscape and topography. We imagined architecture that felt already present: forms emerging from the ground like trees, allowing dense living within nature. The original design took the shape of flower bracts, with apartments as "petals," each with balconies and vertical gardens, appearing as green structures embedded in the forest. After height restrictions, the project evolved into The Wall – not a barrier, but a protective, collective form, conceived like a lava-formed rock in which homes and gathering spaces are carved, as if part of the land for centuries.

ORGANIZATION/GOAL/SETUP

We're in the process of establishing a local architecture studio in Tirana that will oversee all our ongoing and future projects in Albania, from concept to execution, ensuring a seamless process and exceptional results. Our goal is to create a long-term presence, not just as external collaborators but as an integral part of the architectural landscape. We aim to build deeper relationships and deliver projects that are rooted in the culture and environment of the region.

SETUP IN RELATION TO LOCAL OFFICE

Our work in Tirana is different from our previous projects in Europe and Asia. This stems from the current Albanian approach to design and construction quality. For our projects in Tirana, we were required to sign agreements that commit us to remaining involved throughout all phases, right up until completion. This setup aligns with our philosophy of maintaining a high standard of quality and ensuring that our vision is realized as intended.

OPPORTUNITIES/CHALLENGES

Albania is a land brimming with opportunities for architects. As a rising economy with a population eager to build a better future, it stands out in a continent that, in some ways, may have lost its drive for innovation. In this sense, Albania has become the flower of Europe, offering fertile ground for ambitious and forward-thinking architecture.

One of the key factors contributing to this environment is the involvement and commitment of the PM and the government in shaping the projects being developed. This level of engagement creates a unique balance between the economic incentive to maximize square footage and urban needs that call for thoughtful, high-quality design.

The challenges lie in maintaining this balance while navigating a rapidly evolving market. However, with the right partnerships and a shared vision, these challenges can become opportunities to create projects that not only meet economic demands but also elevate the urban fabric and cultural identity of Albania.

HOW TO INTEGRATE GREATER RESPONSIBILITY FOR QUALITY IN PROJECTS

The first step is ensuring that architects remain involved throughout all project phases, from design to completion. This continuity allows for consistent oversight, ensuring that the quality of construction aligns with the original design intent.

Additionally, implementing a system of quality assurance criteria within the permitting and approval processes could be transformative. Tying construction approval to meeting predefined quality benchmarks would help ensure that the built results adhere to both the required standards and the architectural vision.

Together, these steps would create a framework where quality becomes a shared responsibility and is a fundamental part of every project.

BALANCING QUALITY AND DENSITY/INVOLVING STAKEHOLDERS

I believe density can enhance the quality of life in cities. Some of the greatest cities in the world – Paris, New York and London – are incredibly dense, yet they thrive because of how they've integrated design, infrastructure and urban life.

The key to achieving quality in density lies in thoughtfully mixing uses and programs within city blocks and neighborhoods. This means integrating residential, commercial and public spaces alongside robust public transportation systems and amenities like proper sidewalks, bicycle lanes and parks.

Ultimately, the responsibility for ensuring quality in dense environments isn't just on architects. Municipalities play a central role through the urban master plans they develop and the standards they enforce on private developers. By collaborating closely with these stakeholders, architects can help shape environments where density and quality coexist harmoniously, improving urban life for everyone.

EXAMPLE/INSPIRATION

Tirana Tower by Oppenheim sets an example of how great architecture is influenced and provoked by local traditions, materiality and textures. Being a single high-rise tower in the midst of an older low-rise neighborhood, it had the potential to be alien to its surroundings. Instead, it seems to be naturally growing from the city. From afar, its rust color, triangular pattern and different layers of transparency make it look natural in front of the mountainous background.

Albanian patterns

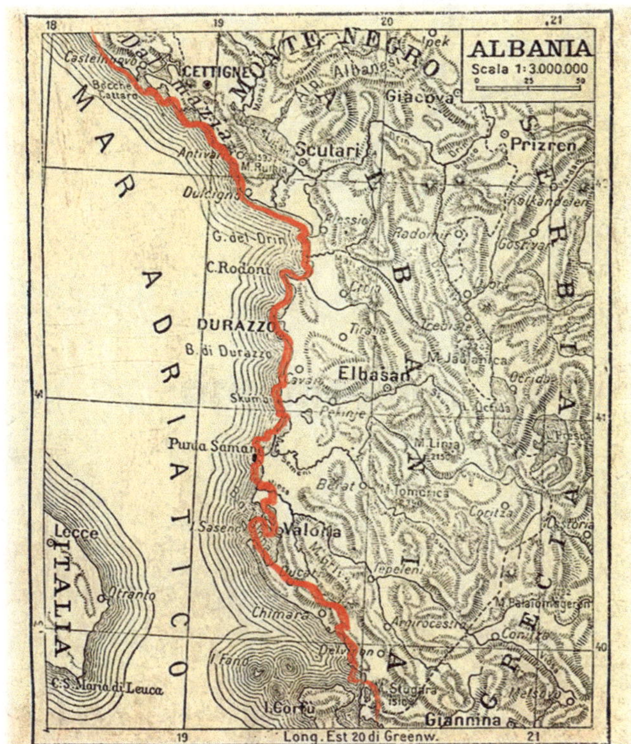

Map of Albania

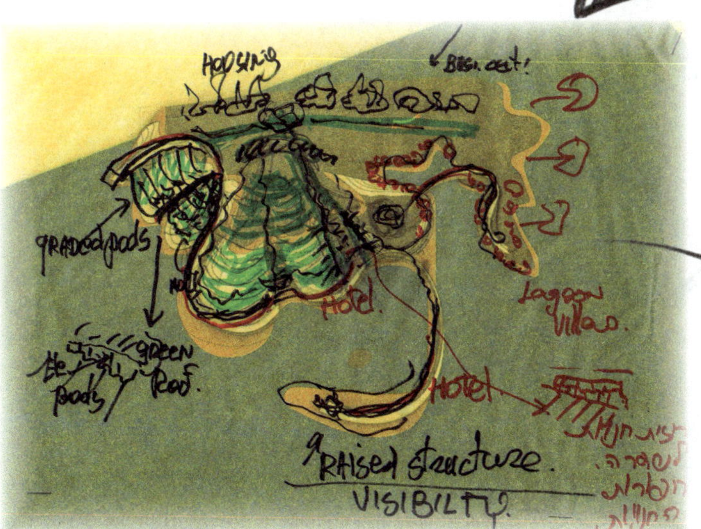

Site plan

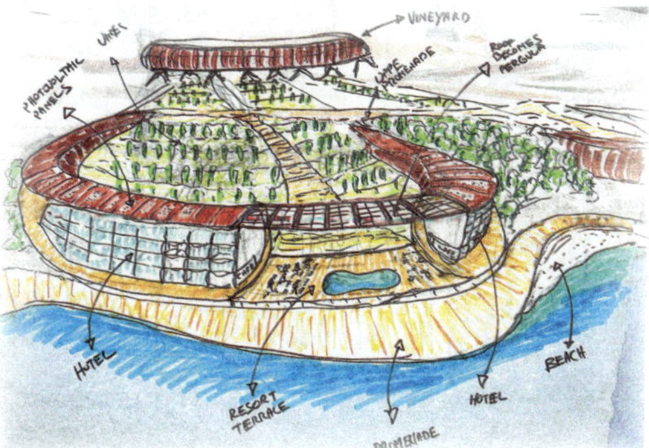

Perspective

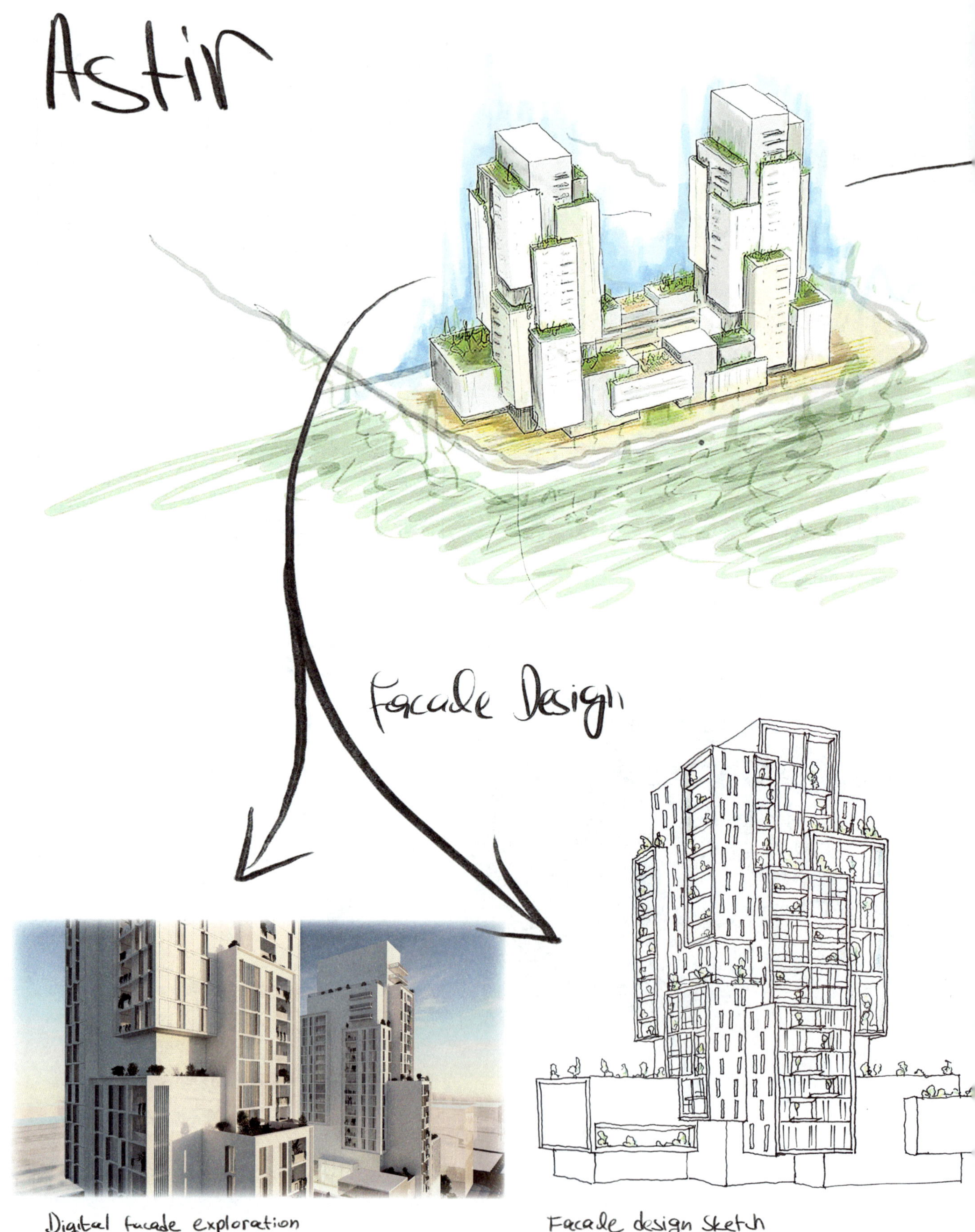

Digital facade exploration

Facade design sketch

Physical Model

Elevation

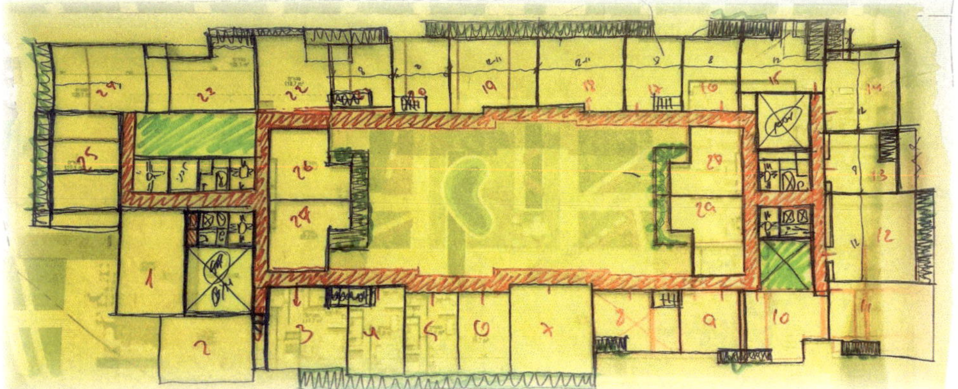

Plan

Circle One

Bryce Canyon

From Inspiration

to sketch

Initial sketch

then Massing

Physical model

& Site Plan

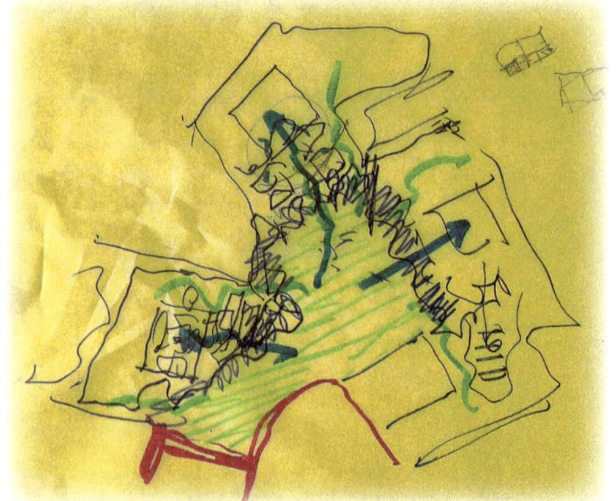
Site plan

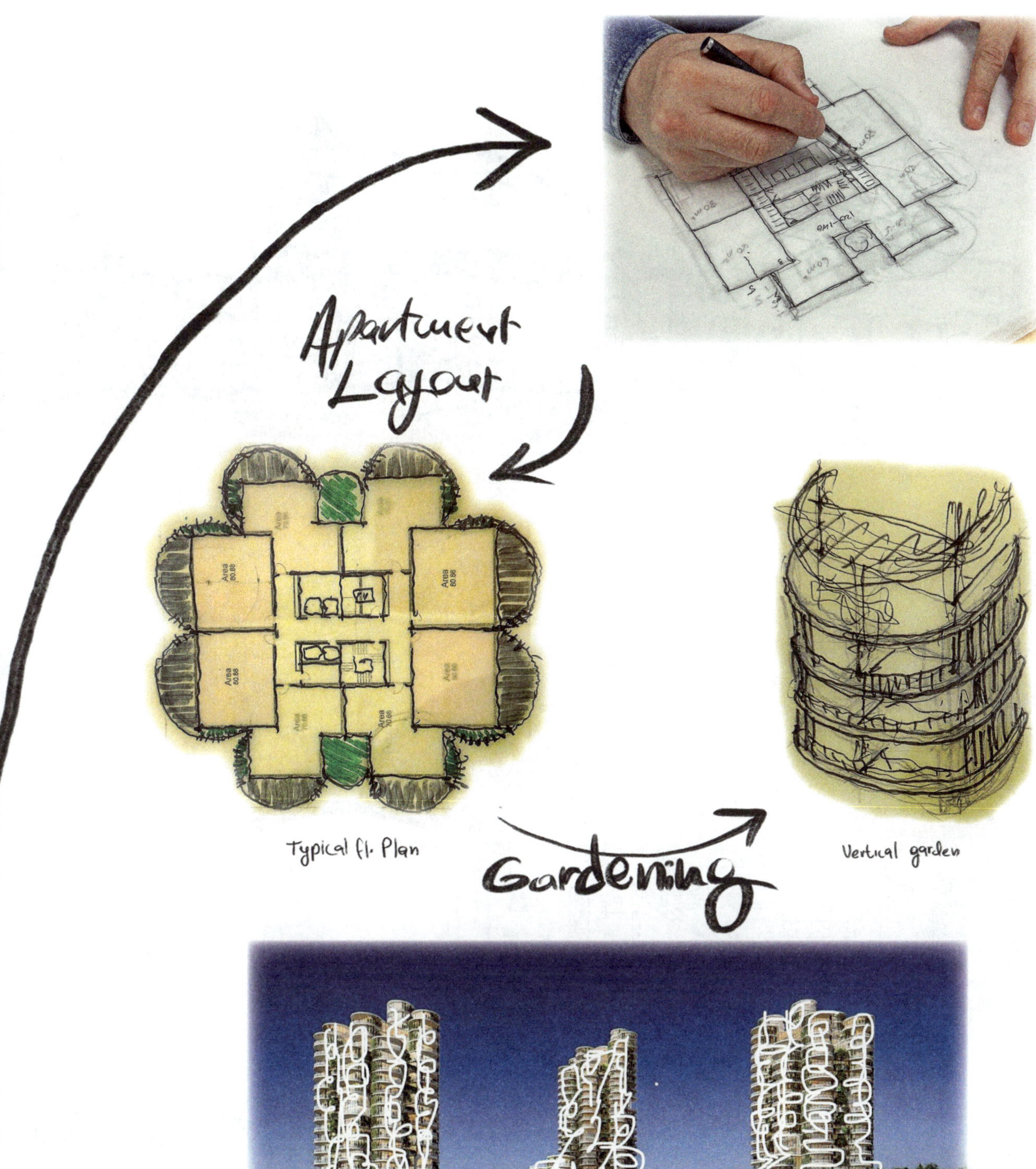

"this is the music coming out of the project"

Sketch and quote by PM Edi Rama

Initial sketch of the design development

Lower Facade

Below

The WALL

Upper Facade

Elevation

The WALL as an active circulation Element

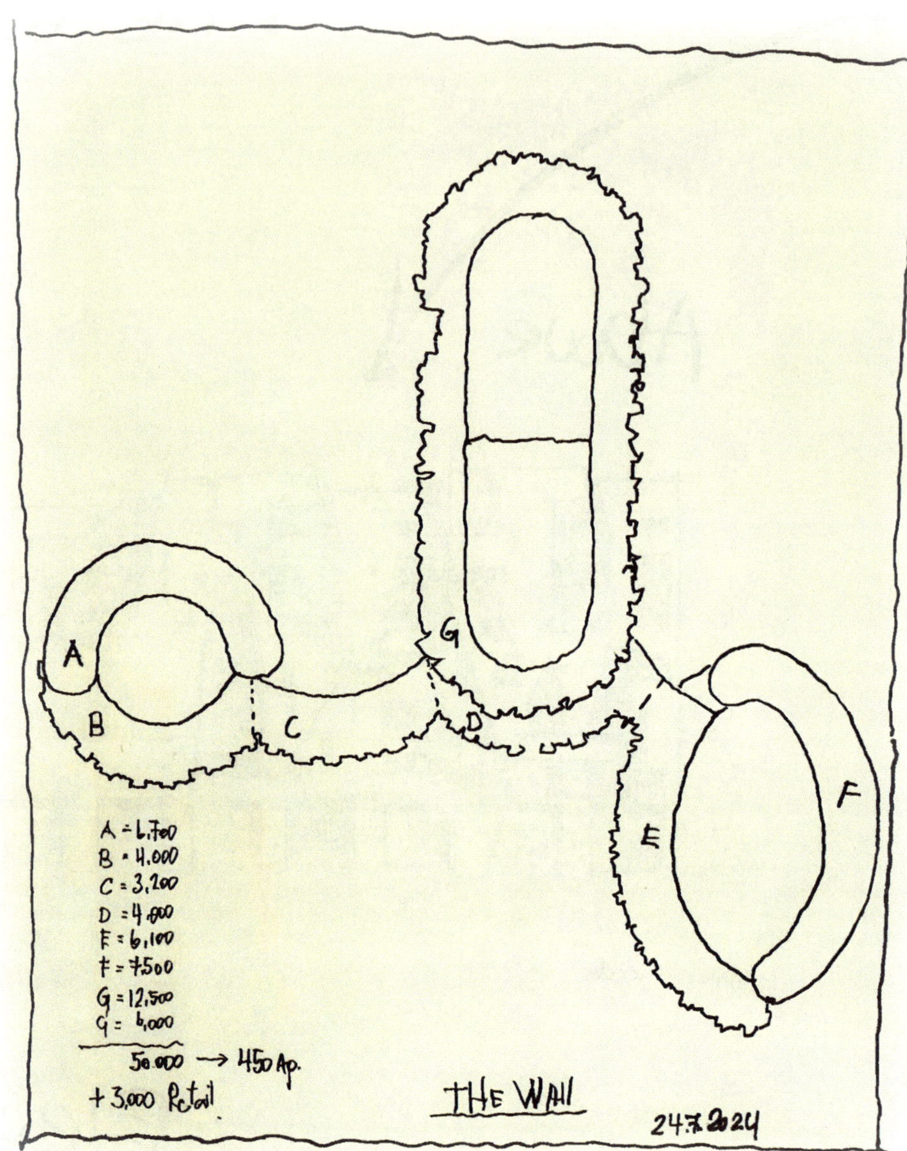

Site plan

Project render

LIST OF PROJECTS

START	NAME PROJECT	LOCATION	DEVELOPER	PROGRAM	PUBLIC/PRIVATE	PHASE
2024	The Wall	Tirana	Anchor Investments	Residential, commercial, medical facility	Private	Permit phase
2024	Astir	Tirana	Anchor Investments	Residential, commercial, medical facility	Private	Permit phase
2024	Media City	Tirana	Anchor Investments	Residential, commercial, medical facility	Private	Design development
2025	TEG	Tirana	INDRIT shpk	Residential, commercial, medical facility	Private	Permit phase
2025	Selit	Tirana	Anchor Investments	Residential, commercial, medical facility	Private	Design development

NAME OFFICE

BAROZZI VEIGA

DATE	PLACE	WORKING IN ALBANIA SINCE
2025	Barcelona, Spain	2024

PRINCIPALS

Fabrizio Barozzi
Alberto Veiga

PROJECT TEAM

Andrea Bergamini
Paola Calcavecchia
Chen-Hsin Chang
Francesco Crocchini
Caterina Delaini
Martin De Pablo Esteban
Marta Grządziel
Alicia Hernanz
Pieter Janssens
Cristina Lopez
Eduardo Lopez
Claudio Triassi
Diletta Trinari
Verena Recla
Eduard Resina
Cecilia Rueda
Maria Ubach
Cristina Vergara
Siyuan Xi
Xianjun Zhou

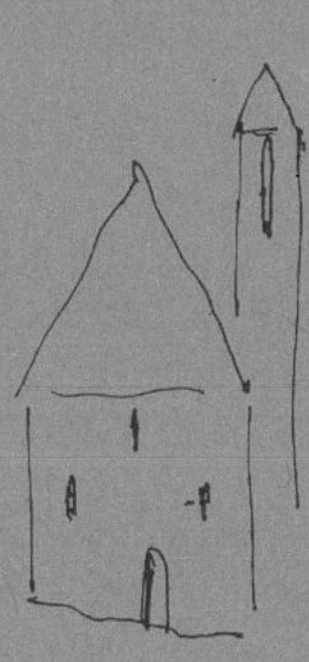

MAIN CONTEXT VS. ALBANIA

We work internationally, with the majority of our projects currently underway in Europe and the United States. Each country has its own regulations that impact both the design and the construction of architecture. While we have not yet gained sufficient experience within the Albanian context to fully describe its specific differences and similarities, we perceive a certain freedom that could allow the possibility of working in an experimental way, in terms of both typology and construction. We believe that the dynamic environment of the country presents an exciting opportunity to create unique architecture.

ORGANIZATION/GOAL/SETUP

We are still at the beginning of our journey in Albania, and our team currently consists of ourselves, our local architect and the client.

SETUP IN RELATION TO LOCAL OFFICE

Years of collaboration with diverse teams of professionals have provided us with a comprehensive understanding of the critical elements involved in developing a project abroad. We believe that to accurately identify and address the true needs of a project, it is essential to establish an active, collaborative dialogue with all stakeholders. Our approach to project development prioritizes maintaining this dialogue and involvement throughout all phases, from concept to construction.

OPPORTUNITIES/CHALLENGES

The freedom we mentioned earlier is, on one hand, exciting; on the other hand, the combination of freedom with time pressure can turn it into a risk. Places and transformations require reflection and time to develop naturally. Finding the balance between control and allowing things to unfold is one of the key challenges. Furthermore, Albania offers many opportunities, particularly due to its beautiful natural landscapes, which have become one of the country's most valuable assets. Our challenge lies in understanding what truly needs to be built and what doesn't, while proposing a respectful intervention that provides architectural value and preserves the stunning existing land.

HOW TO INTEGRATE GREATER RESPONSIBILITY FOR QUALITY IN PROJECTS

An architectural project has a long lifespan, and in this context it is crucial to approach it with a broader vision that not only considers the present but also operates with comprehensive planning.

How to approach the development of the country, addressing not just individual site-specific issues solved by proper buildings but the bigger picture, is essential for uniform and solid growth. Moreover, an architectural project is not simply about constructing a building and assigning a function. The moment something is built – whether it is a private or public project – it begins to belong to the collective. It is important to share this perspective as a common vision for Albania.

BALANCING QUALITY AND DENSITY/INVOLVING STAKEHOLDERS

As architects, we have a responsibility to observe the site, understand it, explore its potential, and to communicate these insights to our clients and the relevant authorities to establish dialogues. Cultural activities, such as the making of this book, play an important role in sharing these reflections.

EXAMPLE/INSPIRATION

Unfortunately, we have not yet gained enough experience to fully understand or explore, not only through publications but also through firsthand experience, many of the projects built in Albania. Nevertheless, we hope to have the opportunity to do so soon during our trips to Vlora.

Exploring Albania

Hereafter we propose a series of analogies for the future.
Albania today is a promising European country capable of creating opportunities for growth and capturing the attention of an increasing number of visitors attracted by the unspoiled landscape and local culture.
As has often been the case in the world, rapid growth, tourism and a strong desire for the future bring with them an architectural development which sometimes disregards the native characteristics of the place.
Through a series of analogies with our way of working, specific values of Albania are highlighted, making some key concepts explicit as possible references and guidelines for sustainable and specific growth in continuity with the country's identity.

Locus

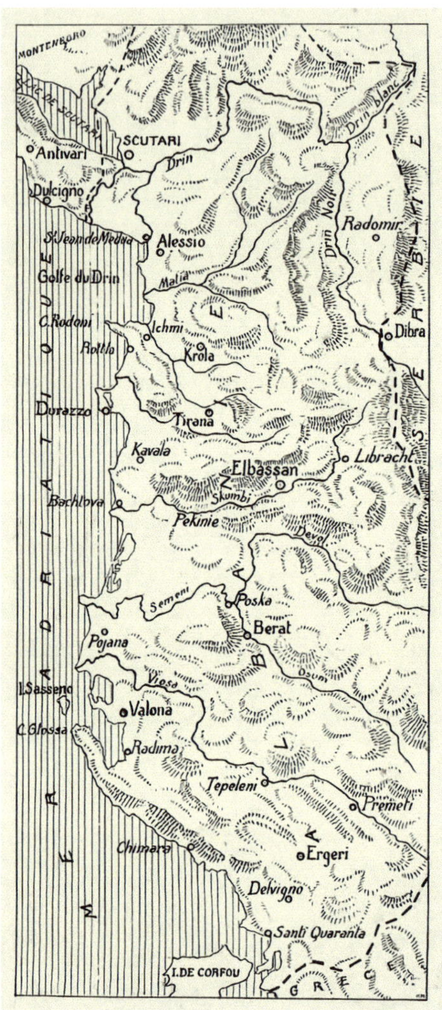

What exists, or, in a broader sense, reality, is always the point of departure for our work.
Our designs are singularizations of their surroundings;
they originate from the interpretation of a physical, imaginary or sensorial reality
that we draw out and intensify.
We consider that the notion of context continues to hold value.
All preexisting elements, whether they are ruins or geography, hold the same significance.
They define a reality upon which to construct a design that helps change and
transform things, revealing unexpected scenarios.
Through the exploration of the existing landscape of Albania, of the dialogue between
coasts and mountains, we aim to reveal the unsuspected and the unexpected.

Tone

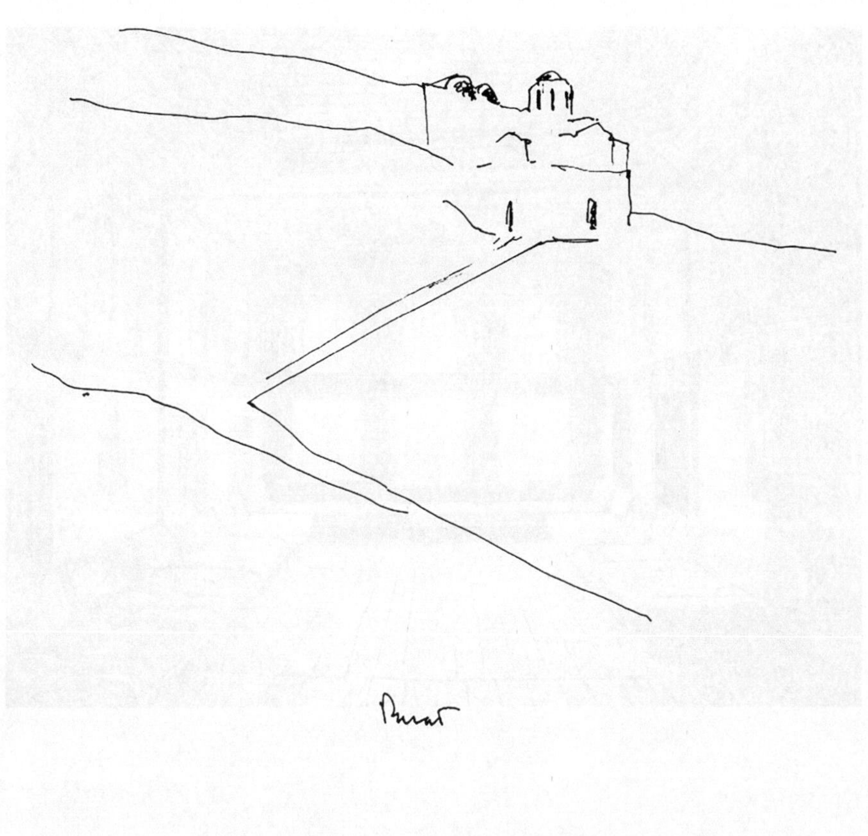

In painting, *tonalism* refers to a quality in artworks where fusion between the subject and its surroundings is achieved by using scumbling techniques to create a misty veil effect. Likewise, in architecture we understand this concept as a mechanism for relating buildings to their landscape, just as the Holy Trinity Church relates to its surroundings in Berat. We imagine the context as a painting by Giorgione or Titian, striving to define architectures without definite outlines, capable of generating a unitary composition modulated by ambient light intensity. We work with a fascination inspired in us by the discovery, through these values and via architecture, of the nonliteral meanings of a given setting.

Memory

Associating the term *memory* with contemporary architectural thinking might seem to be out of place. However, many of our works spring from a recollection, from a reencounter with a memory of a situation or a space. From that point on, we begin to reveal a new situation, a new reality and a new design project, in continuity with our initial perceptions. For us, working with memory means feeling like part of history, part of a tradition that is continuously evolving. The memory of the *oda* – a large room in Albanian traditional housing typology for receiving and entertaining guests, where much culture has been transmitted orally for generations – inspires us to redefine contemporary spaces for sharing culture.

Public

A common theme in our work is the construction of public space.
The urban sphere always takes center stage in our architecture,
which takes its shape from that realm in order to become its framework
and a backdrop for public life.
We understand public space as the cornerstone of all civic architecture.
It is the element that gives it its sense and meaning.
Albania's climate and culture allow public space to be the binding element
between the increasingly rich constellation of architecture elements
that characterize its territory, with the potential of affirming and
consolidating the identities of the place and of the people who live in it.

Tradition

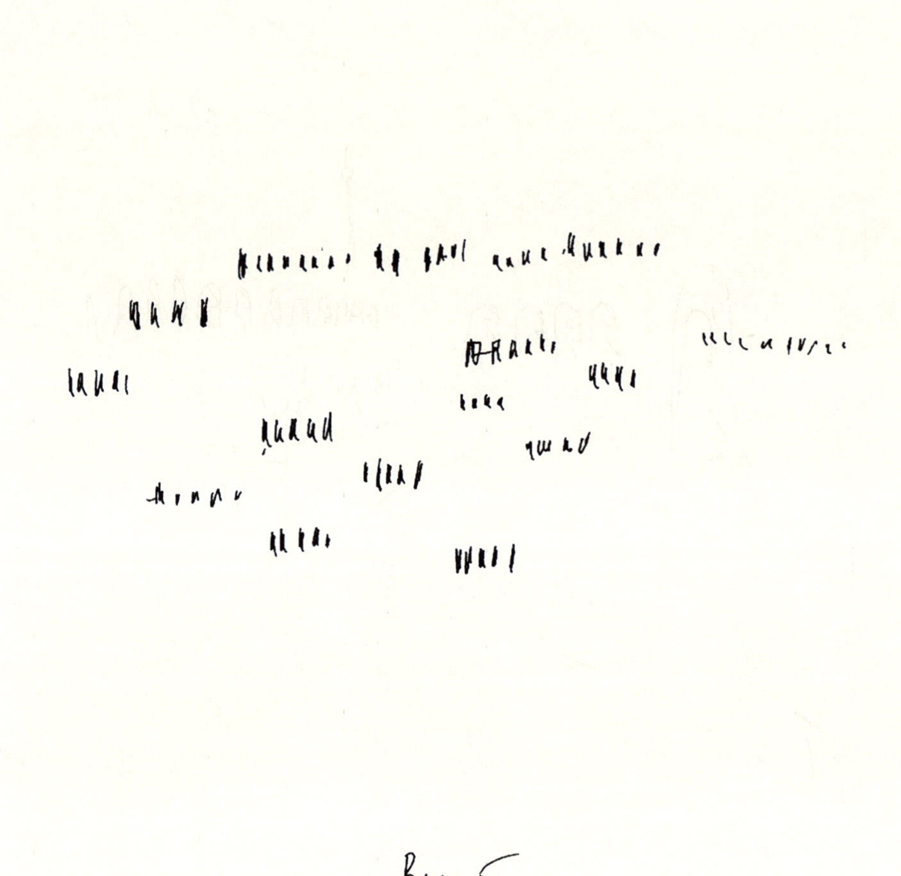

Processes of change have always been either a continuation or a negation of a tradition, all within a system of relationships and influences of a mainly local nature. However, nowadays we work within a context where globalization has fragmented and atomized this set of relationships and thus these influencing factors. This new sphere of action allows and legitimizes experimentation regarding which tradition should be "chosen" and given continuity, thus enhancing its diversity, its uniqueness and its richness. Traditions can be read through the architecture of a place and/or through the local crafts and customs, which are not separate things, but rather the result of a specific way of thinking.

Specific

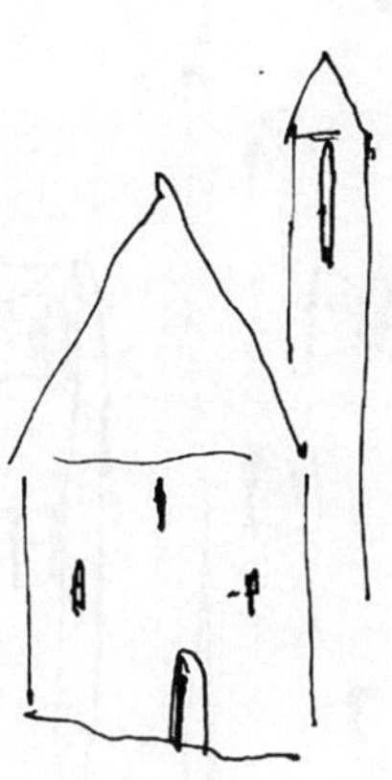

From our very beginnings as a studio, the notion of specificity has been central to our reflections. Specificity is understood as that which is capable of inextricably associating a certain atmosphere with a certain architecture. This is what we can read in the Roman Catholic church at Fushë-Theth.

Following the path of the specific gives us distance from the generic, which we believe has standardized and stagnated current architectural thinking.

Seeking what is specific in architecture means reviving the uniqueness of things, reencountering and preserving the diversity and culture of each place. This is the key to bringing together what starts out as an autonomous approach – the defining idea behind a design project – with the contingencies and the tangible reality of a place.

Artifice

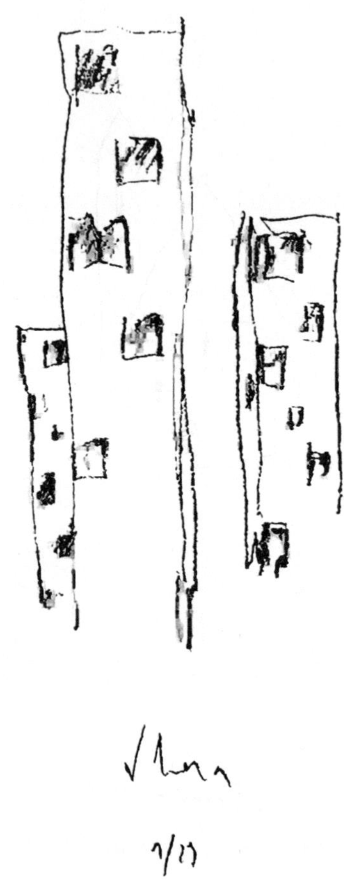

All architecture stands in opposition to nature. Architecture is the construction of an artifice that inhabits the world and makes it a livable place.
The Vlora natural coast profile does not ask for extensive, land-consuming intervention. How can we provide residential spaces without having an improper impact on what exists?
Our proposal for a project in Vlora investigates the possibilities of working on the residential typology to create a new artificial landscape.
We strongly believe that architecture fundamentally has to aspire not only to construct an object, but also to thoughtfully create a meaningful place.
This design reveals the mechanism that simultaneously enhances architecture and nature: the contrast between the artificial character of the former and the organic traits of the latter.

START	NAME PROJECT	LOCATION	PUBLIC/PRIVATE	PHASE
2024	Residential project	Vlora	Private	Concept

NAME OFFICE

BAUKUH

DATE
January 28, 2025

PLACE
Milan, Italy

WORKING IN ALBANIA SINCE
2004

PRINCIPALS
Paolo Carpi
Vittorio Pizzigoni
Giacomo Summa
Pier Paolo Tamburelli
Andrea Zanderigo

PROJECT TEAM
Lorenzo De Pascale
Alessandra Paparcone

COLLABORATORS

CITY CENTER DEVELOPMENT, KORÇA
Favero & Milan
YellowOffice

METROPOLITAN STRATEGY, DURANA
List
Space Caviar
Abkons

RENOVATION TIRANA STUDENT CITY
F&M Ingegneria
List
Bodà
Abkons
Space Caviar

CITY HALL, TIRANA
Johnston Marklee
YellowOffice
Bollinger+Grohmann
Abkons
Matilde Cassani

EXPO ALBANIA
l'AUC
dUCKS scéno
Bollinger+Grohmann
Studio Mathieu Lucas
Studio Raphael Hefti
UDV Architects
Adriatica RC
atmos lab

ROZAFA HOTEL TOWER
l'AUC
Bollinger+Grohmann
Studio Mathieu Lucas
UDV Architects
atmos lab

LIFT TOWER
Sam Chermayeff Office
Muoto
YellowOffice
atmos lab
Arkimade
Simon Boudvin
Bollinger+Grohmann

CIVIC LAND CENTER
Sam Chermayeff Office
Muoto
YellowOffice
atmos lab
Arkimade
Simon Boudvin
Bollinger+Grohmann

SELMAN STËRMASI STADIUM
OFFICE Kersten Geers David Van Severen
ARQUITECTURA-G
YellowOffice
Ne Arkitektët
Bollinger+Grohmann

INTRODUCTION TO ALBANIA

One of the partners, Pier Paolo Tamburelli, was introduced to Albania as a student of the Berlage Institute, via Elia Zenghelis's studio on Albania.

MAIN CONTEXT VS. ALBANIA

baukuh has been working in many different contexts, ranging from Italy and other European countries to North Africa and the Middle East. Each context is specific, while also sharing many similarities with other contexts. It's difficult to generalize the main characteristics of one context compared to another, because even inside a given context there might be so many differences in the building processes, according to the specific occasion. Nevertheless, it is somehow true that in Albania there is a sense of lightness permeating the building process, which is very refreshing and simultaneously a bit scary. Everything is fast, compared to the slow steady speed of processes elsewhere; if it's not fast, it does not happen.

ORGANIZATION/GOAL/SETUP

Albania is close to Italy, just a narrow and shallow sea dividing them. As such, when needed, we simply travel there often, or remain there for longer, in order to get things done. We have gotten to know many people there over the years, so it's relatively easy to find the right persons to get help from. At the same time, it is true that so far we have never had the opportunity to really control a building site, so we never felt the need to establish a long-term partnership or to set up an office over there.

SETUP IN RELATION TO ALBANIAN PARTNER

The general attitude in the office is to share, when the possibility arises. We are ideologically more inclined to this setup.

OPPORTUNITIES/CHALLENGES

Amidst some down moments, over the last twenty years Albania has been a hot spot for architecture, a place where established offices and start-ups have found fertile ground for testing and delivering. But the important aspect is another: Not only did Albania need a lot of architecture after the demise of communism, but it's one of the few places around where architecture still matters.

HOW TO INTEGRATE GREATER RESPONSIBILITY FOR QUALITY IN PROJECTS

Good juries and cultured developers.

BALANCING QUALITY AND DENSITY/INVOLVING STAKEHOLDERS

In order to enhance quality without disrupting the feasibility of a project, the architect can only stress and highlight the special conditions which are already there: politics which favor architecture, a society in which interest in and familiarity with decent architecture is growing over time, and very specific economic conditions where the price of land acquisition has not yet devoured the possibility for architecture to matter.

EXAMPLE/INSPIRATION

An obvious one, Skanderbeg Square.

TOOLBOX ALBANIA FUTURE

Collaboration as the perfect nest for nurturing creativity.

kuh in Albania, a provisional chronology

4, March
a student at the Berlage Institute Rotterdam, Paolo Tamburelli (PPT) takes part in design earch on the Tirana metropolitan region rdinated by Elia Zenghelis. First trip to Tirana neet then-mayor Edi Rama. Rama receives lents at the city hall and tells terrifying anec- e about Venetian merchants daring to refuse anian hospitality.
4, June
ults of the research are presented in erdam to mayor Rama: the "Durana" ropolitan region is born. Rama asks PPT, you want to make buildings in Tirana?"
4, late summer
kuh is contacted by mr. Agron Ajipullari and Roland Jegeni to design a mixed-use build- in Rruga Myslym Shyri. baukuh designs an edibly simple neo-modernist building, which uilt in 2009. The project is quite a failure, as simplicity requires unrealistic (considering context back then) precision in the execution.
5, winter
Agron Ajipullari and mr. Roland Jegeni request baukuh design a mixed-use building in Rruga stafa Matohiti. The project will not be built.
5, winter
kuh is contacted by mr. Artan Gaçi to design ixed-use building in Rruga Xhezmi Delli. time baukuh's project is very sculptural and ally impactful, opting for a simultaneously nger and more cautious strategy. The project pproved.
6
plot (and the project) in Rruga Xhezmi i is sold to a new investor. baukuh's project uilt without the architects knowing.
6
ga Myslym Shyri #2.
7
tin Sobota tells baukuh that the building in ga Xhezmi Delli is under construction. baukuh tacts the new developer and proposes some istments. The building is completed in 2009.
8
npetition for Skanderbeg square, baukuh es to 51N4E (who will end up realizing of the most beautiful European projects ne early 2000s).
8
npetition for Tirana Military Airport, baukuh es to CITYFÖRSTER.
9
npetition for the master plan of the city ter of Korça with YellowOffice. baukuh loses BOLLES+WILSON.
3, August
er winning the parliamentary elections, na invites a group of architects (among them kuh) for a brainstorming session on his re prime ministry. We walk with Rama on Durrës beach, followed by a crowd of socialist supporters in swimsuits; the day after, the right-wing papers write that Rama gave all the Albanian coast to his foreign friends.
2014, September
Andrea Zanderigo organizes for the magazine *San Rocco* a summer school in collaboration with Atelier Albania and Epoka University. Twelve new schools/community centers are designed by students tutored by a bunch of international architects.
2014, fall
Competition for the Durana metropolitan strategy, baukuh loses to l'AUC.
2015, spring
Competition for the Tirana Student City, baukuh wins. The competition presentation takes place in the auditorium of the Hilton Hotel. In the lobby of the hotel baukuh meets Def Leppard; they will give a concert at the nearby stadium the day after.
2016, April
Master plan for the Tirana Student City is delivered.
2017
Housing in Rruga e Kavajës, not built.
2019, June
baukuh receives a commission for the new General Directorate of State Police and Academy of Security.
2019, October
baukuh receives a commission for the new Forensic Science Department of the Albanian State Police. For some reason the building should resemble the Northern Ireland Forensic Science Department. PPT visits Belfast together with staff from the Albanian Ministry of the Interior.
2019, December
Definitive projects for the General Directorate of State Police and Academy of Security and the Forensic Science Department are delivered.
2020, July
Competition for the new Tirana City Hall, baukuh participates with Johnston Marklee, Matilde Cassani and YellowOffice. The competition will not be assigned.
2024, January
Competition for EXPO Albania with l'AUC. baukuh loses to Steven Holl.
2024, July
Competition for the Rozafa Hotel Tower in Shkodra, baukuh and l'AUC lose to selgascano.
2024
Double competition for the Civic Land Center and the Lift Tower, baukuh win together with Sam Chermayeff Office, Muoto and YellowOffice.
2025
Competition for the master plan and renovation of the Selman Stërmasi Stadium, baukuh participates with OFFICE Kersten Geers David Van Severen, ARQUITECTURA-G, l'AUC, YellowOffice and Matilde Cassani. Loses to OMA.

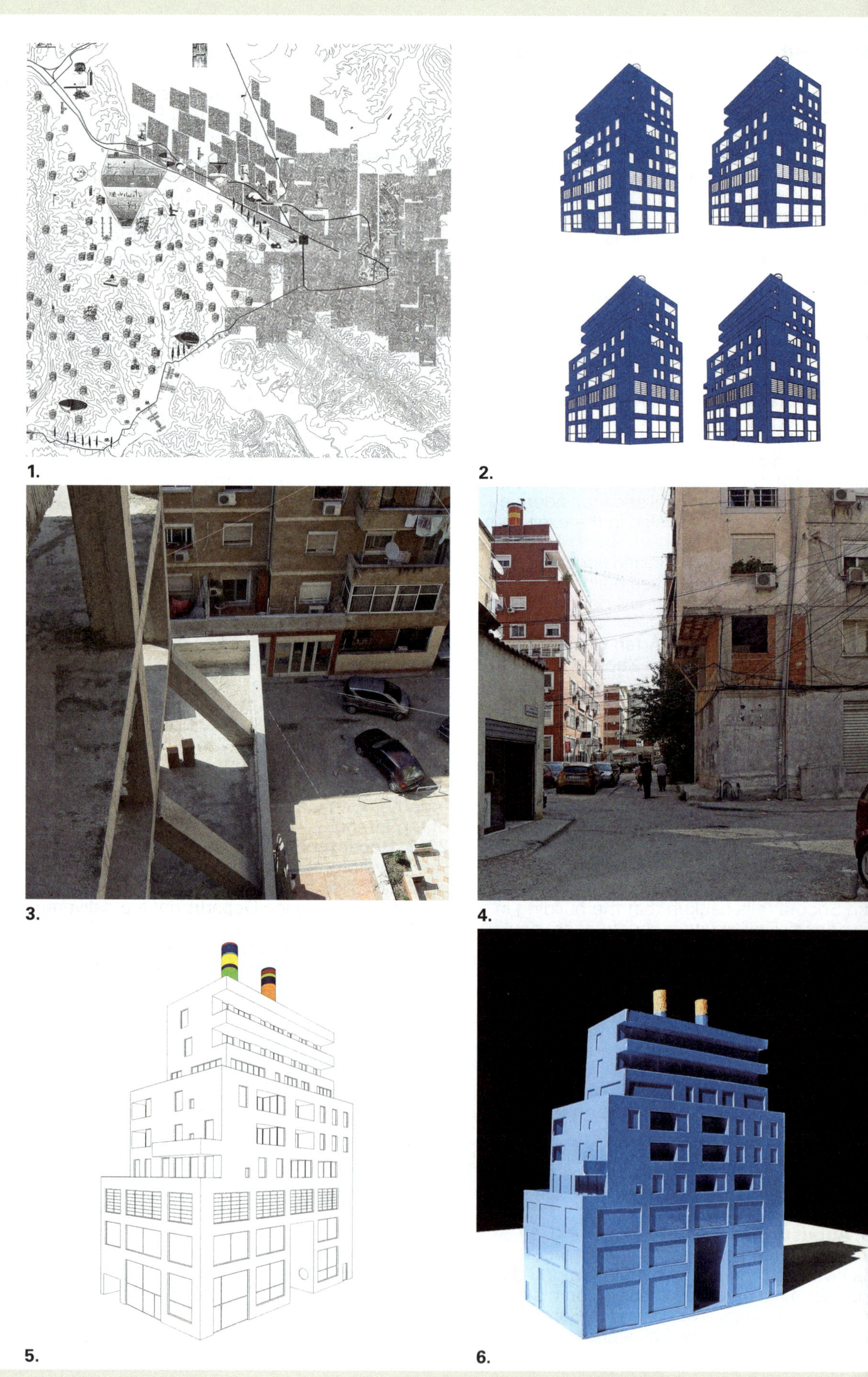

1.

2.

3.

4.

5.

6.

STUDIM URBANISTIK PJESOR I TIRANES (0-9) VITI 2005 SH.1:500
GEN PLAN

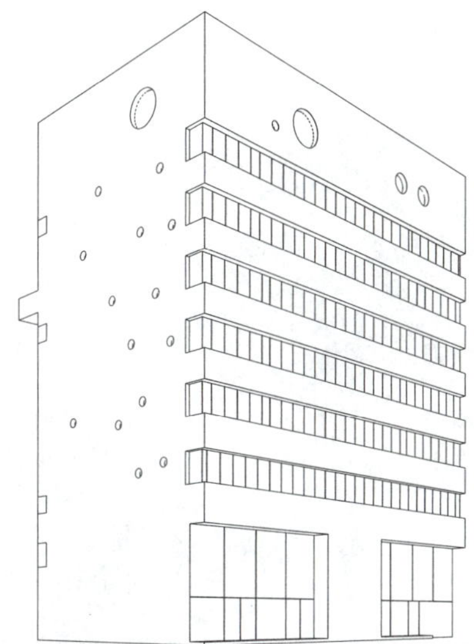

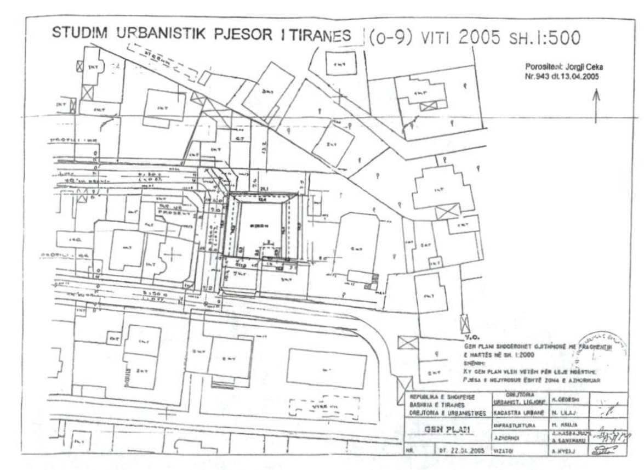

8.

10.

12.

13.

14.

15.

16.

17.

18.

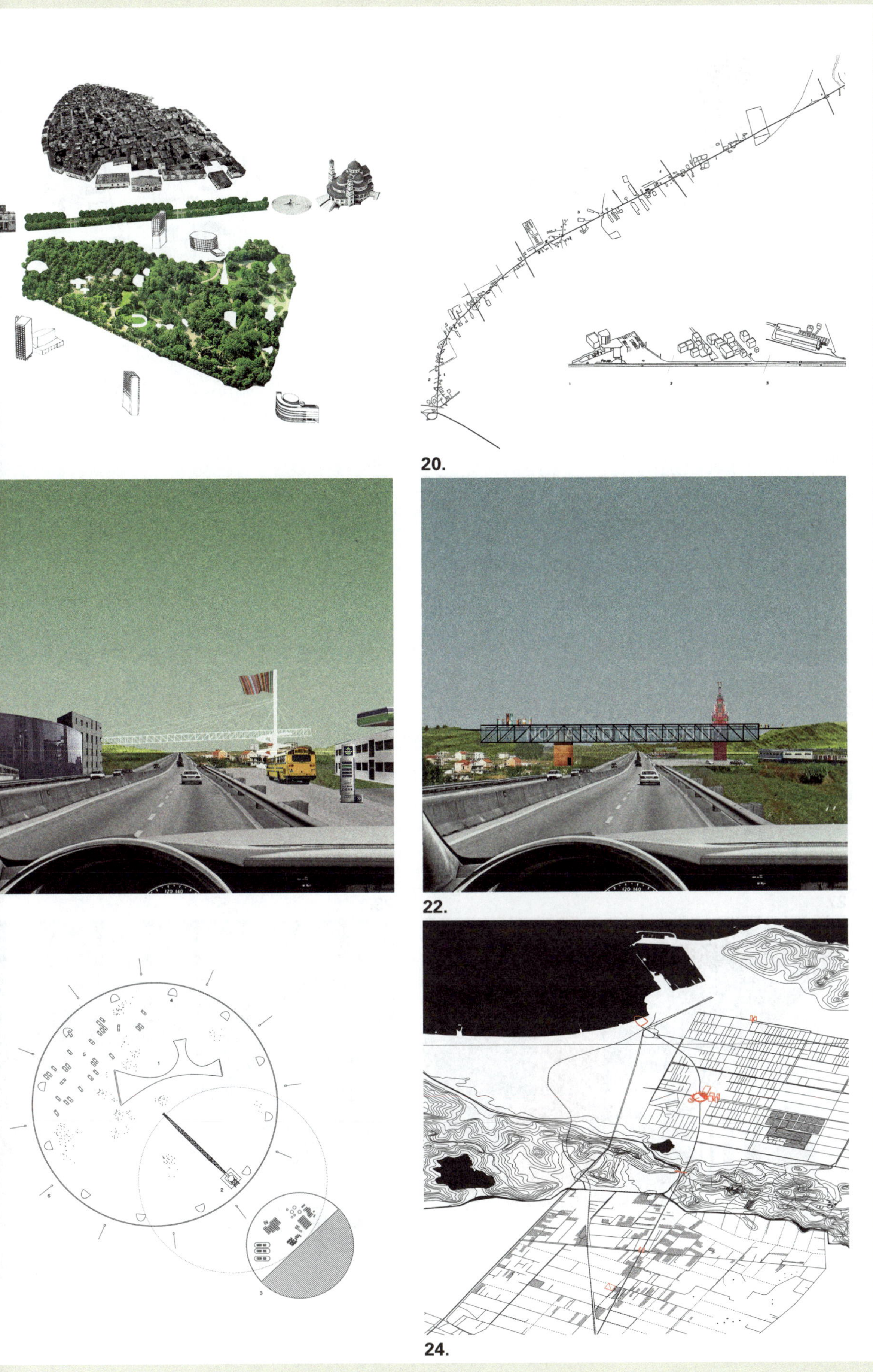

20.

22.

24.

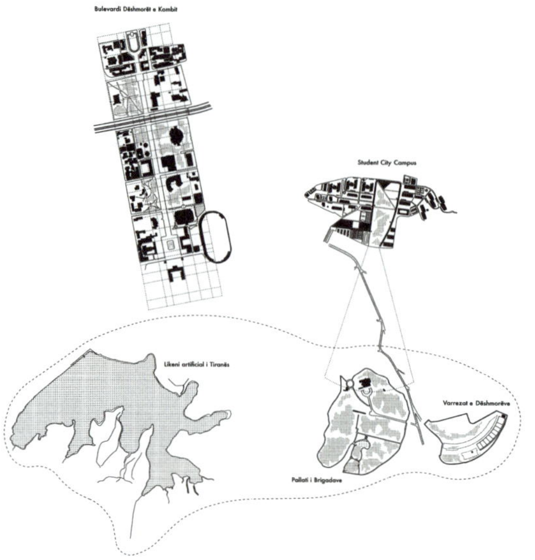

Bulevardi Dëshmorët e Kombit

Student City Campus

Liqeni artificial i Tiranës

Varrezat e Dëshmorëve

Pallati i Brigadave

25.

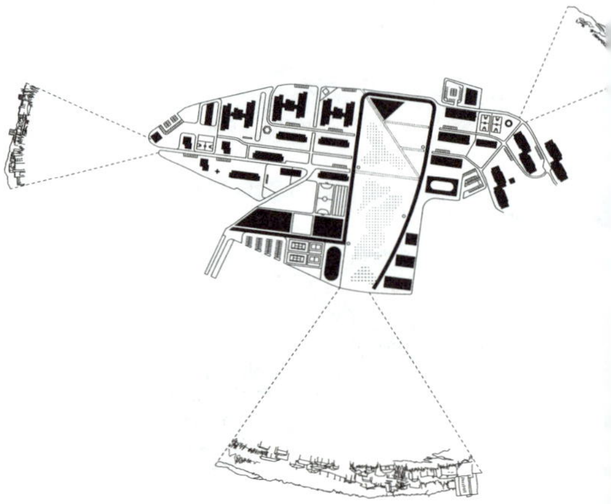

26.

27.

28.

29.

30.

32.

POLICIA POLICIA POLICIA POLICIA POLICIA POLICIA POLICIA

34.

POLICIA

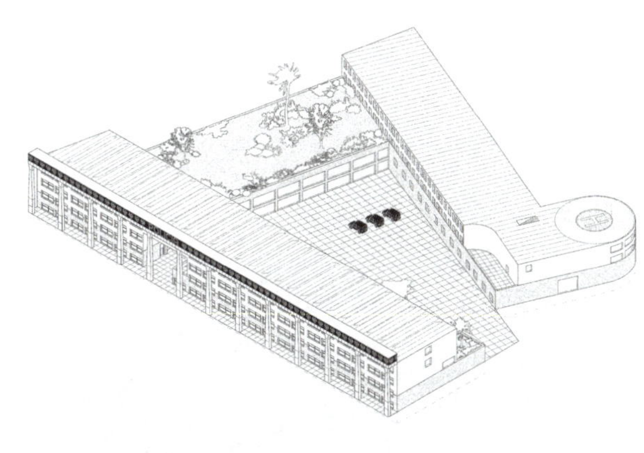

36.

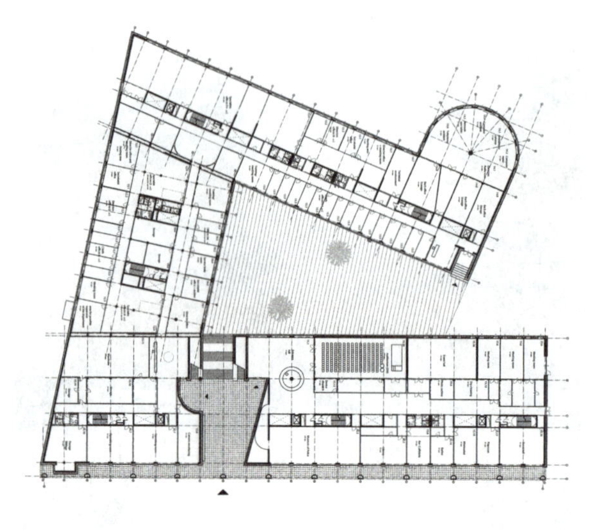

37.

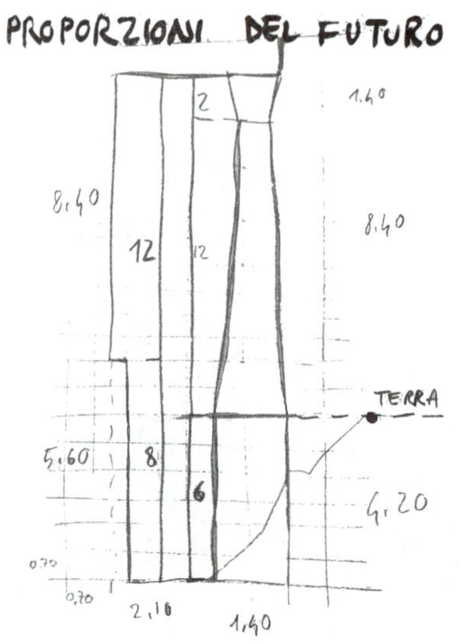

38.

39.

40.

41.

42.

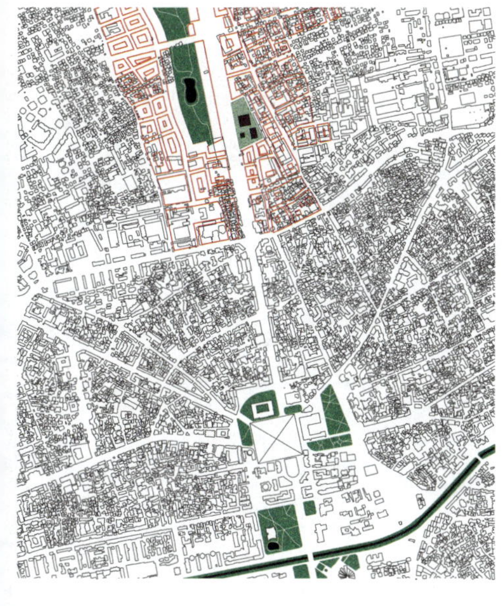

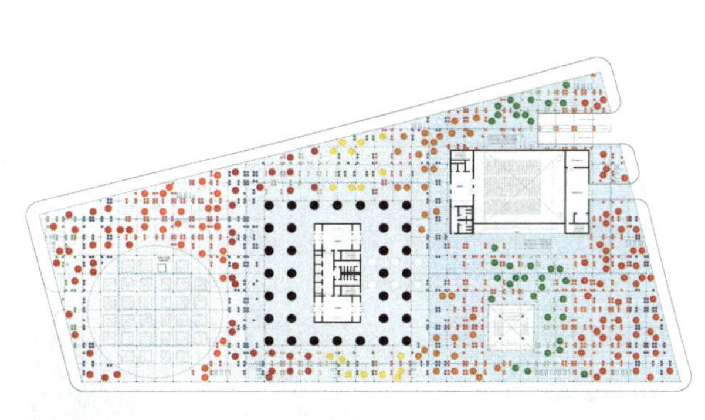

44.

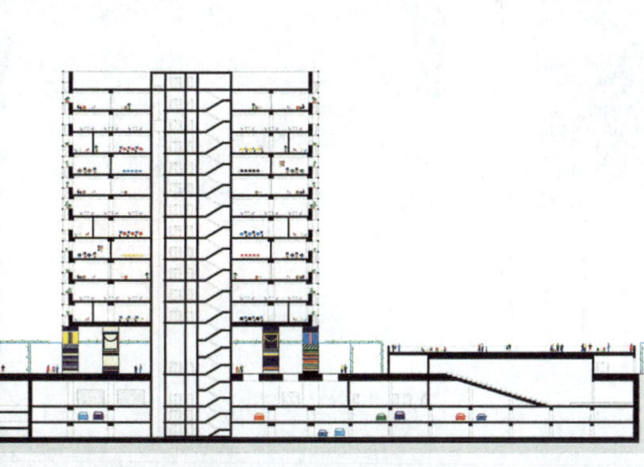

46.

48.

49.

50.

51.

52.

53.

54.

56.

58.

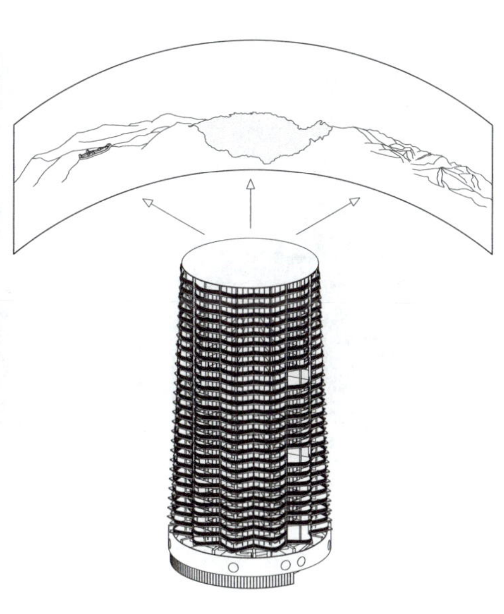

60.

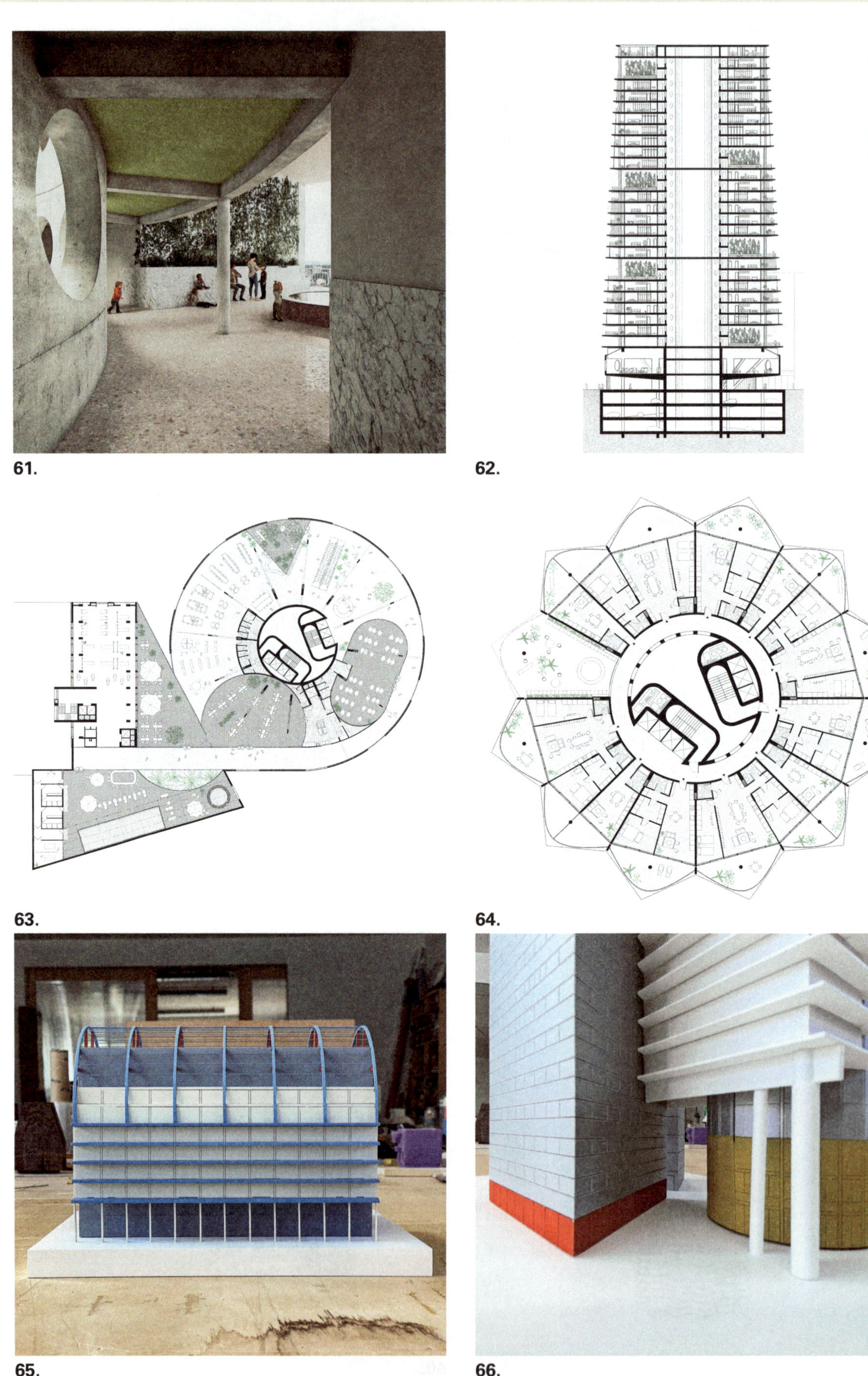

61.

62.

63.

64.

65.

66.

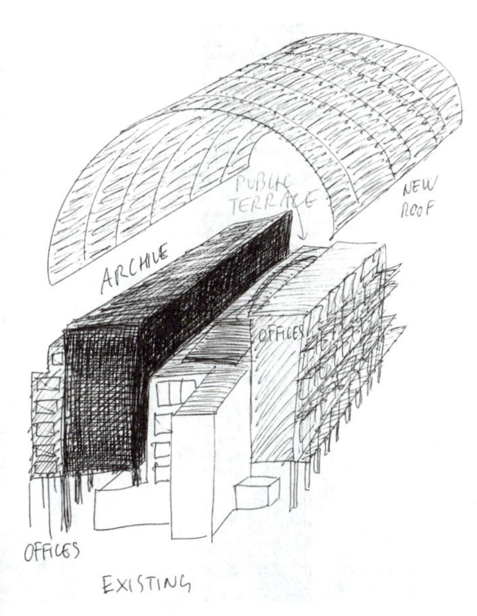

68.

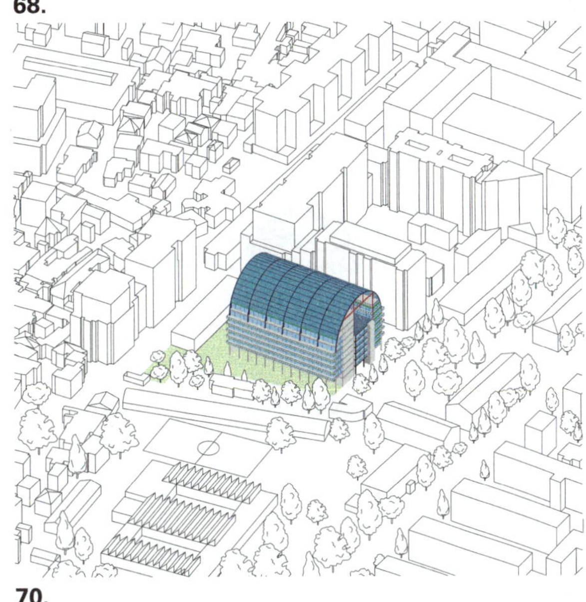

70.

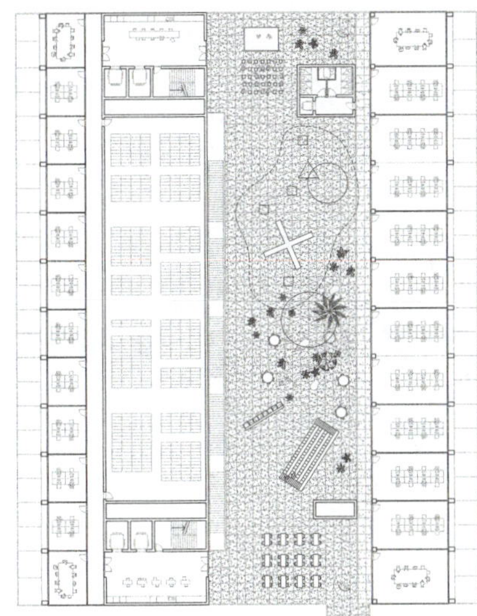

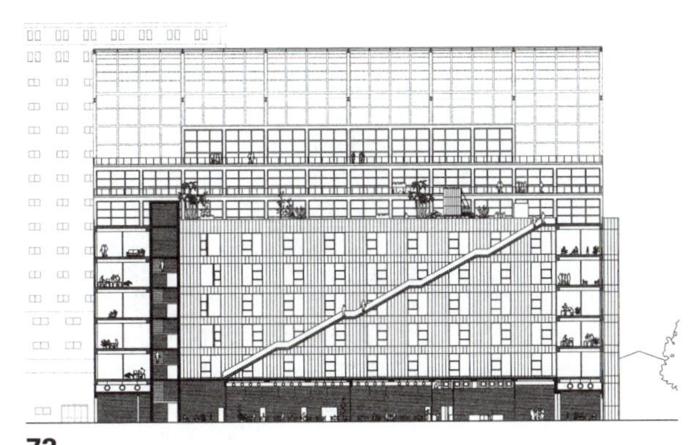

72.

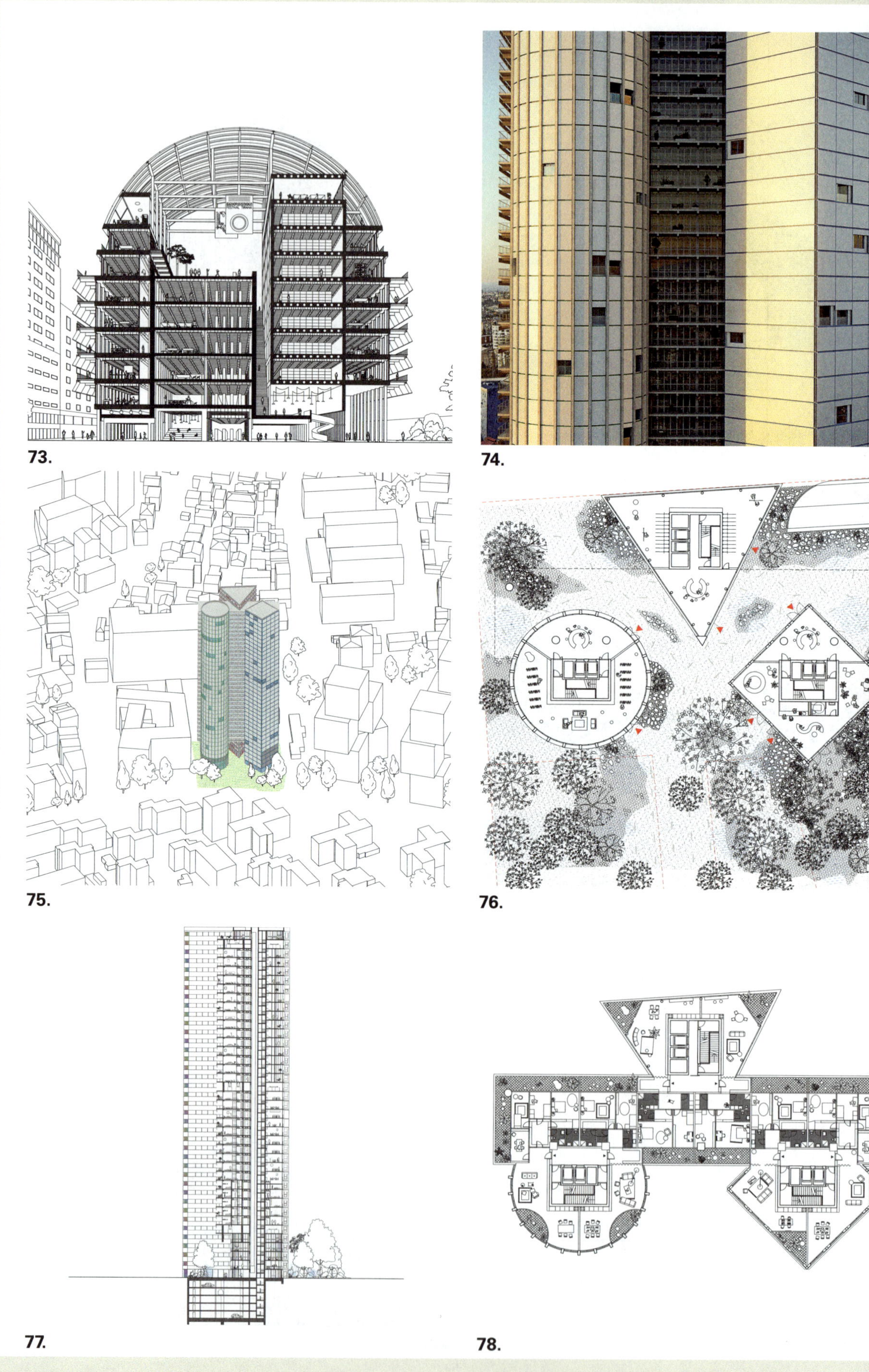

73.

74.

75.

76.

77.

78.

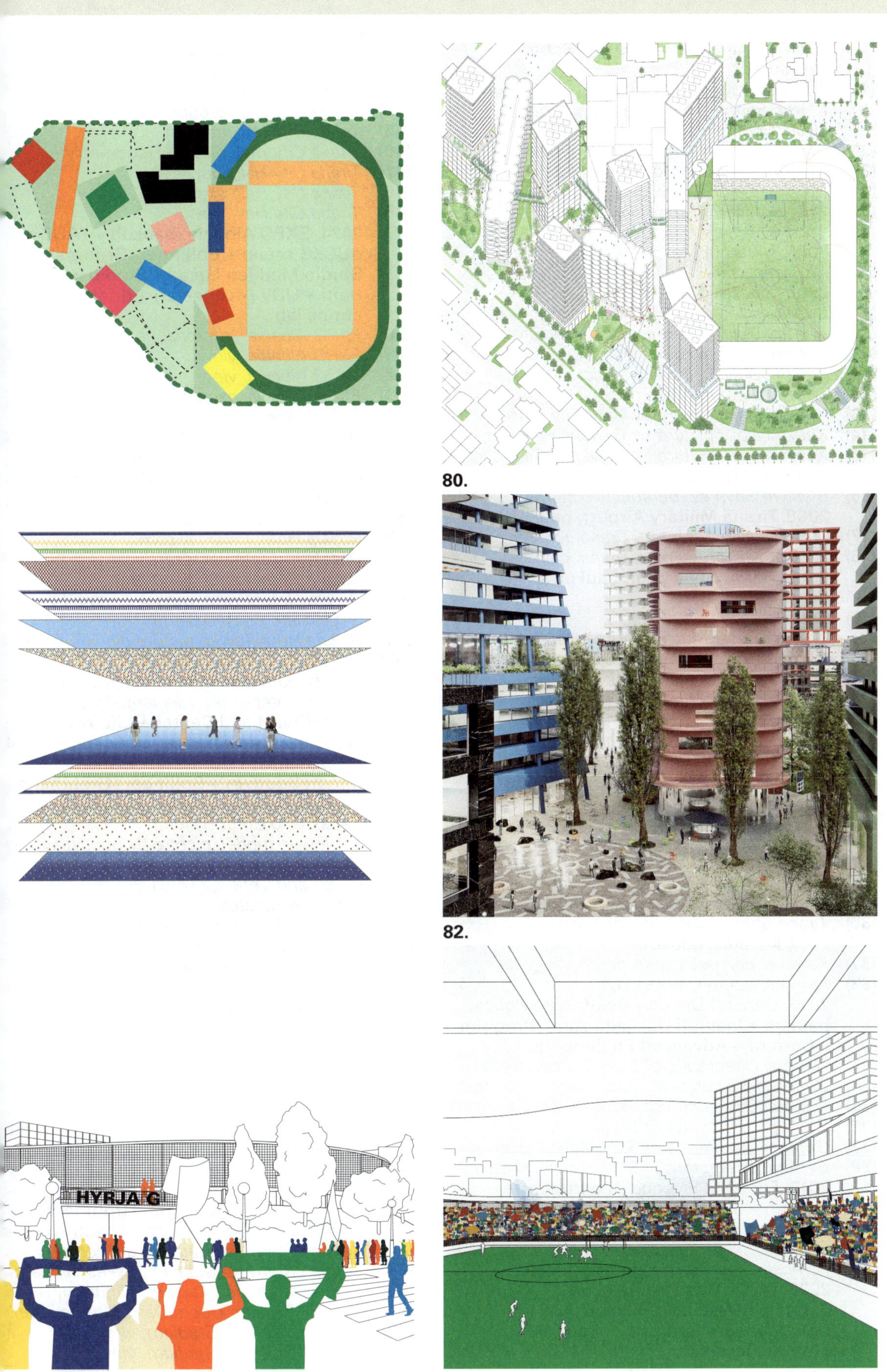

80.

82.

84.

2004, Durana, Nürnberger + Sobota + Tamburelli
(1) *Durana, drawing by Pier Paolo Tamburelli, Martin Sobota and Alexa Nürnberger*
2004, Myslym Shyri #1, baukuh
(2) *Myslym Shyri #1, perspective studies*
(3) *Myslym Shyri #1, picture by Victoria Easton*
(4) *Myslym Shyri #1, building site picture*
(5) *Myslym Shyri #1, perspective study*
(6) *Myslym Shyri #1, model*
2005, Mustafa Matohiti, baukuh
(7) *Mustafa Matohiti, perspective study*
2005, Xhezmi Delli, baukuh
(8) *Xhezmi Delli, cadastre plan with the project*
(9) *Xhezmi Delli, picture by Giovanna Silva*
(10) *Xhezmi Delli, building site picture*
(11) *Xhezmi Delli, building site picture*
(12) *Xhezmi Delli, collage*
(13) *Xhezmi Delli, picture by Giovanna Silva*
(14) *Xhezmi Delli, picture by Giovanna Silva*
(15) *Xhezmi Delli, picture by Giovanna Silva*
2006, Myslym Shyri #2, baukuh
(16) *Myslym Shyri #2, perspective study*
2008, Tirana Military Airport, baukuh
(17) *Former Military Airport, Tirana, master plan*
(18) *Former Military Airport, Tirana, plan*
2009, Korça city center, baukuh + YellowOffice
(19) *Korça city center, collage*
2014, Durana metropolitan strategy, baukuh
(20) *Durana metropolitan strategy, diagram*
(21) *Durana metropolitan strategy, view*
(22) *Durana metropolitan strategy, view*
(23) *Durana metropolitan strategy, diagram*
(24) *Durana metropolitan strategy, diagram*
2015, Tirana Student City, baukuh + LIST + Space Caviar + Bodà + F&M Ingegneria + Abkons
(25) *Tirana Student City, diagram*
(26) *Tirana Student City, diagram*
(27) *Tirana Student City, perspective*
(28) *Tirana Student City, model*
(29) *Tirana Student City, model*
(30) *Tirana Student City, model*
2017, Kavajës, baukuh
(31) *Kavajës, perspective study*
(32) *Kavajës, perspective study*
2019, General Directorate of State Police, baukuh + Instituti Dekliada-Alb + Broggini e Carrera + Advanced Engineering
(33) *General Directorate of State Police, sketch*
(34) *General Directorate of State Police, axonometry*
(35) *General Directorate of State Police, view*
(36) *General Directorate of State Police, view*
(37) *General Directorate of State Police, plan*
(38) *General Directorate of State Police, sketch*
2019, Forensic Science Department, baukuh + Instituti Dekliada-Alb + Broggini e Carrera + Advanced Engineering
(39) *Forensic Science Department, sketch*
(40) *Forensic Science Department, model*
2020, Tirana City Hall, baukuh + Johnston Marklee + YellowOffice + Bollinger+Grohmann + Abkons + Matilde Cassani
(41) *Tirana City Hall, view*
(42) *Tirana City Hall, view*
(43) *Tirana City Hall, master plan*
(44) *Tirana City Hall, ground floor plan*
(45) *Tirana City Hall, section*
(46) *Tirana City Hall, pillars, axonometry*
(47) *Tirana City Hall, view*
(48) *Tirana City Hall, sketch*
(49) *Tirana City Hall, view*
2024, EXPO Albania, baukuh + l'AUC + dUCKS scéno + Bollinger+Grohmann + Studio Mathieu Lucas + Studio Raphael Hefti + UDV Architects + Adriatica RC + atmos lab
(50) *EXPO Albania, territorial perspective*
(51) *EXPO Albania, view*
(52) *EXPO Albania, view*
(53) *EXPO Albania, axonometry*
(54) *EXPO Albania, axonometry*
2024, Rozafa Hotel Tower, baukuh + l'AU
Studio Mathieu Lucas + atmos lab + Bollinger+Grohmann + UDV Architects
(55) *Rozafa Hotel Tower, view*
(56) *Rozafa Hotel Tower, axonometry*
(57) *Rozafa Hotel Tower, sketch*
(58) *Rozafa Hotel Tower, sketch*
(59) *Rozafa Hotel Tower, panorama*
(60) *Rozafa Hotel Tower, model, picture by Sebastiano Conti Gallenti*
(61) *Rozafa Hotel Tower, picture by OUT OF RA*
(62) *Rozafa Hotel Tower, section*
(63) *Rozafa Hotel Tower, hotel lobby plan*
(64) *Rozafa Hotel Tower, residential plan*
2024, Civic Land Center + Lift Tower, baukuh + Sam Chermayeff Office + Muot
YellowOffice + atmos lab + Arkimade + Simon Boudvin + Bollinger+Grohmann
(65) *Civic Land Center, model, picture by Sebastiano Conti Gallenti*
(66) *Lift Tower, model, picture by Sebastiano Conti Gallenti*
(67) *Civic Land Center, sketch*
(68) *Lift Tower, sketch*
(69) *Civic Land Center, picture by Fusão*
(70) *Civic Land Center, axonometry*
(71) *Civic Land Center, plan*
(72) *Civic Land Center, section*
(73) *Civic Land Center, perspective section*
(74) *Lift Tower, picture by Fusão*
(75) *Lift Tower, axonometry*
(76) *Lift Tower, ground floor plan*
(77) *Lift Tower, section*
(78) *Lift Tower, residential plan*
2025, Selman Stërmasi Stadium, baukuh
Ales Construction + OFFICE Kersten Gee
David Van Severen + ARQUITECTURA-G
l'AUC + YellowOffice + Matilde Cassani + Ne Arkitektët + Bollinger+Grohmann
(79) *Selman Stërmasi Stadium, confetti scheme*
(80) *Selman Stërmasi Stadium, axonometry*
(81) *Selman Stërmasi Stadium, Sykes diagram*
(82) *Selman Stërmasi Stadium, picture by OFFICE Kersten Geers David Van Severen*
(83) *Selman Stërmasi Stadium, view*
(84) *Selman Stërmasi Stadium, view*

START	NAME PROJECT	LOCATION	DEVELOPER	COMMISSIONER/CLIENT	PUBLIC/PRIVATE	PHASE
2004	Mixed-use building	Rruga Myslym Shyri, Tirana	Aurora Konstruksion		Private	Executed
2005	Mixed-use building	Rruga Mustafa Matohiti, Tirana	Aurora Konstruksion		Private	Unbuilt
2005	Mixed-use building	Rruga Xhezmi Delli, Tirana	Artan Gaçi and ABG		Private	Executed
2006	Mixed-use building	Rruga Myslym Shyri, Tirana			Private	Unbuilt
2008	Skanderbeg Square	Tirana	Albanian government		Public	Lost competition
2008	Former Military Airport redevelopment	Tirana	Albanian government		Public/private	Lost competition
2009	City Center Development	Korça	Albanian government		Public	Lost competition
2014	Metropolitan strategy	Durana	Albanian government		Public	Lost competition
2015	Renovation Tirana Student City	Tirana	Albanian government		Public	Partially built
2017	Mixed-use building	Rruga e Kavajës, Tirana			Private	Unbuilt
2019	General Directorate of State Police and Academy of Security	Tirana	Albanian government	Instituti Dekliada-Alb, Broggini e Carrera, Advanced Engineering	Public	Unbuilt
2019	Forensic Science Department of the Albanian State Police	Tirana	Albanian government	Instituti Dekliada-Alb, Broggini e Carrera, Advanced Engineering	Public	Unbuilt
2020	City Hall	Tirana	Albanian government		Public	Competition not assigned
2024	EXPO Albania	Tirana	Albanian government		Private	Lost competition
2024	Rozafa Hotel Tower	Shkodra	Rozafa Group		Private	Lost competition
2024	Lift Tower	Tirana	Albanian government		Public/private	Procurement
2024	Civic Land Center	Tirana	Albanian government		Public	Procurement
2025	Selman Stërmasi Stadium	Tirana	Albanian government / Ales		Public/private	Lost competition

NAME OFFICE

BIG

DATE
September 2025

PLACE
Copenhagen, Denmark

WORKING IN ALBANIA SINCE
2017

PRINCIPALS
Bjarke Ingels
Catherine Huang
Giulia Frittoli

PROJECT TEAM
Adrianna Karnaszewska
Alberto Menegazzo
Alex Bogdan Ritivoi
Alexander Dennis William Niemantsverdriet
Álvaro Novas Filgueira
Anastasia Suzdaltseva Kazakova
Anastasiia Nakonechnaia
Andreas Bak
Anna Wozniak
Annette Birthe Jensen
Anton Malthe Ling
Arvin Nadimi
Carmen Simone
Charles Vidal
Chiara Kuhn
Christopher Taylor
Claudia Bertolotti
Connor Forecast
Danyu Zeng
Denzil Ricci
Desislava Georgieva
Eleonora Niccoli
Eva Seo-Andersen
Ewelina Woloszyn
Fabiana Cortolezzis
Federica Fogazzi
Federico Martinez De Sola Monereo
Felipe Chacón
Filippo Dozzi
Finn Nørkjær
Gilana Antonova
Giovanni Salvatore Bitonti
Guanxin Luo
Hui Chen
Hung-Kai Liao
Ipek Akin
Izabella Banas
Jacek Baczkowski
Jean Kekoa Charlot
Juras Lasovsky
Karim Muallem
Kateřina Krchňáková
Keyao Liu
Li Ka Yiu Karry
Loc (Finn) Quang Nguyen
Lucas Stanley Carriere
Marcela Dominika Rydalska
Marco Antonio Paz-Garcia
Martyna Kloda
Mateusz Płudowski
Mats Milan Kolmas
Matteo Dragone
Matteo Pavanello
Mauro Saenz de Cabezon Aguado
Milyausha Garaeva
Molly Hsiao Rou Huang
Monika Dauksaite
Norbert Nadudvari
Paula Joanna Tkaczyk
Philipp Weisz
Pol Marck
Riccardo Piazzai
Rihab Soukkarieh
Rihards Dzelme
Romain Thijsen
Santiago Palacio Villa
Satvika Kedia
Seda Yildiz
Seonhwan Kim
Stanisław Daniel Rudzki
Stefan Plugaru
Tangina Ahmed
Tobias Hjortdal
Tomas Rosello Barros
Tomasz Jakubowski
Tyrone James Cobcroft
Weronika Zaborek
Xavier Thanki
Yanis Amasri Sierra
Yunus Alperen Basak

ALBANIAN PARTNERS

EXECUTIVE ARCHITECT
SON Engineering & Construction
Impuls Architects
AGIKONS

MEP ENGINEER
HYDRO & ENERGY
HMS
IDT Engineering shpk

STRUCTURAL ENGINEER
LEAL CSE
HSC Studio
Dhimitri Papa

ELECTRICAL ENGINEER
Elteknik Engineering & Consulting

Albania has given me, as an architect, a particular toolbox for giving form to the future – one that revolves around the idea of creative leadership. Under the leadership of the Albanian government, and undoubtedly shaped by Prime Minister Edi Rama's background as an artist, there is a profound understanding of the transformative power of creativity.

It is no secret that when the Iron Curtain fell and the Berlin Wall opened, Albania was the poorest country in Europe – and, at the time, the second poorest country in the world. What followed has been an extraordinary transformation, driven not only by economic reform but by the articulation of bold, aspirational ideas – ideas made tangible through physical space.

When Edi Rama served as mayor of Tirana, there were no resources for large-scale renovation. Instead, he turned to painting buildings in vivid, unexpected ways. If economic transformation was not yet possible, then at least the perception of cultural transformation could be. By inviting artists such as Thomas Demand and Olafur Eliasson to participate, this became an artistic act of defiance – a declaration to the world: We may lack economic means, but we possess will, imagination and the courage to envision a different future.

That spirit of leadership has endured. Tirana, and Albania more broadly, has become a laboratory for exploring how art, architecture and design can be leveraged to imagine – and actively construct – a new world. Crucially, this has not required erasing the past. On the contrary, Albania has taken unusual ownership of its history, including its darker chapters. When you visit the House of Comrades or the prime minister's office, you encounter not only renovated spaces and gestures like the timber vertical garden, but also a carefully curated narrative of the country's past – both its achievements and its traumas. History is preserved not as nostalgia, but as instruction and caution.

What strikes me most is the capacity of art, design and architecture to crystallize political and cultural moments into built form – to materially manifest an invisible transformation so that it becomes physically present and collectively experienced. This is a lesson I have carried into other projects. In the Mindfulness City we are designing in Gelephu, Bhutan, for example, we are translating the nine parameters of Gross National Happiness – rooted in Vajrayana Buddhist principles – into urban design strategies. The aim is the same: to ensure that values are not merely abstract ideals, but physically embedded in everyday life.

In this sense, Albania's urban transformation places it at the forefront globally – not because of scale or wealth, but because of its willingness to use design as a cultural, political and imaginative instrument of change.

Our Role as Architects

extracts from a letter by Bjarke Ingels to the Danish magazine Politiken in 2020

. . . I first visited Albania in the spring of 2011. Like many others, I knew almost nothing about the country. A former communist state, it had been in near-total isolation since breaking away from the Soviet Union in the 1960s and was one of Europe's poorest nations. So poor that scenes from the film *Borat*, intended to depict Kazakhstan, were actually filmed in Albania. And of course, it was the homeland of the villains from *Taken* – the characters who kept kidnapping Liam Neeson's daughter.

Yet something interesting had started happening in Tirana. Artists like Olafur Eliasson, Ann Edholm, Dominique Gonzalez-Foerster and Franz Ackermann had been invited to rejuvenate the city with colorful decorations. Without the funds for costly renovations, the city's young, socially liberal mayor, Edi Rama, a visual artist himself, discovered that transformation could be achieved with a bucket of paint and creativity. It felt radical and refreshing.
We were invited to a competition to design the city's mosque and a Museum of Tolerance. The idea was to give the Muslim faith a visible presence in Tirana's cityscape, equal to Christianity and Judaism. Post-communism, Albania began to embrace its unique position as a cultural bridge between north and south, east and west. Promoting a coexistence of major religions seemed like a bold and timely move in a Europe facing increasing ethnic and cultural polarization.

We won the competition despite an unrealistic timeline, a tiny budget and a laughable fee. But we felt there was something genuine here, and we owed it to the Albanian youth to contribute.
However, a municipal election was just around the corner . . . The new conservative leadership scrapped our project, opting for a traditional mosque with domes and minarets. It's remarkable how intense the conflicts are in this young democracy, but it's also understandable that new political freedoms are taken so seriously, with a passion far beyond what we are familiar with in Denmark, where we often take them for granted.
I was deeply disappointed (and a bit relieved) that our contribution to Albania's nation-building ended abruptly before it even began.

. . . In 2015 we were invited back to Tirana. We talked about the many plans they had for the city and were encouraged to explore some of the emerging opportunities. They were working on revitalizing the city's decaying center.
. . . During our visit, we met the people from Fusha shpk – the local contractor working on Skanderbeg Square. We agreed to pursue one of the upcoming public projects together. In the fall of 2017, we signed a contract with Fusha to design a theater as part of a city block featuring various urban functions.
We toured the existing theater building. It lacked an under-stage area and a fly tower. It had no side wings. It was not suitable for theater because it was not designed for that purpose. Instead, it was built to entertain Fascist soldiers during Albania's occupation by Mussolini's Italy from 1939 to 1943. The building was neither listed as a heritage site nor considered architecturally significant.

Neither my colleagues nor I are experts in Fascist architecture, but one can never be too careful with historical buildings. Therefore, we prepared two different proposals for a new theater: one preserving the existing building and one starting from scratch. The existing building was extremely narrow, only 12 meters wide, which is not nearly enough for a proper theater stage. It needed to be at least three times wider. We found a radical solution to this unsolvable problem. By lifting the stage above the old barracks, we could incorporate the theater machinery as a three-dimensional cross planted in the existing context. A Cartesian coordinate system of pure stage technology. It looked wild and crazy. Mad – or perhaps brilliant. For the second proposal, we designed a theater spanning the site to maximize the theater's function. The cross-shaped theater machinery opened northward, allowing passersby to observe the various productions under preparation – as if the theater's engine room had its hood lifted. To the south, the foyer and two experimental stages opened toward the National Museum's park. The main auditorium bridged the front and back of the house, lifting itself to create a covered plaza facing the street and arching its back to create an outdoor amphitheater on its roof. The two open facades revealed their inner life like a dollhouse to the city. The two closed facades rose as a portal to the neighborhood behind the theater.

In early spring 2018, we were invited to Tirana to present our ideas to the city. The response was that we should forget about the old barracks; they held no architectural or historical significance. Instead, we were encouraged to focus all our energy on creating a national stage for Albania that would be worthy of the performing arts. So, we did.
. . . We have designed a theater that will be a radically transparent and publicly engaging national stage. A raw, simple and straightforward building that can serve as the framework for modern Albanian drama.

. . . It would be narrow-minded and arrogant to dismiss our European neighbor as corrupt, backward and unworthy of collaboration. Despite the challenges and lack of profitability, I believe it is part of the responsibility we bear as architects – or, in plain Danish, as *formgivere* (form-givers). I don't think we can settle for simply sitting here at home, coming up with yet another brick pattern for the next pretty, predictable facade. That's why I will continue to engage in open collaborations with those who have far more at stake than we face here at home – and lend them a hand with their challenges and help uplift their visions as they work to shape their future.

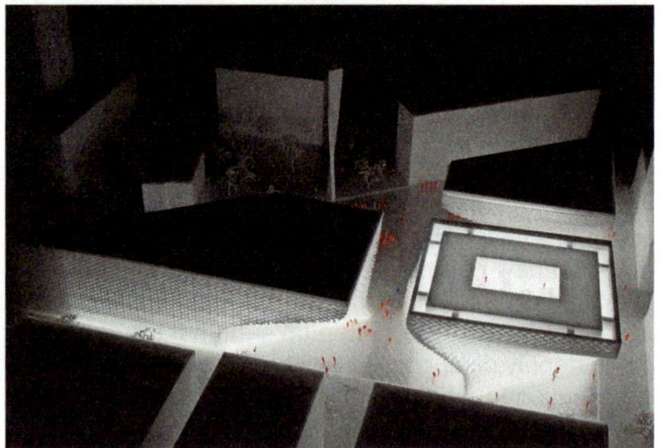

Above, top. View of the plaza.

Above. Pictures of the physical model. The alignment toward Mecca solves the dilemma inherent in the master plan – in its triangular layout, the mosque was somehow tucked in the corner. Now it sits at the end of the plaza – framed by its two neighbors.

NEW MOSQUE OF TIRANA, THE ISLAMIC CENTER AND THE MUSEUM OF RELIGIOUS HARMONY

2011 – idea

Firstly, it is a privilege to contribute to the ambitious rejuvenation of Tirana – especially since it is happening not by the random accumulation of singular monuments, but rather in accordance with a careful and considerate holistic master plan. Secondly, and perhaps most importantly, religious tolerance is one of our greatest challenges today – politically, culturally and even urbanistically. With the construction of the New Mosque of Tirana, the Islamic Center and the Museum of Religious Harmony, Tirana will reestablish the equilibrium by adding a mosque to the newly completed Orthodox and Catholic Cathedrals – making Tirana an example for the rest of the world as a global capital of religious harmony.

Above, top. Visualization of the project from the newly proposed plaza.

Above. The facade expression is bifold, referencing the idea of revealing and hiding the inner workings of a theater with references to the stage curtain and the dollhouse.

Pages 172–173. Pictures of various physical models. The iterative design process has developed with the aid of study models produced with different materials and techniques.

Page 174, top. View of the new public plaza from above. The existing paving continues under the theater with an altered geometry that invites the public to explore the space.

Page 174, bottom. Visualization of the roof terrace. A folding door allows the experimental stage of the black box venue to open to the outside, rendering this space an additional open-air venue.

ALBANIAN NATIONAL THEATER (ZET)

2017 – under construction

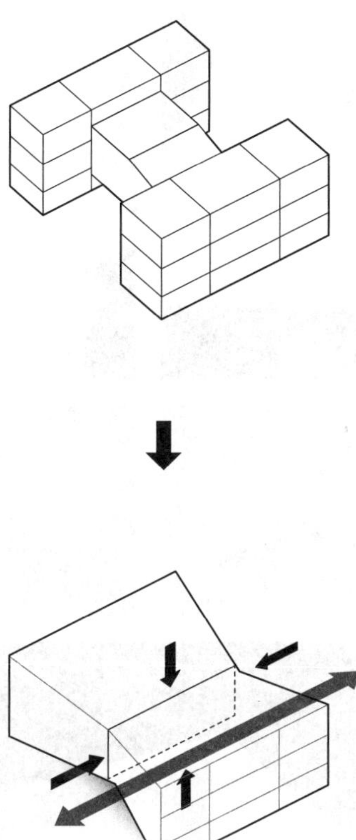

We designed a theater spanning the site to maximize the theater's function. The cross-shaped theater machinery opened northward, allowing passersby to observe the various productions under preparation – as if the theater's engine room had its hood lifted. To the south, the foyer and two experimental stages opened toward the National Museum's park. The main auditorium bridged the front and back of the house, lifting itself to create a covered plaza facing the street and arching its back to create an outdoor amphitheater on its roof. The two open facades revealed their inner life like a dollhouse to the city. The two closed facades rose as a portal to the neighborhood behind the theater.

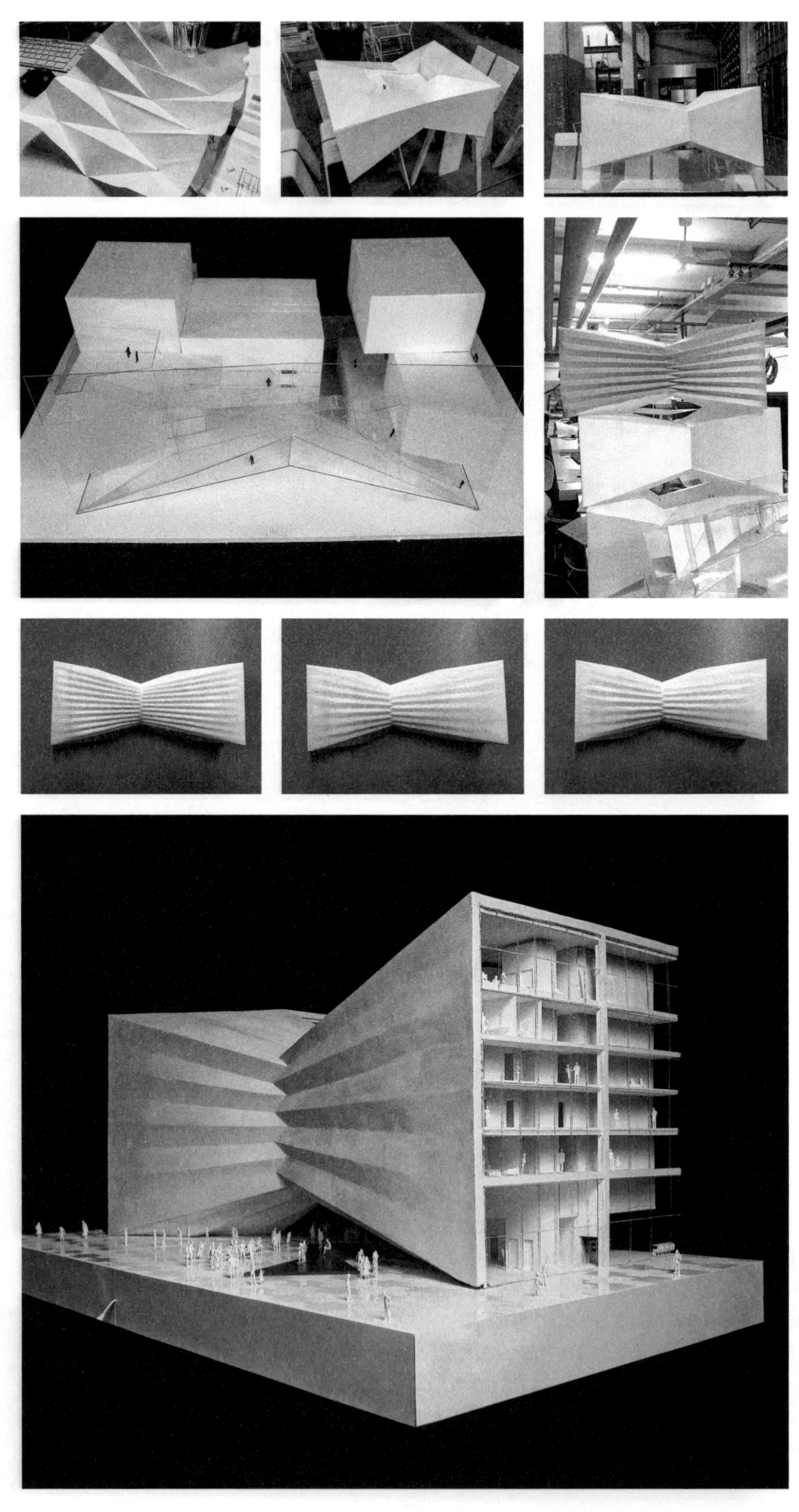

START	NAME PROJECT	LOCATION	COMMISSIONER/CLIENT	PUBLIC/PRIVATE	PHASE
2017	ZET National Theater	Tirana	Agikons	Public	Construction administration
2017	Pixel tower	Tirana	Fusha shpk	Private	Construction drawing
2024	Gateway Residential	Tirana	Kron Construction shpk	Private	Construction drawing
2025	Boulevard Office and Residential	Tirana	Startek	Private	Construction drawing
2025	Faith Park	Petrela	Albanian government	Public	Competition won Concept
2025	The Hillside	Qerret	Marnea	Private	Schematic design

NAME OFFICE

BOFILL TALLER DE ARQUITECTURA

DATE	PLACE	WORKING IN ALBANIA SINCE
2025	Sant Just Desvern, Spain	2022

PRINCIPAL

Pablo Bofill (CEO)
Hernan Cortes (Design Principal)

PROJECT TEAM

Tarás Adamović
Artur Akopov
Belén Alvarez
Carola Bretz
Cristian Camacho
Maria Campos
Andrea Canepa
Graciana De Bernardi
Imenda Dishnica
Alihan Dumankaya
Mariano Esposito
Maria Esteban
Bárbara Fonseca
Victor Galera
Barbara Gimeno
Martina Gjermeni
Javier Guardiola
Javier Irigaray
Javier Jiménez
Patricia Llasera
Martiño Lorenzo
Sofia Martinelli
Guido Martini
Enrique Mascort
Graeme McQuaker
Alborz Mohammadi
Lluis Montoliú
Jorge Muñoz
Ilaena Napier
Carmen Ortíz-Cañavate
Javi Pino
Gabriele Plinio
Jaime Prieto
Alba Peláez
Vivian Rotie
Pablo Saiz
Camilla Sala
Abhishek Sharma
Carolina Tarantino
Silvia Toraño
Maria Uporova
Cuca Vizmanos
Clara Yammine

COLLABORATORS

ARQUITECTURA-G
380-750nm
aei progetti
Arqueha
Buro Happold
Gregori Civera
Maxime Delvaux
MIR
SOCOTEC
Ne Arkitektët, Kristi Tashi, Eri Skendaj
Dalmat Architecture
X-Plan Studio

INTRODUCTION TO ALBANIA

We were first invited by Edi Rama to what we thought was a meeting with a politician. We arrived at a formal building where, quite quickly, it became clear that we were in fact meeting with an artist. Edi took us around the place as if it were an open studio, explaining the history of the city and the country as we went, surrounded by his and others' artworks. We visited the main square and the town hall too that day, talking with the mayor and other politicians in crowded bars, restaurants, streets full of music and life. We returned to Barcelona envious about what we had seen and with excitement about what was to come.

MAIN CONTEXT VS. ALBANIA

We work in different countries, communities and contexts with every project, so this question is difficult to answer. Every place presents a unique building process, and in Albania the overwhelming sensation is a liberty of thought and expression, free from the forces of globalization or dogma.

SETUP IN RELATION TO ALBANIAN PARTNER

We design the buildings ourselves, but we are deeply integrated with the local architects, builders, craftspeople and so on. They teach us about the locality, and hopefully we have taught them something too. We have held workshops for certain painting techniques, for example.

OPPORTUNITIES/CHALLENGES

The opportunities are endless at the moment. We are witnessing the golden age of Tirana, and this energy travels far beyond architecture. Tirana is not constrained by its history. It is fully focused on the future, which presents its own challenges too. Change is happening at such an incredible rate that we must take the time to pause and reflect.

EXAMPLE/INSPIRATION

The entire Skanderbeg Square project by 51N4E. It converts what is essentially an abandoned, ex-communist square in central Tirana into a free space for events, concerts and all sorts of public interaction. There is a real generosity in the open space as well as in the planting, which establishes the square as a garden at the heart of the city. The project is a combined effort, with politicians, planners, architects, landscapers and geographers all playing their part, where art and culture are considered key drivers of transformation.

TOOLBOX ALBANIA FUTURE

To be able to dream, freely.

An explosion of joy following a long tumult.

Tirana has built a creative infrastructure that has made it effervescent, teeming with possibility.

We arrived at an institutional building fronted by a Carsten Höller sculpture at the public entrance. We met Prime Minister Edi Rama there. We arrived to a very formal building, and thought we were going to have a meeting with a politician. But instead, we were surrounded by art and his art, and realized we were meeting with an artist. He took us around the place like an open studio, including the entire history of the country and the city. We visited the main square and the town hall, meeting with the mayor and politicians who were more than just politicians. They were people from the city. A team with an attitude, an eye and a desire for everything. We went to dinner with a friend in a crowded restaurant. It was noisy and packed, teeming with energy under a giant stadium. Their urban planning instilled life among the living. We went to a bar, and then another. Walking through the streets, we passed an electronic music festival. Thunderous volume and waves of people in the city center. So much excitement. From converted concrete blocks to green zones, full bars and occupied buildings. Now a community where the citizens themselves are the founders.

We returned to Barcelona the next day with a real envy of what we had seen and experienced. I grew up in Paris for the first twenty years of my life. I also lived in Barcelona for twenty years. Permanent in them is a topography of nostalgia. It can get invasive. As asphyxiating as worrying about an uncertain future. People obsess over living in outdated, sultry, stuffy eighteenth-century idylls. These are the cities of the past that have cranes for scaffolding and repair. A somewhat blocked creativity. Tirana and Albania have had a history too, but are unconstrained and concentrate on creativity and growth nearing a genesis. It is an amalgam of cultures that makes a country without fear. An immigrant's land.

In motion. Constantly redefining.

An explosion of joy following a long tumult.

To make an attractive city, there must be liberty of thought for all those who think. An ability to express. This expression needs to be at the center of substantial change. If architects and artists follow in this motion, the surroundings will change accordingly. And this has happened here.

This occurred in Berlin decades ago, and it is happening here now. Berlin was the place to be, just as we think of every place's "golden age." However, we are witnessing Tirana's golden age now and its further motion into the future. It goes beyond the city walls and connects all citizens in a special conviviality. It is not engulfed by the tides of globalization or dogma. Tirana is now a destination, unique and ambitious, with a distinct personality. A diverse landscape of natural beauty and cultural richness yet to be fully explored.

Just look at the Skanderbeg Square project by 51N4E. They converted the basically abandoned, ex-communist Tirana central square into a fantastic freedom of ungroomed vegetation, a splayed square for free thought and a dense space for events, concerts and public interaction.

Surrounded by greenery and the urban city, this architectonic reference point is at the city's heart. It is a monument to how a city can be transformed from within its urban core. One that represents a combined effort from politicians, planners, architects, landscapers and geographers. One that allows for inclusion rather than exclusion, contemplative reflection and a combined vision where art and culture stand at the forefront of tangible transformation.

This place is a restless, open-minded body, journeying for a sense of beauty that is unburdened by its past.

To dream here is to pertain to the present and to construct the future.

Pablo Bofill

1

Barcelona Tower

Any addition to Tirana's burgeoning skyline calls for a simple and elegant concept. This is especially true of the architecture being built around Skanderbeg Square, the city's main plaza and cultural heart, where projects must make a bold contribution to the site without confusing its historical identity.

Barcelona Tower serves as a modern landmark, rising 190 meters into spectacular view with a single "twisting" motion. It is both graceful and pragmatic: The twist makes for a more energy-efficient and aerodynamic building envelope (more resistant to wind loads) and combines with a central concrete core to support the overall structure. To create this form, the floor plates rotate around the core by a consistent number of degrees as they ascend and taper off towards the sky – a kind of obelisk – accommodating first offices and then mostly apartments. They are set into a chunky "plinth" containing commercial space at ground level, which works together with the rich red of the concrete pigment to demarcate this architectural world from the one beyond it.

Taller began this project by looking through the Albanian Photographic and Graphic Art Collection as well as its own archive. Twisting and tapering, the formal quality of the traditional fustanella skirt seemed to resemble the stone pillars of La Pirámide and Casa Mont-ras, both built during the 1970s, and felt fitting for a new monument in Tirana.

Location: Tirana
Program: Housing, office and retail
Size: 33,000 m^2
Status: Ongoing project

1 *Danse des Épées* (*Danse Arnaoute*), Jean-Léon Gérôme, 1885

Papuli Tower

In the mid-1970s, the silos at La Fábrica (The Factory) in Barcelona stopped storing cement and were transformed to house Taller de Arquitectura. Today, the vast concrete cylinders take on another purpose, lending their form to a skyscraper in Tirana, stretching 190 meters above the capital and hosting various office, commercial and residential programs.

Papuli Tower is essentially made up of four elongated "silos" (circular in plan) serviced by a central core (square). This geometric purity has a certain beauty to it – the circles as universal symbols of togetherness, their harmonious symmetry around the square – while allowing for the same flexible, practical floor plates enjoyed at Taller's headquarters. A sense of theater and mystery is also carried across, through exaggerated proportions and similar interior palettes to those of The Factory, including deep shades of terra-cotta flooring and oxidized concrete walls. But where the tower starts to really differ from its precedent is in the detailing, particularly in the refined facade texture and fenestration, which combine to create a building that feels animated and contemporary, yet full of original industrial character. This project nods towards Tirana's history as the most heavily industrialized region in the country: At the beginning of the sixteenth century, a bazaar was established to manufacture everything from silk and leather fabrics to ceramics and precious goods.

Location: Tirana
Program: Housing and office
Size: 40,000 m²
Status: Ongoing project

2 Ricardo Bofill Levi at La Fábrica in Barcelona, Spain, circa 1973
3 La Fábrica in Barcelona, Spain, circa 1973

2

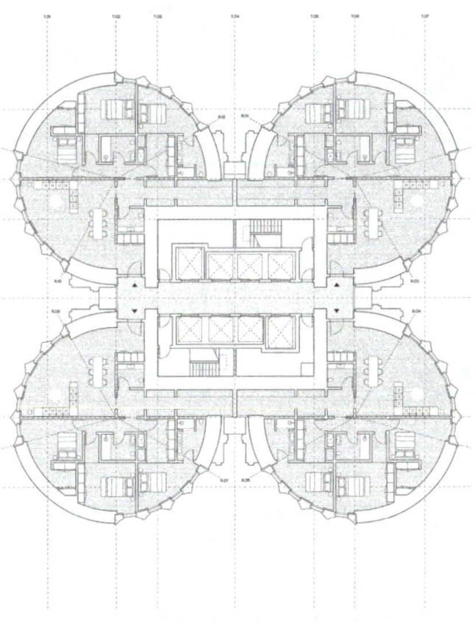

3

4

Villa nr. Red

This project in collaboration with ARQUITECTURA-G revives an abandoned building on the outskirts of Tirana. It is a villa with a unique character – somewhere between monument and ruin – and a spatiality that is defined by the original concrete structure. Its location next to a park sees a merging of the building and its surroundings, with dense vegetation climbing the facades, growing on the roof and hanging from planters.

The villa inhabits the structure in two swift gestures: First, a patio is opened in the middle of nine modules that make up the column grid. Lined with glass, this void illuminates and articulates the four different floor levels while reorganizing the contents of the eight outer modules and integrating nature at their center. Second, the existing hipped roof (found in poor condition) is demolished and replaced with travertine held up by a light metal frame, which juxtaposes the heft of the primary structural work.

Location: Tirana
Program: Villa
Size: 2,520 m^2
Status: Built

4 Exterior view
5, 6 Interior views

5

6

7

Santuario Santa Madre Teresa

By blood, I am Albanian.
By citizenship, an Indian.
By faith, I am a Catholic nun.
As to my calling, I belong to the world.
As to my heart, I belong entirely to the Heart of Jesus.

In this manner, Saint Teresa often spoke about her ancestral motherland as the foundation of her existence. The fact that her family came from Albania is well known and commemorated by the country; Saint Teresa is memorialized in the capital's largest civic hospital, its main airport and one of its finest public squares, as well as in national celebrations that take place every year on September 5. Above all, her principles are embodied in the values of Albanian society.

The Sanctuary is situated on Lapidari Hill, just south of Tirana. To reach the site, worshippers follow a winding road to the hilltop, where a small farm once existed. At this point, the road splits into two paths – one direction offers breathtaking views of the city, while the other looks out towards the sunset – and converges around the site's core architectural components: the church itself, a monument and a pavilion, all positioned on the flattest areas of the landscape. These buildings are connected by smaller footpaths that meander through the gentle slopes, inviting exploration.

The Sanctuary takes visitors on a spiritual journey through five evocative biblical gardens. In each garden, one tree or plant – either specifically identified by the Bible or emblematic of the garden's imagery – is chosen and transformed into an architectonic feature: a sculpture, fountain, monument, coenaculum or walled garden. Altogether, the landscape creates something greater than the sum of its parts; an experience rich with narrative, and with Saint Teresa at its heart.

Location: Tirana
Program: Church, botanical gardens
Size: 18,600 m^2
Status: Ongoing project

7 Biblical gardens

Red Sol Resort

Designing for the Albanian Riviera begins by grappling with the terrain: jagged rocks and sheer mountainsides, undergrowth thickened by the roots of pine and cypress trees. Red Sol Resort takes a rational approach to this landscape, placing a "reticulum" (or fine grid) over the ground plane and creating a framework around which to organize the space.

As a result, the building appears as a series of squares in plan. In section, however, it is free to shift up and down, varying in height to produce the different spatial qualities required by the resort: hotel pavilions, apartments and villas. Zigzagging its way down towards the water, the building has vertical movement akin to that of the mountain, and a materiality closely related to the earth on which it sits. It looks somewhat like a fortress, its various parts connected via a shared network of exterior stairs, bridges and walkways, such that the whole composition appears castellated from afar. Into these travel routes are incorporated pools, patios and viewpoints out to sea, offering space for quiet contemplation or interaction and a greater sense of community life.

A number of Taller's social housing projects from the 1960s and '70s share a similar typology to Red Sol. Located along the Mediterranean, these schemes were modelled on the "kasbah," a historic fortified city or settlement positioned at a vantage point in the landscape (often near the coastline) and further protected by its complex composition.

8

9

10

Location: Dhërmi
Program: Villas and apartments
Size: 10,000 m²
Status: Ongoing project

8 Construction of La Muralla Roja in Calpe, Spain, 1973
9 *Architectural Design*, Taller de Arquitectura issue featuring Walden 7 on the cover, July 1975
10 *Water Orchestra*, Edi Hila, 1985

Taulantia Promenade

Beyond a place for shade and rest, the Taulantia Promenade stands as the symbolic meeting point between the city of Durrës and the Adriatic coast. It plays on features of both the land and the sea – in its architectural form and tone respectively – while stretching 200 meters along the two over a succession of large porticoes.

The geometry of these porticoes comes from the semicircle, a shape which is often chosen by classical architects and artists for its ubiquity in nature, but which feels contemporary and welcoming when constructed in as modern a material as concrete. The repetition of the archway creates the illusion of a barrel vault, giving visitors a guide for their gaze, as well as the appearance of a continuous facade from either side. There is a visual continuity to be found from all angles, in fact: between the changing colors of the water and the blue pigments in the structure; or the shadows made by the roof and by the nearby trees.

Location: Durrës
Program: Public space
Size: 3,750 m²
Status: Ongoing project

11 *The Beauty of Durrës*, 4th century BC. Sketch by Camillo Praschniker, 1918.

11

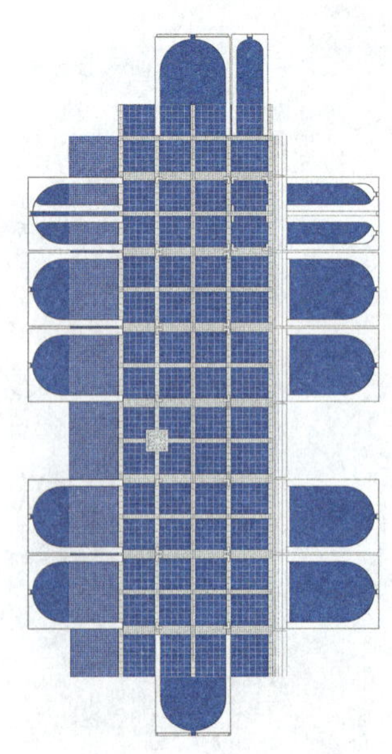

A selection of projects

START	NAME PROJECT	LOCATION	PUBLIC/PRIVATE	PHASE
2022	Barcelona Tower	Tirana	Private	Schematic design
2022	Papuli Tower	Tirana	Private	Concept design
2022	Red Sol Resort	Dhërmi	Private	Detail design
2023	Saint Teresa Sanctuary	Tirana	Public	Concept design
2023	Villa nr. Red	Tirana	Private	Executed
2024	Taulantia Promenade	Durrës	Public	Under construction

NAME OFFICE

BOLLES+WILSON

DATE

January 2026

WORKING IN ALBANIA SINCE

2002

PRINCIPALS

Dr. h.c. Peter Wilson (honorary citizen of Korça)
Professor Julia B. Bolles-Wilson, Dipl.-Ing.

ALBANIAN PARTNERS

ROA Architecture Studio
Vitru Architecture Studio
X-Plan Studio
ATELIER 4
common sense studio
Cristin Development
Ani Panariti
DEA Studio
Andronira Burda
Projection Group

PROJECT TEAM

Kejdi Lulja
Juan González Blanco
Jonas Többen
Franziska Lindner
Ghassan Saleh
Thomas Hall-Thomson
Fabian Holst
Manfred Kieler
Sijie Lyu
Maura Mroz
Yana Pavlova
Dean Piniger
Elena Rivero Lastre
Kristina Schröder
Philip Shelly
Malte Wilms
Christina Schmidt

INTRODUCTION TO ALBANIA

Invited by Mayor Edi Rama for the first international competition.

CONTEXT MAINLY WORKING

Korça and Tirana: buildings, big and small
Regional Planning Studies (ADF)

ORGANIZATION/GOAL/SETUP

We have collaborated with a number of the Albanian facilitating offices but are happiest when working closely with keen young Albanian architects – Vitru or ROA.

For this we have developed an iterative process developing from Peter Wilson's hand-drawn concepts to detail refinement and site husbanding.

SETUP IN RELATION TO ALBANIAN PARTNER

Our designs are elastic and able to absorb input from the local office.

OPPORTUNITIES/CHALLENGES

The challenge is to learn and absorb the DNA of Albanian cities; the opportunity is to think outside the box (this is rarely asked for elsewhere).

HOW TO INTEGRATE GREATER RESPONSIBILITY FOR QUALITY IN PROJECTS

Avoid gags, build simply.

INVOLVING STAKEHOLDERS

Is politically correct, but a ship needs a captain.

INSPIRING PROJECT IN ALBANIA

Our Icon Museum in Korça.

TOOLBOX ALBANIA FUTURE

Ambition, integrity and available technologies.

RECIPROCAL AGENCY IN ALBANIA

I am considered the first foreign architect to be active in Albania; in fact, BOLLES+WILSON were one of the three teams invited to the first international competition. Mayor Edi Rama needed an urban template for the central axis zone that Ismail Kadare had earlier described as a "boulevard without a city."

The French team (Architecture Studio) won. Their impressively formal proposal for lines of towers parallel to the boulevard has since melted due to market forces and planning expediencies into something like our proposed clusters of high-rises. The third team, Mecanoo, reappeared at the planning workshop Edi Rama organized upon becoming prime minister.

What were our first impressions of Tirana? Streets with almost no shops, there were no imported goods to stock a chemist or shoe shop, street stalls sold recycled stuff – plates, clothing, CDs, also bags and rucksacks (necessary for those planning to skip off to Italy). This 100% recycling was ironically exactly what our politically correct wealthier countries would today label as a "sustainable economy." Also notable were the urban blocks with perimeter access but no internal streets. Under communism there were only one hundred cars in Tirana (for party officials). Now traffic is a major problem and the earlier morphology which we at the time sketched as a confetti pattern is now the car-allergic ambition of cities like Paris, Barcelona or Hamburg.

At first one noted that a large number of cars were older Mercedes, reparable analog technology, robust enough for the pot-holed Albanian streets. They may well have been stolen in Germany, but whatever the case they, like 1950s Pontiacs in Havana, were "fit to purpose." One drove us for four hours to win the 2009 Korça master plan competition, it coughed its way up the majestic Albanian mountains and we concluded that it could either ascend or cool us with air-conditioning, but not both.

Skanderbeg Square was by then a sea of traffic, parked buses and elderly gents in hats and winter coats clustering to discuss the rapid changes their country was going through. A grand red Albanian flag stood beside the mounted bronze Skanderbeg. He is today an edge feature of the 2017 elegant 51N4E rescripting of the square. In 2005, for the third French tower competition, we rendered a panorama of the original hot-night Skanderbeg traffic bustle, with our proposed Xhubleta tower lurking in the background. Archea won that competition, although their subtle green facade was absent for years. It was conjectured that the client had run out of money, which may also explain why the other competitors never got their promised fee.

Losing competitions in Tirana becomes a habit, in fact BOLLES+WILSON have never won one. We describe this as "learning by losing." A humiliating experience as juries are broadcast live on Albanian TV. Some losers like Valerio Olgiati, whom I championed as a juror, are immediately snapped up by investors. He now disowns the resulting building beside the Tirana lake, the concrete is painted, not Swiss-haptic.

Dr. h.c. Peter Wilson, Münster, December 2024

B+W tower cluster, 2002

LEARNING BY LOSING

Unsuccessful in the "axis competition," we trooped back to our office. In a book of old Tirana postcards Edi Rama had written *"whatever the result of the competition you are always welcome to stay and work in Tirana."* And true to his word it was not long before the mayor sent an Albanian investor in our direction. An under-construction tower had fallen short of the mayor's expectations, we were to intervene to reconceptualize the facade. As our design evolved, a few more floors with untamed cantilevers appeared, but due to the fact that there were no cranes on site (concrete was carried up on workers' backs – pyramid-style) we were able to simplify the building form above level eight. Below that we legitimized deconstructivist excesses as glazed boxes/monitor screens. This was the Coin Tower, formerly known as Polychromink (our working title).

Before our arrival Edi Rama, an artist by training, had activated aid funds to splash his own polychromed sketches across gray socialist housing. A brilliant strategy that made the gestalt of the city a public issue. The World Bank responded – "we only finance white or gray facades" – to which the mayor reported at a dinner in his favorite illegal restaurant that he *"told the World Bank to eff off."* Following the collapse of communism, public parks and also the banks of the Lana River had filled up with illegal (informal) structures, some five floors high. The mayor had flattened them all, giving the city back its public spaces, for this he became a national hero and at one point also "World Mayor of the Year."

At that time a belt of informal houses had sprung up around Tirana (built by Albanians migrating from the north), many of these were painted bright colors in the hope that the mayor would not demolish them. Much of this spontaneous urbanism has since been legitimized with roads and infrastructure. Many of the new arrivals, having been farmers, planted fruit trees.

Inspired by what we had come across in Tirana, I at the time wrote an open letter to London's *Blueprint* magazine, saying *"if it's color you are after forget Acapulco, Tirana's the place . . ."*

Following the mayor's lead, our Polychromink Tower was wrapped in rainbow striped sun louvers. Unfortunately, last-minute cost-saving omitted every second louver. Now to get the intended effect, one must lie on the pavement at the base of the tower. From the start it was obvious that working in Tirana required an alternative mode of practice, sometimes this involved contributing to the mayor's program of painted facades. One of mine, called "Optimistic Vectors," projected arrows across the facade, pointing from left to right, the *New York Times* published it in a report on Edi's program – it is now said in Tirana that it shows visitors how to exit the city. Another we called "Virtual Air Conditioners" – here we engaged the DNA of Tirana – every building, new or old, is encrusted with satellite dishes, air conditioners and balcony enclosures. The photos we received were speckled with the little cyclops-eyed boxes – our facade graphic simply specified sites for more air conditioners. Red and orange stripes homogenized the building volume, and omitting the middle scale juxtaposed the emancipated building form against thematized detail. It achieved immediate iconic status in Tirana – that is, before the fierce Albanian sun bleached the color. Now when the mayor of Korça asks for color concepts for socialist housing we insist on using long-lasting Keim paint.

Rationalist Apartments

Social housing, facade colors, Korça

Virtual Air Conditioners

KORÇA ACUPUNCTURE

The mentoring phase came to an end with our first commission for a totally new building, which we dubbed "Rationalist Apartments," it stands in the second row behind the 1930s Italian Art Academy. Even here construction was far more open-ended than over-legalized European procedures. At one point Fatmir Bektashi, an investor known for planting vegetables around his buildings (in our case it was olive trees in the street), asked us to incorporate a load of damaged roof tiles he had got for a knock-down price. Thinking on our feet, we used them as the building's plinth – laid horizontally with thick mortar joints like ancient Roman brickwork. The super-haptic result gave us great confidence in labor-intensive Albanian building possibilities that would simply be unaffordable in Europe. For this project the investor brought a crane from Germany.

The operative mode of our Albanian activities went through a phase change with the win of the 2009 international competition for a master plan for downtown Korça. At this moment international aid loans were revolutionizing the Albanian built landscape (such loans also knit a country into long-term debt to a pernicious neoliberal global economy). Already in Korça, aid money had led to below-ground infrastructure renewal and new cobbled streets in the historic center. After this incentive Mayor Niko Peleshi was concerned that people returning from Greece or the US often demolished their family villa to build eight-floor apartment buildings. The master plan was to marshal this threat to the delicate scale of nineteenth-century stone villas. Our proposal prioritized a symbiosis, an interweaving of new interventions within the historic urban morphology. It also removed traffic from the central Boulevard Shën Gjergji, at one end of which an Orthodox cathedral had popped up with the fall of communism. At the other end we placed a campanile called the "Red Bar in the Sky." When, in the Albanian Parliament, the opposition Democratic Party (ex-communists) accused Edi Rama's Socialist Party of ruining Korça with this slim tower, the PM responded with the quip *"that's the first aesthetic opinion I have ever heard from your party."* Not long after, walking in Korça, he said to me, *"I also have a problem with the campanile - it's not high enough."* Politics are destructively polarized in Albania, this we learned with one Korça project where our structural engineer (Democratic Party) absconded with our architect's fee, we as agents of the Socialists were to be unpaid.

Over the last fifteen years we have added more than thirty buildings to Korça, a process of acupuncture, some public (library, city hall, Icon Museum), some for private investors (bus terminal, hotels, housing), also public squares and parks. This process of long-term husbanding would not have been possible without the backup of local facilitating offices, in particular the young but highly capable office Vitru, with whom we evolved an iterative working procedure both in planning and on-site, and from whom we also learned local techniques for stone walls. Trotsky once wrote that developing countries step into the game at a particular moment without the usual long evolution. Albanians took to mobile phones like fish to water, laser-cutting of steel is also no problem.

In the meantime commissions abound in Albania for regional planning studies, here as architects we have in various formats teamed up with economists or tourism experts to tour from village to village, fact-gathering and identifying possible local needs. The role of the architect at this regional scale is marginal, due to international codes of accountability, excessive report writing, stakeholder consultation, etc. The ADF (Albanian Development Fund) often polices these protracted procedures. We are now much happier with direct commissions like the Tirana International Hotel, which today terminates the axis we first studied. Or even the Shkodra Football Stadium and the AFA (Albanian Football Association) headquarters, built on the site of one of our earlier painful competition losses (to an unbuildable Dutch gag). Learning by losing is a technique I would recommend to the droves of international architects now trying to get a foot in the Albanian door. Also along the way they could read my book – *Some Reasons for Traveling to Albania.*

The Red Bar in the Sky, Korça

KORÇA – FIFTEEN YEARS OF ACUPUNCTURE

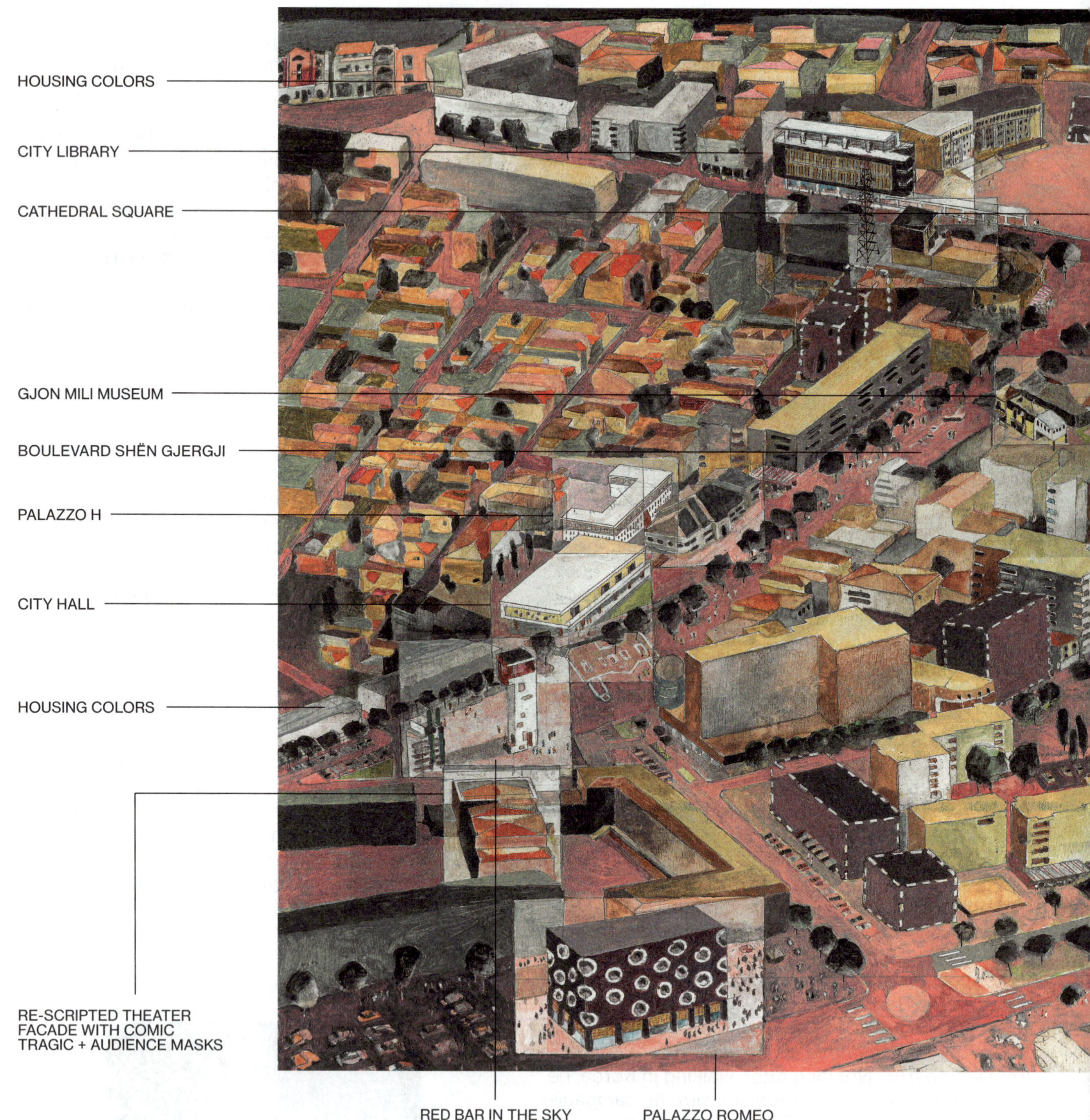

Since the 2009 win of the international master plan competition, BOLLES+WILSON have been engaged in multiple interventions and re-scriptings of the urban fabric of Korça. The intention is to respect the historic scale of stone villas, to ameliorate out-of-scale communist interventions and to add a patchwork of characterful objects that have now caused Korça to become one of the most visited cities in Albania. Collaboration with young local architects (Vitru) engendered iterative design and site procedures. A new Cathedral Square was first raised by three steps to exclude traffic and later framed by a new City Library and the (mixed-use) House of Pine building.

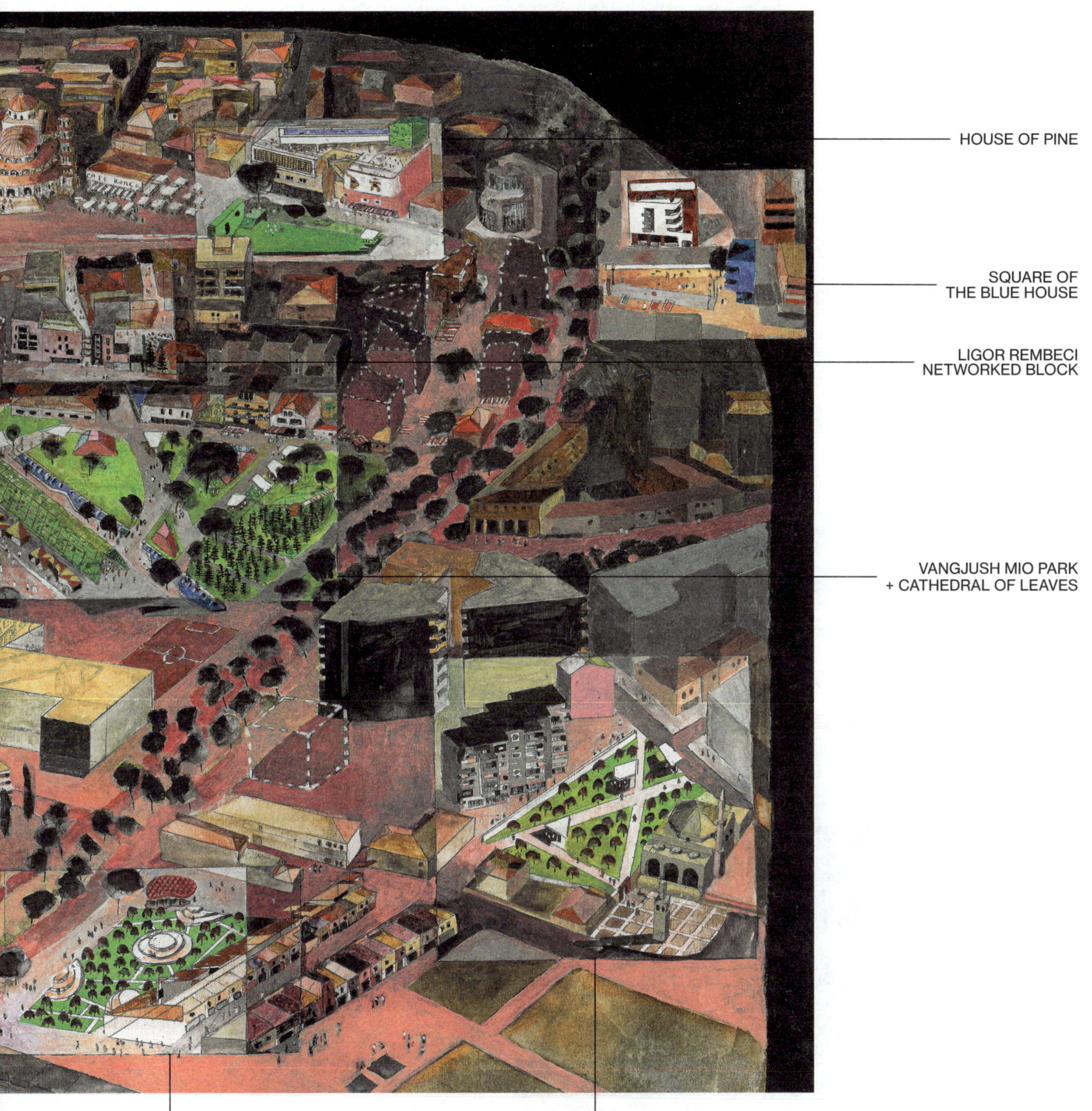

Shop owners at first protested but are now pleased about the removal of traffic from the Boulevard Shën Gjergji, which leads from Cathedral Square to Theater Square – the site of the new Red Bar in the Sky campanile. Four smaller squares have been landscaped: the Blue House and Square, a Paradise Garden for the Iljaz Bej Mosque with plum trees, the Ottoman Bazaar Square and a Cathedral of Leaves, in the Vangjush Mio Park. Other private interventions include Palazzo Romeo and, in the Ligor Rembeci block, the Serenity Residences.

KORÇA THEATRICS

Following the Red Bar in the Sky, a new chapter in the history of the nearby theater was written. The theater originally had a heavy classical facade – a present from the USSR. When Hoxha fell out with the Russians the classicism was removed and replaced by Balkan art deco. This in turn was in 2017 rescripted with the addition of a giant convex tragic and also a concave comic mask (traditional theater signifiers). Audience masks by a local potter were added to each of the 135 existing facade squares. The comic mask is embossed into a haptic black basalt cube (new internal stair). Instruction sketches helped local craftsmen carve the tragic mask with a bread knife from insulation material.

PALAZZO ROMEO, KORÇA

Palazzo Romeo, resulting building

Around the corner from the theater, the Palazzo Romeo (client's name) has become a local landmark.

SCENOGRAPHIC URBANISM – CATHEDRAL SQUARE, KORÇA

Library, Korça

Cathedral Square was the anchor component of the 2009 master plan. To the left of the (post-communist pop-up) cathedral, the new library now collaborates with the ex-communist party headquarters building to frame the public event space. The library's interior is now an intensely used third space for young Korçans.

SCENOGRAPHIC URBANISM – BUS TERMINAL, KORÇA

Bus terminal, street-side

Relocated to the edge of Korça, the new 2019 bus terminal relates as much to the wide landscape as to the nearby city. The concept sketch also co-opts the nearby cooling tower with a Leonidov-quoting graphic. Minibuses cater for long-distance travel in Albania, and bus drivers sleep on the upper floors of the terminal.

CULTURAL SCRIPTING – ICON MUSEUM, KORÇA

Gold Salon with Petersburg hanging

The Kubrick room with two fourteenth-century icons

An existing concrete frame prescribes the volume of this museum sequence – A MUSEUM OF BYZANTINE ART – a treasure house of icons. As Culture Minister Cumbaro said at the opening – "Culture is the new engine of development, and this museum a world window on Albanian culture." The internal "architectural promenade" starts in the high Gold Salon with a dense Petersburg hanging of icons. Then come a White modernist balcony, a Black Labyrinth (medieval atmospherics), a grand Red Salon (Iconostasis – altar screen). Concluding is a White salon (inspired by Kubrick's *2001*) with only two fourteenth-century icons. The PM asked for the facade to be pimped – black plaster was added.

LEARNING FROM KORÇA – RINIA PARK

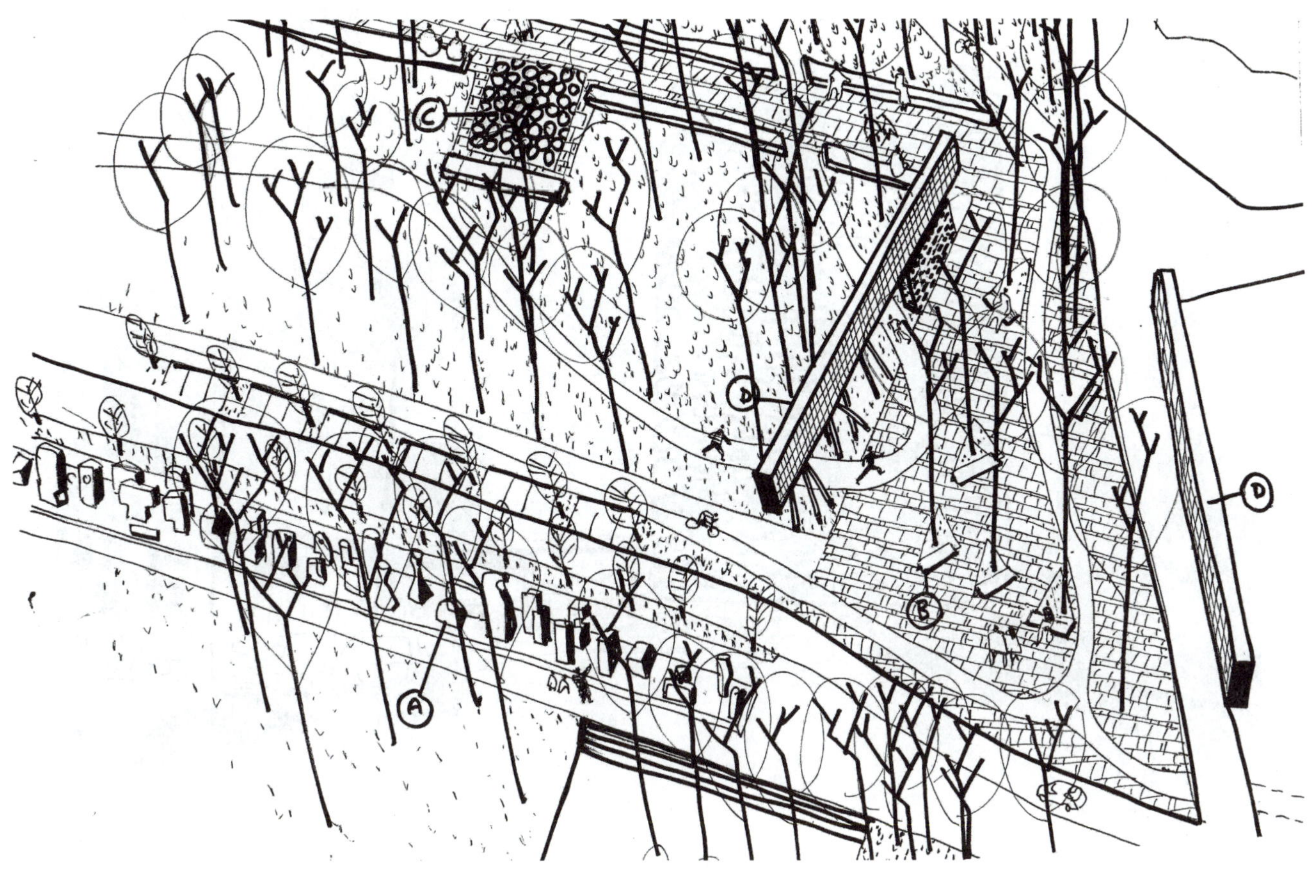

Rinia Park

City hall

The 2015 revitalization of Rinia Park was sketched on a digital tree survey. A light beam was invented, LED chains between glass bricks for softly illuminated crowds to promenade on balmy summer evenings. Elsewhere in Korça, close observation of local architectural syntax has informed Hotel Park Gate. A narrative interpretation of the city's evolution was the first step in transforming the communist library into a new city hall. Existing tiles were integrated.

TWO RELATED TOWERS

TET Tower,
Rruga e Elbasanit, Tirana

The Tirana East Tower (TET) bids farewell to those leaving on the Elbasan Road. Those who drive on will be welcomed by its blue cousin in Vlora.

BETWEEN RESTORATION AND INNOVATION IN ALBANIA

The tilted platform grandstand as background to a spontaneous street market.

The Shkodra Football Stadium had to be ready for the next "turf skirmish" between Serbia and Albania. The five tilted platforms each marshal five hundred visiting fans, a stepped coral with heavy steel handrails. Even in the first sketch, the status of such urban figures was seen as background to everyday life, as it is now to a spontaneous street market. Existing stands with 1,200 seats were given a wind animated screen. From a European perspective, Albania embodies the essential character of otherness. It is still engaged in the construction of identity on the international horizon. Not yet overregulated (except in this case by UEFA), things are possible there that would be unthinkable elsewhere.

CRANE – NO CRANE

CRANE – Tirana International Hotel (Intercontinental), 2016/2024

NO CRANE – Polychromink Tower (Coin), 2004/2008

Seen from Mother Teresa Square, the gold facade of the Intercontinental Hotel anchors the central axis with its noble Mediterranean pines. A black slab lurks behind the visage of gold with its uncompromising grid of windows, each swerving slightly to the left to accommodate illumination. A tower crane was instrumental for the 2016–2024 construction; this was not the case for the 2004–2008 Coin Tower (right). Somewhat to the left of the above perspective are the Rationalist Apartments, the first construction in Tirana to use a site crane.

A GOLD VILLAGE IN THE SKY

Bazaar Gate Tower, under construction

The under-construction Bazaar Gate Tower will be capped by a village of gold penthouses, its tall facade a curtain of bamboo leaves.

AFA TIRANA

Albanian Football Association headquarters

The 2016 Albanian Football Association headquarters building marches confidently across its site. Behind blue and green tinted glass, four levels of open-plan workspaces are backed by glazed team leader boxes.

Coin Tower, Rationalist Apartments, Virtual Air Conditioners (façade graphic), Deputy Prime Minister's office (interior), Rognor Hotel (façade graphic), Hotel Intercontinental (Tirana), Albanian Football Association (Tirana), Football Stadium (Shkodra), Let's-Twist-Again Tower (Tirana), Vasarely Tower (Tirana), House of Moon (Tirana), Bazaar Gate Tower (Tirana), TET Tower (Tirana), Footballers' Hotel – National Team (Tirana) . . .

Master plan Korça, 2009 . . . Red Bar in the Sky, Theater Korça, Palazzo Romeo, Icon Museum, Cathedral Square, Rinia Park, Kids' Activity Center and Sport Park, Gjon Mili Museum, Bus terminal, Cathedral of Leaves, Ligor Rembeci quarter, House of Pine, Serenity Residences, Green Villas, Hotel Park Gate, City Hall, Bazaar Square, Blue House and Square, Paradise Garden, Japanese Garden, Boulevard Republica (façade colors) . . . (all Korça)

NAME OFFICE

CAMILO REBELO

DATE	PLACE	WORKING IN ALBANIA SINCE
July 25, 2025	Porto, Portugal	2023

PRINCIPALS
Camilo Rebelo
Susana Martins

PROJECT TEAM
Carolina Morgado
Leonardo Barros
Patrícia Fernandes
Pedro Pinto Ferreira

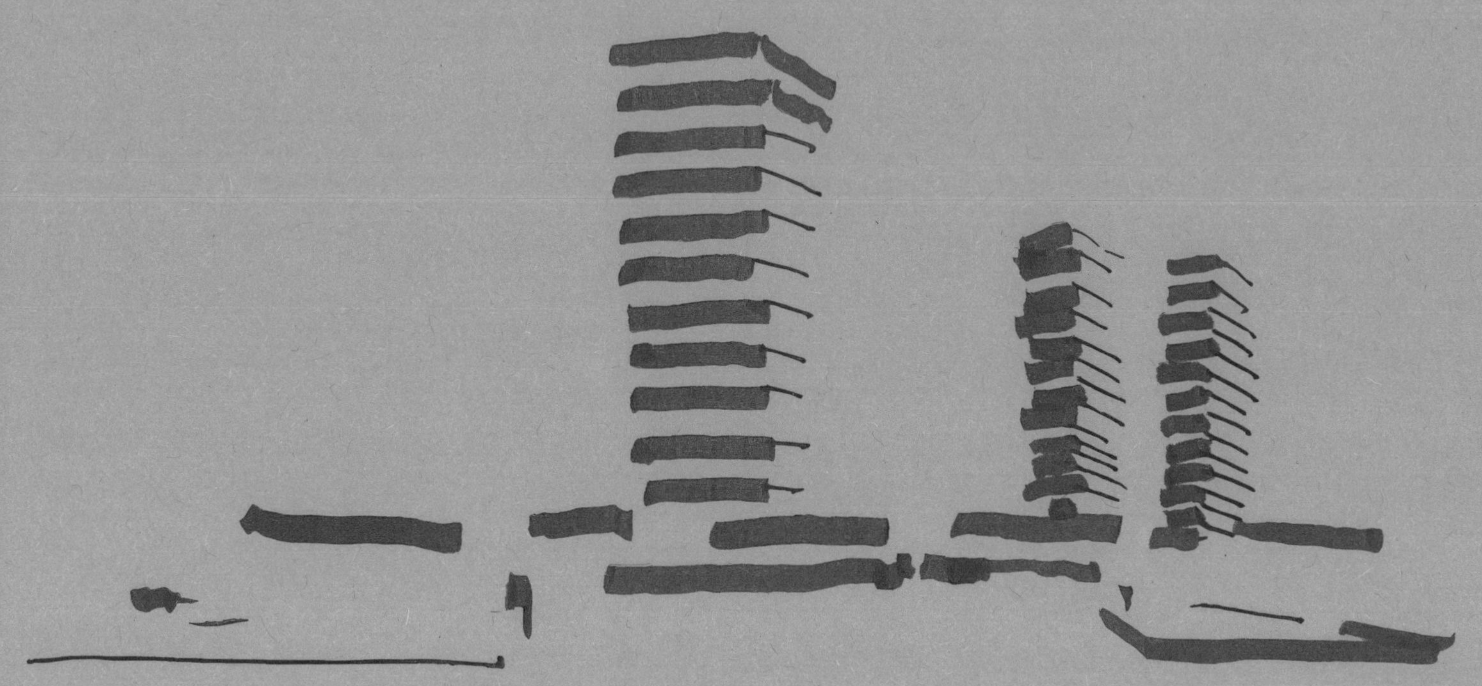

MAIN CONTEXT VS. ALBANIA

We work in different contexts, from urban areas to protected natural areas. Therefore, it is difficult to define a pattern of approach in Albania, as each project is unique. Some present difficulties in urban issues/contexts, related to urban legislation and specific urban construction rules in Albania, while others present challenges due to the natural environment and preserved areas, which require continuous research so that we do not contribute to their destruction.

ORGANIZATION/GOAL/SETUP

Four of our projects are in partnership with Álvaro Siza and with technical consultancy from G.O.P. All projects are discussed and shared to find the most accurate idea and solution for each project.

The Albanian context is no different from other contexts of working abroad, so it is best to have a team with us, from engineers to specialists and architects, whilst also having a strong local partnership in all these areas to have direct contact with the local reality. The combination of our experience working abroad and the fresh and local reality of local partners brings together the strategy and the key to start developing any project.

SETUP IN RELATION TO ALBANIAN PARTNER

From the first idea, we shared everything with our local partners, who immediately became our development partners. Obviously, we share ideas and thoughts about the idea and, later, about the project itself, as they help and advise us in the more advanced stages, such as the construction phase. We expect the participation of local partners, and for us it is important that they are aware of how each project is progressing. Each one is unique in the way we relate to each other as different architecture offices, and with that in mind, we move forward together.

OPPORTUNITIES/CHALLENGES

The opportunity for architects in Albania is the notion that there is an excellent mood, the positive vibe that accompanies each project.

The optimism we find here is unique; we don't find it anywhere else.

Another important thing for us is the climate. We work by understanding the winds, the sun, the shadows – that is, the weather. This is a driving force for ideas and projects, opening new aspects that we can explore. Dealing with this climate promotes new ideas, methods and thoughts.

HOW TO INTEGRATE GREATER RESPONSIBILITY FOR QUALITY IN PROJECTS

The way to take greater responsibility for quality is to allow time for research. Of course, we know that clients want magnificent render images as a commercial product, but sometimes the rendering comes before the idea and the strategy. We know this is an option, but we are not interested in it . . . We work by researching typologies, landscapes and forms, and our images are the result of that research. In our view, quality comes from strong research parallel to project development.

EXAMPLE/INSPIRATION

The project in Albania that is an example is Prime Minister Edi Rama's project for Albania itself, which is ambitious and requires large teams: government agencies, architects with a spectrum of ideas, engineers, landscaping specialists and many more . . . For me, this idea from Prime Minister Edi Rama, followed by the wave of positivity that exists in Albania, provides enough motivation to continue.

FAROL

Year 2023
Architecture Camilo Rebelo + Common Sense Studio
Principals in charge Camilo Rebelo with Susana Martins + Jurtin Hajro
Collaborators Leonardo Barros, Patrícia Fernandes and Pedro Pinto Ferreira + Sindi Balla and Odet Zaimi
Consultant Mina Ghorbanbakhsh
Structural engineering G.O.P Lda. – Jorge Nunes da Silva + HT Construction – Hydajet Tota
Collaborators José Pedro Martins and Francisco Valente
Promoter Gjoka Konstruksion

LAKE

Year 2024
Architecture Camilo Rebelo
Principals in charge Camilo Rebelo with Susana Martins + Jurtin Hajro
Collaborators Leonardo Barros, Patrícia Fernandes and Pedro Pinto Ferreira
Consultant Mina Ghorbanbakhsh
Structural engineering G.O.P Lda. – Jorge Nunes da Silva
Collaborators José Pedro Martins and Francisco Valente

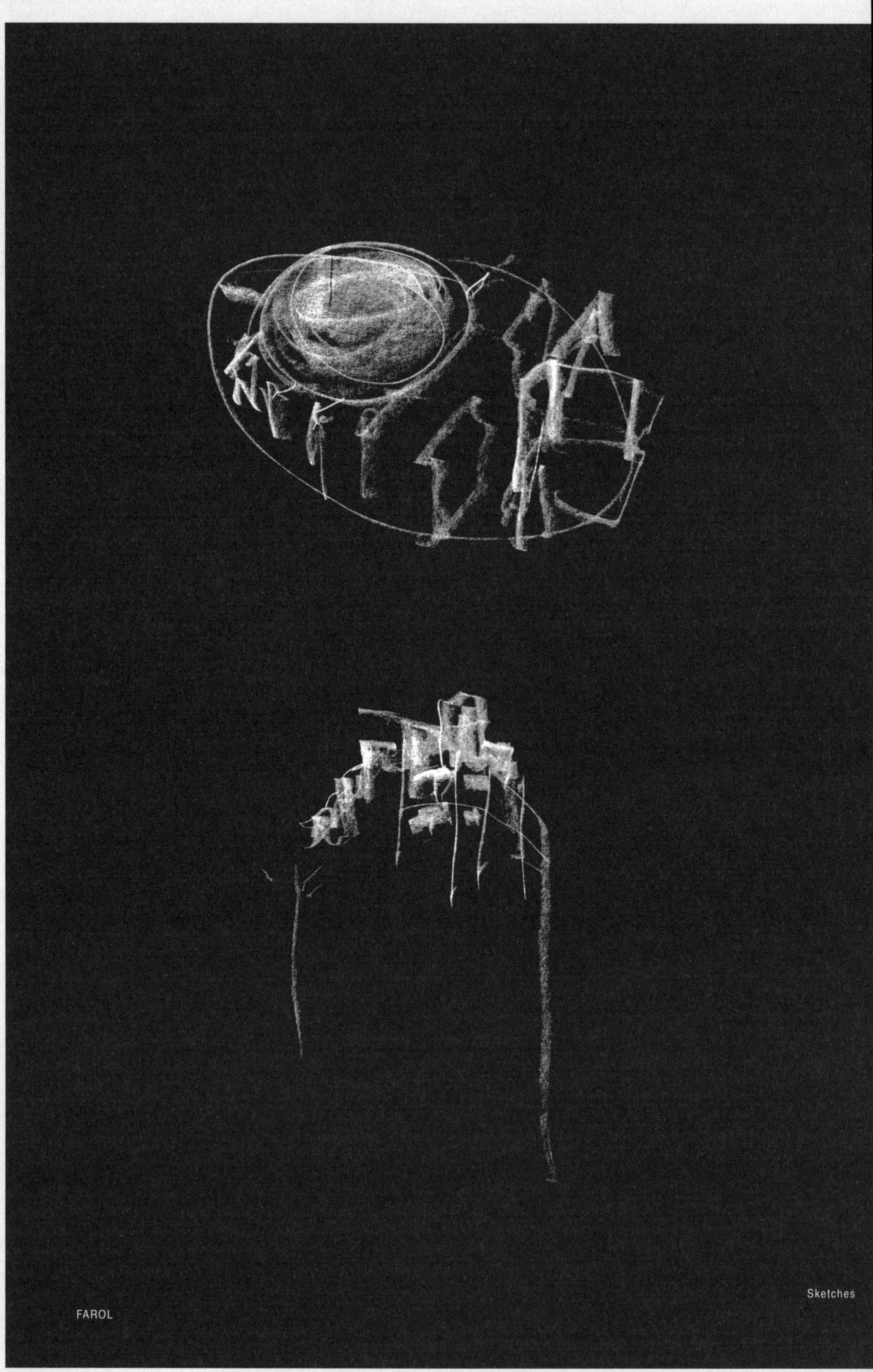

FAROL

Sketches

Collage

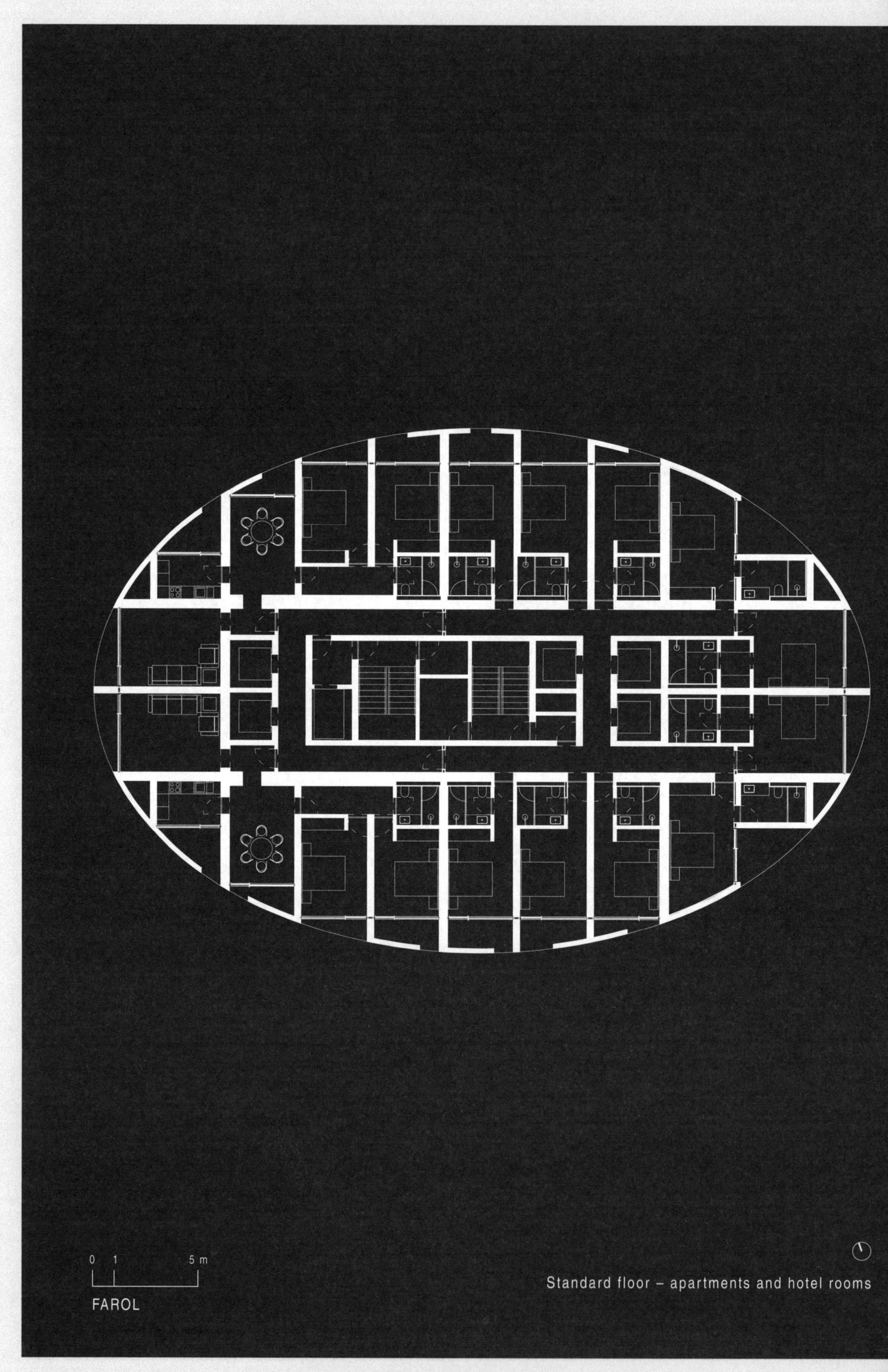

Standard floor – apartments and hotel rooms

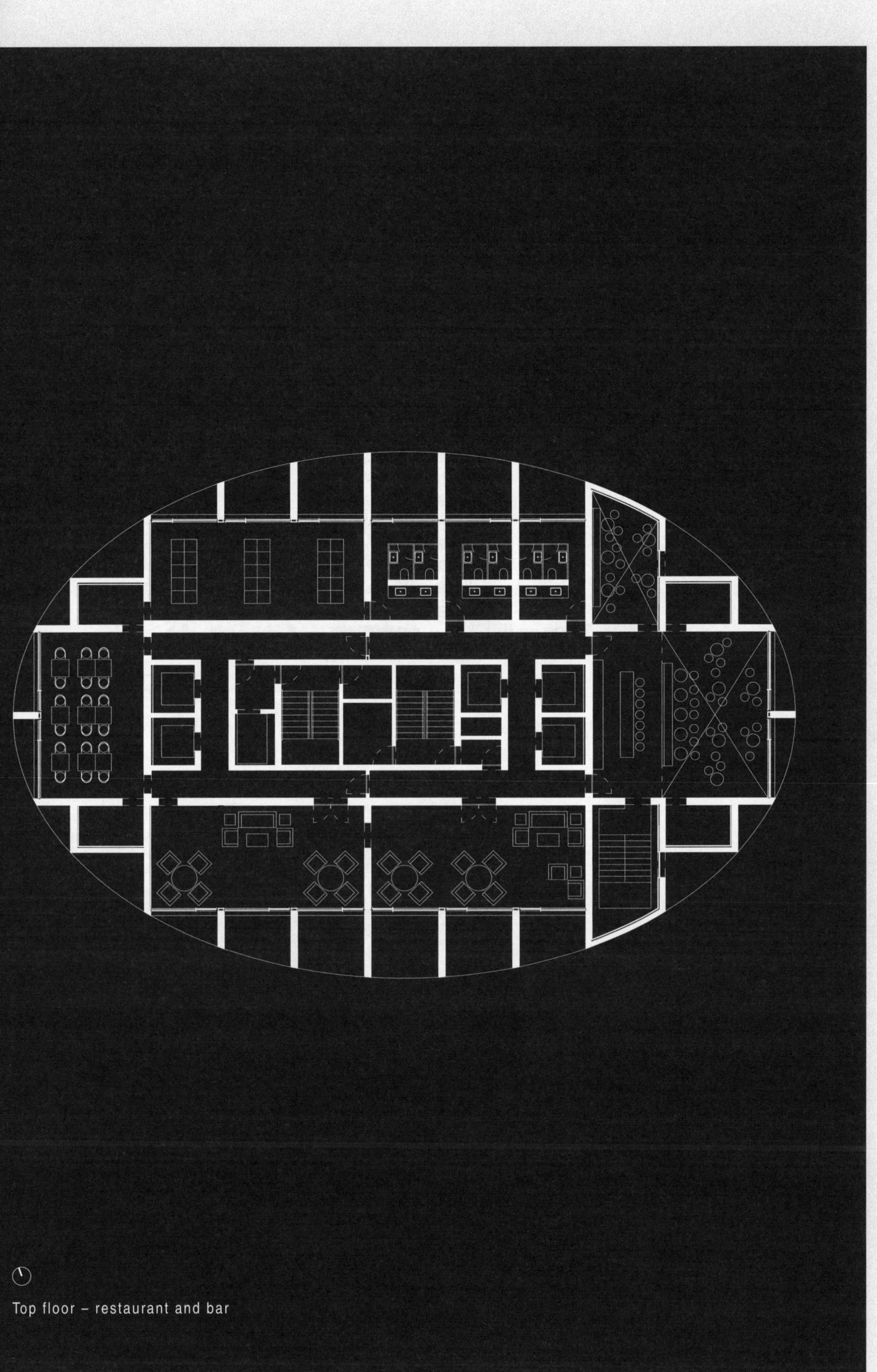

Top floor – restaurant and bar

Sketches

LAKE

Collage

FAROL

The concept for this tower is based on a fusion of three distinct elements – a lighthouse, a column and an ellipse.

Farol is the Portuguese name for *Fari*, lighthouse in Albanian.

Tirana has the intense urban dynamic of a developing contemporary city which emanates energy night and day. This "lighthouse" has a double urban character, a landmark of a city neighborhood into a new centrality, as well as a light stream in the night of lively Tirana.

A column is a statement of culture and time expressed by a combination of structure, geometry and theme. Throughout time, from Karnak, the Doric column and Persepolis to modern columns, we can read history.

As we can see often in the Doric columns, this tower has no base, since for us the common ground and ground zero for its implantation is the city level. The rooftop opens towards the sky, spreading walls, voids and shapes like a chapiter.

A classic column normally has a circular section, however, a circle is a stable dynamic. Therefore, we chose the ellipse, which induces and expresses movement and eccentric dynamics.

This column has a break which represents, in scale, the average skyline of the city of old Tirana. The upper part symbolizes the modern city and its urban statement – in this case, the rebirth of the Don Bosco area.

The plan has an orthogonal grid which is orientated, like in old times, by the cardinal points. Its core has stairs, elevators and shafts, which became the spine of this living structure.

The façade composition is based on horizontal and vertical plans, which are extensions of the inner walls or slabs. They represent stability (horizontal) and progression (vertical) and should be understood as the dynamics or matrix of the living contemporary societies.

The main construction material – white concrete – gives identity and oneness to the vertical system, structure and spaces. Glass and mirrors will be placed to emphasize the theme – stem to the sky – and at night these will provide a lively light beam in the city landscape.

Camilo Rebelo

LAKE

Tirana has the privilege of having lakes in the city center. Nature, natural environments and their landscapes are highly valued when it comes to the quality of life and well-being of citizens and city lovers.

This lake in particular is an immense opportunity for the public and private domain, since its potential is yet to be explored, and it is practically empty of public use. As such, our project considers these two realities; enhancing the natural conditions with the aim of inviting citizens to multiple activities and, at the same time, proposing a new spot: a multilayered program composed of a hotel, a plaza, commercial areas and housing.

Our complex will be located between the city and the lake. This is a first approach to requalifying the lake and the way it is experienced, creating a new public plaza and a gate for the lake and its green atmosphere.

In addition, the lake will be the focus of a landscaping intervention that encourages animal and plant biodiversity in order to increase contact between the lake and the citizens.

Camilo Rebelo

LIST OF PROJECTS

START	NAME PROJECT	LOCATION	DEVELOPER	ENGINEER	PUBLIC/PRIVATE
2023	Farol Tower	Tirana	Gjoka Konstruksion		Private
2023	Vlora Tower*	Vlora	Texas Development, Hel-Pet, Alb-Edil		Private
2023	Ring	Dhërmi			Private
2023	Dune master plan*	Rana e Hedhun	Gruppo IDA	Ilir Trebicka and Klodiana Kucuku	Private
2024	Kulla's Village	Dhërmi	EGEU STONE shpk, ADEL shpk and IMMO-INVEST sha		Private
2024	Lake	Tirana			Private
2025	Trilogy*	Tirana	Gruppo IDA	Ilir Trebicka and Klodiana Kucuku	Public/private
2025	Borsh master plan*	Borsh	Millennium Group		Private

*Projects in co-authorship with Álvaro Siza.

NAME OFFICE

CASANOVA + HERNANDEZ ARCHITECTS

DATE
January 2025

PLACE
Rotterdam, Netherlands

WORKING IN ALBANIA SINCE
2014

PRINCIPALS
Helena Casanova
Jesús Hernández

PROJECT TEAM
Bozhidara Andreeva
Nerea Bilbatua Atorrasagasti
Salva Carta
Mayra Jole Castaniere
Mariachiara Colosimo
Claudio Costantino
Emanuel Dad Khan
Omar Desouky
Maria Dumitriu
Christos Ellinas
Pablo Escuder
Futura Falco
Riccardo Maria Giannelli
Maria Gomez
Mohsen Haghparast
Mohammad Sajjad Hajhosseini
Baoky Huang
Michał Jabłonowski
Jan Ksiazek
Antonio Lorusso
Ilias Markolefas
Daniel Martín de los Ríos
Laura Merchán
Cosmin Mihai Mindru
Luca Misosniky
Alireza Najibi
Luca Natali
Giulia Nencini
Oleksandr Nenenko
Lara Noriega
Irene Portella
Haritsya Putri
Mohanad Qsous
Denisio Ranieri
Fabio Rey Ishihara
Teresa Rodriguez
Irene Sánchez
Jaime Sanz
Nikos Spyrou
Thomas Stathopoulos
Javier Trallero
Stefan Videnov
Denys Yakovenko

INTRODUCTION TO ALBANIA

In 2013, we conducted a research project financed by the Dutch Stimuleringsfonds for Architecture, which culminated in the publication of a book by ACTAR titled *Public Space Acupuncture*. Our research analyzed and compared case studies of innovative strategies for activating city life in nine European cities. One of the selected projects was the artistic painting of façades and the series of playgrounds I Love to Play! in Tirana. Visiting Tirana and studying these strategies, we discovered a fascinating city at the very beginning of its transformation under Mayor Edi Rama. The creativity, energy and determination that he and his team invested in the city's urban transformation were remarkable, often working with limited budgets, but always pursuing ambitious goals. These innovative strategies were highlighted in the book, where Tirana was compared with other forward-thinking cities in Switzerland, Austria, Denmark, Spain and the Netherlands.

One year later, we were invited to participate in an international competition to design the Marubi National Museum of Photography in Shkodra. We won the competition, and since then, we have been deeply involved in projects in Albania.

MAIN CONTEXT VS. ALBANIA

In every context we try to push the boundaries of creativity to get an innovative design. Although the architectural context of Albania shares many similarities with other European countries, its cultural, religious, historical and social differences make it a unique and inspiring place to work. Recognizing and appreciating these differences has been essential to the development of our projects in Albania. Rather than simply adapting global solutions to the Albanian context, we have drawn inspiration from its unique characteristics to create designs with a distinct identity.

ORGANIZATION/GOAL/SETUP

In Albania, we primarily work on public projects, often with cultural programs. For this reason, it is essential to establish strong connections with local historians, ethnographers, archaeologists, restorers and other professionals in the cultural sector. This collaboration provides the projects with a solid local foundation, which is then contrasted with – and often challenged by – the perspectives of international experts, such as curators and specialists in museology, education and communication. This productive tension between local knowledge and global ideas frequently serves as a source of inspiration, sometimes leading to the creation of unique and innovative projects. During the technical phases of the projects, we also collaborate with local engineers and experts to achieve the best solutions, considering the technical and economic context of each project.

Over time, our network of local and international collaborators has grown and been strengthened. Many collaborators have become regular partners, leading to the formation of stable working teams and the development of a working methodology focused on addressing the requirements of each specific context.

SETUP IN RELATION TO ALBANIAN PARTNER

The design is conceived, developed and controlled from the initial concept to the final detail by the office of Casanova + Hernandez Architects in Rotterdam. Each project requires assembling a specific team of local and international experts. In many cases, partnerships are established with local offices of engineers, architects or restoration specialists.

Casanova + Hernandez Architects oversees urban planning, architecture, landscape architecture, interior design and exhibition design, and Jesús Hernández is the partner in the firm who plays the role of team leader of the whole group of experts, traveling frequently to Albania and maintaining direct contact with clients, experts and stakeholders.

We have chosen this setup for working in Albania because such complex projects require a responsible party to ensure coherence across all parts of the project while maintaining conceptual continuity from the beginning to the end of the design process. This approach enables us to adapt every aspect of the project as needed, ensuring the best possible outcome regardless of the circumstances.

OPPORTUNITIES/CHALLENGES

The main opportunity arises from working in a country undergoing a deep social and urban transformation, emerging from the darkness produced by forty years of communist dictatorship and walking in the path of modernization with the goal of integration in the European Union.

The main challenge lies in the absence of established standards to guide this transformation. Far from being seen as a disadvantage, we consider this an opportunity to rethink concepts such as the role of public spaces, museums and cultural buildings in our cities; new models of sustainable tourism; construction systems; environmental considerations; and social sustainability.

EXAMPLE/INSPIRATION

We have worked with several historical buildings in Albania from different historical periods, including Byzantine, Ottoman, Venetian and modernist communist architectural styles. Each of them possesses unique characteristics that influence us in one way or another.

Among them, we find the design of the National Historical Museum in Tirana particularly inspiring, not only as a modernist building with significant architectural value facing Skanderbeg Square, but also as an example of a collaborative design process during the communist period, involving a group of architects, engineers and artists.

Beyond its architectural and artistic achievements, the National Historical Museum is an example for us because it was built during the 1980s, a period when Albania was isolated from the world and experiencing a severe economic crisis. Despite material shortages and challenging circumstances, the construction of this museum reflects the engagement and commitment of many dedicated professionals.

MARUBI NATIONAL MUSEUM OF PHOTOGRAPHY, SHKODRA

MARUBI & AI WEIWEI

The photographs of Pietro Marubi were one of the first things that impressed me most about Albania. They are an intriguing and addictive cocktail of history, ethnography and art. I immediately imagined those photos exhibited in a contemporary art museum, alongside pieces by Jannis Kounellis and Gerhard Richter. More than a collection, I envisioned it as the new Albanian ambassador to the world. We contacted Kim Knoppers, who at the time was curator at the photo museum in Amsterdam, to collaborate on the project and we shared the same addiction. Months after the Marubi museum's opening, a temporary exhibition of Marubi was indeed held at the photo museum in Amsterdam. Two parallel exhibitions were opened that day, Marubi and Ai Weiwei. Just perfect.

MY COLLEAGUE KOLË

Sometimes the fascination with historical figures makes us feel as if they accompany us throughout the design process. Such is the case with Kolë Idromeno, the nineteenth-century architect, photographer, painter and sculptor from Shkodra who designed the building where the museum is located. Seeing his photographs, I sensed an avant-garde and nonconformist quality in Kolë. Referring to him as Kolë conveys a sense of closeness that influenced the project. We carefully restored the original architecture while adding a contemporary extension at the back. This open and transparent volume, articulated around an intimate courtyard, provides natural light and diagonal views between the museum's spaces. It aims to characterize the contemporary museum as a project of our time, while also resonating with the ever-contemporary nature of Kolë Idromeno.

THE HUMAN DIMENSION

A key part of the design process took place in Albania through many casual conversations while drinking coffee or homemade rakia. I recall Lucian Bedeni, the museum director, passionately explaining photographic history while showing old glass negatives, and historian Zef Paci discussing the significance of poses and painted backgrounds in photos. These talks inspired elements like the room dedicated to Pietro Marubi's studio, where a peephole allows visitors to secretly observe others posing like in Marubi's photos. Tourists, students, ambassadors, ministers and all sorts of people pose and take a photo in this room. The design transforms the visit into a memorable experience and a tribute to an era when posing held special meaning.

SHKODRAN SENSE OF HUMOR

After the museum's opening, we had an informal dinner with the client, part of the team and the Dutch ambassador to Albania, Dewi van de Weerd. During the meal, the ambassador asked about the inspiration for the irregular glass façade of the courtyard. Silence fell, and everyone looked at me, intrigued about the answer. I answered that our original design was based on a perfect grid, but the builder made so many mistakes that we kept shifting things to hide them. The ambassador, astonished, asked, "Really?" We all burst into laughter, and I clarified it was a joke. The builder had done an excellent job. The joke played on the reputation of Albanian builders for not always following plans, but also on how foreign architects balance between pursuing strict quality and solving this problem with creativity.

B.1. Chronological exhibition - Room C
FOTOTEKA KOMBËTAR
C1-01
C1-04
C1-07
C2-02
C2-05
A3-02
78
Margjela e Kapedan Pashës
Margjela of Captain Pasha
79
Gorr Jakova me grue
Gorr Jakova with his wife
Thematic-room A: Pjeter Marubi's Photo Studio (Driteshkronja)
Thematic-room B: "Dark Room"
Thematic-room C: Gegë Marubi's Archive
FOTOTEKA KOMBËTARE MARUBI SHKODËR
B.2. Thematic exhibtion - room A: Pjeter Marubi's Photo Studio
INTERIOR THEMATIC-ROOM A
Supervision Phase
Exterior facade thematic rooms A,B and C
A101
Drawing nr.
Phase
Description
Work
801
Detailed Design
Thematic exhibition - overview

08 PHOTOGRAPHIC EXHIBITION
FOTOTEKA KOMBËTARE MARUBI SHKODËR
This is an example of a possible selection of Marubi's photographs to be shown in the photographic exhibition. The final selection of photographs will be done in coordination with the museum staff.
ZEF PAÇI
FOTOGRAFIA SI RITUAL
Marubi
PHOTOGRAPHY AS RITUAL
PRINCI
A3-08
A3-09
A3-10
B1-02
B1-05
B2-03
B3-06
FOTOTEKA KOM
07-11-2014
Date
1:50
Scale
casanova+hernandez architects

BUNA PARK & MUSEUM OF NAVIGATION, SHKODRA

WEAVING THE LANDSCAPE

I have always been in love with Albanian traditional costumes. I am particularly fond of a woman's sleeveless jacket preserved in the historical museum of Shkodra. I especially admire the variety of decorative patterns cleverly used to fill different parts of the costume. This adaptability of patterns inspired the design of the main paths that structure Buna Park. A series of fluid lines adapt to the exterior borders of the site, connecting at tangent points to create stylish shapes in between. The central part of the design is inspired by a specific geometrical pattern used to decorate a traditional Shkodra costume, worn mainly during representative and important occasions. Using the literary personifications I learned from Ismail Kadare, I would describe Buna Park as a beautiful woman dressed in her finest and most elegant attire to celebrate the historical importance of the place.

RECEIVING POSTCARDS FROM THE LAST CENTURY

One day, I discovered an Austro-Hungarian ship sunk near Shaqari Island in Shkodra Lake. I couldn't imagine how this ship had arrived in the lake, but after talking with several historians, I learned that the Buna River was once navigable. In that time Shkodra had an important harbor and bazaar, located where the park was being planned. The story was fascinating, involving many battles and shifting borders as well as the rise of transportation, commerce and craftsmanship, contributing to building the city's identity and refined culture.

This intricate history, now almost forgotten, pushed me to propose a museum to commemorate the place's history. While some were skeptical, historian Zamir Tafilica supported the idea, having studied navigation in the area and knowing the locations of the sunken ships that could be recovered. Some artifacts for the museum were already stored in the historical museum, but more material was needed. Due to the lack of funds, I started collecting some artifacts myself: old books, newspapers and postcards from 1912 to 1940 that depicted the old harbor and bazaar.

Collecting these materials, though far beyond the typical work of an architect, was crucial for the project's development, showing its significance and feasibility. I often bought these postcards online, and each time a new one arrived, it felt like an intriguing message from the past, written in different languages by a variety of people. They were sent from Shkodra to various European cities, and more than one century later they will return to the very place where they were written, closing the circle.

LUNDRA

When we were designing the Marubi National Museum of Photography, I was captivated by some photos from the collection that showed the old harbor of Shkodra with peculiar ships called "Lundra." I found their shape extremely elegant and beautiful. My fascination led me to talk to fishermen and historians and even to travel to Venice, where I met specialists who pointed out similarities between these boats and Venetian gondolas. When we designed the Museum of Navigation, it became inevitable that the ship's stylized shape would influence its design. During the design process, the Lundra gained importance, becoming the museum's most recognizable element. The Lundra became a landmark, evolving from opacity and heaviness to transparency and lightness, becoming a sculptural viewing point to observe the river and mark the position of the former harbor.

Requalification of Shkodra Entrance
1800
185
Museum of Shkodra Navigati

Carte Postale
Kartpostë Shqyptoré
Antonio Baldacci 1885
ANTONIO BALDACCI
L'ERBORISTERIA ALBANESE
Edith Durham (1909)
LA DOMENICA
LA TRIBUNA IL
LA DOMENICA
LA DOMENICA
Le flotte internazionali occupano Scutari in nome delle Potenze
PRIORITAIRE
Jesus hernandez
Lombardkade 24A
3031AH rotterdam
Niederlande
S. SOTIROPOULOS
KREONTOS 71-73
104 43 ATHENS
GREECE

CORRIERE DELLA SERA

Milano — 24 Aprile 1913 — Edizione del mattino

Italia e Colonie, centesimi 5 — Numero arretrato, centesimi 10

Le pubblicazioni che il CORRIERE DELLA SERA offre ai suoi abbonati sono: La Domenica del Corriere — La Lettura — Romanzo Mensile — Corriere dei Piccoli

Scutari si è arresa ai montenegrini
per fame e per mancanza di munizioni
Le Potenze e il "fatto compiuto" - Speranze in un compromesso

(... particolare del "Corriere della Sera")

Rivoluzione negli ospedali

LA DOMENICA DEL CORRIERE

Si pubblica a Milano ogni Domenica — Supplemento illustrato del "Corriere della Sera" — Uffici del giornale: Via Solferino, N. 28 MILANO

23 Febbraio - 2 Marzo 1913. — Centesimi 10 il numero.

La guerra nei Balcani: ostinato bombardamento ed ostinata mirabile resistenza di Scutari alle artiglierie montenegrine.
(Disegno di A. Beltrame).

... ILLUSTRATA

20 aprile 1913 — Anno XXI N. 15

La tragica lotta davanti a Scutari - Il « battaglione della morte »
(Disegno di E. Abbo)

... ILLUSTRATA

... 1913 — Anno XXI - N. 21

Scutari restituita all'Albania. Gli ultimi montenegrini lasciano la città con l'onore delle armi internazionali
(Disegno di E. Abbo)

LA TR...

Supplemento illustrato della "Tribuna"

25 gennaio-1° febbraio 1914

Gl'insorti Albanesi aprono le ostilità contro le truppe del Governo Provvisorio
(Disegno di E. Abbo)

... cade colpito a morte alla testa dei Malissori che muovono all'assalto dei ribelli albanesi
(Disegno di A. Minardi).

...RIERE

... italiani alla dogana.

ALBANIAN CARPET & SHKODRA LAKE MUSEUM, SHIROKA

PUBLIC SPACE AS AN ODA

Someone from Shkodra once told me there was no problem occupying part of the public space because "public" means that it belongs to everyone, and thus also to him. The site was supposed to be a public space, but in reality it was entirely occupied by private constructions, bars and kiosks that blocked the view over the lake. The first idea was simple, to demolish everything without exception to let people see the lake. The second was to design a public space that fosters a sense of belonging, designed as a house with open rooms inspired by the traditional Albanian room for receiving guests known as the *oda*.

ALBANIAN CARPET

I visited Nebije, a woman who runs a small workshop in Zogaj. She makes handmade carpets with other women, using sheep's wool and natural dyes extracted from plants, just as has been done in the region for centuries. One of her carpets particularly caught my attention. It was made from the wool of white and black sheep, without using any dyes. It was simple, modern and beautiful. Our design for Shiroka Square was nearly complete, but when I returned to my office in the Netherlands, I told my team I had found the perfect carpet for the square. I showed them the photo, and we experimented with different designs, scales and fabrication methods. Today, the square is called the "Albanian Carpet" and has received many international awards, all thanks to a brave woman with a beautiful story.

SUNSET AS AN ATTRACTION

Many times, as architects, we are not fully aware of the impact of our designs. One of the open rooms designed for Shiroka Square was conceived as a small open-air theater, oriented toward the sunset. After finishing the construction of the square, a friend from Shkodra told me that the spot had created a new ritual for the citizens of the city. Every afternoon, many people walk from the city along the shore of the lake to watch the sunset, making it a very popular spot, especially in summer.

FISHERMEN'S TALES

Talking with the fishermen of Shiroka and Zogaj, I learned many stories about the lake, such as the names of different types of boats, their specific shapes, designed to adapt to various types of shores, fishing techniques and the rules imposed during communism to prevent sailors from escaping to Yugoslavia. These rules included a requirement for a minimum number of sailors per boat so that one could always act as a spy. These conversations inspired the idea of building a small monument to the sailors, a sculpture crafted from oars that commemorates the fishing culture of the lake.

THE NEST

The Shkodra Lake Museum and Visitor Center was designed as a wooden nest built on an abandoned pier, showcasing the lake's fauna and flora while serving as an incubator for ecological awareness. It features a perimetric public ramp that allows visitors to ascend to the top, where a unique 360-degree panoramic viewpoint offers stunning views of the lake and the mountains. The museum serves both as a tourist attraction and as a tribute to the people who continue to preserve the local culture, including Nebije, Ilir and others.

START	NAME PROJECT	LOCATION	PUBLIC/PRIVATE	PHASE
2014	Marubi National Museum of Photography	Shkodra	Public	Executed
2017	Shiroka Square (Albanian Carpet)	Shkodra	Public	Executed
2017	Shkodra Lake Museum (The Nest)		Public	Detailed design approved, waiting for construction
2018	Ethnographic Museum of Gjirokastër	Gjirokastër	Public	Executed
2018	House Museum Ismail Kadare	Gjirokastër	Public	Executed
2019	Albanian Park	Durrës	Public	Detailed design approved, waiting for construction
2019	Eco Park	Durrës	Public	First phase completed
2019	Museum of the Adriatic Cultures	Durrës	Public	Detailed design approved, waiting for construction
2020	Museum of Albanian Hydropower	Koman	Public	Detailed design approved, waiting for construction
2021	Gjirokastër Castle	Gjirokastër	Public	Detail design
2022	Buna Park	Shkodra	Public	Under construction
2022	Museum of Navigation	Shkodra	Public	Under construction
2022	National Historical Museum	Tirana	Public	Under construction
2024	Valias Experimental Farm and Genetic Bank	Tirana	Public	Detail design
2024	Shkodra Lake Entrance	Shkodra	Public	Preliminary design
2024	Cultural Hotel	Shkodra	Private	Preliminary design
2024	Ethnographic Museum of Tirana	Tirana	Public	Preliminary design

NAME OFFICE

CEBRA

DATE
December 17, 2024

PLACE
Aarhus, Denmark

WORKING IN ALBANIA SINCE
2022

PRINCIPALS
Mikkel Frost (Partner)
Kolja Nielsen (Partner)
Carsten Primdahl (Partner)
Mikkel Schlesinger (Partner)
Thomas Bang (Associated Partner)
Lars Gylling (Associated Partner)
Flemming Svendsen (Associated Partner)
Rasmus Kruse (Associated Partner)
Stefan Rask Nors (Associated Partner)

PROJECT TEAM
Bård Hovden
Cedric Macleod
Henrik Nykjær
Karin Rasmussen
Karoline Bonde
Kazuhiko Yazaki
Klaudio Muca
Magnus Damgaard
Magnus Højgaard
Matias Valsby-Koch
Rasmus Lassen
Robert Zwolinski
Simon Smedsmo
Stine Christiansen
Thomas Bonde
Toke Valum
Trine Gylling

COLLABORATORS
Arup
UNO architects
Nova Construction Group
Naxhi Bakalli
Elvis Uku
Elteknik shpk
Leotec
GeCo
Energy DC
Hydro & Energy
Kejsi-05 shpk
2XKE-Studio shpk
ESDO
Altea Studio

INTRODUCTION TO ALBANIA

Seemingly out of the blue, NOVA Construction Group reached out to us while searching for architects to compete in the design of a new multipurpose landmark in Tirana. They invited us to submit an initial proposal with indicative sketches, along with approximately twenty-five other design offices. We were fortunate to advance to the competition stage and ultimately win, which immediately opened the door to other exciting opportunities in Albania.

SETUP IN RELATION TO ALBANIAN PARTNER

For us, design encompasses all the efforts that lead to the final building. In that sense, we share both the design process and the workload with the local office. That said, our role is typically more prominent during the early stages, when the main idea takes shape. Once the concept is established, we step back a bit and focus on reviewing and providing feedback on plans. The division of work varies from project to project, depending on the specific needs and circumstances.

OPPORTUNITIES/CHALLENGES

Albania's leadership, particularly the prime minister, demonstrates an exceptional interest in and understanding of art and architecture. Urban planning and building design are viewed as powerful tools for transformation and tangible proof of the country's progress. With every completed project, Albania's cities and its overall landscape become more livable and visually appealing.

Working in this environment, where architecture is highly valued and no idea is dismissed on overly conservative grounds, allows our creativity to thrive. We are delivering designs in Albania that many other clients or countries might not even envision. I'm confident that in the years to come, leaders and officials from across Europe will visit Albania to learn from its architectural achievements.

Since none of our projects have completed construction yet, it's a bit difficult to fully assess the challenges. Early on, we were concerned about local fees, but this turned out to be an unnecessary worry. One ongoing question within our office is whether our clients will fully execute our designs as intended and maintain the quality we envision. However, when we look at the work of other architects in Albania, we feel assured that this is achievable.

HOW TO INTEGRATE GREATER RESPONSIBILITY FOR QUALITY IN PROJECTS

Steps are already being taken to ensure that investors deliver on what has been promised through realistic renderings. For example, when a local architect of record submits plans to the municipality for approval, the plans are returned to the design office for review before final sign-off. This helps ensure that the architectural design remains intact and that significant corners aren't cut.

While this protects the overall vision, there is still the risk of poor detailing and subpar craftsmanship. A potential improvement could be to repeat this submission process at later stages, using more detailed drawings to document and safeguard the design ambitions.

Ultimately, the best solution – though it's a long and demanding process – is to change the way investors perceive architecture. Over time, as more sophisticated and well-executed projects are completed, investors may come to appreciate the value of beautifully detailed buildings made from durable materials.

Some level of control will always be necessary, though. A system without any checks is unlikely to work, much like traffic systems rely on highway cameras to enforce rules and maintain order.

BALANCING QUALITY AND DENSITY/INVOLVING STAKEHOLDERS

It's important to recognize that high density isn't inherently negative. Compact neighborhoods may present challenges such as limited daylight and obstructed views, but they also bring significant benefits, like vibrant street life and enough foot traffic to support local businesses – patterns we see in cities like New York and London.

However, there's a fine line, and investors can sometimes push density to the point where plots are overbuilt, compromising overall quality. To address this, authorities play a crucial role in ensuring balance by requiring architects to submit daylight analyses and other documentation that demonstrates the livability of a design.

Fortunately, with advancements in technology, producing these types of analyses has become faster and more accessible. This makes it feasible for such processes to become standard, enhancing transparency and accountability.

EXAMPLE/INSPIRATION

The list of inspiring projects in Albania, both built and unbuilt, is extensive. The transformation of the Pyramid of Tirana is a particularly inspiring example. The surrounding urban park has become a vibrant, inviting space, and the leadership's decision to preserve this monument as part of the city's history is both positive and wise.

The landscape design for Skanderbeg Square and its surrounding areas is another source of inspiration. The use of rough terrazzo for benches and bollards is beautiful and ensures that these elements will age gracefully over time. The Democratic Table, a quirky and conceptual piece of outdoor furniture, is another favorite.

The Hotel Plaza is a delightfully fresh and surprising design, while the Air Albania Stadium and Downtown One add to the city's dynamic architectural landscape. And the momentum continues, with exciting projects like our own Mount Tirana and BIG's theater underway.

TOOLBOX ALBANIA FUTURE

In Albania, we find opportunities to integrate more crafted details and natural materials, such as stone and timber, compared to the off-the-shelf building components we often specify in Denmark. The use of cast-in-place concrete also provides greater flexibility in construction, opening up exciting possibilities for design.

These elements offer a chance to explore a more durable, tactile and authentic approach to architecture – something we're eager to delve deeper into as we develop future projects in Albania.

Mount Tirana

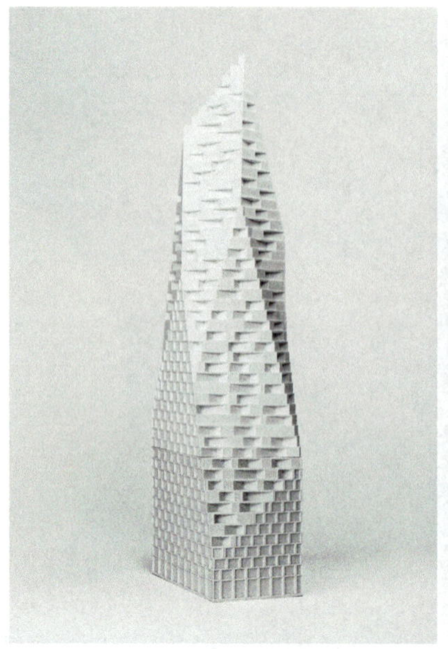

We approach our work in Albania with a deep respect for its history and untouched landscapes. We try to tread carefully, preserving Albania's unique identity while contributing thoughtfully to its development. By working with nature rather than against it, we strive to create spaces that reflect the country's beauty and potential.

Albania, having been under a totalitarian regime until the late twentieth century, experienced limited industrial and infrastructural development, leaving it behind much of Europe in those areas. However, this also meant that vast parts of the country remained pristine, allowing nature to thrive. Today, Albania is one of the few European countries with wild rivers and unspoiled beaches, creating a unique environment that sets the country apart. >

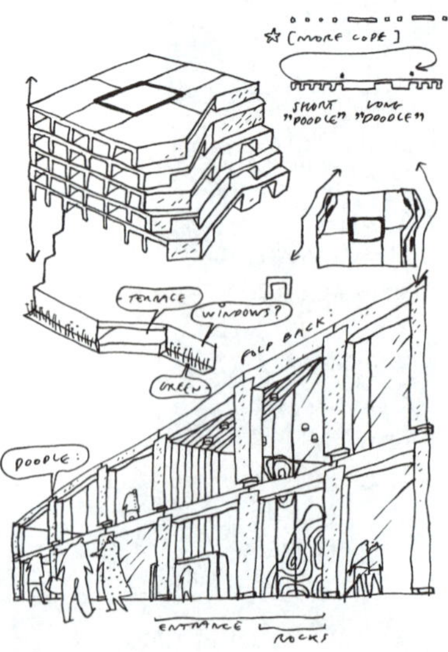

Mount Tirana

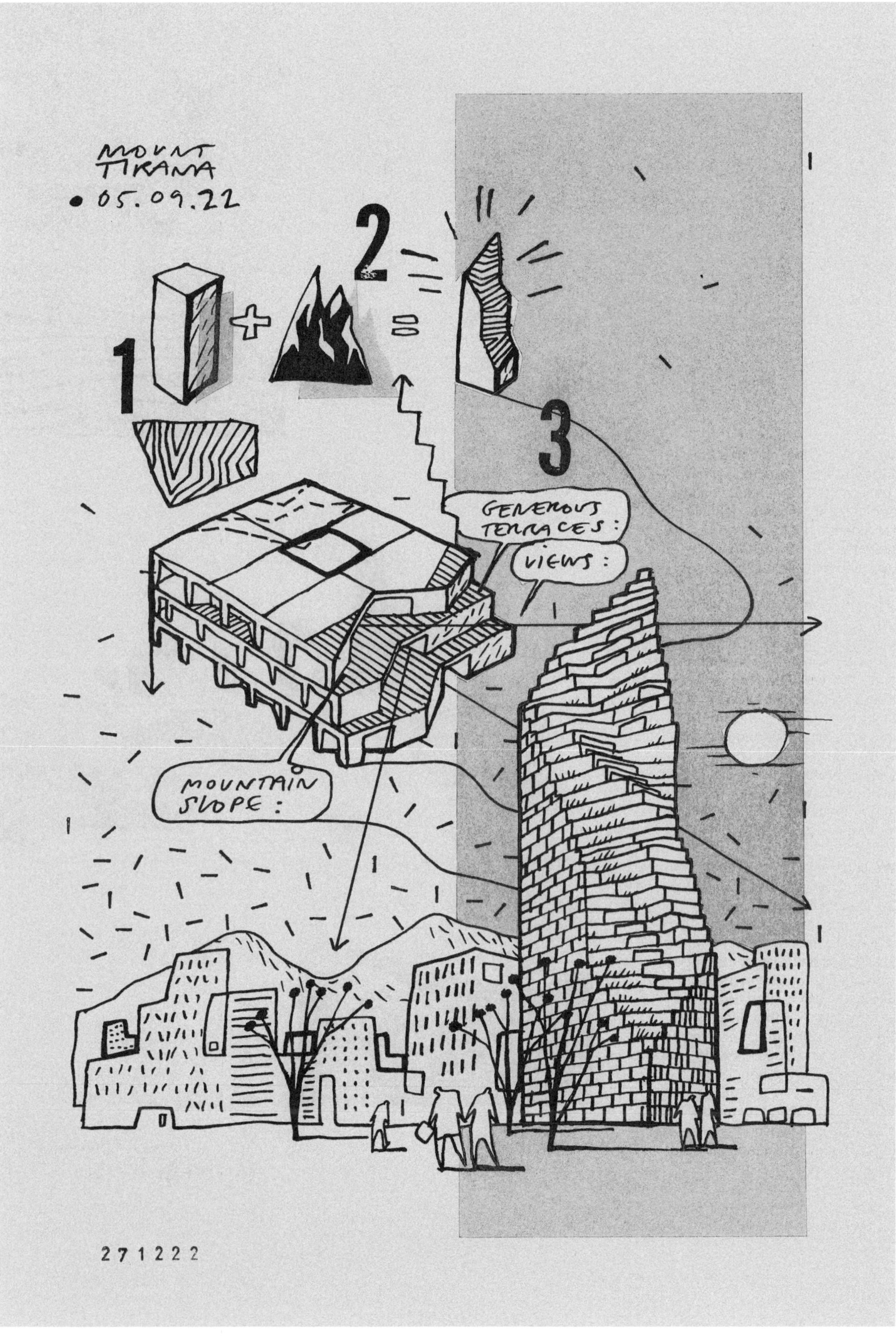

Mount Tirana

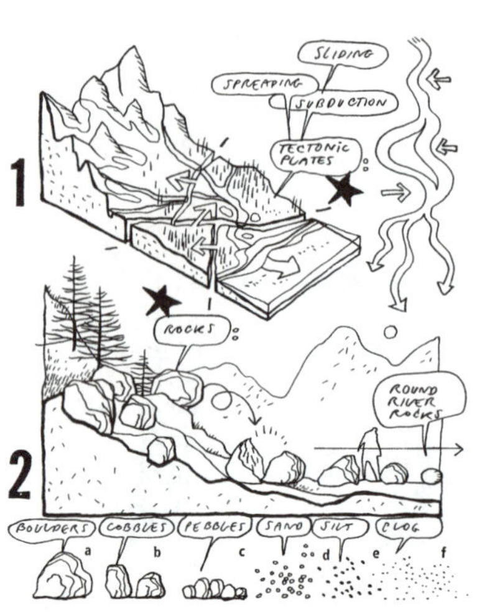

Vjosa Wild River National Park – Europe's first protected wild river – represents a tremendous natural and cultural resource, not only for Albania, but for the world. The fantastic natural scenery of the river ties multiple cultural assets together like pearls on a string into an immersive and educational experience. Our design for the new Multifunctional Center in Tepelenë and Information Stations in Përmet and Vlora will act as "gateways" to this unique national park. The buildings visually blend with the landscape, offering immersive spatial experiences. The project aims to protect biodiversity, attract ecotourism and educate visitors about the care of and appreciation for wild nature.

We find the balance between preservation and development to be fascinating and to carry a deep sense of responsibility. On one hand, the beauty of Albania's untouched nature is something we wish to protect. On the other hand, there is a clear desire for development that aligns with European standards. This creates a delicate challenge: How do we contribute to Albania's growth without compromising its natural and cultural heritage, and without repeating the mistakes of overdevelopment seen in other countries? >

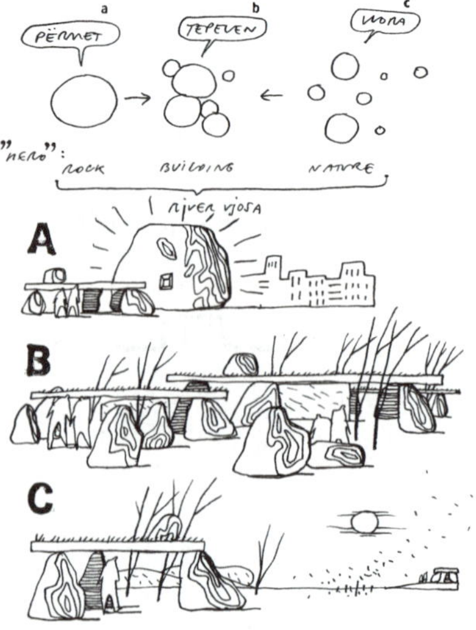

Vjosa River Multifunctional Center and Information Station

Vjosa River Multifunctional Center and Information Station

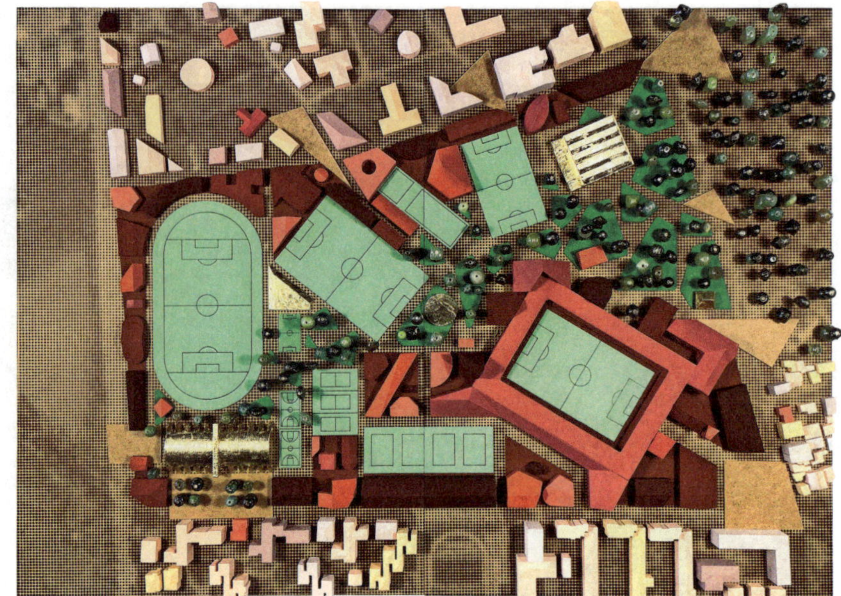

Our approach is rooted in contextualism on multiple levels. We aim to build in harmony with nature and Albania's traditions, avoiding imposing Danish or international "starchitecture." Instead, we seek to blend our designs with the landscapes and urban fabrics, embracing local materials, colors, building techniques and culture.

With our Mount Tirana project, we have chosen to honor the majestic Albanian mountains. Mountains are arguably one of Albania's most loved features. They are a visual embodiment of the forces of nature, frozen in time. Everlasting, awe-inspiring and beautiful, they are the original landmarks. Mount Tirana is a project inspired by Albania's distinctive mountains that will be a new urban landmark in the capital of Albania, Tirana, reflecting the country's national identity and cultural heritage. As one of the tallest buildings in Albania, it symbolizes the connection between Tirana's evolving urban landscape and its natural surroundings.

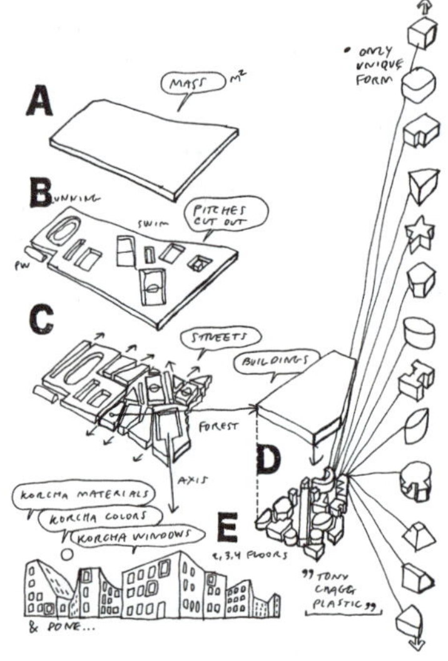

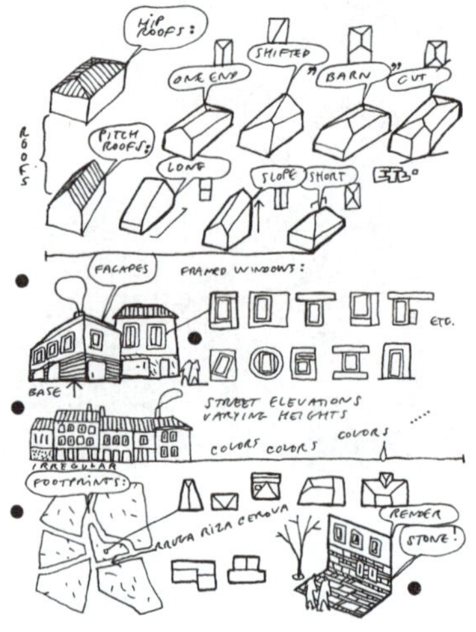

New Skënderbeu Stadium

New Skënderbeu Stadium

New Skënderbeu Stadium

START	NAME PROJECT	LOCATION	DEVELOPER	ALBANIAN PARTNER	M²	PUBLIC/PRIVATE	PHASE
2022	Mount Tirana	Tirana	NOVA Construction 2012	UNO architects, Nova Group, Hydro & Energy, Energy DC, GeCo, Elteknik shpk, Leotec	85,000 m²	Private	Detail design
2022	Eco resort	Near Durrës			1,460,000 m²	Private	Development proposal
2022	TV Klan HQ	Tirana	TV Klan		10,000 m²	Private	Competition proposal
2023	Mixed-use development	Tirana			65,000 m²	Private	Construction permit proposal
2023	Livadh Resorts	Himara		UNO architects	242,000 m²	Private	Development proposal
2023	New Skënderbeu Stadium	Korça	Albanian Development Fund	UNO architects, ESDO, Altea Studio	98,000 m²	Public	Preliminary project idea
2023	Multifunctional Center and Information Stations	Vjosa Wild River National Park (Tepelenë, Përmet and Vlora)	Albanian Government	UNO architects, Kejsi-05 shpk, Energy DC, 2XKE-Studio shpk	2,200 m²	Public	Implementation project
2024	Hotel	Dhërmi		UNO architects	15,000 m²	Private	Construction permit

NAME OFFICE

CHRISTIAN KEREZ

DATE
March 2026

PLACE
Tirana, Albania

WORKING IN ALBANIA SINCE
2024

PRINCIPALS
Christian Kerez

PROJECT TEAM
Ksenia Zivic [1, 2, 3]
Karolina Hajkowicz [1, 3, 4]
Maja Kobal [1, 2, 3]
Bledart Sade [1, 3]
Lucas Almassy [1, 3, 5]
Vico Seeger [2, 3, 4, 5]
Hao Wen [2, 3, 4, 5]
Maciej Wiórek [2, 3, 4, 5]
Ludwig Kissling [3]
Stanisław Rudzki [2, 4]
Mila Allemann [1]
Changshu Chen [1, 3]
Yeliz Abdurahman [3, 5]
Tiago Costa [1, 3]
Davide Fabbro [1]

COLLABORATORS

Catherine Dumont d'Ayot [1, 2, 3, 5]
Bartosz Bukowski [1, 2, 3, 4 (co-lead)]
Adam Górka [1, 2, 3, 4]
Andronira Burda [2, 3, 4]
Marko Shalku [2, 3, 4]
Jung Min Yoo [1, 2, 4, 5]
Kevin Chow [2, 4, 5]

STRUCTURAL ENGINEERS
Archo Studio, Albania [1, 2, 3]
Dr. Schwartz Consulting AG, Switzerland [1, 2]
Elvira Kuri, Albania [4]
B&C Associati, Italy [1, 2]
Emiliano Qosja, Albania [5]

MECHANICAL, HYDRAULIC AND ELECTRICAL ENGINEERS
Echostar, Albania [1, 2, 3]
H & E Energy, Albania [4]
Sokol Shyti, Albania [4]

LOCAL ARCHITECTS
BG Studio, Besnik Grainca [1, 2, 3, 4]
MAD Studio, Taulant Leka & AretaMoço [5]

Projects:
1 Gate of Shkodra
2 Sima Tower
3 Shëngjin Seaside Resort
4 Little Big House
5 Alice

MAIN CONTEXT VS. ALBANIA

Currently I work in China, Switzerland and Brazil. Every context is different from the others. I am excited about the speed in Albania: how quickly developers and politicians are able to make decisions. But this speed is a huge challenge, since many people involved in the process are constantly postponing their work, which makes the planning process not very efficient and very hard to control.

ORGANIZATION/GOAL/SETUP

I do not like to travel too much. I always try to have people from my office that are close to me on the construction sites full-time, to support and control the construction process as much as possible. Because we have several projects ongoing in Albania simultaneously, this month I opened an office in Tirana. I guess I will live and work in Albania for a longer period of time. I am interested in the prospect of not only working in Albania but also living in Albania, and I am confident that this will change my architecture. Architecture in my understanding is not an export or import article. It has to grow out of local technical and economic conditions, to avoid compromises.

SETUP IN RELATION TO ALBANIAN PARTNER

We work on all projects with other architects. Their task is different in every country. In Switzerland they are construction managers. In France or Austria, they provided all execution drawings on our behalf. Here, the role of a local architect resembles rather the role of an architect of record, which is the legal representative and which helps in coordination, mainly with the client and the local authorities. The local architect I work with, Besnik Grainca, is for us rather an accomplice than a supplier, since one of his main roles is to make sure our design will not be compromised during the process of construction. He is in this sense the legal representative of the municipality, which makes his role rather unique.

We are interested in having a close collaboration with construction companies and all specialists in Tirana. In my understanding the design work cannot be separated from the work of building. The only way to control a project on the construction site is to solve all possible problems the construction company and the developers are facing.

OPPORTUNITIES/CHALLENGES

It is easy to make a beautiful rendering; it is always hard to build something beautiful. This is not any different in Albania. We just received several building permits. Some construction sites should start already this year. We have friendly and close relationships with local authorities and the local clients, and we hope we can maintain these relationships through the hard times that will come for all of us.

HOW TO INTEGRATE GREATER RESPONSIBILITY FOR QUALITY IN PROJECTS

Our designs are ambitious and challenge the whole team. We challenge our capacity as architects, and the projects challenge the engineers, developers and construction companies in the same way. To make sure that the buildings keep the promises from the beginning of the design process through the construction permit, it will be crucial to be properly commissioned for construction drawings and site supervision, which is not so clear for some projects. A construction permit is like a script. It has to be improved to create a space which can be experienced only in reality, better than any drawing or rendering.

BALANCING QUALITY AND DENSITY/INVOLVING STAKEHOLDERS

There is a saying that too many cooks spoil the broth (in German: *viele Köche verderben den Brei*). The fewer stakeholders the better. It is great that in Albania the prime minister is personally involved in questions of urbanism and architecture. It is great that architecture and urbanism are not separated artificially from one another. It is exciting that most of the developers run construction companies themselves. The reduction of stakeholders in this country accelerates the process of urbanism, and the question would be if architects can keep up the quality of their design with this acceleration process. To have more freedom as an architect means that we have more responsibility working in Albania. While I can excuse myself in Europe if the outer appearance of a building is not convincing by hiding behind building codes or behind the given master plan, I have to justify every single project in Albania with urbanistic and architectural arguments. Never before have I had the feeling so strongly that architectural design work is in the end driven by urbanistic intentions and public desires as I do in Albania.

EXAMPLE/INSPIRATION

I am more inspired by the energy, the vitality and the courage of this small country that is becoming more and more the focus point of contemporary architecture. I am inspired by the heterogeneity and wildness of the urbanism of Tirana and many other cities in Albania. I am more inspired by the specific context of each project than any singular building done by a famous architect.

TOOLBOX ALBANIA FUTURE

Every generation leaves architecture as their physical legacy for a future generation. When all clothes, furniture, cars and equipment are already out of fashion, architecture remains. It is a miracle that Albania seems to have the only political leader that is aware of this legacy, while in most other countries debates on architecture are fading away, and a general frustration and hatred for architecture – which is purely driven by money-making – is replacing the public debate on buildings and cities. I hope Europe becomes Albanian in this matter before Albania joins the European Union.

July 8, 2024

Gate of Shkodra.

More than 300 apartments at the entrance to the city of Shkodra build a public space instead of occupying the public ground as an object. This space is open to the sky and open to the city on all sides. A space for the public, not only surrounded by private spaces but even covered by apartments. An urban space on the periphery of the city, creating an identity and attraction for the community of inhabitants and for the entire city of Shkodra. A contemporary version of the utopian idea of a Familistère.

November 5, 2024

An Albanian Dream.

Architecture is the most obvious testimony and the longest lasting reminiscence of its time. It is exposed to public view, an explicit reminder that outlives any newspaper, any reviews, anything broadcasted on TV or uploaded on the Internet. It survives the food we are eating and the clothes we are wearing. However, it seems that architecture is relegated to invisibility in many countries, for it is not permitted to communicate anything, not permitted to make an architectural statement, out of fear that it might be subject to debate or, worse yet, open to criticism.

Albania takes a different path. The prime minister Edi Rama has put architecture on his priority list; he attends to it in the only viable way – by being personally involved. This political agenda is radical and unique. Surprising is the fact that it is so exceptional at a time when politicians repeatedly call on the need to pass memory and remembrance on to the next generation, when all they really leave behind are shallow words and unfulfilled promises. Not so the Albanian dream: it will become reality for the next generation.

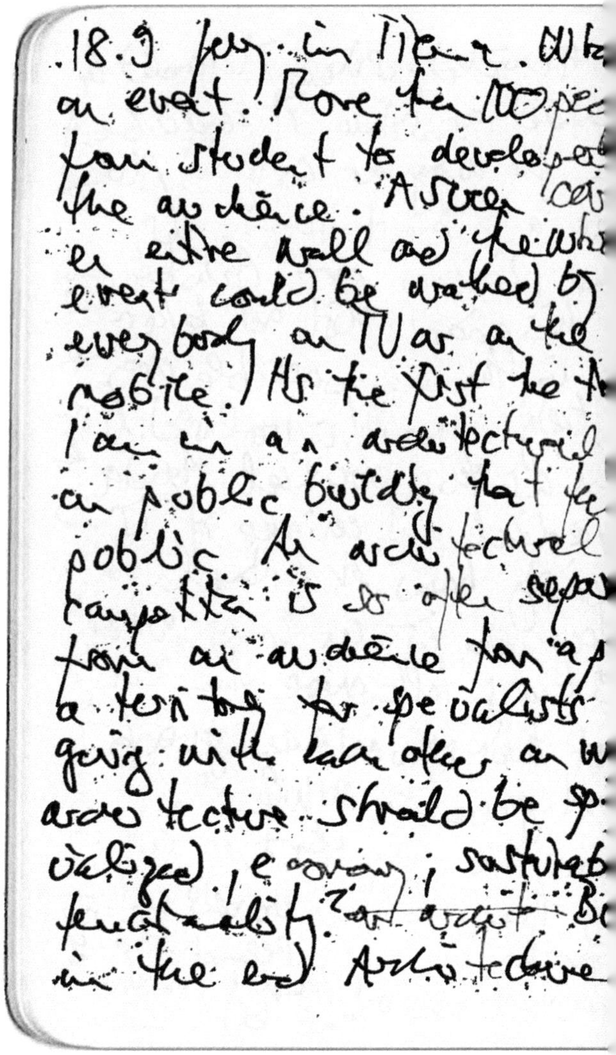

September 18, 2024

Jury in Tirana.

What an event. An audience of over 100 people, from students to developers. A screen that covers the entire wall behind the architects presenting their projects. Everybody in Albania can watch the event on TV or on their mobile phone. It is the first time that I am serving on an architectural jury for a public building in a competition that actually feels public. So often, our competitions are behind closed doors, where specialists in isolation argue with each other about whether the architecture should be focusing on economy, sustainability or functionality. But architecture is, in fact, the most public field of human activity.

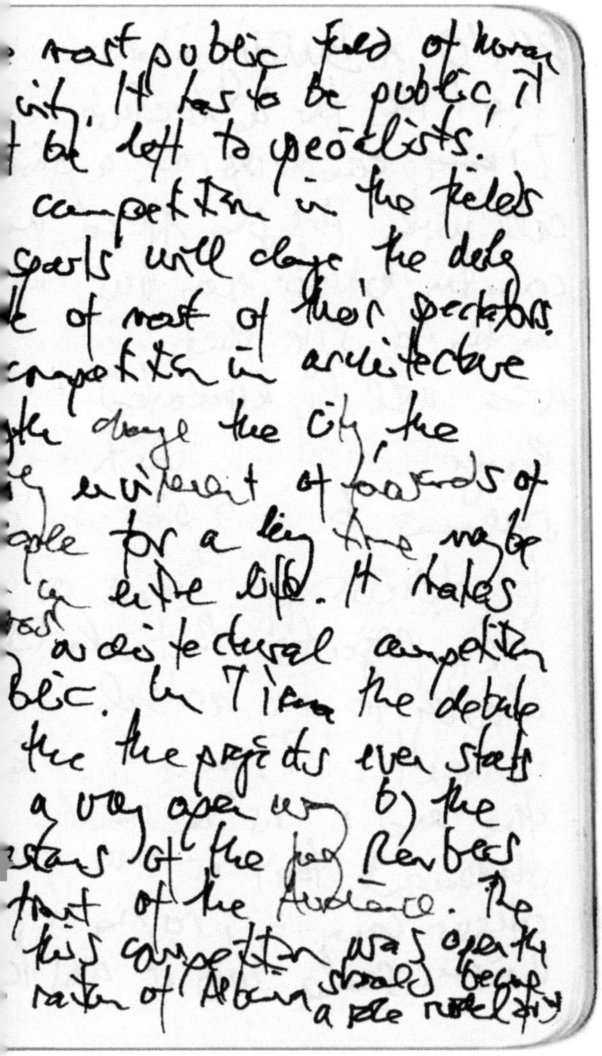
vast public field of human
city. It has to be public, it
be left to specialists.
competition in the fields
sports will change the daily
of most of their spectators
competition in architecture
change the city, the
environment of thousands of
people for a long time maybe
entire life. It makes
architectural competition
public. In Tirana the debate
the projects even starts
a very open way by the
of the jury members
front of the audience. The
this competition was open to
nation of Albania should become
a role model

It must be public; it cannot be left to specialists. No competition in the field of sports is going to change the daily life of most spectators the way a building might impact a city and change the daily environment of thousands of people for a very long time. That makes almost every architectural competition public. In Tirana, debate on the projects starts with jury members openly asking questions in front of the entire audience. The way the competition was open to the entire nation of Albania should definitely become a role model for countries that intend to strive for public interests.

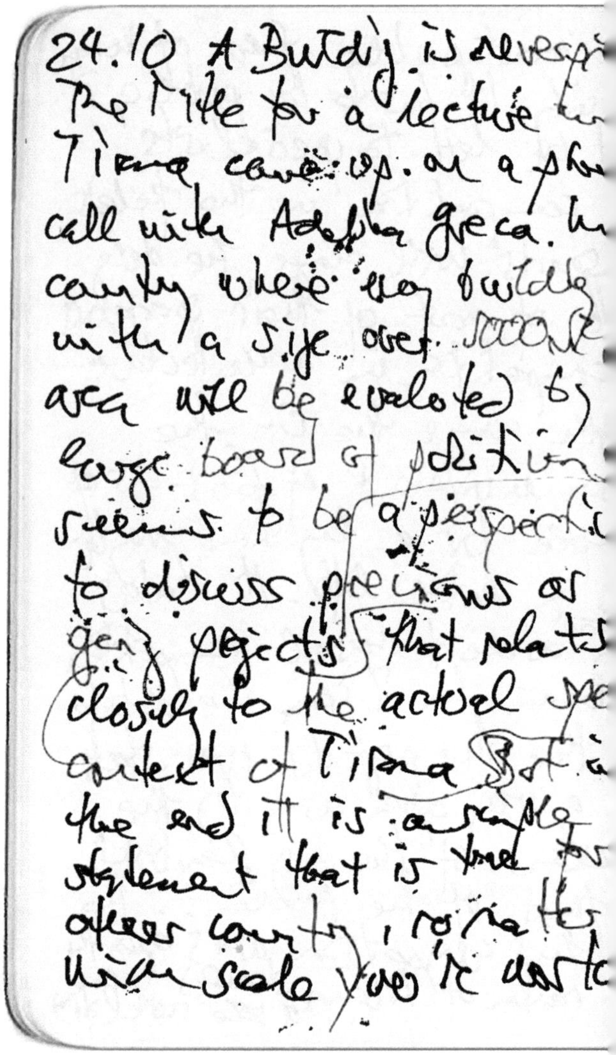

October 24, 2024

A Building is never private.

A Building is never private. A title for a lecture in Tirana came up on a phone call with Adelina Greca. In a country where every building with a size over 5000 m² gross area would be evaluated by a large board of politicians, this title relates closely to the actual and ongoing projects. But in the end it is a simple statement that is true for any other country, no matter in which scale you're working. A Building for an individual family does not only protect its inhabitants from sun and rain but likewise from the views of the people passing by. The protection of the individual to the rest of the community is a public manifestation of the individual that could be articulated in different ways, as a hideout or as a fortress. It becomes in an unavoidable way a public statement; only in this sense is a building more than real estate or private property. Only in this understanding is architecture more than a private interest and could become a topic taught in schools.

December 18, 2024

Shengjin Sea Side Residential Housing.

A terrace is a small and crucial space during the holidays. It is a private space outside the building, in front of the spaces of the apartment. It is an individual space above the public ground, floating in the air. This project will express the individuality of 500 apartments, revealing the individuality of the inhabitants outside the standardized apartment block, offering a new, vibrant experience for the public.

LIST OF PROJECTS

START	NAME PROJECT	LOCATION	DEVELOPER	ALBANIAN PARTNER	ENGINEER	M²	PUBLIC/PRIVATE	PHASE
2024	Gate of Shkodra	Shkodra	AL Invest	BG Studio	Archo Studio, Echostar, Dr. Schwartz Consulting AG, B&C Associati	43,000 m²	Private	Construction permit
2024	Shëngjin Seaside Resort	Shëngjin	Sima & Com Milenium Construction	BG Studio	Archo Studio, Echostar	32,900 m²	Private	Construction permit approved
2025	Little Big House	Tirana	ADI-M	BG Studio	Elvira Kuri, H & E Energy, Shoko Shyti	16,000 m²	Private	Construction permit
2025	Sima Tower	Tirana	Sima & Com, Alb Vizion Construction	BG Studio	Archo Studio, Dr. Schwartz Consulting AG, Echostar, B&C Associati	17,900 m²	Private	Construction permit
2025	Alice	Tirana	Brunes Construction	MAD Studio	Emiliano Qosja	31,700 m²	Private	Concept study

NAME OFFICE

CHYBIK + KRISTOF ARCHITECTS

DATE
September 8, 2025

PLACE
Brno, Czech Republic

WORKING IN ALBANIA SINCE
2022

PRINCIPALS
Ondrej Chybik
Michal Kristof

ALBANIAN PARTNERS
Studioarch4
Loft Architects

PROJECT TEAM

MULTIFUNCTIONAL TOWER TIRANA
Ondrej Chybik
Michal Kristof
Jiří Richter
Radek Satora
Jiří Vala
Ondřej Švancara
Ondřej Mundl
Tea Mersuli
Nertila Aligjoni
Ilya Lebedev
Lukáš Kvasnica
Martyna Bobińska
Magdalena Czopka
Antonin Hampl
Martin Holy
Martin Iglesias

W TOWER
Ondrej Chybik
Michal Kristof
Peter Chaban
Jiří Vitek
Tea Mersuli
Jozef Šefčik
Lujza Hostačná

ODA TIRANA
Ondrej Chybik
Michal Kristof
Jiří Richter
Lucie Skorepova
Jiří Vala
Ingrid Spáčilová
Ilya Lebedev
Peter Chaban
Jan Lebl
Lucija Ritoša
Viktor Makara
Martin Holy
Ondřej Žvak
Martin Iglesias

NICKNAME
CH+K

LOCAL ARCHITECT

We've had the pleasure of collaborating with several talented local architects. Our first partnership was with Studioarch4, whose extensive portfolio includes residential buildings and interiors as well as remarkable projects in the education sector. Additionally, they are working on a tower project on Tirana's New Boulevard – right next to our building.

More recently, for new projects, we've been collaborating with Loft Architects. Initially introduced to us by a client, their diverse portfolio and broad experience across multiple typologies impressed us, as did their attention to detail in execution. This successful collaboration has naturally led to further joint endeavors.

As a studio, we greatly value collaboration and remain open to building relationships with new partners.

MAIN CONTEXT VS. ALBANIA

We primarily work in the Czech Republic and Slovakia, where our office originated, but we have also undertaken projects across Europe and beyond.

A consistent similarity is that we often enter new markets through design competitions, as we did in Albania, which provide opportunities for international studios to bring fresh perspectives. Equally important is our collaboration with local teams, ensuring that each design is rooted in local expertise.

Differences primarily lie in regulations and permitting systems. In Albania, another notable distinction for us is the openness of clients, who appear more receptive to experimentation compared to the more conservative approach common in other markets where we operate.

ORGANIZATION/GOAL/SETUP

Local partnerships are fundamental for our work.

Our commitment extends beyond commercial projects to actively contributing to Albania's positive transformation. By collaborating with municipalities and diverse organizations, we strive to balance commercial endeavors with initiatives that drive long-term social and urban progress.

Additionally, having an Albanian colleague in our Czech studio has enriched our understanding of the local context, culture and regulations. This insight enhances our ability to design and operate more effectively, ensuring our work remains deeply connected to Albania's context.

SETUP IN RELATION TO ALBANIAN PARTNER

In our early projects, particularly the first competition we won in Tirana, we carried out most of the design work independently, bringing local architects on board as consultants. However, as we took on more commissions and built relationships with local architects, we increasingly involved them from the outset of each project. As we continue to establish ourselves in Albania, our goal is to further integrate local architects into the design process and strengthen these collaborations.

OPPORTUNITIES/CHALLENGES

We believe the ongoing urban transformation presents a rare opportunity to rebuild the cities in the spirit of the most modern standards, advanced infrastructure, and relevant environmental solutions, allowing for a significant impact in ways that are not possible in highly urbanized cities. The ability to reinvent and integrate new technologies is a key asset in this case.

However, the cultural differences present a challenge in balancing innovation with local needs. Understanding the market's realities is crucial, making collaboration with local architects essential for successful project execution.

HOW TO INTEGRATE GREATER RESPONSIBILITY FOR QUALITY IN PROJECTS

To integrate greater responsibility for quality, it's essential to emphasize communication throughout the process. Deep involvement with all stakeholders – clients, partners and users – ensures alignment on the vision and quality standards. The more they understand, the more invested they become. A participatory approach, including public consultations, is crucial. This method fosters a deeper connection to the project and should be more widely adopted in Albania to cultivate a culture of quality-driven design.

THE BEGINNINGS

Albania first captured our attention when Skanderbeg Square in Tirana gained international acclaim through its nomination for the EU Mies van der Rohe Award. This bold and transformative project piqued our curiosity: What was the story behind it? To us, the square represented more than architectural ambition – it symbolized a pivotal moment in Albania's transition as a young democracy. By prioritizing shared civic spaces, the country demonstrated the essential role of public space as a foundation for societal transformation.

This idea resonates deeply with us. Since founding our studio in the Czech Republic fifteen years ago, we have been guided by the conviction that public spaces are more than physical constructs; they are the backbone of community life. Our work consistently seeks to restore the relationship between society and public space – a connection often disrupted in the aftermath of systemic change. In such contexts, public spaces frequently exist as paradoxes: simultaneously belonging to everyone and to no one.

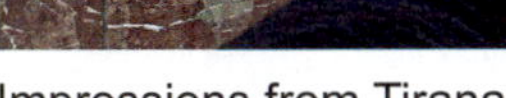

Impressions from Tirana

"If discourse is the foundation of democracy, how can the design of our cities empower and enable it?"

—Richard Sennett

SPACE FOR THE PUBLIC

As Richard Sennett observes in *Democracy and Urban Form*, "If discourse is the foundation of democracy, how can the design of our cities empower and enable it?" Public spaces offer a powerful answer, serving as arenas for dialogue, engagement and collective identity. This philosophy has shaped our master plan projects from the outset, enabling their success by prioritizing public spaces – squares, parks and alleys – within private developments. A recent example of our work, the Mendel Square project in Brno, marks the first stage of a broader revitalization of the city's oldest district and presented a unique opportunity to create an entirely new public square within a historic context. Here, we transformed a neglected transportation crossroads into an efficient hub and a welcoming, functional public space – something that was previously completely missing in this part of the city.

Albania, like the Czech Republic, demonstrates how young democracies can harness public spaces to foster inclusion and social cohesion. This shared belief in the transformative power of public spaces made our work in Albania particularly relevant and has enabled us to contribute meaningfully to its urban evolution.

Tirana's largest master plan, the New Boulevard, exemplifies this approach. By starting with the creation of a public boulevard, it bridges public initiatives with private-sector development. Within this framework, we embarked on our first major contribution: the Multifunctional Tower project, currently under development. Situated in the heart of the city, the project integrates open, walkable public spaces and strengthens connections to key cultural landmarks nearby.

Multifunctional Tower Tirana project, first prize

CRAFTING CHARACTER

An essential part of the journey through young democratic changes is the search for a new identity – one that resonates with the evolving society. This is particularly significant in the context of Albania, where rapid social, economic and urban transformations have unfolded over the past two decades. The early years of this transition were often marked by surges of informal and incoherent development across cities. Now, in the wake of concerted efforts to address and rectify these challenges, our work seeks to contribute meaningfully to the search for a distinct identity and architectural character – a commitment we regard as important. For us, this means crafting designs that are deeply embedded in the local context, rather than adhering to the homogenizing tendencies of the contemporary global style, which imposes architectural repetition across locations – an approach we do not agree with.

Marc Augé's criticism of non-places – spaces that lack identity and fail to foster meaningful relationships – deeply resonates with us. As he writes, "The space of non-place creates neither singular identity nor relations; only solitude, and similitude." Our goal is the opposite: to create architecture that engages in dialogue with its surroundings, with a unique atmosphere emerging from the environment it inhabits.

Achieving this character involves considering a broad spectrum of elements: geometry, scale, texture, materiality, color, light, shadow, craftsmanship and details, and, importantly, the social context. Each project begins with an effort to understand its surroundings. During our first visits to Tirana, we were struck by the city's vibrant character. Its eclectic mix of scales and grids stood in stark contrast to the more conservative and uniform style of Western European city design familiar to us. By observing Tirana's palette of local materials, such as its distinctive natural stones – especially the red varieties – and its urban fabric, we found an architectural language that differs from that of cities in Western and Central Europe. This understanding informs our designs, creating a connection without resorting to imitation.

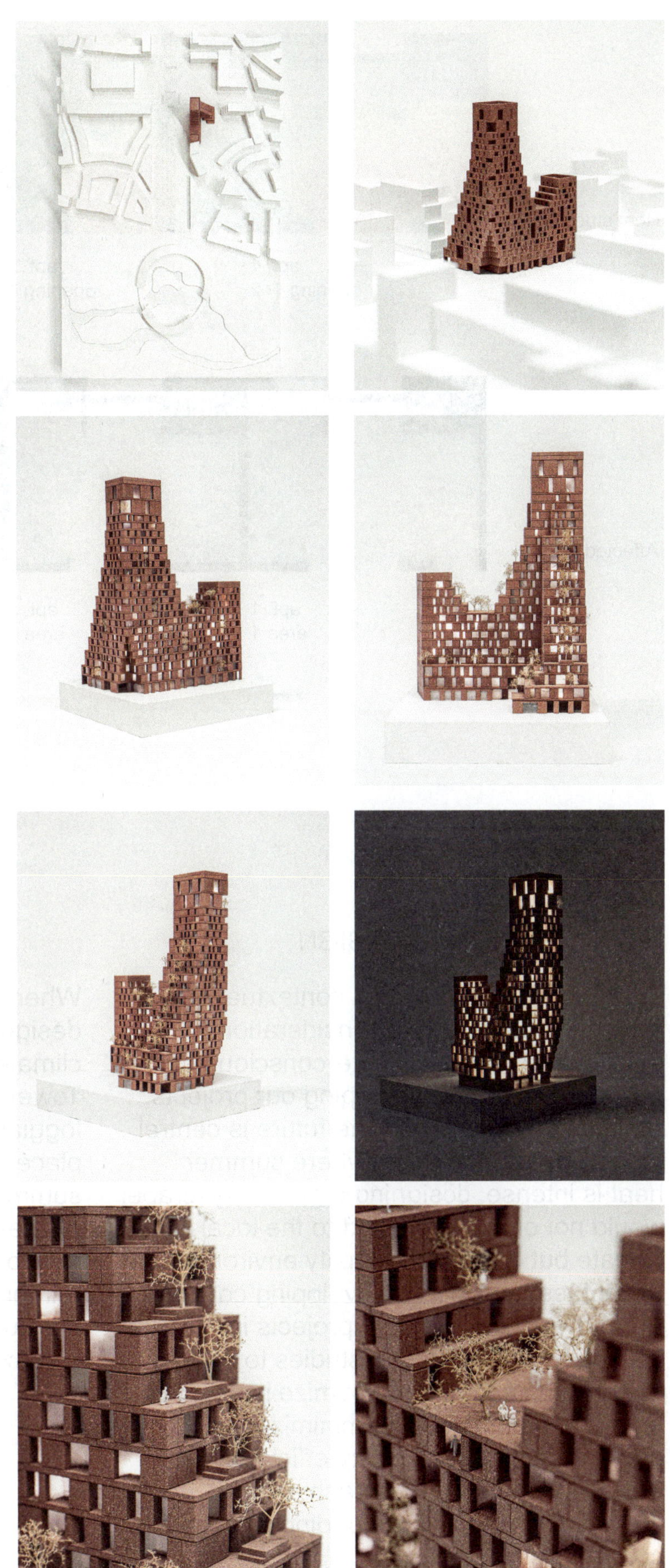

Study models of the Multifunctional Tower Tirana

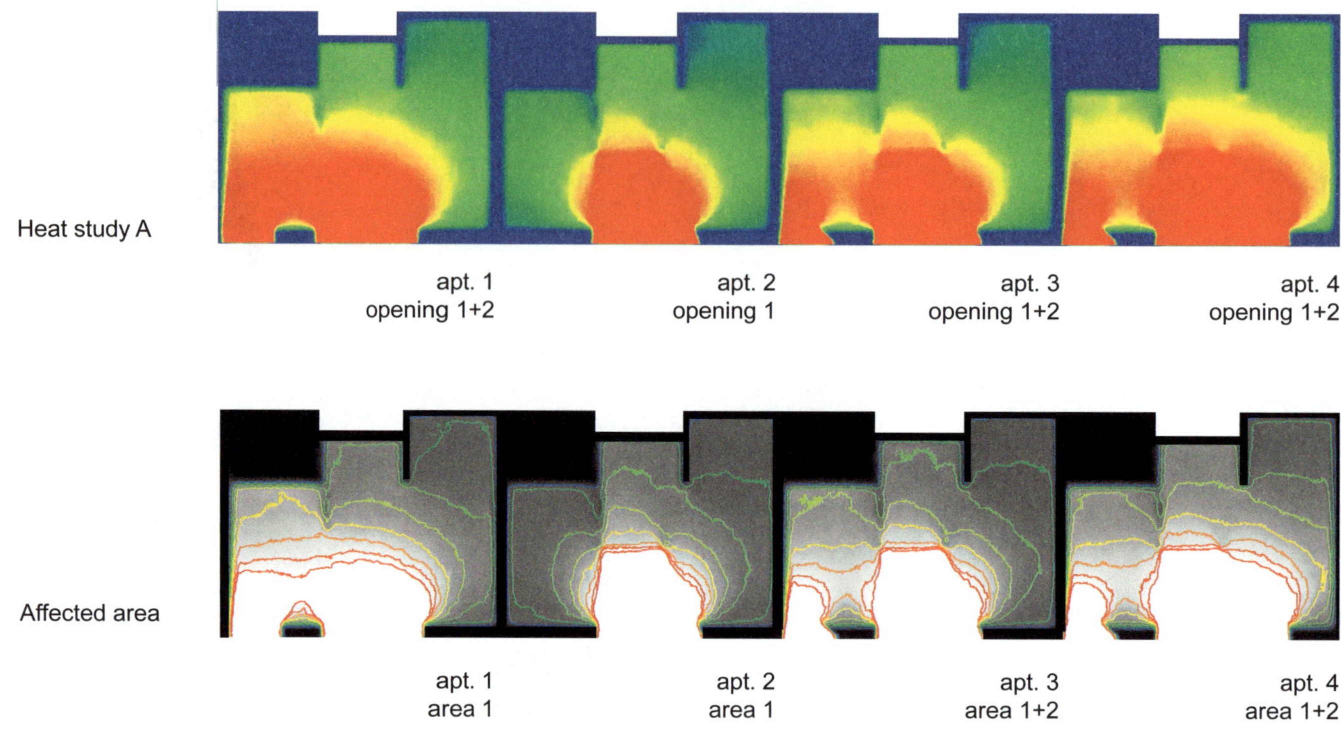

CLIMATE-SPECIFIC DESIGN

This focus on identity and contextual design goes beyond aesthetic considerations.
In cities like Tirana, climate-conscious design plays a crucial role in shaping our projects. Building responsibly for the future is central to our philosophy. Here, where summer heat is intense, designing a glass skyscraper would not only be ill-suited to the local climate but could also amplify environmental impact, especially in a developing country. From the outset in all our projects in Albania, we conduct detailed sun studies to shape the building's form and optimize its layout, ensuring that the design minimizes heat gain and enhances energy efficiency. This climate-responsive approach aligns the building with its surroundings, without compromising comfort.

Wherever feasible, we integrate passive design strategies that respond to the local climate. In the case of the Multifunctional Tower in Tirana, for instance, we introduced loggias for each apartment, strategically placed to shield interior spaces from the summer heat. This thoughtful approach not only ensures the building's sustainability, comfort and energy efficiency but also reinforces its deeper connection to the surrounding environment, making it both contextually and environmentally conscious.

Sun exposure and heat impact analysis

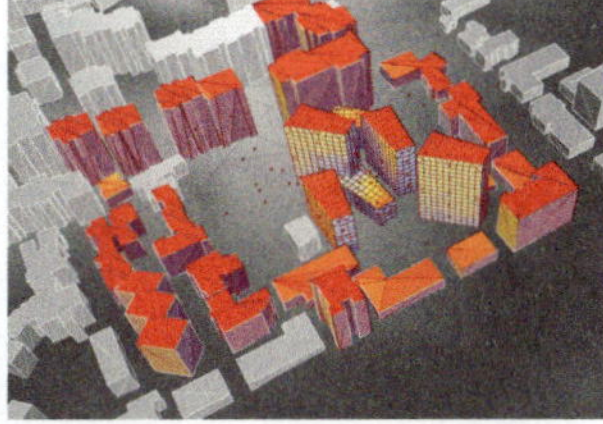

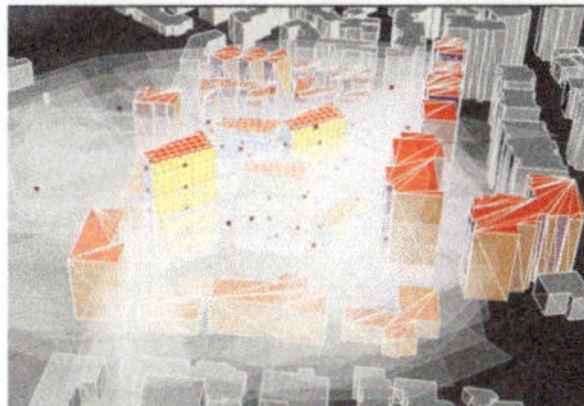

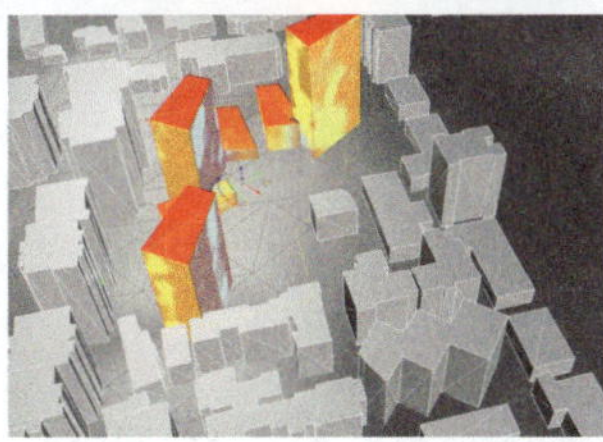

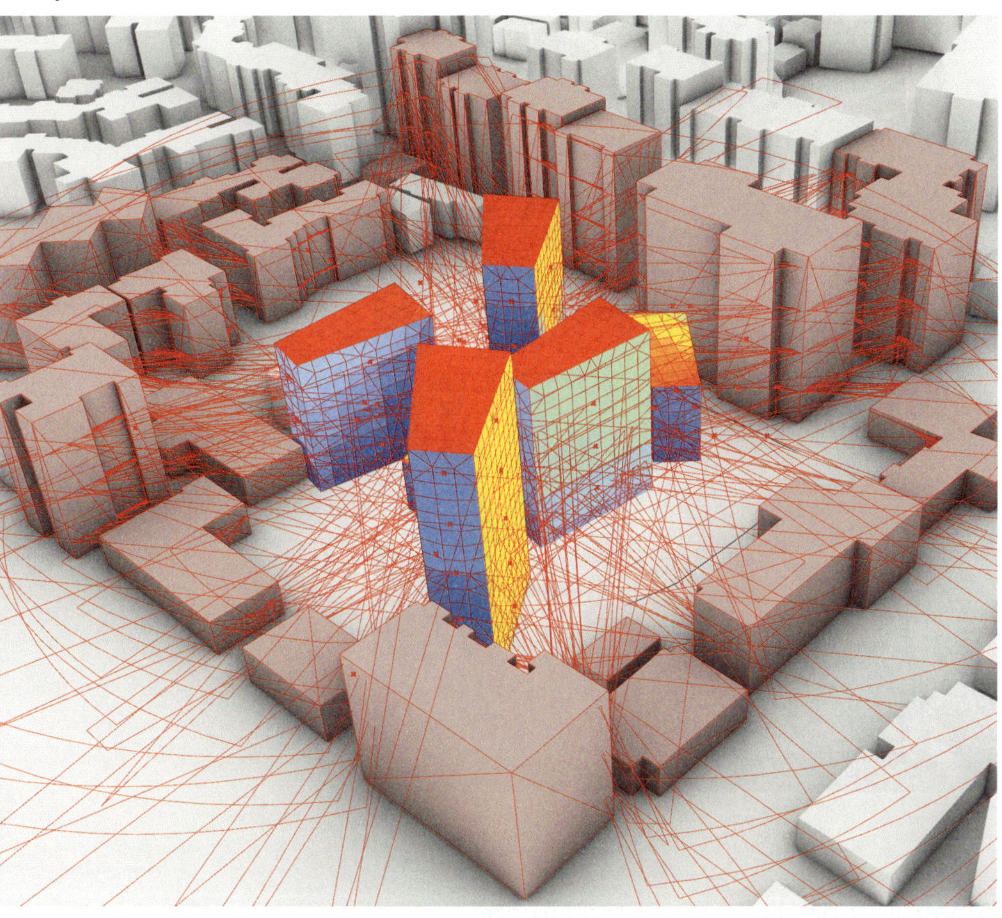

Public square in front of the ODA Tirana project, 2023

Albania's ongoing transformation presents a unique and invaluable opportunity for its future. As it rebuilds, the collective efforts of architects, planners and citizens will shape the country's identity for generations to come. Today, Albania has the chance to continue its evolution by learning from both the successes and the mistakes of similar endeavors across Europe. Mistakes, such as the creation of monofunctional districts – where business quarters become deserted and lifeless after office hours – or the rise of large shopping malls placed around city centers, draining vitality from them, serve as cautionary examples. These are challenges that can be avoided through thoughtful urban planning and the promotion of multifunctionality in new developments. By ensuring that urban spaces are diverse, connected and capable of supporting both social interaction and economic activity, we can help create a livable, coherent urban landscape that serves the needs of all its residents.

Our journey in Albania began with an interest sparked by the transformation of Skanderbeg Square in Tirana. Over time, we have come to understand the broad scope of the country's rebuilding efforts. While many outsiders focus primarily on large-scale developments, towers and skyscrapers, this view overlooks the equally vital work being done in public infrastructure, schools and efforts to rebuild after the devastating earthquakes.

In the context of Albania's ongoing transformation, we believe these efforts should be celebrated as a key part of the future.

START	NAME PROJECT	LOCATION	DEVELOPER	ALBANIAN PARTNER	M²	PUBLIC/PRIVATE	PHASE
2023	Multifunctional Tower Tirana	Tirana	2T + BE-IS shpk	Loft Architects	23,680 m²	Private	Building permission phase (winning competition proposal)
2023	ODA Tirana	Tirana	Albanian government	Studioarch4	135,000 m²	Public	Competition proposal (dual first-prize recipient)
2024	W Tower	Tirana	A&A shpk, Loft Architects		11,000 m²	Private	Architectural study

NAME OFFICE

CITYFÖRSTER ARCHITECTURE & URBANISM

DATE
December 3, 2024

PLACE
Rotterdam, Netherlands

WORKING IN ALBANIA SINCE
2003

PRINCIPALS
Verena Brehm
Arne Hansen
Anne Niehüser
Nils Nolting
Sanna Richter
Oliver Seidel
Martin Sobota

PROJECT TEAM
Piotr Kalbarczyk
Francisco Monforte
Jamie Woods
Valentina Fantini
Jona Fani
Nele Lesemann
Robert Baumann
Philipp Holzer
Michele Guidobaldi
Diogo Zenha
Kristaps Kleinbergs
Anna Savitskaya
Bruno Pereira
Karolina Wrozowska
Sarah Krausslach
Nancy Zimmerman
Tea Hadzizulfic
Christian Moore
Mareike Henschel
Sven Verbruggen
Henri Verhoeven
Hagar Zur
Constanze Hirt
Nina Reckeweg
Eni Ajdini
Henry Endemann
Anamarija Vrzina
Patricia Rodrigues
Rexhina Basha
Jin Myung Lee
Enisa Selmanaj
Shubham Thakur
Isabel Driessen
Kristina Drapic
Andrés López
Quang Minh Huynh
Michał Komosiński
Anaïs Le Grand
Annika Brammer
Edoardo Facchinelli
Justus Schaefer
Ivan Shkurko
Petre Șimonescu
Erialda Zekthi
Valerie Heesakkers
Anna Kurzeja
Sander van Schaik

COLLABORATORS

CO-ARCHITECTS (INTL)
Irgen Salianji, Architects for Urbanity / w. Marina Kounavi
Marina Kounavi, Anne-Sereine Tremblay, Atelier Gram
Luca Moscelli, BUROMOSA
Harm Timmermans, Shift A+U
gruppeomp+g

LANDSCAPE
Ulrike Centmayer
Martin Arfalk, Mandaworks
Philomene van Vliet, Jan Maas, BOOM Landscape
Joost Emmerick
Francesco Garofalo, Openfabric
Peter Veenstra, LOLA Landscape Architects

ENGINEERING
Markus Krauss, Transsolar
Imagine Structure
SWECO
Integration
SRP Schneider + Partner
SRP Albanian Engineering
GAD
Deltares

ARTISTS
Gabriel Lester, PolyLester
Teun Castelein
Elian Stefa

RENDERINGS
Christian Zöllner
CosmosCube

LOCAL ARCHITECTS
Symbiotica
SON Architects
Studioarch4
X-Plan Studio

LOCAL ENGINEERS
PNI 2001
Studio Archimed
Kejsi-05 shpk
Arkon Studio
Dhimitri Papa

OTHER
MVO Nederland
ANVR
Boer Bos
PUM
Sawadee
Alterra
gutundgut
Originate
Paul Gerretsen, Vereniging Deltametropool

INTRODUCTION TO ALBANIA

We came as students at the Berlage Institute with Elia Zenghelis and Pier Vittorio Aureli to work on Visions for Tirana as a Modern European Capital. After the final presentations Edi Rama (then mayor of Tirana) offered us the possibility of working there.

MAIN CONTEXT VS. ALBANIA

We mostly work at the intersection between urban design and architecture in Germany and the Netherlands, as well as internationally. An increasing part of our work concerns consultancy to local and national governments, as well as International Financial Institutions, concerning circular and regenerative economies with the built environment as a focal point.

Albania is and has been our "lab" for many of our concepts and strategies. Following the country and its development – from the poorest nation in Europe to an important driver of the European Idea – for more than twenty years has allowed us to understand the complex playing field. Albania is still very "raw"' in many aspects, which makes processes, forces, and changes readable, even though they are not always easy to chew and swallow.

ORGANIZATION/GOAL/SETUP

We are looking to strike a balance between presence and distance. We have understood over time that our biggest added value is to bring impulses and ideas from abroad and to challenge the local context. At the same time, it is critical to be present and stay involved in projects. For about seven years we have had a formalized presence in Albania with permanent staff. However, we strongly rely on cooperation with local architects, engineers and contractors for all projects and have developed long-lasting cooperations with some of them.

SETUP IN RELATION TO ALBANIAN PARTNER

We find it essential to involve our local counterparts from the beginning and to develop the projects together. This works well when our counterparts have negotiated their contracts well and can afford to invest into a project in the early days. It allows us to adjust our approach to the possibilities and find smart and simple solutions with a soft handover to the later phases of the project. A hard handover on the other side may allow for more radical (innovative?) decisions but is a substantial risk. It can also lead to surprising solutions born out of improvisation, but it is a significant added effort for all parties.

OPPORTUNITIES/CHALLENGES

Albania is still a raw and adventurous environment for architects. Institutions and processes are in constant development and the exception is the rule. This is partly because of the country's turbulent history and its extreme pace of development, which can be a challenge for a profession that prides themselves as Planners, predicting a construction process or urban development and traditionally focusing on avoiding mistakes later by making an effort now. Especially in the early days, with a more volatile political environment, we had to learn the hard way that these efforts are not always appreciated.

HOW TO INTEGRATE GREATER RESPONSIBILITY FOR QUALITY IN PROJECTS

Involve local architects and engineers from the beginning and pay them properly. See above for reasoning.

1. Stick to the (urban) plan. A lot of energy goes into negotiating quantity instead of quality. The plans that Tirana/Albania has are flexible enough to allow for custom solutions.
2. Estimate (realistic) cost (based on transparent statistics) at an early stage to avoid surprises.
3. Require architects to sign off on changes to the projects. Make sure they are paid to review.
4. A bit more predictability of the process, both in terms of timelines and procedures/product, would help to keep motivation and energy up throughout the process.

BALANCING QUALITY AND DENSITY/INVOLVING STAKEHOLDERS

The definition of density and public quality is primarily in the public interest. A good balance needs to be found between protecting public assets such as the natural environment and a healthy living environment (→ low density) with sufficient demand and support for public infrastructures (→ high density). A private investor will always try to externalize part of the cost of his development, be it environmental or infrastructural. This tragedy of the commons cannot be solved by architects in a concrete project, but the rules of the game need to be defined up-front and played along. It is important that these rules are not in choking detail but defined on a strategic level and supervised throughout the process, either by individuals (e.g. supervisors, city architect) or committees (quality teams, design commissions) that advise the bureaucracy.

EXAMPLE/INSPIRATION

Obviously 51N4E's and Peter Wilson's projects have always been great inspirations. The simplicity and robustness of 51's designs such as the TID Tower, using a simple, strong principle (circle to square) and pragmatic solutions, create architectural qualities which become inevitable and can survive a rather chaotic process. Also their use of material, such as terrazzo concrete and the amazing variety of natural stones Albania has to offer, which had been hidden until Skanderbeg Square. Interestingly this variety of stones on the square is the result of pragmatic decisions, not to say improvisations.

From Peter Wilson we have learned that even a small contribution to an ongoing project can make a big difference and that humor is an essential element of a good design.

TOOLBOX ALBANIA FUTURE

The raw and adventurous environment prepares us to understand architecture and planning as open-ended processes we contribute to but which remain collective efforts that don't end when a project is "delivered." In a world facing unprecedented shocks and crises, shifting from a linear understanding of history and economy to a circular one, this is an important skill set.

As architects and urbanists, it's been a privilege to work in Albania over the past two decades. From our beginnings in the old Tirana, with its tattered façades and big dreams, to today's dynamic skyline peppered with household names, our engagement with the country has deeply influenced our practice, offering insights into the intersections of architecture, politics and culture.

It all began with a pivotal introduction, when Elia Zenghelis invited Tirana's then-Mayor Edi Rama to the Berlage Institute in Rotterdam. The presentation Rama gave was unforgettable, even featuring a video in which he performed as part of a local Albanian hip-hop group. Accompanied by a team of young and ambitious municipal architects, his charisma and ambition were electrifying. The vision he expressed felt like a place where our work could truly resonate and where we could perhaps even make a difference.

1. "Architecture without architects": typical development in Tirana, 2004
2. Elia Zenghelis and Edi Rama during studio presentations at the Berlage Institute in Rotterdam, 2004
3. Tirana skyline, 2004
4. Skanderbeg Square with children's entertainment, 2004
5. Typical side street, 2004

Our initial visits to Tirana were intense, revelatory experiences. An artist himself, Rama approached architecture as a medium for collective expression, and he was unafraid to take bold approaches. His project of colorful façade paintings had created quite a buzz on the world stage, while his team of incorruptible "bulldozers without cousins," as Rama called them, had reclaimed Tirana's most important urban spaces as public assets. As the momentum of progress increased he shifted his focus toward a strategy for the whole city, aiming to embed a cultural shift and make the city "a modern European capital" (which was also the title of our studio project).

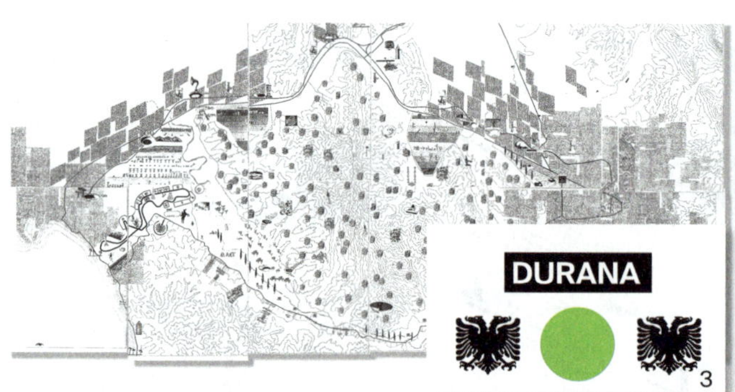

At the time, Tirana was a very poor city. Urban order was only just beginning to return after the chaotic years which had followed the fall of the communist regime. Traffic lights were still a novelty, huge areas of the city lacked paving, and potholes, puddles and open manholes were constant hazards. Municipal services were minimal and there was garbage scattered everywhere. It felt overwhelming, but in hindsight the outlines of an extraordinary strategy were already present.

Today the city is a vibrant European capital, and being part of this evolution remains one of our studio's most formative experiences. We have been fortunate enough to witness a city redefining itself, understanding more of the forces present in urban development and learning how to adapt. In Albania, architecture and urbanism have never been linear processes; they are iterative, responsive and intrinsically tied to the country's broader narrative of development.

1. Altin Gagani, Pier Paolo Tamburelli, Martino Tattara, Reto Durrer, Lu Zhang, Pier Vittorio Aureli and Joachim Declerck on Skanderbeg Square, 2004
2. Audience and TV cameras during the final studio presentation in the central atrium of the National Gallery, 2004
3. Overview map of urban acupuncture along the Tirana-Durrës corridor and the Durana logo, project by Alexa Nürnberger, Pier Paolo Tamburelli and Martin Sobota
4. First site visit with CITYFÖRSTER on Jordan Misja site. Mirror Twins master plan, 2004

Between 2005 and 2013, Albania was in flux as the political order began to change. It was an exhilarating but precarious time for firms like ours. We first began to receive a blizzard of commissions, meeting many of our friends and colleagues more frequently at Tirana's city council meetings than at home in Rotterdam. Rama insisted on public presentations for building permissions, an initiative which fostered open and collegial discourse between local and international architects. These exchanges were frank and free from competition, a pragmatic decision which allowed local firms to benefit from seeing how their international peers approached the work while offering the international firms insight into local discussions.

At the same time it quickly became a sobering experience; as Rama's political star rose, those council meetings became one of the battlegrounds on which the establishment sought to weaken him. In particular, one change to the laws around building permissions enacted to wrest power back to the central government was devastating: Projects stalled, clients stopped paying and contracts held little weight. The work of an architect is always a balancing act, but we were almost too late in learning how to remain stable during such tectonic shifts. Still fascinated by the country, we sought to diversify and soon began to secure public projects like the transformation of Student City 2, which was financed by the German KfW Development Bank.

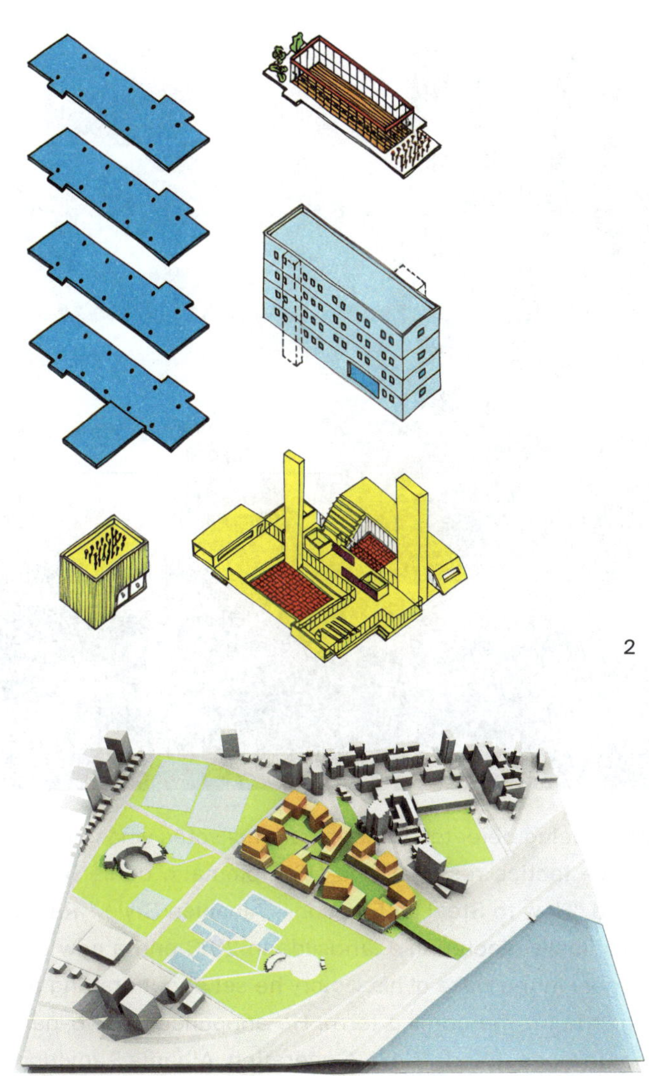

2

3

1

4

1. Commission for a tower in Elbasan, 2006
2. Concept sketch for the renovation of the Socialist Party Headquarters, 2005
3. Project for Lake Park, Tirana, 2005
4. Renovation of Student City 2, Phase 1 completed 2013–2020

After being defeated twice in national votes whose innovative tactics resulted in a US diplomatic cable being titled "How to Steal an Election – Albanian Style," Rama was finally elected in a landslide in 2013 and a new era began. In the wake of his victory he set about drafting an agenda for the coming term. He announced a two-part conference titled "Next Generation Albania," inviting economists and architects to visit the country and discuss their impressions. It was an inspiring moment; we were in the room where strategies were being developed and there was a genuine interest in our opinion, not only on matters of architecture and planning, but also a broader strategic view. As our experiences of the country up to that point had largely been limited to working in Tirana, we also rode the momentum and began to explore more.

A few months later, together with Joni Baboci and Paul Gerretsen of Vereniging Deltametropool and supported by Adelina Greca of AKPT/Atelier Albania, we traveled the country from north to south and met with mayors, urban planners and local entrepreneurs. The people and landscapes we encountered were inspiring, but everywhere we found a built environment which was struggling. Heritage was being disregarded and a lack of urban order affected everything from garbage disposal to tax collection. Agricultural land lay fallow, and large swaths of the coastline had already been concreted over.

1. Welcome speech to the architecture and urban design edition of the "Next Generation Albania" conference, 2013
2. Workshop on Territorial Planning Agenda during "Next Generation Albania" conference. Clockwise from bottom left: Daniel Niggli, Andreas Ruby, Mathias Müller, Minister Dr. Eglantina Gjermeni, Frits van Dongen, Martin Sobota
3. Amphitheater Durrës, with informal buildings encroaching on the second-century AD site

These days the situation is much better; we find many previously blighted areas renewed, architectural mistakes repaired, the urban fabric healed or healing. While the pace of development is still massive, it is a hopeful prospect. The quality of construction and design is getting better every year, mistakes from the past are repaired. There is a constant discourse on the kind of tourism Albania wants to attract and there are so many gems of the country waiting to be uncovered and polished. From the last wild river of Europe, the Vjosa, to the highlands of Kurvelesh. From the traces of Illyrians, Romans and Ottomans to the more recent heritage of communist Albania under Enver Hoxha.

1. Site in Qeparo
2. Rusty bridge from communist times in Përmet
3. Modernist housing in Fier, 2019
4. Scenery of Valbona Valley
5. Site visit with Dhimitër Kote (head of Komuna Xarrë) and Paul Gerretsen (Vereniging Deltametropool), 2013
6. Traditional dry stone wall with spontaneous vegetation
7. Vjosa River valley

Along the way of our country tour, we met with the mayor of Durrës, who had begun investing into public space and proposed a compelling challenge: At the end of the town's long promenade stood an abandoned site awaiting revitalization. The brief was clear yet unusual - create an attraction that is noncommercial, a public space free from consumption. In the context of the post-communist, turbo-capitalist fever we had become accustomed to in Albania, this ambition stood out.

In collaboration with BOOM Landscape, we proposed something elemental: a mountain. Perched atop a future groyne, commanding perfect views of both sunrise and sunset, the terraced landscape would invite visitors to pause, reflect and connect with the horizon, its presence transforming the promenade's end into a natural destination. Sphinx, as the structure is now known, has since gone on to feature in music videos, KFC commercials, memes and countless wedding pictures, and has garnered awards and recognition and been described as Albania's first "European-style" public space.

After the Sphinx and a successful competition in the Albanian Riviera, we soon became involved in other public-space projects that were part of "Rilindja Urbane," the urban rebirth program. These included public spaces in Saranda and on the iconic beaches of Dhërmi and Jala, where the works offered opportunities to celebrate the unique character of Albania's remarkable southern coast. Our approach was grounded in restraint, proposing robust, unspectacular infrastructures to support the coast's development; stabilizing the beach as it were, providing shade and services, delineating public and private realms. We embraced restaurant owners' ad-hoc landscaping and integrated their spontaneous planting into our designs.

At one spot, however, where natural fresh water from a stream originating in the mountains above flows across the promenade and the old foundations of an illegally built hotel, we devised an "Instagrammable" water square with the town's name neatly placed in the frame.

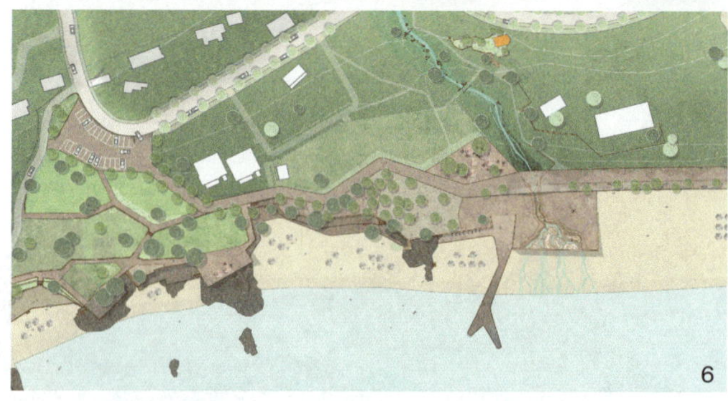

1. The Sphinx, covered with visitors and fishermen
2. Still from one of several music videos shot at the Sphinx - this one is titled "Boom, Boom, Boom"
3. Water square in Dhërmi
4. Mayor Dako shows off a phone cover featuring the pavement pattern from the square surrounding the Sphinx
5. Promenade in Dhërmi
6. Original plan for the Dhërmi "Delta"

Much of our effort in the execution of these works was centered on the work with local stones, reducing concrete to the bare minimum while optimizing conditions for local vegetation. However, one problem which we had to learn the hard way was that finding appropriate plant species proved unexpectedly challenging. Local sourcing was often impractical; vegetation was more easily salvaged from nearby construction sites than acquired from plant nurseries. Ultimately, many plants – including the 316 plane trees which now populate Vlora Boulevard – were imported from Italy or the Netherlands.

1. Dhërmi Promenade, with trees and outdoor furniture merging with the beach
2. Martin Sobota showing a site worker how to scrape mortar from between the stones
3. Three kinds of terrazzo furniture, Vlora Boulevard
4. Bird's-eye view of Vlora Boulevard: first section with crossing
5. Older man walking along extended sidewalk on Vlora Boulevard

1. Walking with a shepherd – testing a future touristic production in Qeparo
2. Master chef Arber Togani presenting his signature dish of local ingredients to workshop participants
3. Discussion between Detjon Prenga, local entrepreneur, World Bank tourism expert Milton Hyun Soo Kal, Paul Bos, farmer and coach, and Irena Toshkallari during the Qeparo workshop

Around 2013 it was clear that Albania wanted to welcome visitors and development, but negative consequences were already being felt in some of the coastal resorts. We were fascinated by questions around how the last undeveloped coast of the Mediterranean could develop a new model instead of falling prey to rapacious mass tourism that ultimately destroys what it seeks. As we became more aware of the untapped potential of the region, we became passionate proponents of alternative models of tourism. In order to substantiate this claim and create an exchange of ideas, we launched an initiative which the Dutch government supported financially, inviting local and international tourism experts to meet with local entrepreneurs, farmers and others.

Through two missions and an intensive one-week workshop, we documented the situation, mapping trends and proposing new models for tourism, agriculture and local supply chains. The outcome, which was published as "The Traveller and the Olive Grove," examines a range of paths by which the tourism and agriculture sectors could be helped to continue their strong development without being trapped into unsustainable trajectories. Looking back, we are happy and a little proud to see that many of the business models proposed in that book have since become reality.

The passion and persistence of Auron Tare, whom we had also met during the first mission and who is a strong advocate for and expert on the hidden wonders of Albania, also led us to work in Nivica. At the time it was a remote mountain village four hours by jeep from the coast, but Auron saw Nivica's potential as an ideal year-round tourism destination combining Albania's coast and mountains, and he was pushing for a road to reduce travel time to one hour. At the time, the government's 100 Villages program had recently been launched, which funded model infrastructure projects in remote areas. Auron needed a document to help persuade villagers and politicians to follow his vision. He guided us to some of his favorite rural development examples, and we later brought urban planning and archaeology students to work together with local Albanian students.

Through our research and work it became evident that missteps in style and misguided interventions were rarely driven by bad intentions, but more often by a lack of clear direction. With this lesson in mind we developed a master plan which sought to channel the Albanians' immense energy and will to develop, steering it toward a more thoughtful, sustainable path. The plan didn't require legal status; it was simply a guiding framework, a tool to shape the future without the rigidity of official decree.

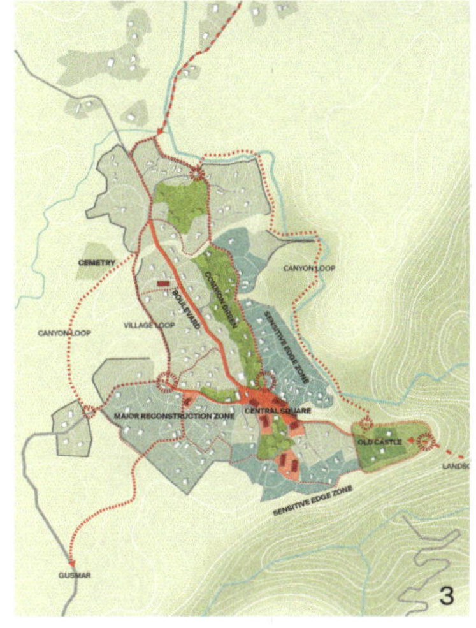

1. Adventurous hike from the village of Kuç
2. Cocreation workshop with Albanian students
3. Master plan for the village, determining areas of special attention, views to protect and limits to development
4. Investigations into typical local construction methods (here: stone roofs)
5. View of Nivica (Kurvelesh), with canyon and Mount Këndrevica

2

3

When we received a commission to reimagine a large touristic development on a beachfront site in Drymades, one of the best-known beaches on the Albanian Riviera, the brief prompted reflection. Could tourism on this scale be compatible with our earlier ambitions? Do the incentives of tourism leave room for interesting architecture at all?

We were initially presented with a template of semidetached houses, each with its own parking and pool. It was a clear nod to the success of the Green Coast development by Mane TCI in Palasë, but we questioned the archetype and embraced the client's desire to increase density, seeing the potential to move toward something more cohesive and sustainable. Given the site's position near the beach, we realized that density could be supported as a strategy for accessibility. Not only could residents easily walk down to the beach, but by integrating pathways inland and embedding essential functions, the project could extend activities in Drymades beyond the summer season – a true village.

The challenge therefore lay in achieving this density without compromising the informal, layered structure of a village, creating a touristic development whose interest is not "urbanity" or modern architecture but nostalgia, emotion and relaxation. In this sense we saw the limits of our control over the outcome of the project as potential, and conceived a modular system – an architectural toolbox allowing future owners to create and customize spatial units and select from a curated catalog of openings and roof forms. The elements drew on the vernacular of Mediterranean architecture, inspired by its simplicity and adaptation to the climate.

With this system established, our efforts turned to optimizing the available views and activating the public spaces between buildings. We designed a circulation system in which central staircases were deliberately omitted in favor of a layered access system. By providing each apartment with its own direct external entrance, each home retains a sense of individuality with varied levels of privacy, while the chance encounters and overlap of village life are still encouraged.

The material strategy also embraces locality and tactility. Windows feature locally crafted wooden shutters to mitigate heat gain while introducing a Mediterranean warmth. Uniform window colors across apartments allow for straightforward maintenance and repair. Sills are absent, as is common in traditional Greek island homes, where façades are refreshed every few years with limewash. Over time this process imparts a patina – a living texture that reflects the ongoing engagement of residents and builders alike. Rather than aiming for permanence and solitude, the architecture embraces imperfection and renewal, embedding a rhythm of repair and transformation that mirrors the rhythm of a true village. The result is an urban density within which communal spaces connect clusters of private homes.

4

1. View along axis connecting the two "urban" squares
2. Diagram showing different angles of sea views
3. Presentation model, February 2021
4. Detail of lime plaster and wooden shutters

1

Our housing projects on the other hand are deeply rooted in our early observations of urban sprawl – a persistent issue where market dynamics continually push the city outward. The allure of a quiet, safe neighborhood just outside the city center remains an irresistible narrative, memorably expressed by Kurt Tucholsky as having "the boulevard at the front door and the beach at the back." For developers, such communities of gated, low-density sprawl represent the perfect vision to market, but they're a poor use of space and resources; from an urbanist's perspective, they are a disaster. In response, our projects aim to reconcile the qualities of suburban living – a green, tranquil environment, and a sense of neighborhood and community – with the efficient density of the city. By combining these seemingly opposing attributes, we strive to reimagine urban living without compromise.

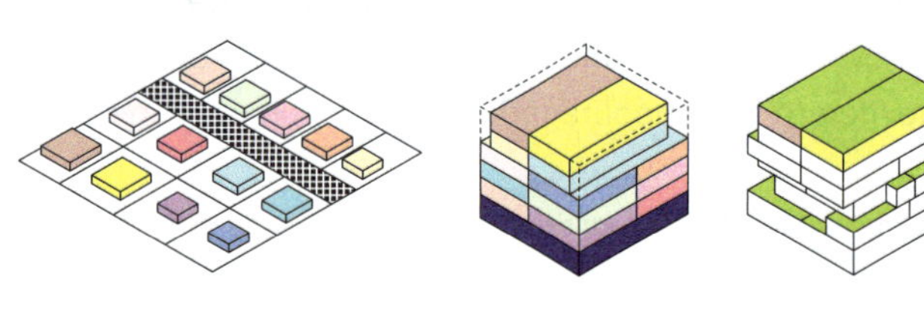

2

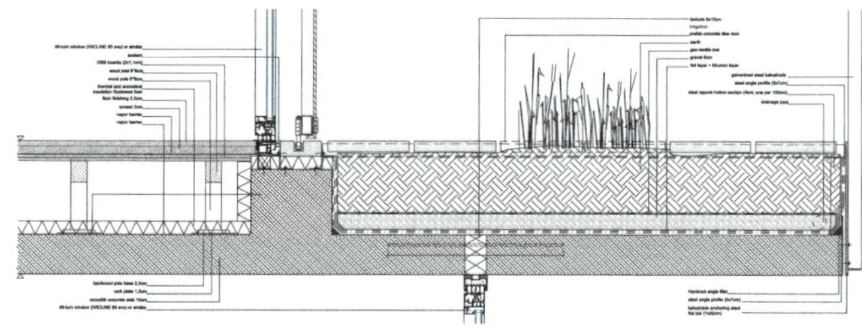

3

4

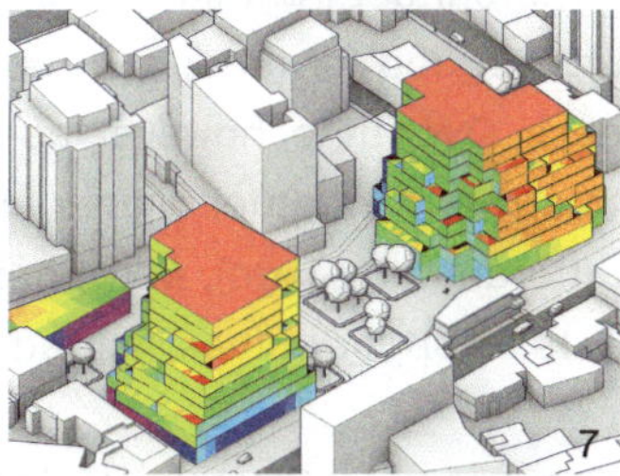

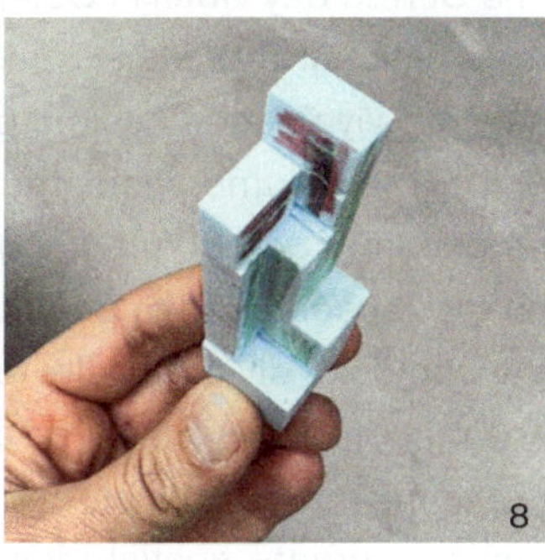

An example of this is our penthouse tower, which draws inspiration from Tirana's 1990s mid-rise typology in which constructions known as "penthouses" proliferated. Similar to the ad-hoc additions seen in Chinese skyscrapers, these rooftop extensions often resemble single-family homes set atop nondescript apartment blocks and bring a suburban quality into the center of the city. We multiplied this approach through a series of setbacks, granting this luxury to more than one unit.

The form of this tower evolved first through a meticulous analysis of setback regulations and daylighting constraints, alongside the client's density ambitions, and was shaped further by the overarching urban plan. When the design process reached an impasse, the client secured an exemption to height restrictions through KKT approval. This opened up possibilities for a more dynamic composition: an active commercial base with a cluster of towers rising above, culminating in twenty-seven bespoke penthouses. The materiality of the structure is intentionally understated, with external sunshading serving as both a defining architectural feature and a simple yet highly effective tool to reduce energy consumption and enhance living quality.

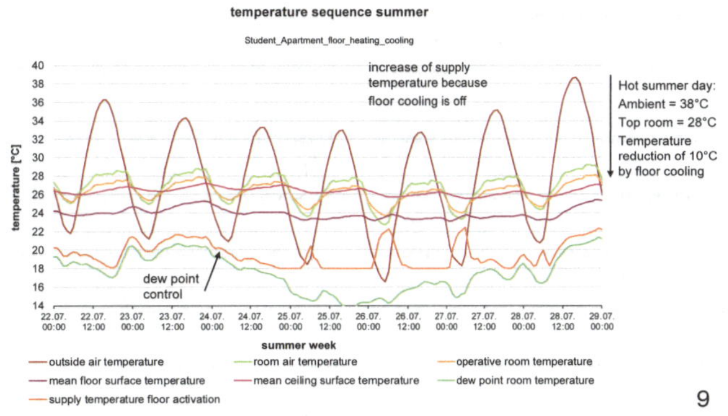

1. View of Embassy Residences render, with neighbors meeting on a Friday afternoon
2. Concept diagram, stacked villas
3. Detail of balconies and external staircase with planting substrate
4. Partial floor plan
5. Frontal view of Pazar i Ri Tower
6. Penthouse 5
7. Solar analysis of early envelope study
8. Model for the terracing
9. Thermal simulation (of Student City 2 project), proving indoor comfort through external shading combined with moderate floor cooling

In recent years we've noted a rise in requests from private developers asking for help with "fixing" their projects. At first these requests felt insulting – a challenge to the identity of contemporary architecture. The client often already has a design, likely one that has stalled in the approval process. The brief to us is typically vague: Provide better renderings, perhaps suggest new materials. The implication is clear – this is cosmetic surgery, not architecture. Initially we rejected these sorts of jobs and argued for a deeper approach, usually without success. Over time, however, as similar inquiries also began to arrive from other clients elsewhere (though framed in different language), we began to reconsider these projects as opportunities instead of frustrations.

The Durrës Bay Hotel in Golem in particular prompted us to rethink our attitude to such projects. The client didn't have a fully fledged design, but had a clear understanding of the volume, indicated by the building's efficient functioning. So our intervention focused almost entirely on the façade and the position of the core. We adjusted the angles of dividing walls to orient rooms toward views and minimize noise. Inspired by the beauty of Skanderbeg Square's paving stones, we used a pattern of natural stone to create spatial identities referring to Albania's diverse regions.

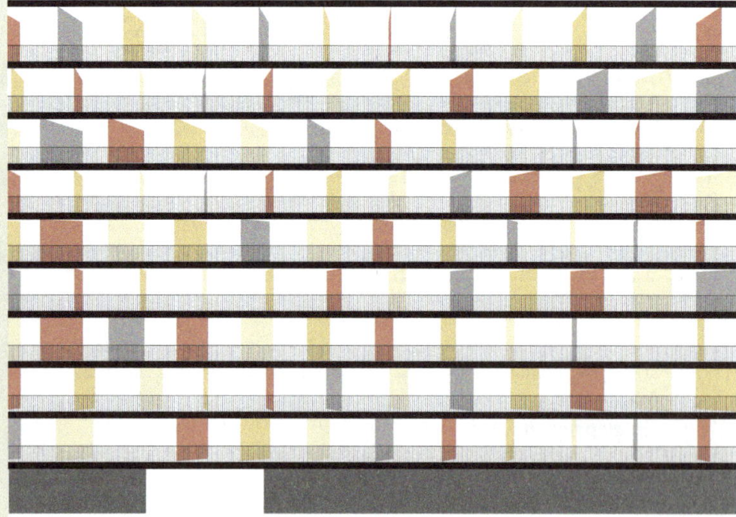

1

1. Elevation diagram showing distribution of different types of local stones
2. Durrës Bay Hotel, poolside view

But then, abruptly and not long before completion, the project shifted. A Chinese investor was repurposing the building – ironically designed in collaboration with Architects for Urbanity – as a call center. A radical shift, but a function which we actually welcomed among the monofunctional developments in Golem. The change was simple. Bathrooms were locked, every second wall removed, and the pool filled with sand. The rational layout adapted seamlessly and brought into practice what we advocate in our most sustainable projects – architecture adaptable for future possibilities.

Some years and a pandemic later, the building returned to its original function as a hotel. It is exemplary for the lessons we can learn from Albania. Resilience and adaptability are common sense here, something we have often lost in our drive for efficiency and predictability. Where a context changes so rapidly this is a more relevant strategy than overly detailed engineering.

2

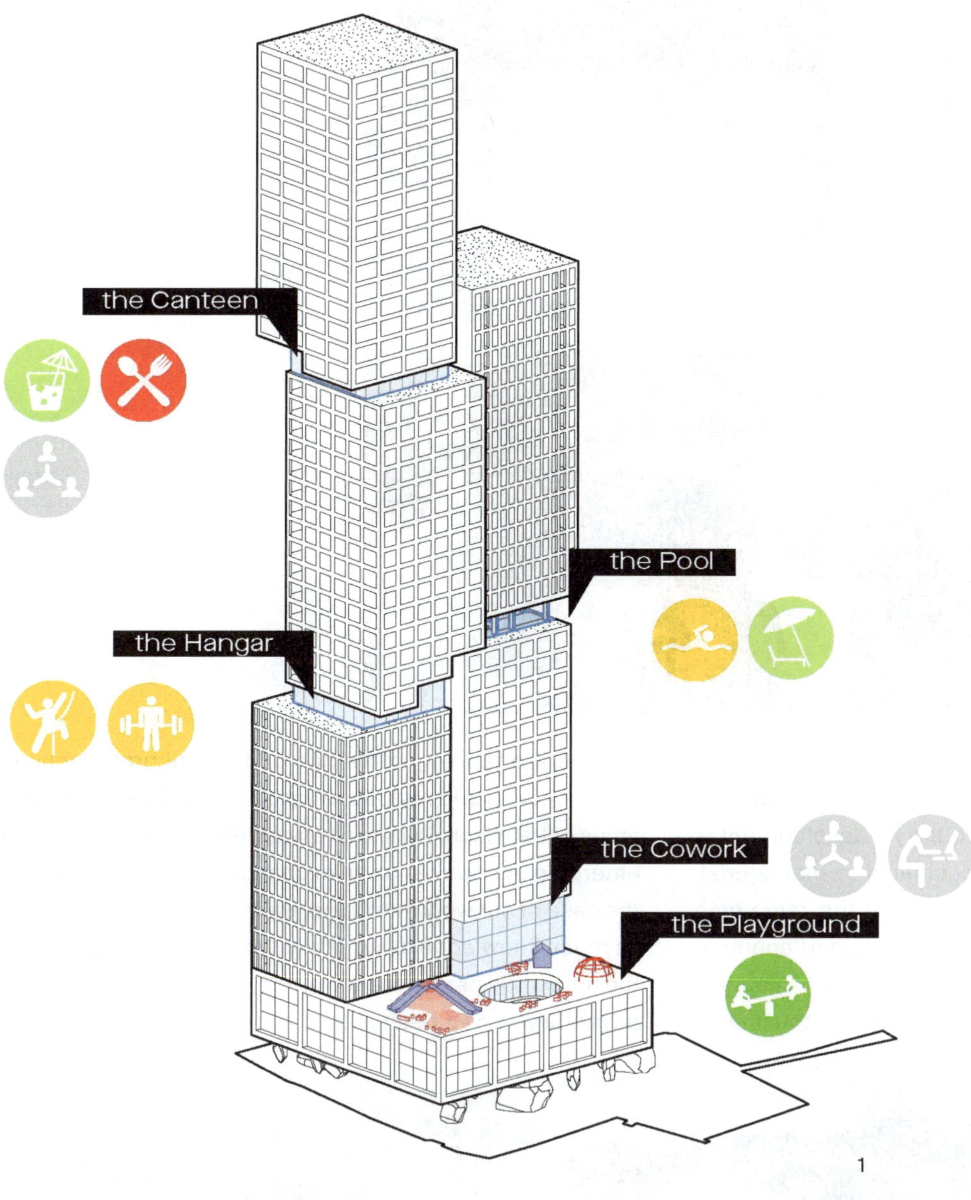

1. Schematic diagram of Reshit Petrela Tower, showing public program

In a second project, a collaboration with atelier GRAM, the challenge is still ongoing. It began as a typical request for a façade redesign, but we soon found that the problem was deeper; the building's proportions were all wrong. In a meeting which felt like a lesson in architectural theory we explained that a squat, low-rise building isn't made more beautiful simply by changing its color. The building also had two blind walls - a compromise apparently agreed upon with the neighbors because it stood very close to the property line.

Although the brief focused on façade architecture, we proposed a more refined solution: a combination of three elegant towers structured by programmatic insertions that not only gave the building character but also imbued it with a civic dimension. Up to that point height limits had been hotly debated, and had in fact killed an earlier project called Park City, but when we inquired about the possibility of increasing the height, we were surprised to learn that there were no limits at all. Instead we were encouraged to go taller and make the building more graceful. During preliminary consultations with the "beauty commission," the main concerns were the integration into the neighborhood and the need to create openness in the ground floor. To respond to the challenges of heavy loads and little natural light, we invited LOLA Landscape from Rotterdam, and together developed a design which radically lifts the building from the ground, providing an attractive public space under the building that is themed around rocks and water.

1. Investigating dead palm trees in Vlora to see how we can turn them into sculptures, 2017
2. Martin Sobota (on the right) meeting Rexhep Uka, the country's foremost botanist, 2016
3. Excursion in Kurvelesh on a typical rainy Albanian day, March 2016
4. Typical Riviera treat: roasted lamb and lots of raki, 2024
5. At Auron Tare's site – a hut in Nivica, 2022
6. Car crash on the way to a site visit in Jala, 2018
7. Mock-up for Durrës façade painting, Francisco Monforte and Di Fang, 2016
8. Next generation CITYFÖRSTER reviewing Rinia Complex in Fier, 2016
9. Working lunch on the way to Drymades, Valentina Fantini and Kristi Doka, 2014
10. Arriving in Tirana on the first direct Amsterdam–Tirana flight, May 2017

The architecture industry's rigidity can sometimes feel limiting, and this makes working in Albania exhilarating and addictive. The pace of the country's development is impressive in all aspects, from technical to managerial, political, jurisdiction, culture and more. At the same time there are strong traditions of family bonds and common sense deeply rooted in the turbulent history of the country, with its repression, shocks and crises. We have the feeling that we are tapping into a rich pool of cultural practices full of lessons and recipes which feel apposite for our own times of transition. People often politely describe working in emerging economies as an exchange of knowledge, but in the case of our work in Albania, we truly continue to receive as much knowledge as we bring. On top of that we cherish the numerous personal encounters, crazy projects and real adventures we've been able to experience. It's a ride!

START	NAME PROJECT	LOCATION	DEVELOPER	PUBLIC/PRIVATE	PHASE
2005	Mirror Twins master plan	Tirana		Private	Master planning
2005	House 1	Tirana		Private	Executed
2005	Lake Park	Tirana		Private	Master planning
2005	Renovation of the Socialist Party Headquarters	Tirana			Concept, partially executed
2008	Park City			Private	Competition, 1st prize, unfollowed
2009	ANA Residential Complex	Tirana	Kontakt shpk	Private	Executed
2013	The Traveller and the Olive Grove	Qeparo	Kingdom of the Netherlands	Public	Executed
2014	Unveiling the Riviera	Saranda – Konispol region	Albanian Ministry of Urban Development and Tourism / Office of the Prime Minister		Executed
2015	Cape Square Durrës	Durrës	Municipality of Durrës	Public	Executed
2016	Central Park Elbasan	Elbasan	Municipality of Elbasan	Public	Executed
2016	Dhërmi & Jala Waterfront	Himara	Albanian Development Fund / Municipality of Himara	Public	Executed
2017	Vlora Boulevard	Vlora City	Municipality of Vlora / Albanian Development Fund	Public	Executed
2016	Sphinx Lofts	Durrës		Private	Under construction
2017	Durrës Bay Hotel	Golem		Private	Executed
2013	Renovation of Student City 2	Tirana	Ministry of Economy, Trade and Energy	Public	Executed
2017	Bar Center Fier	Fier		Private	Executed
2018	Embassy Residences	Tirana	Private	Private	Executed
2018	Rinia Complex	Fier	Private	Private	Under construction
2018	Dhërmi Plaza Hotel	Dhërmi	Private	Private	Executed
2019	Tirana Municipality Building	Tirana	Municipality of Tirana	Public	Competition, 2nd phase – undecided
2020	Drymades Village	Drymades	Gjikuria shpk	Private	Under construction
2021	Drymades promenade	Drymades	Gjikuria shpk	Private	Detailed design
2022	ONI Tower	Tirana		Private	Under construction
2023	Buna Delta Blue / Green City master plan	Shkodra	Netherlands Enterprise Agency	Public	Executed
2023	Underwater Center	Saranda	& Zip Line Përmet, Albanian Development Fund	Public	Under construction
2023	Reshit Petrela Tower	Tirana		Private	Site permission granted
2025	Bogë Mountain Resort	Shkodra		Private	Concept development

NAME OFFICE

COLDEFY

DATE
December 2025

PLACE
Paris, France

WORKING IN ALBANIA SINCE
2024

PRINCIPALS
Thomas Coldefy
Isabel Van Haute
Zoltan Neville

ASSOCIATE ARCHITECTS
ATELIER 4
Artech
SON Architects
UNO architects
Vaeku

PROJECT TEAM
Thomas Amarsy
Martin Mercier
Leonardo Ronchi
Vincent Vaulot
Gabriel Vorbe
Pierre Louis Noez

ARTIST
Jacopo Foggini

INTRODUCTION TO ALBANIA

In recent years, friends who traveled to Albania shared stories of its striking natural beauty, from mountains to the sea, which sparked our desire to discover it both personally and professionally. What truly captured our attention, however, was speaking with fellow architects already working there. They described Albania as a genuine laboratory for innovation and introspection, deeply shaped by its history and culture.

MAIN CONTEXT VS. ALBANIA

Our practice is rooted in France, with experience in Asia and other developing contexts marked by rapid growth and transformation. In Albania, we see a convergence of these experiences: a strong understanding of Western architectural values combined with a speed and ambition reminiscent of Asia a decade ago, while remaining deeply connected to a rich cultural identity. This dynamism creates a stimulating environment for architecture and urban design. By contrast, France offers fewer opportunities to challenge the existing context, where change is often resisted and innovation is confined to new districts. In Albania, architecture is welcomed as a discipline that integrates art, social responsibility, environmental awareness and the creation of meaningful spaces that enrich daily life and cities.

ORGANIZATION/GOAL/SETUP

Today, our design team is based in Paris and works closely with local partners in Albania. This collaboration allows us to maintain rigorous design standards while benefiting from essential local knowledge. Beyond individual projects, our long-term ambition is to build true coalitions with Albanian and international architects, fostering mutual learning and shared growth.

SETUP IN RELATION TO ALBANIAN PARTNER

We regularly organize design workshops to create open dialogue around sites, ideas and challenges. This collaborative approach integrates local insights early in the process, resulting in designs that are both innovative and contextually grounded. We believe this exchange strengthens our work, and we see this dialogue deepening further in the future.

OPPORTUNITIES/CHALLENGES

One of the main challenges lies in navigating Albania's fast-evolving context, where construction methods and regulations change rapidly. While this requires constant adaptability, it also presents a remarkable opportunity. Albania embraces architecture and art as tools to improve quality of life, which aligns with our core understanding of the discipline.

HOW TO INTEGRATE GREATER RESPONSIBILITY FOR QUALITY IN PROJECTS

A key way to integrate greater responsibility for project quality is by empowering well-trained professionals within urban departments. When knowledgeable individuals with the right mindset are given authority to review and approve projects, they can ensure accountability among investors, developers and contractors. This oversight promotes higher construction quality and fosters a culture of responsibility across the industry.

BALANCING QUALITY AND DENSITY/INVOLVING STAKEHOLDERS

By clearly communicating how quality and density can coexist, architects can guide clients, developers and authorities toward more sustainable outcomes. Expanding the process to include citizens, planners and policymakers through participatory approaches helps integrate diverse perspectives while protecting the city's quality and identity.

EXAMPLE/INSPIRATION

Recently we discovered the Eden project by Studio Precht, which sets a high statement on the idea of living in good and sustainable architecture in closer connection with the natural elements.

TOOLBOX ALBANIA FUTURE

Albania offers a dynamic toolbox: rapid urban transformation, ambitious visions and openness to experimentation. This context enables architects to shape better cities and create forward-thinking architecture rooted in local culture and nature.

Tirana's potential is intrinsic to its polarized identities, its culture, its vision of the future, its heritage given by folk clothing & artisanal crafts as well as the nature that is present in an overwhelming way in its cityscape, testifying to the constant urban evolution.

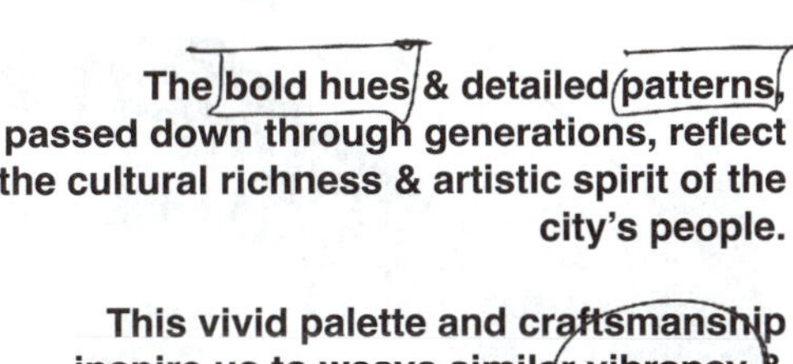

The bold hues & detailed patterns, passed down through generations, reflect the cultural richness & artistic spirit of the city's people.

This vivid palette and craftsmanship inspire us to weave similar vibrancy & texture into our architectural approach.

How can we embody the strong image and Albanian culture in large buildings in the heart of the city with the simplicity of a space that is both welcoming and easy to access by the community?

Wandering through the city as a learning experience to shape our design and pondering how to assimilate its cultural heritage.

How to shape a city in evolution?
How to respect the intrinsic beauty of the city made by people?

VILLE
URBAIN
STRUCTURE

NATURE
FLUIDITÉ
MOUVEMENT

How to balance competing priorities while safeguarding the quality and identity of the city, Tirana as a beautiful chaos?

How can quality and density coexist to create sustainable & livable environments that are able to embody the city of tomorrow while still remaining part of the present?

Tirana for us is a vibrant capital, a unique example of a city at the crossroads of multiple cultures and histories.

With a blend of Ottoman, Italian & modern influences, its urban fabric reflects a dynamic evolution that mirrors its ambition for the future.

We want to highlight in an unprecedented way the connection between art and architecture, because they share the ability to stimulate the senses & convey universal ideas.

Art & architecture take us into worlds we have never seen or heard of and provoke the open-mindedness necessary for humanity.

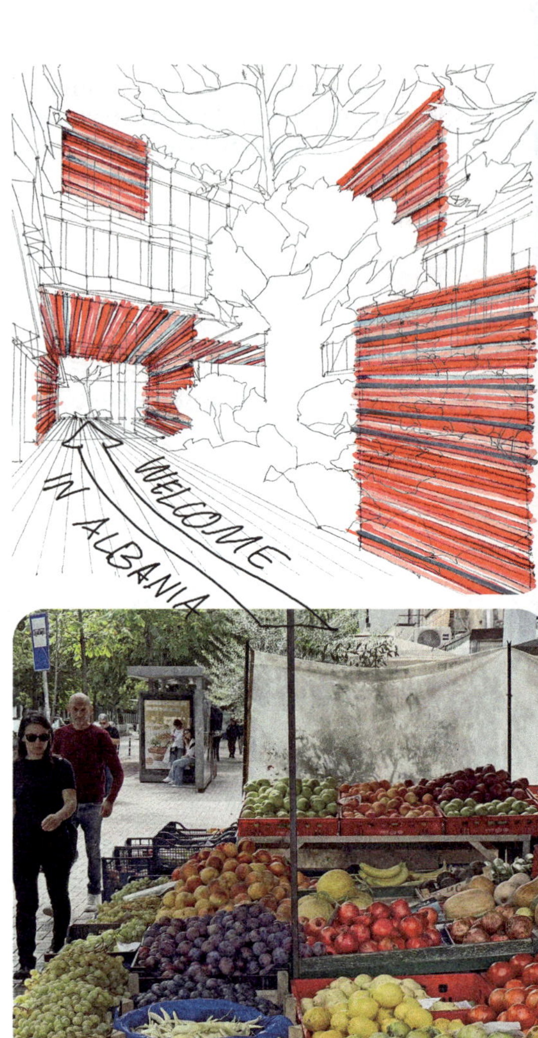

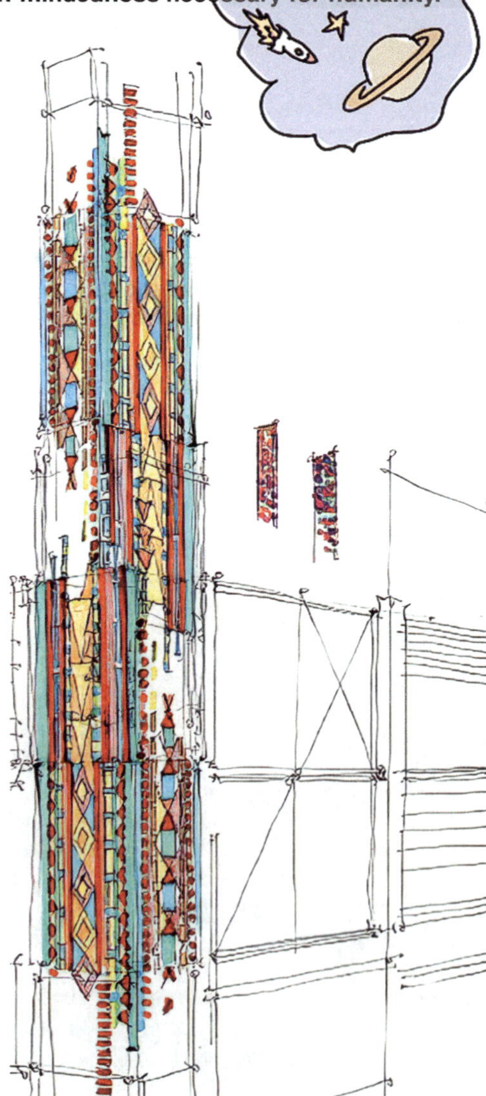

Patterns, colors, scents perfectly define the soul of the city. An evolving reality but with solid roots in its artistic cultural heritage.

We were fascinated by its street art, for its strength of reaction and its sense of need for people to make art. In Tirana you feel this instinct, the intrinsic need to leave a sign.

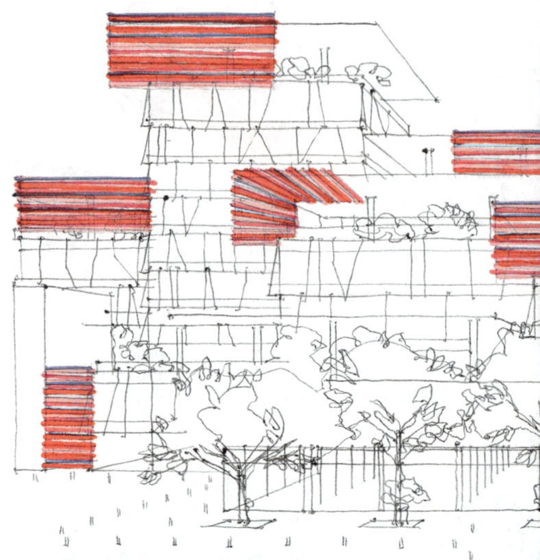

Here everything is transparency, fluidity and serenity. It's about welcoming, it's a whole symbol of conviviality in the image of the Albanian spirit, which is transcribed here through an architecture.

The goal is always to design not just one building among others but rather to research different ways of how to make it become a public space.

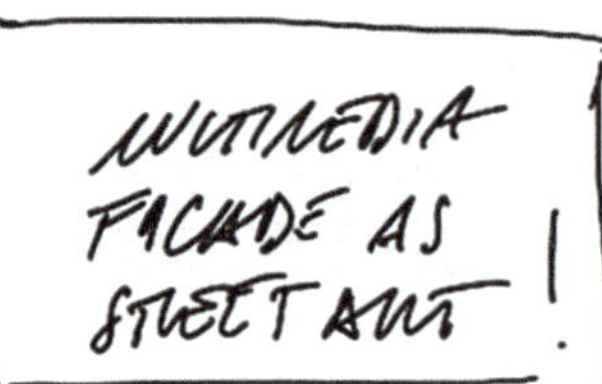

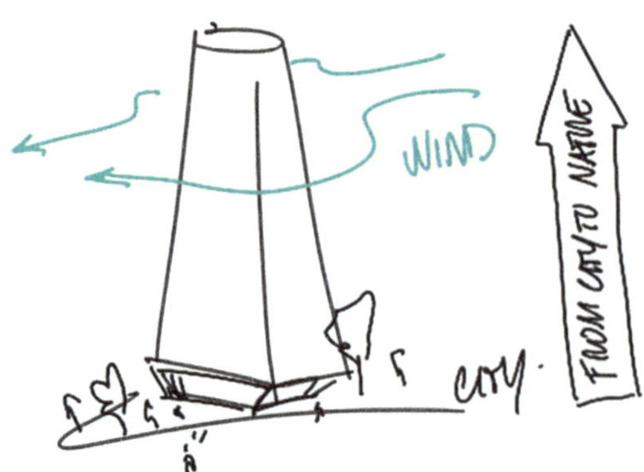

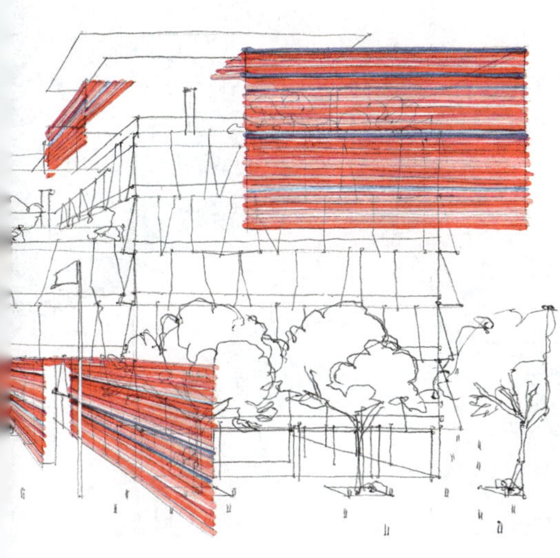

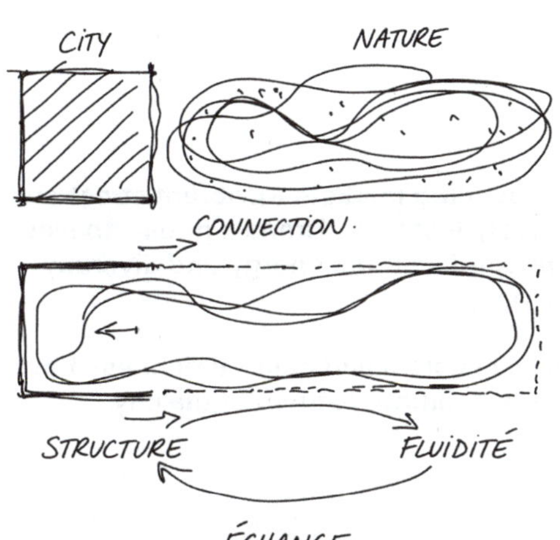

Albania provides a dynamic toolbox, including a rapidly evolving urban landscape, ambitious development goals and a willingness to embrace innovation.

This context allows us to experiment with new ideas, contribute to shaping growing cities, and create spaces that are forward-thinking while deeply connected to local culture & landscape.

From bustling markets to vibrant street art and lively festivals, Tirana's public spaces are infused with the energy and diversity of its people.

This eclecticism and cultural richness have become defining features of the city.

START	NAME PROJECT	LOCATION	DEVELOPER	PUBLIC/PRIVATE	PHASE
2024	Public Administration Cluster	Tirana	AIC	Public/private	Schematic design
2024	Former airfield site	Tirana	Ultratech & Lunor	Private	Schematic design
2024	Mixed-use tower near embassy	Tirana	Ultratech & Lunor	Private	Schematic design
2025	Mixed-use towers near Rruga e Kavajës	Tirana	Glob-3X	Private	Schematic design

NAME OFFICE

DAVIDE MACULLO ARCHITECTS

DATE
January 20, 2025

PLACE
Lugano, Switzerland

WORKING IN ALBANIA SINCE
2016

PRINCIPALS
Davide Macullo
Aileen Forbes-Munnely
Lorenza Tallarini

PROJECT TEAM
Andrea Carlotta Conti
Antonello Scala
Alberto Gullà
Valentina Perazzolo
Carla Ciavarella

ALBANIAN PARTNERS

STRUCTURAL ENGINEERS
Gentian Lipe
PNI 2001, Arian Lako
G+A Projekt, Alier Cara
Rezart Pogaçe
HT Construction

MECHANICAL ENGINEERS
Artan Dersha

ELECTRICAL ENGINEERS
Elteknik shpk, Armand Shkëmbi

ARCHITECTS OF RECORD
Orion Construction
S&L Studio
ERE Architecture & Construction

LOCAL ARCHITECT
Edlira Basha

INTRODUCTION TO ALBANIA

The first time I came to Tirana was for a public competition as project architect for Mario Botta. This was a long time ago. Then, about ten years ago, I was asked by a young Albanian architect to join his team and work in Albania, and we are still collaborating with him today.

MAIN CONTEXT VS. ALBANIA

We constantly draw from context. Meaningful and sustainable architecture emerges from curiosity, a love for life and the transformation of emotion into space. Design begins with self-questioning, grounded in scientific, humanistic and personal research.

Every space shapes human experience and carries a responsibility beyond sustainability: to nourish the spirit. Building in harmony with nature also means honoring human nature and creating conditions for individuals to thrive.

Our studio flourishes through cultural exchange across disciplines, linking the specificity of place with the universality of spatial psychology through a local-meets-global approach.

ORGANIZATION/GOAL/SETUP

Architects are citizens of the world, guided by universal values that adapt to different eras and local contexts. A core part of their role is to translate these shared human principles into specific places, moving beyond abstract space to create environments that are intimate, personal and collective at once.

After ten years in Albania, we have become part of an internal network shaped by exchange and mutual enrichment. The country's emerging cross-cultural dynamic brings together local and global perspectives through deep mutual respect, supporting healthy cultural and economic growth.

We never work for someone, but with them. Each project responds to the needs of its place, transforming those needs into opportunities for individual and collective development.

SETUP IN RELATION TO ALBANIAN PARTNER

From the start, we have placed collaboration at the center of our practice, within the studio and beyond. We are often approached by local architects years later because of our inclusive way of working, rooted in the joy of creating. Without joy, a project cannot succeed.

Our work considers human life in deep connection with the natural world over time. We approach this through what we call human ecology – engaging psychological, anthropological and philosophical dimensions – while also addressing broader ecological factors such as history, geography, climate and economics.

This openness enables a continuous exchange of ideas without rigid roles, allowing each participant to grow through the process. By resisting egocentric expression, we create space for unexpected artistic outcomes and amplify the collective potential of the project.

OPPORTUNITIES/CHALLENGES

Architecture is driven by curiosity and engagement with change. While we have worked in many rapidly transforming contexts, Albania stands apart for the scale and speed of change across the entire country, shaped by its geography, history and political momentum.

Our work seeks the soul of a place, creating architecture that operates on multiple levels. As a Mediterranean culture, Albania resonates deeply with our own ethos, offering a rare opportunity to engage with ancestral values and living heritage.

In the end, architecture is about people, not buildings. We have been shaped by the relationships formed in Albania, learning through exchange and contributing to a shared vision for the country's future.

HOW TO INTEGRATE GREATER RESPONSIBILITY FOR QUALITY IN PROJECTS

Alongside nurturing the soul of communities and addressing the psychology of space, ecology and sustainability are core responsibilities toward life on earth. Architecture in Albania can fully benefit from its climate by embracing passive design principles: shaded spaces in summer, solar gain in winter, thermal mass and natural ventilation. This allows us to move away from over-engineered solutions toward a more contemporary and sustainable way of building.

A project becomes meaningful when it is conceived as a layered system of reasons – capable of being read and reinterpreted over time. Albania's young entrepreneurs and professionals embody this potential. Their education, energy and commitment to their country are extraordinary, and supporting this generation is, in our view, the strongest guarantee for the healthy development of Albania's built environment.

BALANCING QUALITY AND DENSITY/INVOLVING STAKEHOLDERS

Architecture endures when it listens to its moment and place. A building becomes a place through humility, generosity and the ability to absorb and translate the soul of a context. Each work is a faithful portrait of its client and society, and this fidelity is its value.

As the architect becomes part of an increasingly complex system shaped by AI and interdisciplinary collaboration, their role shifts toward preserving beauty through a contextual, philosophical approach that integrates ecological, cultural and human dimensions.

As Byung-Chul Han writes in *Saving Beauty* (2015): "Any form of coercion or necessity deprives action of beauty. Beautiful are those things or activities not dominated by necessity or utility. The forms of life of the free human are all a luxury insofar as they deviate from the necessary and the useful, that is, they detach from them."

EXAMPLE/INSPIRATION

In my view, the most representative work is the Albanian Project – a collection of initiatives stemming from Edi Rama's macro artistic vision at the start of the millennium. Each project that followed continues this vision. Assigning distinctions to individual works does little to foster open dialogue about their impact. True appreciation lies in community engagement: a project's influence on quality of life and its ability to be embraced by inhabitants. Projects driven by purpose, joy and passion achieve the greatest involvement and connection with their users.

Thinking Albania

In 1935, Albert Einstein entered the USA with an Albanian passport. And that is a fine detail. And did you know that the Albanian language has no roots other than its own, even though the Romans, Turks, Russians, Chinese, Italians and now the English have all passed through? Fresh off the back of a ferocious communism, and the mess they were thrown into when it ended, today the Albanians are taking back their freedom in record time. In 2000, Edi Rama, who was mayor of Tirana at the time, started painting the now famous Soviet-style buildings in bright colors, which gave the city international recognition and its citizens a civic sense of respect for art. Today, Rama can celebrate a "futuristic future" that goes beyond the industrial revolution, something that never took place in Albania. Instead, the country is immersed in the technological revolution, which is in full swing, as evidenced by the extraordinary energy he's injecting.
The Albanians, raised on the courage of Skanderbeg, the hero who stopped the Turkish conquest of the Balkans and perhaps later of Europe, grew up on the border between the Eastern and Western Roman empires, cradling Christianity, choosing between the Catholics and the Orthodox. From the twelfth century, they almost became a real State; they resisted the Goths, the Avars, the Slavs, the Bulgarians, the Normans, the pressure from Venice, the Kingdom of Naples, the Byzantine Empire and the Great War.
Having managed to survive Stalin's follower Enver Hoxha, they continued to pass down and live by an ancestral code of honor: "The Kanun of the Albanian mountains cannot distinguish one person from another. We are all equal, soul for soul, in the presence of God." The present-day Albanian revival, now booked at the European table, is facing an epochal crossroads in which to decide whether or not beauty will save their world.

Tirana has been quietly included in the list of capitals dressed in art and contemporary architecture, environmental and economic awareness. The avenues are greener, the monuments are brighter, and the infrastructures, the parks, the public buildings and the new neighborhoods, designed by the best international architects, with a healthy competition, adorn the body of a city in which the spark of Western civilization flows eccentrically. Albania is fully engaged and ready to face the challenge of a new era.
The beginning of our involvement in Albania, about ten years ago, has brought many satisfactions and tangible results of true quality for the region. Over the years, we have come to know each other, and I am grateful that you have valued design principles that are important to us in the creation of space, which I prefer to define as places for people to live. The iconic strength of the completed projects and those still under development is represented by a design that does not fear time, but rather, with time, will release the values of joy, passion and purpose that nourished it.
Working in Albania means merging our ideas with local ones, not imposing our principles, but exchanging proposals in an open and free dialogue. Our lack of preconceptions, combined with Albania's freshness and proactivity, makes it possible to work in a stimulating and prosperous environment.
Over the past decades, we have witnessed rapid expansion and contributed to the development of prosperous economies, where architecture has played a crucial role in symbolizing and reflecting cultural engagement. As Albania opens up to the world, it navigates between architecture driven by dogma and a growing awareness of humanity's connection to its senses and nature.

odern architecture often seeks to dominate nature, ewing it as something separate, without considering e most important aspect: Nature is life. Now is the time plant seeds of quality that focus on the soul of this ountry, enriched by its climate, nature, human resources, aditions and history. Our spaces are meant to be perienced, not just observed. The buildings are gentle olumes embedded in the ground and partly suspended, otective from the outside but permeable from within. ey follow the natural slope of the land, respecting its orphology, and represent not just a structure, but a home, refuge, a temple.
ese passions, enthusiasms and purposes are released from e lines, now turned into a new space: the **Vet Hospital** Tirana, where the smooth and calm shapes of the outside d the rationality of the plans give us new sensations of onder and pleasure.
is marvel signifies a shift from a static mindset to an open, ejudice-free attitude, capable of creating a place – rather an spaces – where people love to live. With humility and mbition, this place embodies the unique characteristics the nature and cultures that have flourished here. buildings are designed with love, they will express love. e strength of architecture lies in its sincerity, because eyond beauty is the feeling of being at ease, and the nses never lie. The true mission is to build a habitat that ositively influences people's lives – following their needs ther than imposing them, because we're not making omes, they are. **The Eagle** of Tirana expresses the values of nation, eliciting the history of Mediterranean architecture, om classicism to the dynamism of the Baroque, passing rough the purity of the Renaissance and Gothic geometry the present, rising to the challenge of sustainability. e nation that granted the passport – and thus wings – Albert Einstein has taken flight into its future. It epitomizes, one volume, our belief that architecture is the link etween the DNA of a place, its present and its future.
Tirana deserves a true eagle, a symbol of strength and pride in belonging to a great civilization. Coming from the airport, entering town in the Lana district, the eagle flies free as an icon of the country, embedded in a dynamic volume that expresses lightness in harmony with its symbolic power.
River Residences is designed to allow private living and participation in the life of the community at the same time. The transition between public life, private life and intimate life is calibrated so that the degree of detail increases rather than decreases. Thus, we have an interior space that dissolves into the exterior space, and the outside enters our homes, so there is no longer an inside and an outside; nature (my park, my city) never ends, and home never ends either. We build to ensure that new residents feel comfortable, paying attention to every moment of daily life, using time as a tool for the design. Individuals and groups come together in community in shared social places. The importance of creating friendly environments for new generations lies in the concept of architecture as an entity that evolves not only in space but also in time. We envision families returning home from school or work, with parents holding their children's hands and proudly surveying their home.
River Residences, in addition to taking care of its inhabitants, tells us about Albania's Mediterranean tradition with its fortifications and stone partitions lost in the country's green nature, in a dialogue between built and natural geometries. The interplay of light and shadows decorates a volume rich in surprises, designed to continuously amaze us and change expression with every movement that allows us to shift our point of view.
Seemingly, **Park Avenue** acts as a sort of Mediterranean central park – a meeting point for and gateway to the city. This unique living experience captures the highest potential of the place, beginning with light that illuminates the built volume and merges it with the park, the element closest to humanity. The project is rooted in the principles of ecology

– both environmental and social – placing people and their comfort at the center of the built environment. Located in an expanding city with ambitious urban goals, the building respects the ideal solar orientation and the urban footprint while creating an organic connection to the city of Tirana. The spiral movement of the masses lightens the visual impact, evoking a precious marine fossil along the Mediterranean shore. The facades, designed with a natural embroidery-like refinement, take full advantage of the city's Mediterranean light. This compositional experience is carried from art to architecture, with every stroke of the building's structure treated like a gesture traced with an artist's brush. The expressive columns branch upwards, creating a building that adapts to new colors, seasons and times of day, all while enhancing the experience of those who inhabit it. Pedestrians circulate freely through fluid spaces marked by elements of surprise, designed to validate humanity's ability to enjoy emotionally significant spaces. The building's overall image reflects values offered by nature, presenting a permeable, respectful and warm architecture, full of love.

Space is a journey into emotions, experienced rather than merely observed, allowing the gaze and senses to flow freely. The new **Dhërmi Resort** offers unique spaces where humanity is at the center. The perception of a green area within the dense construction reflects our sensitive attention to the environment, serving as a green lung of rest and respect. The resort's resemblance to an ancient village, the historic agricultural terraces and the native vegetation give residents the illusion of living in a dream. The soft and unexpected sensations inspire a deep connection with the place, making guests feel as if they are in an ideal world, crafted just for them. Each room is proportioned to evoke different feelings, always enhancing the guest's comfort. The approach along a tree-lined road heightens the sense of anticipation, leading to an enveloping spac where one can enjoy the view of a landscape steeped in history, mythology and heroes, all while feeling protecte in the richly detailed interior of this new world. At the new Dhërmi, every space is surrounded by enticing green patic that filter the strong Mediterranean light. The valley and its vegetation embrace the new living spaces, creating a seamless blend between nature and architecture. The complex is uniformly camouflaged in native vegetatic making it impossible to see the buildings from the beach, while affording breathtaking views of the sea from every residence, in total privacy. We are not just constructing buildings; we are creating places – organisms that breathe and harmonize with the landscape, filters that accommodate and welcome us as part of nature, in symbiosis with it.

The design of **Green Valley** invites nature into our homes, guiding us from intimate spaces to the surrounding environment. The buildings, simple yet magnificent, derive their beauty from a complex interplay of factors. They are never fully enclosed; the walls form a sequence of wings that don't completely meet. Spaces are open in all directions, ensuring privacy while maintaining a connectic to the surroundings. In each apartment, the neighbor's wa feels like an extension of one's living room wall, creating the illusion of being alone, surrounded only by nature. The layers of columns and trees intersect in a continuity that stretches the sense of property, making all the surrounding to the hills and horizon, part of the inhabitant's life. We embrace the gravity that binds us to the earth with primar forms, while opening up in all directions. This approach provides inhabitants with both a sense of protection and continuity of space, ensuring they never feel confined

but always have a route to escape. These projects speak of an extraordinary attitude, one that is a forerunner of a collaboration aimed at strengthening internal forces and making them an integral part of the design outcome. This is an attitude to which we have all committed ourselves, developing a code of understanding and design cross-pollination, where the result is the synthesis of a process, and the buildings are true stories of a slice of life in a nation undergoing cultural growth.

Architecture is the seed that allows us to organize our thoughts, not by prioritizing elements but by recognizing that each component in building human habitats plays a crucial role in humans' behaviors. Architecture is imbued with a fundamental and universal value: humanity's ancestral needs, current conditions and future aspirations.

At its core, a seed is about designing spaces that evoke emotion and influence people's moods, contributing to the sustainable and spiritual growth of humanity. The project pushes the boundaries of respecting nature by understanding human nature, creating a place where individuals can perceive harmony with their surroundings, rather than the feeling of entrapment inherited from our prehistoric past. Every project serves as a manifesto on the human condition, emphasizing our ability to restore balance to the earth through sensitive technology and a deep connection with nature's intelligence. The architecture facilitates balanced transitions, fostering social cohesion and promoting a daily life rooted in mutual respect. **Rezi Dream-Hotel** in Vlora represents, as do all our projects, humanity's transition from childhood to puberty, embarking on a significant phase of evolution filled with opportunities and choices that shape our future on the planet. Although the journey toward mature and conscious living is still long, this stage presents us with pivotal moments for reflection and growth. This work allows us to go beyond superficiality, reflecting the profound significance of architecture and building today, serving as witnesses to the spirit of our time.

START	NAME PROJECT	LOCATION	DEVELOPER	PUBLIC/PRIVATE	PHASE
2019	Green Valley 1, 2	Tirana	Orion Construction	Private	Executed
2019	River Residence 1	Tirana	Orion Construction	Private	Executed
2019	River Residence 2	Tirana	Orion Construction	Private	Construction documents
2019	Green Valley 3	Tirana	Orion Construction	Private	Executed
2020	Park Avenue 1	Tirana	Orion Construction	Private	Executed
2020	Park Avenue 2	Tirana	Orion Construction	Private	Construction documents
2020	Dhërmi Villas Resort	Dhërmi	Orion Construction	Private	Construction documents
2020	Vet Hospital	Tirana		Private	Executed
2024	White Hotel	Tirana	ERE Architecture & Construction	Private	Construction documents
2024	Rezi Dream-Hotel	Vlora	Minaron09 shpk	Private	Construction documents
2024	The Eagle	Tirana	ERE Architecture & Construction	Private	Construction documents
2024	The Stele	Tirana	Prespa Invest Development Company	Private	Concept design
2024	Valona apartments		Joti & S.T. shpk	Private	Final design
2024	Hotel Apartments Velipojë	Shkodra	NewEra Construction shpk	Private	Final design
2024	Farkë Lake apartments	Tirana	ERE Architecture & Construction	Private	Design development
2024	Farkë Hills apartments	Tirana	ERE Architecture & Construction	Private	Schematic design

NAME OFFICE

DILLER SCOFIDIO + RENFRO

DATE	PLACE	WORKING IN ALBANIA SINCE
January 6, 2025	New York City, USA	2024

PRINCIPALS

Elizabeth Diller
Charles Renfro
Benjamin Gilmartin
Ricardo Scofidio

PROJECT TEAM

LAKE DIAMOND TOWERS

Ellix Wu
Christopher Hillyard
Ellen Wood
Michael Sluchevsky
Munjer Hashim
Alfred Wei
Yushiro Okamoto
Mike Robitz
Spencer Hotelling

EMBASSY TOWER

Holly Deichmann
Charlie Blanchard
Ching Ying Ngan
Christopher Hillyard
Dino Kiratzidis
Furui Sun
Matthew Ostrow
Michael Samoc
Alfred Wei
Madeline Ju

ALBANIAN PARTNERS

LAKE DIAMOND TOWERS

ATELIER 4 (Collaborating Architect)
aei progetti (Structural Engineer)
Hydro and Energy, FISHTA electric shpk (MEP Engineers)
Gevers Landscape Architecture (Landscape)
Voltaire Lighting Design (Lighting)

EMBASSY TOWER

X-Plan Studio (Architect of Record)
Dhimitri Papa (Structural Engineer)
GROSS. MAX. landscape architects (Landscape)
Arjan Coka PF (MEP Engineers)

INTRODUCTION TO ALBANIA

Stefano Boeri informed us that he is doing a variety of projects in Albania and has a studio there. We then quickly discovered what a hidden gem Albania is with its burgeoning capital, dramatic mountains, rugged coastline and aquamarine clear seas.

MAIN CONTEXT VS. ALBANIA

In Albania, we have found that time goes simultaneously faster and slower than we are accustomed to in New York. Tirana is changing at an unprecedented pace, with construction at every corner. At the same time, people take their time to really get to know each other and form a partnership over an extended eight-course lunch.

ORGANIZATION/GOAL/SETUP

We strive to make buildings and spaces that prioritize public space, contribute to the city and add to the architectural discourse. In order to make projects that will endure and be extraordinary, everyone on the team needs to be fully invested. We work closely with our local partners on what is being conveyed from the beginning to the end of the project. We rely on locals to provide local knowledge and handle the approvals. DS+R is involved in all aspects of the building, with an emphasis on the public spaces and the facade.

SETUP IN RELATION TO LOCAL OFFICE

While the majority of the design work is done by DS+R, the local architect certainly contributes – especially when it comes to transferring local knowledge.

OPPORTUNITIES/CHALLENGES

With so much construction in Tirana and a large projected increase of inhabitants, it places stress on the public parks, urban infrastructure (water & power supply, data, sewage systems), road networks and public transportation that will prove challenging.

With such optimism and zest for life, we see a great opportunity for elevating the status of Albania in the world.

HOW TO INTEGRATE GREATER RESPONSIBILITY FOR QUALITY IN PROJECTS

The role of the architect during construction is critical to maintain the quality of a project. The architect's role is to observe the construction and review that the constructed building follows the construction documents.

EXAMPLE/INSPIRATION

We love how the Lion Residence's undulating balconies activate the city and incorporate a greening of the city through planted balconies. Dense cities often end up barren, and creating a vertical green city helps clean the air, provides cozy outdoor spaces within the city and makes a city that is literally alive.

TOOLBOX ALBANIA FUTURE

Albania still has a freshness and newness that allows for experimentation and thinking outside the box.

Albanians are accepting and open, which is quite refreshing in our current environment and something we can all learn from.

SITES

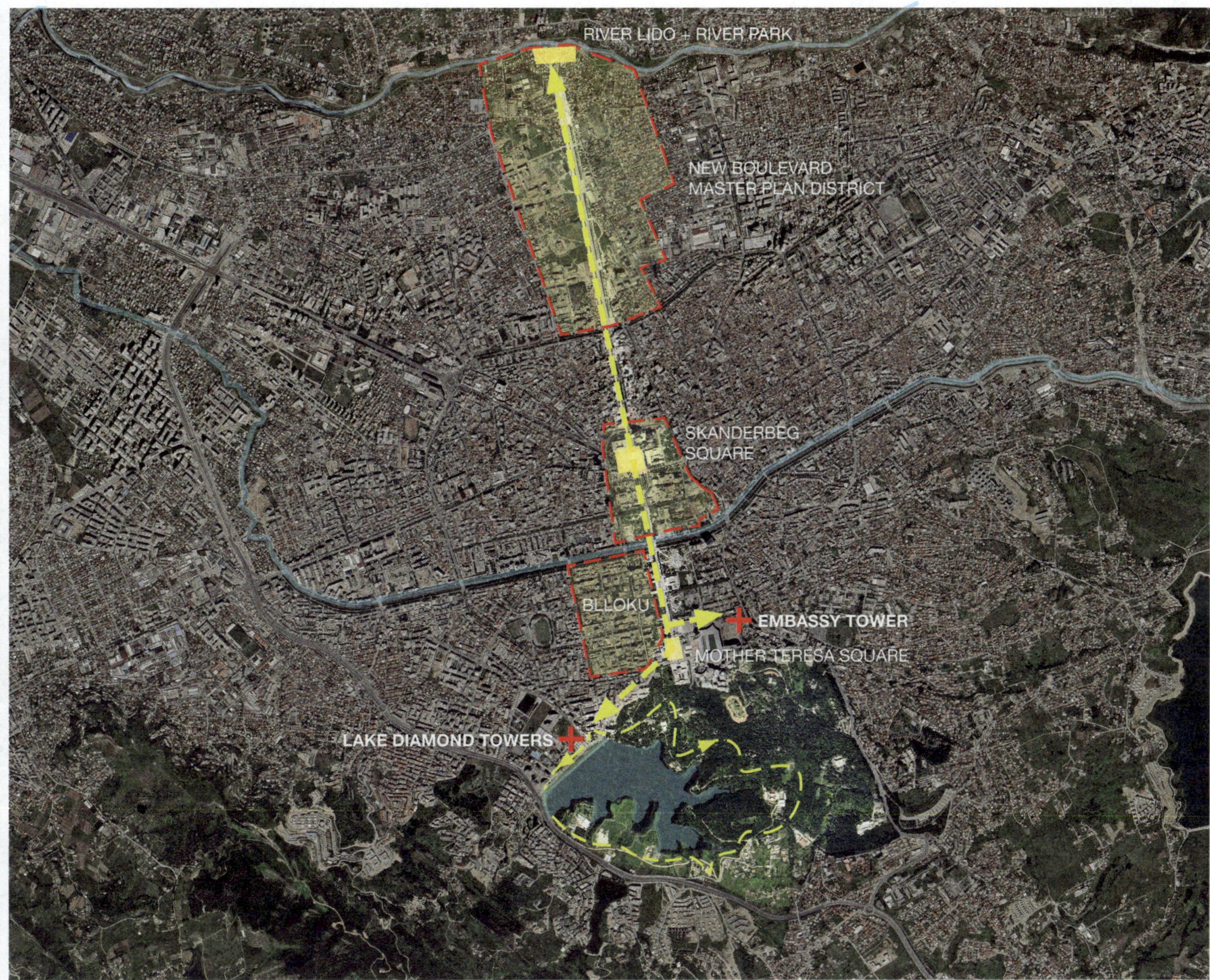

Public space axis

Urban/park interface

SKANDERBEG SQUARE
EMBASSY TOWER
MOTHER TERESA SQUARE
TIRANA PARK

LAKE DIAMOND TOWERS

Segmented icon

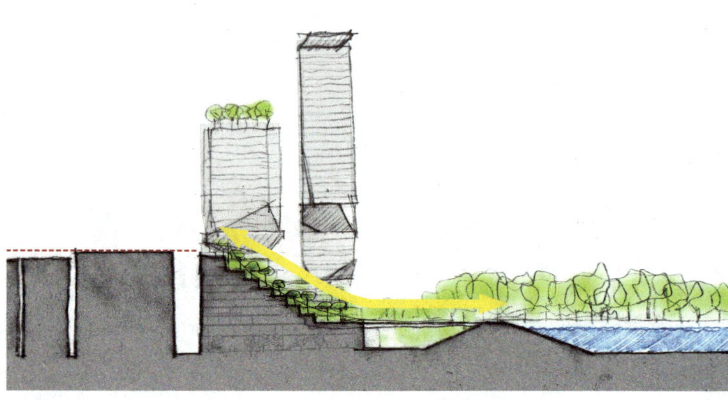

Connector

Ensemble

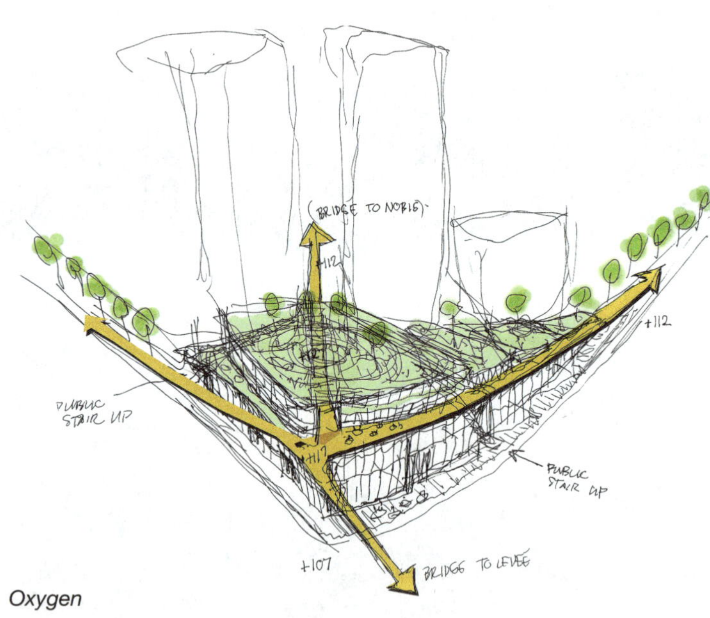

Oxygen

GREEN BASE

The verdant ecosystem of Grand Park and the lake extends into a vegetated tower base of contoured terraces.

STICKY SPACE

Activity from the street level runs up the multilevel base, encouraging the public to stop inside to eat, drink, shop and enjoy cultural programming.

CONNECTOR

The base performs as public infrastructure, bridging over a vehicular road to the lakefront promenade at the crest of the levee.

ENSEMBLE

Each tower atop the base has a unique identity, yet is unmistakably of a family with shared DNA.

SEGMENTED ICON

The stack of volumes maintains both an urban-scale iconicity and street-scale intimacy in perfect balance.

OXYGEN

Each apartment, office and shop owns a piece of the outdoors at the interface of public and private space.

Sticky space

Green base

EMBASSY TOWER

SAMPLING ALBANIA

The stratified landscape climbs the tower, tracking Albania's ecological diversity, from its lush valleys to its alpine mountains.

SYSTEMATIC RANDOMIZATION

The tower is organic, not homogeneous; bespoke, not uniform; fluid, not fixed.

ANIMATED GROUND

The ground floor is a living part of the city with parks, restaurants and shops for visitors and residents.

WELCOME INTERRUPTIONS

Shared amenities throughout the tower dilate within the language of wavy units into swells and breakers.

IDENTITY OVER ANONYMITY

Every resident can recognize their home from across Tirana.

FUZZY FORM

A lush vertical landscape of outdoor terraces for each resident produces a green silhouette on the skyline.

Welcome interruptions

Animated ground

START	NAME PROJECT	LOCATION	DEVELOPER	PUBLIC/PRIVATE	PHASE
2023	Lake Diamond Towers	Tirana	Texas Development shpk, Daton shpk, Green Living Company shpk, Vistas Enterprise shpk	Private	Construction documents
2024	Embassy Tower	Tirana	Hanxhari Group	Private	Design development

NAME OFFICE

EAA – EMRE AROLAT ARCHITECTURE

DATE
Founded 2004

PLACE
Istanbul, Turkey

WORKING IN ALBANIA SINCE
2019

PRINCIPALS
Emre Arolat (Design Partner)
Gonca Paşolar (Managing Partner)

PROJECT TEAM
Ezgi Su Gül
Ruyet Sefercioğlu
Deniz Kösemen [1]
Eylül Büyük [1]
Öner Demircan [1]
Anas Mahli [1]
Helin Akkurt [1]
Yasser Bunni [1]
Ezgi Tokgöz [1]
Pelin Türker [1]
Yağmur Koca [1]
Sait Onur Edes [1]
Osman İshakoğlu [1]
Alper Tüzünoğlu [1]
Çağlar Barış [1, 2]
Ecem Ezmeci [1, 3]
Leyla Kori Velioğlu [1, 3]
Meyssam Seddigh [1, 3, 6, 7, 8]
Zeynep Özkan [2]
Sezin Koç [2]
Şule Camadan [2]
Ece Erdemli [2]
Damla Sakarya [2, 4]
İdris Ayar [2, 3, 6, 7, 8]
Doğukan Salman [3]
Eda Yazkurt [3]
Haldun Bozkurt [3, 4]
Uygar Yüksel [3, 4]
Özge Hocalar [3, 6]
Pelin Yalçın [3, 6]
Natali Tombak [4]
Tuba Bilgiç [4]
Naz Atasoy [4, 6]
Yahya Abdoullah [5]
Mustafa Demir [5]
Can Aktoluğ [5]
Can Binan [6]
Selin Yıldız [6]
Mert Tabak [6]
Berfin Bozfırat [6]
Emre Arda [6, 7]
Zeynep Seyhan [6, 7, 8]
Batuhan Akdemir [7]
Sıla Özkan [7]
Helin Tan [7]
Berfin Bozfırat [7]
Gökalp Alaca [7]
Begüm Sude Kurt [7]
Zehra Bektaş [7]

ALBANIAN PARTNERS
UTS-01 [4]
Meka-Pro shpk [4]
Kejsi-05 shpk [4]
Guust Selhorst [1, 3, 4, 5]
Artech [5]
Dhimitri Papa [5]
Lediana Dila, HMS [5]
Krenar Çaushi, Electroplus Engineering [5]
Libohova Architecture [2]
Boraj Mimoza [2]
Alma Velaj [2]
Deshira Mena [2]
Seed Consulting [2]
Blerta Foto [1]
Aurora Baba [1]
Uejda Nikolli [1]
Brixhilda Maka [1]
Iva Bogdani [6]
Sefedin Sanxhaku [6]
Laert Klema [6]
Ndriçim Allkaj [6]
Marsela Kocllari [6]
Marenglen Toci [6]
Kejsi Lushnjari [7]
Doris Shehu [7]
Romina Sahiti [7]
Agim Marku [7]
Aurel Xhumbi [7]
Tony Leça [7]
John Rufino [7]
Idlir Frangu [7]
Nadjya Mandic [7]

INTERNATIONAL COLLABORATORS
GMD+Moskay [6, 7]
Etik Teknik [6]
Makpa [6, 7]
HB Teknik [6, 7]
DS Architecture [6, 7]
Başak Atalay [1, 6]
Studio Apostoli [6]
Yapı Teknik [7]
Jackson Daly [7]
Muza Lab [7]
SEY Akustik [7]
Onsecon [7]
ERKOC [7]
Planet-FB [7]
Starpool [7]
FEC International [7]
Light Company [7]
Ethnic Technologies [7]
ION Solutions [7]
Focus HC [7]
ByLift [7]
Soliday [7]

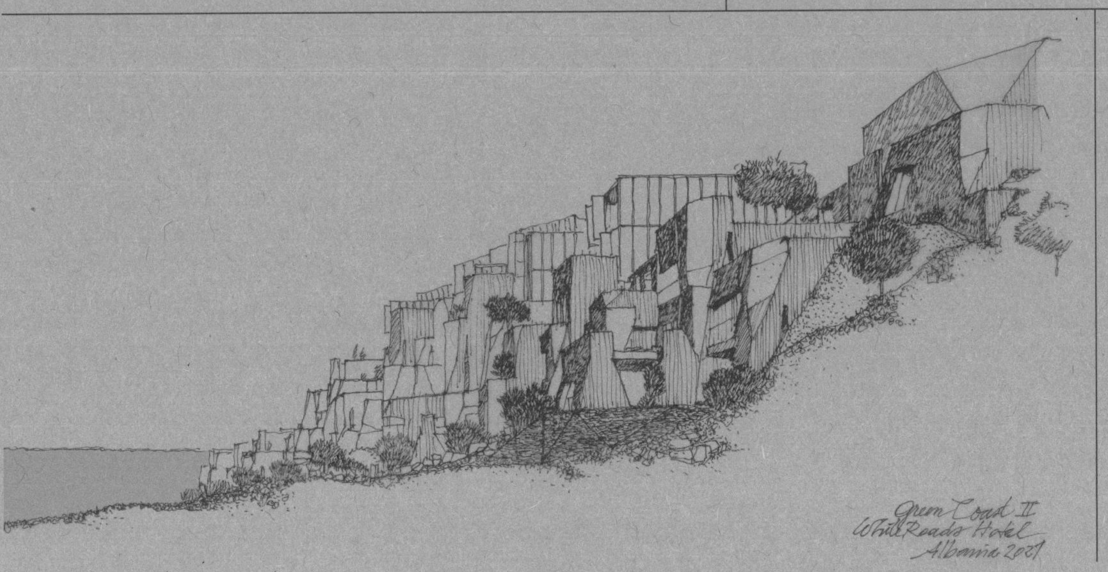

Projects:
1 Lura 5
2 Green Coast III
3 Green Coast Village
4 Green Coast Plot E
5 Green Coast B-Resort
6 Delta Palasë Resort
7 Grand Hyatt Palasë Resort & Spa
8 Ionian Heaven Resort & Casino

MAIN CONTEXT VS. ALBANIA

In Albania, the construction culture shows both distinct traits and familiar patterns. Compared to places like Italy, the United States, Saudi Arabia, the UAE, Georgia and Kyrgyzstan, it closely resembles Turkey's construction culture from twenty-five years ago. This is evident in the tendency to maximize buildable area, sometimes at the expense of architectural quality, and in construction approaches that overlook the natural landscape – patterns that echo discussions I encountered in Turkey decades ago.

ORGANIZATION/GOAL/SETUP

For our projects in Albania, the concept design and schematic design phases are managed through our Istanbul or Florence offices. Following these stages, for some projects we collaborate with local architectural offices, working with them on the design development and construction documentation while providing design supervision. We make an effort to collaborate with local architectural firms to ensure construction implementations from an architectural perspective. In certain projects, we work entirely with local teams for structural, mechanical, electrical and infrastructural engineering, as well as with consultancy services for landscaping, signage and lighting. In some cases, we stimulate collaborations between international firms and local teams to integrate global expertise. Looking ahead, if several of our large-scale projects proceed as planned, we are contemplating the establishment of a branch office in Tirana.

SETUP IN RELATION TO ALBANIAN PARTNER

As part of our collaborations with local offices, we occasionally attempt design partnerships, provided they align with the main architectural concept of the project. However, I must admit that we have not yet made significant progress in this area.

OPPORTUNITIES/CHALLENGES

The relative novelty of the construction sector in Albania presents both opportunities and challenges that are not always easy to foresee. Specifically, the lack of well-established regulations concerning construction and zoning can be seen as a kind of opportunity, creating an intriguing gap in architectural design. However, I must emphasize that these gray areas often generate significant tension between architects striving to develop their designs within the framework of environmental sensitivity and investors aiming to profit from every extra square meter produced by a project. Undoubtedly, considerable progress has been made in this regard by various official institutions since the day we designed our first project in Albania, in 2020. However, the lack of site-specific, high-quality and detailed zoning regulations – particularly in coastal areas – still stands out as a major issue.

HOW TO INTEGRATE GREATER RESPONSIBILITY FOR QUALITY IN PROJECTS

An architect must unconditionally prioritize environmental sustainability and contextual sensitivity in every endeavor. Whether working for private investors or government institutions, it is crucial to foresee rational and forward-thinking developments for the future rather than focusing on short-term gains. Instead of limiting their responsibility to the plot of land on which the project is built, an architect should imagine the finished structure from a much broader perspective, considering the environmental impacts it will create in the short and long term.

BALANCING QUALITY AND DENSITY/INVOLVING STAKEHOLDERS

Long-term strategies and zoning conditions prepared in line with holistic planning principles tailored to different regions can be seen as an ideal scenario. Truth be told, such comprehensive approaches appear to be challenging to achieve in the context of Albania. Though even in processes that seem to be past the point of no return, intervening early and rationally can yield effective solutions. Instead of conventional holistic solutions, carefully designed acupuncture-like interventions, or localized zoning plans that also incorporate the existing fabric and engage multiple layers, can indeed produce unique, one-of-a-kind solutions. I believe the most critical aspect to focus on at this point is ensuring participatory processes; including as many diverse constituents of society as possible in decision-making is vital to fostering equitable decisions.

EXAMPLE/INSPIRATION

If the question refers to a completed building among the projects realized in Albania in recent years, I'm not sure I have a particularly strong answer. What has truly inspired me instead are the many structures and settlements from different periods scattered across the country, places like Berat, Gjirokastër, or traces such as Qeparo and Butrint.

TOOLBOX ALBANIA FUTURE

The atmosphere in our projects along the Albanian Riviera bears a striking resemblance to what I encountered some fifteen or twenty years ago along the Aegean and Mediterranean shores of Turkey. A similar sea, a familiar topography, near-identical vegetation . . . winds that arrive sometimes from land, sometimes from sea, often unpredictable and occasionally wild enough to take you by surprise . . . the sun that can be brutal in July and August, yet deeply rewarding the rest of the year . . . and rains that appear with no warning, sometimes so intense they trigger localized flooding.

Then there's the developer landscape: clients who in the early stages of the project will enthusiastically declare, "of course, we'll do it, don't worry about the budget," only to later dwell endlessly on cost issues, construction difficulties, material availability and labor shortages. Some are impressively sensitive to the environment, while others display an almost baffling indifference.

Within this framework, I can easily say that rather than needing to expand my toolbox, it's mostly been about putting the existing tools to good use, and perhaps more importantly, bringing back into rotation those that had been buried deep at the bottom of the bag. Some required a bit of dusting off, some a light polish to become usable again, and a few needed small adjustments to be fit for today's conditions. But all in all, it's been less about invention, more about recollection and refinement.

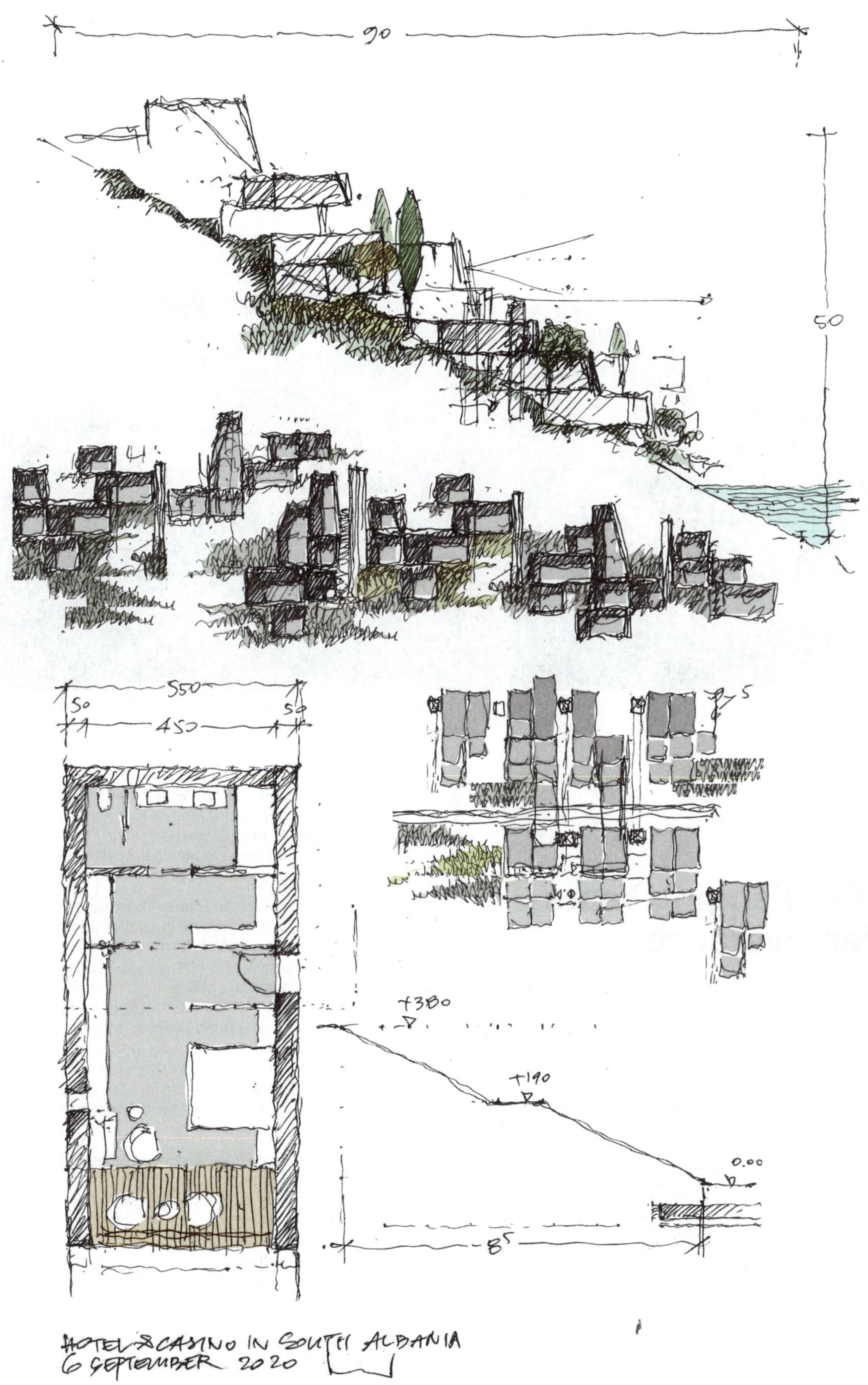

Conceptual studies for Ionian Heaven Resort: Blending into the topography.

B-Resort, Green Coast Village: Dissolving into the context.

Six Challenging Years of Perseverance

In February 2023, the Albanian Ministry of Culture organized a concept project competition for the Besa Museum, which was to be built in an area in the center of Tirana that contains a building from the Ottoman era. At the time, I was at the Tirana Opera House, ready to give a presentation as part of the Share Tirana event. That's when I first heard about the competition.

What followed was quite an adventure . . .

It was a two-stage competition. In the first stage, we submitted a file that presented our initial ideas for the site. The file included various approach diagrams, sketches and a written piece. It began as follows:

"This city has almost become my second home in recent years. It's been more than five years since my first visit. When I spent hours stuck in traffic on the way from the airport to the city, and then got caught in a downpour, I thought Tirana hadn't welcomed me very warmly. I was wrong . . .

"Since then, I've made more than twenty visits. While most were for business, each time I've felt a strange peace, a gradually growing sense of belonging, and a kind of love for this city that I still find hard to fully understand. If you don't think I'm exaggerating, I'll say this: Over time, I've come to feel that if I ever had to leave Istanbul, Tirana could be one of the places I'd want to live.

"This time, I'm here for the Share Albania event. I'm feeling similar emotions again. The weather is beautiful, as if we've captured the first day of spring here. As I sip my coffee in the columned space of the Opera House, which opens onto Skanderbeg Square – one of the city's main social centers – I'm mentally preparing the talk I'll soon give inside. In this country that calls itself 'Europe's last unturned stone,' we've been working on many projects for years. Most of them are in coastal areas, untouched by human hands, with challenging topography. In these places, we create sensitive and contextual designs, preserving the natural environment as much as possible. Somehow, though, we've never done a project in Tirana . . ."

The file we submitted for the first stage of the Besa Museum competition received the highest score among all the participating offices. We were excited for the second stage and worked very hard. We made our presentation to the jury at the same Opera House. The other finalists presented as well. It was a remarkably transparent environment, open to an audience from different professions in the city. The international jury, some of whom I knew very well, gathered to make their decision the same day. The results were to be announced at the site where the museum would be built. We chatted with the other finalists. The weather was hot, and excitement was at its peak. The jury arrived much later than the announced time. The Minister of Culture took the stage. After a thank-you speech, she personally announced the results. We lost . . .

Sketch of Besa Museum by Emre Arolat. When we were selected as one of the finalists with the highest score in the first stage, we became quite hopeful. The result was disappointing. But that's how competitions are . . .

Residential unit, study for Green Coast Village.

First site visit to Lura 5, Lalëzit Bay, 2019.

No, we didn't manage to complete a project in Tirana. But no matter, we've been working on dozens of projects along the exciting coastlines of this beautiful country for years. I can say I've explored the coasts inch by inch. As a sea lover, the natural landscapes I've seen have mesmerized me every time. Unfortunately, the same cannot be said for what has been built by human hands.

They're waiting for me in the meeting room at the Istanbul office. They arrived a bit early, so I wrap up my previous meeting and go straight to them. They smile warmly while speaking. "This is my daughter," he says with a sweet expression. His English isn't great. It's clear his daughter will be translating. After a short Google Earth tour, we find the Lalëzit coast. He's built many structures there before. They look like familiar vacation homes. They've been built at different stages, but all the building groups have conventional settlement plans. Lura 1, 2, 3 and 4. There's also a hotel under construction. He says the construction is actually much further along than it appears on the screen. It seems to be a wooded and wet coastline, but the previous projects seem to have covered up this reality. There are no trees or water left in the built areas. "We wouldn't do it like that," I say. "We need to preserve the trees and avoid intervening too much in the wetland." "Don't worry, I'll build it however you want; however you design it," he says. And so begins our Lura 5 adventure . . .

"To protect the trees I fell in love with at first sight, we used a highly organic planning strategy."

Concept studies of Lura 5 by Emre Arolat.

Emre Arolat with the investor at Lushnjë quarry for natural stone selection.

The project phase was relatively easy. To protect the trees I fell in love with at first sight, we used a highly organic planning strategy. What followed was a grueling process. Some habits are so ingrained that getting certain things constructed differently is like making a camel pass through the eye of a needle. I won't drag this out; otherwise, this text would fill an entire book. The construction is still ongoing. Amidst much conflict, we are doing our best to ensure the design is followed as closely as possible. Although the client isn't very happy to see us there frequently, we continue to provide a service that wasn't requested but is essential to maintaining the architectural and construction quality of this project, which includes villas, townhouses and a hotel.

Green Coast Village apartments: Forming a dialogue with the topography and blending in with nature.

Volumetric study for a resort project in Durrës.

Volumetric studies for the Delta Palasë Resort & Village. Once again, fragmentation, volumetric composition and human scale.

Tourism is poised to become one of the most important driving sectors of Albania's economy. The ongoing infrastructure and superstructure projects across the country seem likely to strengthen this reality. At this critical stage, it is crucial to thoroughly analyze the advantages and disadvantages of tourism and to learn from the mistakes made in this context in other regions. It is essential that not only regulatory and supervisory authorities but also every single investor firmly believe in the importance of preserving this beautiful country's natural and historical wealth, rather than sacrificing it for short-term gains.

The phenomenon of "Being Mediterranean" has been the primary focus of design in all the projects we've done along the coast. Our second project in this beautiful country is in the Saranda region, an urban-scale development. This settlement, shaped around a marina, embodies the true spirit of the Mediterranean. Fragmentation, an alluring volumetric composition and human scale were the guiding principles in shaping the project. In addition to the marina, it includes homes, boutique hotels, small-scale commercial spaces, food and beverage venues, residences, hotels and open communal spaces. Shady narrow streets, pedestrian alleys cutting across the slope and opening to the sea, green corridors and natural materials are the characteristic elements of this project. Four years have passed since the concept project stage. There's still no movement on the investor's side . . .

"The phenomenon of 'Being Mediterranean' has been the primary focus of design in all the projects we've done along the coast."

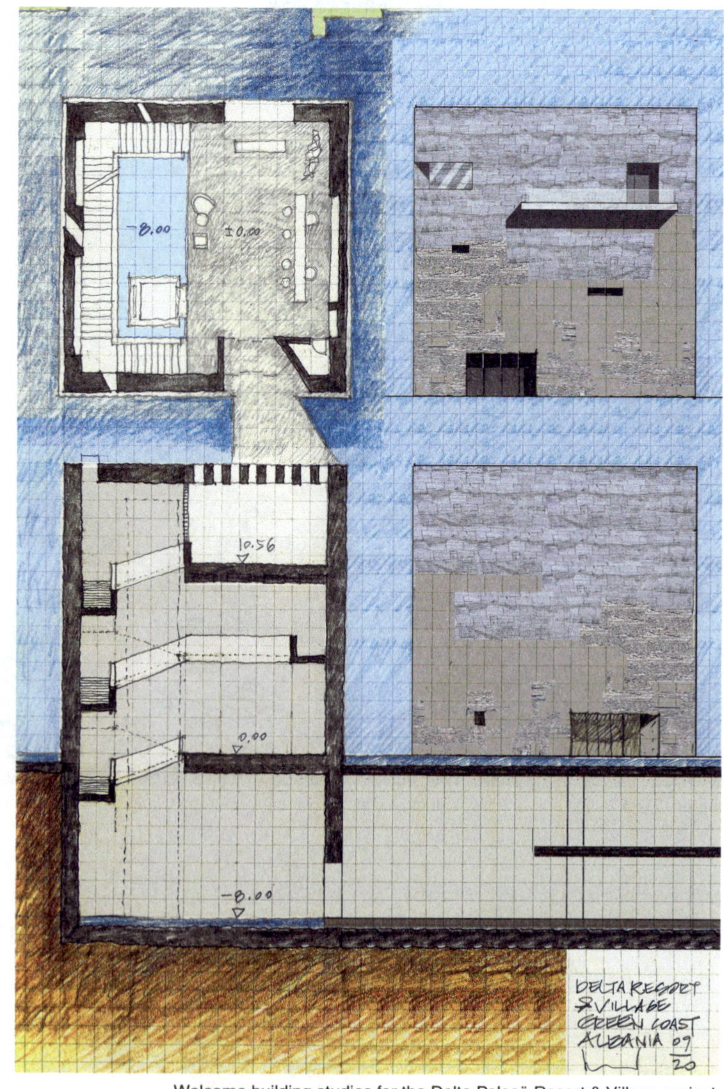

Welcome building studies for the Delta Palasë Resort & Village project.

Grand Hyatt Palasë Resort & Spa, Albania, 2021.

Studies for Grand Hyatt Palasë Resort & Spa: Sculpting natural formations.

Façade mock-ups for Grand Hyatt Palasë Resort & Spa.

On the other hand, the Green Coast Village project, which is similarly shaped by the Mediterranean theme and spans approximately 60 hectares, is progressing rapidly. After a comprehensive master plan that we created for this area, we are now working with a dozen different investors on 28 different parcels, a complex and challenging but also highly enjoyable process.

Projects like Delta Palasë Resort & Village, Ionian Heaven Resort & Casino, Delta Panorama, Himarë Resort, Prestige Resort, Kavaja Resort Complex, Grand Hyatt Palasë Resort & Spa and Les Villages d'Azur in Ksamil are either progressing rapidly or still dormant despite having completed and approved concept projects.

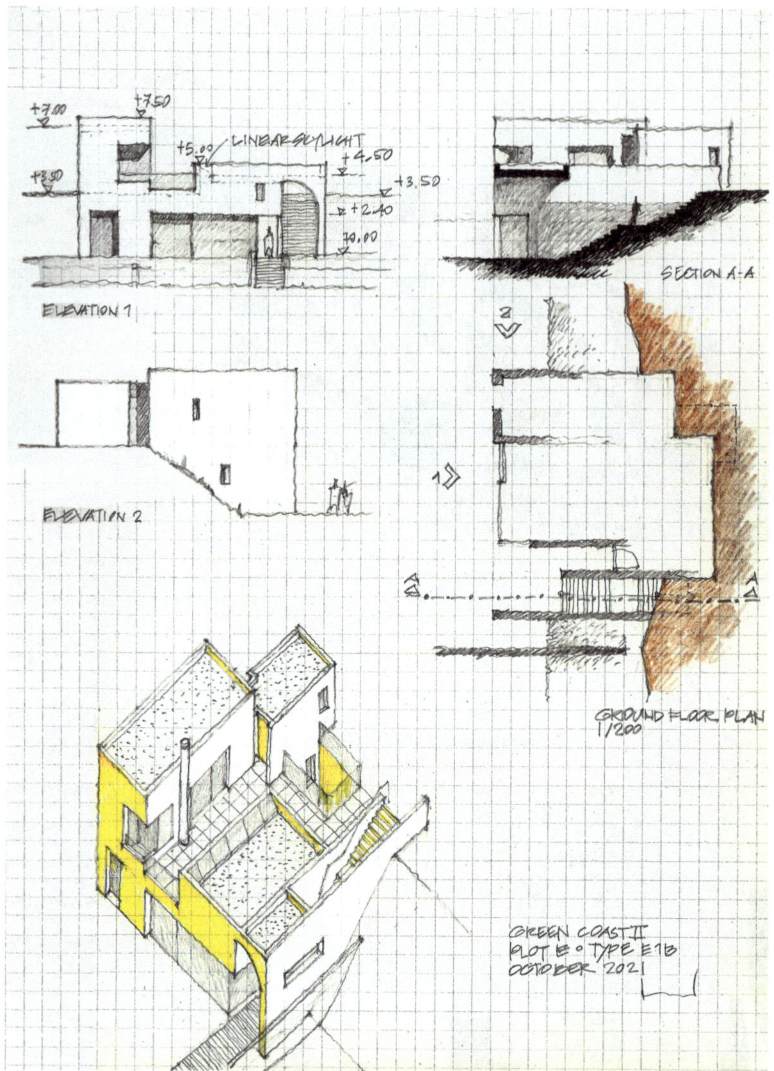

Green Coast Village, plot E, volumetric studies, October 2021.

Truthfully, it hasn't been easy trying to break the bad construction habits I mentioned earlier in most of these projects. The processes involve starting with how to protect the neighboring shrub vegetation while excavating, moving on to matters like the formwork systems for reinforced concrete production, how to pour roof slabs, what density of thermal insulation to use, why it's healthier to use mechanical fasteners for cladding natural stone, or how to water green roofs – things that should be universally acknowledged truths, but are still gray areas in Albania's construction sector. These are topics that are repeatedly discussed with investors, and every time, without exception, we must patiently explain why increasing building density is not a good idea.

But I'm not complaining. In doing all this, we meet new people and continue to learn. I always say that the Albanian people don't feel very foreign to me. Just as many Albanians live in my country, there are also many cultural similarities between the behavioral patterns of both countries. I wouldn't be wrong in saying I don't feel out of place here. Similar stories, similar characters, informal approaches that remind me of each other, surprisingly chaotic but just as alluring lives. Unbelievably delicious crudos, irresistible Primitivo wines . . .

We also had an EXPO Albania adventure during this time. Let me end with that. This complex was to be located in a very rural area on the outskirts of Tirana. For the first stage of the competition, we proposed a solution that presented itself as a public park. Apparently, our design didn't resonate much with the selection committee, as we didn't make it to the second stage this time. I'm curious about how the winning project will manifest in that area.

We still don't have a single project in Tirana. However, my opinion on one thing hasn't changed. This city still seems very attractive for living.

Emre Arolat
September 2024

EAA's proposal for EXPO Albania, blending the building into the context and creating a public park.

START	NAME PROJECT	LOCATION	DEVELOPER	PUBLIC/PRIVATE	PHASE
2019	Lura 5 Hotel & Residences	Lalëzit Bay		Private	Under construction
2020	Marina Saranda Limion master plan	Saranda	Marina Limion shpk		Concept
2020	Green Coast Village master plan	Dhërmi	Green Coast	Public/private	Under construction
2020	Ionian Heaven Resort & Casino	Konispol		Private	Concept
2020	Delta Palasë Resort & Village	Dhërmi	Delta sha	Public/private	Under construction
2021	Kavaja Resort Complex	Kavaja	Shipaku shpk	Public/private	Ongoing
2021	Grand Hyatt Palasë Resort & Spa			Private	Under construction
2023	Les Villages d'Azur master plan	Ksamil	Onhezmi Marina	Public/private	Ongoing
2023	Besa Museum	Tirana	Albanian government	Public	Competition entry
2024	EXPO Albania	Tirana	Albanian government	Public	Competition entry

NAME OFFICE

ELEMENTAL

DATE	PLACE	WORKING IN ALBANIA SINCE
September 2024	Santiago, Chile	May 2024

PRINCIPALS
Alejandro Aravena
Diego Torres
Gonzalo Artega
Juan Cerda
Víctor Oddó

PROJECT TEAM
Suyin Chia
Chiara Consigliere
Mara Cruz
Cristián Martínez
Génesis López

NICKNAME
The Messenger of Sagrada Albania

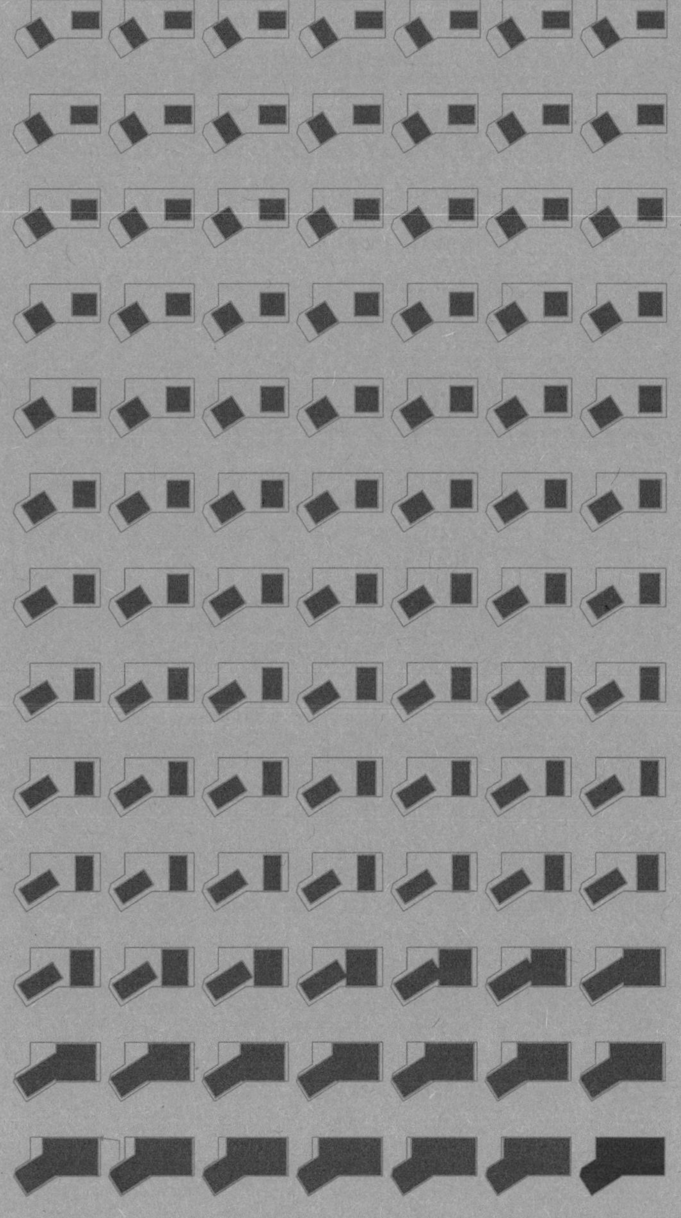

INTRODUCTION TO ALBANIA

Benedetta Tagliabue texted me asking if I was OK with having my contact number shared with Albania's prime minister. I said, of course. Five minutes later I was contacted by the PM, asking if I could come to Tirana to discuss the possibility of a project. Chile is very far away from everywhere, so I said the best thing would be to make a stop in Albania during my next trip to Europe. That was going to take place in two weeks' time, due to a construction site visit to the EDP Building in Lisbon. So in the last days of May, I managed to spend something like twenty-four hours in Albania. Since then, I've been back four times.

MAIN CONTEXT VS. ALBANIA

Chile and Albania are second world: We have to deliver architecture with first-world standards but produce it with third-world resources. So even though before May 2024 I had no clue what Albania was about, when I got there, it felt familiar.

ORGANIZATION/GOAL/SETUP

We haven't organized ourselves yet; that will be the question for this year.

OPPORTUNITIES/CHALLENGES

Given the nature of the projects, all of them towers, we anticipate that our approach of the last years, in which the structure is the architecture, will be more radical. When you have 400,000 tons rising 300 meters from the ground, we would like for the architecture to be almost finished when the structure is finished. It's not only a question of being efficient with resources, but a healthy starting point to stand the test of time.

HOW TO INTEGRATE GREATER RESPONSIBILITY FOR QUALITY IN PROJECTS

Well . . . we postpone "wanting" as much as possible; we don't jump into an answer (design) until we have understood what is the question. It is only when the forces that will inform the form of the project have been identified that we jump into the void of the blank page. The moment you start by listening, observing and understanding the constraints, projects have a greater chance to be pertinent. Pertinence is a way to integrate responsibility and quality.

BALANCING QUALITY AND DENSITY/INVOLVING STAKEHOLDERS

The first thing to agree with stakeholders is what are the problems that need to be addressed; there is nothing worse than answering the wrong question well. Those problems range from very concrete, tangible and measurable ones to abstract, symbolic and hard to grasp ones; often they also pull in opposite directions. But when the starting points are the problems and not the solutions, design integrity takes care of itself. In any case, what you are asking refers to the project itself; the challenge is what happens with the sum of the projects. It is known that individual actions, even if well intentioned, cannot guarantee the common good. So coordination more than money is the scarcest resource in the built environment. The architect's role is to present to and discuss with the authorities that have agency, the measures to be taken to mitigate and eventually compensate for the impact of an isolated project in the overall picture.

EXAMPLE/INSPIRATION

I am not knowledgeable enough yet to name one.

Previous Ideas
Testing Massing
How Many Towers?
How to Fill the Lot's Shape?

Given that this book is about sharing the "cooking" of a project, let's go back to square one:

Architecture is about giving form to the places where people live; it's not more complicated than that, but also not easier than that.

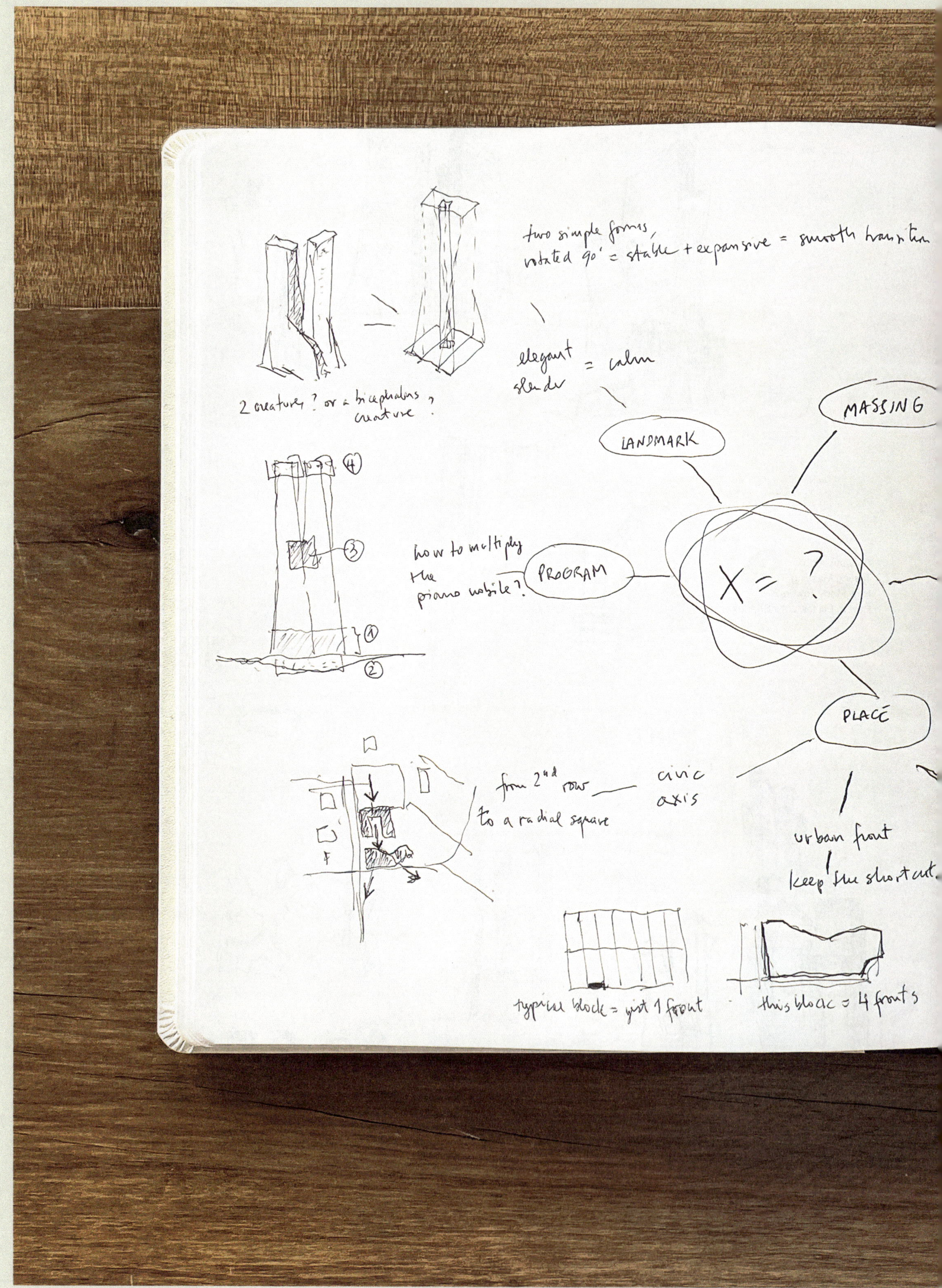
two simple forms,
rotated 90° = stable + expansive = smooth
2 creatures? or a bicephalous creature?
elegant
slender = calm
LANDMARK
MASSING
how to multiply
the
piano nobile?
PROGRAM
X = ?
PLACE
from 2nd row — civic axis
to a radial square
urban front
keep the shortcut.
typical block = just 1 front
this block = 4 fronts

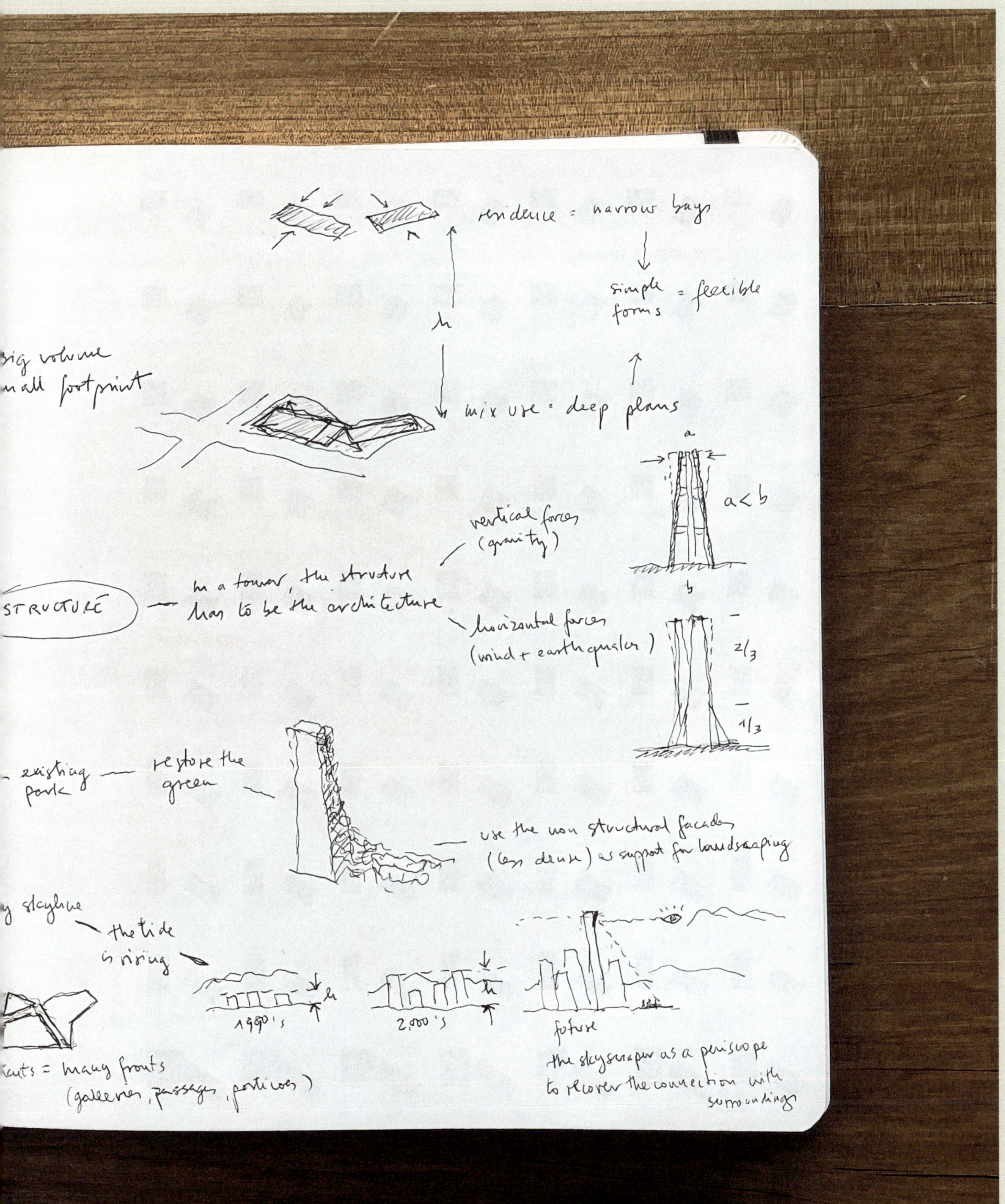

So, the question is, what *informs* the *form* of such places? Or, in other words, what are the forces at play that will be relevant to shape the design? Our starting point is X = ?, where X is the form and the question mark refers to the fact that at the beginning, we don't (want to) know what the project will look like; we don't want to arrive to a form too early. We actually work in several versions of the question and iterate back and forth to design's synthesis and back again to the question until we have identified and distilled the key drivers. In this case of the Tirana Society Towers, we have identified (for now) five relevant forces.

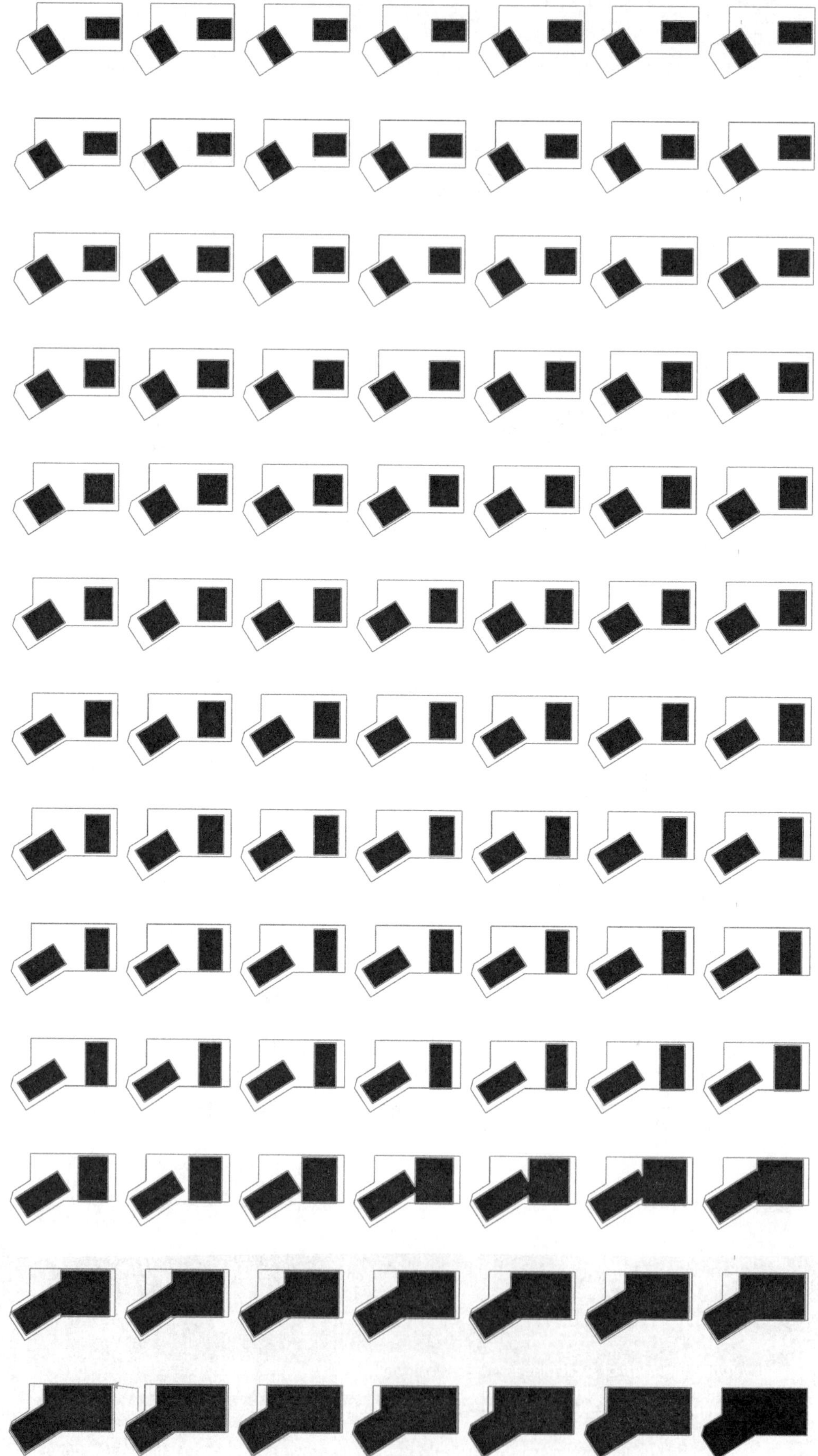

1. The Massing

One of the challenges of this project is that it has to accommodate a **big volume** (165,000 m²) **in a small plot** (4,500 m²). The first consequence is that the resulting massing is vertical, **very vertical**. Then, in order to accommodate the requested programs, there are two different logics that need to be followed: narrow bays for apartments and deep plans for mixed use.
For both logics, it is desirable that **the floor plans have simple shapes**. Such simplicity allows for an easy **adaptation to changes** (offering a dynamic capacity of reaction to a shifting demand). Actually, for projects of this scale, it is known that they have to be flexible in their development and evolution for various reasons (economic, regulatory, society's input). Our challenge was to find the simplest possible geometry within a rather irregular (almost chaotic) plot, so that when the form is required to change, the concept remains.

Big volume
small footprint

2. The Structure

The vertical massing results in a 300-meter-high volume or in other words, 400,000 tons. With such height and weight, **the structure has to be the architecture**; the vertical (gravity) and horizontal (seismic and wind) loads are of such magnitude that the form should follow the forces. The proposed structure follows three principles:

- At least two sides of each tower follow a slightly **buttressed shape** through which loads are carried without interruptions from the top to the foundations; we connect the opposite facades so they balance each other, widening their base.
- On the other two sides of each tower, we follow a dual strategy: In the lower third, we use a **leaning plinth** to truss the structure. The upper two thirds are counter leaning in order to compensate the loss of area due to the buttressed shape; in that case we use a lower density structure to reduce unnecessary weight.
- We use **regular plans** in order to reduce rotations and torsions; vertical forces (gravity) always come from the same direction, but horizontal ones (earthquakes and wind) are unpredictable and dynamic, so regular forms are more efficient at providing lateral stability. In addition to structural efficiency, this approach addresses the necessary flexibility for the inevitable future changes.

Finally, we opted for concrete for three reasons: It offers the lowest carbon footprint for this height, it lasts longer without the need for maintenance and it's a more available technology among local providers.

1. Two parallel vertical walls

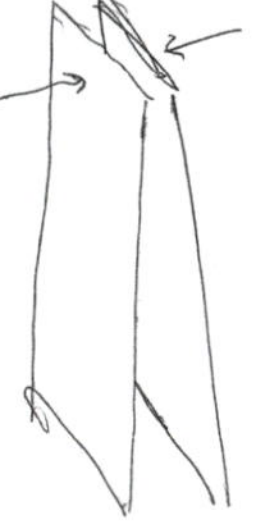

2. Slightly tilted towards the inside

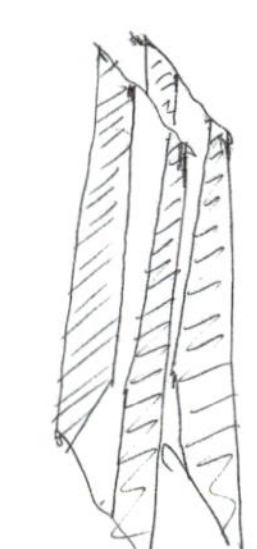

3. Cut with a silhouette with a counterslope

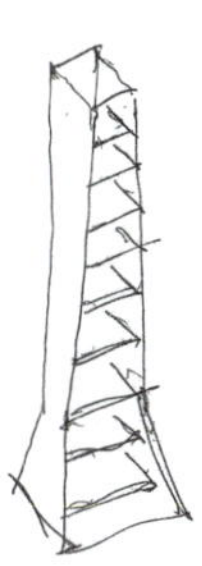

4. Connected by the slabs

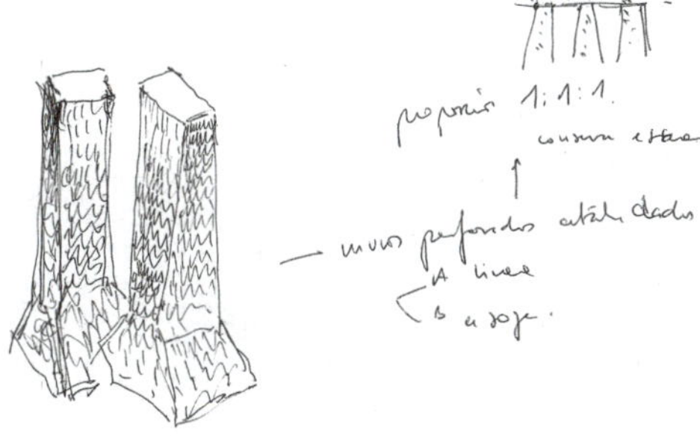

5. Then the walls are perforated with windows (or they are a field of columns)

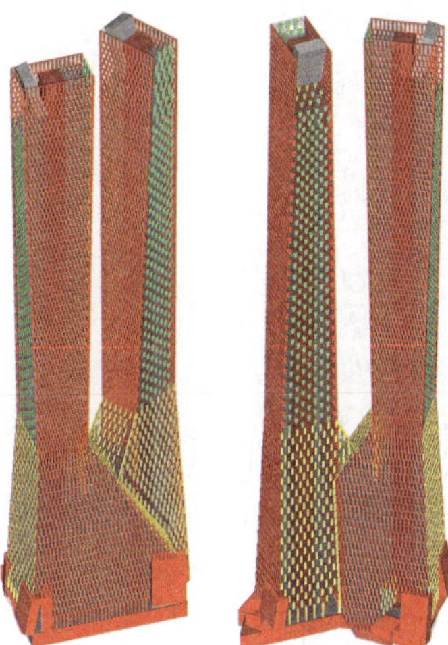

Loads on buttressed walls = continuous from top to bottom
Low density for counter-leaning facades
Forces in leaning plinth

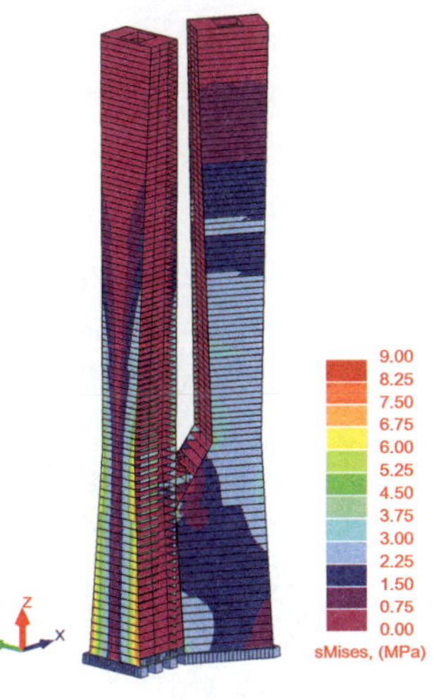

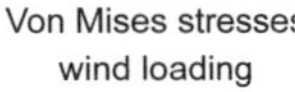

Von Mises stresses
wind loading

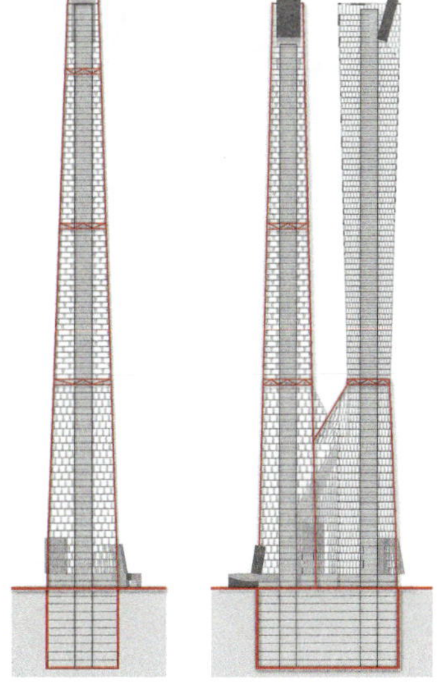

Section aa

Section bb

3. The Place

The context in which this project will be located has to consider at least four levels:

A. Restore the greenery
Even though the plot is private (and therefore developable), nowadays it is a de facto green public space. So, the new project should consider at least a mitigation of any greenery elimination. Given that the project allows for a gap between the structure (external facade) and the enclosure (inner facade), the space in between the two, especially the least dense facades, is suited to hold such greenery as a very simple planting space able to be maintained from inside.

B. Recover the connection with the surroundings
The trend in Tirana is that of an increasing height, one that has gone from a couple of stories to tall buildings to skyscrapers. It's as if a tide is rising (in this case an urban tide) and the people at street level are sinking, losing the connection to the surrounding geography. Whenever we walk by a skyscraper, looking up is almost inevitable but we get very little besides the view of a structure with a dramatic vertical vanishing point.
So, we thought, what if we use the facade as a reflective surface that with the right angle can work as a **periscope** to reconnect with the missing surroundings?

C. Keep the shortcuts
In a typical urban plot, the most valuable side is the one facing the street. Unless you are in a corner lot, only one out of four sides benefits from that condition. In the case of this plot, all four sides have an open front, creating an unusually valuable condition both for the owner and for the city.
On the other hand, given that the plot is unbuilt, pedestrians cross it diagonally in several directions. Hence, it would be desirable to keep the shortcuts, because we would not only preserve the natural flows, but could use them to expand the linear meters of commercial front into the core of the block.

D. New civic axis
Despite the prime location, this site is in a kind of second row of the most important square in Tirana. Actually, the shortcuts marked in the lawns reflect on the one hand an intense and lively use, but also that people have to go around the Opera House. It is a pity that in such a privileged location, the U-shaped opera is used for parking. So, we thought that a low-hanging fruit in urban terms is to allow the great portico of the Opera House to be trespassed so that a new civic axis can develop **through the buildings** beyond the square (and not just around them).

The southeast boulevard

4. The Program

There are two weak points that are typical of any vertical structure: On the one hand, the vital exchange between the building and the city tends to be confined exclusively to the ground level; and on the other hand, the mechanical repetition of floors leaves little room for spaces with a more public vocation to be distributed throughout the whole height.
So, we thought of some strategies in order to overcome such weaknesses and expand the “piano nobile” beyond the street level:

- **Porticoes** all around the perimeter to increase the porosity and therefore the urban exchange at the ground level.
- A series of **galleries** that take advantage of and consolidate the existing shortcuts.
- In between the irregular shape of the site and the regular footprint of the building, we introduced **exterior slopes** and sunken gardens with water features in order to bring natural light and urban exposure to lower levels.
- In the convergence of the towers and the plinth we introduced **elevated atriums** of several heights each.
- The crowning of the towers also introduces multiple-floor sky lounges in order to multiply the uses that can benefit from the unique views.

Finally, the challenge of any mixed-use building is how to differentiate the entrances and cores for the diverse functions. As an intuitive way-finding and orientation strategy we propose that several monoliths circulations to the multiple underground parking levels.

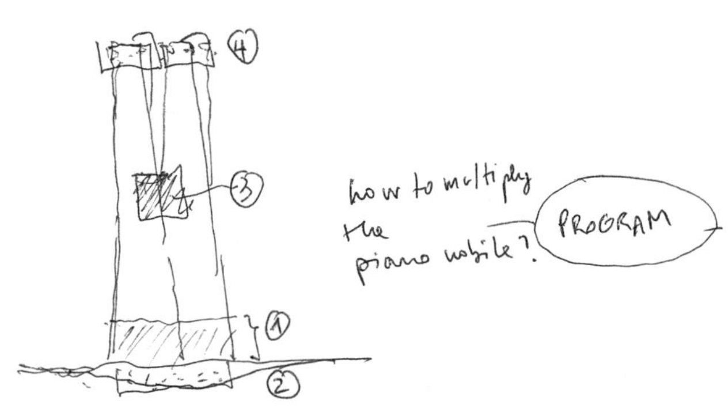

Elevated atriums

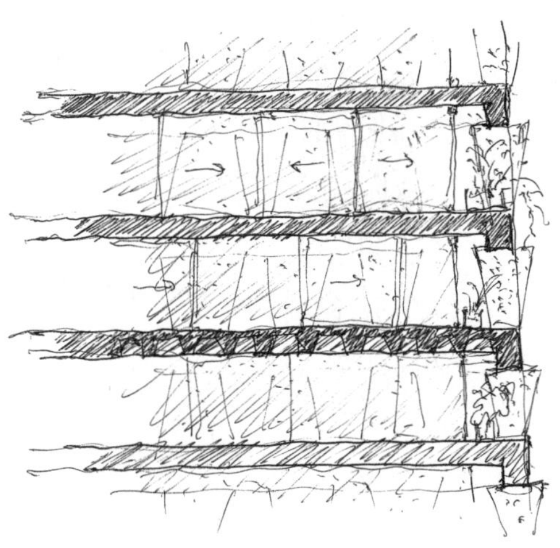

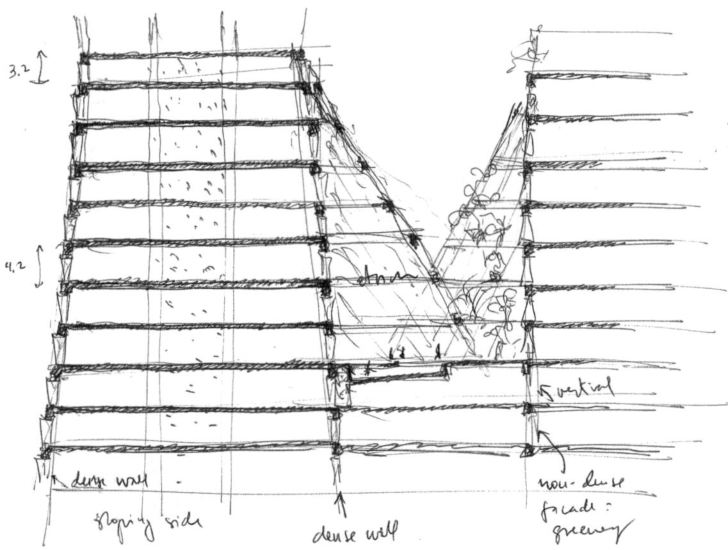

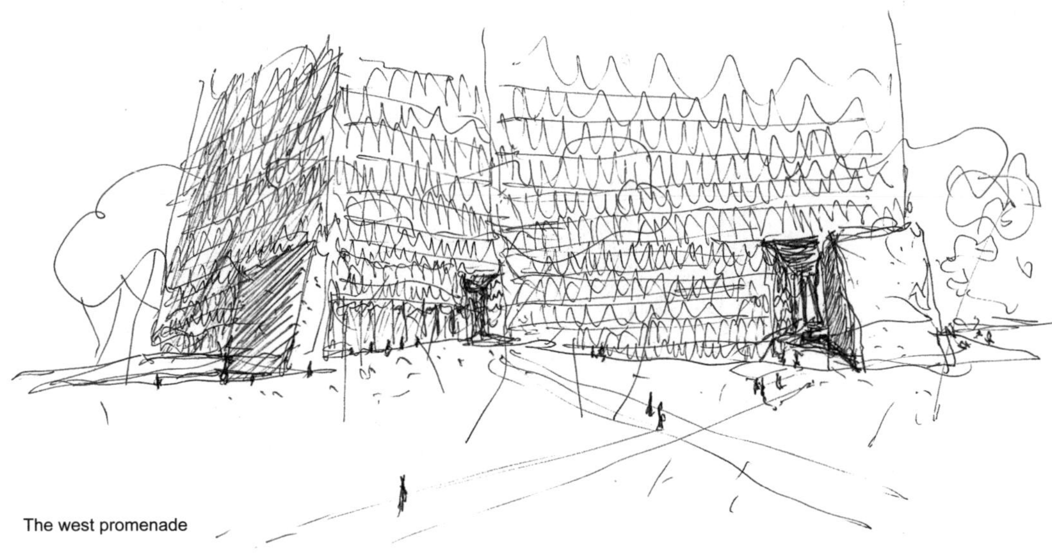

The west promenade

5. The Landmark

The search for elegance was a request from the client. The massing leads naturally to a slender pair of silhouettes, but we thought that two more things had to govern the form: a certain classical calm and a sense of unity.

That is why among all the possible moves and articulations of the volume, we opted for the most simple one, almost only following the structural logic. Then, given that the plinth had to be rather high, we thought of treating it as in Brancusi's or Giacometti's work, where the distinction between pedestal and sculpture has been blurred.

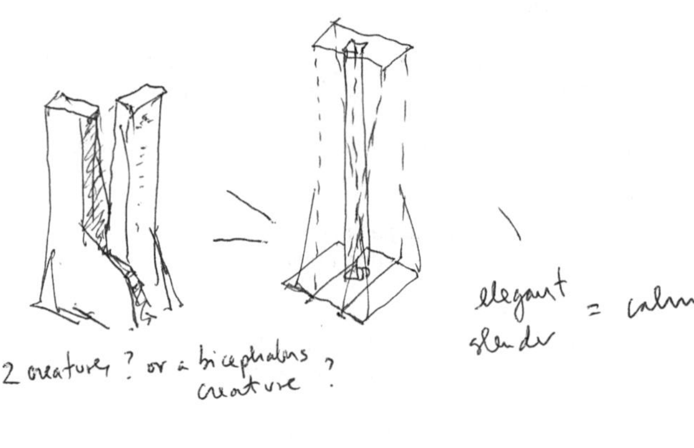

two simple forms, rotated 90° = stable + expansive = smooth transition

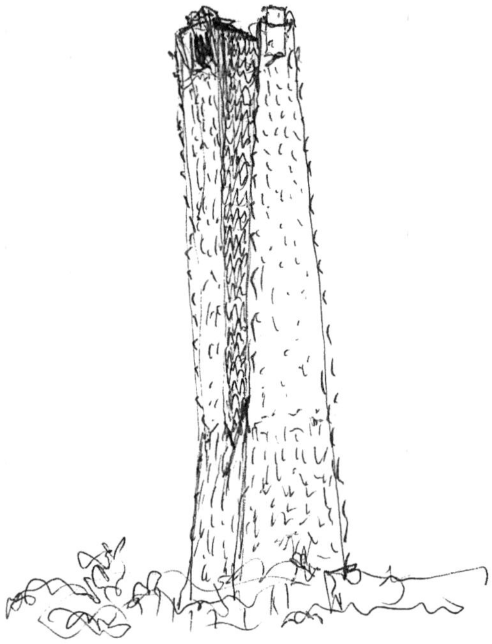

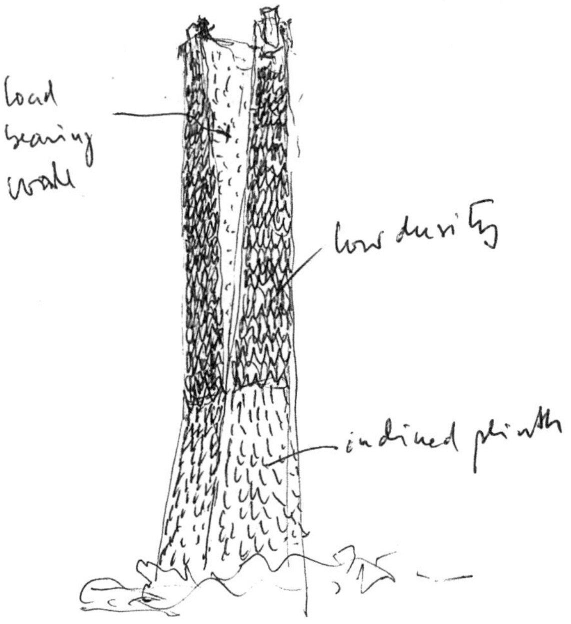

load bearing walls

low density

inclined plinth

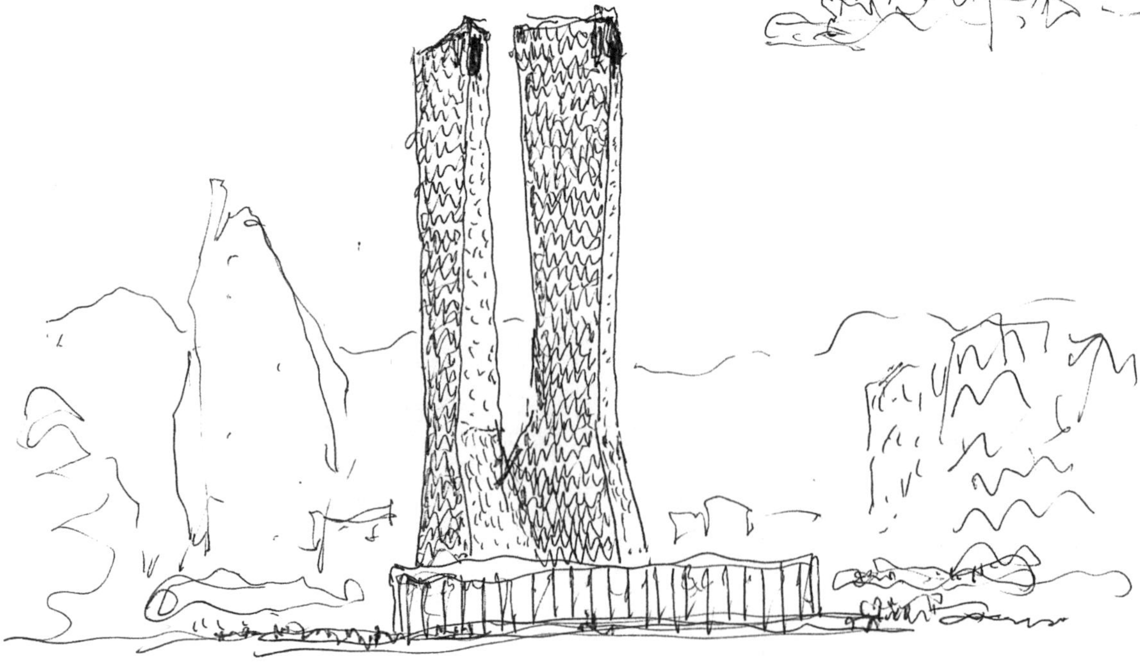

START	NAME PROJECT	LOCATION	PUBLIC/PRIVATE	PHASE
2024		Tirana	Private	First vision approved, about to finish concept design
2024	TST Tirana Society Towers	Tirana	Private	Competition winner, working on contract to start schematic design

NAME OFFICE

ENSAMBLE STUDIO

DATE
April 2025

PLACE
Madrid, Spain

WORKING IN ALBANIA SINCE
March 2023

PRINCIPALS
Débora Mesa Molina
Antón García-Abril

ALBANIAN PARTNERS
BG Studio, Besnik Grainca
IMPULS&CO, Arvjen Lushaj
ArchCo Studio, Dhimitri Papa
MVM Architecture, Alket Meslani

PROJECT TEAM
Javier Cuesta
Borja Soriano
Alvaro Catalan
Veeravalli Vikram
Javier Martin
Vaishnavi Bhartia
Chetan Anand
Nikolay Maslov
Nikolaj Exner
Andrea Varone
Rachit Somani

MAIN CONTEXT VS. ALBANIA

Our practice operates internationally, with projects currently underway in the United States, Barbados, South Korea and Spain. Working across diverse geographies and cultures has consistently enriched our approach, challenging us to adapt, listen and rethink architecture in context.

When we began our work in Spain in 2000, the country was experiencing a moment of intense urban development and collective optimism – marked by open competitions and real opportunities to shape public infrastructure and cultural institutions. We recognize a similar energy in Albania today: a willingness to build meaningful architecture and an openness to engaging global perspectives in the construction of its future. Albania also confronts two defining architectural challenges of the twenty-first century: housing and the relationship between architecture and the landscape. These are precisely the conditions in which architecture can reclaim its highest role – not as a financial asset, but as a cultural act capable of inspiring society, shaping collective identity and elevating shared life.

ORGANIZATION/GOAL/SETUP

We hope that our work in Albania will be long-lasting – like any good relationship! As newcomers, we are in the process of building trust and establishing meaningful collaborations with a wide range of stakeholders, from government leaders to local developers, contractors and citizens. Understanding the specific context of development is a priority for us. Only by doing so can we ensure that our architectural visions are aligned with the realities of each place in which we intervene, and capable of growing through collaboration.

SETUP IN RELATION TO ALBANIAN PARTNER

Projects are developed through continuous dialogue with local architects and clients from the outset. As projects progress into subsequent phases, this collaboration naturally expands to include a broader network of local experts and stakeholders, deepening a shared understanding of regulatory, technical and implementation frameworks. Our objective is to cultivate an integrated way of working in which knowledge and expertise are openly shared. In this way, we do not simply work in a place, but become local through collaboration.

OPPORTUNITIES/CHALLENGES

Albania has a unique opportunity to confront ecology and climate change as it develops, while preserving its mountains, rivers, coastline and landscapes. Ecological awareness needs to be integrated as a core principle of development, rather than treated as an afterthought. Architects play a central role in shaping this approach, engaging governments, developers and contractors to help balance ambitious visions with practical realities.

At the regional level, urban planning, architecture and nature can operate in continuity, reflecting cultural and even spiritual relationships with the land – as explored in our Vlorëst proposal, an architectural forest that celebrates the area's ecological identity. At the scale of the building, architecture can resonate with nature while accommodating urban growth and economic viability. At the industrial scale, materials and technologies can be developed to optimize energy performance, reduce embodied carbon and respond to local conditions. Together, these scales form a framework for ecological thinking in Albania.

HOW TO INTEGRATE GREATER RESPONSIBILITY FOR QUALITY IN PROJECTS

Architecture is, at its core, an act of celebration. It reflects the spirit of its time and captures moments of transformation and growth.

The path of an architect is rarely easy. The simplest route is often to conform to market standards and follow established industry protocols. This frequently results in soulless architecture – automated solutions that reinforce existing systems without questioning them. Unfortunately, this approach is common in many developing contexts, where efficiency and repetition tend to prevail over creativity.

With all the challenges, beauty and energy of the Albanian context, however, the stakes are different and expectations are uniquely high. Architecture here is called to rise above the ordinary and respond to the artistic and cultural richness of its environment. In this context, architecture becomes more than building: It is an act of cultural and artistic expression, a celebration of possibilities and an enduring reflection of the spirit of its time.

BALANCING QUALITY AND DENSITY/INVOLVING STAKEHOLDERS

Albania's rapid development and limited resources invite an approach in which architects mediate between spatial quality, construction logic and urban intensity – transforming constraints into opportunities to strengthen local craft traditions and building knowledge – much like Spain in the 1990s. Albania offers flexibility and an openness to innovation, allowing quality to be framed as a guiding principle rather than a residual outcome.

Materials and their natural origins play a central role. By grounding architectural decisions in material logic and place, quality becomes tangible and legible to clients, authorities and builders. This shared understanding enables a broader group of stakeholders to maintain design integrity: Developers and contractors optimize resources and execution, while public institutions help create conditions for experimentation, density management and long-term value.

An open and collaborative process allows experimentation to coexist with control, leading to higher-quality and more ecologically responsible outcomes. Innovation often emerges not from new technologies but from rethinking methods and expanding the circle of responsibility. In this sense, Albania offers a rare opportunity to reinforce the architect's role as both designer and cultural mediator – ensuring that density enhances, rather than diminishes, architectural quality, sustainability and collective life.

The Balcony is a three-dimensional structure that unites diverse programs into an interconnected urban whole.

March 2023
First encounter with Albania

The Balcony

Congress center in Tirana

A porous urban block with diverse programs that frames the landscape and embodies a dynamic urban vision

November 2023
Journey across the Vjosa River

The Immersive Museum
Tepelenë

Vjosa Museum

Multifunctional Center and Information Stations in Përmet, Tepelenë and Vlora

A series of landscape infrastructures complementing the river

Qyteza e Kulturës (The Cultural Citadel)
Vlora

The Floating Museum
Përmet

November 2024
Larger urban developments

Vlorëst

Master plan to develop a vibrant urban environment in Vlora

A series of mixed-use developments that grow out of the ground like a forest in Albania

July 2024
Private development in Vlora

Belvedere

A cascading residential complex

A terraced building nestled within the slope of a mountain, forming a new ground as an extension of the existing slope

The Floating Museum is a landscape bridge that crosses the Vjosa River in Përmet. It functions as both an infrastructural intervention and a dynamic portal into the river's story.

The Landscraper is a sculptural elevated ground that supports gardens and homes. It is inspired by the organic imperfectness of the terrain on which it rests to create a broken and earthly connection.

The **Belvedere** is a reimagination of the Landscraper, creating a sprawling urban definition in the form of large buildings that are broken into a series of cascading terraces that overlook the sea or vast courtyards in between.

Vlorëst is an urban forest that brings together diverse architectures with distinct landscape features that are special to the Albanian heritage, to create a new master plan strategy.

Our project in Albania is bringing the landscape into architecture, where the hybridization of the natural and the artificial provokes meaningful living experiences and a profound integration of architecture in the environment. This endeavor manifests in different buildings and sites:

START	NAME PROJECT	LOCATION	DEVELOPER	ALBANIAN PARTNER	M²	PUBLIC/PRIVATE	PHASE
2023	The Balcony	Tirana	Usluga shpk		130,000 m²	Public/private	Competition submission (concept design)
2023	Vjosa Museum	Vjosa River (Vlora, Tepelenë, Përmet)			60,000 m²	Public	Competition submission (concept design)
2024	Albaforum	Tirana		MVM Architecture	50,000 m²	Public	Competition submission (concept design)
2024	Energizing Cities: Dual Call for mixed-use projects	Tirana			45,000 m²	Public	Competition submission (concept design)
2024	Landscraper	Vlora	QuadPlan	BG Studio	25,000 m²	Private	Concept design
2024	Belvedere	Vlora	QuadPlan	BG Studio	35,000 m²	Private	Design development
2024	Vlorëst master plan	Vlora		BG Studio	130,000 m²	Private	Master plan concept design

NAME OFFICE

ESTUDI D'ARQUITECTURA TONI GIRONÈS

DATE
December 5, 2025

PLACE
Barcelona, Spain

WORKING IN ALBANIA SINCE
April 2024

PRINCIPALS
Toni Gironès Saderra, PhD architect

ALBANIAN PARTNER
UDV Studio,
Dhimitri Jano & Kostandin Jano (Co-Founders)
Bleona Dhamo (Project Manager)
Alba Golemi (Senior Architect)
Renato Hamza (Senior Architect)
Erestina Jaupi (Senior Architect)
Andi Hoxha (Junior Architect)

PROJECT TEAM
Yasmina Pérez (Senior Architect)
Guillem Elvira (Senior Architect – by projects)
Candela Botta (Junior Architect)
Pere Joan Cladera (Junior Architect)
Roger Garcia (Architecture Student)
Maria Fonti and Mónica Soto (Communication)
Francesc Batlle (Human Resources)

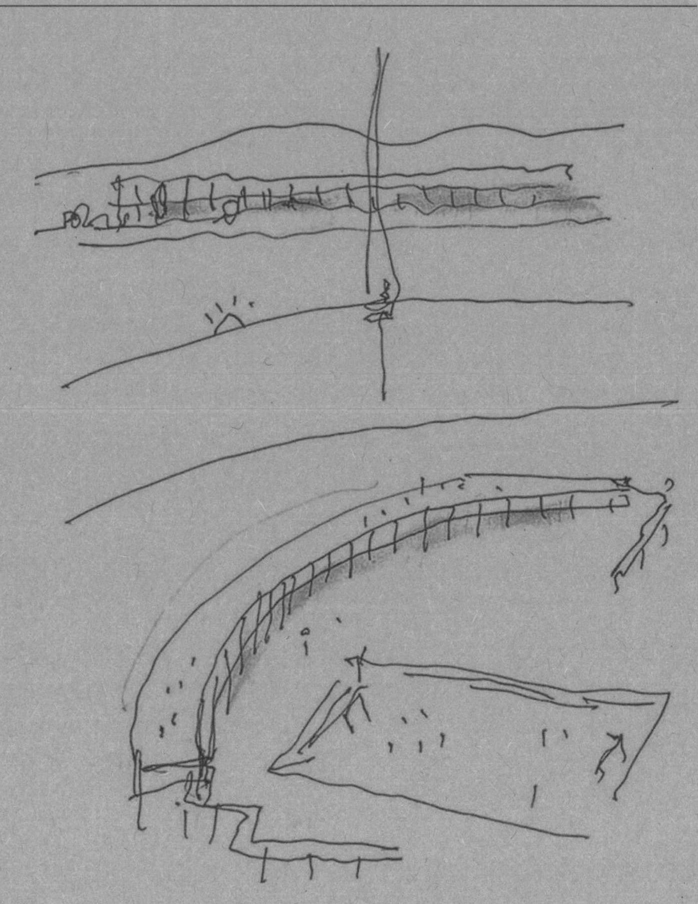

MAIN CONTEXT VS. ALBANIA

The context in which I usually work is based on a certain physical proximity to the processes/projects I develop. The native condition of each place is very important to me, and that's why, in the case of Albania, empathy and the idea of forming a team with the local studio are essential.

ORGANIZATION/GOAL/SETUP

In each project process, we collaborate with an Albanian architecture studio, as I believe that the combination of local knowledge and the objectivity we can bring from a broader perspective is essential and, at the same time, mutually enriching. The projects are approached as processes of research and shared/mutual learning.

The goal is to process and activate good practices related to human dwelling in a country like Albania, which is currently undergoing an extremely accelerated development process. I understand that these processes need to be regulated and produced – trying, as much as possible, to avoid repeating mistakes that have already manifested in other places over the past fifty years.

In this sense, we currently have, to summarize very briefly, two realities: On the one hand, globalization has led to a polarized and speculative economic system, but on the other hand, a certain critical awareness of our species seems to have been emerging in recent times, proposing a change in habits that, from individual awareness, can lead to collective change. In this regard, a certain pedagogical work aimed at current and future generations is fundamental.

SETUP IN RELATION TO LOCAL OFFICE

The premise has been that we must lead the various processes, and in my case, I don't understand leadership without achieving team cohesion by sharing a common goal. Personally, I believe that this goal is to activate the needs of human dwelling in relation to the native condition of the place, establishing the maximum number of harmonious relationships with the different natural elements that determine human (biological) dwelling on the planet, while also optimizing resources to the fullest.

From the beginning of the project to its activation/materialization, we share the entire process with the local team, understood as a way of working that exchanges knowledge.

OPPORTUNITIES/CHALLENGES

In these eighteen months that I have been working in Albania (since April 2024), I have identified as an opportunity the fact that there is space for cross-cutting thinking in the face of widely accepted dynamics of speculation and business around the world. The challenge is to remain clear-sighted in the proposals and, at the same time, to apply them with ethics and a sense of responsibility.

HOW TO INTEGRATE GREATER RESPONSIBILITY FOR QUALITY IN PROJECTS

The quality of projects lies in conveying a common objective regarding human dwelling to all members of the team and achieving it. This team is understood in its broadest sense: architects, professionals from other disciplines (ecologists, biologists, anthropologists, sociologists, engineers, agronomists, geographers, economists, lawyers and especially politicians, understood as a profession that works like the others, with a vocation of service to civil society). Also, and perhaps most importantly, I believe it is essential to incorporate the client, whether public or private, as part of the team.

BALANCING QUALITY AND DENSITY/INVOLVING STAKEHOLDERS

I believe that to maintain quality in density, porosity is essential. The quality of designing transitions between programs at different scales, and the "breathability" of the planetary skin (the soil and subsoil) in relation to the different living beings (the sense of touch), is what determines quality and harmony in dwelling. The key to a good project lies in the void as the articulator of matter.

I believe that for a design to be of quality, it must be open to change over time. The ability to adapt, especially in an uncertain and changing future like the one ahead, is crucial. Making a mathematical analogy, I think what we design/project are equations, not results. The result is determined by the value of the unknowns (*a*, *b*, *c*, *d*, *e*, . . . *x*, *y*, *z* . . .), and these are in turn determined by something that is in constant change, as what we design is a support for life.

And yes, this way of framing can be expanded, involving more parts.

EXAMPLE/INSPIRATION

Skanderbeg Square, and continuing with what was mentioned in the previous question, I think it is a well structured "equation," with a central multipurpose space that functions as a support for different uses throughout the year and a tree-lined perimeter space that in the warm seasons activates much-needed shadows at that time.

TOOLBOX ALBANIA FUTURE

I believe that mutual trust and respect are key, although they need to be worked on daily.

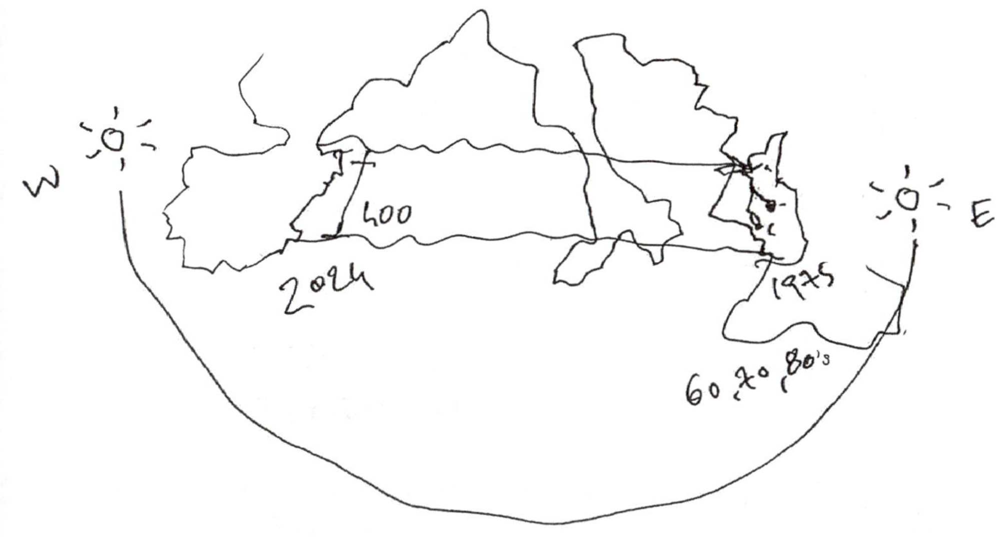

..."TO DO SOMETHING OR MORE THAN SOMETHING IN ALBANIA"... THAT WAS THE SENTENCE THAT ENDED THE WHATSAPP THAT EDI RAMA SENT ME WHEN HE CONTACTED THE ARCHITECTURE STUDIO...

...THAT "MORE THAN SOMETHING", APART FROM A PRIME MINISTER CONTACTING YOU IN SUCH A DIRECT WAY, WAS WHAT CAUGHT MY ATTENTION THE MOST....

...OVER TIME AND IN PARALLEL TO THE KNOWLEDGE OF THE COUNTRY, ITS PEOPLE AND ITS CIRCUMSTANCES, I HAVE BEEN UNDERSTANDING IT.

...AND THAT KNOWLEDGE HAS ALWAYS BEEN PRODUCED FROM INITIAL QUESTIONS THAT IN THE FORM OF STATEMENTS HAVE BEEN ADRESSING AND QUESTIONING THE DIFFERENT PROJECTS.

...IN THE COAST OF LALZI, WAS THE INITIAL QUESTION, IN ITS GEOGRAPHICAL CONDITION OF MEDITERRANEAN CLIMATE COAST THAT CONTINUES INLAND AS A PLAIN OF FULL WETLANDS WHOSE WATER COMES FROM THE "TOPOGRAPHIC RAIN" ORIGINATING IN THE NEARBY MOUNTAIN RANGE....

...THIS CIRCUMSTANCE REMINDED ME IN PART, WHAT HAPPENS IN THE CATALAN COAST (MY PLACE OF ORIGIN), AND MORE SPECIFICALLY THE AREA OF AMPURDAN COAST WITH ITS WETLANDS AND AGRICULTURE STRUCTURE... ANALOGOUS SITUATIONS OCCUR....

...WHEN MEASURING THE LONGITUTE OF THE CATALAN COAST, WE SEE THAT IT HAS A VERY SIMILAR MEASURE TO THE ALBANIAN COAST, SHARING ALSO THE SAME LATITUDE....

.... BARCELONA AND TIRANA ARE IN 41º LATITUDE....

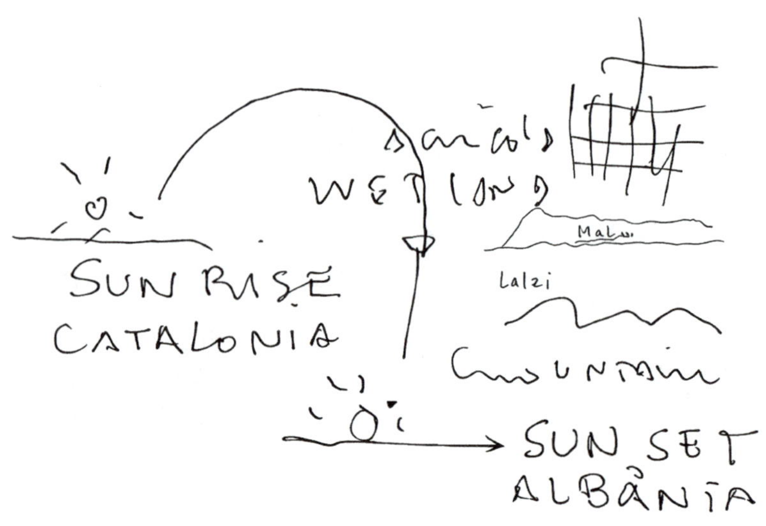

...., ONE COAST IS ORIENTED TO THE EAST AND THE OTHER TO THE WEST, BUT THERE IS A DETERMINING DIFFERENTIAL FACTOR, ALBANIA MAINTAINS IN GREAT PART OF ITS COAST AND INTERIOR THAT AUTHENTICITY AND CONDITION OF ITS OWN PLACE THAT WE HAD IN THE 60s/70 AND THAT PREVAILED IN GREAT PART UNTIL THE END OF THE 90'S, ... AND THAT I CONSIDER, IS A HIGH PATRIMONIAL VALUE, ... THAT, FOR ME, IS THE "SOMETHING, OR MORE THAN SOMETHING" TO WHICH WE REFERRED AT THE BEGINNING.

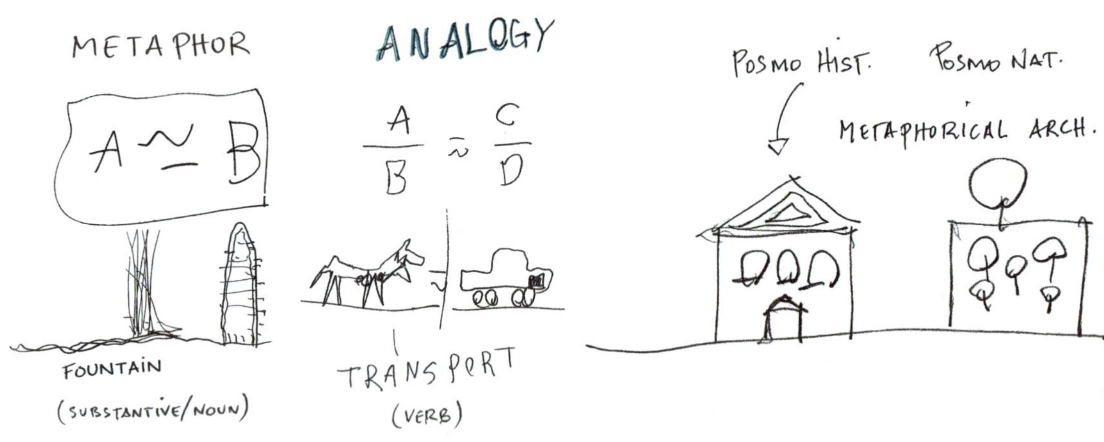

THE CHALLENGE OF "DRAWING WITH WORDS" BRINGS US CLOSER TO THE REAL CONTENT OF EACH PROPOSED PROCESS, THINKING AND QUESTIONING FROM ANALOGICAL MENTALITY, AND DISTANCE US FROM ANY POSSIBILITY OF SUPERFICIAL METAPHORS.

... A SITUATION IN TIME THAT LEADS TO INTERVENE FOR THE FIRST TIME IN A PLACE, SURPASSING BY FAR IN SCALE THE FAMILIES OF FISHERMEN AND AGRICULTURIST THAT POPULATED IN A BALANCED WAY THIS COAST AND THIS WELL-WATERED PLAIN UNTIL NOT LONG AGO.....

... THE NEW NEED OF THE TOURISM RESOURCE, DESERVES A BALANCE THAT GOES THROUGH UNDERSTANDING THE GEOGRAPHICAL AND CLIMATIC CONDITION OF THE PLACE, UNDERSTANDING THE TOPOGRAPHY AS A HARMONIC MOVEMENT IN WHICH THE EMPTY PREVAILS OVER THE FULL AND OF COURSE THE DIFFERENT IDENTITY ELEMENTS GENERATED BY DECANTATION OVER TIME ...

... STRATEGIES IN THE OPTIMIZATION OF THE SUCCESSIVE TOPOGRAPHIC MOVEMENTS, AND ABOVE ALL IN ITS LAYOUT BASED ON AN EXPERIENCE THAT AIMS THE RELATIONSHIP AND AWARENESS OF THE MARITIME HORIZON ..., SMALL TERRACES WITH CHANGES IN ELEVATION OF 50 CMS AND ANALOGOUSLY TO THE NATIVE DUNE SYSTEM, MATERIALIZE THIS TASK, AND IN TURN INTERACT AS INTERMEDIATE SPACES WITH THE MEMORY OF THE FRUIT TREES OF MEDITERRANEAN CLIMATE IN THE ALBANIAN COAST....

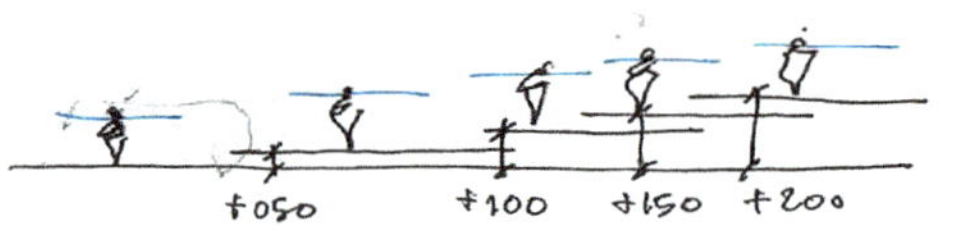

.... TRANSITIONS FROM INSIDE TO OUTSIDE WITH DIFFERENT INTERMEDIATE SPACES THAT ALLOW TO EXPERIENCE THE DIFFERENT PARTS OF THE HABITAT/HOTEL ADAPTING IT TO THE REAL ALBANIAN IDENTITY....

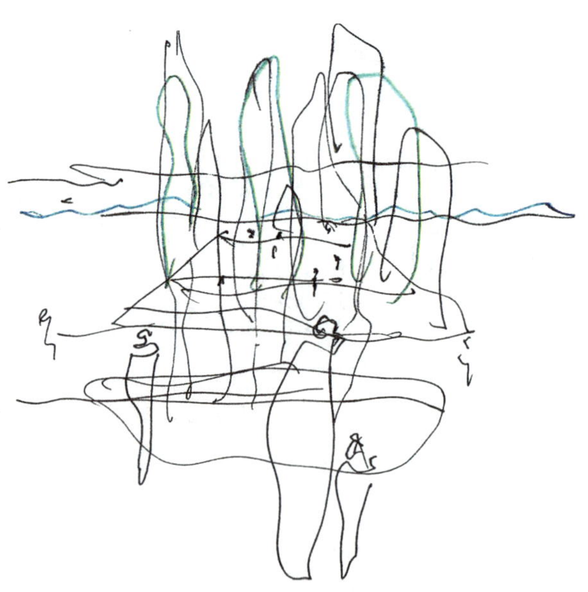

... BUILDINGS, GARDENS AND OPEN SPACES COLLABORATE AS A COHESIVE AND INTERCONNECTED HABITAT. THE BUILDINGS ARE EXTENSIONS OF THEIR NATURAL SURROUNDINGS, AND THE TREES AND GARDENS PLAY AN IMPORTANT ROLE IN THE ARCHITECTURAL FRAMEWORK, TURNING EVERYDAY ENCOUNTERS INTO ENRICHING EXPERIENCES...

... THE COASTLINE IN ALBANIA EXTENDS OVER 300/400 KMS...

... SOME RIVERS AND THEIR DELTAS ARE MANIFESTED AND MODIFY THE COASTLINE OVER TIME....

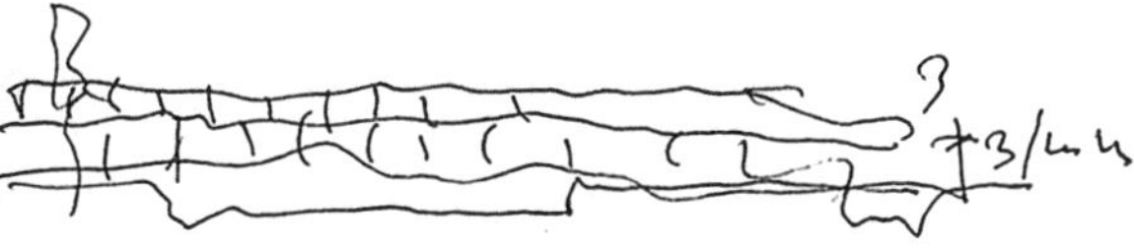

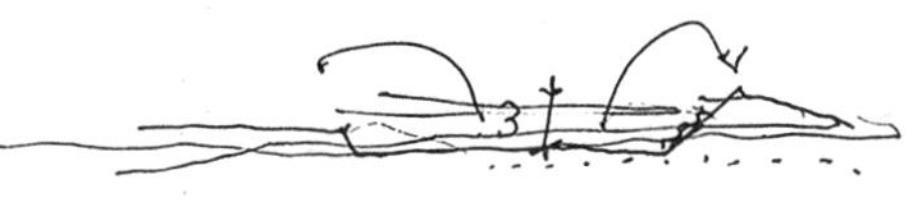

... THIS EPHEMERAL CONDITION IN TIME, IN PERMANENT MOVEMENT, AND SPECIFICALLY IN THE DELTA OF THE SHKUMBIN RIVER, MOTIVATES THE SUCCESSIVE TOPOGRAPHIC CHANGES THAT COMBINING EXCAVATION AND TERRACING, ARE SHAPING DIFFERENT SPACES LINKED TO SPORT, IN SOME CASES HIGH PERFORMANCE....

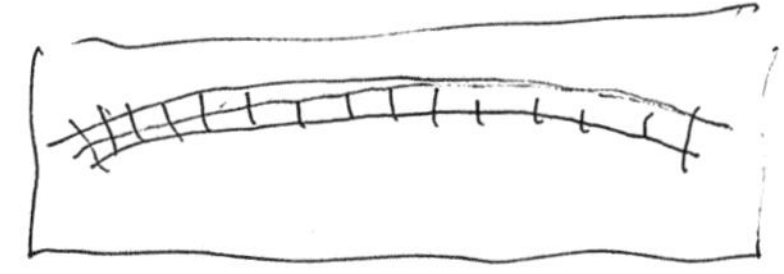

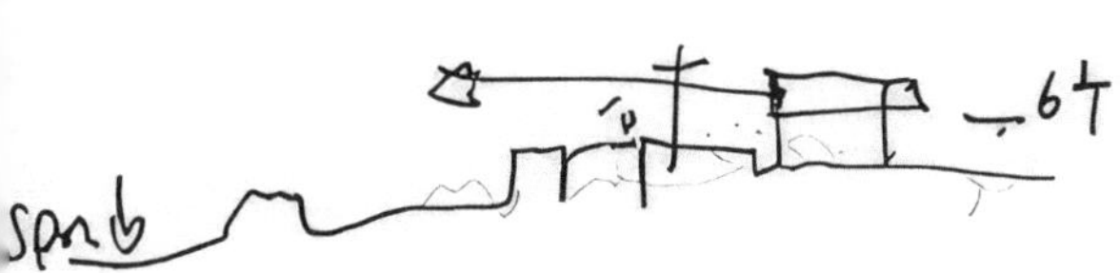

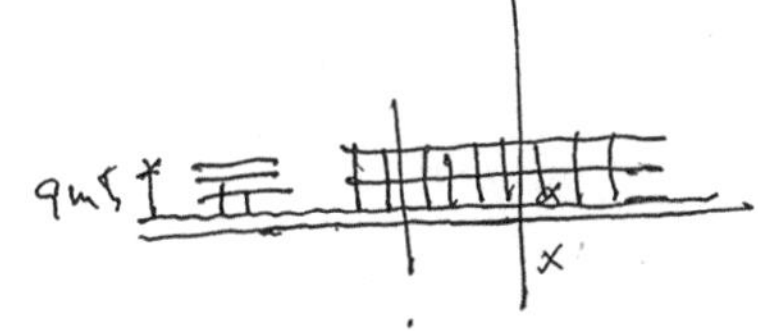

... A DOUBLE HORIZON..., ONE THAT CONFIGURES LOOKING FROM THE SEA A NEW PALAFITIC STRUCTURE PARALLEL TO THE EPHEMERAL DELTAIC COAST, ... AND ANOTHER ONE THAT FROM THE CONVEXITY OF THIS STRUCTURE, DISCOVERS IN A DETAILED AND REPETITIVE WAY, THE HORIZON OF THE SETTING SUN....

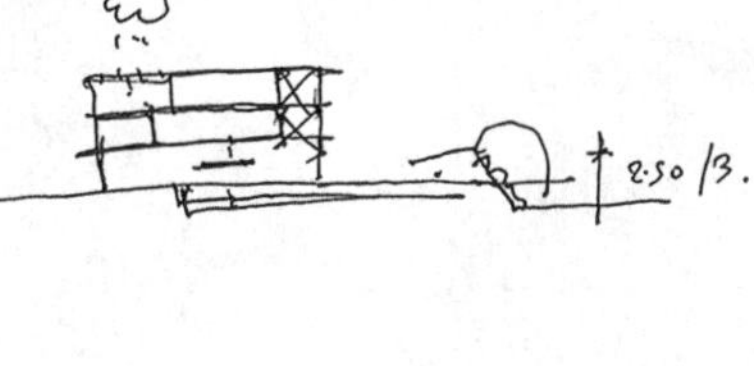

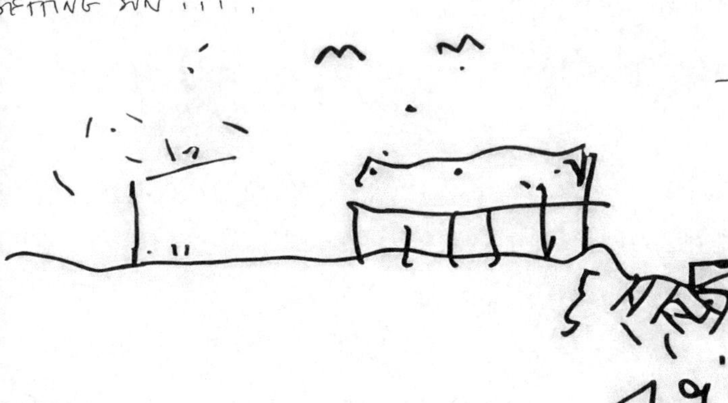

... WE UNDERSTAND ARCHITECTURE AS AN ELEMENT OF MEDIATION THAT ALLOWS OPTIMIZING AND RECONCILING THE ATTRIBUTES OF EACH PLACE, PROPOSING FROM THE DIFFERENT PROJECT PROCESSSES A COEXISTENCE THAT INTERACTS IN HARMONY WITH THE FOUR NATURAL ELEMENTS...

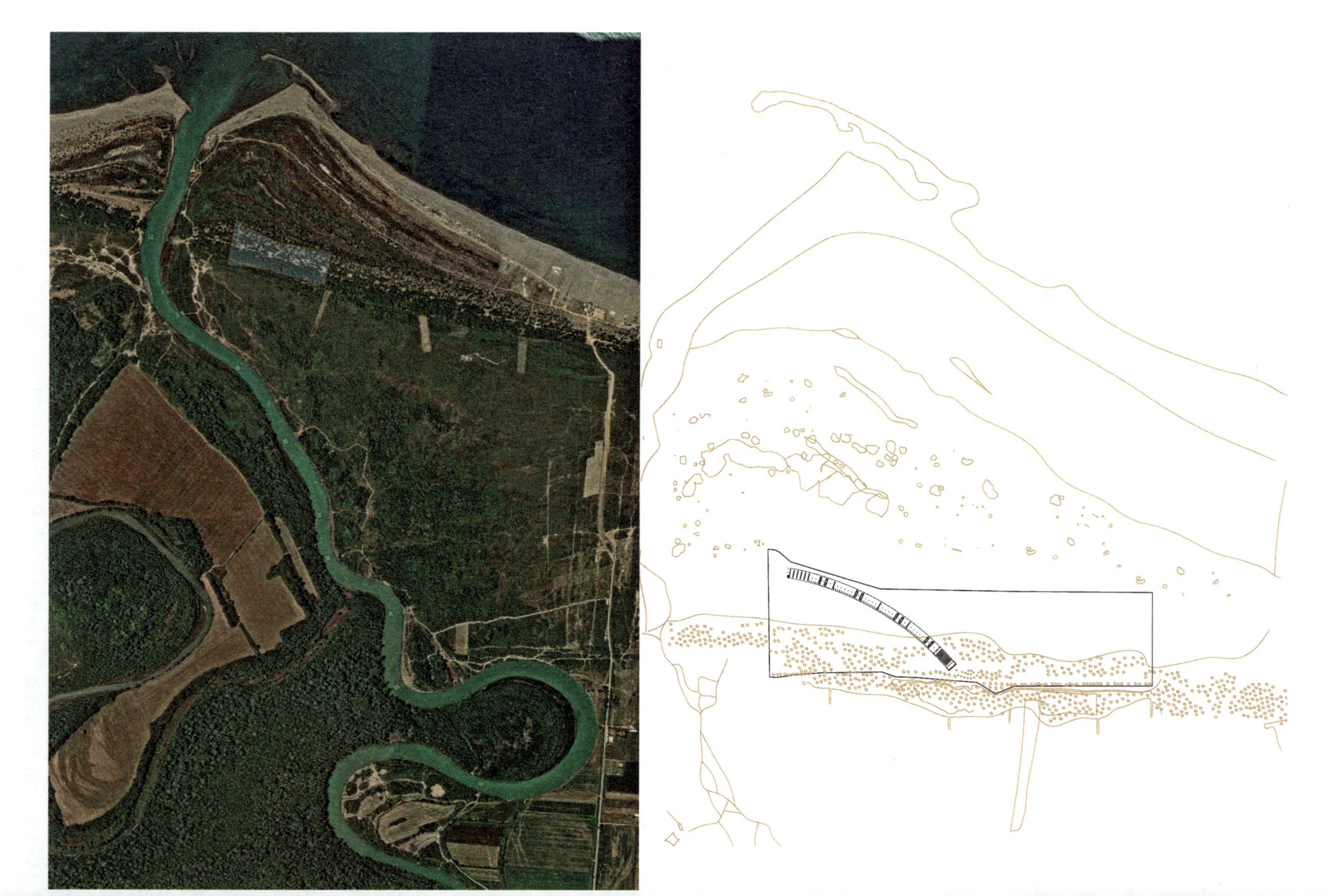

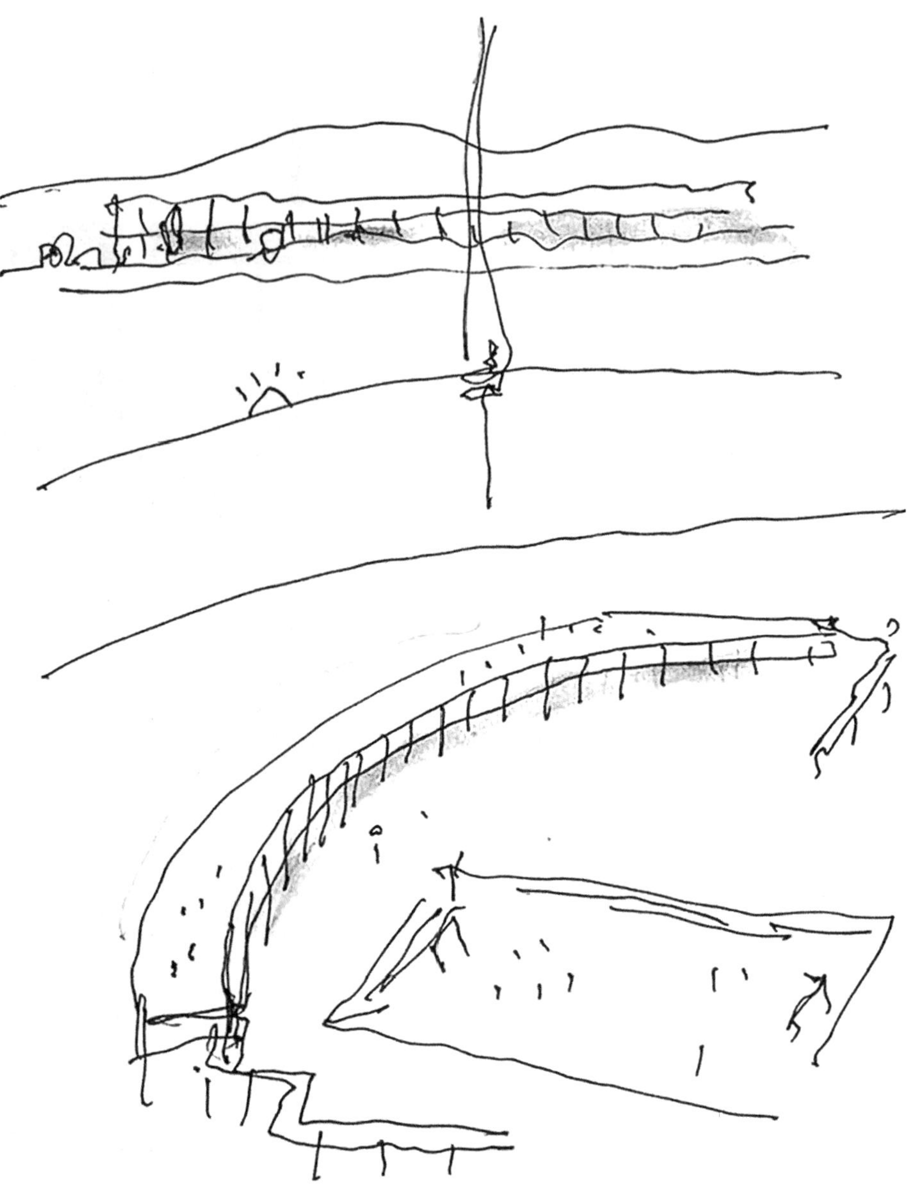

... IT IS NOT SO MUCH THE WORD ARCHITECTURE AS A NOUN THAT INTERESTS US, BUT THE VERB INHABIT BECAUSE IT IS WHAT GIVE IT MEANING. THIS IS HOW WE UNDERSTAND LIVING HUMAN, AS THAT WHICH DERIVES FROM EXPERIENCE AND IS NOT THE PRODUCT OF ONE THEORETICAL SPECULATION OR ANY PREVIOUS STRATEGY, AND THIS IS BECAUSE WE FEEL LIKE AN EXPERIENCE BORN TO BE LIVED AND SHARED FROM WITHIN, AND CONSEQUENTLY, DRIFTS INTO EMOTION AND THOUGHT

... THANKS TO THE DIFFERENT LOCAL TEAMS FOR THEIR GOOD WORK IN THIS NOT EASY CHALLENGE ....

16 0· 20

START	NAME PROJECT	LOCATION	DEVELOPER	PUBLIC/PRIVATE
2024	Lalëzit	Lalëzit Bay	Insifa 6 Vellezerit	Private
2024	Saranda 1	Saranda	Horizon Light Investments	Private
2024	Saranda 3	Saranda	S.E.G-Ahmeti	Private
2024	Durrës	Durrës	Egnatia Football Club	Private
2024	Gjergj Kastrioti School	Durrës		Public

NAME OFFICE

GG-LOOP

DATE
February 9, 2026

PLACE
Amsterdam, Netherlands

WORKING IN ALBANIA SINCE
2024

PRINCIPALS
Giacomo Garziano

ALBANIAN PARTNERS
A+ Architecture
Arthouse
Artreum Generation
Focus Architecture shpk
Impuls Architects
UNO architects
UNS architects
Urna Architects
X-Plan Studio

PROJECT TEAM
Rebaz Ali
Mohamed Abdelhady
Fabián Banuet
Matteo Bettoni
Bogdan Chipara
Daniele Colombati
Aykut Dağ
Edoardo Maria D'angelo
Esra Doğan
Mahdi Eghbali
Mohammad El-Ghandour
Hanieh Farhad
Hossam Hesham
Mafe Maldonado
Arek Seredyn

NICKNAME
"GG" (or "the Samurai")

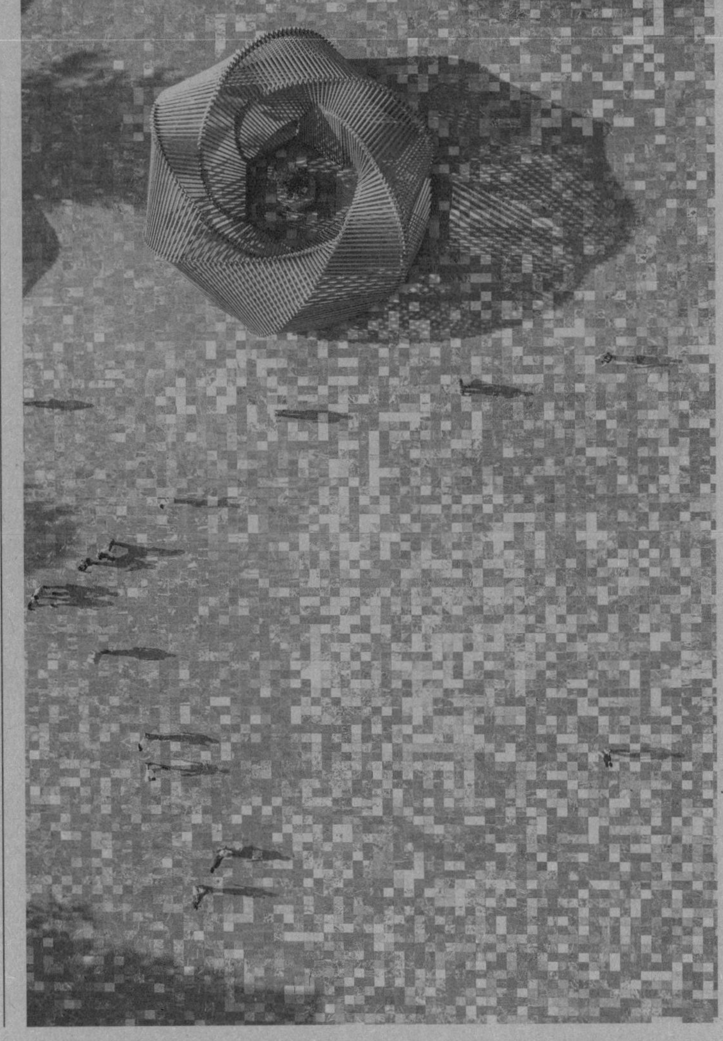

MAIN CONTEXT VS. ALBANIA

I mainly work internationally, across Europe and the Mediterranean, on projects that combine design ambition with real-world constraints. In Albania, the key difference is the level of direct dialogue and collaboration with local stakeholders and institutions. There is trust when you show seriousness and competence, and that creates room to bring experience from other contexts while staying anchored in local knowledge, regulations and construction realities. The fundamentals of the building process remain the same – coordination, clarity, quality – but the pace and the pragmatism can be noticeably different.

ORGANIZATION/GOAL/SETUP

Although GG-loop is relatively new in Albania, the ArchArmy has created a powerful platform for collaboration and exchange between local and international architects, with real cultural impact, as seen through initiatives like the Bread & Heart Festival. We organize our work through daily partnerships with Albanian architects, engineers and local stakeholders, bringing international experience while staying grounded in local knowledge and construction realities. Our goal is long-term, to contribute not only to private developments but increasingly to the public domain, which is why we engaged with themes like Faith Park. In parallel, we are developing a research track that maps the energy lines crossing the country, as an experimental tool to explore how landscape and heritage can inform planning and future development.

SETUP IN RELATION TO ALBANIAN PARTNER

The ArchArmy brings together expertise from different countries, so the collaboration naturally works in both directions. Local partners understand the Albanian context, needs and constraints far better than anyone arriving from abroad, and we learn a great deal from that knowledge.

In practice, we usually lead the conceptual phase to define a clear design direction and overall vision. Local architects then take a stronger role in the technical development and execution, since they navigate the local regulations, documentation and coordination on the ground. We stay closely involved throughout, supervising key steps and decisions to keep the original intent consistent while integrating the expertise of the local teams.

OPPORTUNITIES/CHALLENGES

Interestingly, the biggest opportunity and the biggest challenge are often the same. Albania is moving fast, and that creates room for ambition, experimentation and real impact. At the same time, the speed raises the bar for architects to bring structure, responsibility and long-term thinking into decisions that can otherwise become short-term. The core task is to bridge growth with a more sustainable, conscious approach to development, balancing urgency with care, and transformation with identity.

HOW TO INTEGRATE GREATER RESPONSIBILITY FOR QUALITY IN PROJECTS

Set clear, measurable quality standards from the start – environmental, durability and public-realm criteria – and then enforce them through transparent checkpoints and independent reviews from design to construction.

BALANCING QUALITY AND DENSITY/INVOLVING STAKEHOLDERS

The architect can lead by making quality and density measurable, not just aesthetic goals, and by turning them into a shared framework from the first concept onward. We use internal tools that track key design choices against projected performance and environmental footprint, and we are introducing this approach to clients and partners so decisions stay informed rather than purely market-driven.

Yes, the process can expand. If developers, local architects, engineers and authorities work with the same indicators and review moments, design integrity becomes a collective responsibility, not something the architect defends alone.

EXAMPLE/INSPIRATION

The Faith Park competition is probably the strongest example for me. The idea that a country can create a shared public space that acknowledges multiple religions, beliefs and traditions, without collapsing them into one narrative, is rare. It reflects something very specific about Albania: a lived culture of coexistence, and the courage to give it architectural form. If realized with care, it can become more than a project, it can be a lesson to the world about how space can hold difference with dignity.

ALBANIA'S LEGACY

"Albania is a magical place," my paternal uncle would often tell me upon returning from his humanitarian visits in the early 1990s. "The nature, the landscapes, the dignity and pride of the Albanian people are unmatched."

A RENAISSANCE ROOTED IN RESILIENCE

While Italian television showed a population struggling under hostile conditions and seeking refuge, my childish imagination held onto an almost fairy-tale image of a land just across the Adriatic from my native Puglia, inhabited by a special people.

Many of these people sought a more peaceful life in my country, in my region and in my hometown during the 1990s. Over time, many became friends, and this personal proximity kept feeding the idea of Albania as a place of natural beauty, culture and layered history.

In recent years, many of these friends have returned to their homeland because, they say, "the conditions are far better now!" And the tone in their voices has shifted from survival to possibility.

Despite this deep connection and interest, I did not visit Albania until relatively recently. What brought me here was work, the chance to contribute, with humility and discipline, to the intense architectural transformation the country is living through. Over the last two years, through several projects across Albania, that childhood image has become something more real, more complex and more demanding, a daily dialogue with places, people and constraints.

The change is felt immediately, even before the city, in the infrastructure, in the pace, in the confidence of movement.

But what has changed? Everything, and in some ways nothing.

1. Tirana Archaeological Museum

While wandering through the Tirana Archaeological Museum, I came across this bronze hand, a relic from the first to second century AD. It's intriguing to think that it was once used in the worship of Sabazius, a deity who bridged cultures from the Balkans to Anatolia, eventually becoming part of Roman religious practices. The hand, decorated with sacred symbols, was possibly carried on poles during processions or placed in sanctuaries, connecting people to their divine rituals.

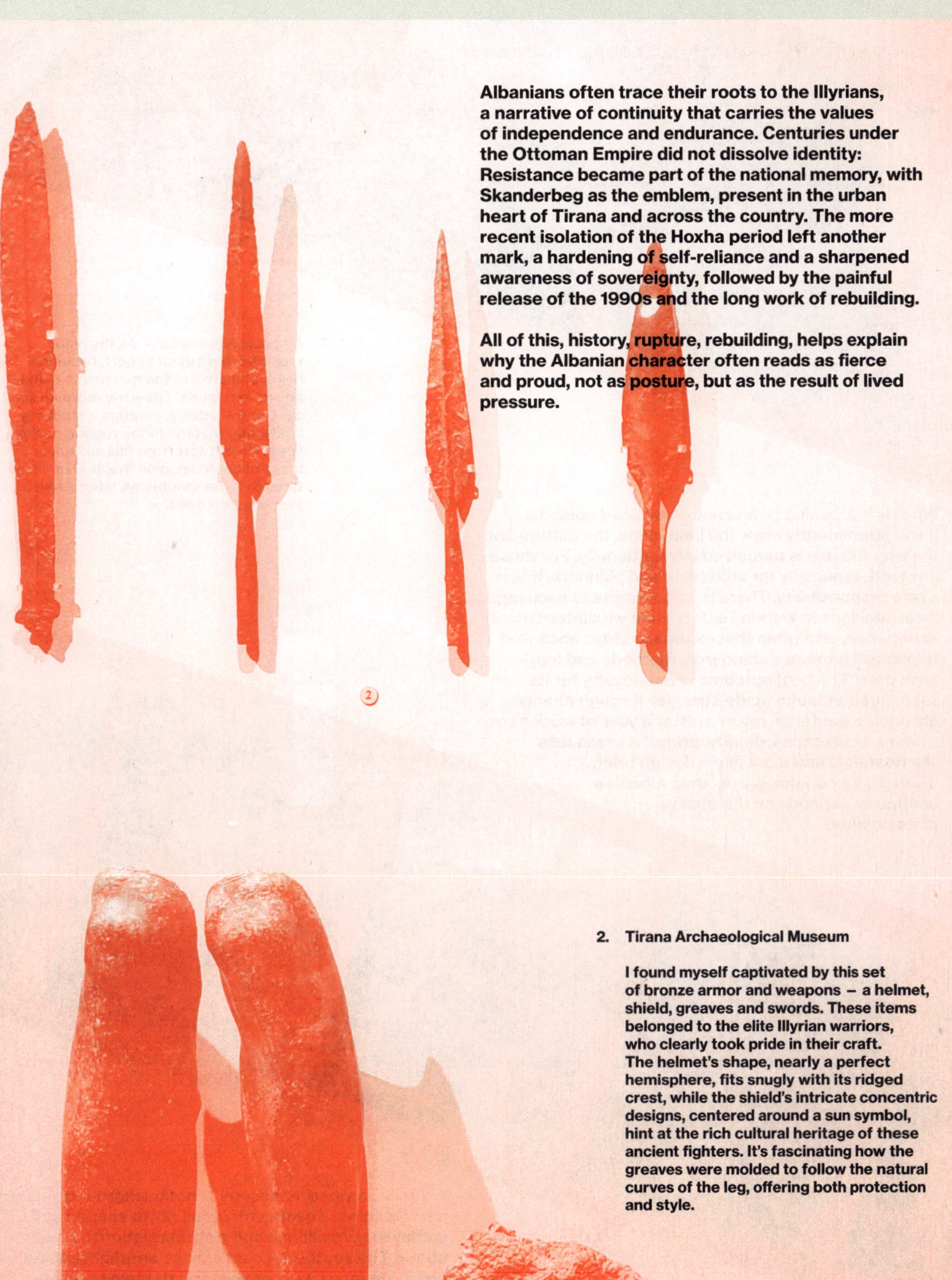

Albanians often trace their roots to the Illyrians, a narrative of continuity that carries the values of independence and endurance. Centuries under the Ottoman Empire did not dissolve identity: Resistance became part of the national memory, with Skanderbeg as the emblem, present in the urban heart of Tirana and across the country. The more recent isolation of the Hoxha period left another mark, a hardening of self-reliance and a sharpened awareness of sovereignty, followed by the painful release of the 1990s and the long work of rebuilding.

All of this, history, rupture, rebuilding, helps explain why the Albanian character often reads as fierce and proud, not as posture, but as the result of lived pressure.

2

2. Tirana Archaeological Museum

I found myself captivated by this set of bronze armor and weapons – a helmet, shield, greaves and swords. These items belonged to the elite Illyrian warriors, who clearly took pride in their craft. The helmet's shape, nearly a perfect hemisphere, fits snugly with its ridged crest, while the shield's intricate concentric designs, centered around a sun symbol, hint at the rich cultural heritage of these ancient fighters. It's fascinating how the greaves were molded to follow the natural curves of the leg, offering both protection and style.

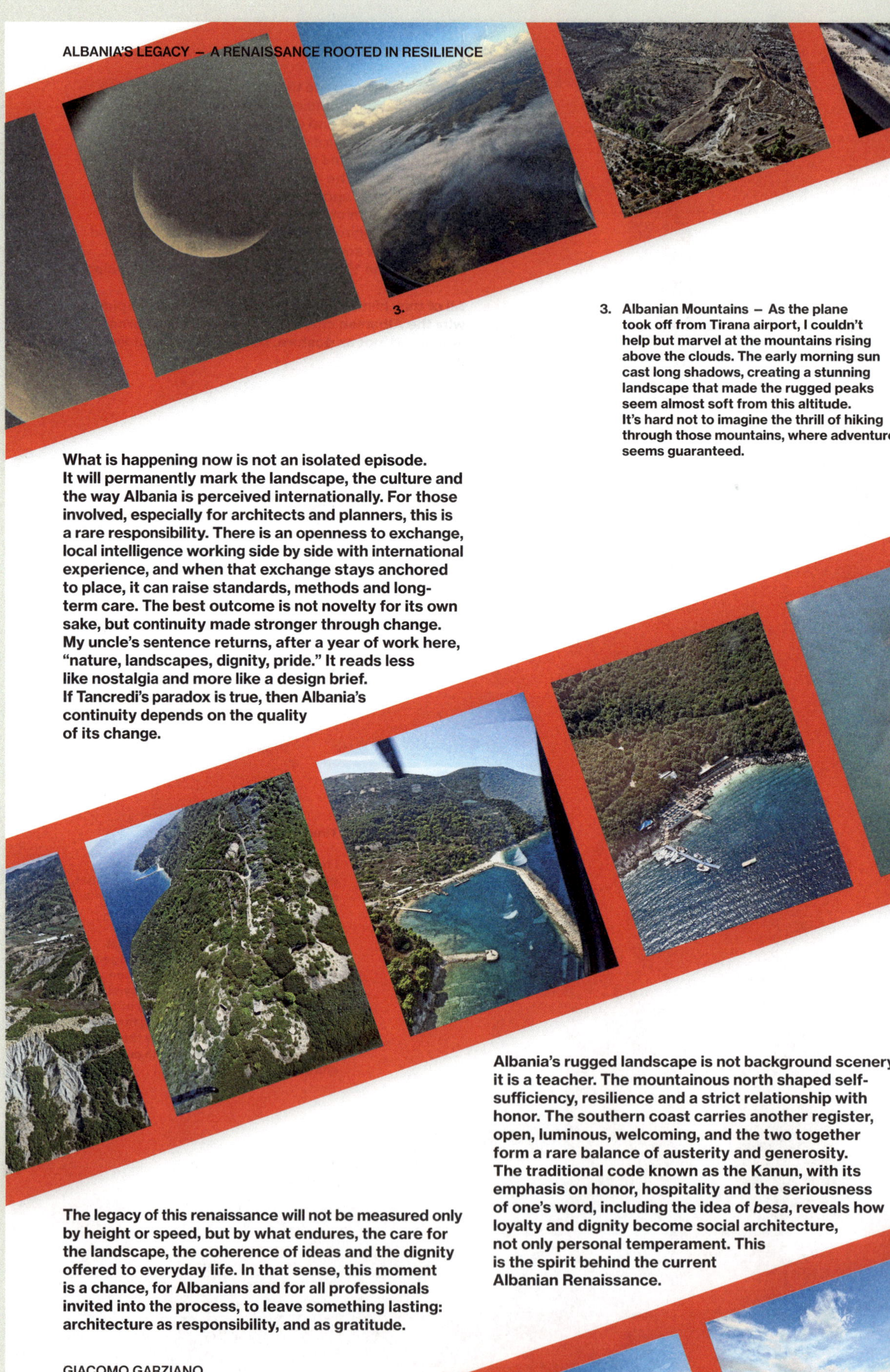

3\. Albanian Mountains – As the plane took off from Tirana airport, I couldn't help but marvel at the mountains rising above the clouds. The early morning sun cast long shadows, creating a stunning landscape that made the rugged peaks seem almost soft from this altitude. It's hard not to imagine the thrill of hiking through those mountains, where adventure seems guaranteed.

What is happening now is not an isolated episode. It will permanently mark the landscape, the culture and the way Albania is perceived internationally. For those involved, especially for architects and planners, this is a rare responsibility. There is an openness to exchange, local intelligence working side by side with international experience, and when that exchange stays anchored to place, it can raise standards, methods and long-term care. The best outcome is not novelty for its own sake, but continuity made stronger through change. My uncle's sentence returns, after a year of work here, "nature, landscapes, dignity, pride." It reads less like nostalgia and more like a design brief. If Tancredi's paradox is true, then Albania's continuity depends on the quality of its change.

Albania's rugged landscape is not background scenery, it is a teacher. The mountainous north shaped self-sufficiency, resilience and a strict relationship with honor. The southern coast carries another register, open, luminous, welcoming, and the two together form a rare balance of austerity and generosity. The traditional code known as the Kanun, with its emphasis on honor, hospitality and the seriousness of one's word, including the idea of *besa*, reveals how loyalty and dignity become social architecture, not only personal temperament. This is the spirit behind the current Albanian Renaissance.

The legacy of this renaissance will not be measured only by height or speed, but by what endures, the care for the landscape, the coherence of ideas and the dignity offered to everyday life. In that sense, this moment is a chance, for Albanians and for all professionals invited into the process, to leave something lasting: architecture as responsibility, and as gratitude.

GIACOMO GARZIANO

In daily collaboration, the same spirit from family stories reappears: pride without theater, determination without complaint, and a desire to earn a position in the world through action. This temperament feels shaped by history, but also by landscape, by the constant presence of mountains, by the memory of thresholds, crossings, isolation, return.

4. As I look at this almost decade-old photo, I can't help but wonder how different the city will look in another twenty years. It's a snapshot of a city in transition, evolving yet always connected to its natural surroundings.

5. Dajti Mountain – Even from the heart of Tirana, the silhouette of the surrounding mountains is ever-present, serving as a constant source of inspiration. I noticed this while walking along one of the city's main arteries, where our project Ora will stand; no matter which way you look, there's always a mountain standing tall in the background. It's fascinating to see how the city's architects have embraced this connection to nature, drawing on the landscape for their designs, ensuring that Tirana feels like a place where the natural world is never far away.

As Tancredi famously said in *The Leopard*, "If we want things to stay as they are, things will have to change." Albania is moving fast, yet the core is recognizable. In Tirana, the streets overflow into congested traffic, cafés and restaurants stay full, cranes rise around vast blue wrappings, almost Christo-like, temporary skins stretched over permanent ambition. The sound of the city is metropolitan and restless, but the genius loci still comes through, persistent, proud, unmistakably Albanian.

5.

4.

I arrived in Albania with an inherited image of a "magical place," and I found a nation moving fast, with the rare courage to reinvent itself without apologizing for its identity. The speed is real, the ambition is real, and so is the responsibility. Tancredi's paradox follows us here, continuity demands change, and change demands care.

For GG-loop, being part of this renaissance means working with a simple discipline:

listen to the genius loci before drawing;
let landscape set the rules of form;
grow projects with local intelligence, craft and partners;
use international know-how to raise standards, not volume;
design for decades, not for renders.

If Albania's transformation is to become heritage, then architecture must do more than stand out, it must stand up – for culture, for nature and for the people who will call these places home.

GIACOMO GARZIANO

References collected while working in Albania, 2024–2025.
They informed projects such as Incantyra, Kulshedra, Undaria, Centaurea, Abies.

AETHRA

**GG-loop pavilion created for the 2025 Bread & Heart Festival in Skanderbeg Square, Tirana.
Named after Aethra, archetype of refuge and care.
A sculptural shelter shaped as a spiral embrace, an homage to Albanian hospitality, echoing the cultural DNA of identity and belonging.**

START	NAME PROJECT	LOCATION	COMMISSIONER/CLIENT	PROGRAM	PUBLIC/PRIVATE	PHASE
2024	Ora*	Tirana	A&E development	Residential towers + commercial plinth + hotel	Private	Definitive design
2024	Gurana	Tirana	EBG	Residential master plan + commercial plinth		Preliminary design
2024	Centaurea*	Tirana	Bega-07	Residential master plan + commercial/ utilities building + landscape	Private	Definitive design
2024	Nautilus*	Kavaja	Artreum	5-star hotel + landscape	Private	Definitive design
2024	Abies*	Tirana	Mark-02	Residential tower + commercial plinth	Private	Preliminary design
2024	Kinomaja*	Tirana	Tre & co	Residential tower + commercial plinth	Private	Preliminary design
2024	Altisora*	Kavaja	Klajdi & RE	Hotel	Private	Preliminary design
2024	Kulshedra*	Vlora	ADRIATIK CENTER	Residential tower + commercial plinth + hotel	Private	Definitive design
2024	Siempre Viva*	Tirana	EB construction	Residential tower + commercial plinth	Private	Definitive design
2024	Doradilla*	Tirana	EB construction	Residential tower + commercial plinth	Private	Definitive design
2025	Undaria	Tirana	S. AG	Residential master plan	Private	Preliminary design
2025	Serendra	Shëngjin	Dimension Construction	Residential tower + hotel tower	Private	Preliminary design
2025	Viridia	Tirana	Bega-07	Residential building + commercial plinth	Private	Definitive design
2025	Lisindra	Tirana	Bega-07	Residential building + commercial plinth	Private	Definitive design
2025	Incantyra	Kavaja	Bonita Konstruksion	Hotel (Hilton)	Private	Definitive design
2025	Orphyria	Tirana	EB construction	Residential tower + commercial plinth	Private	Definitive design
2025	Aethra	Tirana	EB construction	Pavilion for 2025 Bread & Heart Festival	Private	Built
2025	Narea	Kavaja	Grand Brillant	Residential master plan + hotel tower + commercial plinth	Private	Definitive design
2025	Seastra	Kavaja	Grand Brillant	Residential master plan + commercial plinth	Private	Definitive design
2025	Valundra	Vlora		Landscape	Public	Preliminary design

NAME OFFICE

GROUPWORK

DATE	PLACE	WORKING IN ALBANIA SINCE
September 26, 2025	London, United Kingdom	2024

PRINCIPALS
Amin Taha
Alex Cotterill
Dominic Kacinskas
Nerissa Yeung

COLLABORATIONS
UNS architects
Focus Architecture
Webb Yates

ALBANIAN PARTNERS
AL-Point
Lorenc Gjikuria
Jani Zbogo
Ilir Trebicka

INTRODUCTION TO ALBANIA

GROUPWORK were invited to judge an architectural competition for the design of the Tirana Tower in 2024.

MAIN CONTEXT VS. ALBANIA

In all our work we aim to minimize embodied carbon by using sustainably sourced bio-mass materials. While the Albanian context shares similar construction challenges with much of Europe, one of its key differences lies in its potential for local stone and timber to be deployed structurally at scale, as both materials are in abundance and the construction industry offers a great openness to innovation.

ORGANIZATION/GOAL/SETUP

Our goal is to produce buildings and generous public spaces that are thoughtfully detailed, appropriately scaled and carbon negative. To ensure a low amount of embodied carbon, we are particularly focused on advancing the use of sustainably sourced structural stone and timber hybrid structures and have done so by establishing partnerships with universities, research bodies and forward-thinking suppliers. Over time, our setup in Albania has evolved from individual collaborations into longer-term relationships with industry and government partners.

SETUP IN RELATION TO ALBANIAN PARTNER

To ensure our proposals minimize embodied carbon – with sustainably sourced timber and stone specified – and to guarantee buildings can operate with low carbon emissions, we typically do not share design work with local partners. This allows us to protect the integrity of the carbon reduction strategy and material innovation.

OPPORTUNITIES/CHALLENGES

Working in Albania offers architects the opportunity to help shape both urban and rural landscapes in a context that values innovation and experimentation. At the same time, for us the country's rich biodiversity and cultural heritage present the challenge – and privilege – of designing in ways that are sensitive, sustainable and low-carbon, supporting growth while respecting and nurturing local traditions and ecosystems.

HOW TO INTEGRATE GREATER RESPONSIBILITY FOR QUALITY IN PROJECTS

As a practice we operate as an employee ownership trust, ensuring that architects, landscape architects and engineers are equal partners in decision-making. This structure reflects our belief in collective responsibility and fosters a collaborative environment that prioritizes both social and environmental considerations.

BALANCING QUALITY AND DENSITY/INVOLVING STAKEHOLDERS

To ensure neither design quality nor suitable density nor environmental considerations are compromised throughout the design and construction process, there should be a high level of collaboration between material suppliers, local authorities, the client body, and main and sub-contractors.

EXAMPLE/INSPIRATION

More so than contemporary developments, we draw particular inspiration from ancient settlements such as the village of Dhërmi in Vlora County, which was recorded in the late sixteenth century but inhabited since antiquity. We are inspired by its density and its buildings constructed with local load-bearing stone and timber, embodying both material efficiency and cultural heritage.

TOOLBOX ALBANIA FUTURE

Albania offers architects the opportunity to work in a context where innovation and tradition can work in tandem. Its natural resources – abundant stone and timber – provide a great toolbox for developing truly low-carbon, locally rooted architecture. The willingness of the Albanian construction industry to experiment and innovate allows us to rethink construction systems, expand the market for structural stone and timber, and create buildings that are carbon-negative while honoring local cultural practices and the environment.

DESIGN PHILOSOPHY: POETRY IN MATERIAL + STRUCTURE
Our buildings have earned multiple RIBA Regional and National Awards, with several short-listed for the RIBA Stirling Prize and the EU Mies van der Rohe Award. Our philosophy emphasizes maximizing the functions of all materials, whether structural, as internal or external finishes, or as active components of environmental control. We have a holistic approach to material and structure that goes beyond aesthetic considerations and efficiency, translating the cultural narrative embedded in the site heritage context while allowing for contemporary adaptation and reuse, and designing for negative embodied carbon in the life cycle of a building.

SUSTAINABILITY VISION: NEGATIVE AND LOW EMBODIED CARBON BUILDINGS
For more than twelve years our studio has been researching and building with sustainable construction methods. Over the past three years, together with the educational institutions Harvard, Yale, UCL and RCA, and the sustainability and civil engineers Arup, Buro Happold, Eight Versa and Webb Yates, we have been developing a carbon calculation tool, using the globally agreed method for measuring embodied carbon across a building's lifespan – DIN EN 15978.
Our approach includes the use of traditional, locally sourced and carbon-sequestrating materials such as structural stone and timber. In combination with modern methods of construction, our designs have proved to achieve a negative VE CO_2 footprint in materials and construction. GROUPWORK co-curated the New Stone Age exhibition at the Building Centre in 2020 and remains a long-term collaborator with the Design Museum's Future Observatory in educating about and promoting low-carbon construction. We are committed to meeting and exceeding the 2030 RIBA target for reducing operational energy demand and heating by enhancing the building's fabric to the greatest practical extent. By optimizing sun paths to control solar gain, maximizing daylight where necessary, super-insulating where appropriate and using solar chimneys to promote natural ventilation throughout the building. By significantly lowering operational energy requirements, we aim for renewable to not only meet but exceed the building's energy needs. Our dedication to these targets will extend the lifespan of our buildings and result in substantial long-term cost savings.

WORKING IN ALBANIA
We are delighted to contribute as part of the creative teams working to reimagine both the urban and the rural landscapes of Albania. This is a unique opportunity to engage with a country that embraces innovation and experimentation while maintaining a deep respect for its rich biodiversity and natural habitats. We are honored to play a role in shaping a low-carbon future that celebrates cultural heritage, nurtures the environment and fosters sustainable growth.

Farkë Lake, Tirana

Olympic pool, villas, apartments, towers, piazzas, gardens, gallery, retail, hotel and multiuse

-91,072,477 kg CO_2

Dhërmi, Vlora County

Villas, residential blocks, hotel, retail and club

-4,600,796 kg CO_2

Farkë Lake, Tirana

Farkë Lake, Tirana
2024
Public and private

A new district of Tirana composed of

villas
apartments
towers
piazzas
gardens
pools
hotel
retail and multiuse areas
and gallery spaces

bordering Farkë Lake, Tirana,
serving as an exemplar for sustainable,
ethical development.

Generous public piazzas
pathways
and pools
are ensconced in indigenous
vegetation.

Woodlands, piazzas, pools . . .

New neighborhoods,
natural extensions of Tirana's community,
are interspersed with planting and public spaces.

Buildings are strategically located to avoid as much excavation as possible and to benefit from the lakeside location and the biodiversity offered by the vertiginous hillsides.

. . . and micro-neighborhoods

Extensions of both Tirana
and the ground.

Thoughtfully scaled,
ethically designed,

buildings are built of the earth with
locally sourced timber and stone
in a range of colors and finishes.

Dhërmi, Vlora County

Dhërmi, Vlora County
2024
Public and private

Flora, forest paths

Built of the earth

Glimpsed from the Ionian Sea,
partly shrouded by cypress trees,
a cluster of buildings borders the Albanian Riviera.

Low-density construction
the use of local, natural materials
and energy-efficient systems
to balance real luxury with ecological responsibility.

Forest paths meander between the stone buildings,
positioned to avoid disturbing the indigenous
vegetation.

Public spaces, a piazza and beach club,
interspersed with generous gardens,
provide a space to meet before sailing off
or climbing the Ceraunian Mountains.

From the beach to the sky, natural materials such as stone and timber are used to construct classically proportioned and sensitively scaled architecture.

START	NAME PROJECT	LOCATION	DEVELOPER	ALBANIAN PARTNER	M²	PUBLIC/PRIVATE	PHASE
2024	Farkë Lake	Tirana	AL-Point	Ergen Agalliu	270,000 m²	Public/private	Planning stage
2024		Durrës		UNS architects	135,000 m²	Public/private	Planning stage
2024	Dhërmi	Vlora County		Focus Architecture	68,000 m²	Public/private	Planning stage
2025		Himara			20,000 m²	Public/private	Planning stage

NAME OFFICE

HERZOG & DE MEURON

DATE	PLACE	WORKING IN ALBANIA SINCE
December 2024	Basel, Switzerland	January 2024

PRINCIPALS

Jacques Herzog & Pierre de Meuron (Founding Partners)
Olga Bolshanina (Partner in Charge)
Simon Demeuse

CONSULTANTS

Schnetzer Puskas Ingenieure AG (Structural Engineering)
LOLA Landscape Architects (Landscape)
Friedli Facades (Façade Consultant)
LDK Consultants (MEP Consultant)
Lighting Planners Associates Inc. (Lighting Consultant)
Studio Sabine Marcelis (Artist)

PROJECT TEAM

Ilia Tsachev
Luke Willis
Roel Schiffers
Kyungmin Cho
Ciarán Grogan
Clara Rasines Mazo
Jinsu Park
Emanuel Sánchez Pinela
Mateusz Kiercz
Alessandro Musolino
Lorenzo Maccacaro
Yi Ji
Iwona Bogusławska
Travis Gerhardt
Iza Saelens
Eric Turner
GeunHo Min
Sarah McLaughlin Œnder

INTRODUCTION TO ALBANIA

Firstly, it's important to note that Switzerland is home to a large population of Albanians as well as people with Albanian heritage; it's said that Albanian is the second most common non-native language spoken in Switzerland, after English. We were introduced to Albanian culture before being introduced to Albania itself! However, we did not have a professional link to Albania until we were approached by the client through a mutual Basel connection, and our first official trip to Albania confirmed our decision to collaborate on this project.

MAIN CONTEXT VS. ALBANIA

We work across many typologies and countries, always beginning without preconceptions and prioritizing a deep understanding of local context. This approach, rooted in our work with ETH Studio Basel, informed the book *The Inevitable Specificity of Cities*, which examines cities such as Naples, Belgrade, Nairobi and Beirut.

Our portfolio spans scales from territorial studies to towers, but each project demands a high degree of specificity shaped by site, climate, culture and construction conditions. This results in projects without a fixed trademark – Tirana Tower being a clear example.

ORGANIZATION/GOAL/SETUP

When working outside of our own region, we typically work with a local architect – a so-called Executive Architect. While we lead the design of the project for the team, they advise us on codes, regulations, local practice, cultural specificities, from the first concept phase onward. In this specific case, the local architect is part of the client team, which is somewhat unusual.

SETUP IN RELATION TO LOCAL OFFICE

This setup allows us to work closely with the greater team, cultivating strong local relationships based on mutual trust and respect. Our work with the local architect is always a collaboration. We see it as an opportunity for knowledge building and exchange. We bring a lot of expertise to the table, and it is often a first-time experience for the local architects to work on a project of such scale and complexity. The learning process clearly goes in the other direction as well – when working in a new environment we need local expertise. The leveraging of each team member's strengths results in the best outcome for the project itself, the client, the city and its inhabitants.

OPPORTUNITIES/CHALLENGES

We don't know yet! Our approach begins with observing, learning and understanding the context – a process that never really ends. In Albania, we see growing opportunities for architects, a stronger emphasis on quality, and clear ambitions to develop Tirana and the country more broadly.

At the same time, many questions remain, as in any rapidly developing city: population, mobility, density, social mix and construction capacity. What is unmistakable, however, is the enthusiasm and ambition driving Tirana's transformation. This contagious energy, and the promise of a high-quality urban future, is what led us to take on this project as our first Albanian venture.

HOW TO INTEGRATE GREATER RESPONSIBILITY FOR QUALITY IN PROJECTS

The responsibility for quality is shared between architects, engineers, clients, politicians and the construction sector.

Architects and engineers need to design thoughtfully, but also in a simple and uncomplicated way, with an emphasis on quality, and with the people and public space in mind. Clients must make timely decisions and understand the balance between profit and quality – sometimes a small investment can give something huge back to the community and increase the quality of the project exponentially. The government has a responsibility to support the team in their tasks, while still maintaining the formal processes necessary to facilitate approvals; they can also request this commitment to quality and monitor it over time. The city oversees investing in social infrastructure, public transport, public space and a robust programming of these public buildings and public spaces over time to guarantee success. The construction sector has a responsibility to learn and evolve with each new opportunity, being curious about new technologies and more sustainable construction methods. The future of our cities depends on all of this and more – not the least of which would be economic and political stability.

BALANCING QUALITY AND DENSITY/INVOLVING STAKEHOLDERS

Normally, multiple stakeholders are in a dialogue to achieve the right balance. It's essential to have a comprehensive urban vision, such as a strategic plan or plan guide, which can be flexibly updated over time. While targeted developments can quickly rejuvenate specific city areas, maintaining a long-term perspective is crucial. This must include landscape, mobility, existing and future built environments, density, multifunctionality, social infrastructure and economic sustainability. Without a clear and communicated vision, balancing density and quality while providing guidance and rules is challenging, regardless of the client's expertise or good intentions.

Developing such a vision requires collaboration from various stakeholders, including politicians, urbanists, architects, landscape designers, mobility specialists, engineers, economists, sociologists, statisticians, and representatives of the population and future users.

EXAMPLE/INSPIRATION

We find the historical Boulevard to be an amazing public space. While the institutional programs predominate, the boulevard's green, inviting and lively atmosphere highlights the power of well-designed public areas. Tirana Tower will have a major public square at its base, with more public features as one moves up the towers, a sort of vertical extension of the boulevard. Given that the project is at the center of Tirana's New Boulevard, we aim for it to become a lively, well-used gathering spot and connector – a part of the city that enhances and fosters public life.

“Tirana is a city spanning between natural elements, where contrasts of public and private, historic and modern, grand and intimate seamlessly converge”

Pierre de Meuron, 2024

READING TIRANA

Urban green structure

Green Structure

Tirana is a city surrounded by green and mountains, embraced by natural reserves, water reservoirs and parks. This creates a profound visual and physical connection between nature and the urban fabric. The cityscape is woven together by boulevards lined with pine trees, planted streets, larger parks and pocket gardens. These green elements provide a rich diversity of inviting and shaded public spaces, essential for enhancing residents' quality of life and mitigating the effects of a warming climate. The project must focus on creating ample green, permeable and shaded spaces – accessible to all and designed with flexible layouts to encourage diverse activities, fostering both social interaction and environmental sustainability.

Neighborhoods and urban centers

Neighborhoods and Program

Tirana's urbanism is multi-nodal, with one predominant axis. Its urban fabric reflects the city's evolution through various historical periods, resulting in a rich diversity of architectural styles. Today, Tirana is a city in transformation, characterized by a contemporary clash and cohabitation between low-rise (historic) and high-rise (new) developments, alongside a dynamic mix of programs. This vibrant urban complexity is a defining characteristic of contemporary Tirana and has been a source of inspiration for our project.

READING TIRANA

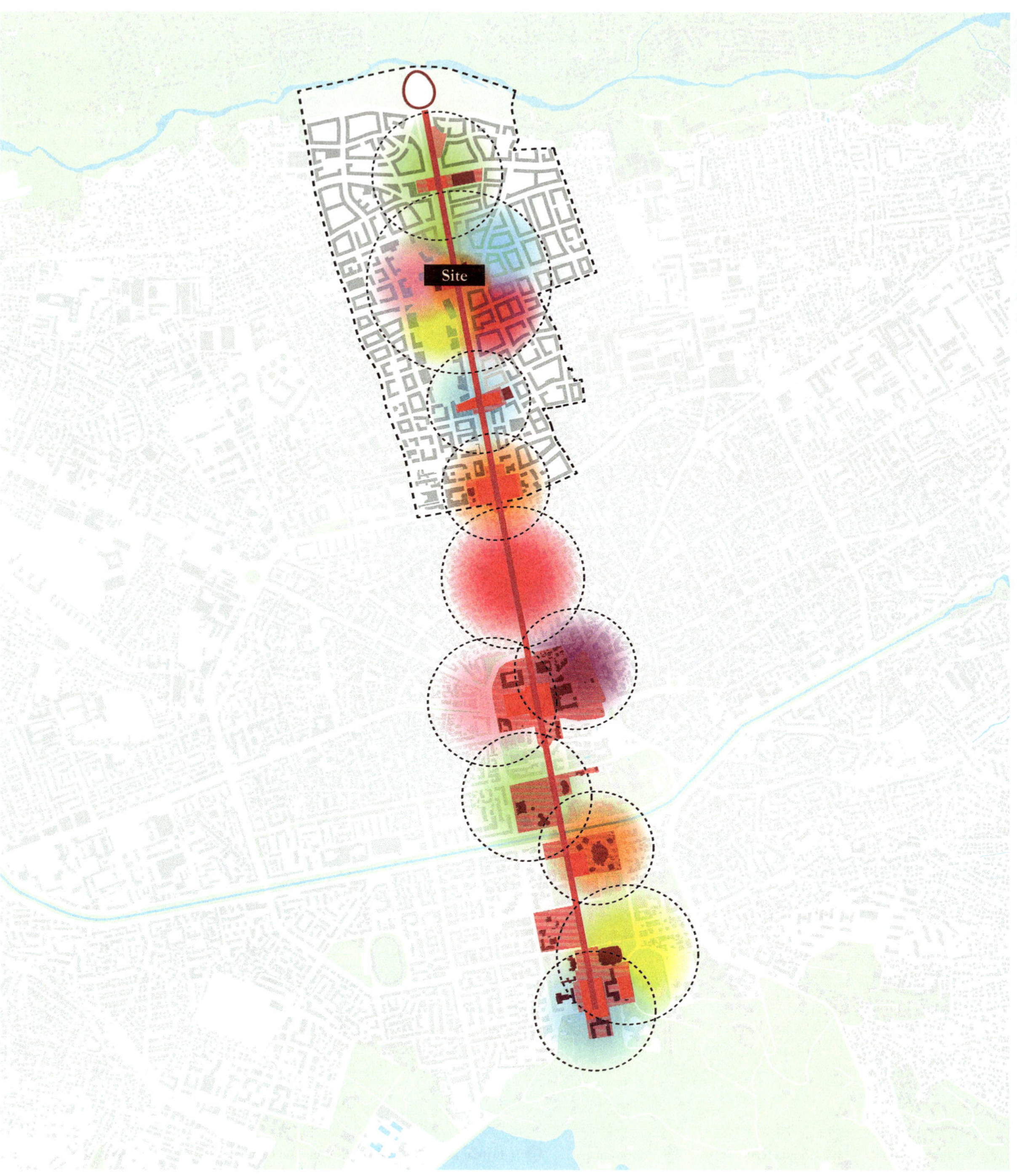

Main axis & urban plazas

Public Space

Tirana's historical boulevard, punctuated by a series of plazas, exemplifies the city's success in creating vibrant public spaces. Despite the predominantly institutional programs along the boulevard, its green, inviting and lively atmosphere highlights the power of well-designed public areas. New Boulevard, envisioned as a sequence of future plazas, offers a significant opportunity to build on this legacy. To ensure these plazas thrive, projects at these strategic locations must prioritize careful design and robust programming of buildings and functions. These elements are essential for activating and sustaining the vitality of public spaces, reinforcing their role as hubs of urban life.

SITE APPROACH

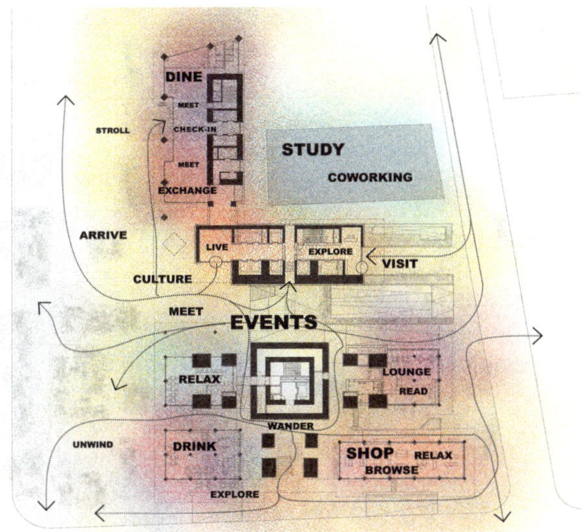

Permeable public space & program-activated ground level

Expanded public space & landscaped podium

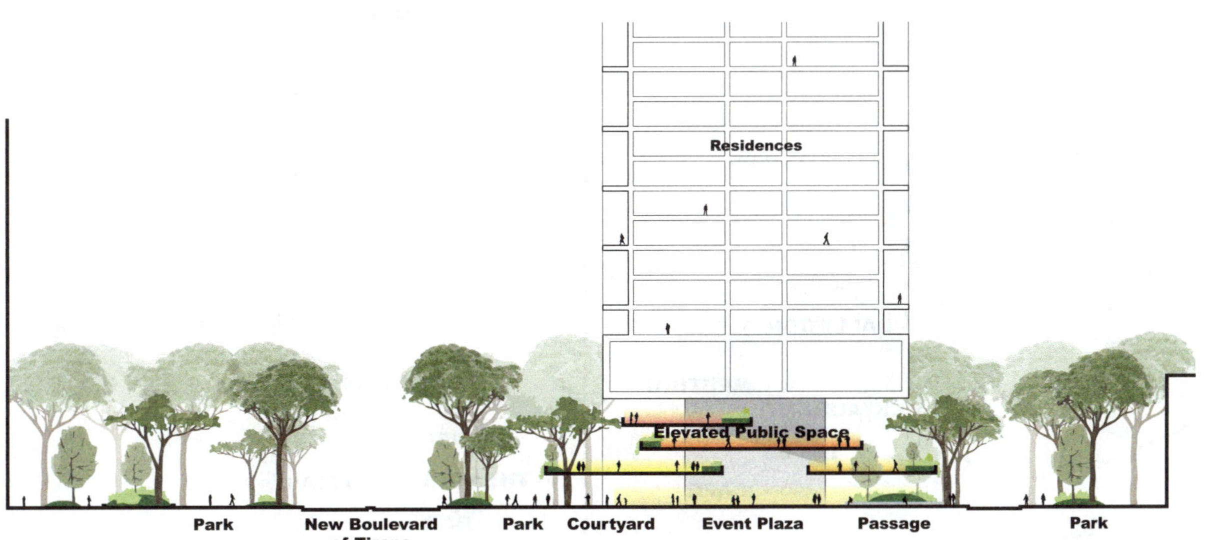

Seamless public space and landscaping throughout the site

Permeable Public Space

The concept of the project is to encourage and amplify the connective potential of the site. The residential and hotel program is split into two towers which are lifted from the ground, allowing urban activities to flow through the site and under the towers. The public ground floor thereby becomes a fully permeable public space, framed and activated by low-rise mixed-use buildings which define an urban datum at the pedestrian scale of the urban blocks along the boulevard. At the heart of the site a multipurpose public plaza will host various cultural events for the city and the neighborhood, such as concerts, dance performances, open-air cinema, fashion shows and book fairs, as well as everyday activities and pop-up markets.

ELEVATED PUBLIC SPACES

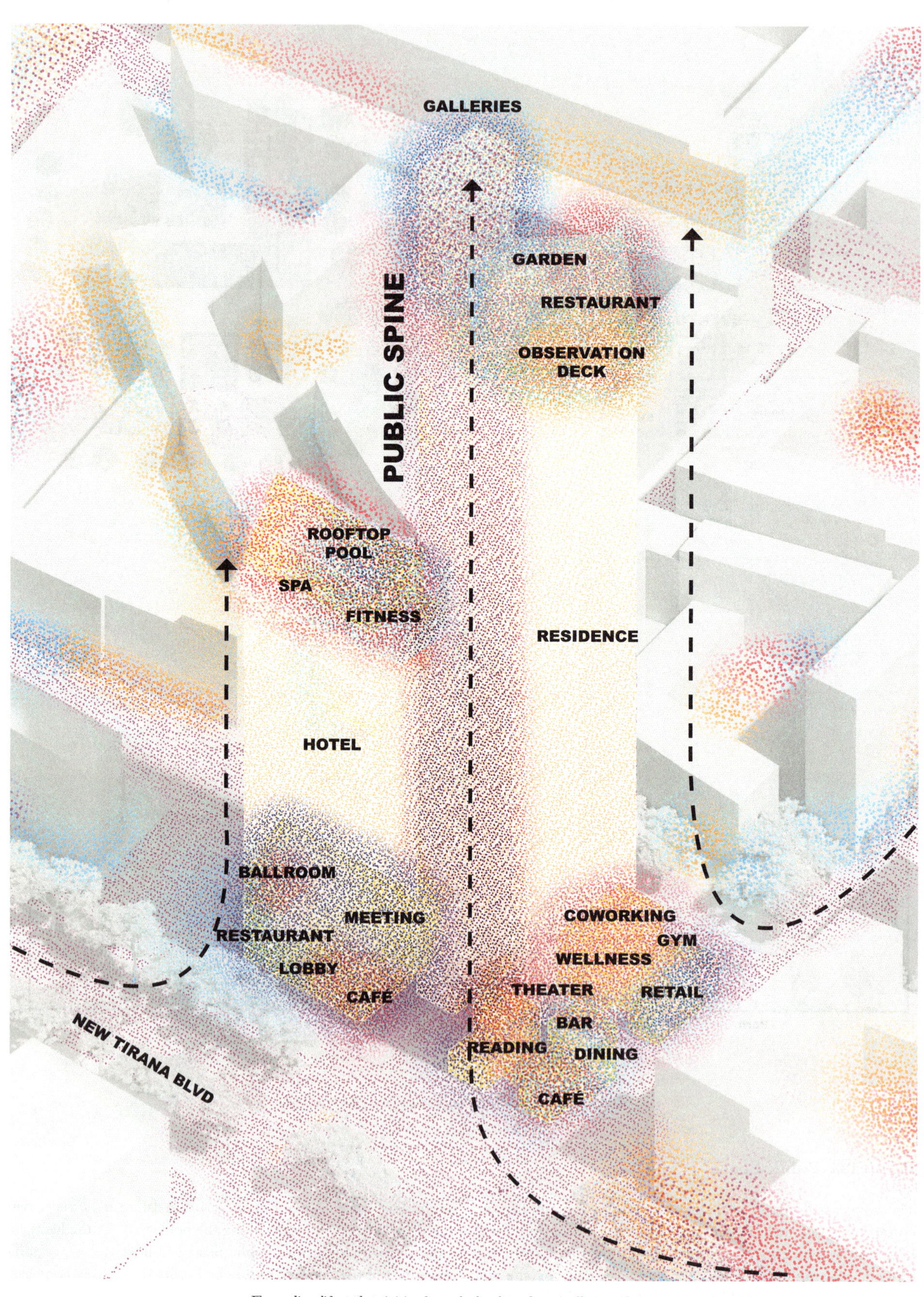

Extending life and activities from the boulevard vertically into the tower

Rooftop observation deck

Landscaped podium and public space

This cluster of vertical volumes addresses the urban scale of the boulevard,
while floating slabs at street level and the inhabited façade create architecture at the human scale

START	NAME PROJECT	LOCATION	DEVELOPER	PUBLIC/PRIVATE	PHASE
2024	Tirana Tower	New Boulevard, Tirana	KLAR	Private	End of schematic design, starting design development

NAME OFFICE

IBUKU STUDIO

DATE	PLACE	WORKING IN ALBANIA SINCE
September 2025	Bali, Indonesia	2025

PRINCIPAL
Elora Hardy

COLLABORATORS
Orion
Tekne Lab

MAIN CONTEXT VS. ALBANIA

My architectural roots were entirely in Bali, where we worked on bamboo innovation for over a decade. In the past five years, we've been invited to work on projects around the world, and have opened up to a broader palette of materials. In each new location, we approach materials as collaborators, exploring what is possible within the context of local sourcing, craftsmanship, technology and building codes.

In Albania, we're just beginning to understand the context and form, letting the site guide us before choosing materials that feel like they truly belong. This project brings new challenges for us – the size and density of 120 rooms on a 15,000-square-meter site is greater than we've done before – but it also feels familiar. The speed of development along the Albanian Riviera reminds us of the growth and increasing tourism in Bali, a story that has shaped our work for years. In Bali, we've woven green, artisanal visions of what the best future could look like into the rapid evolution of its architectural identity.

ORGANIZATION/GOAL/SETUP

For this project, we're collaborating with Tekne Lab to bring computational design into our process. Their tools complement our artisanal and conceptual strengths, allowing us to explore ideas quickly and stay flexible as the design evolves. With computational design, fluidity and change are built into the process rather than being something we have to fight against. This lets us lean into the naturally chaotic nature of ideation, where ideas grow, shift and reshape as new information is gained.

At the same time, we're holding onto what's tangible – using physical models and processes we developed to communicate with craftsmen and keep the project grounded in reality.

Many buildings today are conceived entirely in digital spaces, skipping the tangible and tactile. It's like skipping the womb if they were humans. I'm curious: How can we bring technology in as we conceive and birth a building that feels alive, rooted and real?

SETUP IN RELATION TO ALBANIAN PARTNER

We will be working with Orion's in-house architects from concept through completion. They've been immersed in this site for years now, planning and designing the residences next door, and they will be there to care for the details after we've wrapped out stages. We need balance between external creativity and internal stewardship.

OPPORTUNITIES/CHALLENGES

The opportunity here is connection – bringing Albania forward to the world and drawing people in to discover something they didn't realize they were missing. With PM Edi Rama's creative vision, there's a real energy around using architecture to inspire and lead. As a designer, I hear a strong conviction to create the right conditions for meaningful ideas to take root. It's rare to see this level of intention and opportunity.

HOW TO INTEGRATE GREATER RESPONSIBILITY FOR QUALITY IN PROJECTS

Design quality means holding on to the purpose as the project evolves. It's about remembering what the space should feel like and how it belongs to the larger story the design is telling.

It's easy to lose track when things get complicated, but when everyone – designers, collaborators and clients – stays connected to that purpose, the decisions feel aligned. That's how you keep the design meaningful, and how it feels like it truly belongs.

BALANCING QUALITY AND DENSITY/INVOLVING STAKEHOLDERS

An architect's responsibility is to act as the oracle – looking into the future and seeing how decisions made now will shape people's experience of a space. The trust we earn – and how well we honor it – shapes the outcome.

Balancing quality and density isn't just about numbers or efficiency. It's about imagining places where life feels real, where people naturally gather and connect, and then having everyone believe that. When people feel connected to the design, they help protect its integrity.

EXAMPLE/INSPIRATION

I want to learn more about Albania's deep history – its ancient language roots, its resilience and how its culture was shaped over centuries. Beyond the insular, traumatic century of its recent past, I'm curious about the stories that shaped the culture in the centuries before. How can these layers – its ancient settlements, fortresses and forgotten crafts – help us understand Albania today?

The Zekate House in Gjirokastër stands out. Its blend of defensive strength and domestic life reflects a balance of identity and adaptability. The way it embraces the steep terrain feels like a lesson in working with the land rather than against it.

Today, we may no longer need fortresses, but they still reassure us. They remind us of a resilience deeply woven into the identity of this place. It makes me wonder: How can we hold on to the identity of strength without needing to be defensive?

TOOLBOX ALBANIA FUTURE

Albania offers natural inspiration, cultural depth and openness to new ideas. The dramatic landscape at Dhërmi calls us to design with respect for its contours and story.

Beyond the physical setting, Albania's layered history – a story of resilience and transformation – offers lessons for shaping its future. It's a place where tradition and innovation don't compete – they strengthen each other. There's a sense of possibility here – a country calling for creativity as a way of expressing and shaping its identity. For an architect, this creates a rare opportunity to help express and shape a country's identity.

Belonging. Connection. Place

We design for a future that remembers we are part of nature.

Architecture is about connection –
between people, the land and the stories we share.

This is a conversation. A series of interlinked insights.
It's about curiosity and discovery.

We don't design things; we shape experiences.
It's about how what we sense and see can make us feel.
So let's ask how a place can invite us to belong.

Should it seem as though it was always meant to be there,
or can it also take us beyond?

Elora's mother, Penny Berton, danced in a bamboo geodesic dome built by Buckminster Fuller in Ubud, Bali, in 1980, the year before Elora was born. Bali captured her parents' hearts because it was a place where they could make real their imaginations. Two decades later they began innovating with bamboo.

Listen. Experience. Touch

We begin by listening – to ourselves, to each other
and to the land.

Belonging isn't just an idea;
it's something we feel in the body.

Beyond the way light filters through,
the way the path curves or the way a material makes you
want to reach out and touch it. What else?

We lean into curiosity. What stories from the past should
be carried forward here?
We ask what we want people to do here, and feel here.

Then we shape to be connected, grounded and alive.

There's something about the pebbles on the beach at Dhërmi. They graduate in size,
some as big as the palm of your hand, some ground by the sea into fine sand.

Uncover, Patience, Persistence

What if the site doesn't need to be conquered?
Rather than placing our ideas onto the land,
we ask what's already possible,
valuable, and what needs to be understood.

We must move beyond the seductive impulse
to make form for its own sake
and instead ask what wants to happen there.

How can we dive into the place?

The site leads, it is our first guide.
It is the landscape of the dream.

Dhërmi is between the mountains and the sea, we want both at once.

Trust, Tension, Life

Materials aren't tools –
they're collaborators, each with their
own voice, character and limits.
Our role is to listen and respond,
celebrating what they bring
while respecting their limits.

Working with bamboo has taught us
that when materials are coaxed
into doing something near their edge,
the structure feels alive.

There's almost a breath.

When we approach a building
we intuitively interpret its posture,
as we do with people.
There is tension, compression in the way
that load is distributed across it.
The pose and attitude signals who it is,
and suggests what can happen next.

A structure is part of life, part of time.

The bamboo grid shell of a structural model in process.

On the beach the water sorts the pebbles into gradients. On the land people have arranged the pebbles into a wall.
Under the earth, time is compressing pebbles into stone.

Evolution, Fluidity, Creativity

Ngurah creating a structural model.

Time also reframes. Craftsmanship and
technology aren't opposites.
Every model begins in human hands,
and technology extends
what those hands can create.

What we do with our hands began in our minds.
How can the future amplify artistry,
bridge precision and poetry?

We step forward, experimenting,
inevitably in response to tradition.
Computational tools let us iterate quickly,
but still we carry our humanity.

Design isn't about perfecting our vision –
it's a process where
we work to keep ideas alive.

Adaptability is at the heart of creation.
Can we keep pace with the pulse?

Hands and machines worked together to realize Tilem yoga at Alchemy Bali
and The Arc, the gymnasium at Green School Bali.

Dialogue, Balance

Here on Earth, there are always layers. Between all things, there is air or water – sometimes visible, always in motion.

At Dhërmi, clouds drape the sky, winds nudge the sea, echoes of water mark the sand, and the pebbles keep tumbling until they become sand.

This world is never static. Everything laps at everything else, shifting what is possible.

If we can design to discover rather than to impose, we create places where people can belong.

Growth

From process to design, shaping our first project.

Rooms are arranged like wave-swept pebbles.

Laneways between them recall the old hillside towns.

Along the terraces, each room sees the sea,
while staying low to the land.

The olive grove was here long before us,
so 120 reduced to 80 rooms.

At the core, a valley – not a paved street but
a green heart – branching into paths and laneways,
open to the mountains behind and the sea ahead.

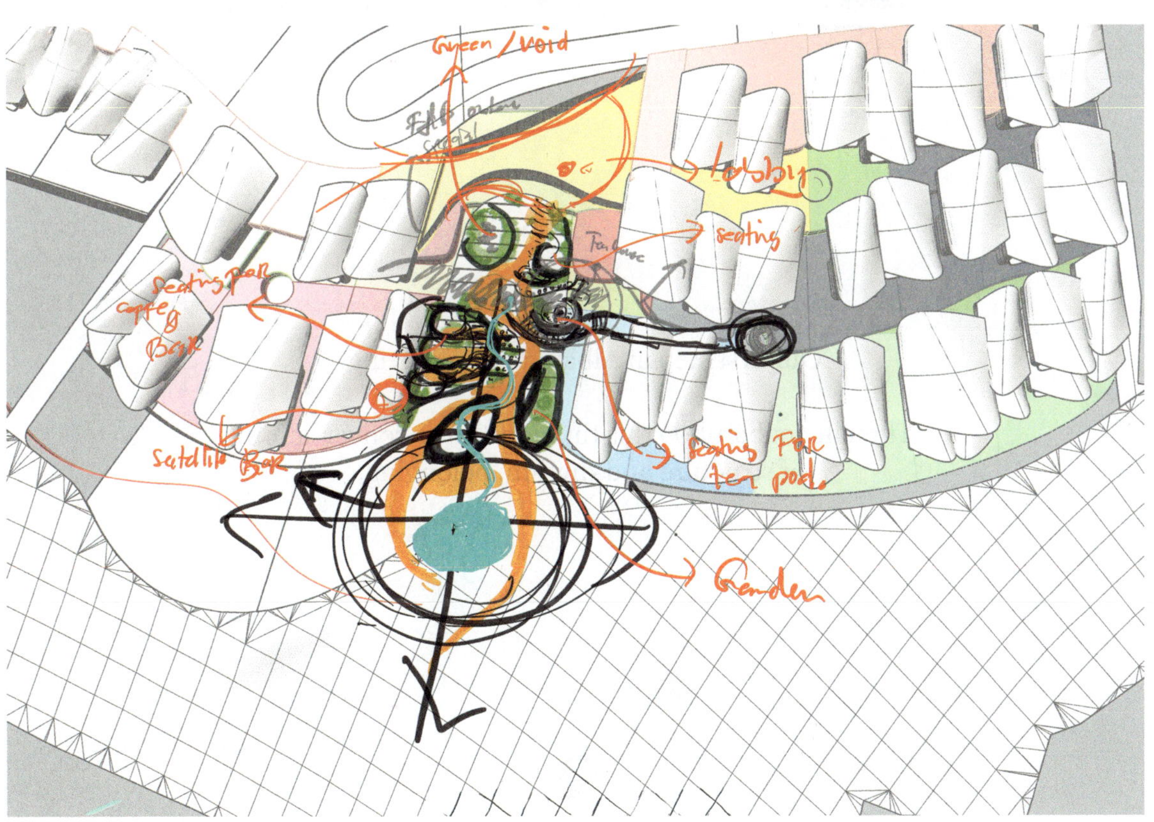

The first trace of the flow of life moving through the site – water, shade, gathering, retreat.

Our first step in Albania, still evolving.

Though not bamboo this time; the same conversation
of structure and rhythm, belonging.

LIST OF PROJECTS

START	NAME PROJECT	LOCATION	DEVELOPER	M²	PUBLIC/PRIVATE	PHASE
2025	Dhërmi Resort	Dhërmi	Orion	12,000 m²	Public	Concept design

NAME OFFICE

KENGO KUMA & ASSOCIATES

DATE
September 2025

PLACE
Tokyo, Japan

WORKING IN ALBANIA SINCE
2023

PRINCIPAL
Kengo Kuma

PROJECT TEAM

BUTRINT NATIONAL PARK VISITOR CENTER
Kengo Kuma
Anteo Sanada
Andrea Toccolini
Wai Yu Man
Sarah Wellesley
Natalia Karhaltseva
Orges Guga
Martina Volonte
Leo Tseng

ART GARDEN
Kengo Kuma
Anteo Sanada
Andrea Toccolini
Wai Yu Man
Natalia Karhaltseva
Sabina Shaiakmetova
Federico Stefanoni
Kotryina Bajorinaite

ALBANIAN PARTNERS

BUTRINT NATIONAL PARK VISITOR CENTER
CHWB (Local Architect)
Ervin Paci (Engineer)

ART GARDEN
SON Architects (Local Architect)
Dhimitri Papa (Engineer)

INTRODUCTION TO ALBANIA

Our office won the competition for designing the Butrint National Park Visitor Center in 2023.

MAIN CONTEXT VS. ALBANIA

Albania has a long history which dates back to the Byzantine and Roman times. I first saw Albania from a helicopter on the way to Butrint, which allowed me to see the land topography from the sky. I found it very exciting as most of the nature is untouched – nobody has added anything to the natural condition. In the contemporary world, especially Asia, it is very difficult to find a project in such "virgin land." It is a big opportunity for us to create, but at the same time, because the condition is so natural, naked and sensitive, we have to do our design carefully.

ORGANIZATION/GOAL/SETUP

In the twentieth century, the countryside was abandoned, and I think in the twenty-first century, architects should show a new model for the countryside, and this new life in the countryside should be based on a new type of economy. We hope to bring about this new type of economy in Albania through our architecture, to help find a solution for the burgeoning countryside.

SETUP IN RELATION TO LOCAL OFFICE

In our Albanian projects, we try to bring our expertise to the local architects, and we also try to learn from the local craftsmen. So we both teach and learn from each other.

OPPORTUNITIES/CHALLENGES

For our project in Butrint, as it is close to the Roman ruins, we should preserve the environment carefully. We don't want to destroy nature; we want to create architecture that can be in harmony with its neighbors and nature. We try to insert a new topography to the place, and this new topography will work with the original topography together in this beautiful natural setting where people can enjoy encountering the beautiful ocean, mountain and monuments together at this special point. Our architecture will serve as a bridge between nature and the artifact, as well as a bridge between history and contemporary culture.

EXAMPLE/INSPIRATION

I saw many projects in Tirana, and it is a unique place in the world as a field of experimentation. But more than that, I was inspired mostly by the beauty of nature in the countryside. There is real history left in the countryside and it is amazing and inspiring. I already got many hints from it, and we can bring this kind of hint to other projects in the world. To work with real history and real nature is a unique experience for us.

TOOLBOX ALBANIA FUTURE

As we sometimes use AI as a tool for design, combining AI and the local craftsmanship and local materials is a good encounter. We feel Albania can be the new platform for showing the possibility of AI plus natural materials.

Learning from the mountains and the sea

Albania is situated in an area that is the boundary between mountains and the sea.

These two natural environments of the mountains and the sea have enabled people to obtain various things and taught people a number of invaluable lessons.

The country of Japan, where I was born, is also situated between mountains and the sea.

Mountains protect us from a wide range of things and provide a link between us, and the sea is a place that connects us to various things and opens up an entire world of possibilities.

How to use these two kinds of places effectively is an important question.

The people in both Albania and Japan have continued to ponder this question over tens of thousands of years, and repeated a process of trial and error.

Today, Albania is attempting to open a new page with a strong new leader.

At a time which is a turning point in history, when the role served by architecture is very large, it is important to examine the form of this new age: the types of relationships which are being created with nature, the quality of these relationships, and the space and experiences that they provide to people.

The reason for this is that architecture gives us specific answers to all of these questions.

Butrint National Park Visitor Center

Connection between natural environments

This project represents an opportunity to establish new connections between the local communities and the expected archaeological site visitors.

The designated area for the visitor center is located in a nodal and strategic position: First, it represents a dense crossway between the trails that, starting from the mountain paths, connect to the wetlands on the Vivari Channel and the moorings on Lake Butrint; second, the panoramic location overlooks all the estuary and the lake.

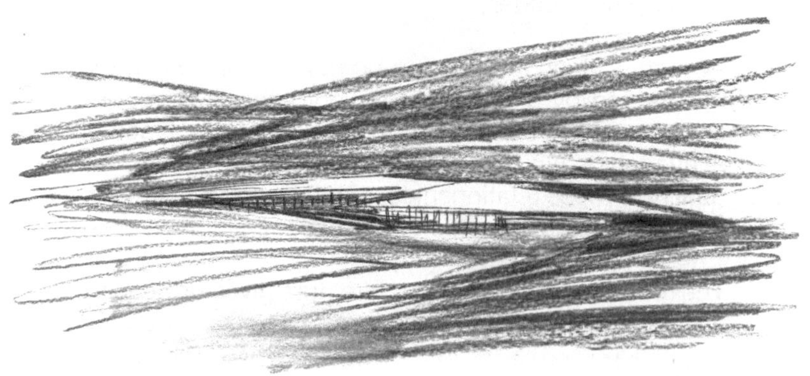

Mountain Bridge – Visitor Center, Butrint

Butrint National Park Visitor Center

Connection between natural environments

Bridge in the clouds, Hokusai

Mesi Bridge, Albania

A&D Visitor Center, Butrint

Butrint National Park Visitor Center

Connection between communities

Our proposal is to create two centers, one above that would act as a "mountain gate," welcoming the visitors and connecting them with the most natural part of the site, the second an "archaeological site gate" that connects the mooring on Butrint Lake to the one on Vivari Channel and creates a public space, an inclusive plaza where the local community and the visitors meet.

The goal is to create an architecture that is able to welcome visitors and enhance their experience while at the same time establishing a dialogue with the local inhabitants, creating new opportunities.

Entrance gate, Butrint

Butrint National Park Visitor Center

Connection between communities

Floating Bridge, Hokusai

Stone bridge, Gjirokastër

Archaeological gate, Butrint

Art Garden, Petrela

Connection between memories

This specific answer consists of making people feel at ease and giving people hope.

Therefore, turning points in history become an age of architecture. Furthermore, the age of transition in Albania is also the age of a considerable transition for the entire world.

In an age when a large transition is required because of a global environmental crisis, Albania can present the world with a new form of cities and architecture, and a model for the entire world.

I feel that having the opportunity to do work in Albania in this age is one of the happiest times in my life as an architect.

Art Garden, Petrela

Art Garden, Petrela

Connection between memories

Ryōan-ji, Engawa, Kyoto

Old bazaar, portico, Tirana

Covered art space, in between old and new, Petrela

Aerial view, Butrint

LIST OF PROJECTS

START	NAME PROJECT	LOCATION	DEVELOPER	PUBLIC/PRIVATE	PHASE
2023	Butrint National Park Visitor Center	Butrint	The Butrint Management Foundation	Public	Design development
2024	Art Garden	Petrela	The American Bank of Investment sha	Private	Under construction

NAME OFFICE

KUEHN MALVEZZI

DATE
December 2024

PLACE
Berlin, Germany

WORKING IN ALBANIA SINCE
2024

PRINCIPALS
Johannes Kuehn
Wilfried Kuehn
Simona Malvezzi

PROJECT TEAM
Konstanze Beelitz
Katarína Bendíková
David Butler
Maria Cacciapuoti
Robert Elert
Margherita Fanin
Karin Fendt
Alexander Garber
Janis Kaisinger
Jakob Naujack
Susie Ryu
Rafael Vindel
Wassily Walter
Johannes Wigand

PROJECT PARTNERS
Artech Studio, Tirana
Bollinger+Grohmann, Frankfurt
List, Paris
Adrian Paci, Milan
SON Architects, Tirana
Transsolar, Stuttgart
Varka Architecture, Tirana
Yellow Office, Milan

INTRODUCTION TO ALBANIA

We were first introduced to Albania through the competition for EXPO Albania. Soon after, we started working on three private realization projects for sites in Tirana.

MAIN CONTEXT VS. ALBANIA

Museums and public spaces are the focus of our practice in general, where we often work together with artists and curators. For the EXPO Albania competition we also collaborated with the Albanian artist Adrian Paci, and we appreciate the curatorial approach to architecture put forth by Prime Minister Edi Rama, who is curating Albania like a complex relational field of architecture, similar to an exhibition. This approach makes even private projects a part of public choices and directs the market dynamics when it comes to the public good.

ORGANIZATION/GOAL/SETUP

We appreciate the cooperation with local partners, and we nurture these connections. It is the local architects who must be empowered to become an authoritative voice on architecture in the near future, and we are interested in interacting with and participating in Albania's growing architectural sphere.

Although Kuehn Malvezzi work from Berlin and Paris, our projects are mostly elsewhere. Designing and building in Albania is no different in that it is not about foreignness, but about interaction and the richness in the relations we build.

SETUP IN RELATION TO ALBANIAN PARTNER

We are the lead architects, and the design responsibility is entrusted to us, as authorship is not something you can melt down. At the same time, we involve specialist planners such as engineers, landscape architects and climate engineers, as well as local architects, from the outset. We do site visits together, discuss choices, materials, building technologies, engineering, and the local offices, both architectural and technical, are crucial in client and political relations.

OPPORTUNITIES/CHALLENGES

In our work we have always opted for Curatorial Design as a principle which we pursue in all the projects we do. Curatorial choices are value choices. They appear undemocratic at times, because curatorial decisions are not based on representation, but on quality, or relations. However, when it comes to the democratically elected statesman as a curator, there is a rare sense of conflation of democratic political power and curatorial decision-making.

HOW TO INTEGRATE GREATER RESPONSIBILITY FOR QUALITY IN PROJECTS

Although most of the projects that we are currently working on in Albania are commercial, for us the challenge is to find a way to win public space out of them, be it through accessible and generous ground floor spaces, semipublic places like roof gardens and panorama terraces on higher floors, or other architectural typologies built into the projects.

That said, this negotiation and pressure from private clients is no different in Albania than elsewhere. It is the political alliance to counteract it that makes the difference.

BALANCING QUALITY AND DENSITY/INVOLVING STAKEHOLDERS

We believe we should question the dichotomy of quality and density as well as public and private, and rather think about this kind of in-between space, its uses and the enablement that people feel in those spaces. That can be done architecturally, and that is our task as architects. We work on those in-between moments or thresholds where in the ambiguities of space we have the chance to reach people where they are. Thus, quality can arise from density and public good from private investment as well. On the other hand, more stakeholders could also entail more political compromise which once again would be contrary to curatorial choice.

EXAMPLE/INSPIRATION

Skanderbeg Square by 51N4E was an inspiration to us long before we started working in Tirana. It demonstrates the importance and potential of public architecture beyond the built object.

TOOLBOX ALBANIA FUTURE

It is empowering for architects to work in Albania. Working closely together with the Territorial Development Agency and the government, rather than only with private clients, means that projects there are informed by the curatorial decisions described earlier. This could become a model for the future in other places if the quality produced in these years not only generates iconic buildings but also more outstanding public spaces. We are confident this is going to happen, given the experiences made so far and the architects involved.

CURATORIAL DESIGN

Pushing the boundaries of architecture as a discipline is a prerequisite for reflecting on and expanding our own practice, and one of the reasons why we firmly believe in collaboration. Working with artists and curators has been a central part of our work from the very beginning. We use strategies and tactics that have been transferred from the production and exhibition of art to architecture and apply them to the conceptual approach in our designs. From the outset, it has been just as important to think outside the box of our own discipline as it has been to exchange ideas with landscape architects, urban planners and specialists, especially when we are working in unfamiliar contexts, as is the case for us in Albania. Local partners at all levels are crucial as well.

Our entry for the EXPO Albania competition for Tirana in early 2024 was developed from the outset in close collaboration with the artist Adrian Paci, landscape architects YellowOffice, urban planners List, and local architects Varka. Landscape and contemporary art thus became the starting point for our design. The embedding of the exhibition grounds in the existing olive groves on-site formed the basis for an exhibition venue that was to grow out of the context of Farkë, at the interface between urban and rural areas in Tirana. With the aim of creating a cultural space open to both production and presentation, the idea of creating a shaded and ventilated outdoor area under a large canopy that extends over the entire plot was the guiding principle behind our design. A local environment is created alongside the large exhibition venues by placing a bazaar-like ring of dried clay brick pavilions underneath the canopy: places of hospitality with studios for artists-in-residence, workshops and coworking spaces. A space for mainstream culture and mass participation, but also a space where underground culture, research practice, experimental art and critical thinking can continuously develop and grow.

A space for large commercial events, but also a space for sophisticated practices and intimacy.

A space for international artists and young creatives, but also a friendly space for local families.

A space for modern technology and artificial intelligence, but also a space for nature and traditional craftsmanship.

An energy-efficient and highly efficient structure, planned together with the climate engineers from Transsolar and the structural engineers from Bollinger+Grohmann, thoroughly explored the development of sustainable exhibition venues.

The topics explored for the EXPO Albania competition, in terms of a multifaceted collaboration, a complex relationship with the existing context and a conscious climatic and structural approach to limiting the carbon footprint during both construction and use, form the basis for the following three projects for Tirana, which we have developed with various partners and teams and which are to be realized from 2025.

VASIL SHANTO TOWER

PORTICO
The three-story portico marks the hotel entrance, but above all expresses the public vocation of this location in the city. By opening up the ground floor to the street as an active space for urban life and as a café terrace that welcomes both guests and locals, a place is created for public events, art installations and performances as well as informal encounters.

EXOSKELETON
The glass skin, which climatically separates the interior from the exterior, sits well behind the exoskeleton finished with polished terrazzo, protecting it from sunlight and heat gain. The façade, which grows in width towards the top, forms an ever-increasing brise-soleil that protects the glass volume behind it.

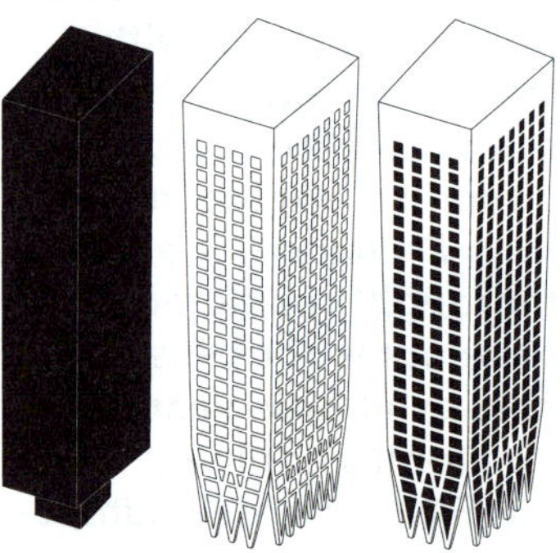

SKIN EXOSKELETON

Above, on three floors, a series of work and conference rooms as well as wellness and spa areas form the public base of the Vasil Shanto Tower up to the 6th floor. Residential flats, each with their own corner loggia, follow from the 6th to the 12th floor. The concrete structure of the Vasil Shanto Tower forms an exoskeleton that reveals its tectonics and resists the layered façade of a curtain wall by placing its skin behind the structure.

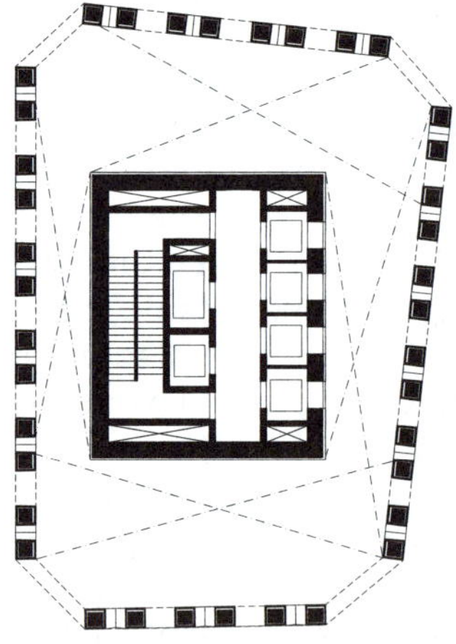

The Vasil Shanto Tower, which renews and updates the legacy of the Hotel Classic in Tirana, will be an element of density in the rapid development of the city.
A six-story base is dedicated to the public and semipublic program. The spacious hotel and residential lobby is part of the portico.

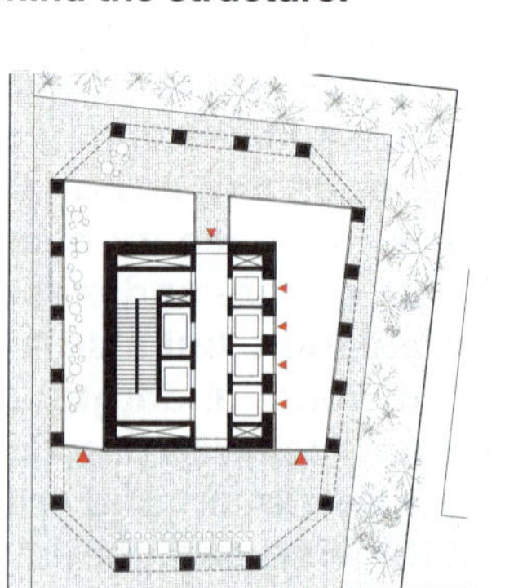

The structure on top serves as a publicly accessible space connected to the loggia on the ground floor. The rooftop restaurant and bar provide sweeping panoramic views of the surrounding landscape and cityscape.

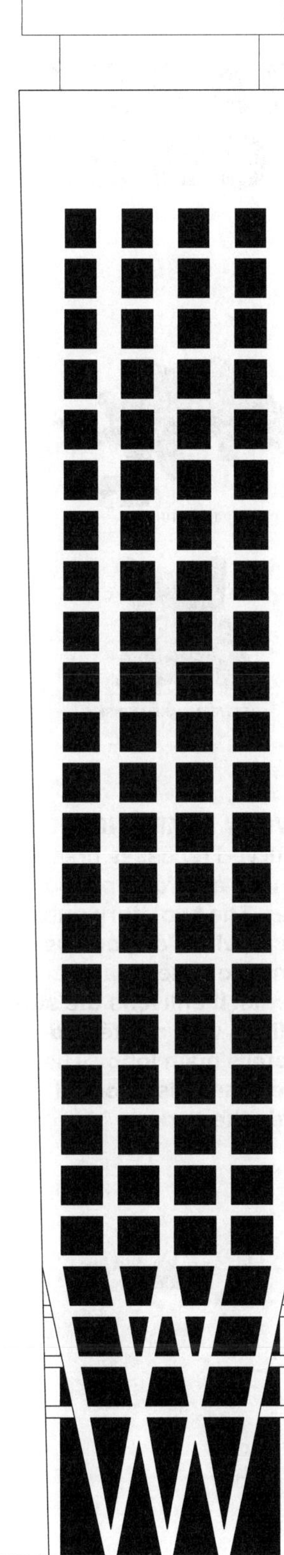

GARDA TOWER

The Garda Tower is a new hinge between the landscape and the city. Situated at the interface between the university district and Parku i Tiranës, the new tower is a high point from which the urban landscape becomes visible. A slender new player in Tirana's skyline, its figure is achieved through the interplay of geometric structure and flowing form.

LAKE TIRANA

BETWEEN LAKE AND SKY

The public space continues on the 26th floor with a sky bar located in the overlapping area between the crown-like glass volume and the mineral façade structure. As a striking feature of the building, the gastronomic floor with its outdoor terraces offers sweeping views of the city.

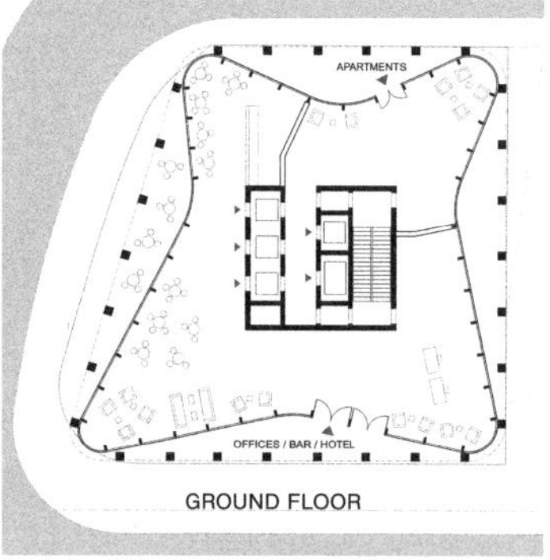

GROUND FLOOR

BETWEEN LAKE AND SKY

The curved recesses create entrances and form public loggias. The two-story public plinth provides a spacious entrance for guests and residents. It enlivens the surroundings with a café and the hotel's main lobby. The main entrance is oriented towards the park.

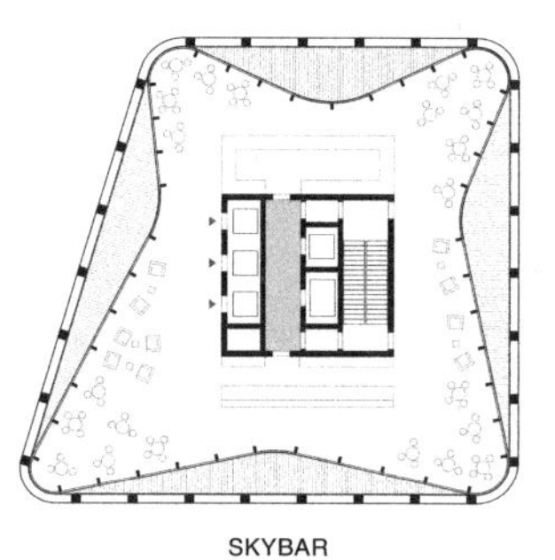

SKYBAR

The tower forms an ensemble with the newly planned buildings opposite, creating a spatial field between them. The relation between urban space and building is expressed as a spatial sculpture: A mineral structure and a curved glass volume intersect. Together, the two elements create structured open spaces that foster an active city life.

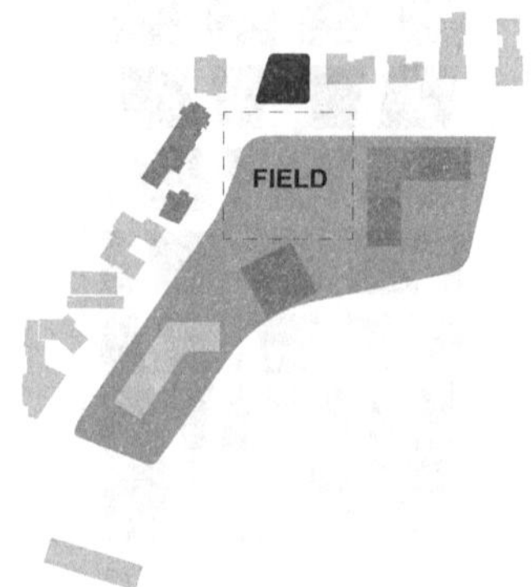

Above this, six hotel floors complete the project. The load-bearing structure becomes a visible façade element, creating a noticeable but serene elevation with generous loggias for all apartments and large windows to maximize natural light and ventilation.

LIQENI I THATË

From the city's edge in the foothills, the site overlooks the lake in the foreground and offers an expansive panorama in the distance. It combines hotel, retail and residential space and connects the rolling hills with the lakefront. The program is organized into three buildings connected by a base, creating a sheltered open space where the buildings, inhabitants and landscape come together.

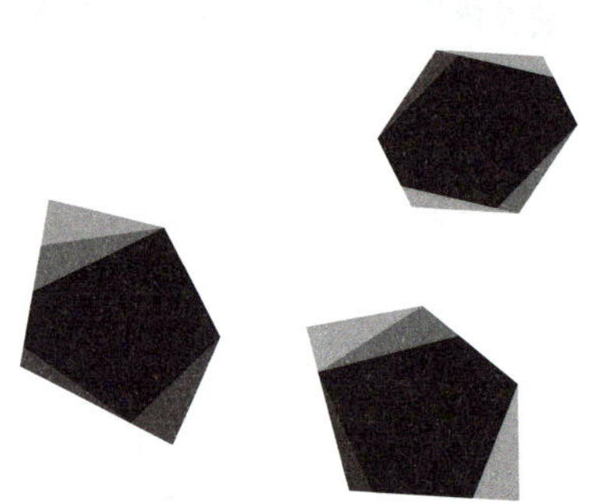

The courtyard of the new buildings frames a secret garden constellated with a green island of trees and underwood vegetation. The goal is to create an open-air room, conceived as a microclimatic garden where residents and hotel users can gather, surrounded by plants, in a suspended moment of relaxation.

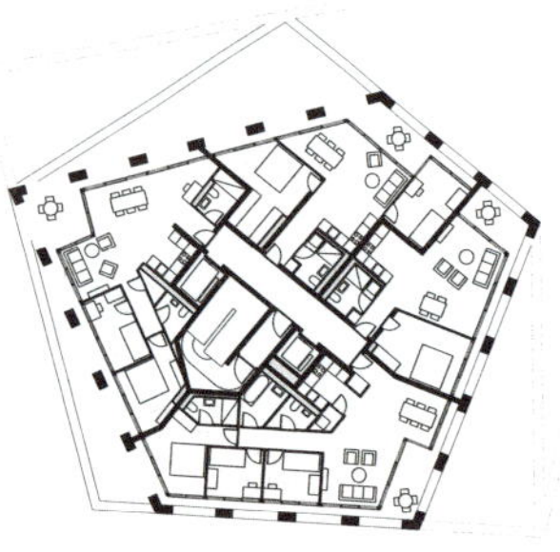

SOUTH BUILDING, 10TH FLOOR

Buildings and green spaces naturally link the site's topography, creating a harmonious transition of landscapes and livable spaces. From the lake, the waterfront plaza opens towards the water landscape through a theater of steps and terraces, creating a peaceful place to rest and enjoy the view.

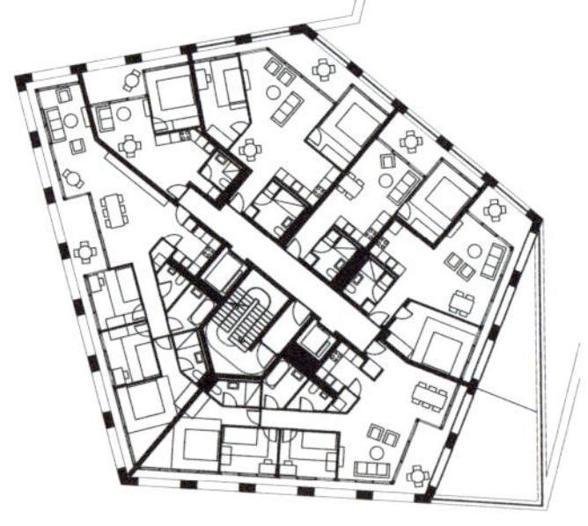

SOUTH BUILDING, 7TH FLOOR

The polygonal volumes rise from the landscape and gradually taper upwards through triangular recesses that form terraces. These recesses and varying heights allow all three buildings to offer unobstructed views of the lake, while creating different silhouettes from each angle. The landscape project acts as a sequence of scenarios that leads from the wooded hills directly to the water landscape of the lake.

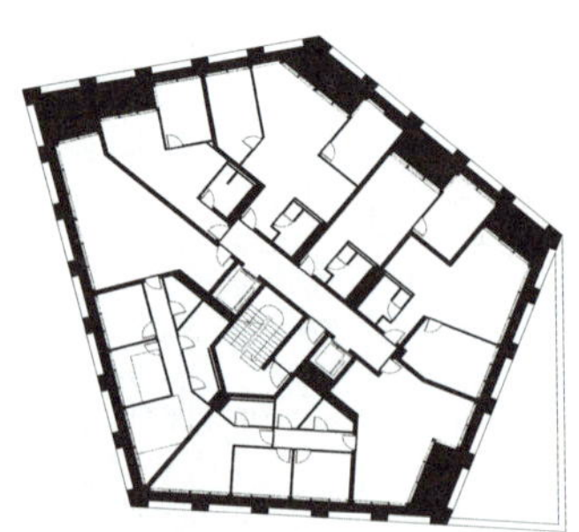

SOUTH BUILDING, LOGGIAS

From the secret garden begins an ascent to the hill, where a belvedere is reachable through a set of wooded terraces crossable by climbing small stairs.
On the roofs, a green filter of shrubs and herbaceous plants delimits the private space of the residential buildings from the public space of the hotel.

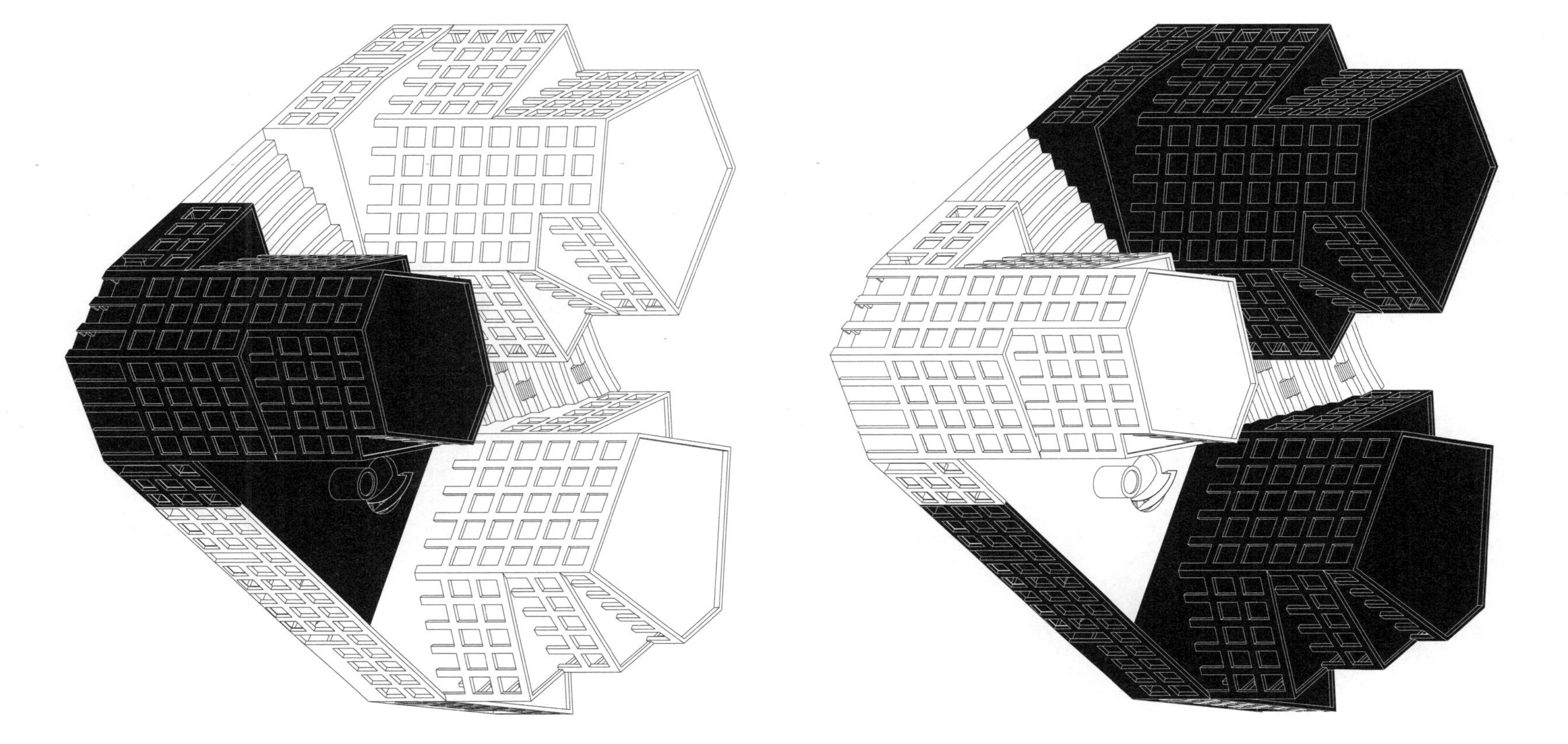

EXPO ALBANIA, VISUALIZATION

START	NAME PROJECT	LOCATION	DEVELOPER	PUBLIC/PRIVATE	PHASE
2024	EXPO Albania	Tirana	Albanian government	Public	Competition
2024	Rozafa Hotel Tower	Shkodra	Rozafa A Ltd	Private	Competition
2024	Vasil Shanto Tower	Tirana	ITAL Project shpk	Private	Design development
2024	Garda Tower	Tirana		Private	Design development
2024	Liqeni i Thatë	Tirana		Private	Design development

NAME OFFICE

LINA GHOTMEH—ARCHITECTURE

DATE
February 4, 2026

PLACE
Paris, France

WORKING IN ALBANIA SINCE
2024

PRINCIPAL
Lina Ghotmeh

ALBANIAN PARTNERS
pOint arkitekture
Ardian Haxhiu Architects
Dhimitri Papa civil engineering

PROJECT TEAM
Alexandru Musteata
Marco Falasca
Michela Garau
Nicola Alessandroni
Nour Karray
Valère Hoguait

OPPORTUNITIES/CHALLENGES

I think that the processes of design, development and construction are not conventional. There are many new developers in the field. It is both an opportunity to innovate and a challenge sometimes in transmitting an architecture culture.

HOW TO INTEGRATE GREATER RESPONSIBILITY FOR QUALITY IN PROJECTS

I think taking time in the design process and ensuring there is urban and social relevance to the project in regards to the future of the cities where projects are happening.

EXAMPLE/INSPIRATION

What inspires me most in Albania is nature, culture. The history of the country and the multiple facets of traditional/vernacular architecture.

I also find Prime Minister Edi Rama to be of great inspiration and drive for art and architecture in Albania.

TOOLBOX ALBANIA FUTURE

Inventiveness, responsibility, timeliness.

Vlora – Mixed-Use Building

2024
Vlora, Albania

Towers in architecture go beyond mere tall structures; they combine functionality, symbolism and innovation. Historically, they served as landmarks and fortifications, while today they reflect the power and ambition of cities.

These buildings maximize space in densely populated urban areas and symbolize humanity's quest for innovation. Culturally, towers can symbolize the connection between the earthly and the divine, or represent power. They bear witness to a city's history and periods of prosperity.

Furthermore, the construction of towers raises questions of sustainable urban planning, integrating ecological elements and smart technologies. In short, towers are witnesses to our evolution, expressions of creativity and symbols of our aspirations.

Vlora
—
It is one of the most significant cities of southern Albania and the region of Labëria, which is traditionally noted for its culture, traditions and folklore.
—

—

Vlora's rich religious history echoes centuries of cultural exchange and resilience across diverse faiths.

—

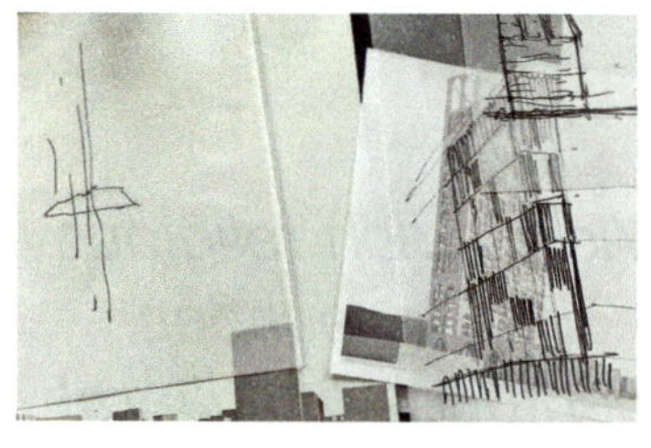

Vlora is geographically and culturally encompassed in the historical region of Labëria, extending from the Albanian Adriatic and Ionian Sea coasts to the mountainous region of southeastern Albania.

—
The city offers a variety of residential areas starting at the coast and going inland. The area is suitable for industrial and environmentally friendly development.
—

—

Vlora is a vibrant coastal city with a well-developed and modern housing infrastructure.

—

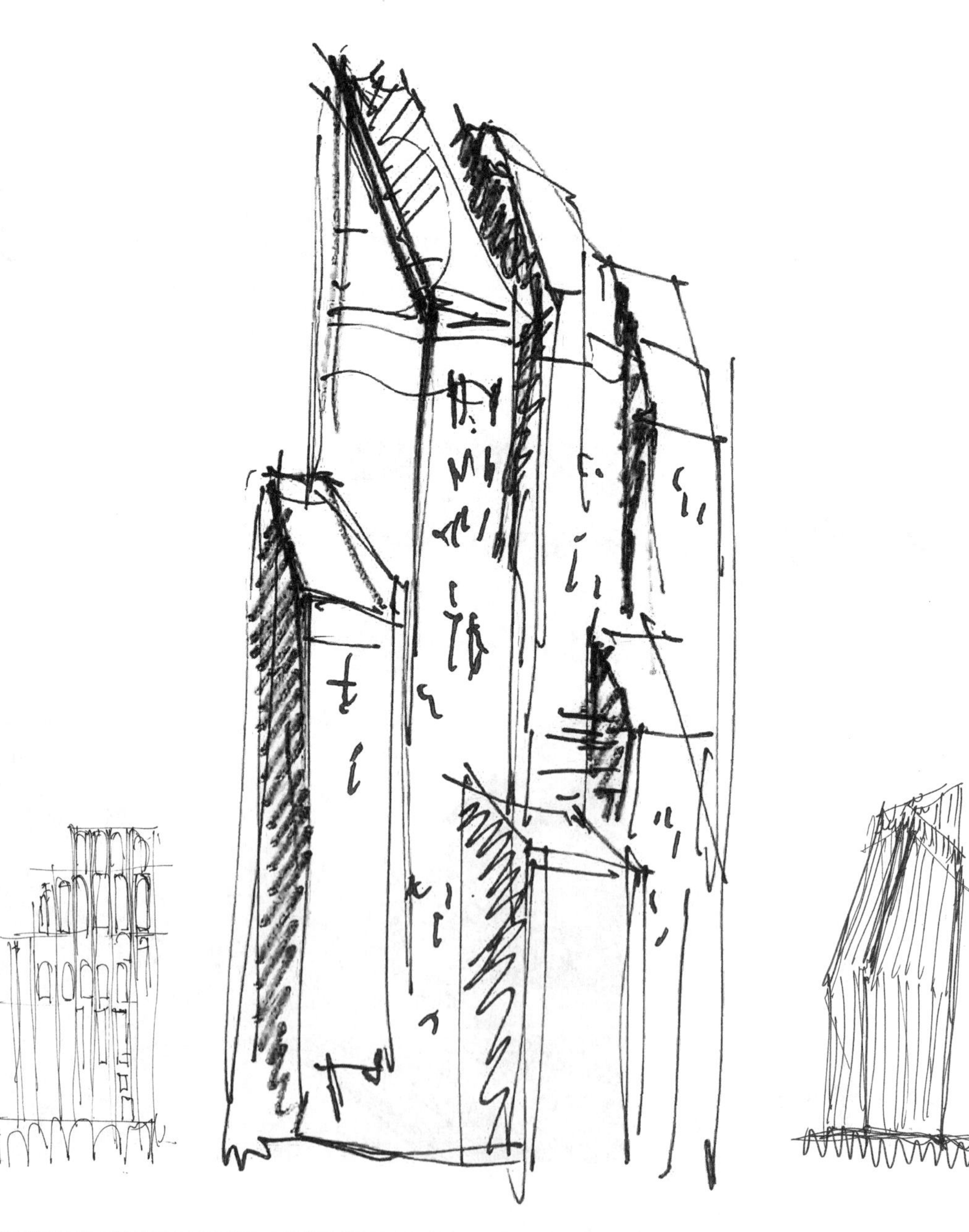

NAME OFFICE

LUCA DINI DESIGN & ARCHITECTURE

DATE
January 13, 2025

PLACE
Florence, Italy

WORKING IN ALBANIA SINCE
2023

PRINCIPALS
Luca Dini

COLLABORATORS
SON Architects
DALMAT Architecture
ICE shpk
HASKONING
M3 Monaco
ATM Company
Maffeis Engineering
IBS Progetti

MAIN CONTEXT VS. ALBANIA

Great architects have been coming to Albania for a long time, bringing their projects and their talent. We've just arrived, and we look at everyone with admiration, drawing inspiration from all.

Our inspiration begins in Albania itself – in the local culture and the genius loci of the places where we've been invited to work.

One of the key characteristics that sets our studio apart is that it's split in half: 50 percent focuses on yacht design, while the other 50 percent is dedicated to architecture and hospitality. These are similar fields, yet at the same time profoundly different.

The nautical world is all about precision, focusing on the smallest details, whereas architecture often takes a broader view – the approach to materials, for instance, is quite different. In yacht design, everything is centered around the final client: We deal with people who come to us to dream, where business considerations often take a back seat.

There's a sense of enthusiasm in Albania that we haven't found elsewhere – a full-circle commitment at every level. Entrepreneurs, the government and others all seem to share one common goal: to build a contemporary, forward-thinking country. At the same time, there's a strong desire to protect the country's natural beauty and a passion for staying current and innovative. This kind of collective effort is rare in other places, where each stakeholder often just focuses on their own part, without striving to build a true collaboration.

ORGANIZATION/GOAL/SETUP

We entered Albania in 2023, and my goal is to establish a permanent office there. So far, thanks to our close proximity to Albania, we've been able to manage operations with week-long trips and a few team members who are based there. As the projects start to take shape, we're making plans to open a local office that will allow us to oversee all developments directly from the country.

We operate through a network of local collaborators, which allows us to understand how best to realize our projects in accordance with Albanian regulations.

SETUP IN RELATION TO ALBANIAN PARTNER

We are currently collaborating with several local offices, all of whom have shown great interest in working with an architecture studio like ours. We've been welcomed like family.

We take full responsibility for the design process, and once the project is approved by the authorities, we share it with the local office, which handles the more technical development phases under our supervision – a process I like to define as *guardianship*. This ensures the project maintains its quality and stays true to our clients' original goals.

If budget-related issues arise, we always strive to find a solution. There is a level of flexibility in reaching an agreement whenever challenges emerge during the construction phase.

OPPORTUNITIES/CHALLENGES

For an architecture studio, working in this country is an incredible opportunity, as both Tirana and Albania as a whole are undergoing a major transformation aimed at improvement and becoming globally competitive.

Having the chance, here in Europe, to contribute to the transformation of an entire nation through architecture is a challenge not to be missed.

It's essential to surround ourselves with skilled professionals, and to clearly understand the limits and possibilities of what we can achieve with these projects.

HOW TO INTEGRATE GREATER RESPONSIBILITY FOR QUALITY IN PROJECTS

In this context, quality is a fundamental aspect. An architecture studio that comes from the world of yachting – where perfection is paramount – brings with it a very specific *forma mentis*. Quality holds as much value as the idea itself or any other aspect of the project; there must always be experienced professionals involved in each area.

As is our usual approach, we send our own specialists – experts in their respective fields – to supervise quality and manage the project teams on-site.

BALANCING QUALITY AND DENSITY/INVOLVING STAKEHOLDERS

As we've seen in every country undergoing transformation, it's natural for entrepreneurs to focus primarily on business. However, we stand against this being the only approach.

Protecting an idea also means thinking about people – thinking about those who will live in and experience these spaces and buildings.

For us, building on every last square centimeter is simply not acceptable. We believe that spaces must first and foremost be livable, and that quality of life should stand at the top of the podium.

As Italians, we are especially attentive to this aspect – sometimes even at the risk of losing projects – because we believe that living well is the foundation of our design philosophy.

EXAMPLE/INSPIRATION

A prime example of a country's successful regeneration is undoubtedly Dhërmi, which has been completely redeveloped from the ground up. Initially, it was essentially an abandoned village, but thanks to a well-executed redevelopment project, it has been completely revived.

Today, it has become an attractive tourist destination, thanks to the introduction of small shops, bars and restaurants that have brought new life to the narrow streets of the town, recreating the typical vibe of Mediterranean villages.

FLORENCE
HEADQUARTERS
FORTE DEI MARMI
OFFICE & SHOWROOM
ATARA
COLOSSEUM 339 TIRANA TOWER
LIFE MARINA COMPLEX
KRORËZ
Our design studio comes from the world of luxury yacht design. A universe we know deeply, where elegance and precision are fundamental.
But we realized that the sea offers much more than just yachts. The sea is an immersive experience, a place where the soul can breathe freely.

KRORËZ MASTER PLAN

Our project goes beyond creating a tourist site, offering an immersive experience that fosters personal and spiritual growth. Starting with luxury and entertainment, the journey deepens into a connection with nature, Albanian culture and self-reflection through sports, local culture and art.

LIFE MARINA COMPLEX MASTER PLAN

The master plan covers seven kilometers of nonlinear coastline with distinctive coves, divided into various functional zones including two large marinas, a village, hotels, retail, casinos and discos. The architecture recreates Mediterranean coastal villages with an exclusive vibe, immersing visitors in Mediterranean culture while honoring Albanian tradition.

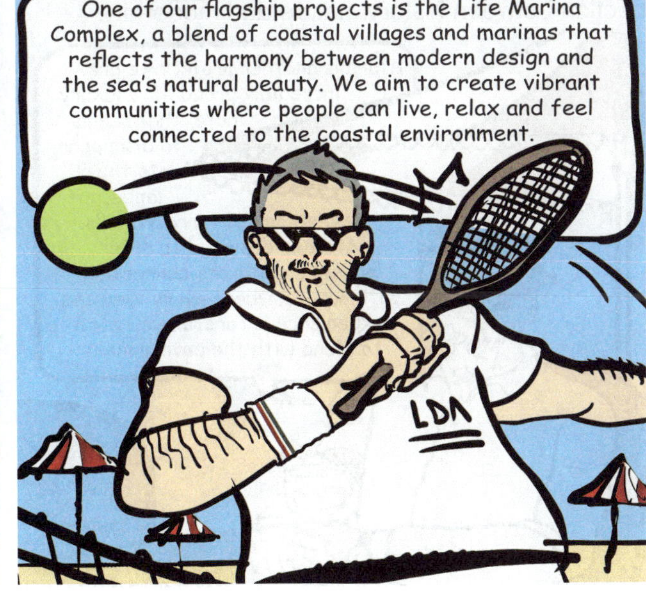

ATARA MASTER PLAN

The Atara project draws inspiration from the ancient ruins of a lost civilization and the region's historical terracing and olive groves. Anchored by the majestic Atara Crown, the project integrates nature, water and architecture in a seamless blend. Life-giving streams from the Atara Gate flow into the Water Garden and Green Park, creating lush environments that honor local traditions. This transformative design breathes new life into the landscape, offering a harmonious connection between history, nature and modernity.

The hotel's terraces recall the region's ancient agricultural practices, making the property a natural extension of the landscape.
Atara is not just a place to stay, but a retreat that combines luxury with landscape, offering an experience deeply rooted in the natural beauty of Albania.

COLOSSEUM 339 TIRANA TOWER

The Colosseum 339 tower in Tirana draws inspiration from de Chirico's metaphysical cityscapes and the dynamic tension of modern society. The design reinterprets surrealist paintings through the architectural archetype of the round arch, which seamlessly integrates façade, interior spaces, and terraces. Influenced by traditional Albanian fortifications and medieval Italian towers, the project bridges cultural heritage and contemporary form, creating a deep connection between Albania and Italy, while embedding human presence into its striking architectural composition.

And in the heart of Tirana, we are bringing a new level of sophistication with the Colosseum Tower, a skyscraper inspired by the metaphysical art of Giorgio de Chirico.

The tower reflects both the classical grandeur and the surreal beauty of de Chirico's works, combining art and architecture in a unique and striking structure.

Hospitality, Shëngjin

Luxury villas, Tirana

SOME OF OUR LATEST PROJECTS

Residential/Hospitality, Durrës

Residential master plan, Durrës

We have 17 projects in Albania under our belt, and many more proposals that we plan to develop in 2025 and in the future.

START	NAME PROJECT	LOCATION	PUBLIC/PRIVATE	PHASE
2023	Life Marina Complex	Albania's southern coast	Private	Concept master plan
2023	Atara master plan	Lukova coast	Private	Detail master plan
2024	Krorëz master plan	Krorëz coast	Private	Concept master plan
2024	Colosseum 339	Tirana	Private	Detail design
2024	Farkë master plan	Farkë Lake, Tirana	Private	Concept master plan
2024	Shëngjin Hotel	Shëngjin	Private	Concept
2024	Pine Residences	Durrës	Private	Detail master plan
2024	Durrës Tower	Durrës	Private	Detail design
2024	Tirana Villas	Tirana	Private	Detail design
2024	Shëngjin master plan	Shëngjin	Private	Concept master plan
2024	The Veil Tower	Tirana	Private	Concept
2024	Fafa Hotel	Durrës	Private	Concept
2024	Dhërmi Hotel	Dhërmi	Private	Concept
2024	Dhërmi Apartments	Dhërmi	Private	Concept
2024	Skalitur Tower	Durrës	Private	Concept
2024	Saranda Resident Hotel	Saranda	Private	Concept master plan
2025	Residential building	Tirana	Private	Concept

NAME OFFICE

MANUELLE GAUTRAND ARCHITECTURE

DATE
September 2025

PLACE
Paris, France

WORKING IN ALBANIA SINCE
January 2025

PRINCIPLES
Far from any standard, we imagine architecture that is rooted in its site and its history, that is at once contextual, ecological and expressive, an architecture that conveys beauty and poetry. We are storytellers, and each of our projects tells a story and takes you on a journey that should remain in your memory.

ALBANIAN PARTNERS
X-Plan Studio
Artech Studio
UNIT STUDIO

PROJECT TEAM
Manuelle Gautrand
Quentin Blaising
Auriane Bonnault
Javier Díez Cerro
Armando D'Alterio
Delphine Fournier
Talia Gassin
Vittorio Perotti
Pierre Axel Petit
Thomas Plantier
Zimo Zhang

INTRODUCTION TO ALBANIA

I was invited to be part of the jury for the international competition for the Tirana Society Tower(s) in August 2024. There I met Edi Rama, Adelajda Roka and Adelina Greca. It was my first trip to Albania. I had never experienced such a warm welcome in any country. And I discovered people who were truly passionate about architecture, with a political vision of what architecture can profoundly bring to a city, to an entire country. It was a magical experience for me.

MAIN CONTEXT VS. ALBANIA

The main difference I see to most countries, including France, is the fact that there is a real "desire for architecture": a desire for projects that truly leave their mark on the country's landscape and history, through their ecological and innovative nature, their aesthetic and poetic qualities, and their desire to strengthen certain crafts and local industries.

This desire translates into a rich, constructive dialogue, making the greatest things possible. Here, architecture is a political determination; it couldn't ask for anything better. It is literally carried forward. And that is rare today, at least in Europe.

ORGANIZATION/GOAL/SETUP

Our projects in Albania are important to me: They are a welcome breath of fresh air for the studio, where on many of our other projects, though always ambitious, I don't feel the same appetite for architecture. The relationship with politicians and with my clients is fundamental for me: An artist always needs to share when he creates, he needs to feel supported. Here in Albania, like all my colleagues, I feel supported by a political vision that I subscribe to, and which motivates me to the utmost. My partnerships are growing and I want to establish in-depth, long-term relationships: with architectural and political institutions, with clients and with Albanian colleagues with whom I share our projects, with the greatest respect.

SETUP IN RELATION TO ALBANIAN PARTNER

Architecture is quite a collective adventure; it cannot be undertaken alone, unless you are willing to risk failure. On the contrary, you have to bring everyone along with you on a journey that lasts several years! This requires sharing, both generously and demandingly. It requires the ability to listen, but also to convince. It requires energy and tenacity that must engage everyone, and that can only happen once you've convinced them of the beauty of the project.

HOW TO INTEGRATE GREATER RESPONSIBILITY FOR QUALITY IN PROJECTS

A project is not just a sketch with beautiful images: We work tirelessly on it, and the design process doesn't stop with the sketch – it continues throughout the design and construction phases. New ideas are constantly emerging which need to be discussed, shared and incorporated. And the quality of a project also depends on the way in which we involve craftsmen and contractors, who are only too willing to go the extra mile if they feel part of the process. For me, a worksite is always an opportunity to bring craftsmanship into architecture: to revive special, original techniques that are sometimes in danger of disappearing. I like to reveal them so that they stay alive.

BALANCING QUALITY AND DENSITY/INVOLVING STAKEHOLDERS

Urban planners could play a slightly broader role upstream, by establishing some guidelines and limits to excessively homogeneous densification. The aim would be to protect a certain number of urban or natural areas from excessive density. Some areas can accommodate a high level of densification, while others, which are more fragile and sometimes rarer, must be absolutely preserved.

For example, it must be possible to control coastal areas, not only to avoid excessive densification, but also to prevent urban fragmentation, which makes it impossible to maintain the large ecological corridors that are so necessary for biodiversity. It would be better to work with contrasting areas, some of which are heavily urbanized while others are left untouched and natural.

It may also be necessary to accompany any densification of built-up areas with a densification of landscaped areas: protecting existing trees, but also encouraging the planting of relatively large numbers of trees, the creation of parks and gardens in the heart of blocks, and the creation of generously planted roofs.

EXAMPLE/INSPIRATION

The overall project in and around Skanderbeg Square is an extraordinary starting point: It seems to have launched a dynamic, and set the tone for a unique ambition and level of architectural and urban quality. I'm particularly inspired by this example because architecture plays only a small part in it: It's the public spaces, magnified, that create a new, generous and lively setting.

For me, public space is fundamental to a city, and its vibrancy – or lack of it – reflects the quality of life in this city. Here you can feel the enormous energy, with all generations coming together to share these open, permissive spaces.

TOOLBOX ALBANIA FUTURE

Albania gives me a vision of architecture, a vision that I embrace and share.

It brings together a community of people, institutions, politicians and architects who are ready to share in this collective adventure.

It brings a rich culture, which is an endless source of inspiration for me: a culture and history that are deeply European, thanks to the country's geographical location at the crossroads of so many migratory movements and flows . . .

We must now work with this rich matrix, the political vision, the men and women who share it, and there are so many of them, and finally their history . . .

A rich palette that I must now translate into bold, memorable architecture that is full of meaning.

OUR INGREDIENTS

As a good "chef," I first of all like to know who I'm cooking for: I want to prepare the best dish there is, the one that feeds you, but much more than that . . . the one that leaves a lasting impression on you and leaves you with an unforgettable memory: the memory of an emotion.

Here I "cook," I "design," in Albania, a country that I'm discovering a little more of every day. My first impression was of a magnificent Mediterranean country, for me the most beautiful region in the world, the region where I was born. But this country is first and foremost European, much more so than some other European countries.

It is not geographically on the edge of Europe, somewhat isolated and protected from demographic flows like some other countries. It is "in the middle," as it always has been: in the middle of cultural, linguistic, human and historical mixing.

And today it arrives at an alchemical moment, precious and fragile, one of extremely rich balance between different cultures, lines of thought, religions, histories and traditions. It is like a mille-feuille, my favorite French cake: made up of layers, each one gradually revealing itself, each one complementing the previous one and contributing to the richness that it displays today. Alchemy, then.

So here are my recipes, and I want them to be gourmet!

CELEBRATE A SITE

To celebrate a site, I first have to look at what already exists, what's around me, the strengths and weaknesses of what's already there, what's visible and what's invisible: its history, the culture in which it has been immersed, the geology beneath its feet, the scars of its past, the climate that has already shaped its existence, its orientation to the sun, its light, its "atmosphere."

And I draw it, as a first form of reinterpretation, a way of entering into its most intimate characteristics, of making it my own, almost physically. It's my "raw material," and when the project is delivered, I want this raw material to be highlighted, praised and celebrated by my architecture.

REVEAL LOCAL MATERIALITIES & KNOW-HOW

I enjoy working with materials extracted from the site (or nearby) and consider them as genuine resources, along with the techniques associated with these materials: Working with local craftsmen often allows us to rediscover ancient techniques. There's a fine line between craftsmanship and art, just as there is between architecture and art. In this case, it is touching to see how our projects can contribute to maintaining local industries and strengthening skills that might otherwise have disappeared. The human aspect is very present, reminding us of the essential role of the craftsmen who build what we have designed, and how much we owe them.

Here, the sand from the seashore is one of my resources: Used in concrete and coatings, it will shape the project like a sandcastle, like the ones we used to build by the sea when we were children . . .

ARCHITECTURE AS AN EXTENSION OF PUBLIC SPACE

Public space is the most precious ingredient of a city: It is the foundation of our culture. It brings inhabitants together, gives them a sense of belonging to a community and a feeling of social cohesion. I dream of building projects that open up these public spaces in the most permissive and porous way possible. In fact, all architecture takes up space in the public arena and, in a way, reduces its size: it must therefore compensate by giving something back to this reduced public space. It must be like a filter that allows the public space to sneak into our architecture and extend itself as generously as possible.

I want my architecture to become like a walk, a journey. I want it to become like a theater, the theater of our lives.

CREATE URBAN MARKERS

Architecture is designed for the long term; it is built to last. Here, it must therefore reflect the extraordinary alchemy that has taken shape in Albania. Ultimately, what we build today will become our heritage tomorrow. It must not be generic, but rather an expression of this culture, which it must literally celebrate.

I want my projects to seek perfect symbiosis with the sites that host them: The more sensitive and profound this symbiosis is, the more powerful and memorable the result can be. This is how each project can have a symbolic impact, because it will have succeeded in anchoring itself in the landscape in which it is invited to take its place.

We must create urban landmarks that every inhabitant can be proud of, capable of lasting and forming the heritage of tomorrow.

ADAPT TO THE CLIMATE

Wherever the project is located, the geography of the site, its topography, climate and orientation towards the sun and wind are fundamental factors. I like to think of the site as a matrix with which we need to establish a fertile dialogue.

We always study the path of the sun: It's important for the design of the project, but it's also important in terms of its impact on the spaces around us. Minimizing the shadows cast on the surrounding spaces is always a challenge for me. Making sure that our architecture doesn't make the winds worse, that it doesn't degrade the context in which it's set: The more we respect the site in which we're setting up, the more that site will reveal our architecture in return.

EMBRACE NATURE

When the landscape is exceptional, here thanks to its natural character and because it is still wild in parts, I want our architecture to disappear into it, to blend in, like a chameleon. I want to use the same ingredients that this landscape offers us: layers of limestone, rock formations, terraced fields, olive groves, fragrant scrubland, a palette of unique colors that are so Mediterranean. It is an entire atmosphere to be recreated in our architecture, to settle future inhabitants seamlessly into this landscape and teach them respect and contemplation. They must rediscover direct contact with nature, sharing their living space with it.
Yes, architecture can be expressive and iconic, but sometimes it must be more silent, delicately and discreetly embedded in nature. Its preexistence commands respect, the kind we generally have for an ecosystem that preceded us, in which we must take our place with humility.

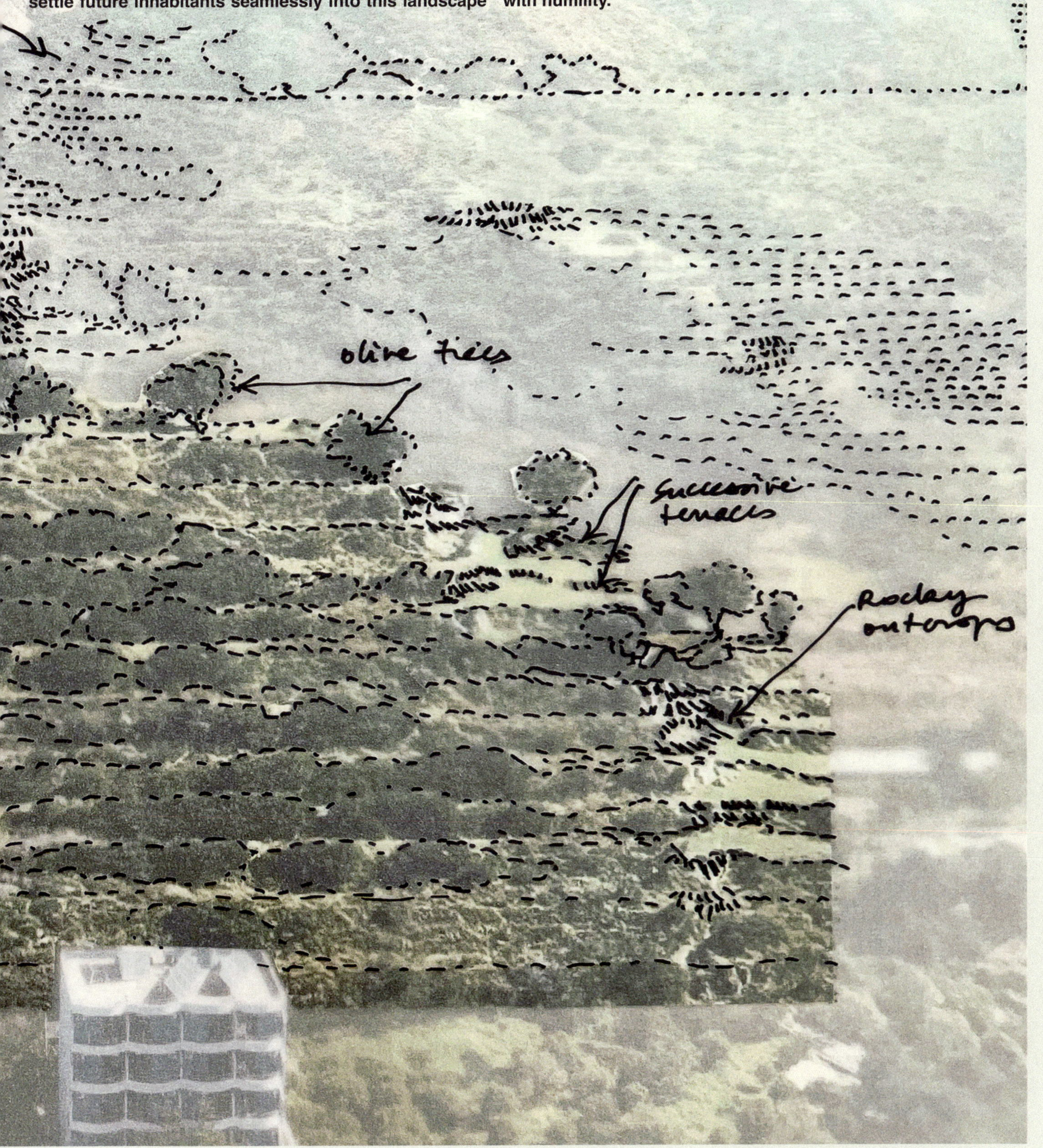

NEVER FORGET THE CULTURE!

We must never forget the cultural facet of each site, the one that is the most difficult to grasp and describe because it is almost subjective: the one that appeals to our emotions . . . There's this notion of "atmosphere": How do you respect the atmosphere of a place? How do you respect its collective memory?

It's often by looking at works of art that I'm able to analyze the unique atmosphere of a particular place, to understand at the deepest level what has made it special, often over the centuries: far beyond its architecture, a place has a color palette, a skyline, skies – in short, this notion of atmosphere that makes it comparable to no other.

LIST OF PROJECTS

We've had a great start to all of them since spring/summer 2025. Three of them were approved at the KKT meeting, the other the other one have not yet been. Two projects, Tirana Jardins and Lalëzit Bay, have reached the schematic design stage.

START	NAME PROJECT	LOCATION	DEVELOPER	ALBANIAN PARTNER	PHASE
2025	Tirana Jardins	Tirana	XHAJS TIRANA	X-Plan Studio	Schematic design
2025	Upper East Tirana	Tirana	Glob-3X Group	Artech Studio	
2025	Lalëzit Bay	Lalëzit Bay	XHAJS TIRANA	X-Plan Studio	Schematic design
2025	Golem Beach	Golem Beach	3A CONSTRUCTION	UNIT STUDIO	

NAME OFFICE

MASS STUDIES

DATE
January 20, 2025

PLACE
Seoul, South Korea

WORKING IN ALBANIA SINCE
September 2024

PRINCIPAL
Minsuk Cho

CONSULTANTS
Eden Structure, Hyung Jong Jeon (Structural Engineer)
HANA Consulting Engineers Co., Ltd., Sangrak Chang (MEP Engineer)
Artech Studio (Local Architect)

PROJECT TEAM
Junkoo Kang
Bumhyun Chun
Hyeseong Kim
Saecheol Oh
Yeonsu Hong
Tamooh Edelbi
Shinhyuk Kim
Junghun Park
Betty Bo Ra Kim
Donghee Yang
Heegon Kim
Youngung Kim
Yurim Lee
Euna Jeong

MAIN CONTEXT VS. ALBANIA

Our works have been mostly in South Korea. Although it's a small country, it has offered quite diverse and rich natural and cultural contexts. Each project has been a rigorous exploration of specific architectural opportunities for a given location. Our task in Albania obviously offers a completely different context that requires a lot more effort to learn, yet our attitude remains the same.

ORGANIZATION/GOAL/SETUP

Since we are still in the early stages of the project, we are in the process of establishing partnerships for our task. Despite the differences and distance, our goal is to make successful architectural contributions through collaboration with users and specialists, working as a single team. From our previous experience, we know that close communication is key to achieving a certain level of intimacy.

SETUP IN RELATION TO ALBANIAN PARTNER

It is important to work in close collaboration with the local team throughout the design process, aiming to create a built environment that is truly suited to Albania.

OPPORTUNITIES/CHALLENGES

We were deeply inspired by Albania's mountainous landscapes, which offer both a significant opportunity for innovative architecture and a challenge for achieving harmonious construction.

HOW TO INTEGRATE GREATER RESPONSIBILITY FOR QUALITY IN PROJECTS

We believe that achieving quality ultimately depends on the design architect's continuous involvement throughout the project – from the initial design phase to construction completion – in close collaboration with local architects and specialists.

BALANCING QUALITY AND DENSITY/INVOLVING STAKEHOLDERS

It is essential for the design architect to gain the full trust of government officials and the client through a strong vision, a serious and dedicated effort toward the endeavor, and firm relationships with all parties involved.

EXAMPLE/INSPIRATION

We find the transformation of Skanderbeg Square in Tirana by 514NE and the mountain village of Vuno in Vlora County both inspiring.

TOOLBOX ALBANIA FUTURE

The sensible coexistence of human settlements with challenging topographic conditions is the toolkit Albania provides us as architects to shape the future.

lora Calligraphy

/hen we first visited Tirana in late August 2024, delajda "Ada" Roka, the general director of AZHT, troduced a few potential projects we could get in- olved in, suggesting that we might take on more than ne. However, as we were new to Albania, we wanted focus our efforts. Instead of pursuing projects in irana, we chose to engage in a smaller-scale project: low-rise development on the seaside hills of Vlora. /e also quickly realized that one of the exciting simi- .rities between Albania and South Korea is that both re very mountainous countries. For us as architects, ne challenge and focus has long been how a moun- in can sensibly become a human settlement.

ne of the sites presented – a 2.8-hectare moun- inous terrain at the southern tip of an oceanfront hotel and residential development in Vlora – seemed like a fitting choice for our potential contribution. That same afternoon, after the meeting, we headed straight to Vlora, a beautiful Adriatic seaside city with dramatic rocky hills, to meet our client and visit the site.

Upon arriving at the stunning site, our client informed us that the site had expanded to over four times its original size, now spanning more than 13.4 hectares. The elevation had also increased significantly, rising from a 105-meter level difference to 210 meters above the oceanside access road.

The site itself is taller than any tower we have ever designed.

View of the Adriatic Sea from the site

It was somewhat comforting to realize that the site's vertical dimension, at less than 300 meters, is comparable to Namsan Mountain in central Seoul. Our office sits at around the 100-meter level there, so we were already quite familiar with the challenges posed by such terrain from our daily experience.

We managed to climb 35 meters from the base of the site, where we encountered a dramatic sandstone cliff rising more than halfway up the site's total height – around 135 meters. Unable to see beyond the cliff without mountain-climbing gear, we were fortunate that our client had brought a drone, which he skillfully piloted in real-time using his mobile phone. Above the cliff, informal villages sprawled around the site, while within its boundaries, we spotted a grid-like farm field with goats grazing peacefully.

Extremely exciting and challenging at the same time.

The following day, accompanied by Ada and Mas Studies partner Junkoo Kang, we met Prime Minist Edi Rama at his office. Upon discovering that w were from South Korea, the prime minister remarke that Albania was once referred to as the "Nor Korea of Europe" due to its isolation and poverty b fore the 1990s.

I shared with him that I belong to a South Korean ge eration that, until the late 1960s, was actually poor than North Korea and also lived under autocratic ru until the early 1990s. As a result, I have witnessed wide spectrum of dynamic political, economic an sociocultural changes and progress throughout m life, along with the demanding responsibilities place on architects and architecture during such transfo mations. Because of this experience, I feel a certa familiarity with what Albania has been going throug – fortunately, under his remarkable leadership.

View of the sandstone cliff within the si

also expressed my hope that when North Korea ventually opens up – coexisting peacefully with outh Korea and integrating into the larger world architecture will serve as a powerful tool for ommunication between people with differences. lbania stands as an inspiring example for this aspi- ational future.

his vision was a key motivation for us to become volved and to closely observe Albania's current ansformative moment, allowing us to learn and repare to contribute meaningfully to an optimistic ture for the Korean Peninsula.

s a gesture of appreciation, I presented the prime inister with an exhibition catalog from the 2014 enice Biennale's Korean pavilion, which I curated. he project required me to envision the first-ever rchitectural exhibition representing both North and South Korea, made possible through a collaborative effort involving contributions from many other nations, as direct engagement between the two Koreas was not an option at the time.

The prime minister inquired about the amount of floor area our client had requested for the site. After hearing our response, he quickly did the calculations in his head and remarked that it was likely too much for the site. He emphasized that what truly matters is what we as architects believe to be an appropriate amount of built area for the context.

I found his perspective both encouraging and inspiring – the notion that there could be an alternative to market-driven speculative development, one that grants architects a more meaningful and demanding role in shaping responsible and thoughtful environments.

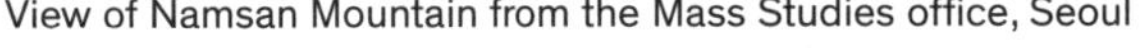

View of Namsan Mountain from the Mass Studies office, Seoul

A week after our return to Seoul, our client sent us a digital modeling file containing detailed topographic measurements of the site. From this, we were able to determine the areas where construction was feasible, based on the steepness of the hillside and other site conditions. We quickly recognized that the most sensible and economical way to build on such challenging terrain was to compress elements creatively, blending architecture and infrastructure in innovative ways. This strategy allows us to maximize the value of the "unbuilt" – the desirable existing natural features like the sandstone cliff, forest and water passage – while preserving them in the process.

It is like calligraphy: an act of being conscious of the negative space – the untouched landscape – while making precise strokes on blank paper.

We also considered ways to share the experience o this stunningly dramatic vertical site, with its breath taking Adriatic Sea view, with the broader publi – transforming it into a common space. This coul be achieved through minimal interventions, such a smaller structures at various locations accessible vi elevators, a hillavator and interconnected passage that form a three-dimensional network. In doing s the site would become much more than just a gate community with a hotel.

Although this project is still in its early stages an will continue to be demanding, we are determined t approach this challenge with commitment and hope

Minsuk Cho, Mass Studies, January 2025

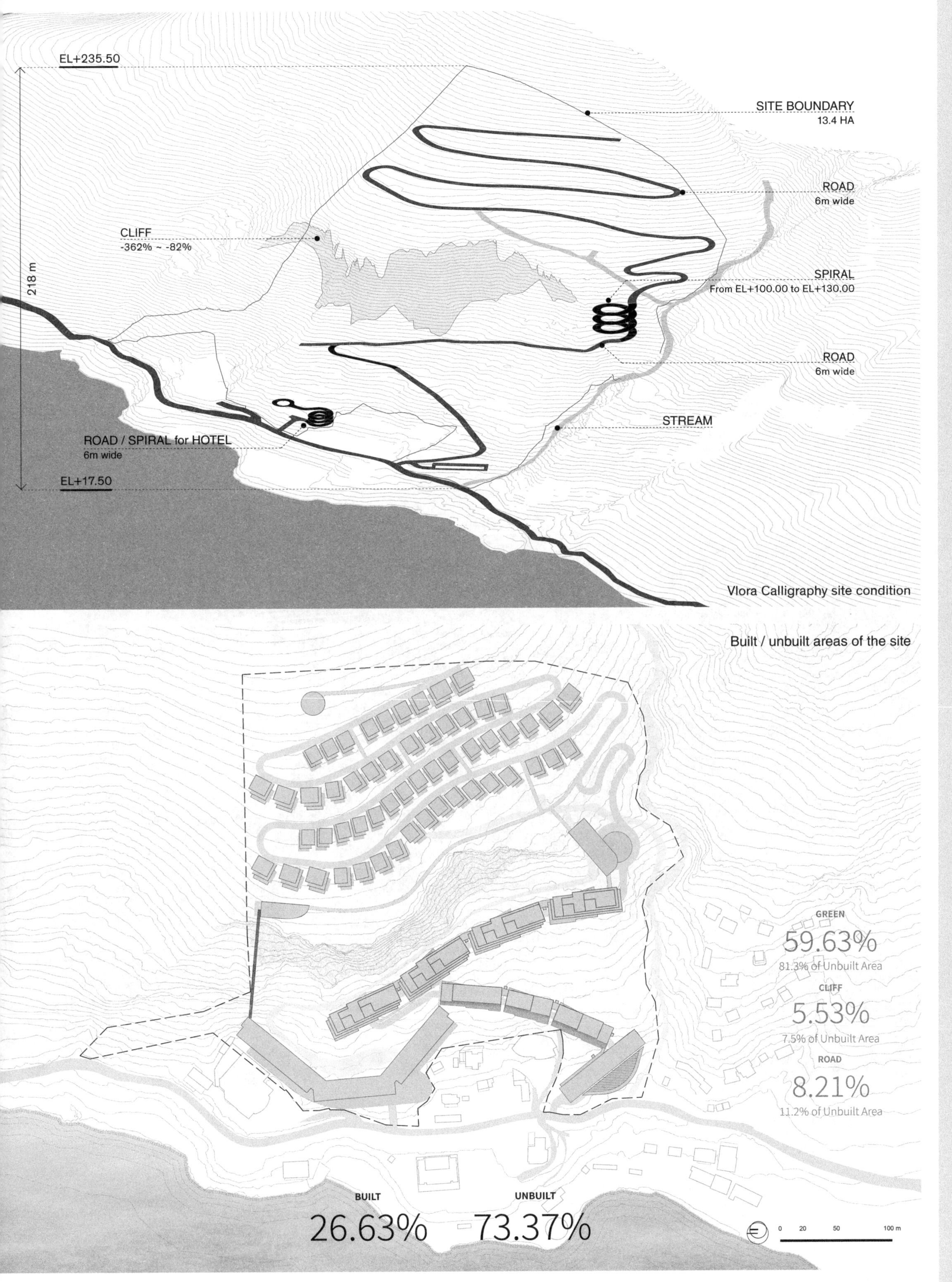

Vlora Calligraphy site condition

Built / unbuilt areas of the site

View of Vlora Calligraphy from northwest

View of hotel lobby in Vlora Calligraph

START	NAME PROJECT	LOCATION	DEVELOPER	PUBLIC/PRIVATE	PHASE
2024	Vlora Calligraphy	Rruga “Sali Vranishti,” Jonufer, Vlora	Fortis Beton CO + Hanxhari Group	Private	Concept design

NAME OFFICE

MCA – MARIO CUCINELLA ARCHITECTS

DATE
December 16, 2024

PLACE
Bologna, Italy

WORKING IN ALBANIA SINCE
2014

PRINCIPAL
Mario Cucinella (Architect & Founder)

PROJECT TEAM

MET BUILDING
Mario Cucinella
Tommaso Bettini
Elena Giugni
Eurind Caka
Paolo Greco
Lucrezia Rendace
Marco Dell'Agli
Michele Roveri
Angelo Ungarelli
Kseniya Shkroban
Marta Bordi
Marta Torsello
Francesca Fochi
Luca Vernocchi
Laura La Mendola
Michele Olivieri
Giovanni Sanna
Francesco Visco
Alberto Menozzi
Andrea Rossi (R&D)
Elena Biason (R&D)
Alessia Monacelli (Visual Artist)

EKSPOZITA BUILDING
Mario Cucinella
Tommaso Bettini
Elena Giugni
Marco Dell'Agli
Eurind Caka
Biagio Amodio
Kseniya Shkroban
Antonino Cucinella
Laura La Mendola
Michele Olivieri
Giovanni Sanna
Yuri Costantini (Model Maker)
Andrea Genovesi (Model Maker)
Alessia Monacelli (Visual Artist Coordinator)
Francesco Cerulli (Visual Artist)

ALBANIAN PARTNERS

MET BUILDING
Arben Shtylla (Local Architect)
Erjon Petriti (Structural Engineering)
Archimed (MEP Engineering)
FISHTA electric shpk (Electrical Engineering)
LAND (Landscape Design)

EKSPOZITA BUILDING
Ekoplan, Viktor Dhimgjini (Local Architect)
Henars Engineering, Helidon Kokona (Structural Engineering)
A2N termoklima, Nuri Njeraku (MEP Engineering)
Elteknik shpk (Electrical Engineering)

INTRODUCTION TO ALBANIA

MET Tirana Building: The client contacted us thanks to a connection with a university professor.

Ekspozita Building: The client contacted us thanks to the MET Tirana Building project under construction.

MAIN CONTEXT VS. ALBANIA

The majority of our projects are based in Italy, our home market, where we have established a deep understanding of the building process and its cultural nuances. However, working in a new country, such as Albania, requires adapting to its unique business practices and construction dynamics to achieve our goals.

This adaptability is what makes operating as an international architecture firm so rewarding. Every project becomes an opportunity to engage with new customs, cultures and methodologies, enriching our perspective while working toward a shared vision of high-quality, impactful design. The core values of collaboration and sustainability remain constant, regardless of the context.

ORGANIZATION/GOAL/SETUP

Our projects in Albania are realized through a collaborative working group that combines MCA's architectural expertise with the skills of local technicians. MCA oversees the architectural design, while technical offices in Tirana manage structures, mechanical systems, and administrative and urban planning supervision. The construction phase is handled by local teams, with MCA providing artistic supervision through scheduled site visits.

This approach ensures a seamless integration of global design principles with local expertise, fostering a balance between innovation and context-specific solutions. Over the past decade, this setup has proven effective and remains consistent, allowing us to build strong partnerships while achieving our goals of high-quality, sustainable architecture in Albania.

SETUP IN RELATION TO ALBANIAN PARTNER

We actively collaborate with local technicians, leveraging their expertise to enhance our projects. This approach is driven by their proven skill and enthusiasm for working on complex buildings, as well as their deep understanding of the local context. Their knowledge of Albania's rapidly evolving development and management dynamics is invaluable in ensuring that our designs are not only innovative but also responsive to the unique challenges and opportunities of the territory. At MCA, this partnership allows us to blend global design excellence with local insights for truly impactful results.

OPPORTUNITIES/CHALLENGES

Over the past decade, Albania has emerged as one of the most dynamic construction markets in Europe, with Tirana experiencing unparalleled growth in built volumes among European capitals. This rapid development presents both opportunities and challenges for architects.

One key opportunity lies in the willingness of both public and private developers to prioritize high-quality projects. This commitment to excellence has been matched by significant investment in achieving elevated construction standards, creating an environment where ambitious and innovative designs can flourish.

For MCA, this focus on quality aligns with our philosophy of creating architecture that is sustainable, impactful and deeply connected to its context. The challenge lies in maintaining this momentum while balancing the demands of rapid urbanization with the need for thoughtful, long-term planning. However, the progress made over the past decade demonstrates that Albania is well-positioned to continue leading with bold, high-quality architectural statements.

HOW TO INTEGRATE GREATER RESPONSIBILITY FOR QUALITY IN PROJECTS

Achieving high-quality outcomes in new buildings often relies on a combination of factors. In Tirana, significant investments have elevated the standard of construction, attracting some of the world's leading architectural firms. This has fostered a competitive environment where innovation and excellence thrive.

Equally important is the role of public institutions in championing quality. The local authorities have demonstrated a remarkable sensitivity to promoting unique and impactful architectural expressions, ensuring that every project contributes meaningfully to the city's identity and urban landscape.

BALANCING QUALITY AND DENSITY/INVOLVING STAKEHOLDERS

Rapid building development often risks compromising construction quality. However, Tirana has largely succeeded in mitigating this challenge. To ensure long-term success, maintaining a comprehensive perspective on the city's urban plan is essential, especially in a rapidly evolving context.

Architects play a key role in balancing density with quality, and this responsibility can be amplified by fostering collaboration with diverse stakeholders, including policymakers, developers and local communities. This type of inclusive process strengthens design integrity while aligning architectural goals with social and environmental needs. At MCA, we believe this collective approach is fundamental to achieving sustainable and high-quality urban environments.

TOOLBOX ALBANIA FUTURE

Albania offers an incredibly rich and diverse "toolbox" for architects, one that resonates deeply with our philosophy. Its breathtaking landscapes inspire designs that harmonize with nature, and its cultural heritage and historical layers provide a foundation for projects that respect and reinterpret local traditions while addressing contemporary needs.

Additionally, the country presents opportunities to explore sustainable solutions, leveraging its climate and natural resources to develop innovative approaches to energy efficiency and resilience. Albania's vibrant communities and their aspirations further drive us to design spaces that enhance quality of life while fostering social and cultural connections.

Albania is more than a context; it is a source of inspiration that aligns with our commitment to creating architecture that is empathetic, sustainable and deeply rooted in its environment.

MET Tirana Building

Dëshmorët e Kombit Boulevard

VIEW OF THE TOP OF THE BUILDING

PROGRAM: mixed use (residential and offices)
SIZE: 32,000 m²
STATUS: under construction

The MET Tirana Building is a new residential and office building that was conceived as if a new species of plant had sprung up in one of the most important and central areas of Tirana, along Bulevardi Zhan d'Ark. This strikingly expressive work of architecture is nonetheless characterized by a certain degree of monumentality, as required by the context. The architectural configuration transforms the constraints of urban regulations into an opportunity to experiment with "excavated" volumes, and thus the elliptical shape of the building becomes a play of spiraling terraces. The articulation of the forms, together with the composition of the façade, based on alternating opaque and transparent modules, and the floor-to-ceiling glazing at the ground level, gives the building a sense of elegance and lightness. The project took inspiration from the city of Berat, with its hybridization of nature and artifice. The building is lightened as it goes up by means of a progressive subtraction of volume, so that most of the elliptical plan has been removed at the top floor. This configuration made it possible to create large terraces on the upper residential floors, embellished with planters big enough for trees and large shrubs. The fully glazed walls of the apartments facing the terraces permit both generous amounts of natural light and ample views of the surrounding environment.

The vegetation that "inhabits" the building, consisting of climatically adaptive species, transforms the building into a sort of gigantic tree that changes its appearance according to the seasons.

BERAT, THE TOWN OF A THOUSAND WINDOWS

EXTERNAL VIEW OF THE BUILDING

The playful sculpting of the building's volumes, the rhythmic texture of its surfaces and the environmental qualities of its tree-planted terraces combine to create an elegant work of urban revitalization that fits perfectly into the context of the boulevard.

BUILDING CONCEPT EVOLUTION: PHYSICAL STUDY MODELS

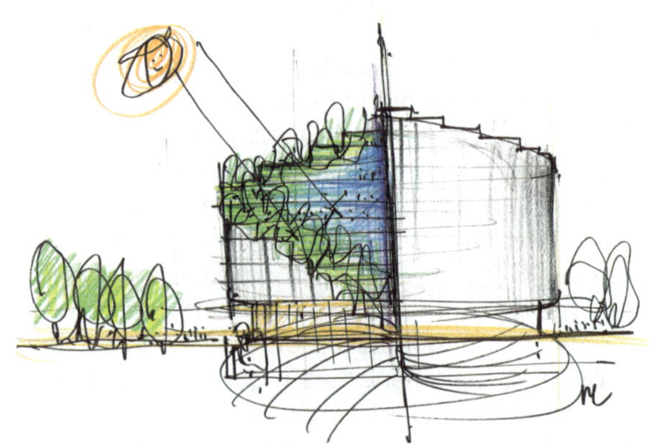

SKETCH OF THE BUILDING BY MARIO CUCINELLA

EXTERNAL VIEW OF THE BUILDING

DETAILED SECTION AND ELEVATION DRAWINGS

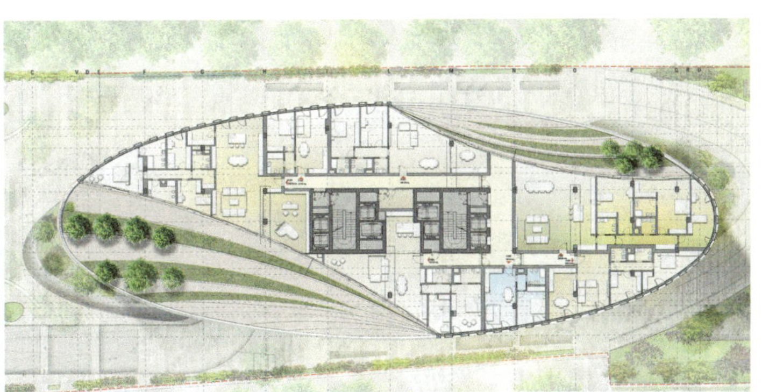

RESIDENTIAL FLOOR PLAN DRAWINGS

FAÇADE OF THE BUILDING

FAÇADE STUDY DRAWINGS

EVOLUTION OF THE BUILDING SITE

Ekspozita Building

Gjergj Fishta Boulevard

A NEW URBAN LANDSCAPE

PROGRAM: mixed use (residential and offices)
SIZE: 38,000 m^2
STATUS: under construction

Even taller and more imposing than the MET Tirana Building, soaring almost 90 meters above Tirana, the Ekspozita Building is a striking mixed-use structure that integrates commercial, residential and public spaces. One of two landmark projects by the renowned Italian firm in the Albanian capital, it stands as a prominent reference point within the city's dynamic urban landscape.

The building's distinctive form and its generous integration of green space, a rarity in this bustling European capital, reflect Albania's rich cultural heritage and natural beauty. The upper floors offer a sense of retreat, evoking the tranquility of a green oasis, while inward-facing openings provide both privacy and protection from the city's vibrant energy.

Occupying three and a half sides of a square footprint, the building opens its courtyard to the south, embracing the tree-lined Gjergj Fishta Boulevard, one of Tirana's key avenues. The tower rises to 24 stories, gradually narrowing as it ascends, with its highest point at the rear, a subtle homage to the nearby Mount Dajti and the surrounding Balkan Mountains.

This unique geometry allows the structure to occupy just 44 percent of the plot at ground level, creating a smaller footprint ideal for residential use as the tower climbs.

The Ekspozita Building is attuned to Tirana's humid, temperate climate, where summer temperatures often exceed 30°C. The building is highly insulated, designed to require minimal heating or cooling during the temperate seasons of fall and spring.

INSPIRATIONAL REFERENCE: TYPICAL SOUTHERN COSTAL LANDSCAPE OF ALBANIA

BUILDING CONCEPT EVOLUTION: PHYSICAL STUDY MODELS

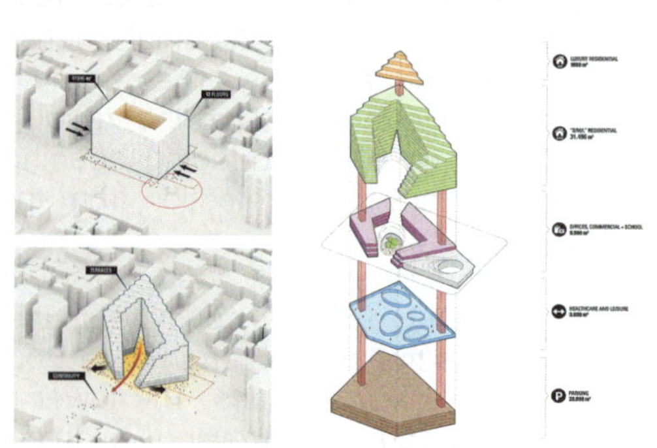

CONCEPT DIAGRAMS

FAÇADE STUDY DRAWINGS

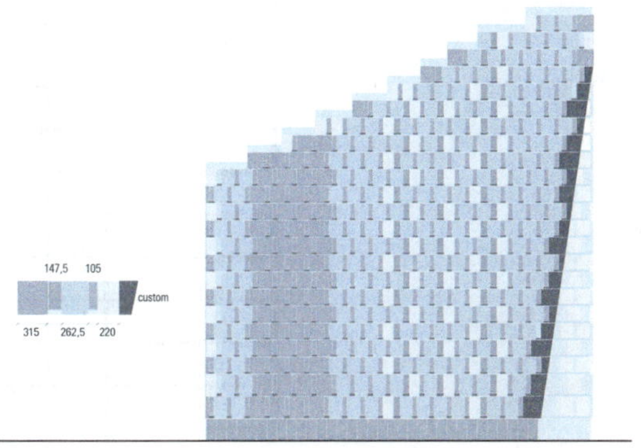

FAÇADE STUDY DIAGRAMS

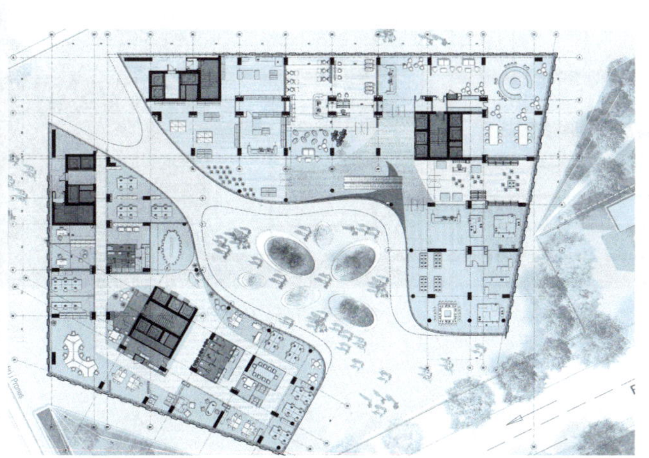

SECOND FLOOR PLAN DRAWINGS

EXTERNAL VIEW FROM THE STREET

GENERAL SECTION OF THE BUILDING

THE BUILDING SITE

START	NAME PROJECT	LOCATION	DEVELOPER	M²	PROGRAM	PUBLIC/PRIVATE	PHASE
2014	MET Tirana Building	Tirana	MET Invest	32,000 m²	Mixed use (residential and offices)	Private	Under construction
2018	Ekspozita Building	Tirana	Victoria Construction shpk	38,000 m²	Mixed use (residential and offices)	Private	Under construction

NAME OFFICE

MIRALLES TAGLIABUE – EMBT ARCHITECTS

DATE
September 2025

PLACE
Barcelona, Spain

WORKING IN ALBANIA SINCE
2023

PRINCIPALS
Benedetta Tagliabue

PROJECT TEAM

PROJECT DIRECTORS
Joan Callís
Marzia Faranda
Nazaret Busto
Bernardo Garcia

DESIGN TEAM
Andres Belderrain
Giulia Pinato
Marco Barani
Tu Bui
Yuke Zhao
Alessia Maurri
Asier Lacarra
Brandon Avalos
Costanza Bardazzi
Daniel Hernán García
Delfina Mascetti
Eleonora Scalia
Giulia Cartechini
Kuan Chia Huang
Ludovica Cucculelli
Sofia Dini
Susanna Risi
Vivien Centelles

NICKNAME
Bene

ALBANIAN PARTNERS

KORAN VILLAGE
X-Plan Studio

HOUSING ZHAN D'ARK
Gazmend Oketa

RESIDENCE VELIPOJË
Geni Marku

MAIN CONTEXT VS. ALBANIA

The context I mainly work in involves projects that often emphasize public engagement and sustainability. In Albania, the context is distinct because of its unique political and historical background. After decades without significant urban or architectural development, there's now a strong need for planning, yet the challenge is to balance this with preserving the country's stunning natural landscapes.

One of the biggest differences in the building process is that in Albania most of the opportunities so far have been with private promoters. This often requires convincing stakeholders to adopt sustainable practices, which is not always their immediate priority. However, a similarity lies in the collaborative spirit – there are incredibly talented and generous architects in Albania, and there's a shared commitment to experimenting and pushing boundaries to create meaningful architecture.

ORGANIZATION/GOAL/SETUP

In Albania, my approach has gradually shifted from collaborations initiated by local promoters to more direct partnerships with local architects. These relationships have been crucial in understanding the country's specific challenges and potentials.

The focus remains on projects that respect Albania's natural beauty while responding to urgent needs for infrastructure and planning, integrating sustainable and innovative strategies even when working with private promoters. Looking ahead, I aim to support a long-term architectural framework that strengthens cultural identity and environmental responsibility through close collaboration with local talent.

SETUP IN RELATION TO ALBANIAN PARTNER

The design process is a collaborative effort. While my team often leads the conceptual design and development phases, we actively involve local offices. Their role goes beyond execution – they contribute valuable insights into the cultural, environmental and regulatory contexts that shape the projects.

I chose this setup because I believe in the power of collective creativity. Local offices bring a unique perspective and an understanding of craftsmanship, materials and techniques specific to Albania. By working together, we can blend innovation with tradition, resulting in architecture that resonates with the place and its people. This partnership also helps foster knowledge exchange, building capacity and inspiring new ideas on both sides.

HOW TO INTEGRATE GREATER RESPONSIBILITY FOR QUALITY IN PROJECTS

Integrating greater responsibility for quality in projects requires a combination of clear standards, strong advocacy and unwavering commitment to principles. One key approach is to establish nonnegotiable benchmarks for sustainability, aesthetics and functionality from the very beginning of a project. This often means being firm in saying "no" when proposals compromise these values.

Another important strategy is education. For example, emphasizing how sustainable materials and thoughtful design can enhance the value and longevity of a project often helps align interests. Demonstrating these benefits through successful case studies can also be persuasive.

Additionally, creating a collaborative design process with local architects and experts ensures that projects reflect both global standards and local knowledge. By encouraging experimentation and innovation while respecting cultural and environmental contexts, we can achieve a higher level of quality that resonates deeply with the place and its people.

BALANCING QUALITY AND DENSITY/INVOLVING STAKEHOLDERS

It's our responsibility to establish a clear vision from the outset and to communicate why this balance matters – not just to developers but also to the communities impacted by the projects. Density doesn't have to mean sacrificing quality; in fact, it can be an opportunity for innovation.

We often work across disciplines, involving urban planners, ecologists or even sociologists in the process, because it's not just about buildings – it's about how people live in these spaces. Opening up the process to more voices helps ensure the integrity of the design.

Sometimes you also have to be firm. There have been moments where I've had to say "no" to certain demands because they didn't align with what I believed was acceptable. But it's also about education – showing developers or the public that in the long run, quality benefits everyone, including them.

EXAMPLE/INSPIRATION

There is one project that I find deeply inspiring: the transformation of the former prime minister's (Mehmet Shehu) residence, now known as the House of Comrades. This building, which once symbolized a particular and painful era, has been transformed into a space for hosting official guests and creating positive impressions of Albania. What struck me was how it embraced its past instead of erasing it. The use of art, photographs and reinterpretations of historical elements made it a project that doesn't shy away from memory but transforms it into something hopeful and forward-looking. It's not just about the physical transformation of a space; it's about emotional and cultural transformation as well.

TOOLBOX ALBANIA FUTURE

Albania's extraordinary natural landscapes demand careful, sustainable design and provide a level of inspiration that is increasingly rare.

Equally important is the resilience and experimental spirit of Albanian architects, craftsmen and builders, whose traditional skills combine naturally with contemporary approaches. Decades of underdevelopment in planning and infrastructure become a motivation to set thoughtful long-term precedents.

Finally, Albania's growing openness to collaboration between local and international actors creates a fertile ground for experimentation, positioning the country as a laboratory for meaningful architectural and urban transformation.

Design and concept for the Koran Village in Pogradec

Design and concept for the residence & hotel in Velipojë

Design and concept for the residence & hotel in Velipojë

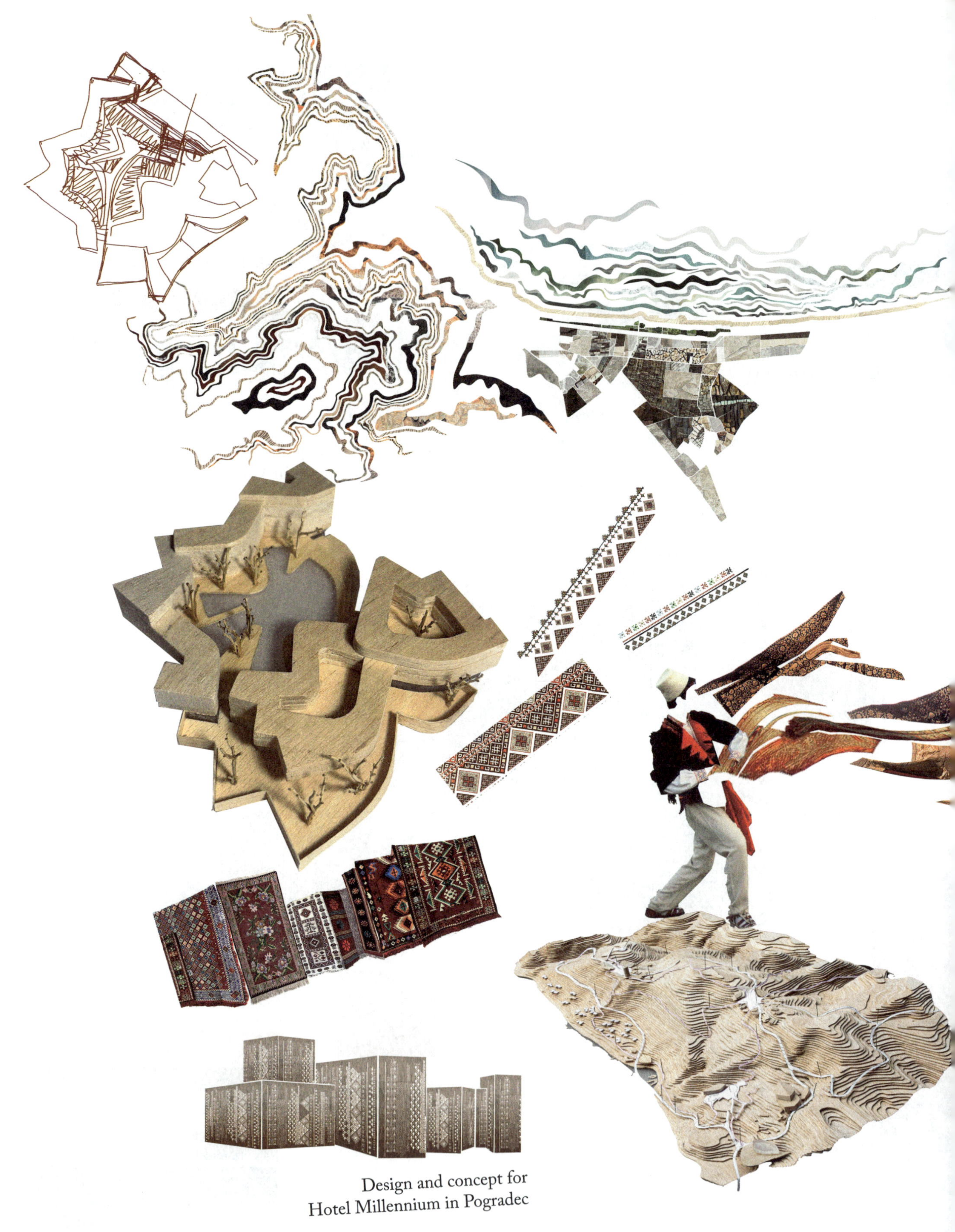

Design and concept for
Hotel Millennium in Pogradec

Design and concept for
Zhan d'Ark housing in Tirana

Design and concept for Zhan d'Ark in Tirana

START	NAME PROJECT	LOCATION	DEVELOPER	PHASE
2024	Koran Village	Pogradec	Arlis Ndërtim	Concept
2024	Housing Zhan d'Ark	Tirana	Gotbek Construction	Concept
2024	Hotel Millennium	Pogradec	Millennium Group	Concept
2024	Residence & hotel Velipojë	Shkodra	Rozafa A Ltd	Schematic design
2024	Zel Melia	Vlora		Concept
2024	Luxury resort	Gjiri i Lalëzit	Mabetex Group	Feasibility study

NAME OFFICE

MVRDV

DATE	PLACE	WORKING IN ALBANIA SINCE
October 2025	Rotterdam, Netherlands	2003

PRINCIPALS

Winy Maas
Jacob van Rijs
Nathalie de Vries

PROJECT TEAM

Winy Maas
Bertrand Schippan
Stavros Gargaretas
Stefan de Koning
Ronald Hoogeveen
Angel Sanchez Navarro
Anna Gasco
Valentina Chiappa Nuñez
Eduart Balla
Afrodite Moustroufi
Agnieszka Thiel
Alberto Carro Novo
Alessandra Carallo
Alex Niemantsverdriet
Andreas Anagnostopoulos
Anna Zoia
Boris Tikvarski
Boudewijn Thomas
Cai Huang
Carlota Sola Gonzalvo
Changqinq Ye
Christina Polyviou
Dimitra Tsitsi
Dirco Kok
Efthymia Papadima
Elien Deceuninck
Esteban Alvarez Ruiz
Francesca Cambi
Francesca Celli
Francesco Mammarella
Pilotti Aielli
Geert Folmer

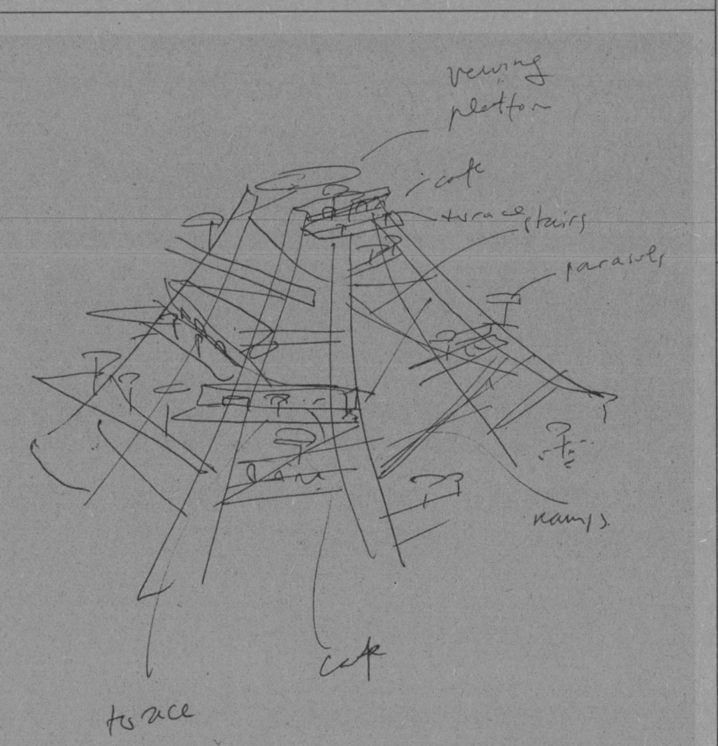

COLLABORATORS

PYRAMID OF TIRANA
iRI shpk (Co-Architect)
TUMO Tirana (Education Partner)
Fusha shpk (Contractor)
AADF (Project Coordination)
Arup, iRI shpk, Nikolin Risilia, Artur Dado, Isuf Kore (MEP)
Daniel Gjoni (Monuments Expert)
Arben Liçi (Environmental Adviser)

SKANDERBEG BUILDING
Sfera Studio (Co-Architect)

TIRANA BOULEVARD
UNO architects, local executive architect (Co-Architect)
Sky Invest shpk and Pajtoni Group (Client)

MUNICIPALITY HQ
iRI shpk, represented by Gent Agolli (Co-Architect)
Topotek1 (Landscape)

FARMMAX
iRI shpk (Co-Architect)
Municipality of Tirana (Other Collaborator)

GREAT RING ROAD (THE ROCK)
X-Plan Studio (Local Architect)

UMEA
MIC-HUB, under F&M Ingegneria coordination (Mobility & Transport Strategy, Environmental & ESIA Specialists)
Deltares (Specialist Subcontractor)

I LOVE VLORE TOWER
UDV Architects and Ada Petrela (Co-Architect)

THE NEEDLE
iRI shpk (Co-Architect)

INTRODUCTION TO ALBANIA

Our introduction to Albania began with a conversation with Edi Rama after Winy Maas gave a lecture in Rotterdam in the early 2000s. At the time, Rama – then mayor of Tirana – jokingly remarked that we would "never dare to come to Albania." This sparked curiosity, and three weeks later, Winy Maas visited Albania. He recalls his first impression of the country as a "beautiful mess," yet full of energy. The vibrant coffee culture on terraces and glimpses of stunning landscapes stood out to him. During that first visit, they had lengthy discussions about architecture and the country's challenges, particularly regarding housing, land ownership and development. These conversations highlighted tasks like organizing property, addressing occupied lands and boosting the economy – issues that demanded a role for architecture to help resolve.

MAIN CONTEXT VS. ALBANIA

We've worked all over the world, gaining experience in many different building processes. We have projects in Europe, Asia and North America, and in most of these places, the process is more streamlined. There's access to quality materials, expertise and established regulations and permit systems. Even narrowing it down to how we work locally in the Netherlands compared to Albania, there are significant differences. Starting up in Albania over twenty years ago came with challenges. The building process often felt improvised, regulations for high-rise buildings were almost nonexistent and there weren't many engineers with the necessary expertise. Once, when new high-rise regulations were introduced following an earthquake, we had to completely adjust a façade design within two weeks. To give you another example of how things were done back then: During the construction of Downtown One, the workers formed a close-knit community. They even slept on the floor above where they were working. The work progressed floor by floor, with the team moving up as each level was completed. While unconventional, it showed the dedication of the local teams.

ORGANIZATION/GOAL/SETUP

When we first started working in Albania, we focused on building strong collaborations with local co-architects, architects and engineers. Since we didn't have an office there, we were often on-site, sometimes on short notice. When things went wrong, we had to be there to sort them out.

As Albania's system became more organized, it became easier to work remotely, and we've shifted from on-site improvisation to a more formal approach. Over time, we've gained knowledge from navigating the local building scene, and now we have a team within our office dedicated to sharing that expertise. Our goal has always been to establish long-lasting partnerships – with clients, local experts and the community. Since we place strong emphasis on public projects, we ensure we're not just working with clients but engaging with the city itself.

SETUP IN RELATION TO ALBANIAN PARTNER

It's a collaborative process. Having local knowledge and expertise involved right from the start is essential. In the early stages, we guide most of the design, but as the project progresses toward the execution phase, the local architects tend to take a more prominent role. We regularly organize workshops in both Rotterdam and Tirana with the involved parties to ensure that the collaboration strengthens the project.

OPPORTUNITIES/CHALLENGES

What sets Albania apart is its openness to new ideas and its willingness to take risks. Prime Minister Edi Rama's belief in architecture as a vital part of the country's future sets the tone, and there's a refreshing directness in how projects are approached. There's a kind of energy and ambition in Albania that's hard to find elsewhere, the unique experience of working in a country that is seeking its place in Europe.

HOW TO INTEGRATE GREATER RESPONSIBILITY FOR QUALITY IN PROJECTS

The key is to make quality a shared responsibility. In Albania, we've seen the shift from improvised beginnings to a more organized system with codes and permit structures. That helps. But rules alone don't guarantee quality. What matters is the culture around it: the idea that everything we build should be done beautifully. That's not just the architect's task; it's something the government, developers, engineers and even the public need to embrace. Competitions, collaborations with local architects and transparent processes are ways to embed accountability. It's also important not to overregulate and kill Albania's energy of invention and curiosity. There should be balance.

BALANCING QUALITY AND DENSITY/INVOLVING STAKEHOLDERS

Densification is a big question in Tirana. The danger is that density simply means "more," but the real task is to make it *better*. The architect has a responsibility to show that density can improve livability, not destroy it. In Albania, we've been able to do that because there is openness, a willingness to take risks and to have direct conversations with politicians, developers and citizens. The architect should act as a mediator between all these groups. And yes, it should be expanded. Involving more stakeholders through competitions, workshops and open discussions makes the process stronger.

EXAMPLE/INSPIRATION

A simple yet inspiring example in Albania is the early transformation of Tirana led by Edi Rama, who has a background as a painter. He started by adding color to social housing blocks and inviting artists to contribute, creating a playful, vibrant city almost instantly. This shows how culture, urbanism and everyday life can come together to refresh a city while respecting its unique history.

Tirana, I love you Albania is one of the fastest-changing countries in Europe. After the collapse of the Hoxha regime, the rise of Edi Rama, first as minister of culture, then mayor of Tirana and later as prime minister, began a turn towards modernization. Edi is an artist at heart. The city was transformed with color. This low-cost approach increased the energy and pride in the city. Following this example, we envisaged the line "Tirana, I love you" on an apartment building in the city center.

Hotel Constantinopoli This villa was originally built by Italians, a consequence of Albania's historical relationship with Italy. It was intended to become a hotel, but it was too small. We proposed to restore the villa and add more program. On top of its pedestal the villa would become more dramatic and beautiful, surrounded by a swimming pool.

Toptani Market Hall At the time the Toptani area, right next to Tirana's "old city," was quite empty. For the competition for a new market hall, we imagined a thick slab for offices and shops, covering the market that would open to the city in four directions. It was a sibling to the early designs for the Rotterdam Markthal, which we started to design around the same time. We won the competition. It was soon discovered that the concrete required was too expensive, so we developed a new iteration. On the outside, there are terraces on each level, with staircases allowing people to climb to the top. Years later, after a long period of silence, we discovered the building was under construction. Somehow, another office had taken over our project and finished it. The façade is quite well developed, although not with the terraces and the stairs originally envisaged. The interior is a bit more commercial, and it doesn't open up completely at the edges as in our original design. But it's still our building, for better or for worse.

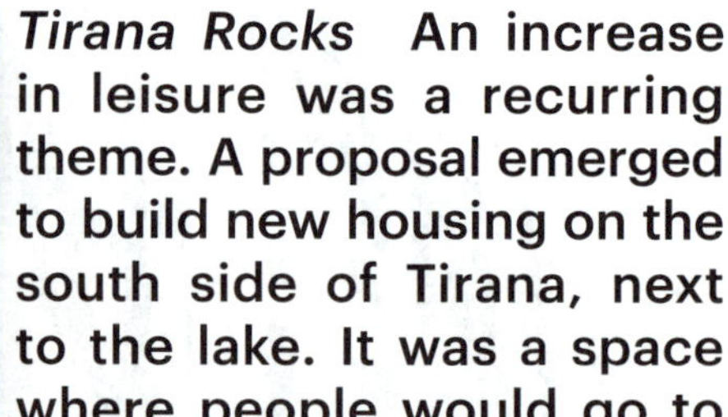

Tirana Rocks An increase in leisure was a recurring theme. A proposal emerged to build new housing on the south side of Tirana, next to the lake. It was a space where people would go to enjoy themselves, and the new development could raise the money needed to improve the amenities. For the new buildings, we started with blocks that were all the same and imagined what we could do with them. Perhaps some are stacked on top of others, or leaning . . . maybe some towers could be kissing? The result was a symbol of diversity. We won the competition, yet the project was never built.

Downtown One In 2015 the area around Skanderbeg Square was really developing fast: The river had been cleaned some years before, and competitions to design towers in the area were popping up a lot. We wanted this collection of towers to have a certain coherence. We rotated the building to face the monument, placing Skanderbeg at the center. The shape echoed the geography and topography of Albania, in a kind of pixelated form. The "push-in, push-out" effect was used to create terraces all the way to the top of the building. Once again, we ran into cost issues. Once again, we had to transform the project. The final design is more modest, but it maintains a number of the same features: It is still turned towards Skanderbeg Square. It still features the map of Albania, so from below people can say, "There, my apartment is in the Durrës pixel." It still has the push-in and push-out with terraces on top, so people can have a barbecue outside and chat with their neighbors on a nearby terrace.

Pyramid of Tirana in 2012

Pyramid of Tirana The Pyramid of Tirana was originally built as a monument and museum to Enver Hoxha. It was codesigned by Hoxha's daughter and her husband. After the collapse of Hoxha's regime, it was used as a NATO base during the Kosovo War, a conference center, a nightclub and a broadcast center for Albanian media. Over time the building fell into disrepair. Numerous proposals were made to demolish it and redevelop the land, whether for a new Albanian parliament, an opera house, or for commercial uses. Historian Ardian Klosi started a petition against the demolition, saying that the building is a symbol of how we have to build on our past, and that the past can never truly be erased. A study published in 2015 suggested that the majority of people in Tirana were against the demolition.

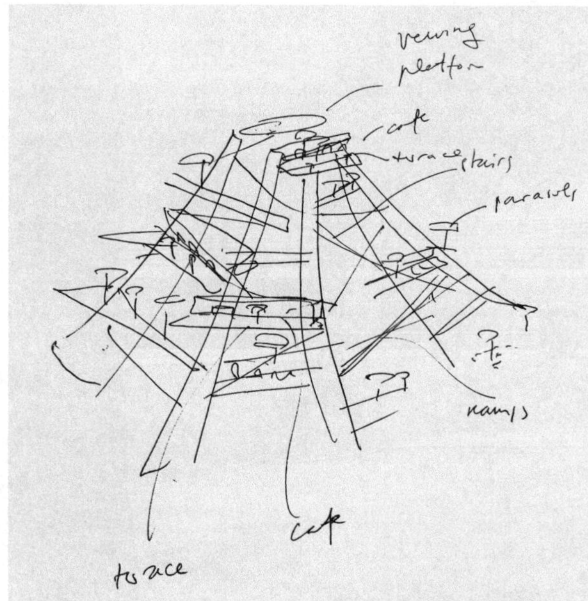

While these debates took place, we took inspiration from a very different group of people: Bored teenagers had adopted the pyramid as a place to hang out. They would climb the concrete beams and slide back down in a rebellious, daredevil act. If you want to understand how the present is built on the remains of the past, there are few better examples than a new generation, with no memory of the regime, using the dictator's monument like a playground.

The Albanian-American Development Foundation, in collaboration with the municipality of Tirana, entered an agreement for the revitalization of the Pyramid of Tirana. As per this agreement, the AADF financed and contracted MVRDV for the design of the architectural project, to transform it into a multifunctional and recreational site. At this moment, we were invited to enter the competition to transform it. We proposed to add steps to the outside, so that anybody could have the experience of conquering the dictator's monument. In one spot it is still possible to slide back down.

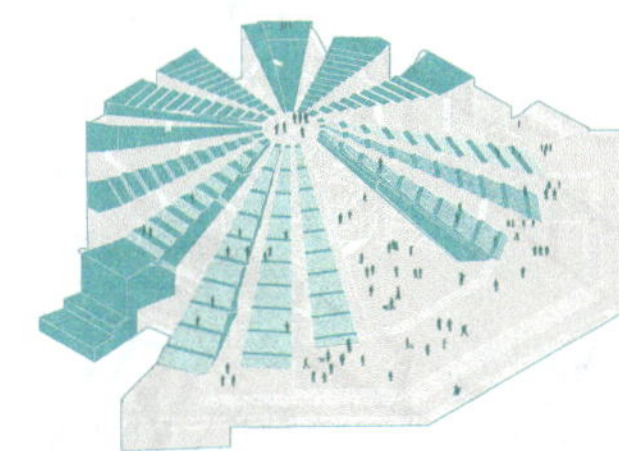

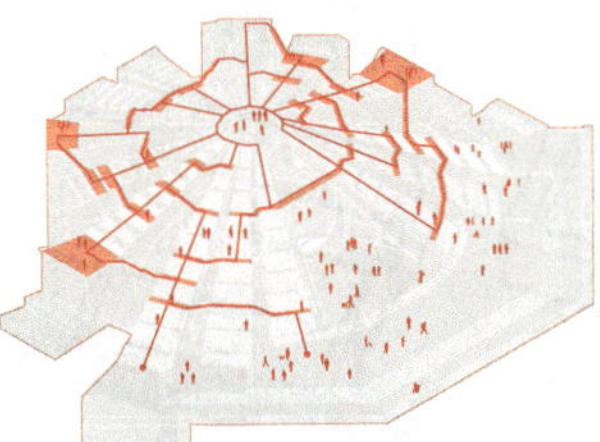

For the rest of the structure, we opened it up. The park continues into the structure, where it is protected from the rain by glass flaps. Inside, we inhabited the space with a stack of colorful boxes that also spill out into the surroundings. Half of these boxes house cafés, restaurants, offices and studios and are accessible to the public. The other half are home to TUMO Tirana, a nonprofit that provides free education in software, robotics, animation, music and film. From a monument to the past, it has become an optimistic symbol of the future.

Gorge(ous) If you fly over Albania to see the mountains and rivers – these areas are beautiful, and vulnerable, and could be considered as part of a new national park program. Meanwhile the coast is basically under construction. Many of these construction projects have questionable quality. For the design of a hotel on a stunning gorge site by the sea, our aim was to set an example for something better. We pushed the building to the back of the gorge. The building is a mirrored beam across the gap. It helps to keep the gorge public and accessible, and connects the natural areas on either side of the gorge. It appears like a jewel on the coastline.

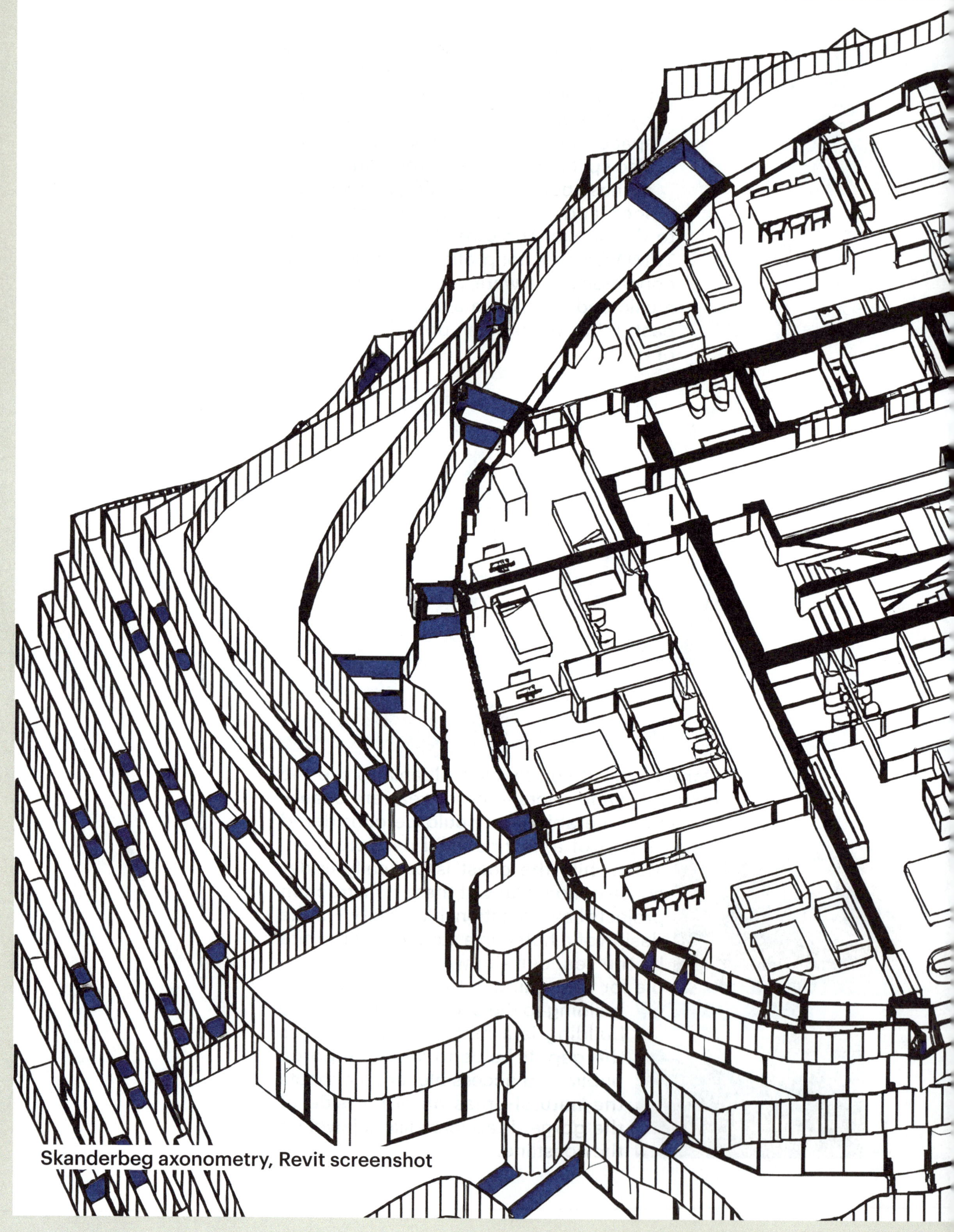

Skanderbeg axonometry, Revit screenshot

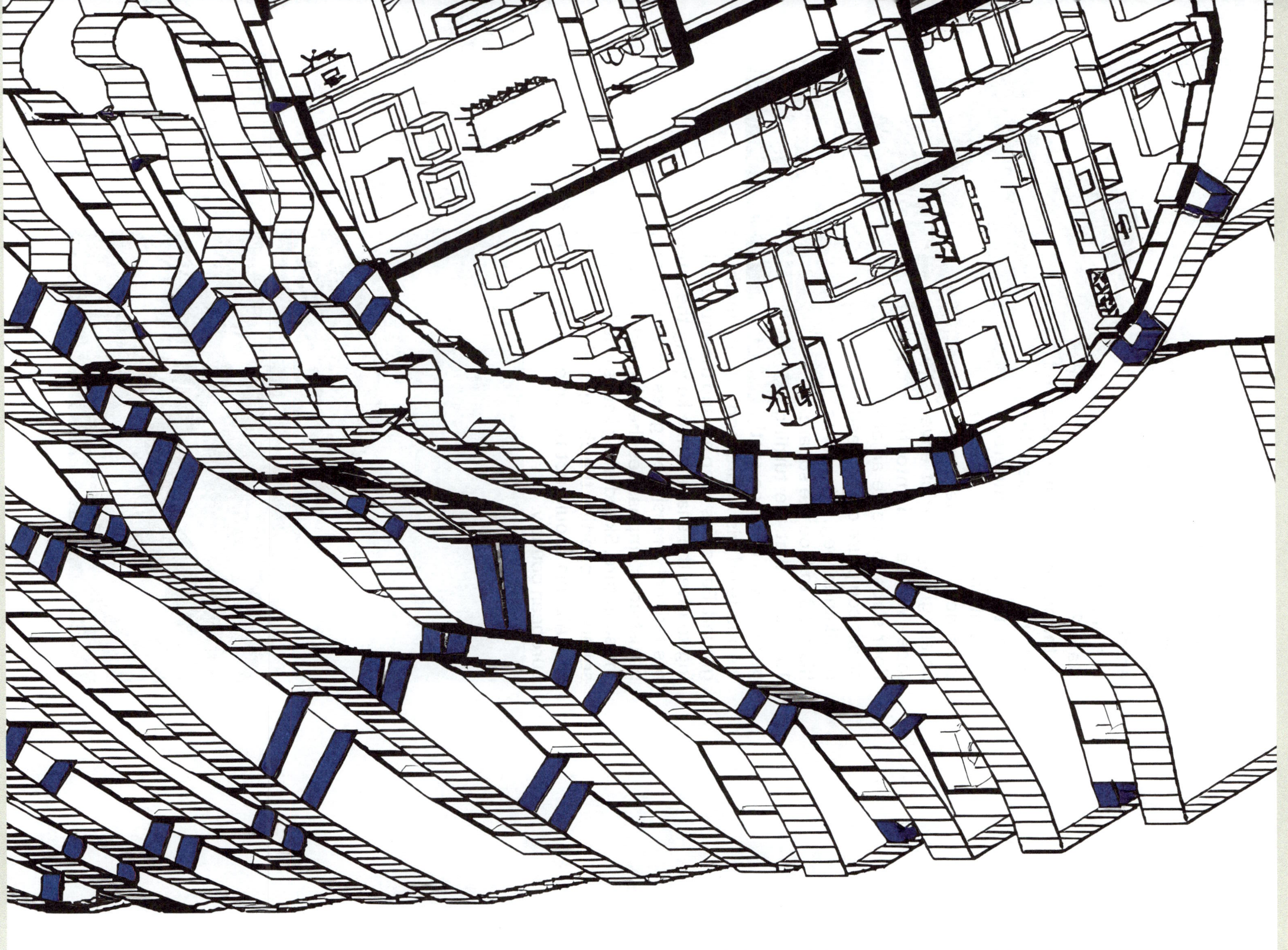

Skanderbeg Building Albania wants to join the EU. As this goal gets closer, how can the country preserve and emphasize its individuality in a unified Europe of many states?

At the corner of Skanderbeg Square, we proposed the idea to give Skanderbeg himself a much greater presence. The site is very small, giving a strict envelope. We carved into the floor slabs to create an abstract sculpture of the head of Skanderbeg. He turns his head to face the square. To ensure that the turning gesture was done correctly, we modeled his entire body underneath the ground. Balconies wrap around the entire building to give the shape while keeping the interiors rational. Translucent glass on the balcony balustrades emphasizes the abstract quality of the sculpture. Skanderbeg keeps watch over his square – supporting the changes while pleading that Albania should not become like any other European country.

Tirana Boulevard Skanderbeg Square and the surrounding area is becoming increasingly refined. Attention has shifted to the next area of the city that needs systematic overview. A new boulevard to the north is under construction. A commission came from a developer for two towers on this boulevard. Behind the site is a park, so we realized that the project needed to become a connector between the park and the boulevard. The program is split into four parts to become a portal. Adding staircases on either side ensures that pedestrians can go through. A colorful urban living room opened up through the middle, like a rift that invites people to explore the other side.

Municipality HQ The city planned a new building to house 1,200 municipal workers. The mayor along with all the administration and other employees would work there. We separated the functions into horizontal bands. Each level steps back so that the building becomes a tribune with a wooden structure. At the foot of the tribune is a public plaza. Floating over the entire ensemble is a pergola, which provides shade and supports solar cells. The plaza monumentalizes the building as a space for the people.

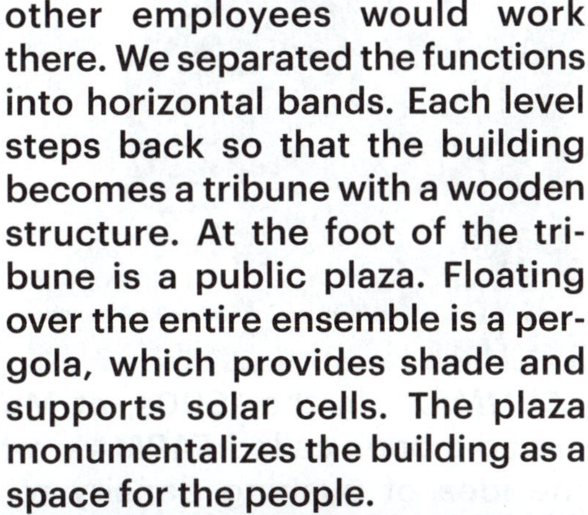

The Halo Our client now wanted to build right next to Skanderbeg. How could we respond to such close proximity with such a building? We imagined the new building as a backdrop, like a screen behind the monument of Skanderbeg. The shape of Skanderbeg is preserved like an imprint in this backdrop. This imprint also opens up a new public space at the foot of the building. The project represents a continuation of the development around Skanderbeg Square. It is an evolving process that changes with each new addition. It creates variety and personality.

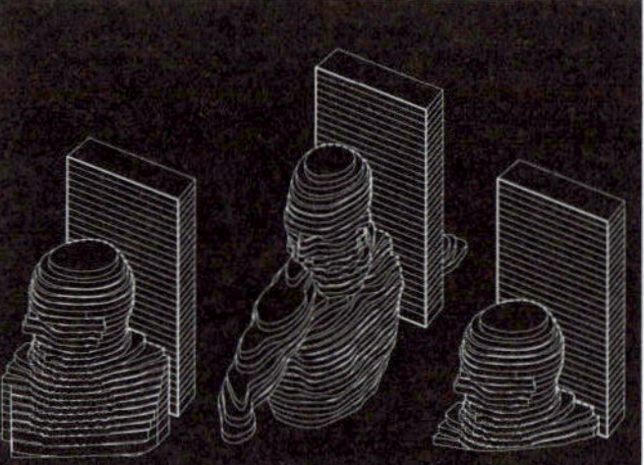

FARMMAX In the 1990s, at MVRDV we produced a book called *FARMAX*, which explored the idea of pushing density to extremes. In Tirana, FARMAX became FARMMAX. The Agricultural University wanted to turn the land around their existing buildings into a new plantation test zone. How can we combine institutional buildings and housing with the maximum density of farm space? The answer was to turn the buildings themselves into an agricultural domain. Their roofs, façades and balconies would be covered in plants. We created a grid across the entire site. All the native species of Albania would be in an alphabetized arboretum, an approach we tested in our design for the 2022 Floriade in Almere, the

Netherlands. In the final design we achieve a floor area ratio of 1.6, even with a carpet of agricultural space covering everything.

Great Ring Road (The Rock) Tirana's infrastructure continues to develop, with a ring road being built around the city. There is space for an eye-catching new apartment building where this road crosses the Lana River, in the northwest of the city. Its location next to the road from the airport means it will act as a landmark welcoming people to the city. We cut into the base of the

slab to create more public space, and cut into the top to give it a recognizable silhouette. It created a form like a standing stone. With the building's rough finishes and rugged balconies, we completed this impression. Greenery covers the balconies from ground level to the top. In this way, the Rock is tied into the natural landscape of the riverside and becomes part of the city's green ambition.

UMEA Once again we were invited to create something on the coastline. This time, a new airport near Vlora was spurring development. The result is UMEA, a large-scale coastal master plan located near the Vjosa River and close to the airport. The developer wanted to create a year-round destination: a place that combines leisure, hospitality and living, guided by the surrounding landscape, within a 650-hectare area. The nature here needs to be looked after, so we made a full investigation of the site's natural conditions. Protecting the wetlands and minimizing environmental impact were the main priorities. How to work with the landscape rather than against it? We avoided building on the dunes and kept construction in the woodland to a minimum. This approach defined the shape of the coastal villages and the roads connecting them. Preserving the site's natural character keeps the place calm and full of nature. Connected, but still far from the city.

I love Vlore Vlora is a seaside city that's really starting to change, and our site sits right in the middle, between the new marina and the old town. The building's scale sits in between too, bridging old and new. It's on the newly renovated boulevard, full of energy, with a park just in front, so the ground level feels open and alive. We broke the volume up to fit the surroundings and to create terraces and elevated gardens where residents can enjoy views of the sea and the mountains. It's part of the city, but it also wants to be noticed. We put a message on it – "I Love Vlore" – a message for the city and its future. It's a landmark, a place people can point to, a symbol of Vlora's future.

The Needle As the city center of Tirana developed, it became necessary for the university area to grow and to reestablish its place in the city. A new building for the European School is under construction, so there is a need for

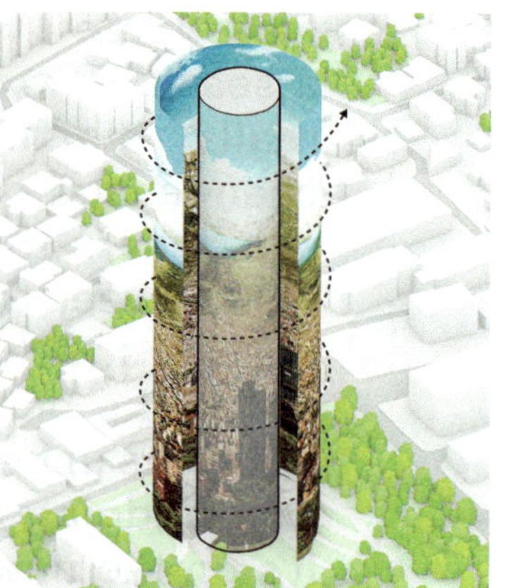

more accommodations. In the center of the campus, a plan to build new housing with a library and commercial spaces provided the opportunity. A 200-meter tower gives the university its own identity-defining centerpiece while maximizing the public space at the heart of the university. Commercial spaces are terraced into the landscape, with bridges connecting directly into the library. The roof offers a viewing platform for the whole city. We proposed to work with local artists to create a print of a stylized image of Tirana. Covering the entire façade, it "reflects" its surroundings, from the street, to the skyline, to the mountains: a snapshot of the city during this pivotal period of its history.

START	NAME PROJECT	LOCATION	DEVELOPER	ENGINEER	PUBLIC/PRIVATE	PHASE
2003	Tirana, I love you	Tirana				Unbuilt
2003	Hotel Constantinopoli	Tirana				Unbuilt
2008	Toptani Market Hall	Tirana	Gener 2 Development	Arup, London, UK / Arup, Amsterdam, NL (lighting)	Private	Executed
2008	Tirana Rocks	Tirana	Gener 2 Development		Private	Competition – unbuilt
2016	Downtown One	Tirana	Kastrati Group	LEAL, Arup, Elteknik	Private	Under construction
2016	Pyramid of Tirana	Tirana	Albanian-American Development Foundation, Municipality of Tirana, Albanian Ministry of Culture	Arup, Gentian Lipe, Luan Murtaj MEP: Arup, iRI shpk, Nikolin Risilia, Artur Dado, Isuf Kore	Private	Executed
2016	Gorge(ous)	Gjipe Beach				Unbuilt
2018	Skanderbeg Building	Tirana	ANA shpk, VI&VI shpk	Structure: LEAL (represented by Ruben Alite)	Private	Under construction
2020	Tirana Boulevard	Tirana		Structural consultancy: Ove Arup & Partners; local structure: Uts-01; local mechanical: Hydro and Energy, local electrical: Kejsi-05	Private	Design development
2020	Municipality HQ	Tirana	Municipality of Tirana	Arup		Competition – unbuilt
2020	The Halo	Tirana	MSA Konstruksion shpk	Structure: LEAL (represented by Ruben Alite)	Private	Design development
2020	FARMMAX	Kodër-Kamëz area, Tirana	iRI shpk			Study
2024	Great Ring Road (The Rock)	Tirana	Albus Invest shpk, Loraldo shpk (part of Pajtoni Group)	Engineering consultancy: Ove Arup & Partners	Private	Design development
2024	UMEA	Vlora	UMEA shpk	F&M Ingegneria	Private	Design development
2024	I Love Vlore Tower	Vlora	Stroytech shpk	Structure: Armeda Gramos; hydro & mechanical: Arta Miraka; electrical: Saimir Saliaj; fire fighting: Ergys Çaushi	Private	Design development
2024	The Needle	Tirana	Frasheri MF		Private	Design development

NAME OFFICE

NOA

DATE
September 19, 2025

PLACE
Bolzano/Bozen, Italy

WORKING IN ALBANIA SINCE
June 2024

PRINCIPALS
Stefan Rier
Lukas Rungger

PROJECT TEAM
Lukas Rungger (NOA founder)
Stefan Rier (NOA founder)
Christian Rottensteiner (NOA partner)
Andrea Dal Negro
Silvia Marzani
Alexander Donà
Franco Zagato
Francesco Padovan
Maddalena Gioseffi
Anna Lena Reier
Alexander Kellner
Niccolò Panzani
Federico Zoller

NICKNAME
The Mediterranean Mountaineers

INTRODUCTION TO ALBANIA

Albania is a land of great openness and opportunities for contemporary architecture; it's hard not to have it on your radar. We were following with great interest what was happening under the leadership of Edi Rama during the last couple of years . . . and one day a spontaneous call by Alban Efthimi for a possible collaboration on a tower in Tirana was the start of a unique journey.

MAIN CONTEXT VS. ALBANIA

Fifteen years ago, we founded NOA in the heart of the Alps, in the bilingual region of South Tirol, which has allowed us to express ourselves freely. Today, we have projects spread across Europe, with a focus on hospitality, offices, retail and cultural buildings. In Albania, we are witnessing an approach to architecture that is open and free from preconceived notions, much like when we first began. Albania has established itself as a vibrant laboratory of ideas, an open kitchen full of changing ingredients, where the vigilant and constant attention to architecture also allows projects to progress faster than in other parts of the world. Particularly the focus on "experimentation" encourages us designers to leave our comfort zone and contribute to a new "face" of the country and its people.

ORGANIZATION/GOAL/SETUP

We were fascinated by the many "facets" of the various Albanian contexts we found. Walking through Tirana, we had the impression of a city that oscillates between order and disorder. Watching the horizon from Gjiri i Midhjeve beach, we reflected on the importance the sea has in the development of this country and how deeply Mediterranean its people are. Our goal within this diverse reality is to remain true to our design principles and propose architectural concepts offering an innovative interpretation of the place in which they are set. In this design journey, we hope for a fruitful and inspirational exchange with many Albanian actors, collaborating together and crafting a partnership that will be beneficial for years to come.

SETUP IN RELATION TO ALBANIAN PARTNER

We have established a good collaboration with ATELIER 4 and with Alban Efthimi, one of its founders. NOA is responsible for the design, while the Albanian studio provides their technical expertise, as well as insights on local regulations. They are also our cultural bridge and gateway to the Albanian way of life, including its past and present cultural evolution. This continuous exchange naturally blurs the boundaries between designing and strictly executing the proposal, making the creation process a fluid journey where the pieces continuously shift to create something unique.

HOW TO INTEGRATE GREATER RESPONSIBILITY FOR QUALITY IN PROJECTS

The complexity of our built environment is high, and carrying out so many big projects simultaneously requires deep understanding and impeccable organization from all the actors involved. There are guidelines and principles to steer the development of these projects, of which we recognize as essential: ensuring affordable housing for everyone, especially considering the young population in Tirana; promoting mixed-use functions to shorten distances that can be covered on foot or by bike; protecting spaces from consumption-only use; guaranteeing public spaces; fostering a synergy between architecture and culture; and creating a positive impact throughout the entire construction sector.

EXAMPLE/INSPIRATION

Our local partner, ATELIER 4, has completed the revitalization of the historic bazaar at Avni Rustemi Square. We consider this an exemplary project for reclaiming historical values and rescuing the site from aesthetic degradation. In 2019, the bazaar was a finalist for the EUmies Awards, which speaks for itself . . . This work represents a multidimensional dialogue, extending far beyond a single urban investment, and beautifully reflects the city's DNA.

SEASIDE

Traveling toward Saranda, where the residential project Berdenesh Hills is set to rise, became a significant source of inspiration. Observing the changing landscape through the car window while leaving Tirana revealed a gradual transformation: The view transitions from a dense urban landscape to a low-density rural setting, where Mediterranean scrub covers gentle hills.

Concentric topography

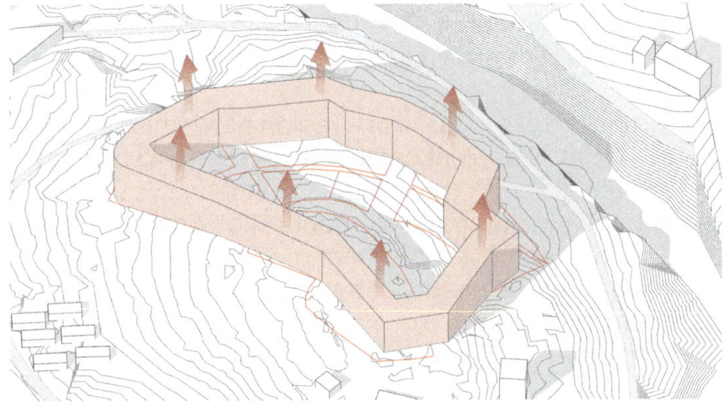

Volume extrusion below surrounding heights

We were deeply impressed by the coastline of this region: It unfolds as an inward-turning spline, marked by continuous inlets, large bays and small coves, all framed by the silhouette of Corfu on the horizon.

Leaving Saranda – a town that has experienced a construction boom since the 1990s – behind, we entered a landscape defined by the interplay of land and water. Jagged cliffs draw an irregular point of contact between land and sea.

Layering of the natural and built landscape

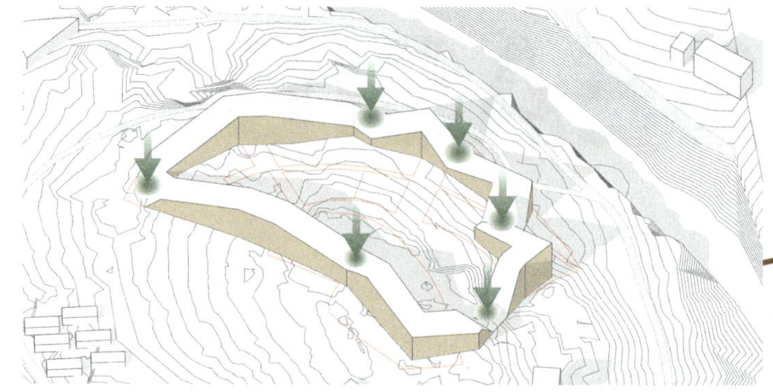

Height variation to allow unobstructed views

We aim to offer surprising interpretations of the spaces where our architecture takes root, ensuring that the landscape and its cultural context always remain the main players.

Rising behind our project site, exposed stone slabs form a tectonic pattern of projections and recesses. This distinct territorial identity plays a fundamental role in shaping the project. Especially in contexts so different from the birthplace of our architectural sensitivity – the peaks of the Alps versus the heart of the Mediterranean – it is essential to read and translate what surrounds us.

The project site is located in a region rich in history, where traces of ancient castles, fortresses and bastions are scattered across the landscape. Our analysis of both the natural and anthropic elements allowed us to define a grammar for a new settlement model – one capable of interpreting the beauty of the place and establishing continuity with its history.

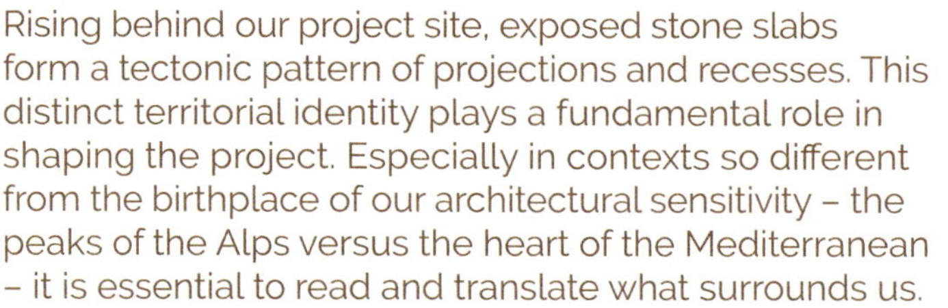

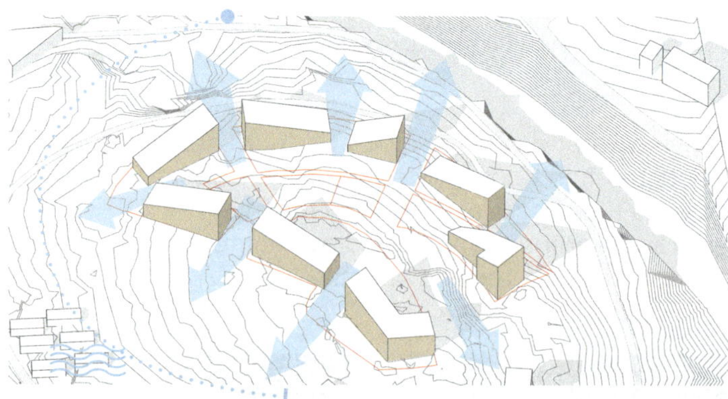

Creation of axes and connections to the landscape

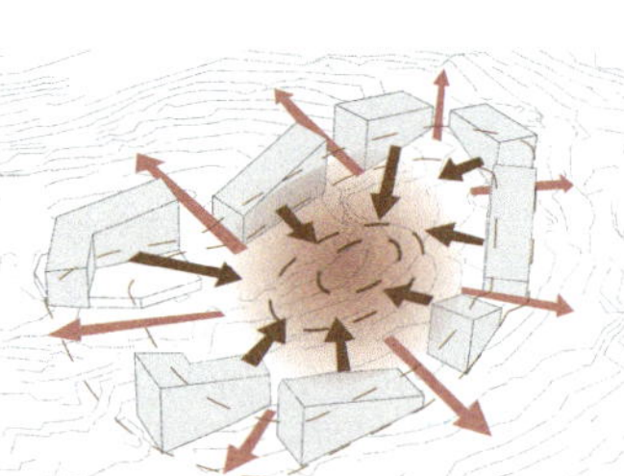

An inverted citadel

Although the predominant architectural typology in the seaside town of Saranda today is the tower, for this project, we sought to reconnect with the traces of the past. We envisioned the creation of a new small neighborhood in form of a citadel. Like its historical counterparts, this contemporary citadel develops around a focal point, the central piazza. However, unlike ancient Greek, Roman or medieval fortresses – the most famous Albanian example being Gjirokastër – its perimeter walls, formed by a variety of buildings, open outward in a continuous search for connection with the external environment. An additional element of integration with the landscape is achieved through the staggered roof planes, which rise and fall to mimic the surrounding topography.

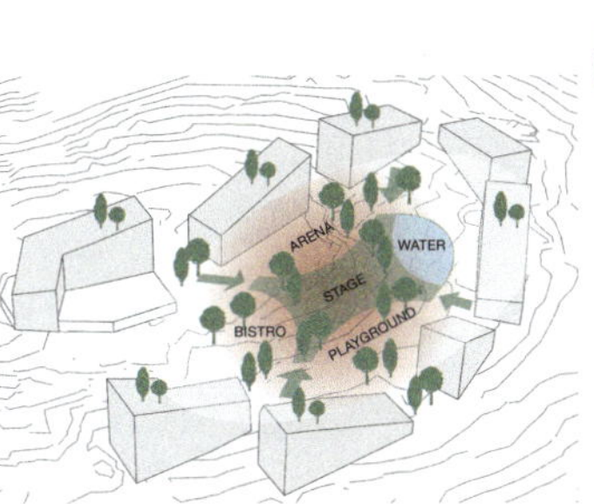

Wide green spaces create a park accessible to all

We practice architecture to tell a narrative. We want to understand the place where we design: trace its history, capture its peculiarities, breathe its atmosphere.

This creates an architectural landscape that blends seamlessly with its natural environment. The varied heights open up new views, consistently framing the true focus of the project: the sea.

The façade features bands of warm, earthy tones that echo the lines of the landscape. These organic lines form a dynamic interplay of protrusions and recesses. The terraces not only provide generous outdoor spaces for residents but also enhance the building's integration with its surroundings, softening its visual impact while maximizing natural light.

Overlaps and recesses

Berdenesh, sea-facing apartments

Puzzle Tirana, inner courtyard

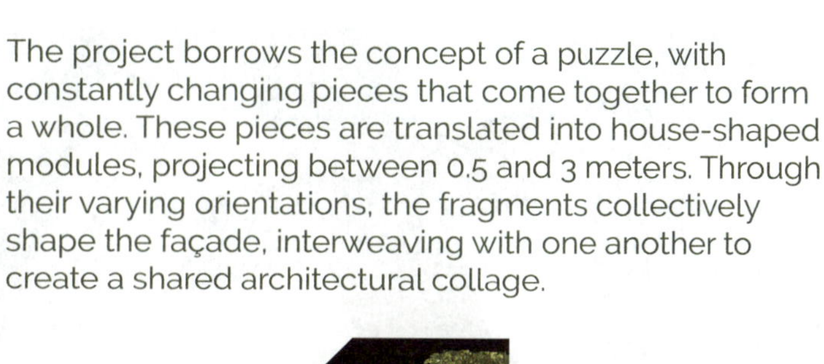

The project borrows the concept of a puzzle, with constantly changing pieces that come together to form a whole. These pieces are translated into house-shaped modules, projecting between 0.5 and 3 meters. Through their varying orientations, the fragments collectively shape the façade, interweaving with one another to create a shared architectural collage.

The building's four façades hold equal architectural value. These are further enriched by grafting local plants onto the projecting sections of the modules. On the first two floors, this hanging garden is complemented by sculptures, creating an artistic pathway along the façade. The void that cuts through the façade on the upper floors adds an element of surprise, evoking the feeling we experienced upon our first arrival in Tirana.

Urban and rural: These two realms have shaped our journey as a studio. Our roots lie in a rural context, where we were free to express ourselves, while our professional training took place entirely in an urban setting. Today, in our practice, we continually strive to bridge the gap between these two worlds.

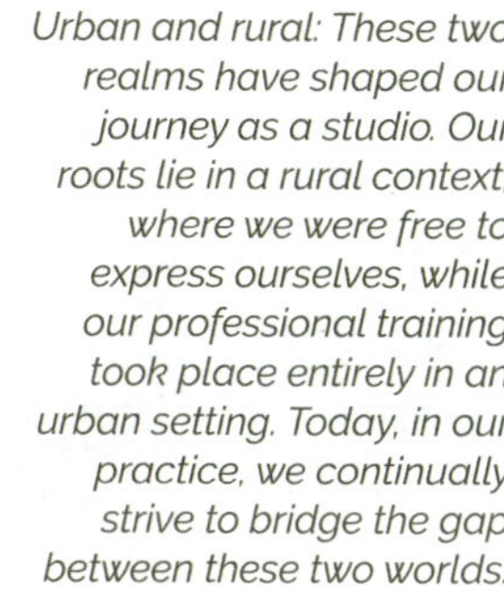

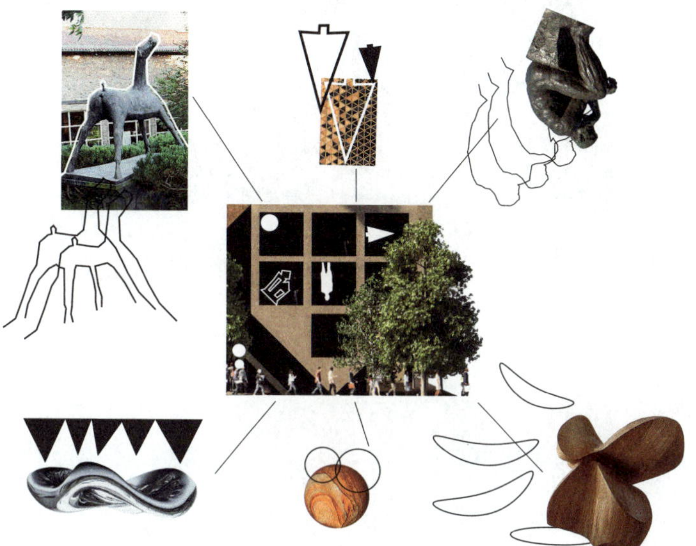

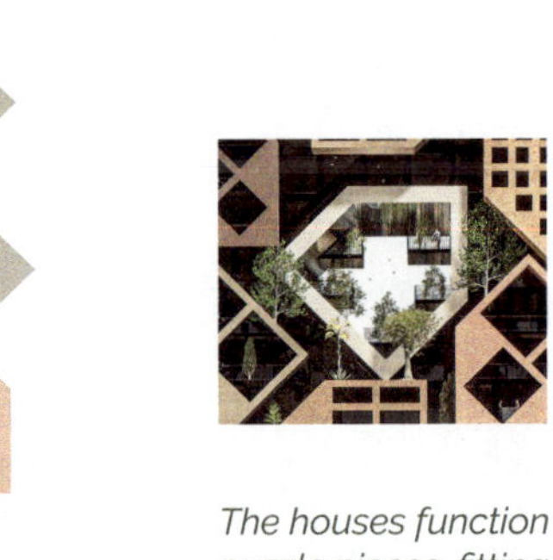

The houses function as puzzle pieces, fitting together and rotating until they "click" into place. A large void, shaped like a rotated house, cuts across the façade from side to side, adding an unexpected element.

Even next to our lot, on one side there is a 20-story-high tower, while on the other side there are single- or multifamily homes with just one or two floors. We were fascinated by this unique coexistence, which inspired

the concept of creating a design that represents the fusion and densification of two contrasting worlds – urban and rural – into a single architectural intervention. The concept envisions a vertical metropolitan village that oscillates between order and disorder, rules and chaos. A highly dynamic façade contrasts with an underlying grid system that rationally organizes the space.

The design is inspired by rural homes, where there is traditionally more freedom to create personalized spaces, blending architectural design with a DIY approach.

CITYSCAPE

Inspired by the rapid transformation of Tirana, the design proposal for Puzzle Tirana develops a dizzying vertical composition that draws on elements from both rural and urban contexts. Upon arriving in Tirana, we observed that the urbanization process was still fragmented, resembling a puzzle, with traces of rural fabric still visible within the city's perimeter.

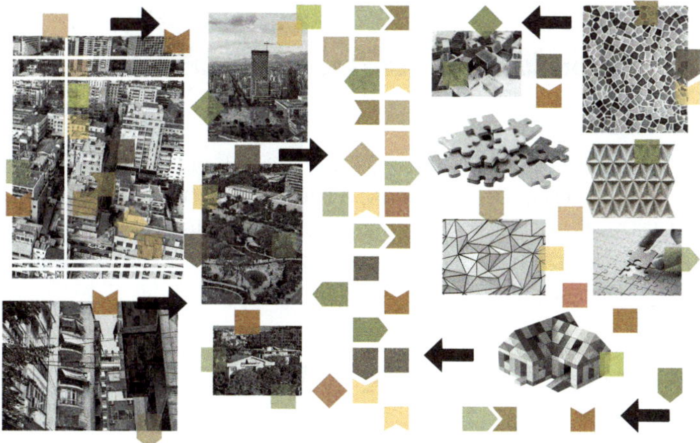

A city with a rich yet turbulent past. It seemed like a kind of puzzle where the old and new worlds coexist in a fascinating interplay of contrasts.

The gabled house is an archetype of the rural world, scattered throughout the Albanian countryside and hinterland, often in an unfinished form. Yet single-family houses can also be found in the center of Tirana.

START	NAME PROJECT	LOCATION	DEVELOPER	ALBANIAN PARTNER	M^2	PUBLIC/PRIVATE	PHASE
2024	Puzzle Tirana	Rruga Medar Shtylla, Tirana	Lunor, Texas Development, Innovex, Daton	ATELIER 4	22,800 m^2*	Private	Final design before building permits
2024	Berdenesh Hills	Berdenesh, Saranda	Lunor, Trust	ATELIER 4	26,000 m^2*	Private	Under construction
2025	The Tailor of Tirana	Ali Demi, Tirana	Sian Buildings Albania	ATELIER 4	47,000 m^2*	Private	Preliminary design
2025	Saukonia	Sauk, Tirana	Karoli Construction	ATELIER 4	23,200 m^2*	Private	Preliminary design
2025	Planters' Place	Rruga Viktoria, Tirana	Agra-Lu, Kamberi Construction	ATELIER 4	15,860 m^2*	Private	Preliminary design
2025	The Stagescraper	Rruga e Kavajës, Tirana	Texas Development	ATELIER 4	21,640 m^2*	Private	Preliminary design

*above-ground floor area

NAME OFFICE

NUNO MELO SOUSA

DATE
September 26, 2025

PLACE
Penafiel, Portugal

WORKING IN ALBANIA SINCE
2024

PRINCIPALS
Nuno Melo Sousa

ALBANIAN PARTNERS
A+ Architecture Studio
Roynsarch Studio, Marsela Volaj
SON Architects
Vaeku Studio, Urim Hoxha

PROJECT TEAM
Ana Arantes
Ana Dias
Diogo Veiga
Hugo Cruz
Inês Montez
I-Hsuan Chu
Luís Formiga
Tiago Amado

MAIN CONTEXT VS. ALBANIA

I work in the small city of Penafiel, 40 kilometers from Porto, Northern Portugal. The main difference has to do with the scale of the projects in Albania, which are very different from the small-scale projects I am engaged with in Portugal. Yet I can see a lot of similarities when it comes to the construction context, in which elementary concrete structures and brick/block walls are the main building techniques. This is in addition to a craftmanship which is still to be found in both countries.

ORGANIZATION/GOAL/SETUP

I've been in close contact with the clients and local architects I am working with, visiting the country every two months to assist and interact with the local dynamics. I've also been traveling through Albania to better grasp its intense growth and speed and to better understand how I can better build my projects.

My goal is to do the best I can by understanding the context where I am now inserted.

SETUP IN RELATION TO LOCAL OFFICE

I share my design work with the local office after it has been developed internally and already has a strong idea. Then we can debate and adjust, aiming to better frame it within the Albanian context. I had to adapt to the apartment size ratios and living aspects to be better accepted within the context. It is not different from the way I work in Portugal, as everything I produce at the office is developed internally, with rare design collaborations.

OPPORTUNITIES/CHALLENGES

The opportunity in Albania is to develop programs and scales that there is no space or development for in our cities. Besides that, there is freedom of expression in these proposals and a slight flexibility when it comes to legislation, which can also better help the designs achieve a certain dose of radicality. And there is joy and hope!

HOW TO INTEGRATE GREATER RESPONSIBILITY FOR QUALITY IN PROJECTS

That is a personal question and really depends on each one's stance. On my side, the answer is to work as intensively as possible on each project and never settle for half. To be happy with what one does whether it is next door or miles away, as in the end, it is always us, our name, our responsibility for what we propose and design.

Of course, clients and local architects have to align with this too. This tango needs three, not only two. And we have to keep raising our concerns on how to build and propose buildable projects with livable and healthy spaces, which can raise the building context bar. We have to be as radical as we are exigent about what we do.

BALANCING QUALITY AND DENSITY/INVOLVING STAKEHOLDERS

We have to ask as many times as possible and we have to create awareness that less is more when it comes to density. It doesn't mean that we will win every one of these discussions, but we shall start with them – and try to commit as much as possible to what is a pleasant and balanced outcome of what we do.

EXAMPLE/INSPIRATION

I really like Skanderbeg Square in Tirana. It is a radical project. A square without lights at night. That resembles a hill. With multiple stones. I like it very much.

TOOLBOX ALBANIA FUTURE

It is a school of thought as much as it is a school of life. First I learn from my colleagues. I grew up looking at most of their books and publications, and now I can talk with them and collect bits and pieces of knowledge about their interactions in Albania. I also look forward to understanding how they manage the same constraints I find in difficult plots, amazing sites, intensity demand and program flexibility. And then we engage ourselves with full heart and body and we try our best.

1. krahu tower, shëngjin
2. dy shkallë, kavaja
3. këndi tower, vlora
4. katër kulla hotel, ksamil

a. ground-floor plan+pastel+scan
b. substrate
c. model
d. collage
e. render+print+pastel+scan
f. print+pastel+scan
g. thoughts

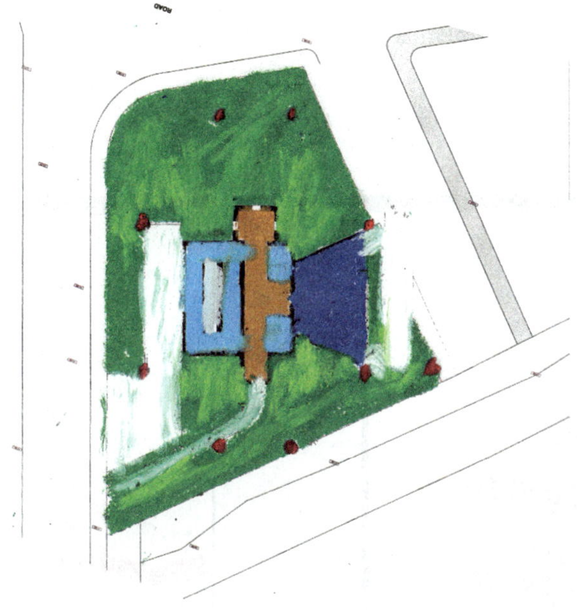

3.g
deviations
one's near-miss trials
I enjoy looking at these
at the end of the process it seems like its essence was there
looking at you since the first drafts
sometimes it comes easier than others
a lobby for a tower is no given thing, as one size needs to fit all
(at least most!) just like snapback caps.
the start of a vertical movement

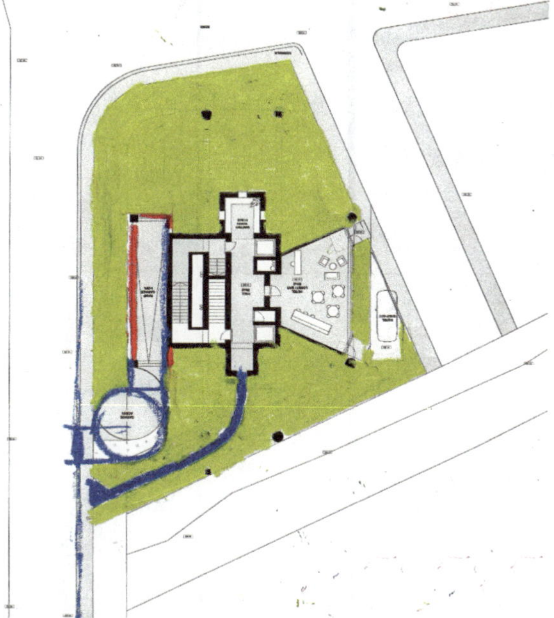

3.g
a difficult plot
open yet blind corners
stretched and compressing the
entrance with verandas facing both
sea and mountain

3.g
the drawing of a plan is to articulate
a choreography
to imagine the movement of bodies,
figures, specters,
through space
to relate walls, pillars and the
walkable surface
a creature with two tongues,
a tail and a fat body

3.a

1.b

3.b

3.c

4.e
3.e

4.e
3.e

2.b

2.d

I hit the road for a week: from car to car, table to table, site to site
expectations always high, no time to lose
rush to head rush
tall towers, mixed-use or hotels and apartments, served with long conversations
miles of inland western movie scenarios, broken high mountains steep
flat seas
flat skies
from no construction to full construction
difficult sites – but those make a project, don't they?
yesterday is to deliver, to propose an idea – an ideal;
and avoid, at all costs, to spoil and risk the future
to keep it (this welcoming), Albania

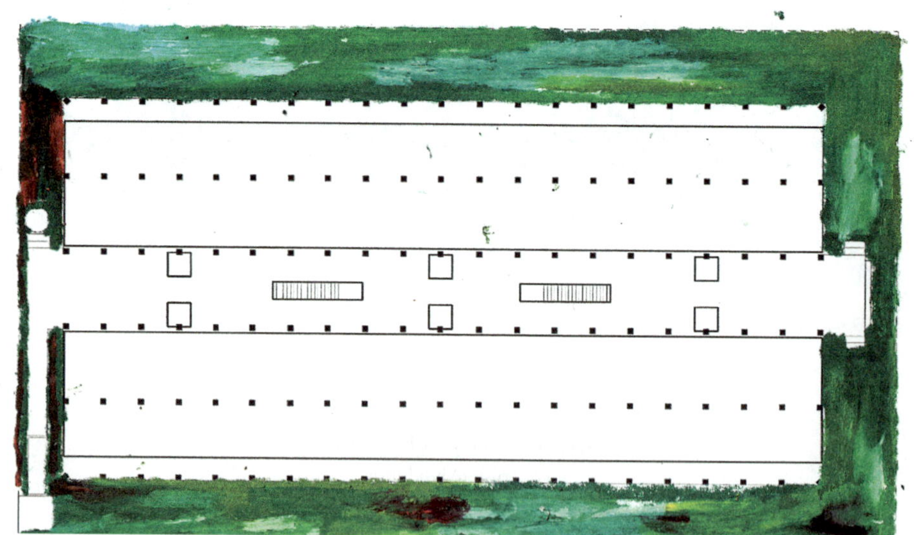

2.f

four-piece composition,
– to be found along the intriguing coast of Albania – recorded live in our studio – cosmos
– 2 basement, vila gualdina, penafiel
during the vigorous winter of 24 to 25,
with cold walks outside,
long stares at the fire burning,
hundreds of prints,
thousand doubts,
full of joy
packed with hope

START	NAME PROJECT	LOCATION	DEVELOPER	ALBANIAN PARTNER	M²	PUBLIC/PRIVATE	PHASE
2024	Krahu Tower	Shëngjin	Ilyonis Constructions	Roynsarch Studio	12,915 m²	Private	Construction permit – processing
2024	Këndi Tower	Vlora	Modeste shpk	SON Architects	10,000 m²	Private	Construction permit – processing
2024	Tre Kopshte	Kavaja	Vizion Property shpk	Vaeku Studio	12,215 m²	Private	Construction permit – processing
2024	Katër Kulla Hotel	Ksamil		SON Architects	1,415 m²	Private	Construction permit – processing
2024	Triada Verde	Himara	Bega 07 shpk	A+ Architecture Studio	7,310 m²	Private	Submitted for construction permit

NAME OFFICE

OFFICE KERSTEN GEERS DAVID VAN SEVEREN

DATE	PLACE	WORKING IN ALBANIA SINCE
December 17, 2024	Brussels, Belgium	March 2024

PRINCIPALS
Kersten Geers
David Van Severen

ALBANIAN PARTNERS
SINGULAR (Local Architect)
"CIVIL-ING" (Structural Engineers)
ITE grup (Electrical Engineer)
Rita Voj (Mechanical and Hydraulic Engineer)

PROJECT TEAM
Kersten Geers
David Van Severen
Valentina Previtera
Elisa Guarnieri

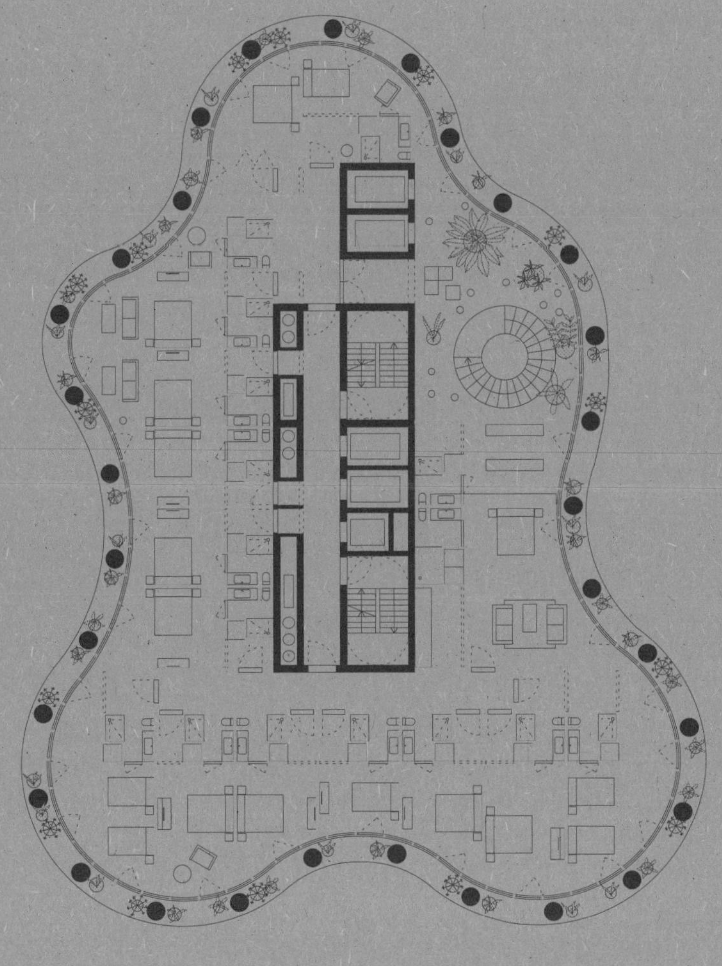

INTRODUCTION TO ALBANIA

We were among the selected teams for the EXPO Albania international competition. We didn't win, but were subsequently commissioned to design something else – two towers.

MAIN CONTEXT VS. ALBANIA

The context changes with every project, really. This depends not only on the project location, but also on the size and complexity of the organization. When working abroad, we team up with local architects, and depending on the project, our designers might either relocate on-site or simply visit occasionally. We always try to collaborate with local companies and resources.

ORGANIZATION/GOAL/SETUP

We are in the early stages of working in Albania, and we need to see how things will evolve. For now, we do have connections with local architects and engineers, and we plan to establish long-term collaborations, so the entire know-how will be local.

SETUP IN RELATION TO ALBANIAN PARTNER

We are the authors of the original design, and thus have the role of the leading architect. But the local office is not simply executing this proposal. They have an important role in adapting the design to the local working conditions.

OPPORTUNITIES/CHALLENGES

It seems things are developing at a fast pace in Albania, from 300-meter-high towers in Tirana to large developments on the coastline. The sheer quantity of building production is certainly an opportunity for architects. The challenge is maybe to not take on too much, and to focus on a few exemplary projects.

HOW TO INTEGRATE GREATER RESPONSIBILITY FOR QUALITY IN PROJECTS

The continuous presence of the architect – from the early sketches of the design to the last detail, and also during the construction. This is the only way to ensure quality, if the architect can take responsibility for the design.

BALANCING QUALITY AND DENSITY/INVOLVING STAKEHOLDERS

A robust set of urban principles would be a great help, sort of a contemporary urbanism that is free and restricted at the same time, enabling different stakeholders to get involved.

EXAMPLE/INSPIRATION

The main square in Tirana, Skanderbeg Square, is a beautiful place and shows that empty space is as important as the buildings.

TOOLBOX ALBANIA FUTURE

The international community of architects coming together in Albania, similar to important architecture schools or events like the Venice Biennale, creates an important opportunity to exchange ideas, experiences and approaches to the context. This is a kind of toolbox in itself: a place to exchange knowledge and ideas.

In Praise of Crude Urban Figures

Architecture is born naked. It has no material, no size, no color and no place. It exists as a formal summary of different intentions. Within itself, it carries a kernel of previous architectures, built or imagined. This is a rudimentary architecture, not more than a type, or a geometrical definition. A tower or a house. A square plan or a round plan. Something big or small. It is malleable; this is an architecture of endless possibilities. What makes such rudimentary and arbitrary form viable architecture, is a self-imposed coherence and a set of axiomatic rules: the grid, the geometric correction, the perimeter, the proportions. Any request thus has to conform to the design principles. The rigidity of the method is paradoxically a prerequisite for flexibility. Once formally established, architecture can absorb any importunities and demands. More square meters? More rooms? More floors? Yes to all. Still, such architecture survives because of its formal DNA. Its high tolerance to complexity is what makes it continuously pragmatic. Its durability combines a fixed shape with an evanescent content. Such abstract form can be anywhere, it has the status of an object. In its mild indifference it somehow always fits. The place is ultimately its sole engine.

Architecture becomes real only when it finds a place, and thus becomes part of the local culture, local climate, local building codes. This is when architecture acquires its materiality, tactility and spatial quality. Its uniqueness relies on the tension between fitting and not fitting its new environment. Any new building is a violent proposition. Its alien condition is modified when it becomes an urban form, an architecture that makes a city – no matter whether in Brussels, or Dallas, or Muharraq or, for that matter, Tirana.

Oblivious abstraction combined with an utmost precision is the only way we can deal with issues we hardly know about, in places we are not familiar with. A manufacturing facility for versatile satellite platforms, a cancer research center, a museum of contemporary art, radio-television media headquarters, offices for the European Commission. Each project comes with a set of guidelines – highly technical or utterly frivolous – and random objectives architecture is expected to accomplish. Amid ruthless profit-motivated ambition, we hopelessly deal in utopian standards, aiming for beauty. Successful architecture finds its reasoning on the fringes, in the added value that surpasses its immediate objectives. Its survival depends on its rudimentary form.

A tower is a clear urban figure, made as a simple stack of slabs. Its formal expression is disconnected from any technology, functions or elaborate facade systems, and thus immune to mistakes. As the technology and functions – both liable to changes – inhabit the crude structure, the finishing of the building is sturdier and less prone to construction flaws. Such a technological facade is not related to anything that happens inside; it is startling for its raw tactility. In a built environment showcasing exuberance, it is the responsibility of the urban figure to remain a repository.

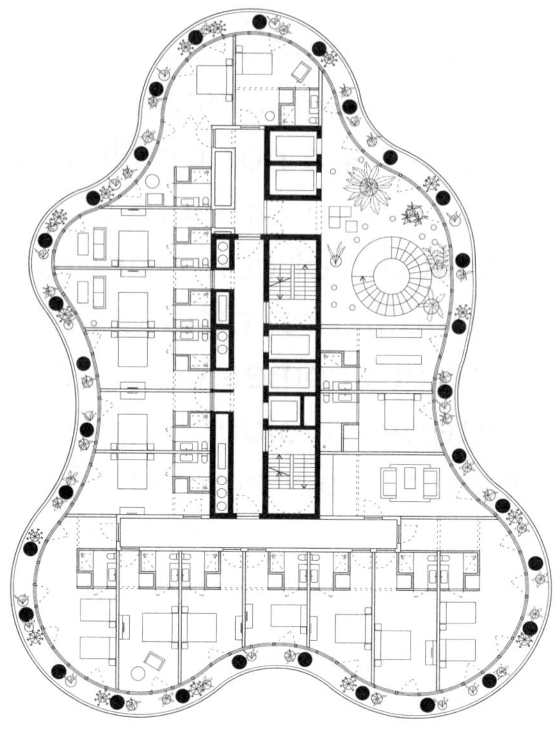

Hotel floor plan +8/+21

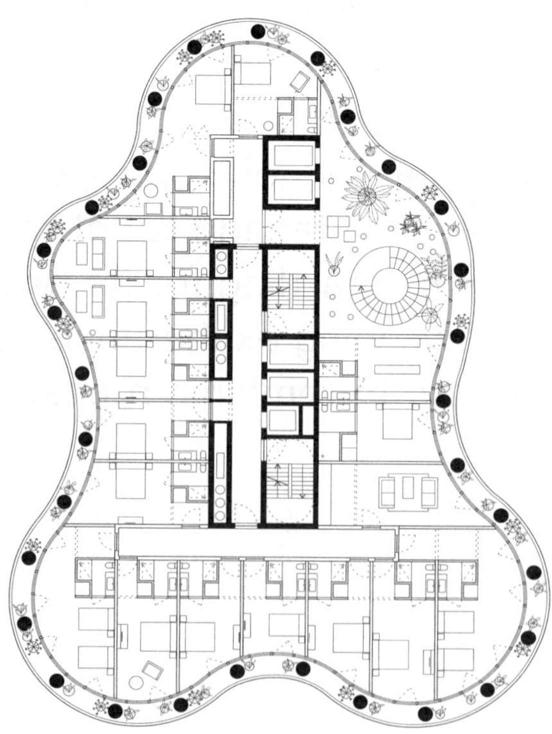

Hotel floor plan +1/+6

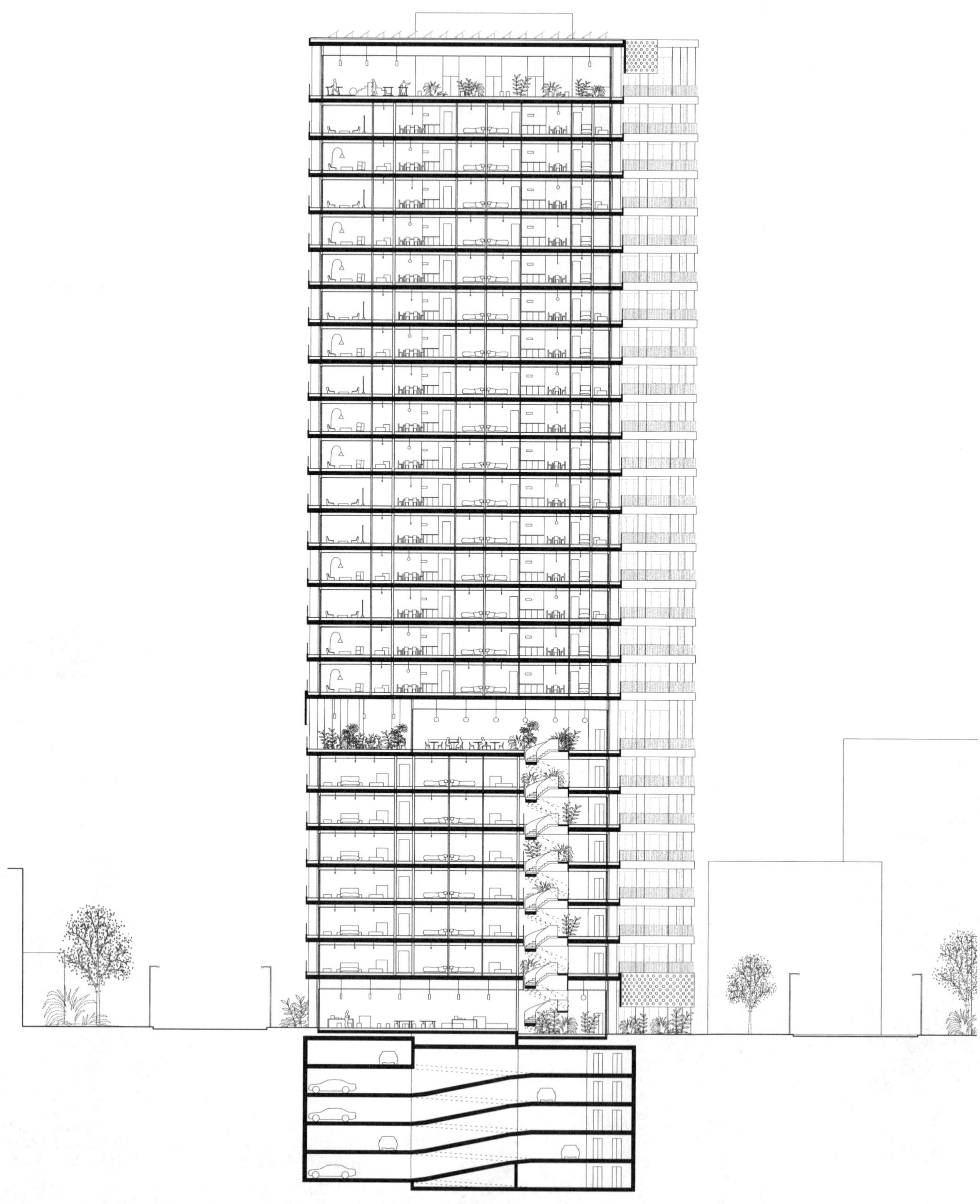

Section AA

NAME PROJECT	LOCATION	PROGRAM	PHASE
Faces of Tirana	Tirana	Mixed-use tower	Pending
Flower Tower	Tirana	Mixed-use tower	Tender
Dunes of Orikum	Orikum	Resort & residences	Pending
Teuta Tower	Durrës	Mixed-use tower	Ongoing – submitting building permit
Super Quadra	Tirana	Residential building	Ongoing – sketch design

NAME OFFICE

OMA

DATE	PLACE	WORKING IN ALBANIA SINCE
March 5, 2025	Rotterdam, Netherlands	2016

PARTNERS

Rem Koolhaas
Reinier de Graaf
Shohei Shigematsu
Iyad Alsaka
Chris van Duijn
Jason Long
David Gianotten (Managing Partner)

ALBANIAN PARTNERS

Kontakt (Local Architect)
LEAL – CSE (Local Engineer)
Archimed S.P.S. (Mechanical Engineer)

PROJECT TEAM

Reinier de Graaf (Partner in Charge)
Roza Matveeva (Lead Architect)
Jad Semaan (Lead Architect)
Michel van de Kar (Lead Architect)
Daan Ooievaar (Lead Architect)
Anton Anikeev
Julian Beqiri
Marco Gambarè
Andreas Karavanas
Francesca Lantieri
Davide Masserini
Barbara Materia
Ferzilet Leti Numani
Ekaterina Nuzhdina
Maria Aller Rey
Joanna Rozbroj
Zheng Zhou

INTRODUCTION TO ALBANIA

In 2016, we received an invitation from Albanian real estate developer Kontakt to design a residential master plan in Tirana.

MAIN CONTEXT VS. ALBANIA

We work wherever interesting propositions present themselves. Like many of the places we have worked before, Albania – and Tirana in particular – is undergoing rapid transformation, and it's exciting to be involved in this process. What was particularly appealing about working here was the opportunity to design a large-scale residential complex for an affordable market – a type of commission that is increasingly rare today.

ORGANIZATION/GOAL/SETUP

We don't follow a recipe. Every project requires a different setup depending on the nature of the commission, so we adopt the most efficient structure for each context.

SETUP IN RELATION TO ALBANIAN PARTNER

For Mangalem 21, the client had an in-house architecture team responsible for the execution.

OPPORTUNITIES/CHALLENGES

Western European architects have been welcomed to work in Albania for a good ten years now. More recently, American architects too. Prime Minister Edi Rama's insistence to put Albania on the map of contemporary architecture has attracted more and more offices, both established and emerging. I think what makes Albania attractive is that projects get built. Of course, construction budgets and the experience of contractors are not the same as in Western Europe or the US, but, as we said, things are changing fast.

HOW TO INTEGRATE GREATER RESPONSIBILITY FOR QUALITY IN PROJECTS

Willingness to question established habits, and architects can be of help in that.

BALANCING QUALITY AND DENSITY/INVOLVING STAKEHOLDERS

Not too many stakeholders, please!

EXAMPLE/INSPIRATION

Skanderbeg Square shows that you can build good quality architecture in Albania today.

TOOLBOX ALBANIA FUTURE

Albania offers not so much a toolbox but just the right amount of freedom for architects to do their job properly.

Objet re-trouvé
Reinier de Graaf / OMA

I still have the relics: two large towels, one with the double-headed eagle flag, the other with a 500 euro bill. The summer of 2016 we spent our holidays in Albania with family and friends – in Tirana, Durrës, Shkodra and Theth National Park. There were bears in the woods, allegedly. The wall of our hotel lobby contained detailed instructions on how to act if you came across them. Each life-saving suggestion came with an illustration. I remember only the most poignant one: a male figure lying on his back. Pretend you're dead!

That is exactly what our business development team did when we received an invitation to design a large housing project in Tirana. The conditions weren't favorable – are they ever? – and one decided to give this one a pass. The invitation ended up in the trash can. I remember coming back to the office, somewhere late in August, and getting wind of the opportunity to work in the country where I had just spent a lazy three weeks. A silly coincidence?

Less than a week later, I made my first professional visit. I got to see a different side of the country: open-minded, innovative and progressive, and more than a little eager to make that known. Europe's most isolated country until 1991 had become decidedly European.

Ambitious in terms of architecture, too. Skanderbeg Square was in the middle of an extreme makeover. New buildings by international architects were being erected around its edges. The square's new pavement radiated a kind of bridal whiteness. Its stone slabs, collected from all over Albania, served as a symbol national unity – or so I was told. Old communist buildings like the Palace of Culture – a gift from Nikita Khrushchev – and the National History Museum seemed to have acquired new vigor as a result of their younger neighbors.

The Enver Hoxha Pyramid was about to be saved from demolition. The huge concrete structure loomed along the Boulevard of the Nation's Martyrs like a voiceless carcass from a bygone age. Probably enjoying the best part of its life – no longer hostage to the ideology that begat it, not yet subject to the playful fantasies of new architects eager to make their own mark on history.

Then again, the same thing might be said of us. I hope we stood the test. For us, Mangalem 21 stands as an adventurous extension of our repertoire: 1,200 affordable homes straddling twenty-four courtyards, their walls and window frames a combination of color and color-blocking alike – a tribute to the colorful transformation of Tirana's communist-era housing blocks. I don't know how it happened, but it did. I'm glad it did. Coincidence or not, I'm deeply grateful for the opportunity.

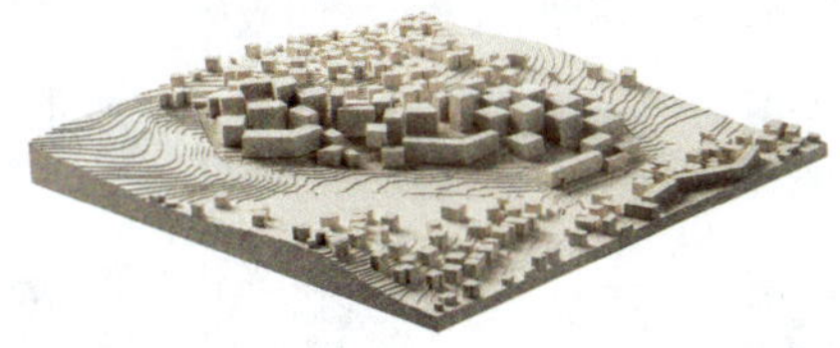

An open letter to Edi Rama
Prime Minister of the Republic of Albania
Rotterdam, March 3, 2025

Your excellency / dear Edi,

Please forgive me for addressing you in this form. You may not remember me; we only met once, and I am merely one of many foreign architects currently working in your country. I am writing to express my gratitude for the opportunity to work in Albania and also my broader admiration for everything you have achieved since you became prime minister a little over a decade ago.

Under your rule, Albania has acquired near model-status. Multiple religious and ethnic groups are peacefully living together; there is an effective separation of church(es) and state; a young working population keeps an economy afloat; labor participation by women is high and steadily on the increase; Albania is actively seeking EU membership and, not to forget, it has excellent taste in architecture.

In an unruly world, Albania is beginning to feel like the hopeful exception: pro-international collaboration, pro-progressive values and, perhaps most importantly, pro-reason – a beacon of enlightenment against the odds.

The purpose of my writing, however, goes beyond flattery. I'm writing to you because I'm worried. At this moment, your party is seeking a fourth consecutive term. I can only hope they succeed. It is difficult to picture a new regime taking care of architects as well as the current one.

Our profession is historically dependent on political patronage and certain somber thoughts have been going through my head lately. What will happen if the Socialists do not win the election? Will this mecca of contemporary architecture abruptly come to an end? Will a seemingly inexhaustible well of work suddenly dry up? Might the ArchArmy have to lay down its arms as expediently as it was mobilized?

I don't say this lightly, but for us architects, it would be best if the upcoming elections were simply called off. I would even go a step further. Given Albania's enduring status as an enlightened architectural patron, our profession would benefit greatly if the country never had another election again, and if you, after your fifth consecutive term as prime minister, would just continue as president for life – maybe even King.

Major historical events are unfolding as we speak. Autocracy is rapidly gaining ground as the definitive form of twenty-first-century government. Hopes of a productive alternative are shattered on a daily basis. We seem to be witnessing the end of The End of History. In that context, my plea is as simple as it is straightforward: In a world of autocracies, may we have one benevolent autocrat with taste?

I know that what I am asking of you is no small sacrifice, yet it is one of momentous importance. I hope you will consider.

Yours sincerely,
Reinier de Graaf

START	NAME PROJECT	LOCATION	DEVELOPER	PHASE
2016	Mangalem 21	Tirana	Kontakt	Executed

NAME OFFICE

OODA

DATE	PLACE	WORKING IN ALBANIA SINCE
January 20, 2025	Porto and Lisbon, Portugal	2022

PRINCIPALS

Diogo Brito
Rodrigo Vilas-Boas
Francisco Lencastre
João Jesus
Julião Pinto Leite

PROJECT TEAM

João Styliano
Inês Monteiro
José Pedro Rocha
André Veiga
Joana Ferreira
Ana Soares
André Lima
Vânia Couto
Marinos Skouras
Antígona Pinto
Luís Ferreira
Vânia Costa
Mónica Baía
Laura Leão
Luís Carlos
João Brás
Mariana Duarte
Axel Fangueiro
Francisca Araújo
Tânia Ferreira
João Queiroz
Luís Garcia
Pedro Costa
Beatriz Robalo
Margarida D'Alte
Vasco Custódio
Mariana Vinha
Isabella Goulart
Noiala Araújo
Renzo Canro
Ana Leite Fernandes
Marina Rodrigues
Nuno Ferreira
Carlos Pereira
Eduardo Sousa
Marcelo Valente
Pedro Mesquita
Pedro Cunha e Costa
Simão Mariz
Lourenço Andrade
Cesare Mazzocato
Inês Silva
Jonás Gómez
Joana Anacleto
João Simões
Ingrid Ori
Eduardo Viana
Tomasz Szymosz
Malte Justi
Emma Træland
Petter Lysgaard
Seontae Park

ALBANIAN PARTNERS

GAS STATION
SON Architects, Ilir Bejleri (Local Architect)
Dhimitri Papa (Structural Engineer)

HORA VERTIKALE
Artech, Genti Shtëmbari (Local Architect)
Dhimitri Papa (Structural Engineer)

BOND TOWER
NOVA Construction Group, Kleant Bibolli (Local Architect)
Dhimitri Papa (Structural Engineer)

NDARJA (THE SPLIT)
Artech, Genti Shtëmbari (Local Architect)
Dhimitri Papa (Structural Engineer)

THE CONCAVE
A+ STUDIO, Anita Beleri (Local Architect)
Gezim Pajo (Structural Engineer)

INTRODUCTION TO ALBANIA

We were invited to apply for a two-phase competition for a multifunctional tower in Tirana, and OODA was selected as one of the five finalists, along with Shigeru Ban, CEBRA, Fuksas and UNStudio. The competition was won by CEBRA. The process was covered by the local media, however, which gave us the chance to showcase our project, approach and profile to a vast local audience, including not only students and local architects but also investors and promoters.

SETUP IN RELATION TO ALBANIAN PARTNER

We see architecture as a team sport: We elevate each other, and the collective effort is, to us, more substantial, profound and productive than the individual work or gesture. This is not only the nature of our practice internally but also what we promote externally. Namely with local architects. We need their involvement, advice and support to ensure that the projects are the best fit for the market, make sense for the place and are feasible within the local conditions. We often like to underline that, to us, architecture should always be specific and adequate. Never generic or replicated. That's why our projects are always different, even within the same city. We are focused on finding the specific ingredients of each site, each program and each place.

OPPORTUNITIES/CHALLENGES

The most prominent opportunity for an architect in Albania lies in the ability to work with fewer bureaucratic hurdles and restrictions, allowing for a more flexible interpretation of the project scope. This unique condition provides architects with greater freedom to express their concepts and achieve creative visions and sensitive approaches, often with fewer constraints compared to other countries or markets. However, this freedom comes with significant challenges.

On the one hand, with increased freedom comes increased responsibility – much like the famous "with great power comes great responsibility" quote. Architects must ensure their projects not only showcase creativity and innovation but also engage meaningfully with the local community, utilize regional suppliers and contribute positively and sustainably to their surroundings. The aim should be to create meaningful, long-lasting impacts rather than merely bold or short-term statements. On the other hand, a major challenge lies in the practical implementation of these creative visions. The local construction industry often struggles to meet the technical demands of more ambitious architectural concepts. While the market allows for bold and unconventional designs, the limitations (as yet) of local building methods and materials can make it difficult to deliver projects that meet expectations and maintain their intended appearance over time. This disconnect can result in projects that fall short of their potential or fail to stand the test of time. Ultimately, architects working in Albania – whether international or local – must strike a balance between creative exploration and practical responsibility, ensuring designs that are not only innovative but also feasible and aligned with the local context and resources.

EXAMPLE/INSPIRATION

Skanderbeg Square, by 51N4E.

TOOLBOX ALBANIA FUTURE

Coming from Portugal, we do see several similarities to Albania: from history to heritage, from cultural to family values, from weather to the richness of nature. However, Portugal became different after its entrance into the European Union in 1986. Being the poorest economical member at that time, a construction boom started that lasts until today and that transformed the country. That boom did not always necessarily involve architecture at its core, however, and we witnessed vast areas of our country undergo massive construction for housing, hospitality and services – especially on the outskirts of the main cities or in the south, in the Algarve. The same happened in regions in the south of Spain, for instance. Albania could learn from this, as it is experiencing similar events and, in fact, architecture could play a significant role to prevent massive wrongdoings and be the anchor of the development of its bright future with more consciousness, more carefulness and inclusivity. And design-oriented, driven by built ideas. As Alberto Campo Baeza notably mentioned, "The history of architecture, far from being a history of forms, is basically a history of ideas, of constructed ideas. Forms are destroyed with the passing of time, but ideas remain, they are eternal." This could sum up the uniqueness that Albania could offer to architects and artists, but also to rulers, teachers, leaders, investors and other stakeholders who are willing to contribute to the future they believe should exist. Building ideas that sustain the test of time and that are meaningful to people.

Diogo Brito, OODA Founding Partner

GAS STATION

We see architecture as a team sport, we elevate each other, and the collective effort is for us more substantial, profound and productive than the individual work or gesture. This belief is not only the essence of our practice internally, but also what we promote externally. We often like to emphasize that, for us, architecture should always be specific and adequate. Never generic or replicated. That's why our projects are always different, even within the same city. We are very focused on finding the specific ingredients of each site, each program, each client and each unique story to tell.

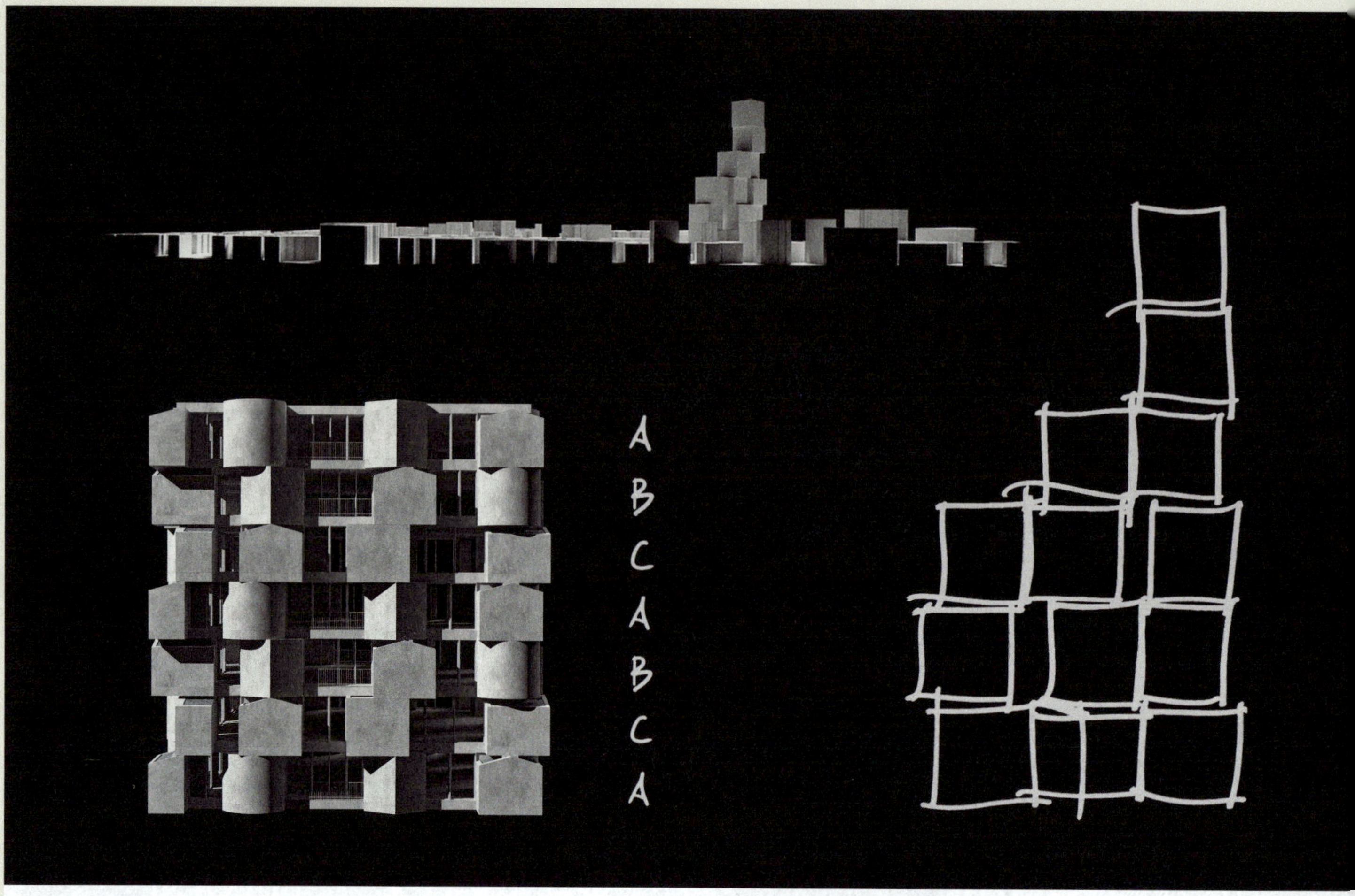

A B C A B C A

HORA VERTIKALE

While expressing their qualities and intentions, the projects should also be thought out and designed to engage with the local community, use local suppliers and ensure that their presence has a meaningful and lasting positive impact on their surroundings.

inspirati

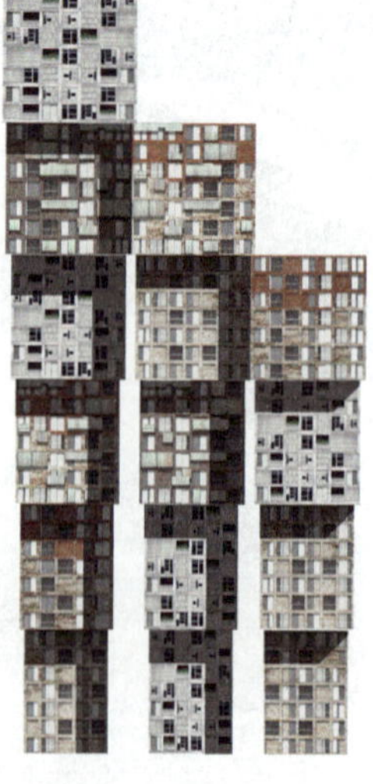

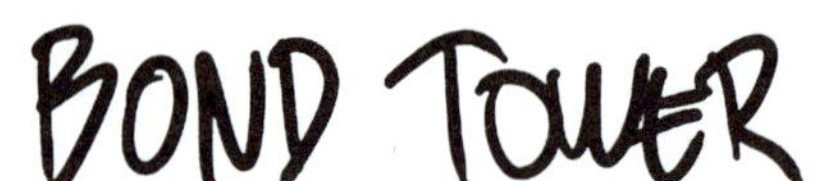

With a process intended to be strongly narrative it's paramount to test several contrasting concepts, overlapping different inspirations, until a focused narrowing-down of options allows us to choose what we believe to be the best answer to the problem to be solved.

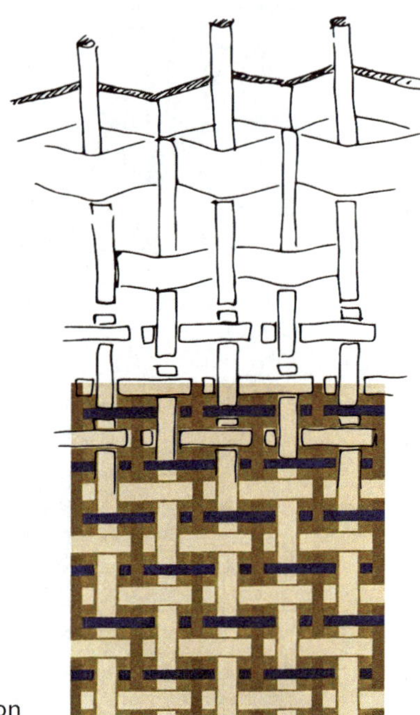

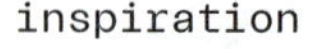

inspiration

We believe that the role of the architect should be to underline inclusiveness, strive for projects that fit Albania's idiosyncrasies and be an example of how inspiring it could be to work and live in a country that is admired for its beauty and history but has also been discovered worldwide through the lens of architecture in all its diversity and pluralism of expression.

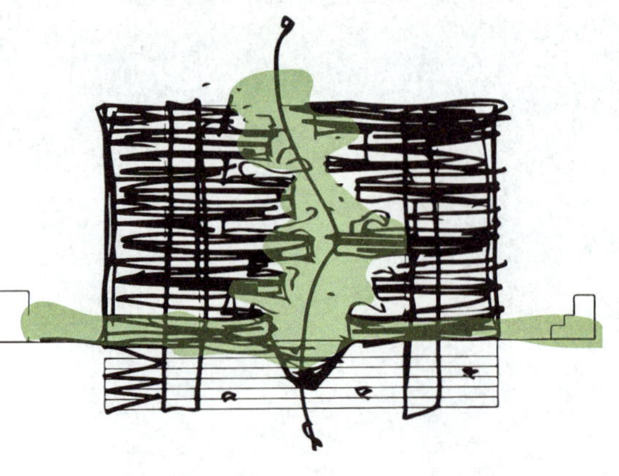

inspiration

inspiration

In Albania, more than constructing buildings, architects have the possibility to build ideas. To create stories that are told through bold designs while leveraging nature and creating a new type of engagement with the public realm.

THE CONCAVE (LLAMAN BEACH)

We have eight projects in Albania, all private.

START	NAME PROJECT	LOCATION	M²	PUBLIC/PRIVATE	PHASE
2022	Gas Station	Kolonje	600 m²	Private	Executed
2022	Klan TV new headquarters	Tirana	10,000 m²	Private	Schematic design
2023	Hora Vertikale	Tirana	46,500 m²	Private	Under construction
2023	Bond Tower	Tirana	43,800 m²	Private	Detail design
2023	Ndarja (The Split)	Tirana	33,500 m²	Private	Detail design
2024	Oricon*	Tirana	61,000 m²	Private	Concept design
2024	5th of May	Tirana	41,500 m²	Private	Concept design
2024	The Concave		5,800 m²	Private	Concept design
2024	Asim Vokshi	Tirana	20,000 m²	Private	Concept design

*Project in partnership with Souto Moura - Arquitectos.

NAME OFFICE

OPPENHEIM ARCHITECTURE

DATE
2025

PLACE
Miami, USA /
Basel, Switzerland /
Tirana, Albania

WORKING IN ALBANIA SINCE
2020

PRINCIPALS
Chad Oppenheim
Beat Huesler

ALBANIAN PARTNERS
Artech
ATELIER 4
common sense studio
CreativA Architectural Design
Focus Architecture shpk
MA Studio
pOint arkitekture
UDV
X-Plan Studio

PROJECT TEAM
Tom McKeogh (Studio Leader)
Rasem Kamal (Design Lead)
Francisca Neto Soares de Moura (Hospitality Design Lead)
Mariana Charters (Interior Design Lead)
Adriana Faísca
Agata Ratajczak
Alexandre Mecattaf
Ana Lopes
Anisa Myftari
Annabelle Peintre
Anya Pankovskaia
Daniela Guerra
Dina Muti
Francesco Marangi
Francisco Ramos
Helena Riesenberger
Igor Coimbra
Inaya Berger
Jephthah Sigg
Joana Sousa
José Urbiola
Joyce Frisella
Julia Zaiser
Junik Balisha
Kelia Sila
Kristijan Marcok
Kseniia Ponomar
Laura Buka
Laura Radics
Lucie Skorepova
Luisa Komisarov
Maria Diego Fernandez
Martino Cucurnia
Natacha Viveiros
Nicolas Ioannou
Olha Tymczuk
Quirin Batsch
Roksana Papakozma
Sabine Ariqat
Samuel Heitz
Sarah Eichkorn
Stefano Lombardi
Stela Velo
Tamara Fajer
Tom Stepins
Tom Walch
Victoire Brem
Ylli Ahmeti

NICKNAME
OA

MAIN CONTEXT VS. ALBANIA

We work in emerging destinations for hospitality and in cities undergoing rapid transformation. Across different contexts, from Puglia to Athens, Abu Dhabi to Basel, we consistently encounter evolving regulatory frameworks and strong local practices and craft traditions. In Albania, decisions move faster and with fewer institutional layers than elsewhere in Europe. That pace creates opportunity, but it also demands clarity. Architecture here is tested quickly through use, climate and daily life, leaving little room for ideas that aren't grounded in construction, material and experience.

ORGANIZATION/GOAL/SETUP

We organize ourselves around being there. That means continuity, presence and shared responsibility. From the beginning, we chose to be in the country often, not at a distance. We respect our local partners and value their accountability, judgment and communication over rigid processes. Being on the ground regularly – and having opened an office in Tirana in 2024 – allows decisions to happen through conversation and trust. Our commitment in Albania is long-term, and we've shaped the way we work around that reality.

SETUP IN RELATION TO ALBANIAN PARTNER

We share design responsibility, but we stay closely involved in design leadership. We set the direction and remain engaged throughout the process, working hand in hand with local partners who understand the cultural context, regulatory reality and how things actually get built. That exchange is essential. When design is disconnected from local knowledge, it stays abstract. When leadership drops away, quality suffers. The work holds together when both are present.

OPPORTUNITIES/CHALLENGES

The opportunity is the chance to make something meaningful and to connect with a community and a nation in transformation, shaping not just individual buildings but entire urban conditions. The challenge is balancing architectural quality with the pressures of density and development. Within these realities, there is a growing alignment between architects, developers and public authorities around public space, material integrity and long-term civic value.

HOW TO INTEGRATE GREATER RESPONSIBILITY FOR QUALITY IN PROJECTS

Quality has to become something everyone expects, not something you try to rescue at the end. That starts early, through material testing, full-scale mock-ups and staying close as the project takes shape. But it also requires vision from clients and from public authorities, an understanding that architecture carries long-term responsibility, not just short-term delivery. When that expectation is shared, it becomes easier to stay accountable through construction and to build work that can last for generations.

BALANCING QUALITY AND DENSITY/INVOLVING STAKEHOLDERS

Whether in dense urban environments or places of exceptional natural beauty, the role of the architect is to manage density with care. In cities, density can support public life, access and continuity when it's shaped thoughtfully. In sensitive landscapes, it requires restraint and precision, an understanding of when to build and when not to. In both cases, density is not an abstract target but a responsibility. Architecture has the capacity to convert pressure into balance, allowing places to grow without losing what makes them meaningful.

EXAMPLE/INSPIRATION

Our Besa Museum is compelling because it doesn't try to explain everything. We weren't interested in turning culture into a symbol or a single idea. Instead, the project creates a framework where memory, stories and everyday experience can sit together over time. It's intentionally part of the city – not an object set apart, but embedded in the urban fabric, open, accessible and connected to daily life. In a context where identity can easily become politicized or reduced to imagery, that restraint feels important. It allows the building to carry meaning without trying to lock it down.

We also deeply respect the restoration of Skanderbeg Square, redesigned by 51N4E. It's visually strong, but its power comes from clarity rather than monumentality. The square absorbs political events, cultural moments and everyday use all at once. Grounded in material, topography and movement, it shows how architecture can hold intensity while remaining open, generous and rooted in place.

TOOLBOX ALBANIA FUTURE

Albania asks a lot of you as an architect. It asks you to be present, to make decisions with incomplete information and to stand behind them. It forces you to think through construction, not around it, and to stay clear about what matters when things move fast. Over time, that builds judgment. It sharpens how you understand place, risk and responsibility. Those lessons don't stay in Albania. They change how you work everywhere else.

Finding the Spirit of Place

Designing in Albania begins with listening. It is an ongoing conversation with the land, its memory and the people who inhabit it. Architecture here does not originate from a fixed formal idea, but from immersion. Walking the terrain, observing its rhythms, sharing meals and engaging directly with those who carry local knowledge becomes the foundation of the work.

What emerges is not imposed architecture, but architecture shaped from within the place itself. Presence is essential. To work here requires building with the land, not placing objects upon it. Through collaboration, exploration and patient iteration, the projects take form as restrained and grounded interventions, inseparable from their context and quietly monumental through their care and precision.

Community-Making

OA visits Berat, 2024

Crafting a community for artists at Folie Village

Inspiring spaces for learning at Shkodra School

Understanding "The Village"

Living/working artist community

Team reconnaissance at Berat, 2024

Pigments of place at Vlora Beach

Materiality of Place

Earth mineral plasterwork at Folie Village

Camouflaged village at Jala Beach

On-site concrete casting techniques at Dhërmi Resort

Excavation as architecture at the Signature Villa

Architecture in symbiosis at The Rock

The Besa Museum

Designing a museum for an intangible concept required us, as foreign architects, to begin by listening rather than interpreting. Understanding the cultural, historical and ethical dimensions of Besa was essential before any architectural decision could be made. This process established a foundation for an experience that speaks to both local communities and visitors, grounding the project in shared understanding rather than symbolic representation.

Besa, meaning *faith* or *word of honor*, describes a deeply rooted cultural commitment to responsibility, protection and moral obligation, often upheld at great personal cost. Rather than attempting to define Besa through form, the project allows this ethos to guide decisions at every scale, from urban presence and restoration strategy to spatial atmosphere and narrative experience.

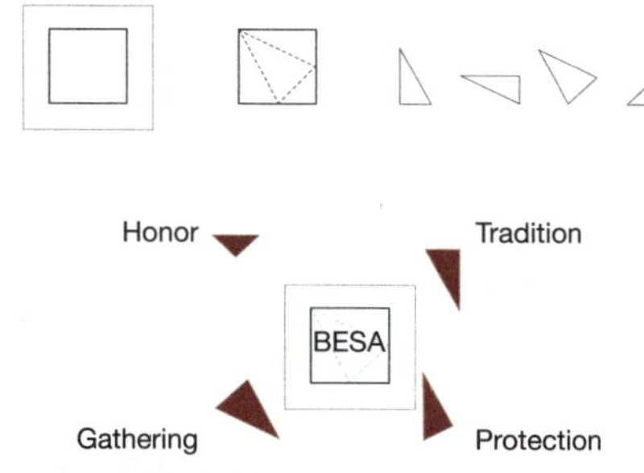

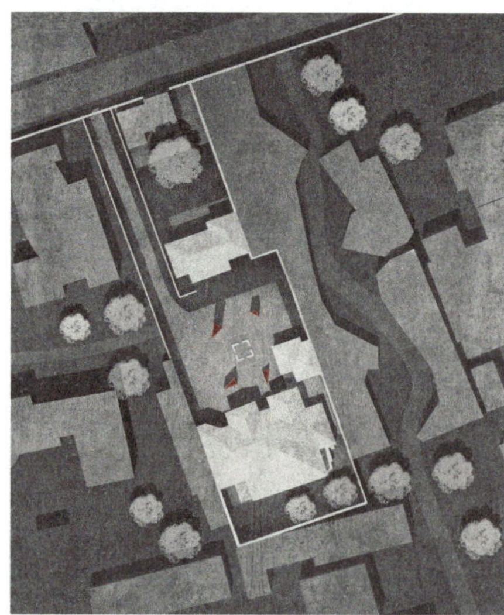

Through research and collaboration with cultural practitioners, four shared values emerged. Tradition, Protection, Gathering and Honor. Rather than remaining abstract ideas, they are translated into four architectural elements positioned across the site. Conceived as light-bearing towers, they provide a guide and illuminate the spaces of the museum. In this way, ethical principles become spatial instruments rather than symbolic gestures.

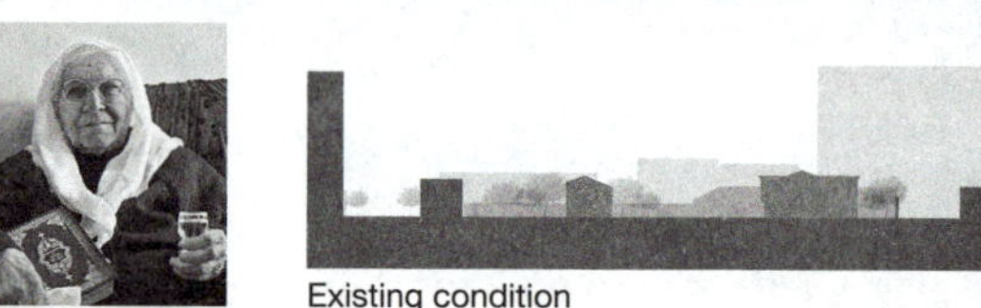
Existing condition

Creation of a new wing underground

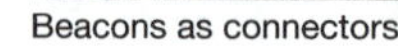
Beacons as connectors

1. Pillars of Besa
2. Toptani residence
3. Back garden
4. Besa courtyard
5. Selamillëku
6. North gate
7. Restaurant/admin

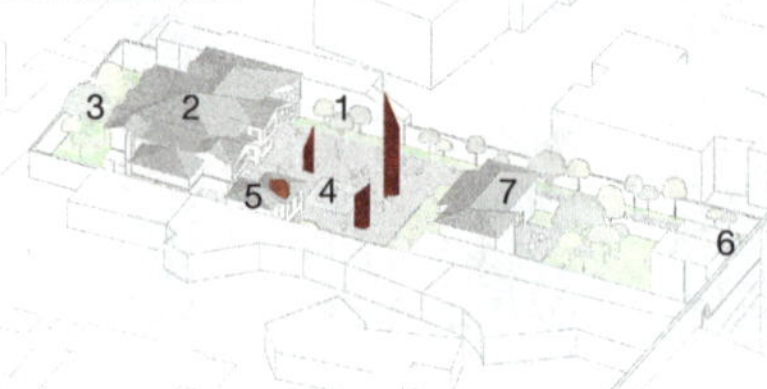

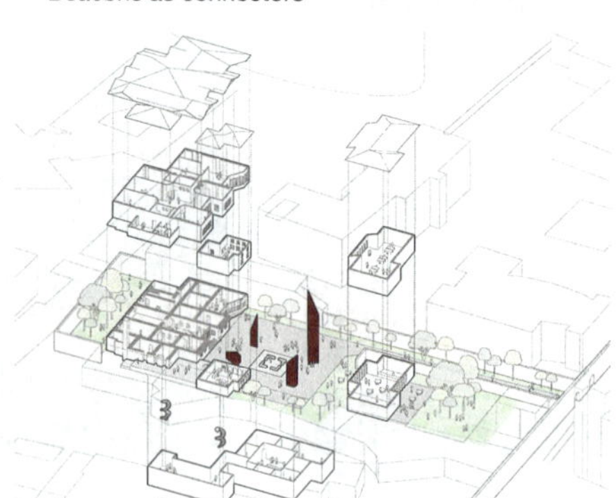

The project centers on the careful restoration of the Toptani House, reimagining it as a functioning museum while preserving its architectural integrity.

With the use of 3D scanning and historical drawings, the building is understood simultaneously in its present condition and original form. This layered reading informs decisions on reconstruction, conservation and selective interventions, including new vertical connections to the underground extension.

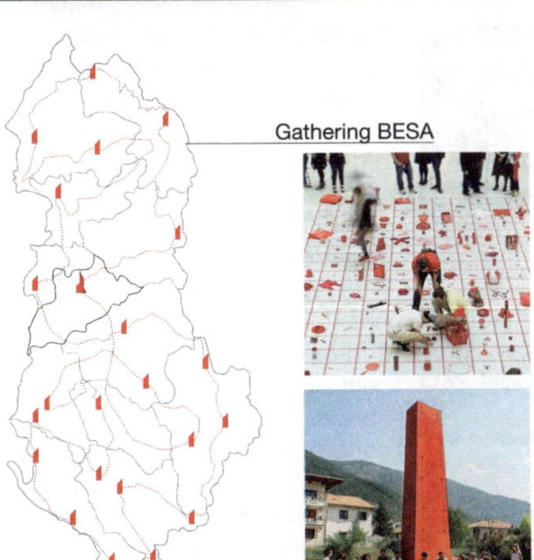

The museum is conceived as a question rather than an answer. How can architecture represent a cultural value shaped through lived experience? Instead of offering a single definition, the project looks to Albanian society itself, understanding Besa as a collective and evolving value.

Besa is conceived as a living archive through a national program titled Gathering, collecting personal stories and objects from communities across Albania and anchoring the museum in shared lived experience.

A mobile museum travels through the country, recording audio and video testimonies and producing 3D scans of objects that individuals identify as embodiments of Besa. These contributions form a central exhibition, grounding the museum in collective memory rather than a fixed narrative.

College of Europe

The College of Europe campus in Tirana stands as a quiet yet confident expression of Albania's evolving place within the European context. Conceived as the institution's first purpose-built home, the project weaves shared European values with the depth of Albanian history and tradition.

Drawing from Tirana's vibrant student life and social culture, the campus is shaped by democratic spatial principles that are open, inviting and designed to foster encounter, dialogue and a shared sense of belonging. More than an academic setting, the campus becomes a living landscape of cooperation and exchange, where ideas of European unity are expressed through Albania's distinct voice. The result is an environment that feels unmistakably European, yet deeply and confidently Albanian.

Research into Tirana's history as a student city revealed that beyond material expression, color and texture, the essence of the city lies in its people and its vibrant social life.

Three buildings, each serving a distinct user group, are positioned along the site's edges and oriented toward a shared central agora. This circular space, conceived as a porous concrete dome referencing Albania's bunkers, houses an auditorium and forms the social heart of the campus.

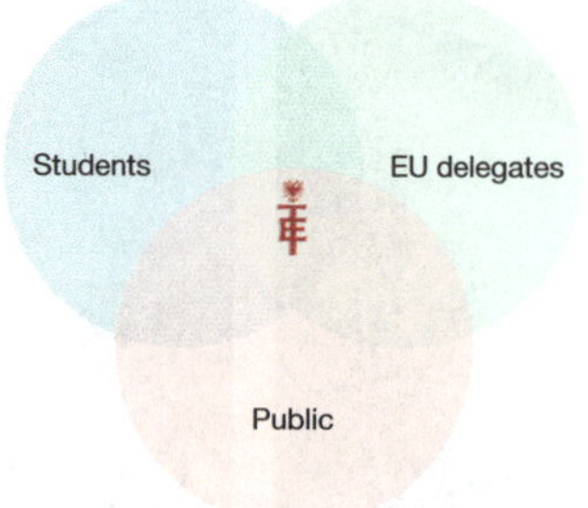

1. Gateway building
2. Agora
3. Diplomat building
4. University building
5. Sports park

The emphasis on social interaction, cooperation and integration extends to the spatial organization of each building.

Inspired by their historic use by students during protests, deep loggias wrap each floor, fostering camaraderie and creating visual and social links between the buildings.

Inspired by the musical structure of *Ode to Joy*, the city-facing facades are rhythmically articulated in textured dark red concrete.

A layered arrangement of structural and nonstructural elements functions as a brise-soleil, regulating the internal environment while making the public foyer more open and inviting.

With people at the heart of the concept, the agora draws inspiration from classical Greek theater, where concentric seating around a central stage reinforces the democratic nature of shared space.

The seating, adapted from ancient Greek senate typologies, reinforces these democratic ideals, fostering equality, visibility and shared experience.

Drawing from Tirana's social fabric, the campus is anchored by a generous ground floor foyer that extends outward as a covered public space connecting the buildings. This approach creates a continuous canopy at ground level and a green terrace above, seamlessly linking the campus to the adjacent sports park.

Tirana: A New Community

Across communities designed in Tirana, the work is guided by a shared ambition to strengthen the city's urban spirit through permeability, connectivity and community-focused ground conditions. Buildings are conceived not as isolated objects, but as integral components of a broader urban fabric. By lifting residential volumes above ground level, the projects dissolve the traditional street wall and introduce porous ground conditions that reconnect each site to the surrounding neighborhoods and major city axes.

Active plinths, integrated commercial programs and layered public spaces extend local streetscape traditions while supporting everyday social interaction. Drawing from Albanian materiality, craft and pattern, the architecture balances contemporary expression with cultural continuity. Facade systems respond to climate, acoustics and daily life, shaping mixed-use environments where private living and public life intersect. Interconnected urban neighborhoods contribute to Tirana as a vibrant and continuous city rather than a collection of isolated landmarks.

The tower facades draw inspiration from traditional Albanian carpet patterns, translating their geometric logic into a system of openings embedded within the building envelope.

These patterned voids generate a dynamic play of light and shadow while embedding cultural references within a contemporary architectural form.

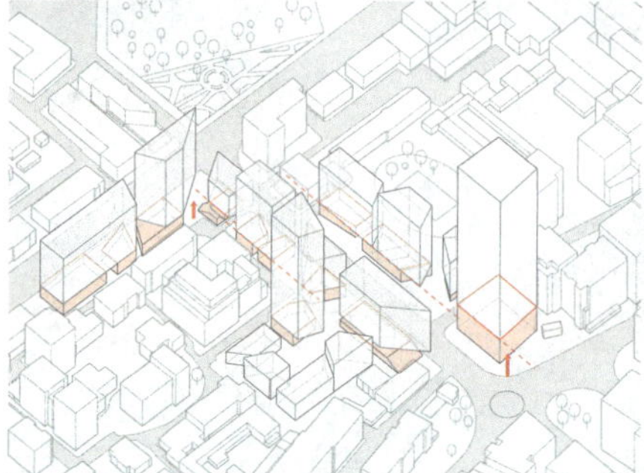

Relationship with master-plan datum

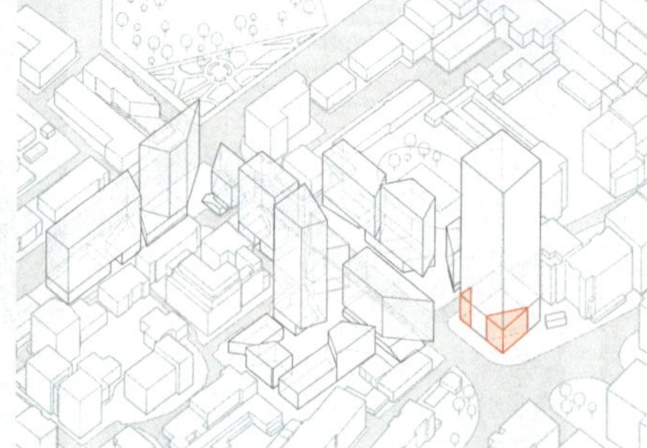

Opening up the corners

Public plaza

The projects' primary urban strategy prioritizes community life, placing shared spaces at the center of the development to encourage social interaction and inclusivity.

Through the integration of public plazas, green spaces and mixed-use programs, this parasitic urban approach activates existing structures, reinforces neighborhood identity and enhances everyday life, aligning contemporary urban living with a broader sense of collective identity.

The facade is an evolving process working toward the final fixed outcome. Full-scale one-to-one mock-ups are produced to test quality, proportion and texture at the scale of the street. On-site testing of concrete mixes and pigments fine-tunes color, texture and performance through direct observation under real conditions. Knowledge emerges through making, with design decisions shaped by observation, testing and learning through doing.

We design with the land, not on it. In Albania, this means engaging the landscape as a living system shaped by geography, history and collective memory. At the scale of territory, architecture becomes an act of calibration rather than imposition, aligning built form with topography, climate, movement and social life. Through this approach, projects such as the Vlora Beach master plan are conceived not as objects in a landscape, but as extensions of it, structuring relationships between land, sea and community over time.

Since 2020, Oppenheim Architecture has built a sustained body of work across Tirana, Vlora, Dhërmi, Jala and Shkodra. The projects range from cultural and educational buildings to hospitality, residential and urban-scale developments. Rather than isolated commissions, this work reflects a long-term commitment to Albania at a moment of rapid political, economic and spatial change.

NAME OFFICE

RCR ARQUITECTES

DATE
January 20, 2025

PLACE
Olot, Spain

WORKING IN ALBANIA SINCE
2024

PRINCIPALS
Rafael Aranda
Carme Pigem
Ramon Vilalta
Joan Puigcorbé

ALBANIAN PARTNERS
Pajtoni Group
Kron Construction shpk
iRI shpk
PAAS architects
Pau Llimona
Natàlia Guillamet (Landscape)
Blázquez-Guanter arquitectes (Structure)
Luan Myraj (Structure)
Meka-Pro shpk (Engineer, Plumbing)
Marsel Pylla (Engineer, Security)
Besart Dalliu (Engineer, Electrical)

MAIN CONTEXT VS. ALBANIA

Since we are at the beginning of the project process, the main difference is the capital role of the Territorial Development Agency of Albania.

ORGANIZATION/GOAL/SETUP

Because the promoter itself has a technical and a construction company, we are working together, sharing knowledge and experiences.

SETUP IN RELATION TO ALBANIAN PARTNER

We share the principles to get a solution that belongs to both.

OPPORTUNITIES/CHALLENGES

To be living now in the most vibrant architectural moment in the world. To get the opportunity to see, to participate in, to live with the desired or chosen level of engagement in which you are interested the most.

HOW TO INTEGRATE GREATER RESPONSIBILITY FOR QUALITY IN PROJECTS

Responsibility and engagement and the pleasure of touching and enjoying the result: That could be the seed for aspiring to greater quality for the next one.

BALANCING QUALITY AND DENSITY/INVOLVING STAKEHOLDERS

Density comes from two different items: fitting more people into a specific area and/or getting more business/money. But density is a box that can be filled with big stones first before then adding successively smaller ones until you put in sand and finally water.

When must we stop? The site offers the answer with its geography (topography, nature, boundaries, neighbors . . .), along with the needs of the people and the expectations of the community (for public commissions). Balancing all these components with the artistic expression of the space gives an answer that could be understood as a guiding principle: to BALANCE. How to define “to balance”? Do not destroy the mood of the natural environment, to reinforce the idea of keeping some air in the box.

But the first step in the building business is to get the land. Let’s think about the cost of the land!

EXAMPLE/INSPIRATION

The capacity of Bulevardi Dëshmorët e Kombit in Tirana to assemble buildings from different periods, streets, rivers and squares and convert all of this into one unified public space.

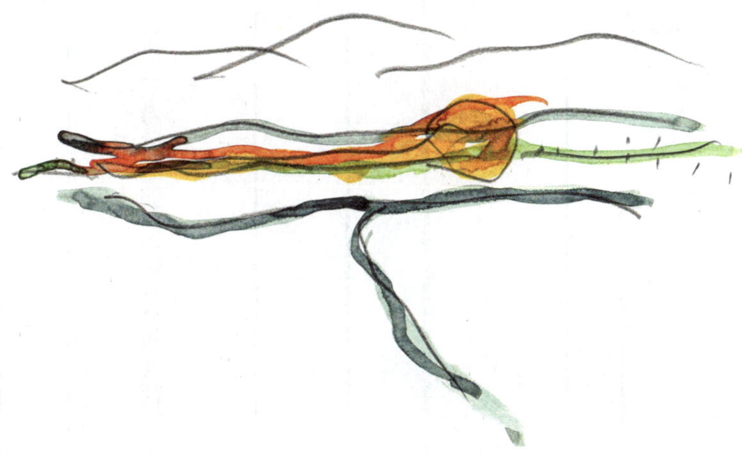

PAJTONI RESIDENCE
HOUSING AND MIXED USE
PAJTONI
RCR ARQUITECTES / J. PUIGCORBÉ
2024 – PRESENT

To **build a city**, and to **build a community**.

A building can be an island, a landmark, a lighthouse. It points out paths, directions, or it observes. Weaving a neighborhood requires knowing, talking, and more than radiating, attracting and absorbing, to gather. Beyond the neighborhood, to belong to the city, which is made up of mixture, human encounters, rhythms and variations. It is an evolution in constant migration; hence the city is complex. It presents stages, uses, continuities, flows, layers, systems. Today perhaps one of the most requested layers is the one which reconnects human beings with their first base, the territory, the original landscape, the nature.

It is also essential today to manage the creation of a system where the previous phases cohabit with the preexisting geography and the current layout to make nature present in the city. To ensure a balance for a new sustainable urban world between citizens and **landscape links** and the necessary systems of energy, mobility, parking, residential, productivity, commercial, recreational use, sports, singularity, administrative and **gathering places** – without forgetting, but revealing and further promoting **the deeper meaning of places** to make a sense of belonging.

START	NAME PROJECT	LOCATION	DEVELOPER	PUBLIC/PRIVATE	PHASE
2024	Pajtoni Residence	Mëzez, Tirana	Pajtoni	Private	Schematic design

NAME OFFICE

ROJKIND ARQUITECTOS

DATE
February 3, 2026

PLACE
Mexico City, Mexico

WORKING IN ALBANIA SINCE
October 2024

PRINCIPAL
Hon. FAIA Michel Rojkind

PROJECT TEAM
Andrea León
Alfredo Hernández
Julián Bermúdez
Carla Castañeda
Adrián Aguilar
Alonso Gordillo
Kennet Berumen
Lucía Castellanos
Marco García
Ignacio López
Jair Vega
Israel Dorantes

COLLABORATORS
Multiplicities
álvarez tello
Amasa Estudio
Chris Luce
Estudio MMX
Taller Territorial De México
Esperon Studio
Vertebral

ALBANIAN PARTNERS
SON Architects
Motus Holdings

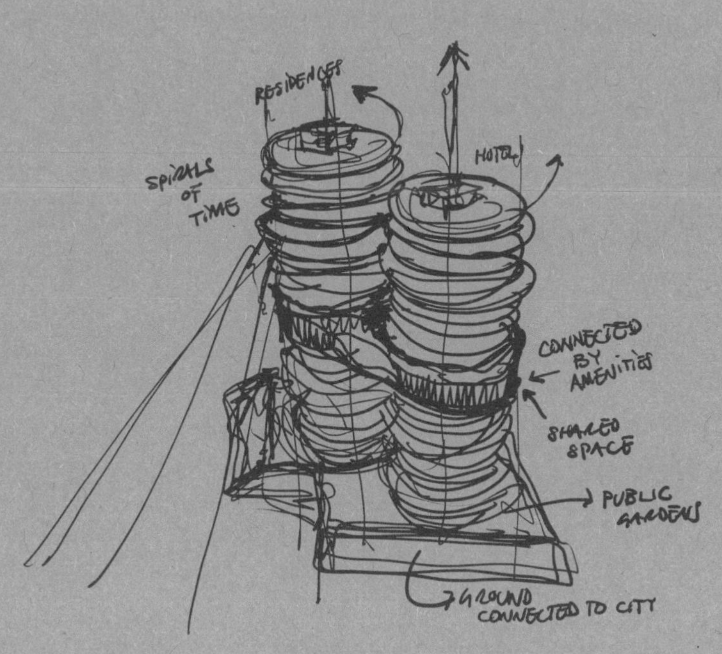

SETUP IN RELATION TO ALBANIAN PARTNER

Most of the time we coauthor from the start, from diagnosis to delivery.

Why:

- Legitimacy and precision: Local codes, procurement, labor and politics shape concepts.
- Integrity: Shared authorship reduces value-engineering drift and protects intent.
- Reciprocity: Digital design + local fabrication requires skills and maintenance know-how; we bring our "fresh eye" approach and also take back home local knowledge.
- Trust: Visible local authorship strengthens community engagement and stewardship.

HOW TO INTEGRATE GREATER RESPONSIBILITY FOR QUALITY IN PROJECTS

1. Set targets at kickoff
   Begin with a performance brief embedded in drawings and specs. Define measurable goals for comfort, ecology, access, durability and maintenance from day one.
2. Prototype before committing
   Require 1:1 mock-ups of critical assemblies (façade depth and shading, acoustics, entrances, wayfinding). Measure on-site and adjust massing and details based on data.
3. Architect-led site supervision
   Engage the design team for construction phase services. Hold monthly site meetings with formal minutes, track decision logs and enforce a design-authority matrix so intent is protected through delivery.
4. Independent quality review
   Use a peer panel to issue sign-offs at concept, design development, mock-up review and pre-handover. Publish short determinations for transparency.
5. Guardrails during value management
   Test every change against the performance brief. If a change lowers performance, add a compensating measure or reject it.
6. Pre-opening verification
   Conduct the final building inspection by the authority before issuing the Certificate of Occupancy and authorizing the building to open to the public.
7. Bind stewardship after opening
   Adopt a five-year stewardship compact that commits owner, operator and municipality to maintenance cycles, landscape and shade care, water systems, cultural programming and post-occupancy evaluation.

ROSE GARDEN MARINA

Location:	*Durrës, Albania*
Type:	*Mixed-use*
Area:	*27,000 m²*
Design Year:	*2024*
Collaboration:	*Multiplicities + SON Architects*
Status:	*Completed schematic design*

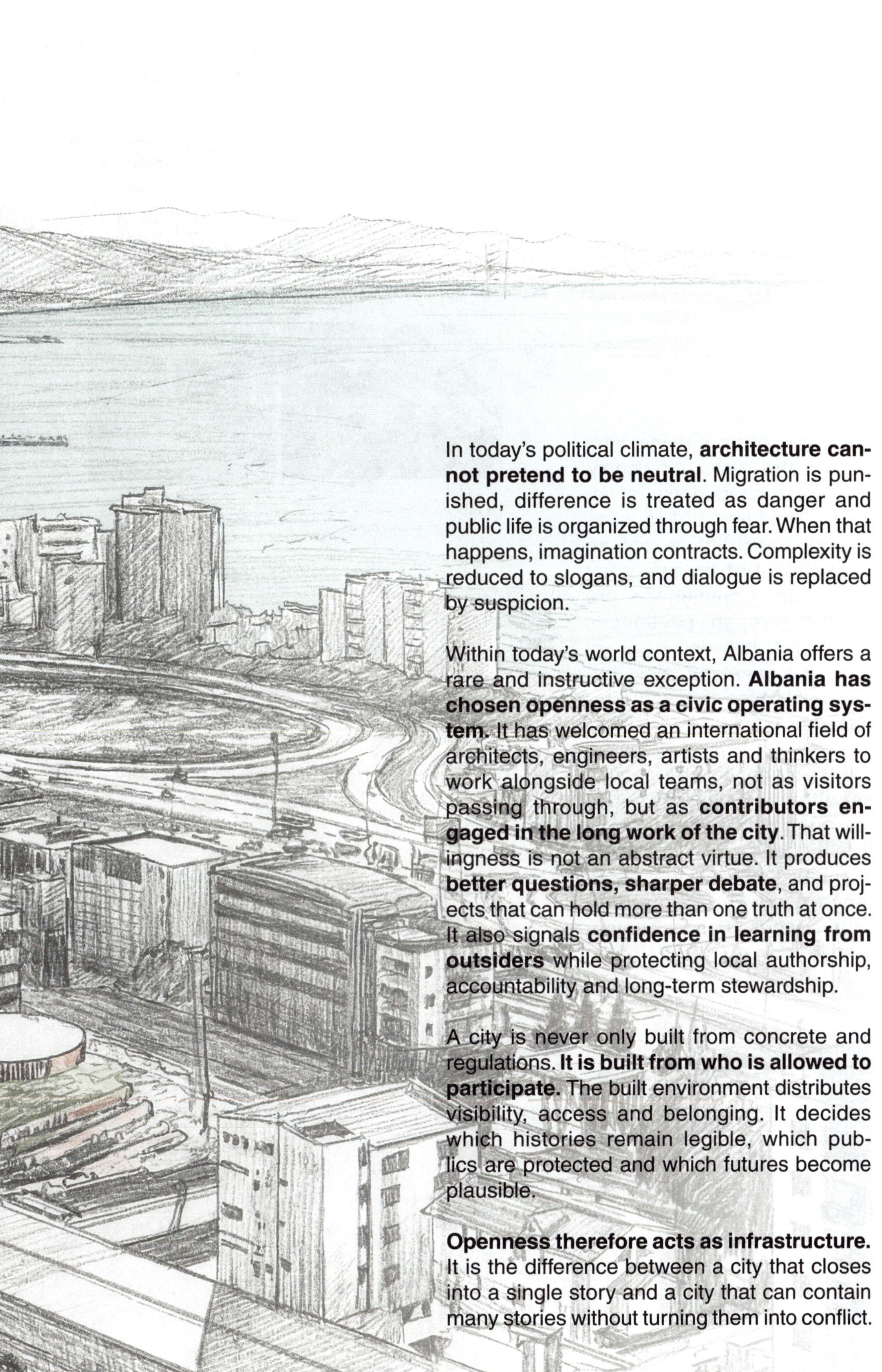

In today's political climate, **architecture cannot pretend to be neutral**. Migration is punished, difference is treated as danger and public life is organized through fear. When that happens, imagination contracts. Complexity is reduced to slogans, and dialogue is replaced by suspicion.

Within today's world context, Albania offers a rare and instructive exception. **Albania has chosen openness as a civic operating system.** It has welcomed an international field of architects, engineers, artists and thinkers to work alongside local teams, not as visitors passing through, but as **contributors engaged in the long work of the city**. That willingness is not an abstract virtue. It produces **better questions, sharper debate**, and projects that can hold more than one truth at once. It also signals **confidence in learning from outsiders** while protecting local authorship, accountability and long-term stewardship.

A city is never only built from concrete and regulations. **It is built from who is allowed to participate.** The built environment distributes visibility, access and belonging. It decides which histories remain legible, which publics are protected and which futures become plausible.

Openness therefore acts as infrastructure. It is the difference between a city that closes into a single story and a city that can contain many stories without turning them into conflict.

"OPENNESS AS A CIVIC OPERATING SYSTEM"

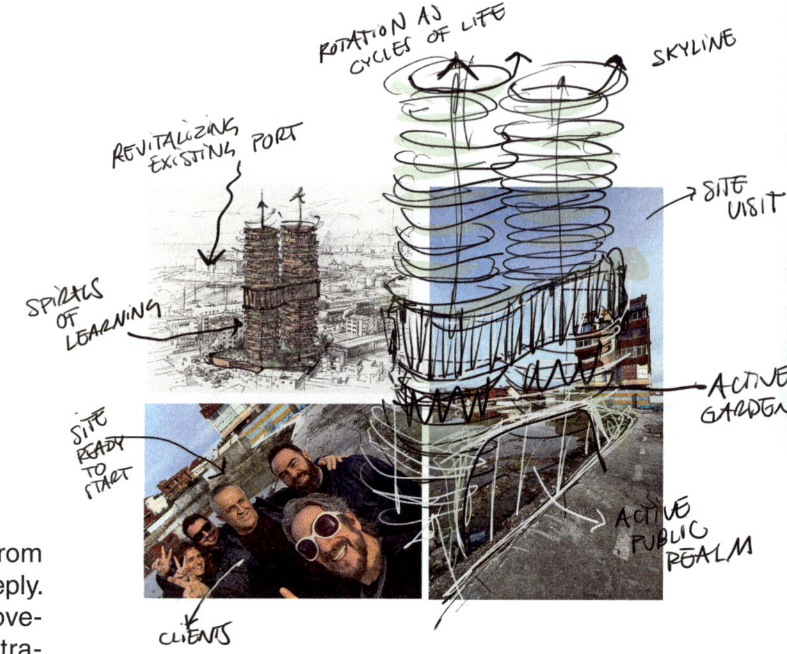

For those of us arriving from Mexico, this resonates deeply. Mexico is shaped by movement, mixture and contradiction. **Hybridity is not an exception but an everyday condition.** Communities are formed through continuous negotiation between what arrives and what remains, between inherited forms and urgent new needs.

That experience sharpens a **sensitivity to diversity** and to the dangers of simplification. It teaches you that identity is accumulation, and that **resilience comes from learning to live with difference** rather than erasing it.

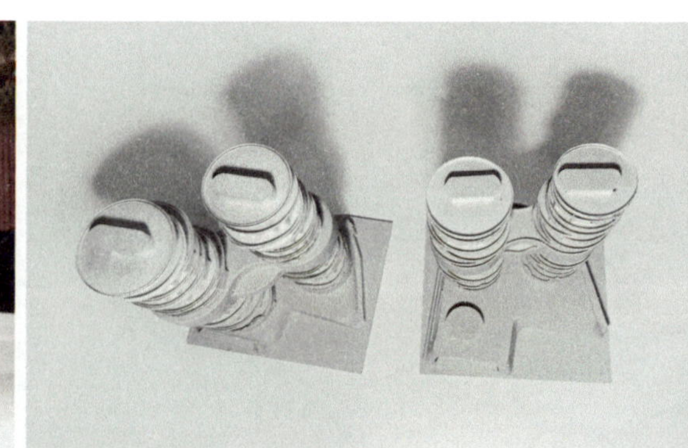

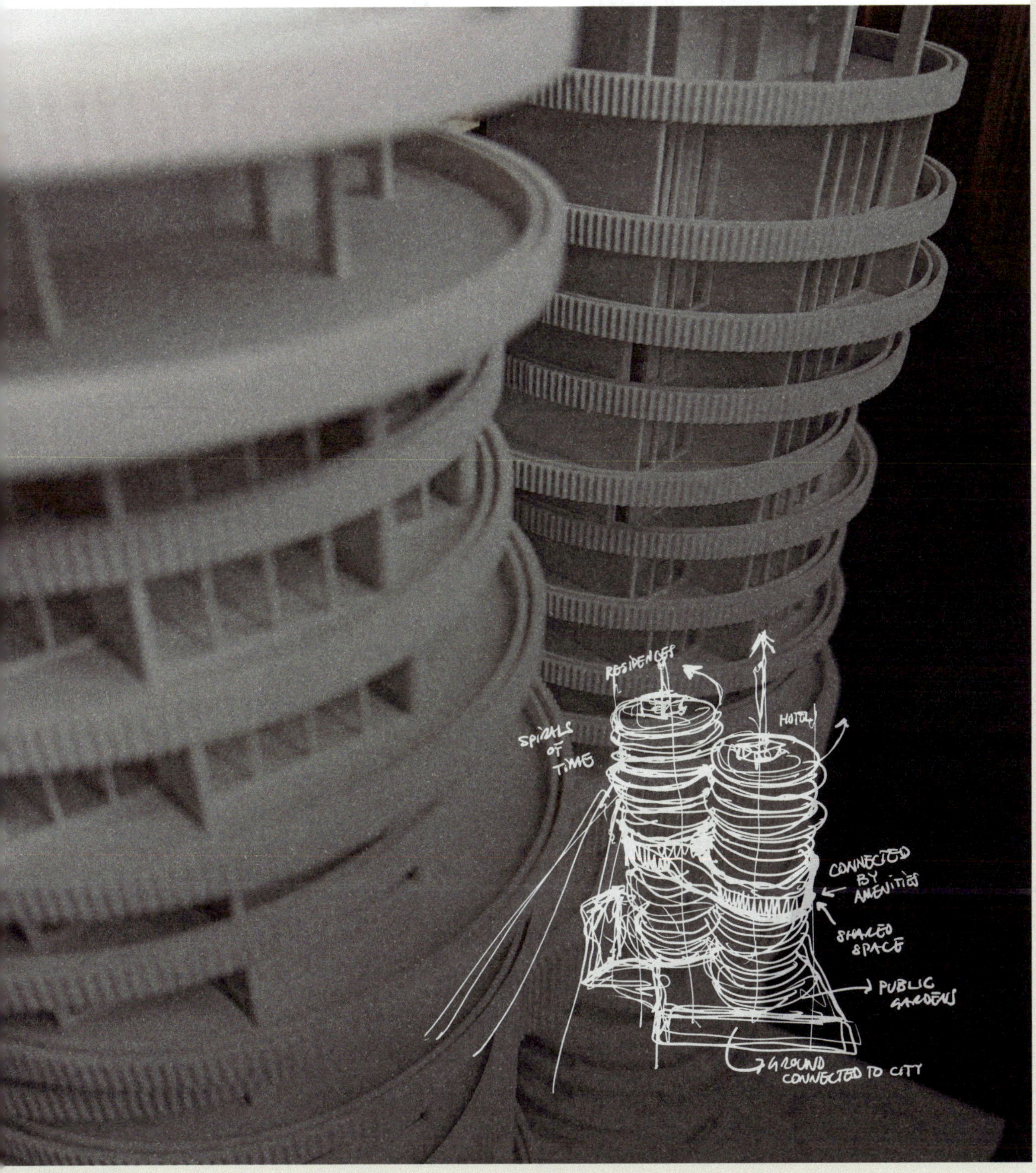

RESIDENCES
SPIRALS OF TIME
HOTEL
CONNECTED BY AMENITIES
SHARED SPACE
PUBLIC GARDENS
GROUND CONNECTED TO CITY

1. Lobby A
2. Lobby B
3. Restaurant
4. Restrooms
5. Reception
6. Store
7. Bar
8. Playscape
9. Café
10. Park
11. Kitchen

Level 2: Public Park

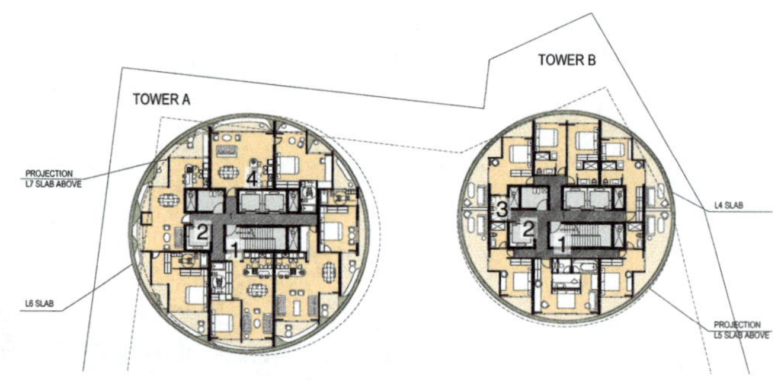

1. Access
2. MEP (mechanical, electricity and plumbing)
3. Hotel Rooms
4. Residences

Level 4: Residences & Hotel

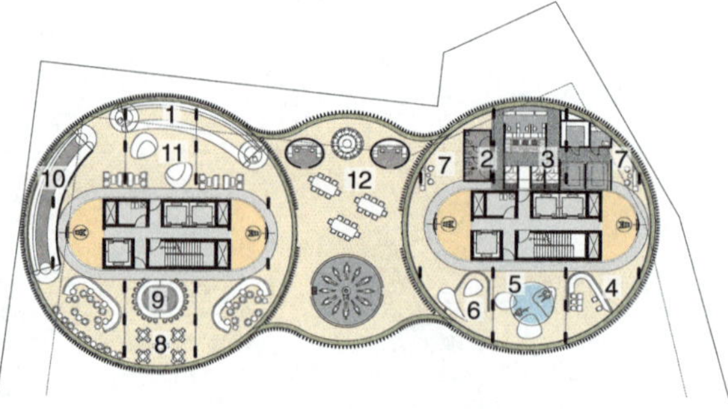

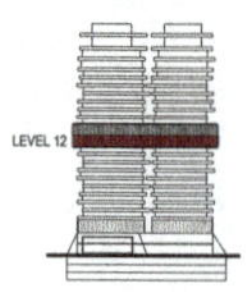

1. Sky Lobby
2. Restrooms
3. Spa
4. Nail Salon
5. Jacuzzi
6. Pre-Treatment
7. Lockers
8. Dining Salon
9. Food & Beverage
10. Kitchen
11. Lounge
12. Event / Expo / Work

Level 12: Amenities

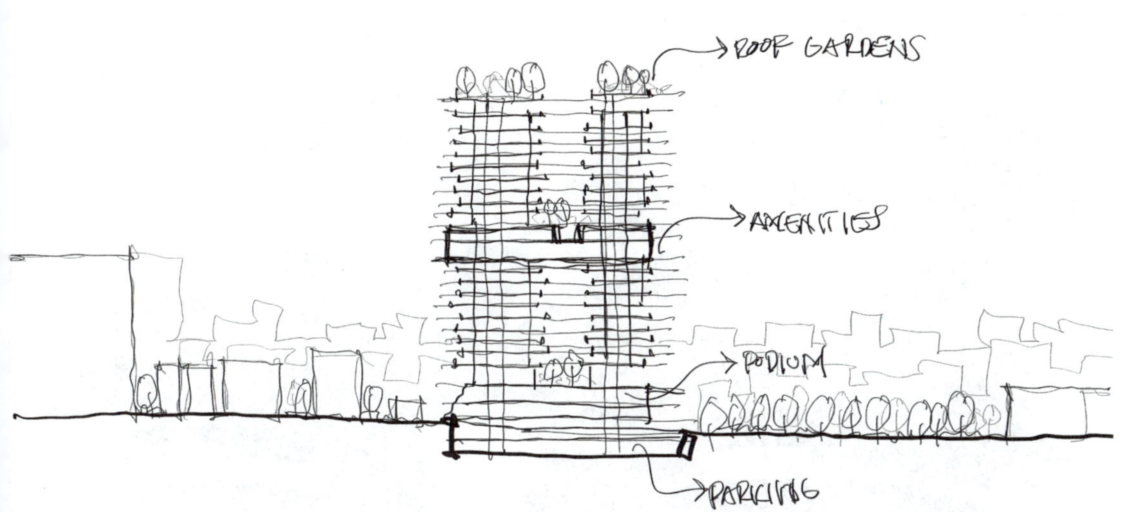

The project's layout is organized into two twin towers with circular floor plans, composed of stacked, offset discs that generate perimeter terraces with vegetation. Built in pigmented, striated concrete, the towers deliberately contrast with the surrounding industrial landscape, establishing a sculptural and contemporary presence that redefines the urban skyline of Durrës. The 12th floor accommodates the amenities and serves as a connecting bridge between the two towers.

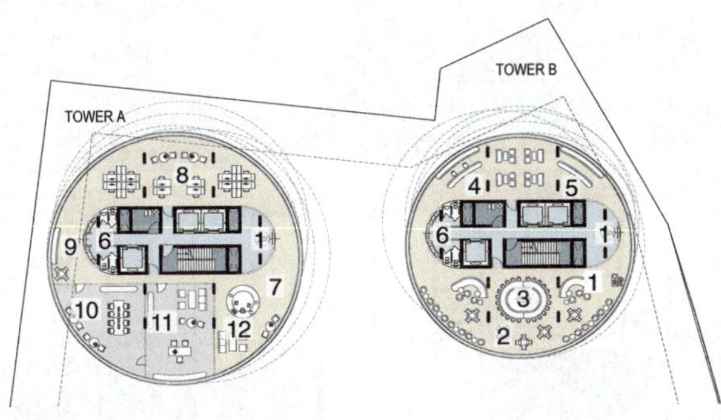

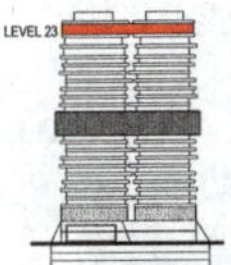

Level 23: Offices

1. *Lobby*
2. *Dining Salon*
3. *Bar*
4. *Sky Lobby*
5. *Kitchen*
6. *Restrooms*
7. *Reception*
8. *Coworking Space*
9. *Coffee Station*
10. *Meeting Room*
11. *Private Office*
12. *Waiting Area*

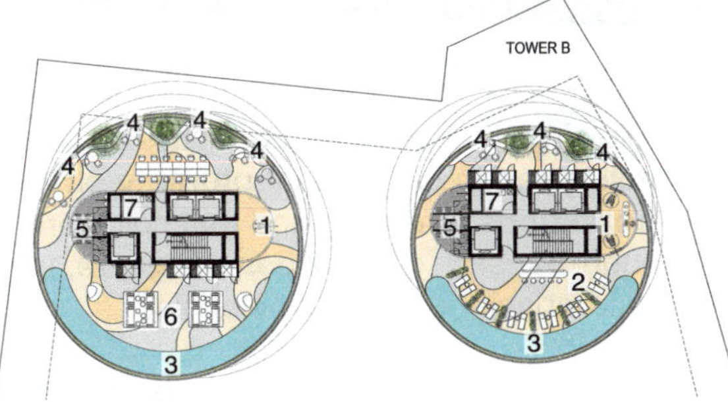

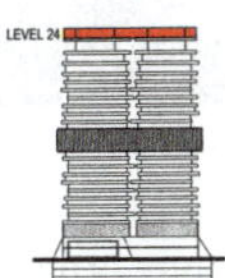

Level 24: Pools

1. *Lobby*
2. *Bar*
3. *Pool*
4. *Seating*
5. *Restrooms*
6. *Lounge*
7. *MEP*

We do not give anyone a voice. People already have one. The responsibility of institutions and of those who build is to **create the conditions where voices can be heard** through transparent processes, accessible public space and a commitment to dignity.

Albania's openness reminds us that borders are political choices, not natural facts. **In a time of fragmentation, choosing openness is a stance.** It says that many minds can share a city, that **plurality strengthens the public realm**, and that collaboration across borders can still generate care, intelligence, and new forms of belonging.

If imagination is a public resource, then defending it is a civic duty. We keep listening, keep making room and never surrender our POWER TO IMAGINE.

START	NAME PROJECT	LOCATION	PROGRAM	PHASE
2024	Vertex	Dhërmi		Concept design
2024	Pjeza	Durrës	Hotel facade	Concept design
2024	Rose Garden Marina	Durrës	Mixed use	Concept design
2024	Komuna	Tirana	Mixed use	Concept design
2024	Ardanë	Vlora	Mixed use	Concept design
2025	Master plan in Elbasan for the Metalurgjiku	Elbasan	Master plan	In progress
2025	Palasë Garden Hills	Palasë	Residential	Concept design
2025	Sauk	Tirana	Residential	Concept design
2025	Borsh	Borsh	Residential and hospitality	Concept design
2025	MNT	Tirana	Residential	Concept design
2025	Hënë Resorts	Dhërmi		Concept design
2025	Henne	Himara	Mixed use	Concept design
2025	Neighborhood	Tirana	Hospitality	Concept design
2025	Shkodra	Skodra	Mixed use	Concept design
2025	Orikum	Vlora	Mixed use	Concept design
2025	Dyrrah	Plazhi San Pietro	Residential / hospitality	Concept design
2025	Lundër	Tirana	Residential / hospitality	Concept design
2025	Piqeras	Piqeras	Master plan	Concept design
2025	Petrela	Petrela	Residential / hospitality	Concept design

All projects done for a private client except master plan in Elbasan for the Metalurgjiku and KOR multifunctional development.

NAME OFFICE

SAM CHERMAYEFF OFFICE

DATE
2026

PLACE
Berlin, Germany

WORKING IN ALBANIA SINCE
April 2024

PRINCIPALS
Sam Chermayeff
Barbara Polakova

ALBANIAN PARTNER
AL-Point
Albanian government

PROJECT TEAM
William Beck
Laura Bertagno
Petra Duriskova
Matthew Lochert
Tommaso Sossi

NICKNAME
Chechen Gangster

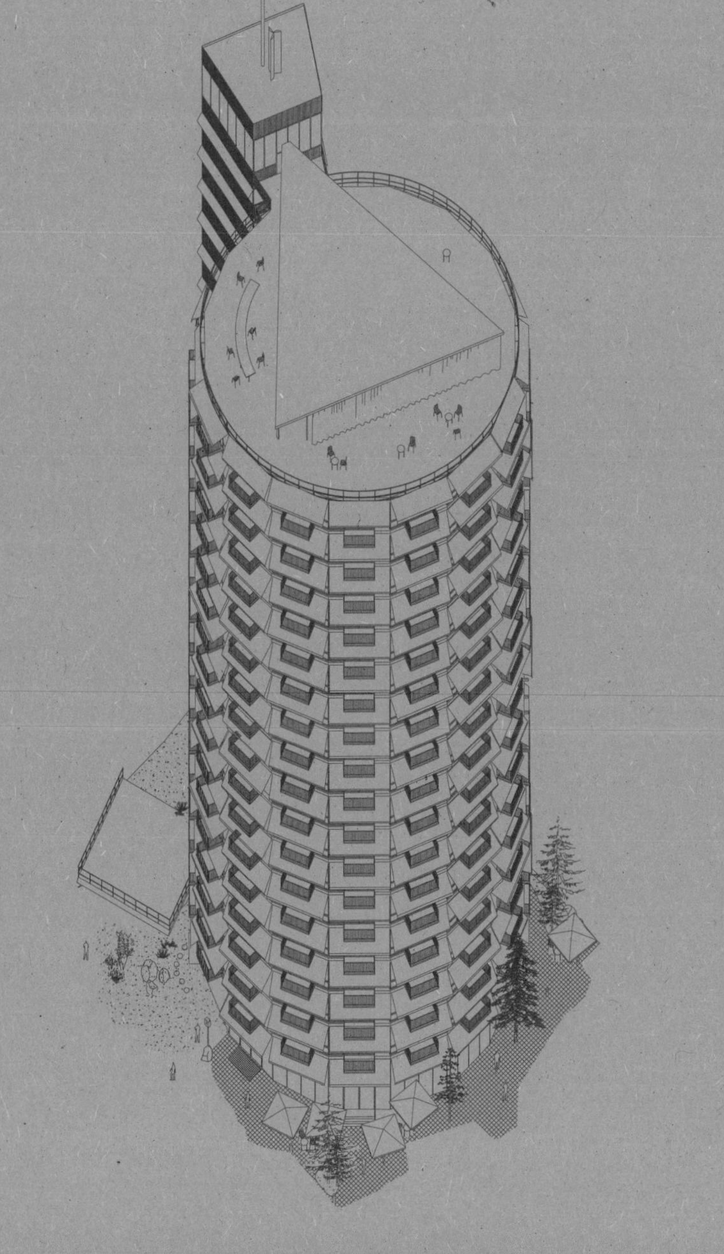

MAIN CONTEXT VS. ALBANIA

We generally work on domestic situations, from kitchen accessories to large housing. We do this in Albania as well. In all cases we're interrogating how people want to live and offering more. In Albania specifically we find that clients and users are potentially more open to new futures. This is to say that people are not looking for what they already know.

ORGANIZATION/GOAL/SETUP

We have too many goals in Albania. Our favorite goal, the clearest one, is that we want to design and build such that truly everyone understands both how to build the projects and by extension how to live there.

SETUP IN RELATION TO ALBANIAN PARTNER

I would not say we choose anything. We are ever feeling it out. Our clients and the local office, the same people most of the time, have experience that we do not have. We both have visions, and they are not precisely the same. We both try to understand, but we do not need to make that vision align. We rather try to understand each way and accommodate each. This cohabitation of parallel visions is unique and makes our projects better.

OPPORTUNITIES/CHALLENGES

The freedom of working in Albania quickly turns into weighty responsibility. There are few oppositional forces so we internalize it. This weight increases though we might have thought the opposite.

HOW TO INTEGRATE GREATER RESPONSIBILITY FOR QUALITY IN PROJECTS

Strangely, we feel the quality is changing already. Our permit applications are coming back with reasonable changes and requests from the authorities.

I would like a master plan. I would like help getting everyone on board. I would like to feel part of a larger vision that others understand. That said, were we in charge of the place during my short time working in Tirana, I would have changed that vision and plan several times. So the dynamism is also appreciated.

BALANCING QUALITY AND DENSITY/INVOLVING STAKEHOLDERS

I believe that it is our responsibility to design projects such that they can be built economically and easily. This is to say we try hard to define our projects agnostic to details, where possible.

More than density, our worry is about what, where and for whom. Recently we have been working on low-cost projects that are meant to be accessible to everyday people, and that is important. For all kinds of reasons architecture should not be for the wealthy.

EXAMPLE/INSPIRATION

Skanderbeg Square is one of the most beautiful public spaces anywhere in the world. It is clear in that you can read it as one good idea. Or you can dig into it and see that it works with at least ten layers of thought. We find it useful to remind ourselves that it is fantastic empirically, rather than in context.

TOOLBOX ALBANIA FUTURE

Because there are not many rules and my clients care very little for the context, we are forced to think through our own values. We think about what we want our projects to say – and, most importantly, to whom. This is of course exhausting and actually hard. We must organize ourselves to make time for this consideration. Of course we want to impress our colleagues in this book. That is the case worldwide. In Albania, our work must speak to a broader audience, an audience that we do not intuitively understand. Somehow in Berlin or New York, for example, the audience and the world of architecture fold together, but in Tirana we pause and think differently. Our clients help with this by keeping a strange but powerful distance.

HAPPY

HAPPY BIRTHDAY MOTHER

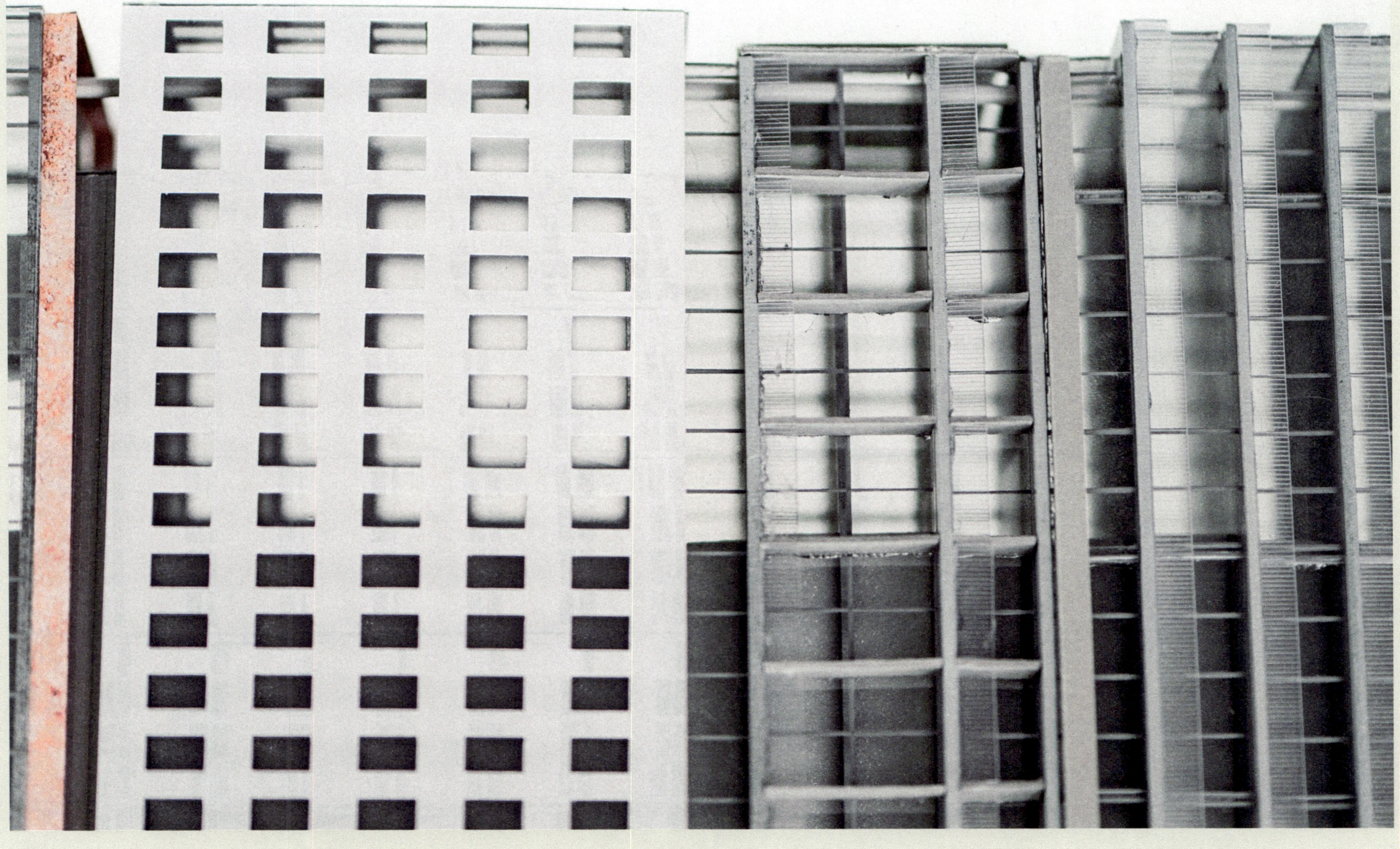

My goodness. Our experience of Albania is truly wild.

On Wednesday, May 1, 2024, a holiday, at 10:00 p.m., my friend Pablo Bofill called me to say that "Edi" was going to call me. We had never discussed Albania beyond me agreeing that it must be interesting in Tirana.

Around 11:00 p.m., Ada called. (Somehow, only several months later did I get her last name, Roka. Now I would say we know each other pretty well. I know her compatriot Adelina Greca well now too.)

In short order we were asked to do two projects in Tirana. One for 30,000 square meters and another for 15,000. Of course I agreed, not really understanding what was happening. This was followed by some short calls with our new clients in the days that followed.

Cut to our first visit to Tirana, several weeks later. We were picked up from the tarmac and whisked off to the House of Comrades. There was no real schedule for our first trip, or for our more recent ones.

We want to talk about the people. Everybody knows Prime Minister Edi Rama here. He's amazing, but we want to talk about our guys. We love our guys. We have four clients so far and they are simply the best clients that we have ever had.

First there is Alex. He is the head of a triumvirate with another man named Alex and a third named Amarildo. These guys are my guys, and I am their guy. Barbara, my office partner, calls them "The Boys." I think that they are forty-six, thirty-eight and twenty-nine. They each have a G-wagon and wear Richard Mille watches and Cartier nails. (As an aside, our office car is also a slightly absurd Mercedes.)

These guys somehow made it happen. They have an architecture office, so they know what we do. They have a furniture company too, also what we do. One of them, Alex, who I have come to understand is actually called Sander, has a wife and two kids. I have not met them, but am sure we will. The other two sound like they are working on families. They are clearheaded and work very hard. We stay up talking and working with them well past midnight. Only one of them speaks English close to perfection, but the other two are learning faster than I learn Albanian. In any case, we understand each other. I trust them and I have the feeling that they trust us.

On our first meeting, Sander, Alex and Amarildo took us to the site of our building in Tirana. (It is an urban infill corner of a block and it is 44 stories tall.) The precise nature of this project is only emerging now. They said that we could do "whatever we want" and as far as we can tell, they meant it. At the same time, at their suggestion, we set back some parts. We respect the neighborhood and there is a sense of care. That said, we are all a little out of our depth. We know it and we are racing along with it together.

This first big tower, now called Sun Moon Star, is perhaps not the point, nor is our second tower, called the Fruit Depot. The point is that our little office and their little office build together now. We were four people in Berlin. Now we are ten. They were a loose affiliation themselves and now they have a big new office full of architects. We even recommend them to our other colleagues. Now, we've been four times to meet them. We're taking our whole office next month and we're expecting a visit from them in Berlin. We stay at a hotel that they own and now we talk on the phone and message more or less daily. I would say that we are friends. They want to start more towers. They want to do something at the beach and so on. We wish for this too. Again, we trust them. For sure they want to turn a profit, but they seem to integrate this desire with a genuine awe for their own place and time.

On the second tower, we were paired with Piro Angjeli, who is a completely different man. He's a tiny bit older than Our Guys and he's happy that we do the second tower with the first tower's clients, who are also the local architects. He, Piro, asks for it to be reasonable and logical, "simple regular apartments." He sees us working very hard and suggests that we should not work so hard, then pauses and says, "The fish is nice here." His colleague rightly asked us to make some small changes to the parking and that was it.

We worked on these two buildings. Then we won two more buildings in a bigger competition: another 40,000-square-meter housing project with a hotel, and a major addition to the Cadaster offices.

(We did this with our colleagues Muoto and baukuh.) The first people to congratulate us were Our Guys. They might even have known that we won before we did (they are paying attention to what happens in Tirana). They wanted to celebrate with us and that is what we did, right before we went back to work on their tower. Of course we talked to them about what the government might be thinking about the competitions. We wondered if they might do it, build it. They brought up lots of questions. They take the time to teach us and we them. They want to change our projects in ways that make complete sense and they do this while respecting our intentions, which is not what most people do, strangely.

This works because right after we met Our Guys we had our first meeting with Edi Rama and he said, "No glass facades . . . whatever you do should be half you [Sam], half you smelling the mountains." This was surprisingly clear. He also asked where I was from and I answered New York. He repeated the question, and the second time I said Grozny. Ever since, he exclusively refers to me as "Chechen Gangster."

This is starting to be a ramble. We're all simply working on trying to figure this place out, trying to smell it but also just trying to design huge projects. We are planning another trip next week. This has changed our lives.

Circle Square Triangle

(This is a new title that no one agreed upon but it might be better than Lift.)

Rruga Muhamet Gjollesha 70, Tirana
Client: to be found
40,000 m^2
37 stories (or more)

Design Architects:
Sam Chermayeff Office, baukuh, Studio Muoto
Executive Architects:
AL-Point (TBC)

Structure:
Bollinger+Grohmann / HT Construction

Landscape:
YellowOffice
Details of many kinds:
Simon Boudvin, artist

Civic Land Center

Rruga Panorama 1001, Tirana
Client: Albania
30,000 m^2

Design Architects:
Sam Chermayeff Office, baukuh, Studio Muoto
Executive Architects:
AL-Point (TBC)

Structure:
Bollinger+Grohmann / HT Construction (TBC)

Landscape:
YellowOffice
Details of many kinds:
Simon Boudvin, artist

Fruit Depot

Rruga Jordan Misja no. 1/1, Tirana
15,000 m^2
18 stories

Design Architects:
Sam Chermayeff Office
Executive Architects:
AL-Point

Structure:
Bollinger+Grohmann / HT Construction

Sun Moon Star

Rruga Reshnit Petreia 10, Tirana
Client:
AL-Point (Alexander Vasily, Amarildo Haruni, Alexander Arredo)
30,000 m^2
44 stories

Design Architects:
Sam Chermayeff Office
Executive Architects:
AL-Point (including Ergen Agalliu)

Structure:
Bollinger+Grohmann / HT Construction

Moon Clock:
Simon Boudvin / Piovenefabi / Onsitestudio

LIST OF PROJECTS

START	NAME PROJECT	LOCATION	DEVELOPER	M²	PUBLIC/PRIVATE	PHASE
2024	Sun Moon Star	Tirana	AL-Point	30,000 m²	Private	Permit phase
2024	Fruit Depot	Tirana		15,000 m²	Private	Permit phase
2024	Free House	Durrës		360 m²	Public	Designing
2024	Lift Tower	Tirana	Albanian government	40,000 m²	Public	Development
2024	Civic Land Center	Tirana	Albanian government	30,000 m²	Public	Development
2025	Satellite	Tirana	AL-Point	50,000m²	Private	Designing

NAME OFFICE

SELGASCANO + FRPO

DATE	PLACE	WORKING IN ALBANIA SINCE
September 2025	Madrid, Spain	2024

PRINCIPALS

José Selgas & Lucía Cano +
Pablo Oriol & Fernando Rodríguez

PROJECT TEAM

SELGASCANO

Paolo Tringali
Juan Muzquiz
Íñigo Riveira
María Andrés
Fabiana Perrogón
Leandra Matas
Inés Olavarrietą
Arjon Kadillari

FRPO

Adrián Sánchez
Victoria Luque
Pilar Corredoyra
Paula Gómez
Álvaro Laviña
Loreto Mazariegos

MAIN CONTEXT VS. ALBANIA

Widely different contexts in Albania: Countryside, Villages, Sea, Cities, Lakes, Houses, Apartments, Villas, Social Housing, Hotels. But everything is in the same cloud that represents Albania – understandable and close for us, as in the end it is a Mediterranean country, as is ours (Spain).

All the processes are pretty similar, but at the same time they depend on many small and big differences related to the site, history, program or climate.

ORGANIZATION/GOAL/SETUP

We are two different studios from Madrid, working together on most of the projects. At the same time, since the beginning, we have had a partnership with the local architect Besnik Grainca, who's a teacher at Polis University. Also, all the engineering is made in Albania, with well-trained local engineers who know all the constraints and local possibilities better than we do.

SETUP IN RELATION TO ALBANIAN PARTNER

We share ideas and spend a lot of time together discussing them, but at the end the initial concept design is developed and drawn at our offices in Madrid. For the construction phases we'll probably need to have some of our people at the local office working together.

OPPORTUNITIES/CHALLENGES

Opportunities are bigger than in any other place in the world right now. It's difficult to achieve that level nowadays, where you can work with absolute freedom – in any other place, where typically everything is controlled by too many committees and project managers, being the architect is just a residual part of that stupidly cumbersome process.

The only challenge is to have good control of the economical part. Economy, as everywhere, is fundamental to every project, and you need to always have that in mind. There is no way that we can propose new materials or construction processes that the clients are not able to pay for or that the industry is not ready to produce to be used there.

HOW TO INTEGRATE GREATER RESPONSIBILITY FOR QUALITY IN PROJECTS

It's up to us: In our experience, the quality in a project comes from a big presence from our side on the construction site, taking care as much as possible of everything. That means bringing people from our office to be close to the site and traveling to Albania a lot, as we already do now – every two weeks or more if necessary.

BALANCING QUALITY AND DENSITY/INVOLVING STAKEHOLDERS

Our experience is that the responsibility is coming from your continuous presence throughout the process. More people involved and more stakeholders are just more waste of time and more difficulties in arriving at the final quality in a project. Of course, the client' respect is fundamental, and we feel that so far, but we need to keep earning that respect continuously.

EXAMPLE/INSPIRATION

It is not about a project, it is the ambience that inspires us. The kind of competitions they are making, where the only important thing is the architectural quality. That transmits a sense of creative tension that enriches us and we hope will enrich the whole country in some years.

TOOLBOX ALBANIA FUTURE

Is freedom a toolbox?

ROZAFA TOWER HOTEL
A top view of the competition model that became the iconic logo of the proposal we presented in Shkodra in July 2024

selgascano + FRPO

COAUTHORSHIP & COLLABORATION The Albanian adventure of our offices (selgascano and FRPO) began in the spring of 2024 with a joint invitation to participate in the international Rozafa Tower competition in Shkodra, which we were fortunate enough to win. As a result of the joint work between two offices with different sensibilities, various projects of varying scales, programs, clients and locations have been developed. The process has been very satisfying for us so far. The collaboration has yielded unexpected riches that we value greatly. All the projects featured here are coauthored by FRPO and selgascano (both offices based in the west area of Madrid), but they also include a thorough collaboration with local offices – whose help has been invaluable! – as well as greatly committed clients and a public administration that is always willing to help. Some of the projects are also a shared work with Estudio Cano Lasso, also based in Madrid. We have chosen six concepts that summarize the intentions and findings of the journey we have taken – free ground, vegetation, slenderness, lightness, geometry and color – and we have illustrated them with images taken from our work folders, to briefly revisit our humble contribution to what we like to call the "Albanian Rush."

LOS BANCALES DE FARKË (Tirana) Shade and coolness in the streets of Himara (pictured). Vegetation is a fundamental part of the Albanian and Mediterranean architectural experience.

SURF & TURF (Shëngjin) The tower is sandwiched between the beach town and the wooded mountain. The base rises up and allows vegetation to penetrate inward.

PYJET E DRILONIT (Tushemisht) The vegetation at the mouth of the Drilon River at Lake Ohrid spreads out between the trembling fingers of the apartment buildings.

AbA2 (Tirana) The walkways leading to the homes run between trees. The shadows cast by the branches and leaves blend with those of the light railings and brise-soleils.

LOS BANCALES DE FARKË (Tirana) Restoring the original landscape. Mediterranean green roofs, gardens full of olive trees, streets covered with vines. The houses are camouflaged under a blanket of vegetation that descends toward Lake Farkë.

FREE GROUND & VEGETATION Less architecture and more nature. Less flooring, walls and ceilings; more trees, shrubs and grasses. The quality of the environments in which we live deteriorates exponentially when they move away from nature. Our projects always give priority to the natural. There is a global collective concern for the renaturalization of built environments. But in a climate of urban growth and construction boom such as Albania is currently experiencing, we must make an even greater effort: The risk of irreversibly damaging the environment is high. The first step is always to free up as much land as possible, occupying the smallest footprint to obtain the largest available planting space. Vegetation and trees form the most important part of our projects. Logically, this is Mediterranean vegetation, in continuity with the areas and ecosystems in which we are working, in order to recover and enhance the direct and simple natural quality of the most popular architecture and the beautiful plant tradition of Albanian streets and towns.

SURF & TURF (Shëngjin) One of the many color studies, with the aim of stylizing the appearance of the small apartment building.

N'MES PISHAVE (Shëngjin) Work process and testing. From the three-dimensional digital model to the physical model.

SKY-K (Durrës) The volume of the small residential building is split in two to lighten its presence among the uneven buildings on Durrës Beach.

N'MES PISHAVE (Shëngjin) The 2024 Shëngjin forest fire calls for the restoration of the pine forest ecosystem. N'Mes Pishave is a residential and hotel tower that rises with extreme slenderness to allow the forest to grow back around it.

TINY MODELS
A collection of small, beautiful objects for the Bread & Heart Festival in Tirana. They all belong to a family of delicate, slender geometries.

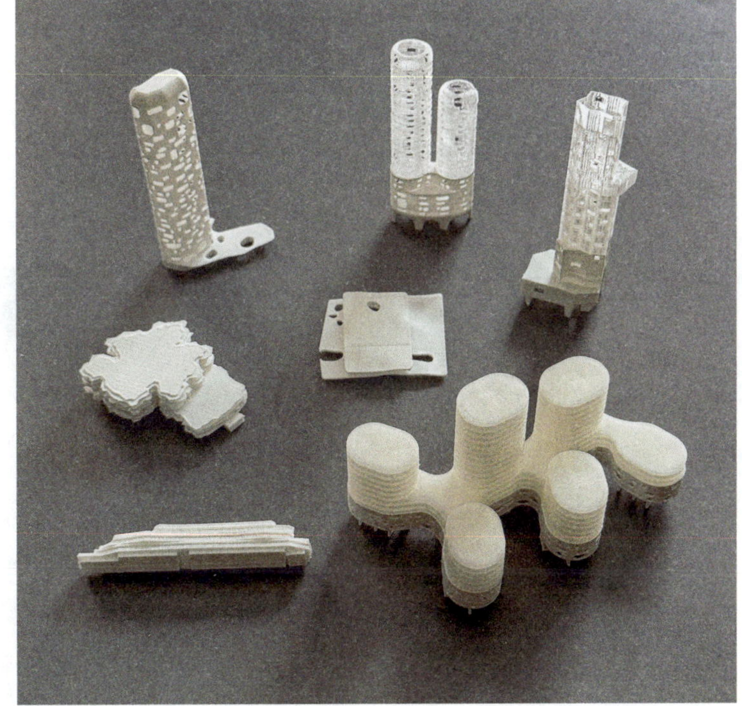

GJIRAFA (Shëngjin) Hotel and residences on Shëngjin Beach. The beautiful views are not limited to the sea, toward the west. Kune Lagoon, to the southeast, is a place of outstanding beauty.

SLENDERNESS & LIGHTNESS *A little thinner! Lift it up! More slender! It still weighs too much . . . it should float! It looks better from here . . . turn it around and refine it!* Our obsession with slenderness and lightness fills our work conversations. We've been working with them for years and we never tire of it. Because the thrill of lightness is the spice of architecture. And because light and slender, delicate architecture leaves more room to enjoy nature, which is always the best protagonist. These conditions apply to major decisions about the layout and volume of a building, but they also guide the details of each small-scale element. Vertically and horizontally, in towers and cantilevers, every time we sit down to work, someone says . . . *make it lighter!*

STRATI DI MARE (Shēngjin) After dozens of versions, the dance of geometries freezes into a layout that frees up floor space, maximizes views and establishes good relations with neighbors.

AbA2 (Tirana) Each level has two or three colors that extend horizontally across all the pieces of the project. Like a horizontal puff pastry of color and shape.

ROZAFA TOWER HOTEL (Shkodra) Overlay and color studies for the competition model. Working with Gilberto, our model maker, is part of the project's thought process.

STRATI DI MARE (Shēngjin) Layers of color facing the sea. Overlapping sheets that vibrate with the changing light and give each of the small hotel and residential towers their own character.

ROZAFA TOWER HOTEL (Shkodra)
Competition model. The imposing scale of the tower in the center of Shkodra is mitigated and softened by the vibration of broken lines, hiding the size of each floor behind sunshades and railings.

AbA2 (Tirana) Model of the final solution. Six small buildings connected by walkways and terraces with changing geometries that adapt to the sloping topography and blend in with the trees.

GEOMETRY & COLOR The world is geometry and color. Hundreds of colors, thousands of geometries. The chromatic and formal richness of nature invites us to explore, to venture into unknown fields that are full of wonderful discoveries. Too often, architecture has renounced them, impoverishing its results in the name of rationalization, hygiene, industry or economics. But the exploration of shapes and colors, of geometries and material nuances, does not contradict simplicity and economy. The journey of discovery is longer, less linear or obvious, but the rational solution is always waiting for us somewhere in this exploration without preconceived paths. The surprise of the unexpected is the reward for a journey whose only compass is intuition.

ENDLESS CHANDELIER
Conceptual model of Rozafa Tower Hotel for the Bread & Heart Festival in Tirana (June 2025)

START	NAME PROJECT	LOCATION	DEVELOPER	PUBLIC/PRIVATE	PHASE
2024	Rozafa Tower Hotel	Shkodra	Rozafa Group	Private	Detail design
2024	One Living apartment building	Vlora	Valeron AEA shpk	Private	Detail design
2024	N'Mes Pishave	Shëngjin	Klajdi Construction shpk	Private	Concept design
2024	Strati di Mare	Shëngjin	Flori shpk, Eark shpk	Private	Concept design
2024	Hotel	Himara	Valeron AEA shpk	Private	Concept design
2024	AbA2	Tirana	Kontakt	Private	Concept design
2024	Pyjet e Drilonit	Tushemisht	Kontakt	Private	Concept design
2024	Pogradec Building	Pogradec		Private	Concept design
2024	360 units social housing	Tirana	Tirana Municipality	Public	Concept design
2024	Kopshti Hotel	Tragjas	Llanaj Ndertim shpk	Private	Concept design
2024	Los Bancales de Farkë	Tirana	Amzo shpk	Private	Concept design
2024	Sky-K	Durrës	IMK shpk	Private	Concept design
2024	Armadillo	Mjull Bathore	ABV Konstruksion shpk	Private	Detail design
2025	Gjirafa residential & hotel	Shëngjin	Alessio Konstruksion	Private	Concept design
2025	Surf & Turf residential	Shëngjin	Alessio Konstruksion	Private	Concept design

NAME OFFICE

SHIGERU BAN ARCHITECTS, JEAN DE GASTINES ARCHITECTES

DATE	PLACE	WORKING IN ALBANIA SINCE
January 15, 2026	Paris, France / Tokyo, Japan	2022

PRINCIPALS
Shigeru Ban
Jean de Gastines

ALBANIAN PARTNER
Matrix Konstruksion

PROJECT TEAM
Taro Okabe
Philippe Sim
Isabella Bönke
Leo Cammilli
Kelly Ann De Gouveia
Yunyu Liu
Anna-Maria Bolok

INTRODUCTION TO ALBANIA

Invited to a design competition.

MAIN CONTEXT VS. ALBANIA

We work in a fast-changing urban context where decisions are made quickly and ambitions are high. Development is intense, and architecture is expected to be visible and expressive.

The building process is less fixed than in Western Europe. This creates uncertainty, but also flexibility. The basic structure of the process is familiar, but adjustments often happen later and more informally. Because of this, architects need to stay involved and responsive.

ORGANIZATION/GOAL/SETUP

We work with local partners who understand regulations and procedures. This is essential to move projects forward.

Our goal is simple: to keep design quality high while making projects buildable. We have been working in Albania for about four years, and our design attitude has not changed. However, since we have not yet experienced the construction phase, our organization will likely evolve once projects are built.

SETUP IN RELATION TO ALBANIAN PARTNER

We develop the concept, design logic and details, and local offices adapt it to local conditions and approvals.

This setup requires clarity. One office defines the architectural intention, the other ensures feasibility. In this context, clear roles help avoid confusion and loss of quality.

OPPORTUNITIES/CHALLENGES

The opportunity is freedom. Architects are expected to propose strong ideas and take responsibility for them.

The challenge is the approval process, which can be slow and unpredictable. This requires patience and a pragmatic attitude. You need to accept this condition and work within it.

HOW TO INTEGRATE GREATER RESPONSIBILITY FOR QUALITY IN PROJECTS

Quality improves when architects stay involved beyond design. Decisions made during construction are critical.

Responsibility should be continuous, not limited to early phases. This requires trust and clear communication with all partners.

BALANCING QUALITY AND DENSITY/INVOLVING STAKEHOLDERS

Quality and density are linked. Higher density requires clearer design decisions.

The architect's role is to explain this logic simply: how space, structure and use make density work. This should be stated early and without ambiguity.

Design integrity is easier to maintain when the main idea is shared with developers, authorities and engineers. When everyone understands the reasons behind decisions, quality can survive change.

EXAMPLE/INSPIRATION

We are inspired less by individual projects and more by projects that take risks and test new ideas. In Albania, experimentation is possible, and that is valuable.

TOOLBOX ALBANIA FUTURE

Albania offers freedom, speed and high expectations.

Because rules are not fully fixed, architects must think clearly, decide quickly and take responsibility. This strengthens problem-solving skills and makes architectural thinking more direct and practical.

High-Rise Tower, New Boulevard

What would Tirana look like if it were expressed through architecture? What if Tirana's past, present and future were all integrated into a single tower? This is a challenging attempt to visualize the dynamism, uniqueness and potential of this city, which is undergoing rapid change.

Impressions of Tirana

We were captivated by Tirana. How colorful and full of vitality it is! The whole city is full of youthful energy. The contrast between old and new, the skyscrapers rising one after another with their distinctive architecture, the characteristic sunlight and clouds – all of these things characterize this city.

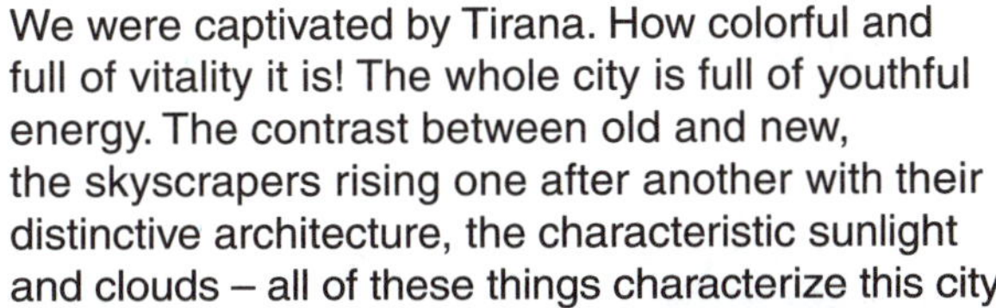

Progress

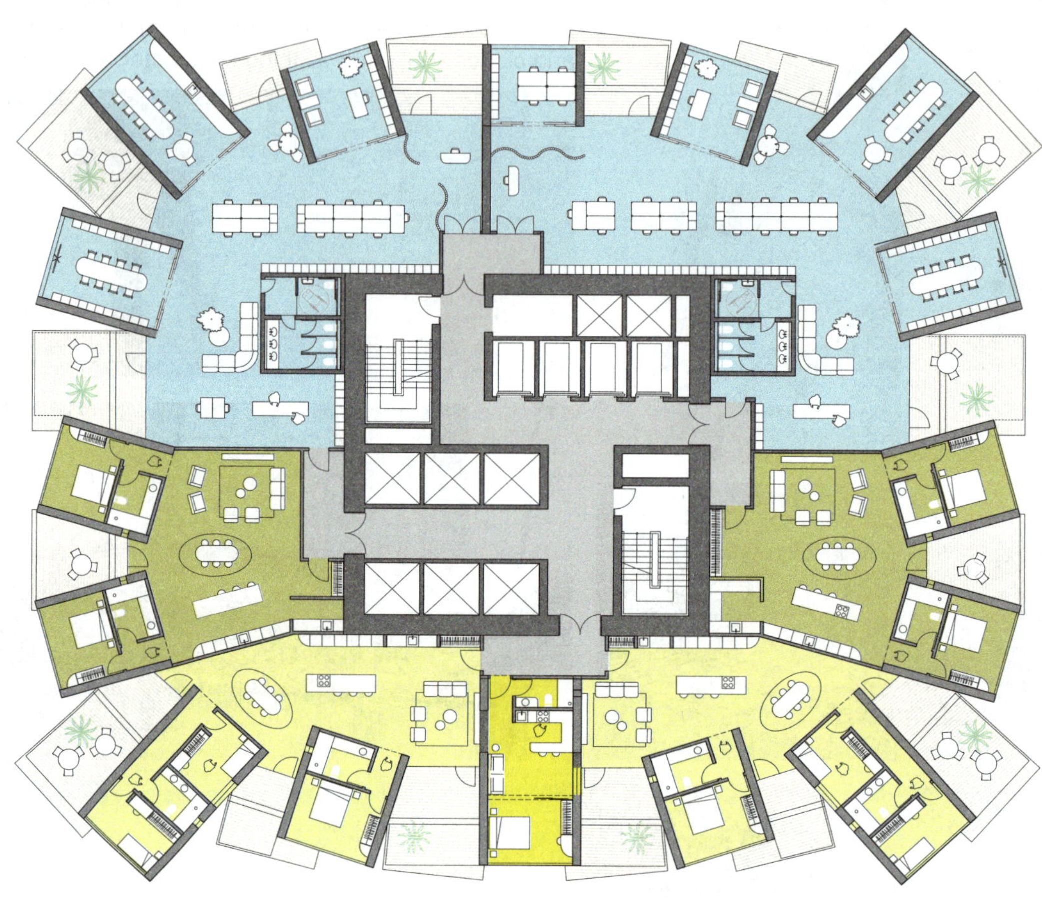

The site where our tower is to be built is located in the middle of a newly developed boulevard that stretches north from the center of the city. While new buildings are springing up all around the site, on our site there are even horses being kept. What a contrast! Working on the design in Paris, far away from Tirana, we can't help but think of the bustling city even when drawing a single line. We can't wait for the day when construction begins and we can walk around inside this tower, which will continue to grow upwards, and smell the scent of wet concrete and wood being cut. And we hope that this tower will eventually become something irreplaceable for the people of this city.

Albania has historically been influenced by various countries and has a "multilayered" cityscape, with its cities having a variety of architectural typologies. Among these traditions, the city of Berat, called the "Town of a Thousand Windows," stands out as an important UNESCO World Heritage Site in Albania.
The proposed tower is a modern version of Corbusier's Unité d'habitation, with all functions, such as commercial space, office space and living space, in a single vertical city, just like stacking up the traditional Albanian architectural typologies.
The low-rise area is an intermediate area where people can enjoy strolling through stores and parks, and where people can naturally relax and enjoy themselves, and where there is continuity with the surrounding green areas and plazas.
In the mid-rise area, the upper floors of the stores will be used as living and working spaces, just like in the city of Berat, with small-scale buildings layered and overlapping each other, creating a collage-like contingent landscape.
The high-rise area is a modern and rational tower: an architectural typology that is neither historical nor traditional, but has a facade that maximizes the use of photovoltaic power as a means of harnessing natural energy, which is the most important issue of our time. Usually, high-rise towers are covered by a closed curtain wall, but in this proposal courtyards, intermediate areas between the interior and exterior that allow natural ventilation, are incorporated throughout the tower to create a high-rise tower that can breathe.

START	NAME PROJECT	LOCATION	DEVELOPER	ALBANIAN PARTNER	M²	PUBLIC/PRIVATE	PHASE
2022	High-rise tower	Midway, New Boulevard, Tirana	Matrix Konstruksion	Matrix Konstruksion	61,655 m²	Private	Schematic design

NAME OFFICE

SOUTO MOURA – ARQUITECTOS

DATE
January 24, 2025

PLACE
Porto, Portugal

WORKING IN ALBANIA SINCE
2024

PRINCIPALS
Eduardo Souto De Moura

PROJECT TEAM
André Tavares
António Dias
Daniel de Castro
Diogo Guimarães
Elisa Lindade
Eurico Salgado
Francisca Figueiredo
Henrique Menezes
Joana Corrêa
João Ferreira
Manuel Campos
Pedro Martins
Pedro Guedes Oliveira
Ricardo Prata
Rita Maia
Tiago Simão

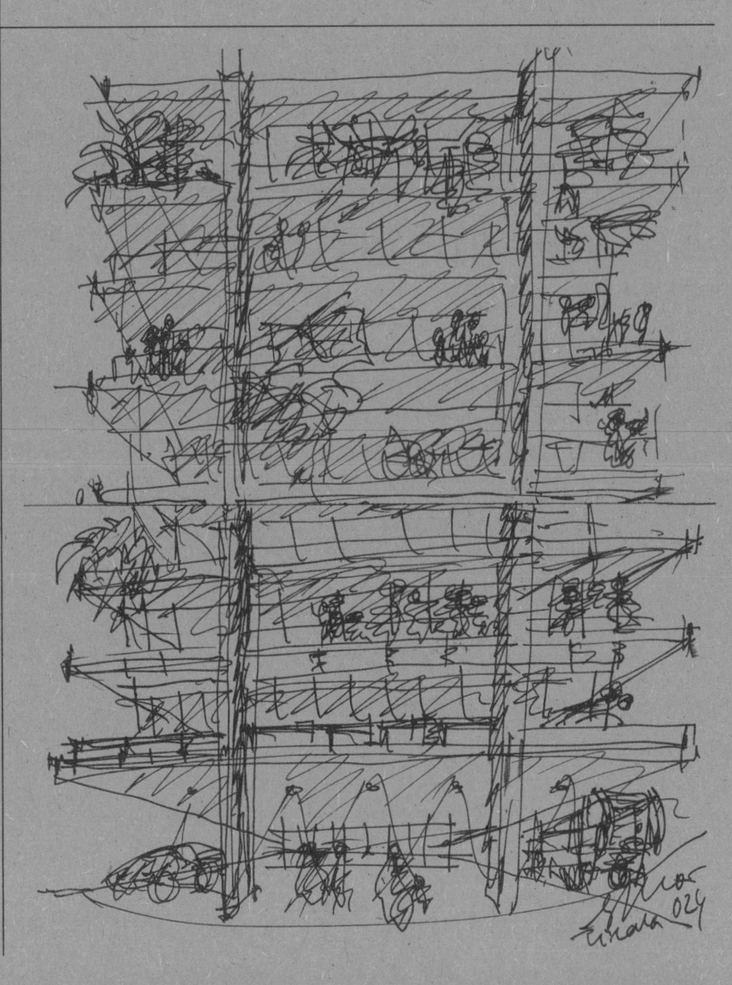

INTRODUCTION TO ALBANIA

I got to know Albania on a trip to Italy and Montenegro after the 25 April Revolution (1974).

MAIN CONTEXT VS. ALBANIA

I believe in the trilogy of material/building system/language, each with its own identity.

ORGANIZATION/GOAL/SETUP

I was invited and partnered with an architect with some experience in Albania.

SETUP IN RELATION TO ALBANIAN PARTNER

He must carry out our proposal. Because he knows the country's reality and culture best.

OPPORTUNITIES/CHALLENGES

It's a country under reconstruction. It must not make the mistakes of its postwar neighbors.

HOW TO INTEGRATE GREATER RESPONSIBILITY FOR QUALITY IN PROJECTS

There should be greater crossover between information and form.

BALANCING QUALITY AND DENSITY/INVOLVING STAKEHOLDERS

We can never let our convictions about the quality of our proposal get the better of us.

More information never hurts anyone.

EXAMPLE/INSPIRATION

The National Theater of Opera and Ballet in Tirana.

TOOLBOX ALBANIA FUTURE

The expectation of being able to practice our profession in another way.

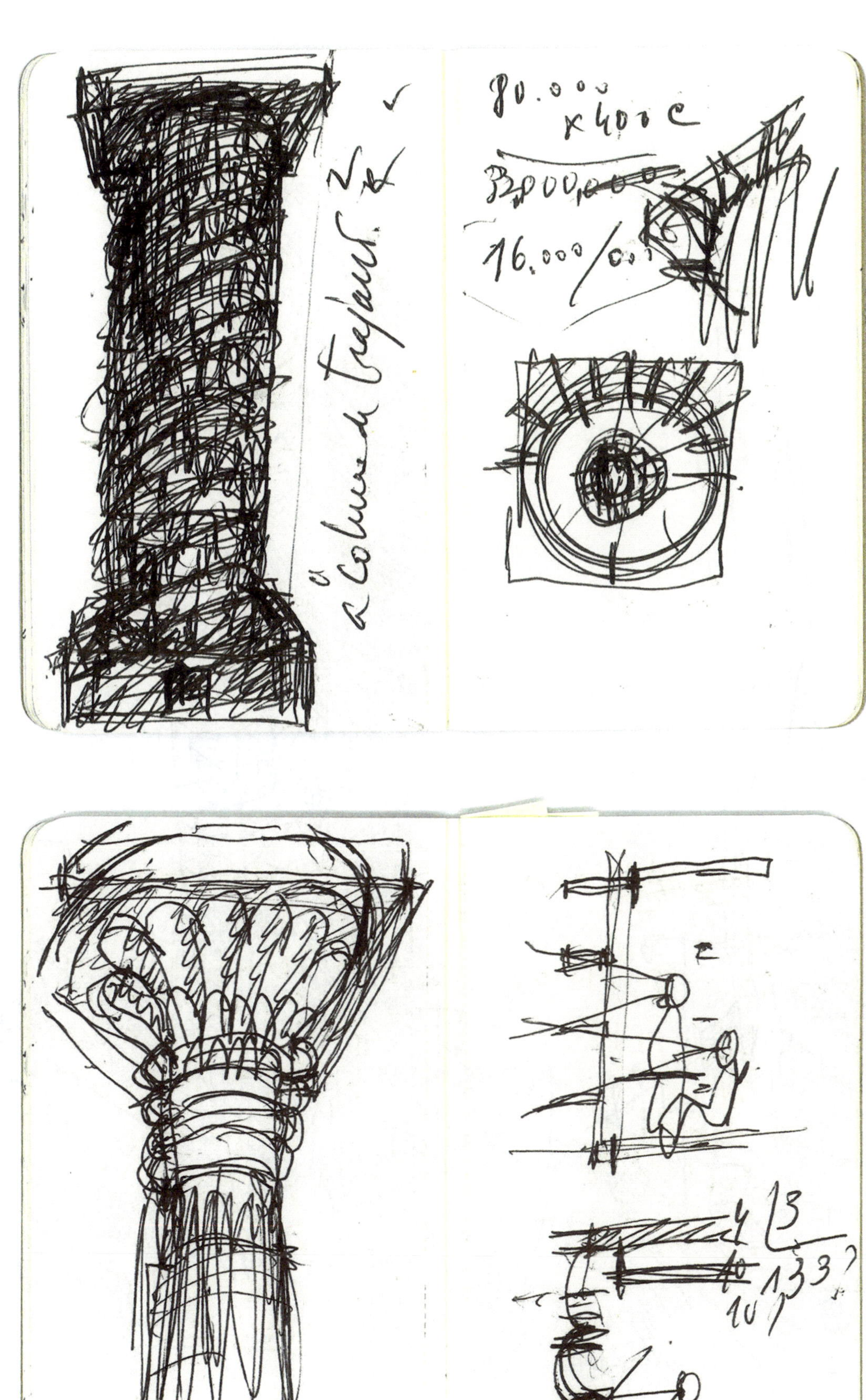

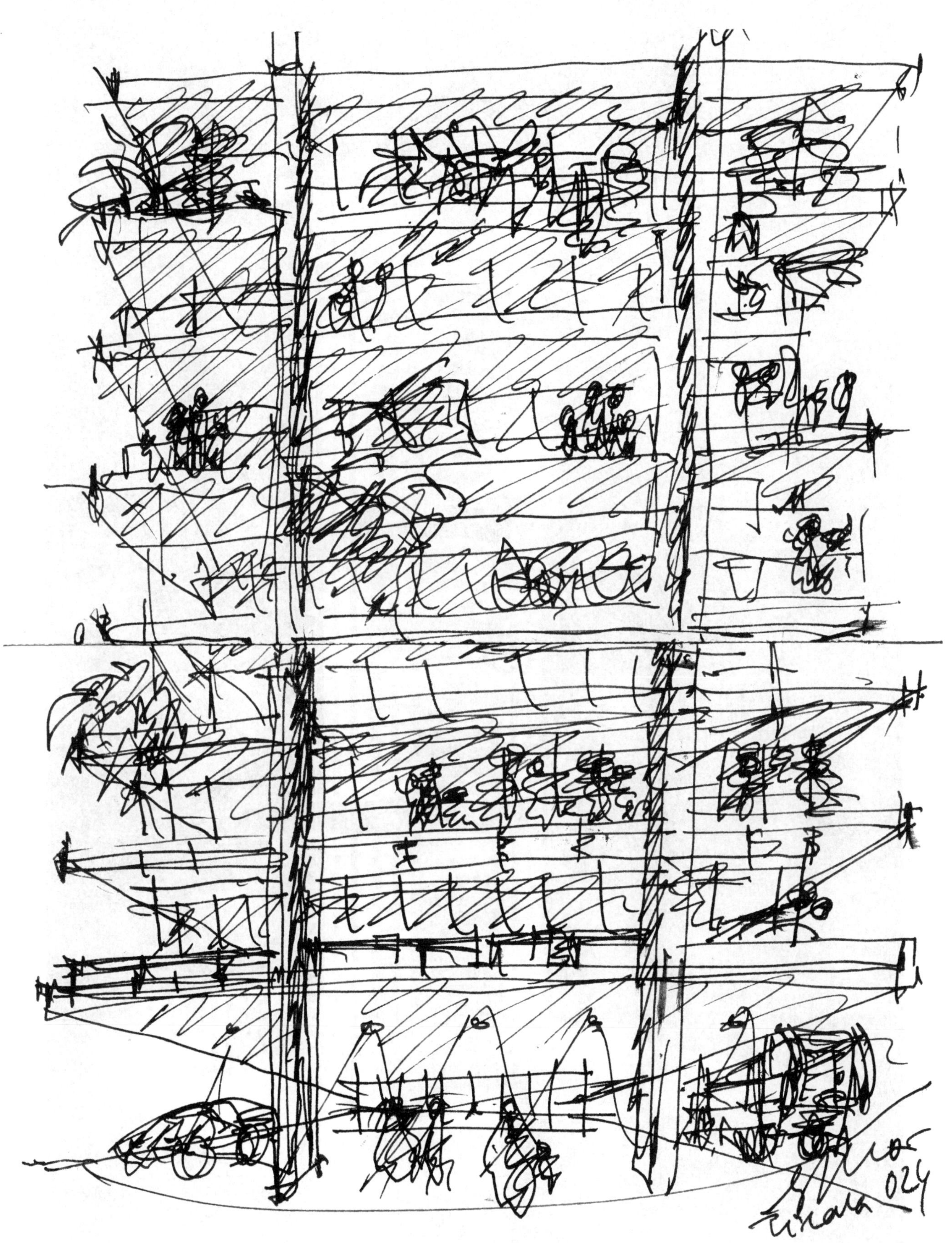

LIST OF PROJECTS

START	NAME PROJECT	LOCATION	DEVELOPER	ALBANIAN PARTNER	M²	PUBLIC/PRIVATE	PHASE
2024	Oricon Tower*	Tirana	Hanxhari Group	Artech	61,000 m²	Private	Concept design

*Project in partnership with OODA.

NAME OFFICE

STEFANO BOERI ARCHITETTI

DATE
September 2025

PLACE
Milan, Italy

WORKING IN ALBANIA SINCE
2013

PRINCIPLES
Urban planning, green and sustainable architecture, urban forestry, nature-based solutions

PRINCIPALS
Stefano Boeri (Partner)
Francesca Cesa Bianchi (Partner)
Pietro Chiodi (Partner)
Marco Giorgio (Partner)

PROJECT TEAM

STEFANO BOERI ARCHITETTI TIRANA
Francesca Cesa Bianchi (Partner in Charge)
Carlotta Capobianco (Project Director)
Andrea Zucchi (Project Director)

DESIGN TEAM 2013–2025
Jacopo Abbate
Jona Arkaxhiu
Orjana Balla
Daniele Barillari
Marco Bernardini
Carolina Bocella
Michele Brunello
Agostino Bucci
Jacopo Colatarci
Tracy Decolly
Laura Di Donfrancesco
Giorgio Donà
Saimir Elmadhi
Linda El Zaher
Moataz Faisal Farid
Yulia Filatova
Sara Gangemi
Besart Gjana
Eleonora Grassi
Federico Godino
Julia Gocalek
Lorena Hasani
Paloma Herrero Ermakova
Sara Koçi
Corrado Longa
Ani Marku
Era Merkuri
Martina Mitrovic
Azzurra Muzzonigro
Hana Narvaez
Jona Os
Federico Panella
He Ruoyu
Paolo Russo
Mario Shilong Tan
Mattia Tettoni
Luca Tognù
Elisa Versari

ALBANIAN PARTNERS
AGIKONS shpk
Albana Kocollari, ANK Architecture
Alca shpk
Alket Kumaraku
HYDRO & ENERGY
Anion EE
Arch. Edmond Alite, Mobycon
Arch. Eranda Shalsi
Arch. Eri Cobo
Arch. Joni Baboci, Layer
Arch. Kreshnik Merxhani
Arch. Vasilika Shtephani
Avv. Florian Xhafa
Elenita Roshi
EMA Consulting
Erin Mlloja
FISHTA electric shpk
Gener 2 shpk
IMPACT shpk
Ing. Artan Dersha
Ing. Bledar Malaj
Ing. Bledar Tole
Ing. Dhimitri Papa
Ing. Diana Brahaj
Ing. Dritan Bradko
Ing. Erjon Alimani
Ing. Ermir Gjoka
Ing. Fatjon Zekaj
Ing. Gezim Tola
Ing. Helidon Kokona
Ing. Ilo Bodi
Ing. Llambi Karaman, Xhenlux
Ing. Malaj
Ing. Niko Lako
Ing. Petrit Hoxhaj
Ing. Rubin Kodra
Ing. Saimir Saliaj, ITE Group shpk
Kreshnik Bajraktari
LEAL CSE shpk
SCE Project S.r.l.
Son-Group
TAULANT shpk
Zavalani Consulting shpk

INTRODUCTION TO ALBANIA

The first time Stefano Boeri was in Albania was in 2001, a few years after the end of the civil war. Public space was basically nonexistent. A wave of illegal buildings – the only way citizens could assert their right to property during the communist regime – had taken over the squares, the streets, even the Lana riverbed.

He came back in 2009/2010, serving as a jury member for an international competition that featured some of the most prominent names in European architecture. The winner was Casamonti (Archea) with the Alban Tower.

Meanwhile in 2008, a few months earlier, Stefano Boeri had written an article for *Abitare* magazine about politicians capable of changing the world, translating their visions into something that citizens could understand and immediately put into practice. Edi Rama, then mayor of Tirana, was one of the three politicians he focused on.

MAIN CONTEXT VS. ALBANIA

We are based in Milan, with branches in China and Albania. Our work spans Europe, and we are also active in Middle East and Asia. Overall, our team includes one hundred architects working across diverse geographic and cultural contexts.

What particularly characterizes the Albanian context is the way many architectural firms have developed distinct approaches, aesthetics and architectural languages. And in the last year, we've noticed a growing number of young architects beginning to define their own unique styles as a kind of autonomous declination of the foreign architectural contributions.

ORGANIZATION/GOAL/SETUP

We started by working on a few projects and in 2013 we won the competition to design the master plan Tirana 2030. Edi Rama's vision was particularly interesting: simultaneous competitions for all major cities in Albania. While we were designing Tirana's future, other teams worked on Durrës, Vlora and beyond.

It's both important and fascinating when a country chooses to imagine its future not through rigid five-year plans, but through a broader, interconnected set of master plans. This wasn't a puzzle-like process, where pieces are made to fit together, but rather an additive one. As we presented our vision for Tirana, others were already presenting ideas for Durrës. It became a way to compare different proposals and approaches, each shaped by its own context.

SETUP IN RELATION TO ALBANIAN PARTNER

We believe it is essential to engage in meaningful dialogue with local architects, sharing expertise, local knowledge, ideas and visions. Our interaction also extends to public institutions and universities, allowing us to transform these exchanges into valuable training opportunities for emerging architects. This ongoing dialogue – this blending of schools of thought, styles and design approaches – is deeply rooted in the country's DNA, shaped by its recent history. It is a cultural asset that should be preserved and further enhanced.

OPPORTUNITIES/CHALLENGES

For us, the opportunity lies in working on projects at many different scales – from residential buildings to archaeological sites, from large master plans to individual public schools. Each project gives us a chance to innovate, introducing new ideas and technical advancements.

For example, with the Blloku Cube, we experimented with a semi-transparent façade that changes with chromatic reflections. With the Vertical Forest in Tirana, we explored a new organization of balconies and plants covering three sides of the building. With the Bonce project we are studying an innovative relationship between greenery and tall buildings, and in the project we are working on to enhance the ruins of the ancient Roman amphitheater in Durrës, we are discovering the still unexplored richness of archaeology present in the Albanian territory.

HOW TO INTEGRATE GREATER RESPONSIBILITY FOR QUALITY IN PROJECTS

We believe the focus should be on an increasingly complex and stratified reality, able to ensure a high social as well as functional mix. It must accommodate diverse modes of transportation and integrate all the technologies and systems needed to optimize energy consumption.

Living nature – trees, plants – should be a fundamental component. Above all, the city must be dense with activities, community spaces and intersection points where different realities, communities and experiences converge. This is what makes a city truly multifaceted. It must avoid becoming homogenized with segregated or ghettoized neighborhoods, which unfortunately are all too common in many rapidly developing cities.

EXAMPLE/INSPIRATION

We have worked extensively with local students and young architects: There is a strong desire to reclaim and renovate parts of the legacy from the past – both the communist era and the post-communist urban development – in order to enrich the openness and unpredictable complexity of public spaces.

In the overall urban design approach, this is the direction that we, as architects, and our colleagues are shaping. We are not only discussing proposals to reuse structures from Hoxha's dictatorial era, as in the case of the Pyramid redesigned by MVRDV, but also considering other periods of twentieth-century architectural history, such as the heritage from the Italian Fascist era.

TOOLBOX ALBANIA FUTURE

From an architectural perspective, the approach underway appears to focus on significant investments aimed at improving citizens' quality of life. For example, the government's plan to build over twenty new school facilities addresses some of the education system's existing shortcomings. And this new philosophy is inevitably attracting quality designers in a virtuous circle of growth. We believe that the three public schools we designed and built in Tirana between 2015 and 2017, at minimal cost but with great attention to ensuring that the collective spaces could be used by the neighborhood communities, demonstrate that urban regeneration policies can yield real results and help reduce social inequalities.

TR030

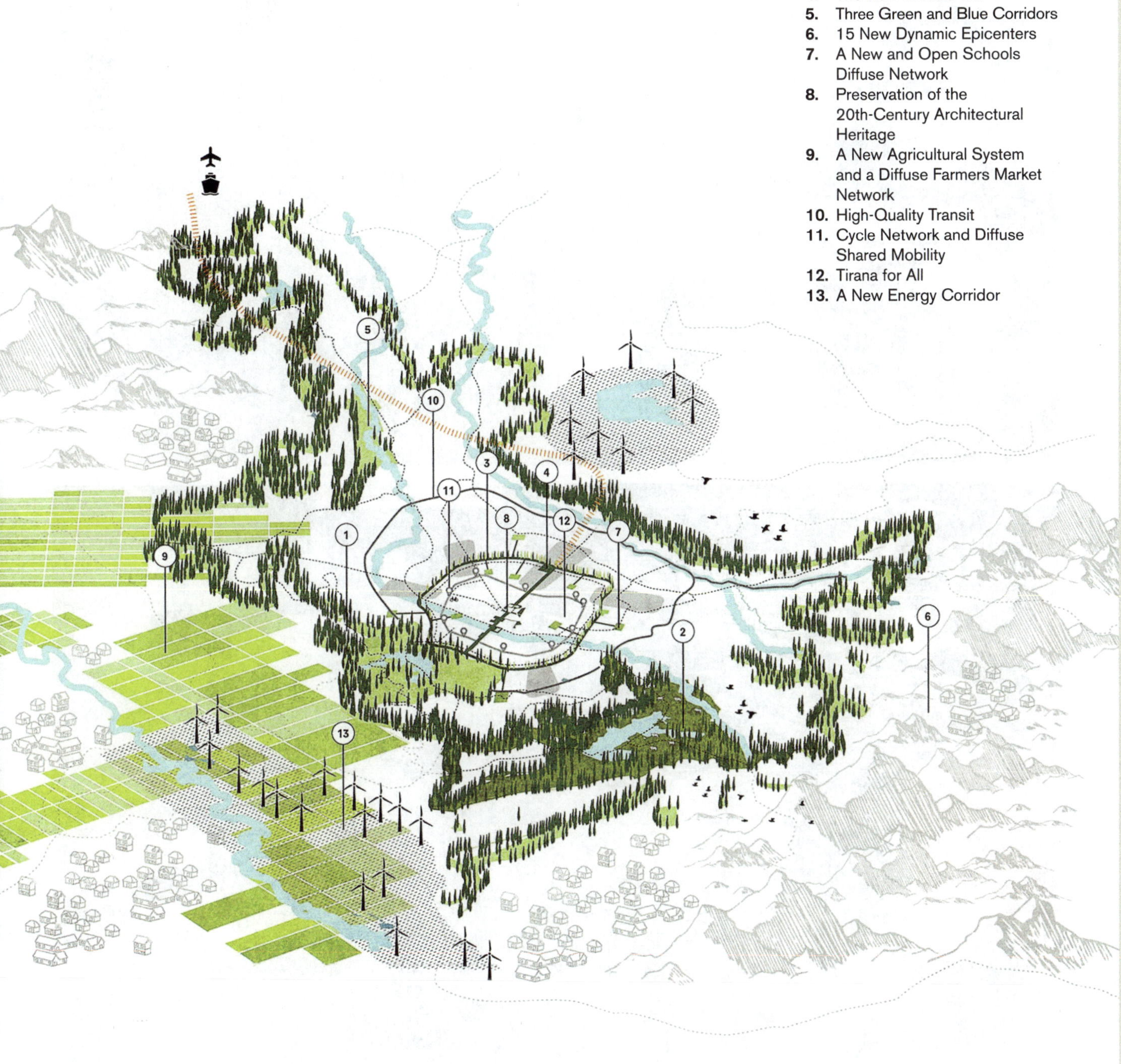

TIRANA 2030. A KALEIDOSCOPIC METROPOLIS: A plan for reclaiming the landscape. The city's green areas triple through a comprehensive intervention that creates a continuous orbital forest system around Tirana. The plan includes the planting of two million trees, the development of parks and protected nature reserves to preserve and enhance local biodiversity, the introduction of new ecological corridors and the creation of a green ring road – the "New 4th Green Ring" – conceived as a linear public space and a sustainable mobility route at the core of Greater Tirana.

Ambrogio Lorenzetti, ***Allegoria ed Effetti del Buono e del Cattivo Governo*** (Allegory and Effects of Good and Bad Government), 1338–1339, series of three frescoes, 7.7 × 14.4 m (room), Palazzo Pubblico, Siena, Italy. Starting from the image of the famous fresco *Allegoria ed Effetti del Buono e del Cattivo Governo*, the theme of the "kaleidoscopic city" is defined as a model for a new balance between city and nature.

TIRANA 2030. A KALEIDOSCOPIC METROPOLIS. Fresco drawings of Tirana 2030 showing the different focal points of the project. Top row, from left to right: A New Orbital Forest; The New 4th Green Ring, A Natural Oasis; bottom row, from left to right: The New World Park; A New Agricultural System; A New and Open Schools Diffuse Network.

Tirana Rhapsody[1]

Stefano Boeri

I started getting to know Tirana in 2009, and later, in 2014, I was involved in designing the city's master plan. Fifteen years later, the Tirana we live in today – where we've opened an architecture studio and started a local business – has changed radically, yet in a uniquely special way.

In some respects, and in certain parts of Tirana, the changes have been so rapid that it seems impossible to believe only fifteen years have passed, while in other respects the city seems to have remained fixed, immobile, even going backward in time.

In fact, time in Tirana does not follow a single direction or rhythm – and that is precisely its urban miracle.

It is a metropolis that, in the early years of the millennium, was still largely undeveloped – almost feudal – and lacking basic services, infrastructure and public transport. In twenty years it has become a modern and kaleidoscopic metropolis (this was both the title and the guiding vision of our master plan), in which, however, alongside the temporal urban modern changes, large medieval niches remain. This happens when the classical yet flexible forms of contemporary European architecture are set cheek-by-jowl alongside rigid Soviet- or Chinese-style buildings, or when skyscrapers emerge vertically from among the little wood and brick houses.

When seen from above, Tirana today appears as a kaleidoscope of historical fragments, spatial elements that feed on the past, present and future of the entire history of this European city.

Next to neighborhood markets, we now find the new stadium and the renovated pyramid, a multicultural and technological center aimed at young people; next to the alleys between Rruga e Durrësit (Durrësit Street) and Rruga e Kavajës (Kavajës Street), there is the spacious Skanderbeg Square; side by side with the neighborhoods of traditional brick-built houses with their dangling electric cables, there are brand-new skyscrapers.

Tirana is a poignant metropolis featuring a disorderly system of spectacular "time shelters":[2] places where time has stopped, entirely shaping the lived spaces in which memory becomes denser and imagination moves faster. Yet there are also places offering potential futures, slivers of time sometimes encapsulated in the remote past.

The challenge in the years to come will not be to slow down these uneven accelerations but rather that of preserving their rhapsodic, non-overwhelming and all-enveloping nature.

Time in Tirana does not have a single direction; in some places it bends and turns back on itself; in others it is immobile; in yet others it accelerates forcefully.

Tirana's metropolitan rhapsody must, therefore, be protected – although, if you think about it, there could be nothing further from the real nature of this wild and courageous city than a protective attitude; a city that is ever more disproportionate, rhapsodic and beautiful.

1 The musical term *rhapsody* is defined as an instrumental composition, often solo, in which several themes, almost always of popular origin, are carried out in free form, with heroic meanings or featuring ethnic and national exaltations, or intended to enhance a particular instrumental virtuosity. It was a favorite form in Romanticism and beyond until the beginning of the twentieth century. Significant examples are those by F. Liszt (Hungarian Rhapsody), J. Brahms, E. Lalo (Norwegian Rhapsody), A. Dvořák (Slavic Rhapsody), C. Saint-Saëns (Auvergne Rhapsody), M. Ravel (Spanish Rhapsody), C. Debussy (Rhapsodies) and G. Gershwin (Rhapsody in Blue, 1924). Entry from the *Enciclopedia Treccani.*

2 Georgi Gospodinov, *Time Shelter*, 2020.

RADURA is a temporary installation — but it is also much more than that. Located in Parku i Piramidës since 2019, it offers a refuge from the chaos of the often frenetic and noisy city life. It is a place where one can sit, rest or wait — in a word, regenerate — engaging in simple everyday actions that are often made difficult by the pace of contemporary urban life, which pushes everything toward movement, impatience and speed.

THREE OPEN SCHOOLS. From top to bottom: Don Bosco School (2021); Kodër-Kamëz School (2024); Shqiponja School (2024). The core of the vision lies in the idea that the school of the future can become an epicenter in the urban life of neighborhoods, a place open to everyone, of all ages, every day of the year.

ARCHITECTURE PROJECTS. From top to bottom: Tirana Vertical Forest (2025); Blloku Cube (2024); West Residences (2025).

TIRANA RIVERSIDE. Stefano Boeri Architetti designed the master plan guidelines based on principles of social and functional mix. The project was then implemented by local architects and companies, building on the studio's framework.

START	NAME PROJECT	LOCATION	DEVELOPER	PUBLIC/PRIVATE	PHASE
2015	Tirana 2030 – A Kaleidoscopic Metropolis	Tirana	Ministry of Urban Development	Public	Delivered
2016	Radura	Parku i Piramidës, Tirana	Municipality of Tirana	Public	Executed
2017	Blloku Cube	Tirana	Invest Society	Private	Executed
2017	West Residences	Tirana	Invest Society	Private	Executed
2017	Vertical Forest	Tirana	Gener 2 shpk	Private	Executed
2017	Three New Schools for Tirana: Don Bosco School, Kodër-Kamëz School, Shqiponja School	Tirana	PPP Agikons Construction Company, Municipality of Tirana	Public	Executed
2020	Tirana Riverside	Tirana	Municipality of Tirana	Public	Delivered
2021	New Boulevard	Tirana	EHW GmbH	Private	Ongoing
2022	Durrës Archaeological Park	Durrës	Albanian-American Development Foundation	Public	Delivered
2022	Domus Cube	Tirana	Domus Group shpk	Private	Under construction
2022	Transport Directory, D.P.SH.T.RR. building	Tirana	D.P.SH.T.RR	Public	Under construction
2023	Petro Nini	Tirana	Domus Group shpk	Private	Ongoing
2023	Tirana Mosaic Tower	Tirana	Domus Group shpk	Private	Ongoing
2024	Bonce building	Tirana	Bonce shpk	Private	Ongoing
2025	Baks Rrjoll master plan	North Albanian shoreline	Gener 2 shpk	Private	Ongoing

NAME OFFICE

STEVEN HOLL ARCHITECTS

DATE	PLACE	WORKING IN ALBANIA SINCE
January 10, 2025	New York City, USA / Beijing, China	2024

PRINCIPLES

Our projects combine sustainable technology and forward-looking approaches to architecture. We see a sustainable approach to design and construction as an obligation to the future of the built environment and are committed to this vision in each project.

COLLABORATORS

Agnieszka Kurant
ATELIER 4
Arup
Atelier Markgraph
Stoss

PROJECT TEAM

Steven Holl (Lead Designer)
Roberto Bannura (Partner in Charge)
Olaf Schmidt (Partner in Charge)
Dimitra Tsachrelia (Project Advisor)
Han-Yuan Chang (Project Architects)
Lirong Tan (Project Architects)
Nour Chahboun (Project Team)
Peiwei Chang (Project Team)
Frank Fan (Project Team)
Maxwell Funk (Project Team)
Hannah Hill (Project Team)

INTRODUCTION TO ALBANIA

We had been following PM Rama's great efforts to invigorate the country and its public institutions. During that time, the Territorial Development Agency reached out seeking our interest to participate in architectural design competitions. The announcement of EXPO Albania created a fitting and positive opening for our firm, given its cultural relevance, social and community-engagement characteristics, and potential to combine art and architecture as a single creative force.

MAIN CONTEXT VS. ALBANIA

Our current involvement in Albania involves two projects of different characteristics: one public and one private. While both offer distinctive opportunities, challenges and work dynamics, what they have in common is a shared vision for architectural excellence, public space integration and a positive contribution to Tirana's urban environment. These efforts align seamlessly with PM Rama's vision that these new developments should be in service to the city's revitalization and modernization.

ORGANIZATION/GOAL/SETUP

As with the large majority of projects undertaken by our firm, working in Tirana involves assembling a team of trusted and like-minded professionals with whom to collaborate. Beyond a professional relationship, we aim to establish true friendships and a collaborative ethos that can span years, in the most fruitful and reciprocal of relationships. These human dynamics within our work help shape our understanding of the country's culture, history and traditions: all aspects that become relevant to and are expressed in the design process.

SETUP IN RELATION TO LOCAL OFFICE

We see our collaborators as valued team members in every stage of the design process. They are involved as part of the design team from the earliest stages of concept design, participating in internal architectural discussions and helping frame the aspirations and design principles of the projects from the outset.

As the design process evolves into latter phases of the design, our collaborators gradually take charge and ownership of responsibilities toward project documentation and site support. During those stages, particularly during the process of design guardianship during construction, we see our collaborators as strong contributors to the design resolution of conflicts arising during construction and toward client turnover.

OPPORTUNITIES/CHALLENGES

Albania is experiencing a unique revitalization, reshaping its identity through art and architecture. Contributing to this transformation is an opportunity that should be approached with responsibility and in service of this visionary period.

Thanks to our past similar experiences in Asia, we are familiar with the challenges this process entails. Institutional shifts, zoning repositioning and ongoing developments in the construction industry are just a few of the variables at play during this process.

Key to succeeding in this shifting landscape is adaptability and responsiveness in the firm's design philosophy and in the project design itself.

HOW TO INTEGRATE GREATER RESPONSIBILITY FOR QUALITY IN PROJECTS

Supporting the participation of the design architect in all stages of the project, particularly during the construction and implementation phases, is key for the project's capacity to retain the integrity of its design intent and driving vision, while providing a dynamic workflow toward the timely resolution of design challenges that only arise during construction.

BALANCING QUALITY AND DENSITY/INVOLVING STAKEHOLDERS

Our firm believes in the sustainable development of a project site. This entails the inclusion of public, landscaped areas in the project that help balance the scale of urban development, while allowing for active community engagement.

We are also strong proponents of sustainability design principles, ranging from passive strategies (project orientation, use of natural light and ventilation) to mature technologies that reduce the carbon footprint of our buildings (geothermal energy, solar energy collection, renewable construction materials). We believe that some of these principles can proactively be written into the zoning requirements of any new site. We look forward to working with the Territorial Development Agency and similar stakeholders in advancing a new vision that sponsors sustainable developments of equitable characteristics.

ARCHITECTURE OF ART: DRIVING URBAN LIFE IN TIRANA

EXPO ALBANIA

EXPO URBAN HOUSING

TIRANA "L" TOWER

EXPO ALBANIA

TIRANA, ALBANIA
2024 –

Art drives architecture: Traversing the rectangular volumes of the expo center, a computer-animated line of LED light continuously signs and resigns the building as a collective artwork

Mass timber trusses spanning 80 meters are positioned at varying heights according to the rhythm set by the "signature line," creating a dynamic, skylit environment

ART SHAPES ARCHITECTURE
EXPO Albania (2024) in Tirana, by Steven Holl Architects with artist Agnieszka Kurant – in collaboration with ATELIER 4 – demonstrates how art shapes architecture. Kurant's "End of Signature" animates a collective community signature in LED light, continuously signing and erasing itself. This dynamic line defines the undulating CLT roof trusses. As a jury member noted, "the art becomes architecture."

ECOLOGICAL & SPATIAL INNOVATION
EXPO Albania integrates geothermal heating and cooling, white solar shingles, and rainwater recycling. Skylights offer natural light with blackout options, while rewilded earth mounds buffer noise. A recycled-water reflecting pool connects the Main Hall and wine hotel, which celebrates Albania's 3,000-year-old wine culture through vineyards and festival spaces. The Main Hall, constructed with hempcrete, balances lightness and grounded materiality.

SITE & CONNECTIVITY
Located on a 6-hectare former military site, the 80-by-120-meter Main Hall interlocks with the Entry Hall and conference spaces, framing the surrounding mountain views. The program includes a 10,000-square-meter main hall, 2,000-square-meter complementary space, 5,000-square-meter outdoor area and underground parking for 500 cars.

Positioned along Tirana's outer ring road, the site offers rapid access to the airport and the Adriatic–Ionian Corridor, supporting Tirana's 2030 urban development goals. Designed to rival regional centers in Belgrade, Zagreb and Bucharest, EXPO Albania celebrates innovation, ecology and cultural heritage.

The winning team includes Steven Holl Architects, Agnieszka Kurant, ATELIER 4, Atelier Markgraph, Stoss and Arup.

Steven Holl Architects' collaboration with artist Agnieszka Kurant develops an architectural language aligned with her *End of Signature* body of work and artistic concepts. The team expands the concept, which was first realized on the Guggenheim Museum in New York City in 2015, into a fully spatial dimension. The signature defines the roofline of the building, while its earthy hempcrete materiality anchors it within the surrounding mountain landscape. Open-glass views at the ground level lift the building in lightness, further enhanced by the water's reflection. The recycled-water pond also plays a crucial role in the ecological design, supporting biodiversity.

EXPO URBAN HOUSING

South of EXPO Albania, new public spaces are shaped by meandering residential buildings.

TIRANA "L" TOWER
KASTRATI GROUP

TIRANA, ALBANIA
2024 –

A hybrid tower of living, working and recreation is envisioned in Albanian stone and stained concrete

Vibrant interlocking spaces are public gardens with art

In the center of the urban fabric of Tirana, a hybrid tower of living, working and recreation is envisioned in Albanian stone and stained concrete. Urban porosity as a central spatial concept organizes public space at grade and is expressed in large green space openings above. The real material is space:

1) the new public space shaped by the "L" form
2) urban porosity via open passages
3) vertical green public spaces
4) public observatory and restaurant at the top
5) ecological design

Geothermally cooled and heated, with ample natural light, fresh air and operable windows, the tower aims for the highest ecological standards.

The total footprint of 3,635 square meters is reclaimed through five sky gardens, which weave along the seam of the "L" geometry. Like interlocked fingers, the voids are as significant as the solids. These public gardens, equal in size to the building's footprint, are spaces given back to the city in this key central urban site. Each garden features distinct Albanian flora, with high meadow grasses in the upper void and seaside succulents in the lower void. Colored cantilevers play with the language of the "L" and extend the biodiversity of the planting themes onto public green balconies. At grade, water gardens activate a new public space, including a special garden court at the existing church. The proposal includes naming this new space after the great Albanian poet and writer Ismail Kadare (1936–2024).

While the "L" cuts modulate scale in the overall form, the polychrome soffits glow with light at night, marking a new central metropolitan destination in Tirana. A 200-room hotel, condominiums, live-work lofts, offices, shops, two restaurants and, at 269 meters, a public rooftop observation and café animate urban life.

Tirana "L" Tower, inspired by interlocking hands

START	NAME PROJECT	LOCATION	DEVELOPER	PUBLIC/PRIVATE	PHASE
2024	EXPO Albania	Tirana		Public	Competition, winning entry
2024	Tirana “L” Tower	Tirana	Kastrati	Private	Concept design

NAME OFFICE

STUDIO GANG

DATE
Founded 1997,
Chicago, USA

PLACE
Chicago, New York City,
San Francisco, USA /
Paris, France

WORKING IN ALBANIA SINCE
2024

PRINCIPALS
Jeanne Gang (founding partner)
Ana Flor Ortiz (design principal and partner)
Rodia Valladares Sánchez (design principal and partner)

PROJECT TEAM

LEPIDOPTERA
Jeanne Gang and
Rodia Valladares Sánchez
with Enrique Orts Costa
Anne-Virginie Sala
Jason Flores
Alfred Klopper
Myriem Rhmari Tlemcani
Melissa Naranjo Barrientos
Charles Curran
Leia Gorra
Austin Sun
Jonathan Rabagliati
Ana Sotelo
Luis Tejeda
Mauricio Sánchez
Mark Schendel
Antoinette De Montille
Dylan King
William Emmick
Austin Chod
Jing Chen-Joyeux
Jay Hoffman

VINE
Jeanne Gang and
Ana Flor Ortiz with
Jason Flores
Sarah Athena Beauchamp
Evdokias
Alan Huang
Steven Meyer
Julien Roy
Mauricio Sánchez
Violante Piccolomini
Neha Harish
Jonathan Chamblee
Meghan Jones
Myriem Rhmari Tlemcani
William Emmick
Brian Hartman
Anne-Virginie Sala
Alfred Klopper
Jonathan Izen
Diana Aguilar Gonzalez
Efi Orfanou
Aria Griffin
Hubert Yang
Luis Tejeda
Colleen Lyell
Sangwon Kim
Jay Hoffman

COLLABORATORS

LEPIDOPTERA
Arup (Design Engineers: Structure, MEP/FP, Facade, Vertical Transport, Environmental Analysis)

VINE
Arup (Design Engineers: Structure, MEP/FP, Facade, Vertical Transport, Environmental Analysis)

ALBANIAN PARTNERS
MA Studio & Partners
Commonsense Studio

LEPIDOPTERA
Pajtoni Group and Uni Group Investment (Client)
KRON Construction shpk (Client Representative)
Artech Studio (Architect of Record)
UTS-01 (Local Structural Engineer)
HMS Studio (Local MEP Engineer)
Denis Latollari (Local HYD/Fire Engineer)
Krenar Çaushi (Local Electrical Engineer)
Pespa Alumin (Façade and Solar Screen Contractor)

VINE
Gener 2 (Client, Architect of Record and Local Engineer)
LEAL (Local Structural Engineer)

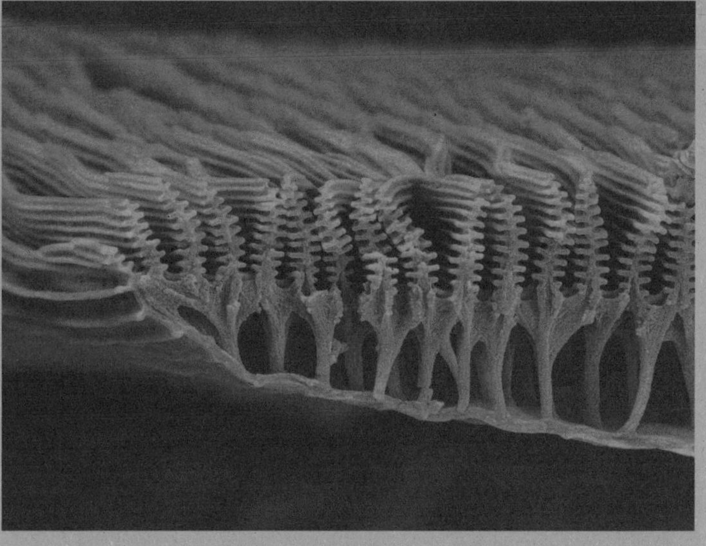

INTRODUCTION TO ALBANIA

We were invited to enter the international design competition for EXPO Albania. When I looked at Albania on Google Earth, I realized I knew almost nothing about this place. I went to eBird, a citizen science app that I use when I travel, to see where Albania was located on the migratory flyways. I was astonished at the variety of the country's landscapes and topographies, and hence its biodiversity. Next I watched a TED Talk given by Prime Minister Edi Rama, who spoke about color and urbanism. At this point, I was hooked, yet skeptical that a paradise like this, so relatively undiscovered, could exist in 2024. We said "yes" to the competition. Later I learned that other architects from around the world, good architects, were already working here. At that point I got on a plane to Tirana.

MAIN CONTEXT VS. ALBANIA

The act of building – that is, construction, which I love – is similar in Albania and North America, where our office began. When design is ambitious yet mindful of the local material and construction capabilities, everyone involved rises to the occasion to make a work of Art. This doesn't mean that we all perfectly agree along the way, but as architects, we love the back and forth with engineers and craftspeople to accomplish our goal in a fluid, mutually enriching way.

The overall design process varies a lot between countries. In fact, it seems the ways in which we can win a project, interact with clients and have our designs approved are different everywhere. For private sector projects, we find that in the US, developer clients have a strong position; in Europe, the government agencies do. Each has its pros and cons, but we don't have enough space to get into it here! The point is that in Albania, it is a bit of both. Private developers have their goals, but the government side has great design leadership and ambition. This system seems to work – after all, there are wonderful buildings being created and high standards being set.

ORGANIZATION/GOAL/SETUP

First, we want to work with Albanian architects. In the long term, the quality of Albanian architects and landscape architects – their education, their experiences in designing and building, their understanding of ecology – all of this will determine the future of the country. No nation can exclusively depend on outside architects. This is why we are excited to collaborate with local architects. So far, we've worked with MA Studio & Partners, Artech and Gener 2, who are all amazing. We've found so many similarities and connections, and I feel like I learn more from them about building in Albania every day. Our goal is to synchronize as if we were one office.

SETUP IN RELATION TO ALBANIAN PARTNER

Our office does most of the design work in earlier phases, but we collaborate closely with our local architects. They're an important voice at the table, and we ask them to bring their knowledge and feedback on more traditional design items – local ways of building, codes and materials – but also about Albanian culture and how people use and perceive things. We want to make sure the new places we're creating will resonate with the local people who will live and work there. Design decisions, of course, take place throughout the process, and we've found that person-to-person communication and direct contact with our collaborators is crucial. As a form of best practice, we like to begin collaboration with the local architect early on, and to stay involved all the way through completion. In addition to local architects and engineers, we also collaborate with an international team of consultants. This is especially important because mixed-use towers are a relatively new building type in Albania.

OPPORTUNITIES/CHALLENGES

The main opportunities are being able to build in an environment that is open to new ideas, and that has a genuine need for new construction because of the long period in the twentieth century when there wasn't much built. For me, this is much preferable to working in certain extremely wealthy countries, where architecture is treated more as a glitzy marketing strategy.

I find the challenges lie in understanding the available skill sets and how to work with them, but this is a challenge in every place. It requires getting to know the local abilities and qualities. In itself, this can be an opportunity to learn something new.

BALANCING QUALITY AND DENSITY/INVOLVING STAKEHOLDERS

For coastal sites, I think it's critical to understand their ecology, and it is the responsibility of the architect to find the right collaborators who can help them understand the natural environment and how their project will impact it. On urban sites, I think the architect has to try to learn about both the existing infrastructural capacities and future plans for infrastructure in order to support a project's density.

EXAMPLE/INSPIRATION

I like MVRDV's Pyramid of Tirana, with its interesting layers of reuse, adaptation and reinvention. The building invites everyone, young and old, to engage with it in different ways.

TOOLBOX ALBANIA FUTURE

One tool that I've really come to appreciate through working in Albania is WhatsApp, as a direct way of connecting with colleagues and peers. Of course I use WhatsApp for personal messaging, but the way it's used in Albania as an open platform for conversation and exchange with peers – including the architects represented in this book – helps you learn about architectural issues and challenges, as well as the personal side of working in a country outside your own. I feel connected on a deeper level. I think this tool could work well to connect architects in any new city where we all have projects and shared aspirations.

Eastern monarch butterflies breed in the US and Canada, then migrate to Mexico for the winter, where they can be seen covering entire trees.

Albania's sun-drenched coasts are certainly postcard perfect, but for me it isn't the geography or weather that has made this place come alive – it is the life itself, and discovering its rich biodiversity. An amazing variety of habitats is found within this corner of Europe. Thanks to the interactions between its varying physical features – geologies and climates, hydrologies and soils, rugged terrains and planted orchards – conditions are right for an abundance of terrestrial life to flourish.

As a birder, my first goal in Tirana was to set out in the early morning, binoculars in hand, to scan the edges of Skanderbeg Square. Almost immediately, I caught a quick glint of whitish blue flash across the leafy background of street trees. It wasn't my intended bird, but rather the gossamer wing of a butterfly.

From the science that I later reviewed, I learned that Albania's many species of butterflies and moths haven't yet been completely documented. Existing evidence does, however, indicate impressive diversity in Albania among this order of insects collectively known as *lepidoptera,* and new studies are underway to document them.

Postcards sent from Albania in 1963 might have used these postage stamps featuring regional butterflies and moths.

How extraordinary, was my first reaction to this new knowledge. But the pleasure was immediately tempered by worries of warming temperatures, pesticide use and habitat loss due to the country's rapid development.

As an architect now working in Albania, I feel a deep sense of responsibility to design in harmony with the environment and act with care for all living things.

And as Tirana sets out on its next phase of architectural growth with optimism and hope, who else but the butterfly – so remarkable, yet so fragile – to remind us of the risks as well as the possibilities of metamorphosis?

A physical model showing the aggregation of Lepidoptera's wing-like sunshades, which seem to perch lightly on the facade. Their design and location pattern synthesizes sun angles, balconies and window placement.

Lepidoptera is a new residence and office for Tirana that is inspired by these delicate, ephemeral creatures. It works with the local climate to offer inhabitants double-height balconies where they can enjoy outdoor living and working in all seasons.

Lightweight brise-soleils protect against strong wind and beating sun, while still allowing pleasant breezes, filtered natural light and sweeping views of the surrounding city. With embodied carbon in mind, the lightweight screens, like a butterfly wing, use minimal material for maximum impact – functional, visual and environmental.

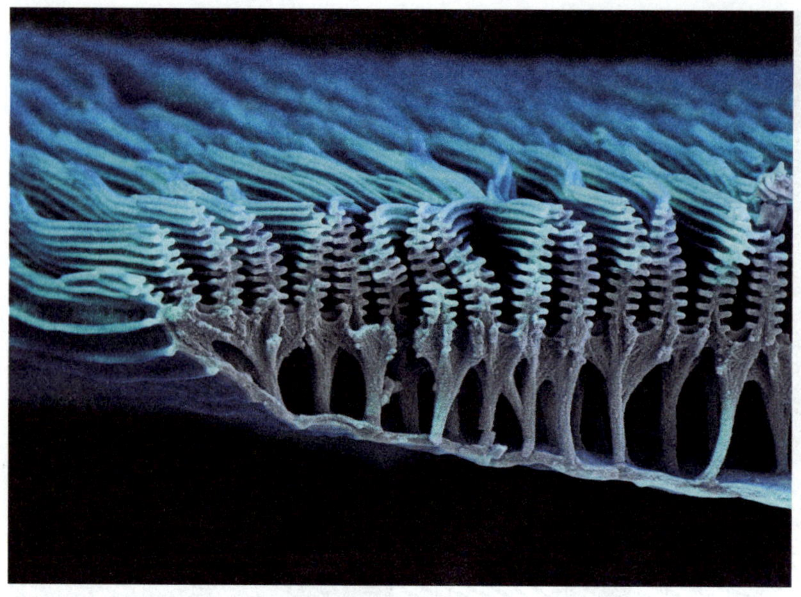

Butterfly wings are stunningly colorful, yet these colors are produced without a single pigment. Their iridescent hues come from the way their nanoscale textures refract light. This "structural color" is what we see.

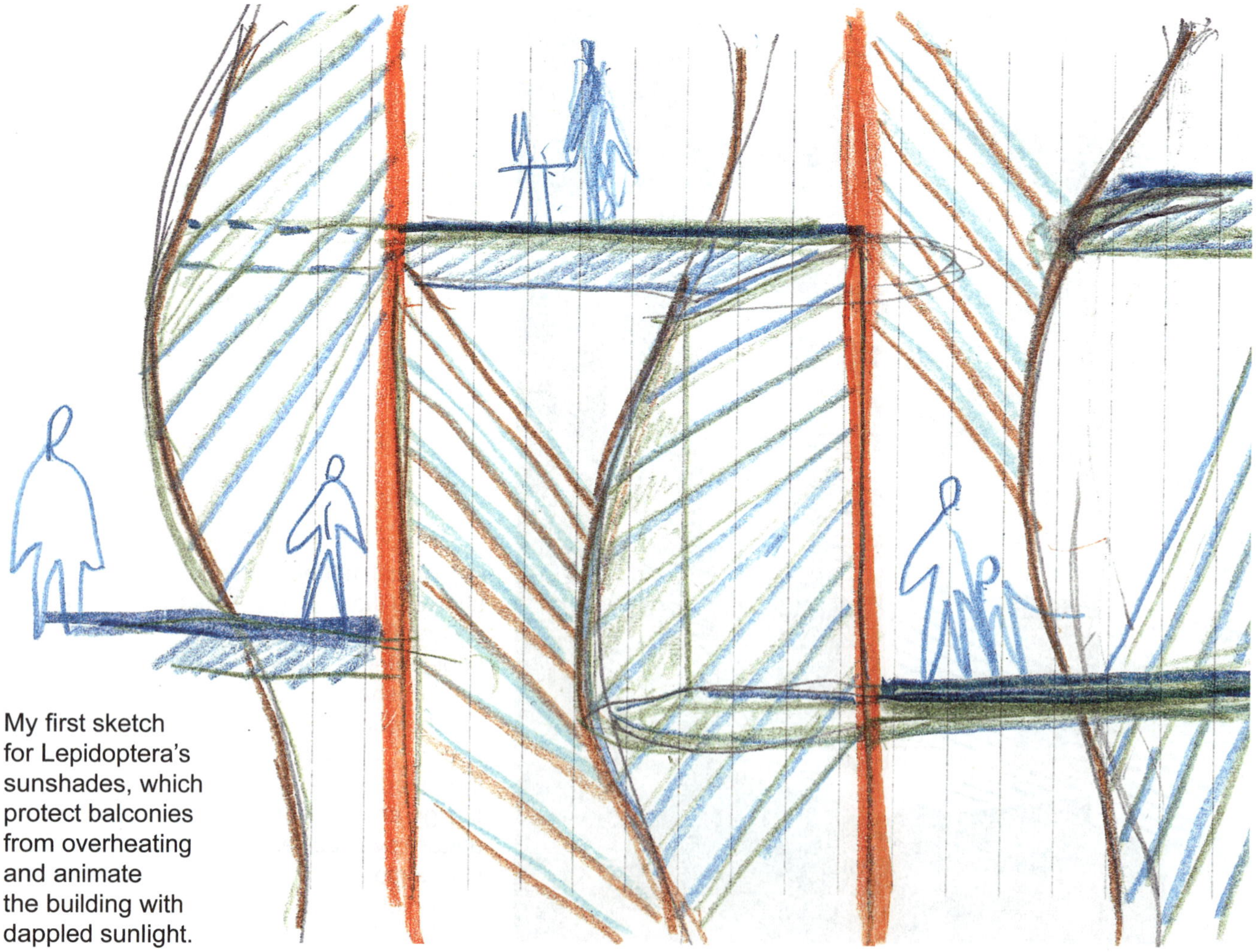

My first sketch for Lepidoptera's sunshades, which protect balconies from overheating and animate the building with dappled sunlight.

Color ignited Tirana's transformation, starting in the 1990s with Edi Rama's polychromatic facades project. Today, Lepidoptera aims to add vibrancy to the neighborhood with its "structural color" and energetic, mixed-use program.

During my first visit to Albania, I met many people and went away feeling like I had made new friends. Whether it was everyday residents, students, government officials or fellow architects – everyone had such a positive mood and generous spirit, and from each I learned a little bit about Albanian life. One aspect that stood out was the importance of sharing a meal and reserving time for family, a value rooted in rural life that I saw is still very much alive in the city. Culturally and geographically, Albania's countryside seems ever-present, which is why it's difficult for me to imagine a previous generation constructing so many bunkers and factories. This building boom included creating over seven hundred artificial lakes with engineered shapes, whose water was meant to serve as infrastructure to power industrial ambitions.

Building on the local transformation already underway, softening the hard edge of the artificial lake and adding recreational amenities and native plantings can create a more ecologically and economically vibrant area.

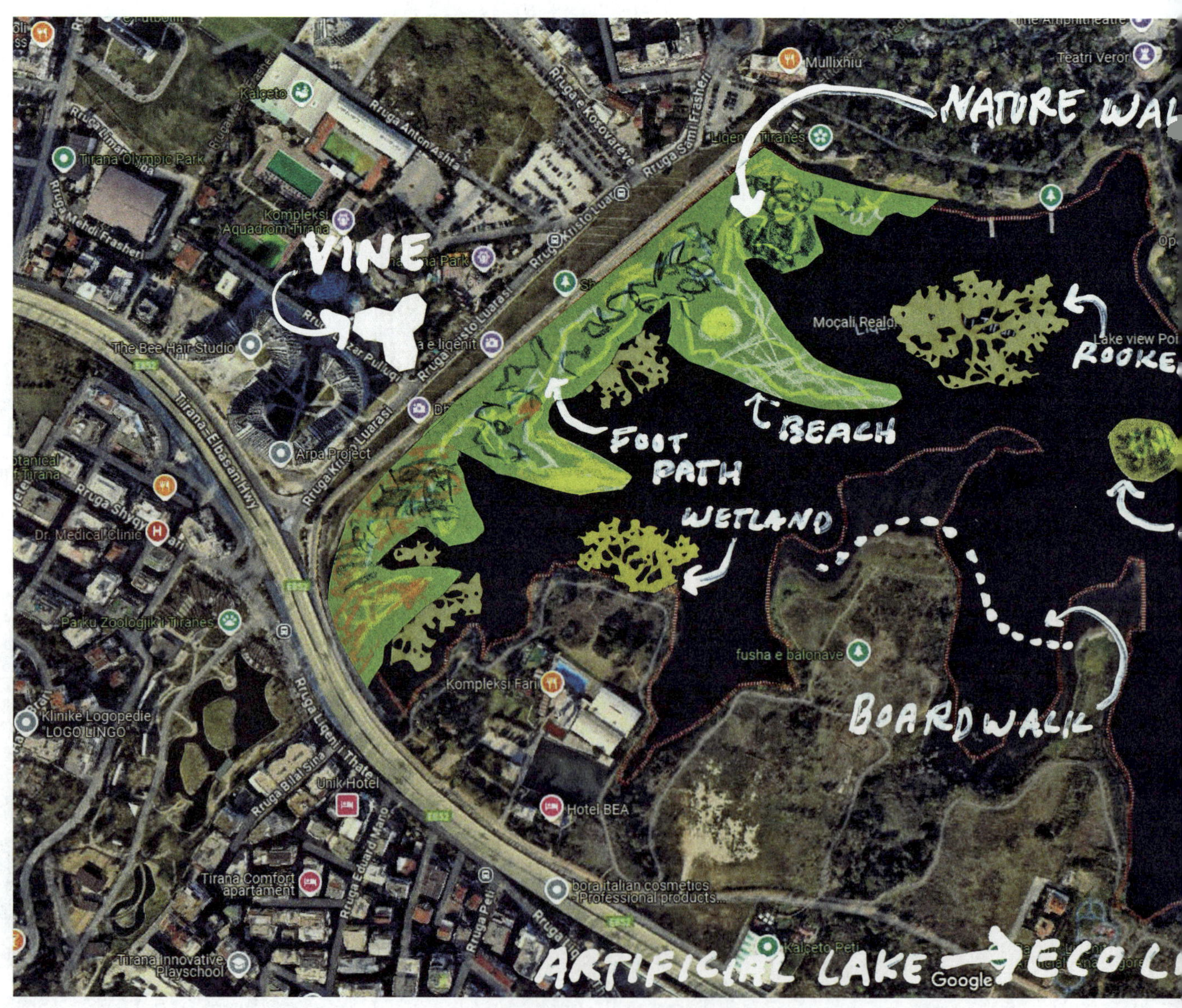

Sketching the Albanian landscape, like these rugged foothills east of Tirana, helps me understand more about the deep history and ecology of this special place.

Today, the man-made lakes are finding new purpose in support of contemporary values and dreams. Our project site borders the long, straight edge of one of these water bodies, a freshwater reservoir in Tirana. It now acts as a public amenity for leisure activities – a place where you can enjoy nature right in the center of the city. It is becoming a new kind of green infrastructure for living. With its prime urban location, and with this evolving green infrastructure, the neighborhood is ready to grow to accommodate more residents and visitors.

An early idea about Vine and its relationship with the adjacent lake.

Digital sketching quickly advances design ideas, developing the facade design and exploring the creation of a biodiverse roof garden.

Vine is a new residence and hotel that looks out over the lake. Working with its triangular plot, the geometry of the building plan resolves into a trefoil – like a plant with three-lobed leaves – with slightly bowed sides and cropped ends. Apartments with large outdoor terraces climb up around the central core in subtly staggered tiers. From afar, Vine will reveal its faceted surfaces in light and shadow, in shades that vary from dark to light.

I can also envision how the adjacent lake can one day grow a bit as well, gaining irregular edges and islands so it, too, can become a more accommodating and immersive urban home – this one for Albania's birds, fish, pollinators and many other species of urban wildlife!

The plan accommodates a variety of apartment types within its triangular site. It also gives every inhabitant great access to sunlight, fresh air and views of the lake or surrounding city.

START	NAME PROJECT	LOCATION	DEVELOPER	ALBANIAN PARTNER	M²	PUBLIC/PRIVATE	PHASE
2024	Lepidoptera	Tirana	Ksamil Seaview shpk	Artech Studio	31,400 m²	Private	Detail design
2024	Vine	Tirana	Gener 2	Gener 2	64,000 m²	Private	Schematic design

NAME OFFICE

STUDIO PRECHT

DATE	PLACE	WORKING IN ALBANIA SINCE
January 2026	Werfen, Austria	2019

PRINCIPALS
Chris Precht
Tang Fei

PROJECT TEAM
Gregor Hoheisel

INTRODUCTION TO ALBANIA

Prime Minister Edi Rama sent me a message on Instagram, asking if I would be interested in working in Albania.

MAIN CONTEXT VS. ALBANIA

The majority of our projects are tourism- and residential-related.

There are not many countries in the world that have a boom in these fields comparable to Albania's. The excitement and development speed are unmatched.

And not many governments are as focused on utilizing architecture and design to develop the country.

ORGANIZATION/GOAL/SETUP

Over the last five years we have developed a network of clients, local partner architects and engineers, and we have gained substantial experience regarding Albania's regulations and permitting process. We have also gained deep insight into the culture and preferences of Albanians. All this helps us to be highly efficient and capable of matching the developer's pace.

As some of our designs are now under construction and many are scheduled for construction to start within 2026 we are currently deepening our relations with our local partner architects and developing our strategy to provide quality control and professional consultancy during the realization phase. This might include opening an office in Albania.

SETUP IN RELATION TO LOCAL OFFICE

We value open discussions and advice, but during the design process we try to avoid "too many cooks working on one dough." In architecture there are always plenty of alternative solutions, many of them equally as good as the one we might propose. But to keep the concepts strong and the ideas and stories told "on point," it is important to have a lead designer with one clear vison.

OPPORTUNITIES/CHALLENGES

The fascinating opportunity is to contribute to the transformation of a nation through architecture and design. Our understanding of the extent of this chance and responsibility is growing fuller with every day that we are allowed to work in Albania.

HOW TO INTEGRATE GREATER RESPONSIBILITY FOR QUALITY IN PROJECTS

The next step in the journey to realizing the vision of Edi Rama and his "army of international architects" is to realize the designs to the highest levels. Therefore, a clear financial outlook is required to give the developers confidence in the required investments, and know-how must be transferred from the best international builders into Albania.

We are trying to contribute to this process by bringing the best Austrian wood builders to Albania to instigate an understanding of the possibilities in timber construction and promote the development of Albanian forestry and timber construction industries.

BALANCING QUALITY AND DENSITY/INVOLVING STAKEHOLDERS

Edi Rama made it very clear that we as architects have an obligation to fight for quality and resist the typical developer's desire for "the most square meters at the lowest cost."

It is a tough battle, especially as every experienced architect will have built an understanding of the financial limits of design over a myriad of dead architectural dreams. The most important factor to enhance quality is to create a safe development environment, giving the developers security that their investments will pay off over long periods of stable value growth. Here the architects can assist by creating environments that will attract tourists for decades to come. By protecting natural assets and resisting the rush to overbuild in a short-lived development fever dream. But that investment climate must be supported by many more agencies, as well as by national marketing, environmental protection and economic regulation. It's a task that needs vision and the support of the country as a team.

EXAMPLE/INSPIRATION

The Air Albania Stadium by Marco Casamonti (Archea) in Tirana is a successful example of a multifaceted approach to revitalizing the city, activating tourism, literally bringing color and vibrancy to the heart of Tirana, taking risks with sound and traffic disturbance, driving massive investments and creating a vibrant landmark. Respect!

But likewise, we admire quieter work, like Oppenheim's Panorama Hilltop retreat near Dhërmi. A gentle complex of building volumes, distinctly contemporary but rooted in the local vernacular. A place where we ourselves would love to spend our holidays. And a place that is not fashionable but timelessly integrated into Albania's greatest gift, its natural beauty.

that day in the mountains

In our studio in the Austrian Alps, surrounded by mountains, nature is more than a backdrop. It becomes central to our way of thinking. Living and designing in such a dynamic environment has taught us to respect the natural flow and this perspective gradually extends to our projects.

Especially for young architects, it's often a challenge to turn ambitious, wishful theories into built reality. But Albania offers a unique opportunity. With the country's focus on development through quality architecture and the involvement of forward-thinking political initiatives, the country has become an exceptional platform for fresh and innovative ideas. It's a place where creativity isn't just encouraged, it's needed.

Albania also holds a special place within our studio. Our 10-meter-long "work-in-progress" wall is a constantly evolving canvas, filled with sketches, models and ideas for ongoing projects across the country. It's a daily reminder of how ideas grow and adapt as we dive deeper into the diverse Albanian landscapes. And as our projects in Albania continue to grow, so does our connection to its land and culture, making every design an opportunity to bridge nature, architecture and culture in meaningful ways.

that day in the park

I like to discover new cities by running. The first day I spent in Tirana, I was heading to the Central Park. I was taken by its vividness. There is something about the energy of the park. Couples sitting by the lake, families laying out their picnic blankets in the shade, joggers weaving with me through the trails. And everywhere, people talking, laughing, connecting. The city's heartbeat.

Since then, I come back whenever I am in town. It's the kind of a place where I can just be. Let my thoughts wander, breath deeply and take in the rhythm of life around me.

So, when Edi Rama asked me to design a place as a meeting room in the courtyard of the Prime Minister's Building, I thought of this feeling.

A park where he and his staff could step away from work for a moment, find a quiet spot under a tree, catch up with colleagues and friends or just reflect. At the same time it should be a symbol for an ecological transformation of the country and for other heads of state to be greeted among local plants, scents and birdlife.

There is also a playful element to the entire garden. The steps are spiraling upwards and take you in a final push above the roofline of the existing building, with a view of the city. It's a reminder of what people in the building are working for: a dynamic city that is constantly evolving. And the garden should reflect that energy.

We were in the middle of Divjakë National Park, and honestly, it felt like stepping into another world.

The path we were walking on was so narrow, and the reeds were towering above us, swaying in a summer breeze. The air was humid, the ground soft underfoot, and everywhere you looked, there were these winding canals. It felt endless, but in the best way – like you could lose yourself here.

And the wildlife? Incredible. If you just stood still for a moment, you'd hear it – the buzzing, the rustling, the calls of rare birds. We even saw some resting on their long migratory journeys. I couldn't help but wonder what stories they'd tell us if they could.

That's the magic of Divjakë.

It's not loud or obvious, but the more time you spend there, the more it reveals itself to you. When we were tasked with designing a state guesthouse in the park, I wanted to capture that feeling of discovery – of getting lost in something bigger than yourself. The design isn't about dominating the landscape but becoming part of it, blending into the reeds and the canals. It's about creating a place where people can stay and really feel the spirit of this other Albanian world.

that day at the sea

that day in the mountains

I love bridges. I always have. There's something almost poetic about them. A bridge takes two places that have been separated forever to connect them.

That moment when the land and the structure meet is magic. It's as if the earth reaches up to the bridge, and the bridge reaches back. And suddenly, there's a path where there wasn't one before.

That's exactly the feeling I wanted to bring to our project on the Vjosa River. It wasn't just about creating a functional crossing, but rather about celebrating the connection itself. The Vjosa is this stunning, untamed river. And the bridge we designed shouldn't just span above it; it should engage with it.

We even added a spa to the concept because I wanted people to linger here, to experience the river and the surrounding landscape in a deeper way.

To me, Albania itself is a kind of bridge – it's a place that connects its rich history with a forward-looking future. And this project feels like a reflection of that.

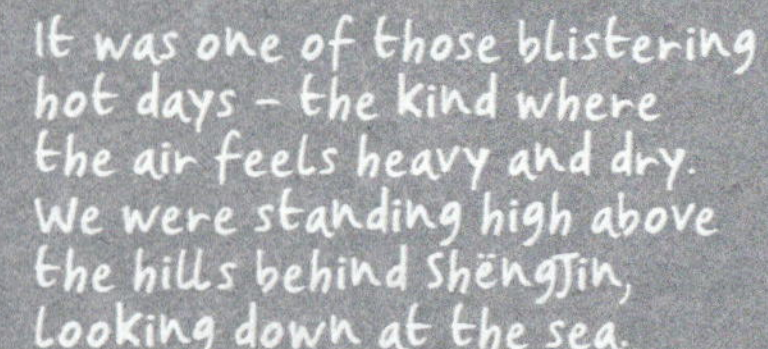

It was one of those blistering hot days – the kind where the air feels heavy and dry. We were standing high above the hills behind Shëngjin, looking down at the sea.

From up there, you could take it all in: the blue Adriatic Sea stretching endlessly before us, the horizon blending seamlessly with the sky.

A warm wind swept up the slope. Beside us, goats climbed the rocky hillsides, while far below, surfers rode the waves.

As the sun rose, its golden rays shimmered on the water, and by evening, the sky was painted with breathtaking hues of pink and orange.

Rising from this steep hillside, 155 meters above the waves, our design seeks to become an extension of the landscape itself.

The structures cascade down the slope in terraced layers, ensuring that the panoramic view remains the protagonist

We reinterpreted the traditional Albanian çardak to create airy, shaded sanctuarie using natural materials, resulting in spaces that feel as organic as the cliffs they rest upon.

START	NAME PROJECT	ALBANIAN PARTNER	CONSULTANT	KEY CONTRACTOR	PROGRAM	PHASE
2019	“Eden” Garden at the prime minister’s offices	Fusha shpk	Mingzhu Nerval (Landscape design), Tragwerkspartner (Structural engineer)	Fusha shpk (General contractor), Holzbau Maier (Timber construction)	Multistory garden in the Prime Minister’s Building in Tirana	Executed
2020	Divjakë regional development study				National park master plan	Executed
2020	Gas station and farmers market	UDV + ABGA Studio	Dhimitri Papa (Structural engineer)	Kastrati	Commercial	Under construction
2020	Mixed-use building with gas station	UDV + ABGA Studio	Dhimitri Papa (Structural engineer)	Kastrati	Commercial	Under construction
2020	Warehouse + Residences + Gas Station	UDV + ABGA Studio	Dhimitri Papa (Structural engineer)	Kastrati	Commercial	Under construction
2020	Vlora Hotel Embrace	Studio B+L shpk			Hotel and apartments	Planning approval
2021	Start Oil gas station				Petrol station	Executed
2021	Tirana 1000 Island Residences	UDV	Dhimitri Papa (Structural engineer)		Residential	Under construction
2022	Bashtovë Seaside Resort and Residences	SON Architects			Mixed use	Planning approval
2023	Bogë Valley Regional Development Study				Master plan	Executed
2023	Cape of Rodon “Prive” Hotel and Residences	MW Plan			Hotel and apartments	Under construction
2023	Lapidari Hospital	UDV + ABGA Studio			Hospital	Planning approval
2023	Lapidari Scenic Restaurant and Beer Garden	UDV + ABGA Studio			Beer garden, restaurant, apartments	Planning approval
2023	Park Apartment Competition				Residential	Executed
2023	Shëngjin Hotel and Casino	UDV / Saas Archstudio	Ideal Project shpk		Hotel arch and interior	Planning approval
2023	Shëngjin Veranda Residences		Dhimitri Papa (Structural engineer)		Residential	Under construction
2023	Shëngjin Village Residences		Dhimitri Papa (Structural engineer)		Residential	Under construction
2023	Shëngjin Northern Apartments				Residential	Construction documentation

START	NAME PROJECT	ALBANIAN PARTNER	CONSULTANT	KEY CONTRACTOR	PROGRAM	PHASE
2023	Uji i Ftohtë Hotel	ABGA Studio			Conference room	Planning approval
2023	Uji i Ftohtë Hotel Spa and Bridge	ABGA Studio			Spa and bridge	Planning approval
2024	Maji Street, Tirana – Residential high-rise	ABGA Studio			Residential	Planning approval
2024	MOOONS, Tirana	UDV	Dhimitri Papa (Structural engineer), Bami shpk Vegetation (Timber construction)	GAC shpk	Exhibition	Executed
2024	The Oval Hotel	ABGA Studio	Ideal Project shpk		Hotel	Construction documentation
2025	Bogë Mountain Resort	Arkpro Architectural Studio			Mixed use	Planning approval
2025	Stand of Albania at the Dubai Hospitality Exhibition		KUBE Studio	Elevations Ltd	Exhibition design	Executed
2025	Palasë Hotel	X-Plan Studio	Dhimitri Papa (Structural engineer)		Hotel and apartments	Planning approval
2025	Tale Regional Development		Arup Structural, Ecology, Services		Urban / Regional development	Concept design
2025	Vlora Hospitality Competition	ABGA Studio	Jeshile Landscape Design		Hotel	Won the competition, project pending
2025	Vlora Public Garbage Bins	Urban utility design				Prototyping

NAME OFFICE

TALLER HECTOR BARROSO

DATE
Founded 2011

PLACE
Mexico City, Mexico

WORKING IN ALBANIA SINCE
December 2024

PRINCIPAL
Héctor Barroso Riba

PROJECT TEAM
Carlos Ruiz Galindo Ripol
Alan Rojas Marín
Gabriel Alfaro Fregoso
Miguel Ángel Ordaz Quiñonez
Myrna Angélica Sarmiento Reyes
Natalia Villada Villada
Nicolás Andrés Silva Soto
Pablo de Jesús Manjarrez Gordillo

ALBANIAN PARTNERS

GLOW TOWER
Artech Studio (Local Office)
Glob-3X Group (Developer)

CHILDREN'S HOME
Studio B&L (Local Office)
Albanian Investment Corporation (AIC) (Developer)

INTRODUCTION TO ALBANIA

Through Ada.

MAIN CONTEXT VS. ALBANIA

We mainly work in city, forest and beach contexts. The construction process in Albania is similar to that in Mexico. In both countries, there is a strong and skilled labor force, with a notable reliance on artisanal building methods. At the same time, construction processes in both places are not highly industrialized.

ORGANIZATION/GOAL/SETUP

I am still learning from Albania, and I believe it takes time to truly understand the different aspects of the country. I am gradually getting to know its territory, climate, culture and working processes, and I see myself continuing to work here for quite some time.

Within our studio in Mexico, we have a dedicated Albania team focused on analyzing, understanding and developing the projects we are working on here. I see the Albanian colleagues I collaborate with not only as partners but also as friends. Every visit to Albania is deeply rewarding – it feels like reconnecting with a culture and people I have known for decades.

SETUP IN RELATION TO ALBANIAN PARTNER

I have always considered myself a good listener. While I lead the design team and guide the decision-making process, this is always done in close dialogue with our local partners. They usually have a deeper understanding of the context, which makes it very valuable to remain open to their recommendations and the solutions they propose. I believe it is more beneficial to be receptive to the many voices and perspectives involved in a project.

OPPORTUNITIES/CHALLENGES

The main challenge is time – we are constantly working against the clock. Architecture requires time, so I always try to find a balance between the deadlines we are given and the time a project truly needs. An architect must also maintain the necessary authority to ensure that the project does not shift during construction, which could put everything at risk.

At the same time, it is essential to remain sensitive to the specific context in which we are working, as it can be different from other places. Architecture must always embrace and respond to locality.

HOW TO INTEGRATE GREATER RESPONSIBILITY FOR QUALITY IN PROJECTS

Responsibility for quality starts with constant dialogue and collaboration among all project participants. Open communication with local partners and artisans helps adapt the design without compromising its integrity. Quality also requires balancing deadlines with the care that materials, detailing and construction demand. Being attentive to the local context ensures the project is well-built and rooted in its environment.

BALANCING QUALITY AND DENSITY/INVOLVING STAKEHOLDERS

The architect's role in balancing quality and density is first and foremost one of listening and guiding. We lead the design vision but must remain receptive to the perspectives of local collaborators who understand the site and its context better. By fostering a culture of collaboration, we can include contractors, artisans, clients and even the broader community in discussions that uphold design integrity. Communicating this responsibility requires transparency, clear reasoning behind design decisions and openness to suggestions. Expanding this process to involve more stakeholders strengthens the project's quality, as everyone becomes invested in protecting the architecture's values throughout construction.

EXAMPLE/INSPIRATION

Every project in Albania is inspiring because it challenges us to understand the context. Each project is a response to a different question, and it is fascinating to see how each one finds its own answer.

TOOLBOX ALBANIA FUTURE

Albania offers a unique set of tools for any architect willing to learn from its context. The country teaches patience, observation and adaptation – understanding local materials, construction techniques and social structures. It encourages dialogue with skilled local labor and a hands-on approach to making architecture, allowing us to rethink and refine designs on-site. These experiences expand our architectural toolbox by reinforcing sensitivity to place, the importance of craftsmanship, and the ability to balance creative vision with practical realities, lessons that are invaluable for future projects anywhere in the world.

GLOW TOWER

A tower that is pure structure; structure as tower.

PERMEABILITY

Dissolved boundary between public and private realms, allowing a seamless flow between both.

FLOW AND CONNECTION

Interconnected voids blur the distinction between inside and outside, enhancing spatial continuity.

URBAN CONTINUITY

A recessed corner opens up a plaza, establishing a direct dialogue with the surrounding urban fabric.

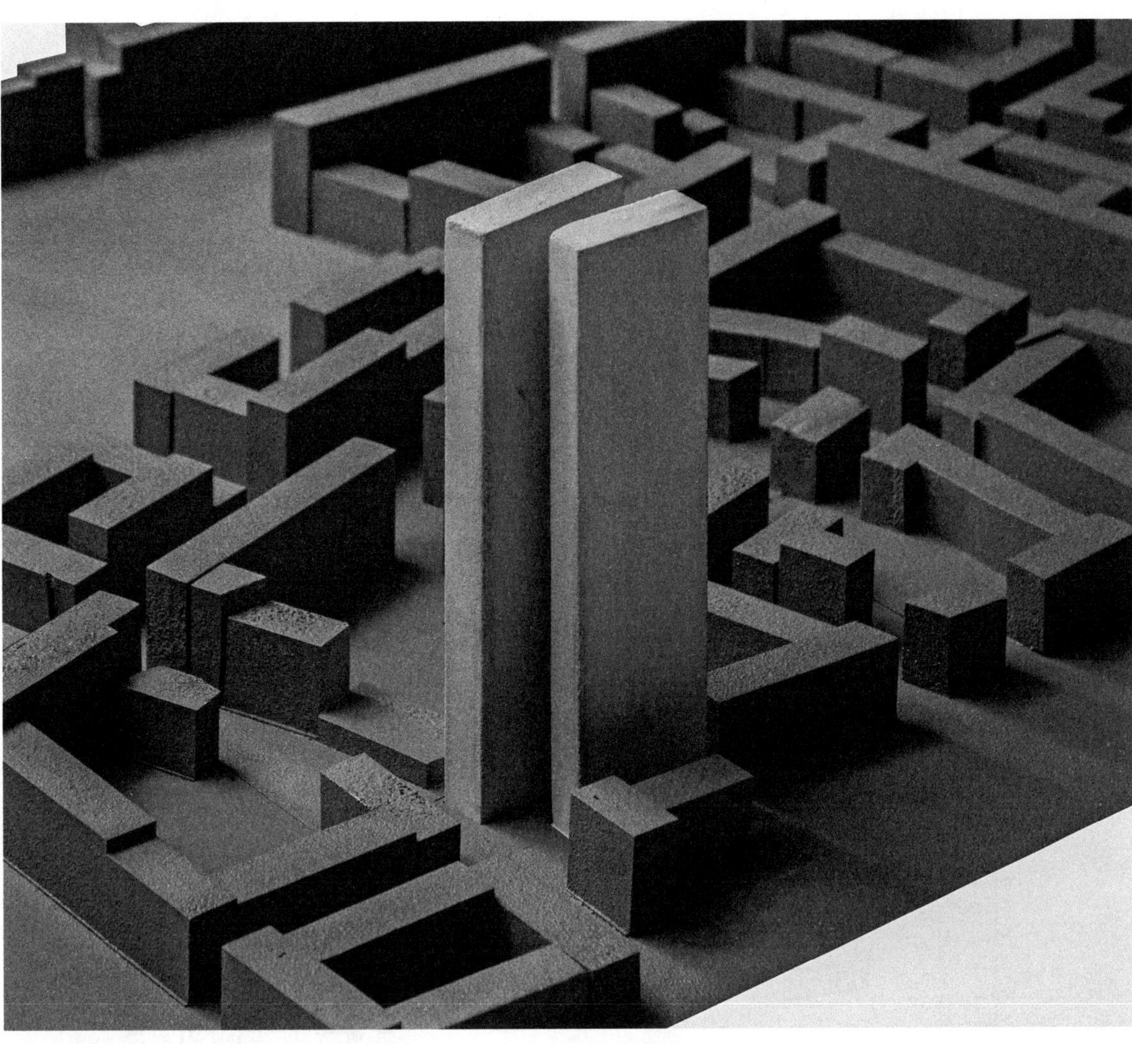

Volumetric model

Volumetric model: Plaza detail

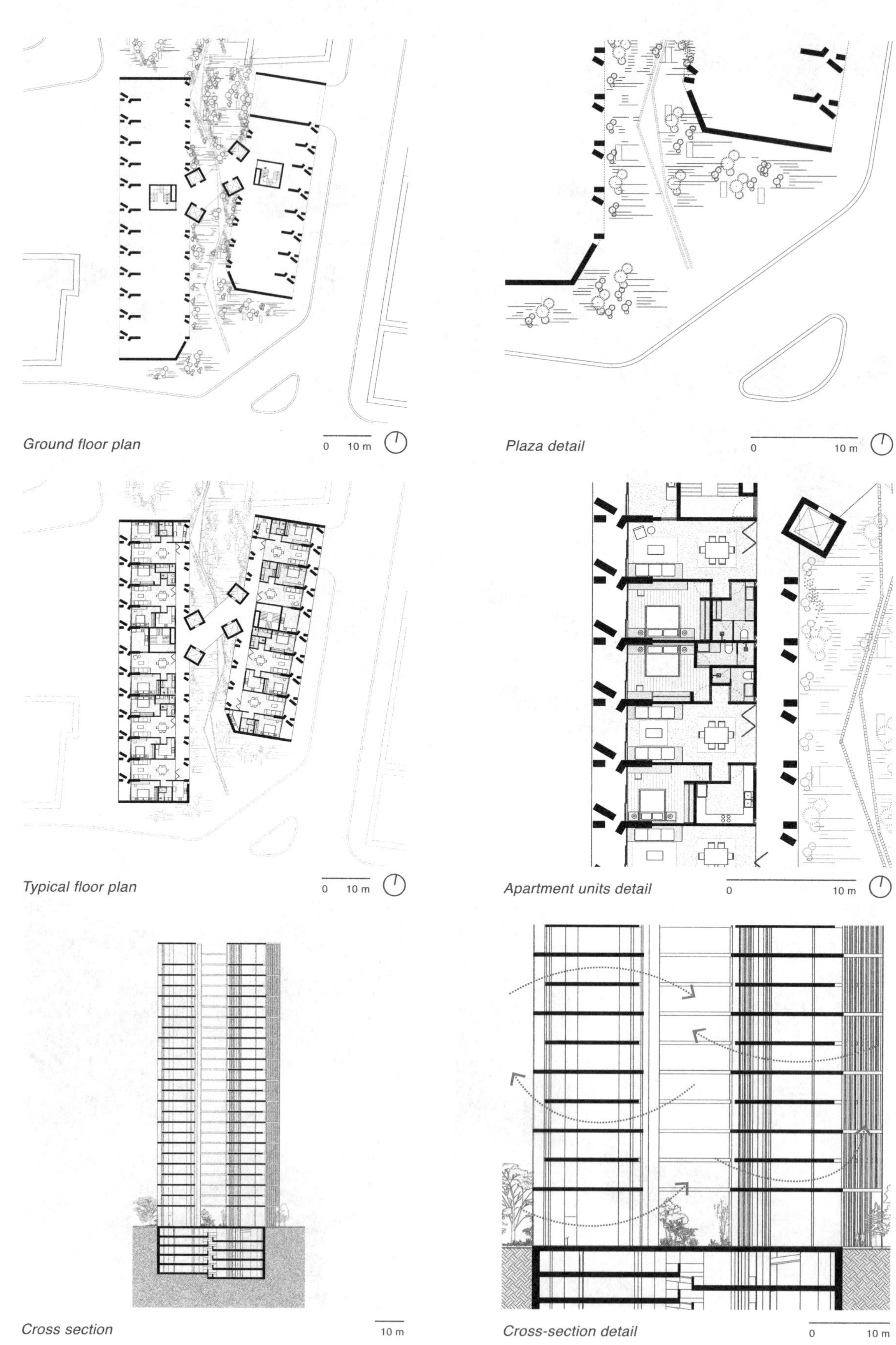

Ground floor plan

Plaza detail

Typical floor plan

Apartment units detail

Cross section

Cross-section detail

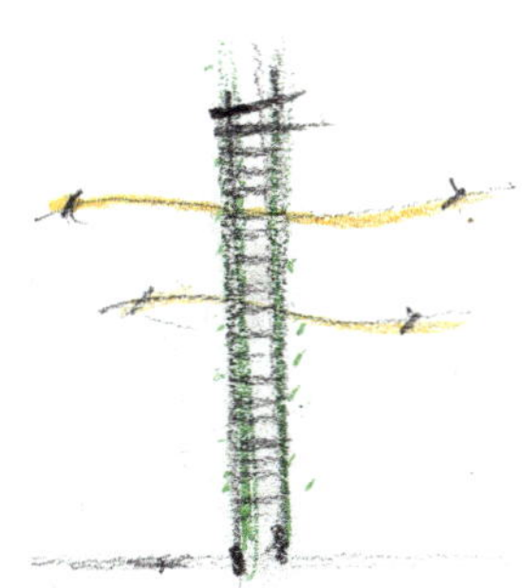

CROSS VENTILATION

The building's porosity allows air and natural light to flow through its volumes, creating a comfortable and naturally lit environment.

Volumetric model

Volumetric model: Detail

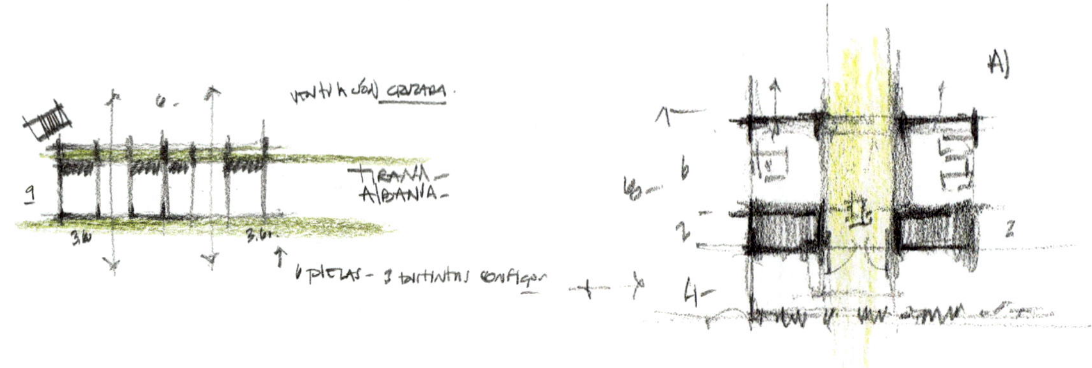
TIRANA-
ALBANIA-

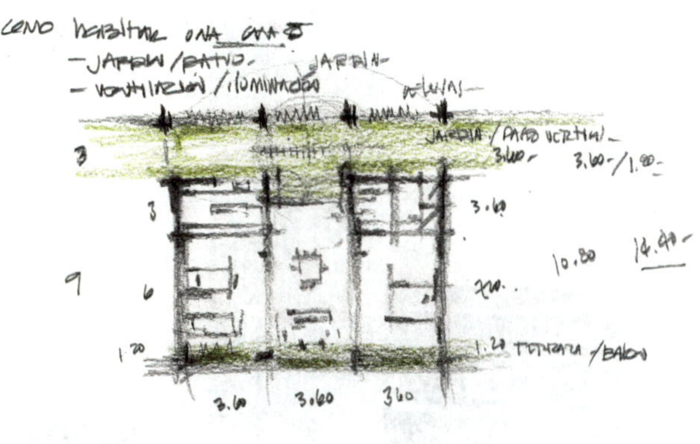

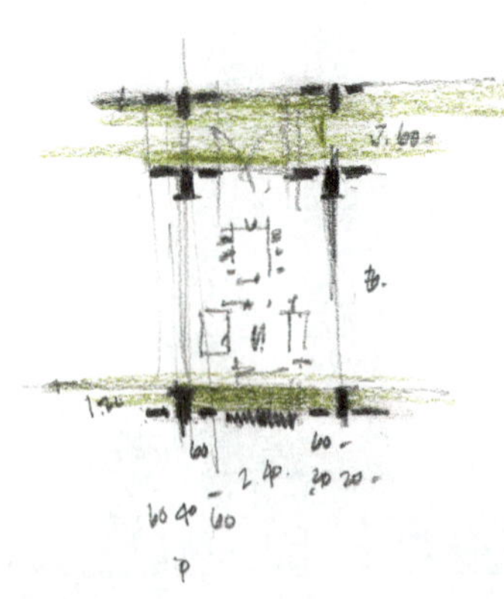

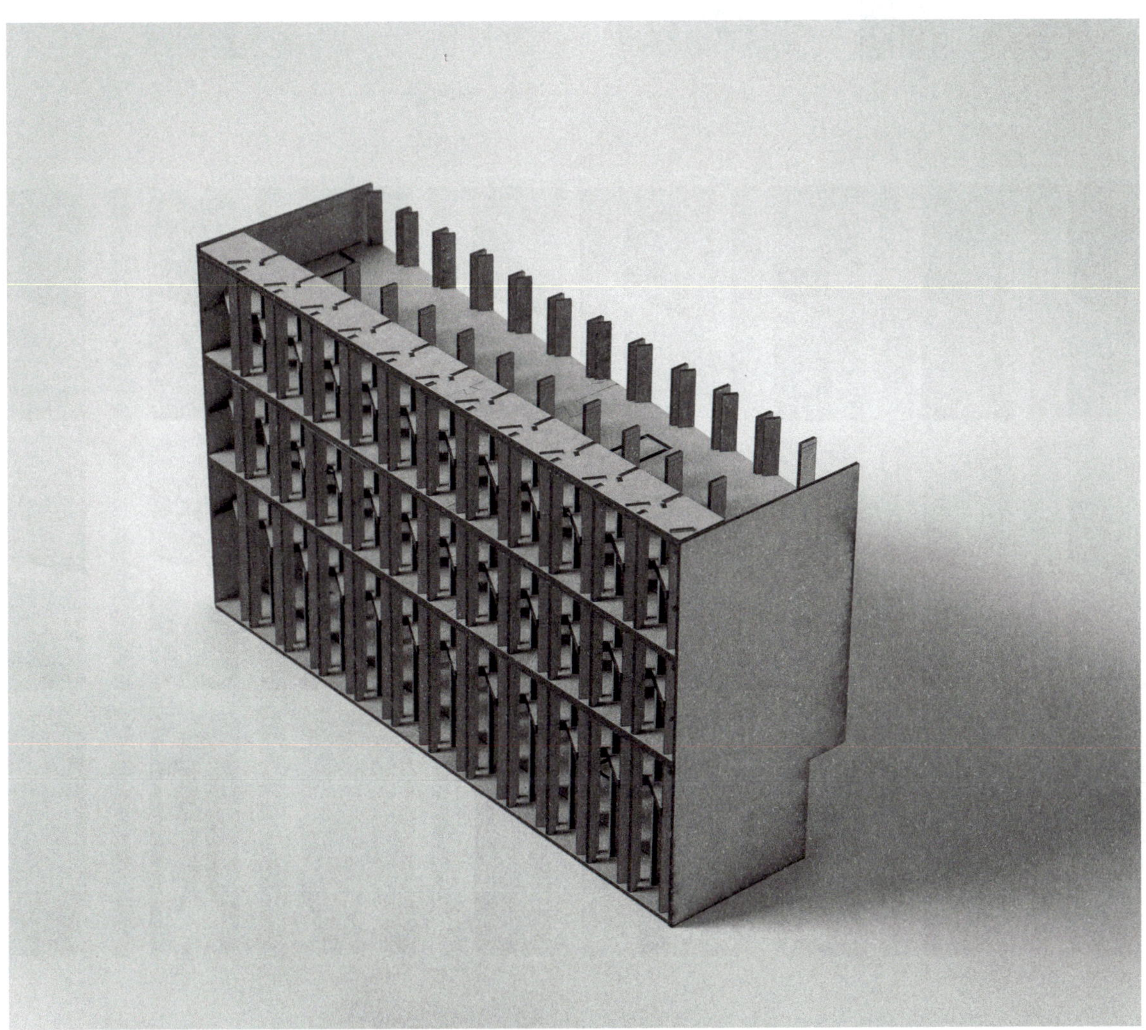

Structural grid model

LIST OF PROJECTS

START	NAME PROJECT	LOCATION	DEVELOPER	ALBANIAN PARTNER	M²	PUBLIC/PRIVATE	PHASE
2024	Glow Tower	Tirana	Glob-3X Group	Artech Studio	42,000 m²	Private	Preliminary design
2025	Lotus Lake	Tirana	KLAR shpk	KLAR shpk	52,200 m²	Private	Preliminary design
2025	General Beach Hotel	Kavaja, Tirana	R2R shpk	BG Studio	4,460 m²	Private	Concept design
2026	Children's Home	Tirana	Albanian Investment Corporation (AIC)	Studio B&L	4,730 m²	Public	Preliminary design

NAME OFFICE

TOYO ITO & ASSOCIATES, ARCHITECTS

DATE
2025

PLACE
Tokyo, Japan /
Barcelona, Spain

WORKING IN ALBANIA SINCE
2024

PRINCIPALS
4

COLLABORATORS
AU Studio (Architecture)
ACPA (Landscape Architecture)
UNS architects (Local Architects)

TEAM
40

PROJECT TEAM
Toyo Ito
Yoko Izumi
Takeo Higashi
Koichi Yamazaki
Shuichi Kobari
Nils Becker
Carlos Gallego

INTRODUCTION TO ALBANIA

I received an invitation to be a judge for a competition for a trade fair in Albania and an invitation from the developer BALFIN to work on a project at around the same time, so I told the staff at the Ito office in Barcelona to go to Albania.

ORGANIZATION/GOAL/SETUP

The project design activities in Albania have just begun, so it is difficult to say for sure, but the goal of the master plan design is to minimize environmental damage and to restore communities that are in the process of being lost. For the Tale project, we are working with a landscape designer from Barcelona to advance the design, but we will naturally need the cooperation of local engineers and architects to realize the ideas.

SETUP IN RELATION TO ALBANIAN PARTNER

I plan to work with a local architect introduced by a developer called UNS architects. Since regulations regarding architecture and construction vary from country to country, foreign architects usually work with local architects. There are things that cannot be done without local help, such as procedures for obtaining building permits, structural calculations, cost management, and selection of construction methods and materials appropriate to the local area.

HOW TO INTEGRATE GREATER RESPONSIBILITY FOR QUALITY IN PROJECTS

Rather than just creating the basic plan and leaving the rest to local architects, we ask them to participate in the detailed design and construction supervision work. We also think it is important to take as long a design period as possible and increase the density of the design by discussing it with various people.

BALANCING QUALITY AND DENSITY/INVOLVING STAKEHOLDERS

Even with high density, it is possible to maintain quality to a certain extent if the design is good. In Japan, density is almost always predetermined by urban planning drawings, so in this Tale project, we did not think that we would be able to discuss building density (floor area ratio) itself through the architecture we were thinking about. Usually, the floor area ratio is determined in advance by land development experts and becomes a major condition for purchasing land, but in the case of Tale, the floor area ratio was decided in consultation between the developer and the government, and the architect helped both parties by creating guide design options.

EXAMPLE/INSPIRATION

Although it is not architecture, there are some similarities between the Albanian coast and Japan, even though Albania is a Mediterranean country with mountains close to the coast. In particular, because of the topography it rains quite a lot, and water seems to be an important element of the natural landscape and the culture of the people.

TALE MASTER PLAN

BETWEEN TWO WATERS: SALT WATER FROM THE SEA AND FRESH WATER FROM THE LAND . . . COASTAL WETLAND

MAT RIVER
IN THE MOUNTAINS

MAT RIVER IN THE
ALLUVIAL FAN

MAT RIVER ON THE
ADRIATIC COAST

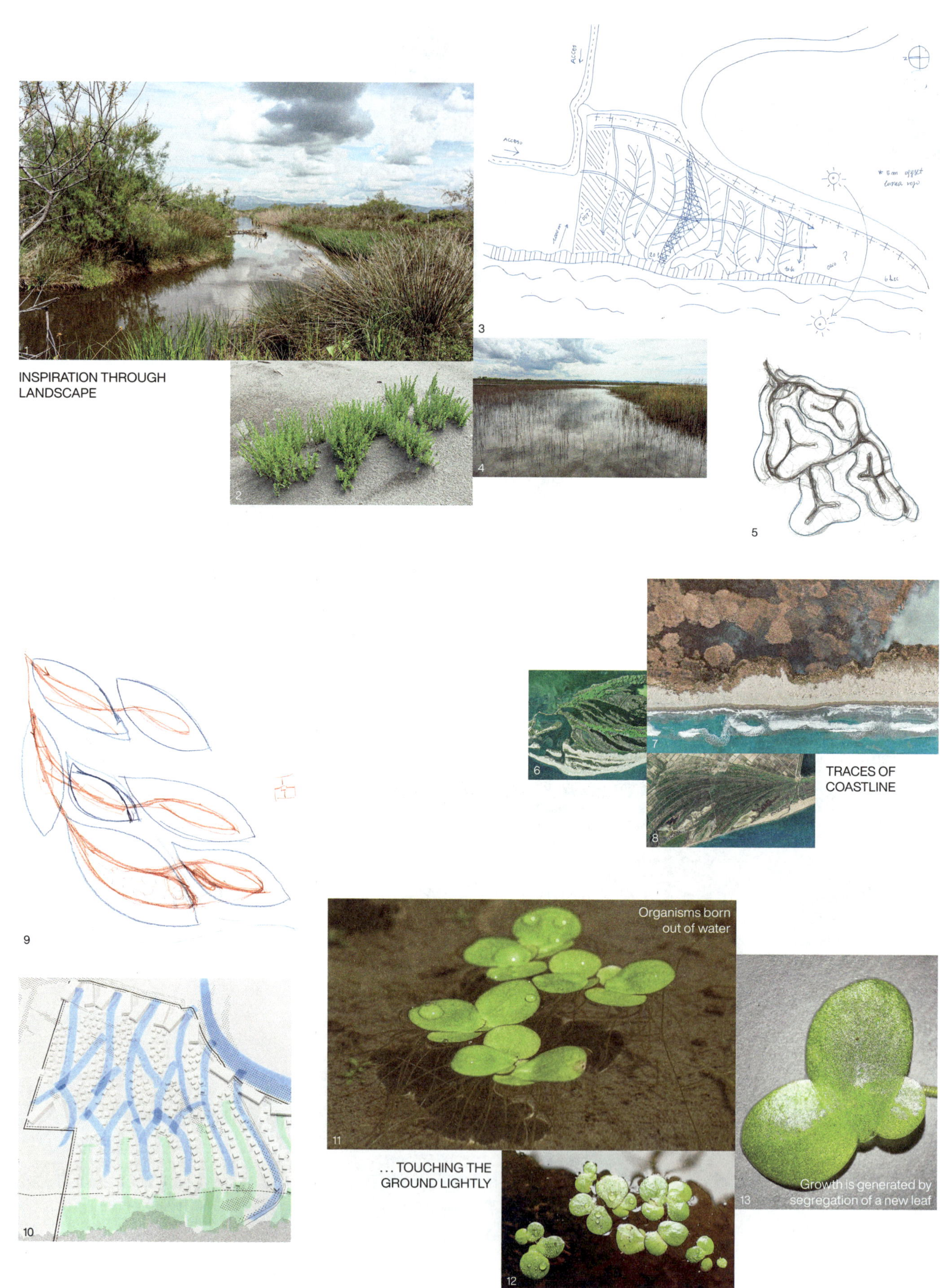
INSPIRATION THROUGH
LANDSCAPE
TRACES OF
COASTLINE
Organisms born
out of water
. . . TOUCHING THE
GROUND LIGHTLY
Growth is generated by
segregation of a new leaf

LOCATION & CONTEXT

FORMATION PROCESS
. . . WORKING WITH
A DYNAMIC
LANDSCAPE . . .
CONSOLIDATION OF ISLANDS

PROGRESSIVE GROWTH
. . . ON THIS SITE WE HAVE
CONSTANT WATER INPUTS
FROM SEVERAL DIRECTIONS.
MARSHES AND WETLANDS
PLAY A CRUCIAL ROLE IN
ABSORBING FLOODWATERS . . .

PLANTING OF SAPLINGS

WE CAN EXPLORE CREATING A
LANDSCAPE THAT CAN ABSORB
THE MOVEMENTS OF THE
WATER, BOTH FROM THE RIVER
AND THE SEA, WITH HOUSING
LOCATED ON FLOOD-PROTECTED
ISLANDS. AMONG THESE
ISLANDS LIES THE DYNAMIC
LANDSCAPE OF THE WETLAND . . .

INFRASTRUCTURE

BUILDING FOOTPRINT

MASTER PLAN

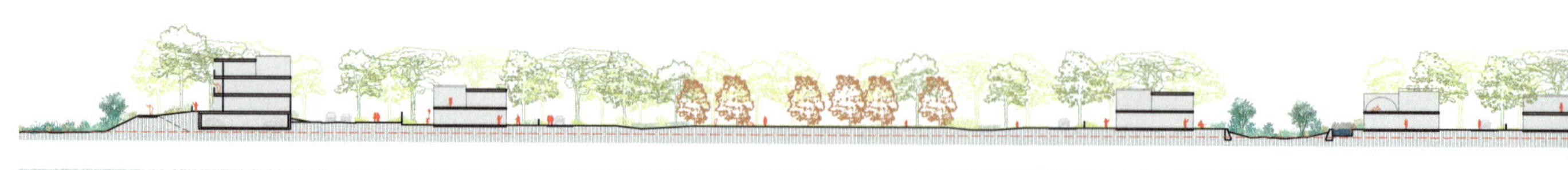
WETLAND
ISLAND
WETLAND

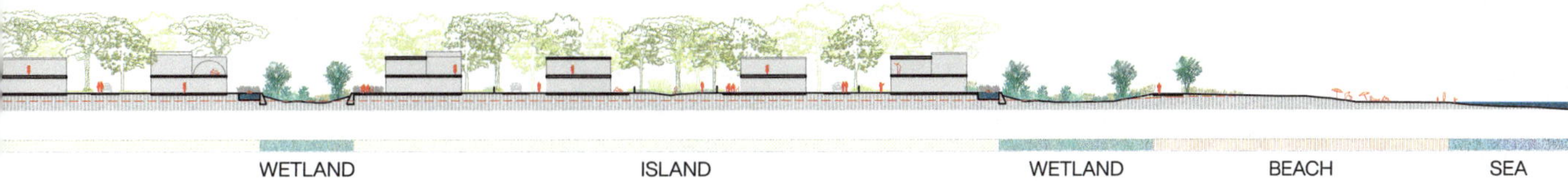
WETLAND
ISLAND
WETLAND
BEACH
SEA

START	NAME PROJECT	LOCATION	DEVELOPER	PUBLIC/PRIVATE	PHASE
2024	Master plan design for Valamar Tale	Laç, Lezha	BALFIN Group	Private	Phase 3, master plan design

NAME OFFICE

VALERIO OLGIATI

DATE	PLACE	WORKING IN ALBANIA SINCE
January 17, 2025	Flims, Switzerland	2003

PRINCIPAL

Valerio Olgiati

The following questions were answered by collaborators of Valerio Olgiati.

INTRODUCTION TO ALBANIA

Valerio was invited to be member of a jury in 2003.

MAIN CONTEXT VS. ALBANIA

The context in which we mainly work is international. Valerio Olgiati works on commercial and cultural projects as well as private houses in Europe, the USA and the Middle East.

The building process is similar to all the other locations we have experienced.

ORGANIZATION/GOAL/SETUP

The organization in the Albanian context follows the same principles we apply to all our projects. During the design phase, we operate in an independent way, fulfilling the client's guidelines and the plot regulations. The idea of a project always comes from inside our office. This approach allows us to develop a project which is cultural and not political. Then, during the development phase, a local architect is involved. Valerio Olgiati is responsible for the architecture in all the phases. The local architect is responsible for coordinating the project until the end of construction, under our supervision. Planners, such as engineers and MEP specialists, collaborate with us closely, following our guidelines to ensure the project's goals are achieved.

OPPORTUNITIES/CHALLENGES

Albania has been developing a lot since the first visit of Valerio in 2003. More and more opportunities are arising thanks to the great vision of the administration.

HOW TO INTEGRATE GREATER RESPONSIBILITY FOR QUALITY IN PROJECTS

Valerio Olgiati's projects are systems that can be understood as a totality. Quality is achieved through meticulous planning and a fully detailed design of the system, finalized before construction begins. The execution plans are also drawn inside our office. To preserve this standard, no improvisation is allowed. The construction team carries the crucial responsibility of faithfully realizing the project exactly as envisioned by the architect.

Tirana, 2003

Tirana, 2004

Tirana, 2005

Albania, 2006

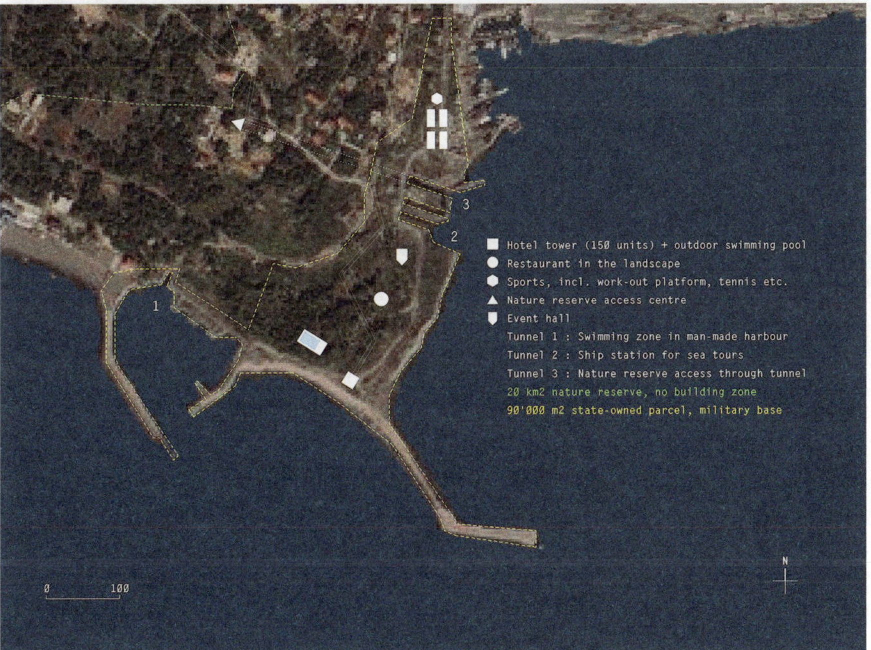

Shëngjin, 2018

No building zone
(existing nature reserve)
Golf club restaurant
Nature reserve (20 km2) for hiking + cycling
18-hole golf course (60 ha)
Residential with 300 units (16 ha)
Pier + restaurant + tennis courts
0
500
Hotel with 150 rooms + support infrastructure (9 ha)
N

Lezha, 2020

Tirana, 2024

Lezha, 2024

START	NAME PROJECT	LOCATION	COMMISSIONER/CLIENT	PROGRAM	PUBLIC/PRIVATE	PHASE
2004	Project at the Intersection of Ring Boulevard and Elbasani Road	Tirana	City of Tirana	Residential, hotel, offices, retail	Public	Competition
2005	Ardia Palace Tirana	Tirana		Residential and commercial complex	Private	Until building permission
2018	Naval Base Lezha	Shëngjin		Hotel, sport facilities, restaurant, marina	Private	Feasibility study
2020	Towers Rana Hedun	Lezha		Resort	Private	Development permit – ongoing
2023	Rruga Adem Jashari	Tirana		Residential, hotel, retail	Private	Construction permit – ongoing

NAME OFFICE

XDGA

DATE	PLACE	WORKING IN ALBANIA SINCE
September 2025	Brussels, Belgium	2005

PRINCIPAL

Xaveer De Geyter

PROJECT TEAM

Doug Allard
David Ampe
Heiner Averkamp
Tom Bonnevalle
Maud Bouhin
Lionel Bousquet
Jérémie Brault
Karel Bruyland
Rémy Carat
Elena Caruso
Antoine Chaudemanche
Pieter Coelis
Beatrice Colaiacomo
Johan Cool
Catherine Cornu
Elisabeth d'Aubarede
Joris De Greef
Thaïs de Roquemaurel
Chloe de Salins
Pieter De Walsche
Hanne Defloor
Nathalie Devoghelaere
Issa Driesen
Nicolas Duerinck
Nenad Duric
Mélanie Evra
Annelotte Herrebosch
Eva Hoffmann
Yasmine Houari
Ingrid Huyghe
Maxime Jaume
Ménélik Jobert
Karla Kovacevic
Solene Le Gallo
Jacqueline De Souza Luduvice
Jonathan Robert Maj
Philip Niekamp
Emilia Ockerman
Federico Pedrini
Julien Picard
Martin Pujol
Anne-Sophie Rouillère
Jelle Segers
Dana Smetankova
Yuichiro Suzuki
Celeste Tellarini
Victor Vacherot
Willem Van Besien
Wouter Van Daele
Catherine Van Driessche
Marie-Pierre Vandeputte
Lode Vanderbeek
Samia Wahbi
Ulysse Zehnlé
Rui Zenha
Ujzë Zhuri

INTRODUCTION TO ALBANIA

In 2004 I was teaching at the Berlage Institute in Rotterdam and one day a tall person came into the cafeteria and introduced himself as Edi Rama, mayor of Tirana. He started talking about his first initiatives to change the city, and one of them was to have a large number of existing buildings colorfully painted according to sketches by different artists and architects. Now that was a striking plan, initiated by a person with a unique combination of qualities: the free thought of an artist and the power of a capital mayor. To this day, these exceptional qualities continue to make many things possible in Albania.

MAIN CONTEXT VS. ALBANIA

Apart from Albania we work mostly in Belgium, France and Germany. The great majority of our projects are the results of competitions. This also used to be the case in Albania, but more recently demands from private initiatives are adding to this.

The crucial difference between working in these countries and in Albania is that here there is a desire for good architecture, whereas in Belgium, France and Germany good architecture is becoming in the best case nothing more than a nice extra on top of lots of other demands. It is a matter of eagerness rather than indifference and apathy.

Of course this eagerness is not present everywhere and at all layers. But the fact that the authorities sustain this ambition forms a shield against all kinds of obstacles.

ORGANIZATION/GOAL/SETUP

The local office is part of our "eyes on Albania": Through them we understand what is going on, what is possible, what is best to avoid . . . in terms of both society and architecture/construction. In that sense they are part of our team. Also, we do not split up a project process into a design part and an execution part – the design continues up until the execution. Strictly speaking, concepts are developed in our Brussels office, and in an early stage they are discussed with both the client and the local office. They evolve from there, and the local office plays a key role in this evolution.

HOW TO INTEGRATE GREATER RESPONSIBILITY FOR QUALITY IN PROJECTS

When working on public projects in Albania, the responsibility of the architect is split between the design and the follow-up of construction. According to law, the tasks are divided into two separate contracts. This means an architect cannot take full responsibility for a public project. We think it is crucial that both tasks can be unified in one contract.

EXAMPLE/INSPIRATION

The "ordinary" concrete skeleton that one finds everywhere throughout the country, the basis for anyone's house. Of course this is not an exclusively Albanian concept. Some consider it a form of pollution of the landscape, although many of them are extremely beautiful. On the one hand they are the product of a "boots on the ground" economic logic, and on the other hand they are poetic frameworks for the future.

House where Albanian Independence was declared, now the National Museum of Independence in the center of the park and waterfront project in Vlora

Lessons from a young democracy

In Albania, making public space in order to reorganize the city proves to be more than just an empty promise. The decision to redesign the entire coastline of the city of Vlora, before any private initiatives were being developed, provoked first of all a turnaround in the public life of the city. What was before an area for illegal construction, private exploitation and a sealed-off harbor became a long stretch of public functions that link the city to a fantastic seascape. A continuous promenade meandering between the waterline and the main road interconnects squares, beaches, gardens, sports fields, a swimming pool and a pier, thus transforming the Lungomare into the bouncing heart of the city.

Vlora waterfront promenade – phase 1

Vlora waterfront promenade – phase 1

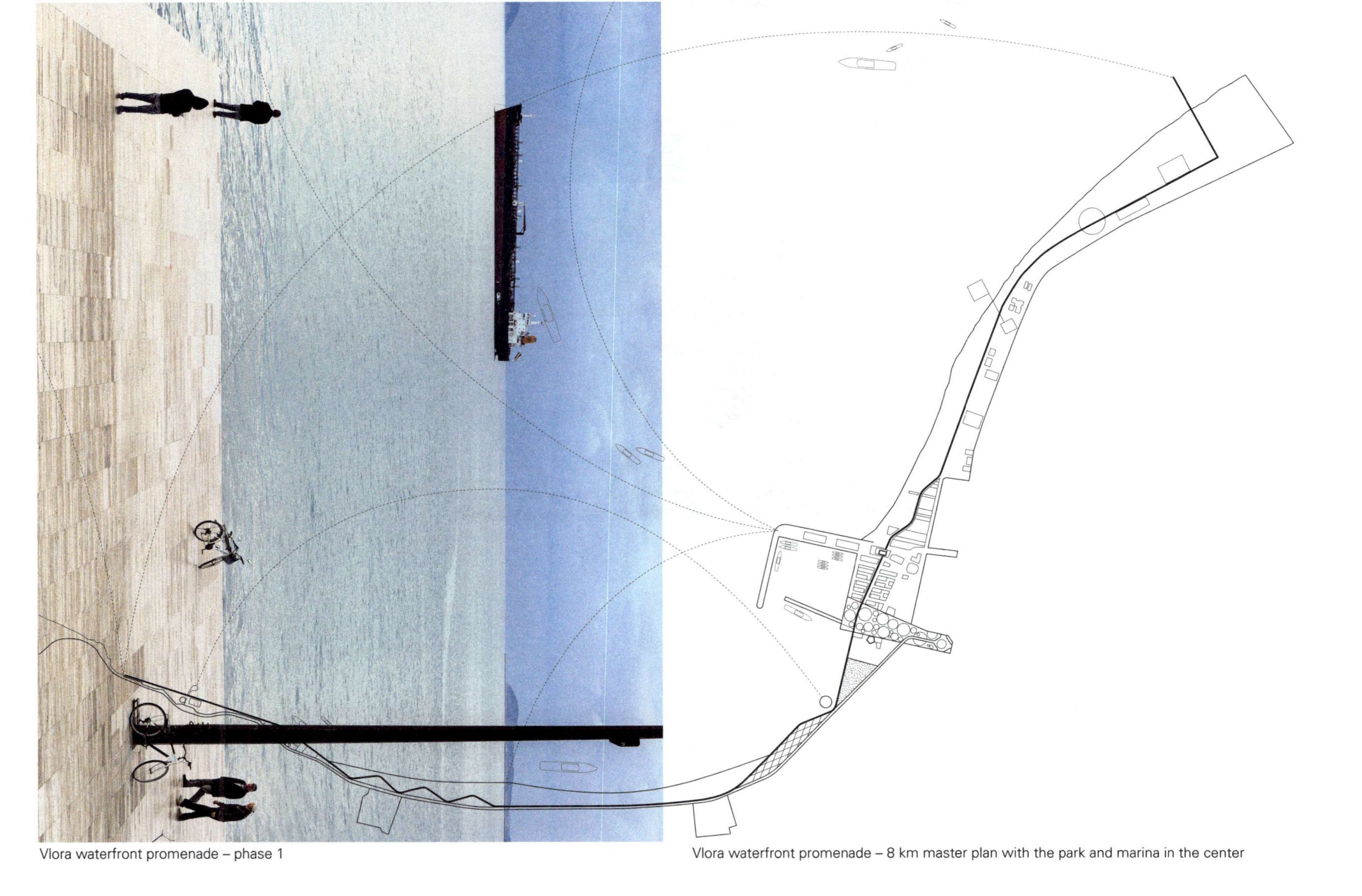

Vlora waterfront promenade – phase 1

Vlora waterfront promenade – 8 km master plan with the park and marina in the center

Secondly, it became a catalyzer for a long series of new private projects, with as a centerpiece the harbor being transformed into a new neighborhood with a park, hotels, housing, shops, restaurants and a marina.

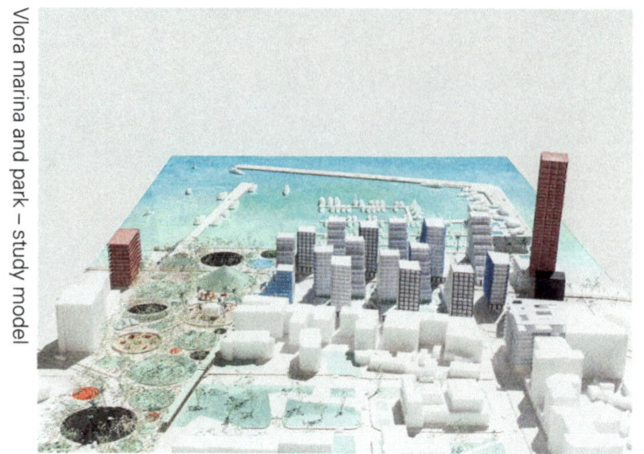

Vlora marina and park – study model

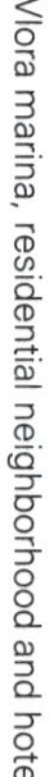

Vlora marina, residential neighborhood and hotel

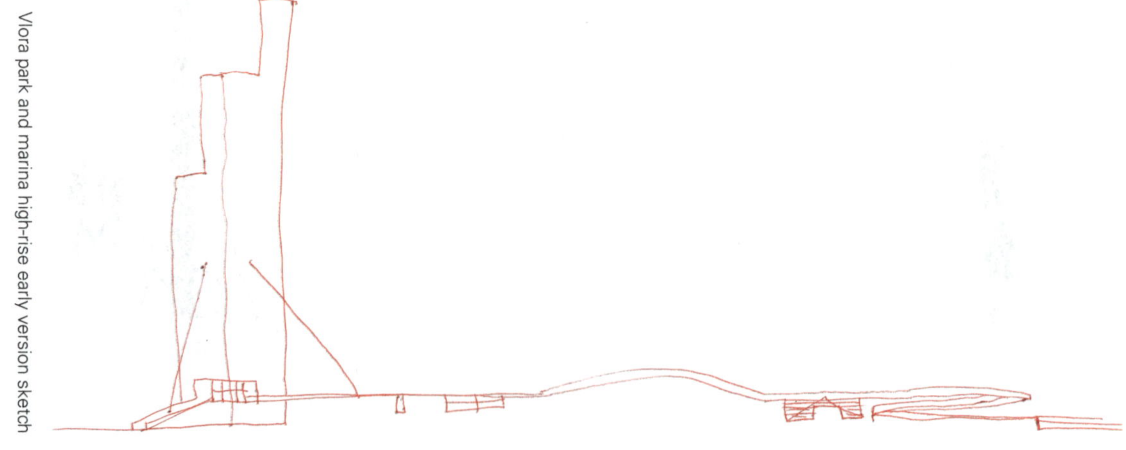

Vlora park and marina high-rise early version sketch

Vlora marina residences – trellis collage

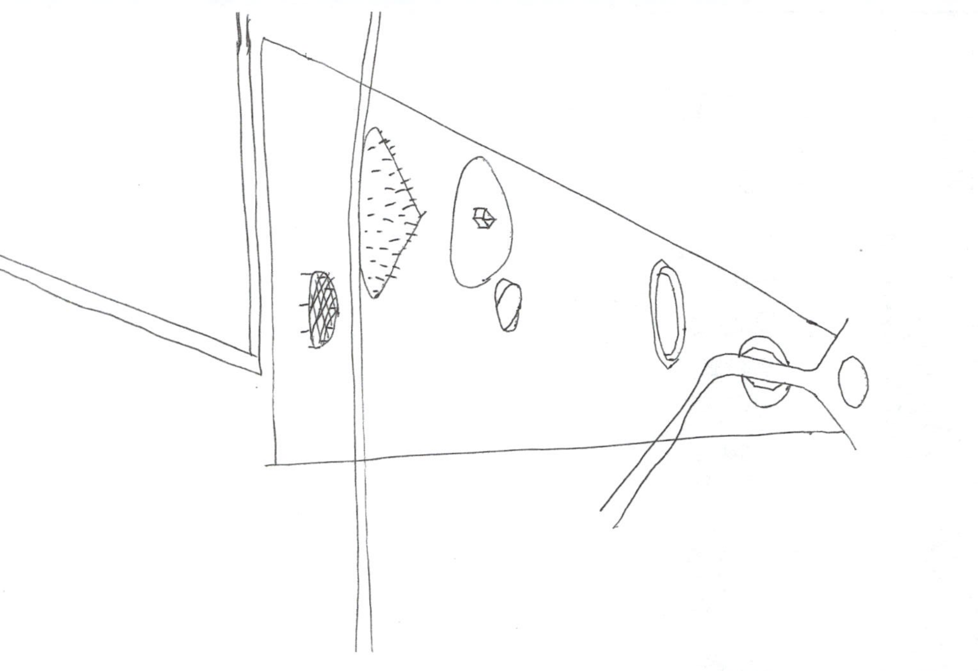

Vlora park of the Independence House, sketch – topographic elements

Topographic feature in the park – construction site photo

Vlora Flag Square, central canopy

Vlora Flag Square – diagrammatic plan of independent and diversified public spaces

Vlora Flag Square and Regional Development Center

Along the central axis of the city, from the historical city center towards the seaside park and marina, a series of (re)new(ed) urban hotspots are being developed. Flag Square and its surroundings are getting restructured through a composition of squared urban elements: a temple-like public roof, a car-free square devoted to the Independence Monument, a promenade towards the military cemetery, and various public gardens.

More surprising, we convinced the authorities not to destroy a huge, derelict concrete structure of 25,000 square meters, but instead to transform it into a Regional Development Center with outside public stairs climbing up its fifteen floors. Finally, on the location of the former stadium, a new football stadium and sports hall will be built, along with a green public space that will be the starting point for the reorganization of the neighborhood. A vast amount of private development is needed to make this possible, but the real lesson here is that a stadium can be an urban catalyzer instead of being built, like anywhere else in Europe, on the outskirts of the city in the middle of a sea of cars.

Vlora Regional Development Center – public stairs under construction

Vlora Regional Development Center – image of the 100 years of independence celebration, using the building as a viewing platform.

Vlora stadium – conceptual collage of the final phase

Vlora stadium – competition model

Saranda port – development concept image and early sketch

Working as an architect in Albania is liberating, provoking a degree of freedom that sometimes leaves us in a cold sweat.

In various situations we must address demands for mass tourism. These are often at a scale that does not compare to what preexists, so mimicry is not an option. Instead our strategy is to propose specific answers that add a layer of a new order to the existing context. In the harbor area of Saranda, a hilly coastal town that is oriented towards the Greek island of Corfu, we propose monumental buildings that offer framed views to the ships and sea from the existing fabric.

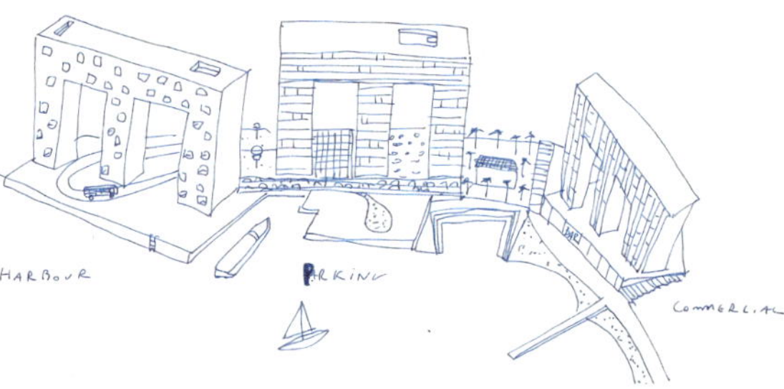

Saranda port – development collage of the framed views to the sea

In Ksamil, a small place with more and more private developments, a three-dimensional promenade that mediates between these infrastructures and the shoreline reinstalls a form of coherence in the chaos.

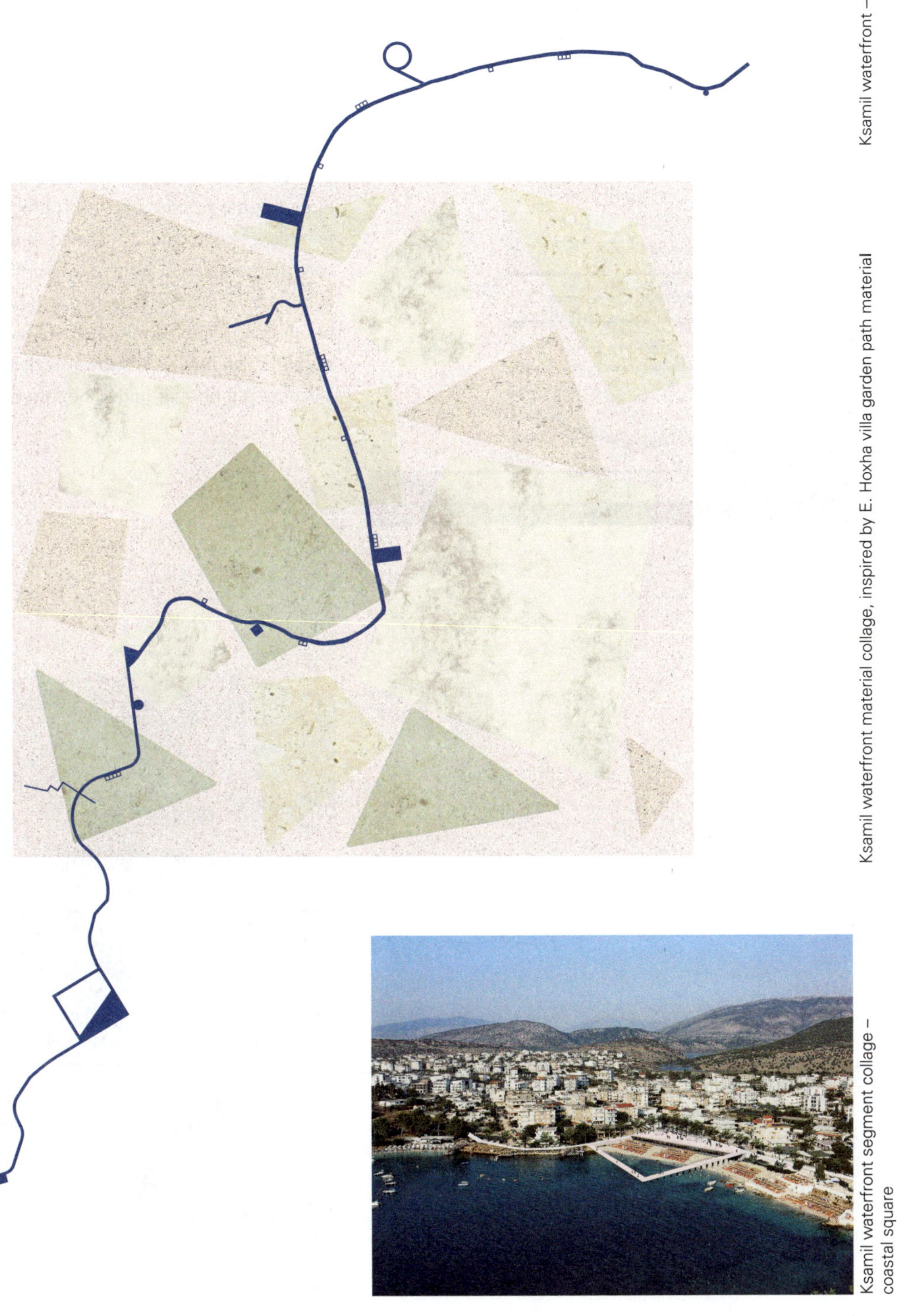

Ksamil waterfront – schematic plan

Ksamil waterfront material collage, inspired by E. Hoxha villa garden path material

Ksamil waterfront segment collage – coastal square

Puppet Theater – model with opened gates

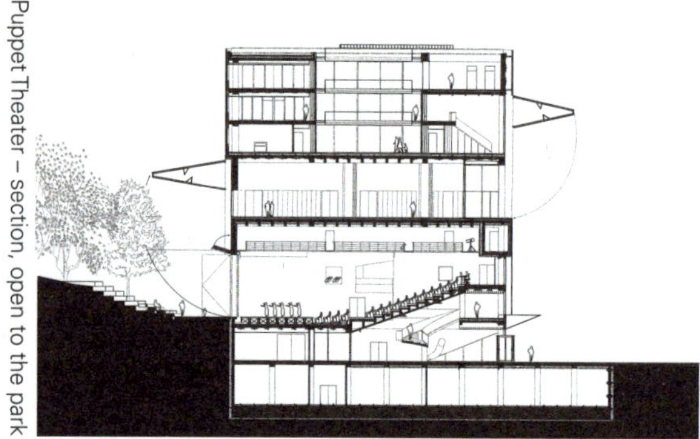
Puppet Theater – section, open to the park

Public space is also the generating factor for the design of a series of three objects in between Tirana Park and the city edge. After a competition about whether and eventually how one ought to build on this border, it was decided to develop a hotel building, the Puppet Theater and the National Library along it. In our proposal each of them develops a specific spatial relation to the park, and together they assure a transparency and a frivolous permeability between city and park. The hotel consists of an L-shaped volume with a huge walk-through outside lobby carved out. The theater stage can be alternatively opened for outside performances towards the ascending park; large folding facades open the cubical volume, just like street theater vans used to do. The library, basically an opaque archive tower with a hooked-on administration and auditorium wing, stands on a plinth that is shoved into the park slope. This slope is continued downwards towards the street through a central public stair under the tower.

Tirana Garda, overall view – hotel, Puppet Theater and National Library

"Spectacle machine" – reference image

Theater in the park – reference image

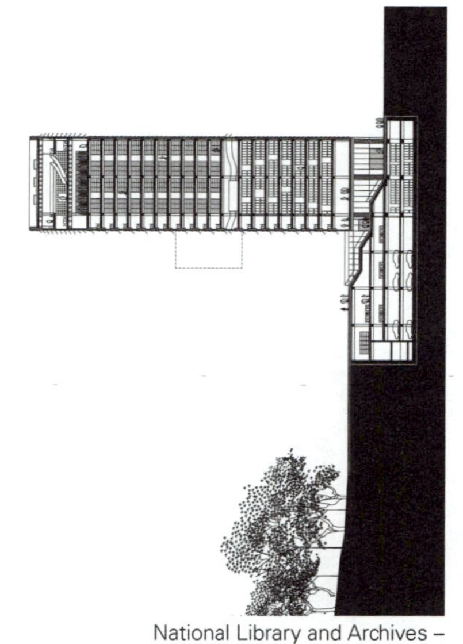

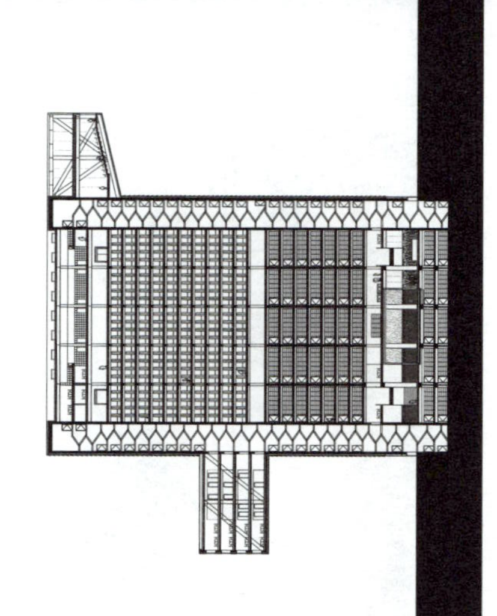

National Library and Archives – cross and long section

National Library and Archives – view from the street

Tirana Park Hotel – visualization of the crossing void

Puppet Theater – main hall construction

START	NAME PROJECT	LOCATION	DEVELOPER	ALBANIAN PARTNER	M²	PUBLIC/PRIVATE	PHASE
2005	Metropol Tower Tirana	Tirana			16,800 m²	Private	Competition
2011	Qemal Stafa Zone "D"	Tirana	KLAN		29,250 m²	Private	Competition
2014	Vlora Waterfront Promenade	Vlora	ADF	MetroPolis	25 ha	Public	Executed
2015	Park entrance	Tirana	Municipality of Tirana	Symbiotica	25,000 m²	Public	Competition
2018	Isa Boletini Park	Vlora	ADF	iRI shpk	30 ha	Public	Prov. delivery
2018	Gas station	Vlora	Kastrati Group		50 m²	Private	Under construction
2019	Sheshi i Flamurit	Vlora	ADF	iRI shpk	15 ha	Public	Prov. delivery
2019	Vlora Marina (incl. Marriott, casino, residences, . . .)	Vlora	BALFIN Group	iRI shpk	300,000 m²	Private/public	Under construction
2019	Garda master plan	Tirana	Municipality of Tirana		30 ha	Public	Study concluded
2020	Lungomare 2	Vlora	ADF, Adhenis	iRI shpk	10 ha	Public	Under construction
2020	Lukova PUITD	Lukova, Borsh, Qeparo, Piqeras	KfW + ADF	iRI shpk	45 km²	Public	Study concluded
2020	Orikum Regional Dev. Plan	Orikum	World Bank + ADF	iRI shpk	15 km²	Public	Study concluded
2020	Tirana New Municipality	Tirana	Municipality of Tirana	iRI shpk	22,500 m²	Public	Competition
2020	Vlora Landmark	Vlora	Feniks Konstr., LAZAJ 2002 shpk	iRI shpk	55,000 m²	Private	Stopped
2020	Pier Restaurant	Vlora	Adhenis shpk	iRI shpk	550 m²	Private	Under construction
2020	Orikum Oasis	Orikum	LAXMI Real Estate	iRI shpk	500,000 m²	Private	Ongoing
2020	Park Hotel	Tirana	Ferrobeton shpk	iRI shpk	45,000 m²	Private	Under construction
2020	Teatri i Kukullave + QKKF	Tirana	Ministry of Culture	iRI shpk	8,500 m²	Public	Under construction
2021	Regional Development Center	Vlora	ADF	iRI shpk	26,500 m²	Public	Under construction
2021	Saranda Port	Saranda		iRI shpk	110,000 m²	Private/public	Ongoing
2022	Plazhi i Vjeter	Vlora	F.A. Alb. Investment	iRI shpk	18,000 m²	Private	Permit phase
2022	SH2 Retail Center	Kamëz	Arkon Studio shpk	iRI shpk	50,000 m²	Private	Stopped
2023	Vlora Park Tower	Vlora	Hanxhari Group	iRI shpk	40,000 m²	Private	Ongoing
2023	Flamurtari Stadium	Vlora	ADF	CMA	200,000 m²	Public	Feasibility study
2023	Projects for integrated urban and tourism development	Orikum, Borsh, Ksamil	World Bank + ADF	iRI shpk		Public	Tendering

START	NAME PROJECT	LOCATION	DEVELOPER	ALBANIAN PARTNER	M^2	PUBLIC/PRIVATE	PHASE
2023	New Boulevard Tower	Tirana	2T shpk		20,000 m^2	Private	Competition
2024	Tirana Expo	Tirana	AIC, ADF, Albanian government		45,000 m^2	Public	Competition
2024	Admiral Abdi Mati	Durrës	T&Xh, Badriklo	iRI shpk	25,000 m^2	Private	Permit phase
2024	Tirana East Entrance	Tirana	HERAL 07 shpk	AK Design	90,000 m^2	Private	Development permit

ALBANIA AS A GEOPOLITICAL SURFACE: 1912–PRESENT
(an ultrashort bibliographic timeline for the purpose of recommended further reading)

Albania's architectural history is not a story that unfolds in isolation. It is a story shaped by its position – small in size, but located at the meeting point of empires, military interests and shifting geopolitical ambitions. Over time, different foreign actors have entered, measured, planned and built across its territory. What emerges is not a single authorship, but a continuous layering of external influences, always adapted, sometimes resisted, never entirely absorbed.

1912–1939: STATE FORMATION, FIRST PLANS, FOREIGN EXPERTISE

Statehood in Albania is entangled with foreign planning expertise (Austrian, Italian) and geopolitical positioning – space emerges as a tool of fragile sovereignty.

Blumi, Isa. *Foundations of Modernity: Human Agency and the Imperial State in the Ottoman Balkans.* Routledge, 2011.
Fischer, Bernd J. *King Zog and the Struggle for Stability in Albania.* East European Monographs, 1984.
Jelavich, Barbara. *History of the Balkans, Vol. 2: Twentieth Century.* Cambridge University Press, 1983.
Pearson, Owen. *Albania and King Zog: Independence, Republic and Monarchy 1908–1939.* I. B. Tauris, 2004.
Vickers, Miranda. *The Albanians: A Modern History.* I. B. Tauris, 1995.

The proclamation of Albanian independence by Ismail Qemali in Vlora in 1912 marked the end of Ottoman Empire rule, but not the end of external influence – rather, its transformation. Spatial development in Albania was from the outset shaped through foreign presence and intervention. During World War I, the Habsburg Monarchy deployed systematic military mapping as a means of control, establishing a territorial framework that enabled the construction of over 900 km of roads in a short period. Mapping here precedes infrastructure: a spatial logic imposed through measurement and administration.

This condition persisted in Tirana, where the emergence of a capital required external expertise to formalize its structure. When Ahmet Zogu commissioned Austrian architect Wolfgang Köhler and engineer Eshref Frashëri in 1923, the resulting plan can be understood as part of a broader engagement with foreign knowledge in shaping the city's early form.

In 1928, Ahmet Zogu declared himself King Zog I, aligning Albania with a westernizing political project already entangled with external actors. The 1925 agreement with Italy and the establishment of SVEA (Società per lo Sviluppo Economico dell'Albania) bound infrastructure and state-building to Italian economic influence. Development was structured through dependency rather than autonomy.

In Tirana, this relationship took spatial form. Armando Brasini's north–south axis (1925) functioned as a political diagram, organizing the city toward a central administrative and royal core. Fragments of this project – most notably the square near the Et'hem Bey Mosque – remain as spatial traces of this ordering. Under Italian influence, the central square was renamed "Piazza Vittorio Emanuele III," embedding political alignment into the urban fabric.

Florestano Di Fausto later extended this axis with a series of ministries arranged symmetrically along the boulevard. Their modest scale reflects economic conditions, while their Neo-Renaissance language operates as a form of translation rather than synthesis. Foreign architectural forms are adapted and re-inscribed into local context, producing a city shaped through relational and asymmetrical exchanges of power.

1939–1945: OCCUPATION, INFRASTRUCTURE, TERRITORIAL CONTROL

Spatial development is militarized – roads, mapping and planning become instruments of occupation.

Fischer, Bernd J. *Albania at War, 1939–1945.* Purdue University Press, 1999.
Fischer, Bernd J. "Albania 1943–1945: A View Through Western Documents." *Tirana Times*, 2012.
Pearson, Owen. *Albania in Occupation and War: From Fascism to Communism 1940–1945.* I. B. Tauris, 2006.
Pojani, Dorina. "Urban Design, Ideology, and Power..." *Planning Perspectives* 30, no. 1 (2015): 67–94.
Vickers, Miranda. *The Albanians: A Modern History.* I. B. Tauris, 1995.

The invasion by Italy in 1939 marked a decisive intensification of these entanglements. With King Zog I in exile, the fascist administration reconfigured Tirana through centralized planning, embedding ideological control within the urban fabric.

Under Gherardo Bosio, the city becomes a field of projection: a site where architecture operates as an extension of political doctrine. Yet rather than a total imposition, Bosio's work operates through transformation – reframing existing structures while incorporating them into a new spatial narrative.

The redesign of Piazza Vittorio Emanuele III (later Skanderbeg Square) exemplifies this condition. The square is not erased but reorganized – recalibrated as a civic and administrative center where infrastructure, finance and ideology converge. This produces a layered urban condition, in which continuity and rupture coexist.

Bosio's 1939 plan further articulates Tirana through a system of axes and flows, extending along the Lana River and radiating outward. The city is reframed as a network of relations – circulation, visibility and control – rather than as a bounded object.

Following the collapse of Italian power in 1943 during World War II, German forces occupied Albania. Yet the more significant shift occurs in 1944, when the National Liberation Movement establishes a new political order. What changes is not the centrality of power within spatial production, but its ideological framing. Space remains an active medium through which authority is exercised, reorganized and contested.

1945–1990: SOCIALIST PLANNING, ISOLATION, IDEOLOGICAL SPACE

Imported Soviet and Chinese models produce centralized planning, industrialization and monumental space, while isolation transforms Albania into a self-contained spatial system.

Abrahams, Fred C. *Modern Albania: From Dictatorship to Democracy in Europe.* New York University Press, 2015.
Biberaj, Elez. *Albania: A Socialist Maverick.* Westview Press, 1990.
Hall, Derek. *Albania and the Albanians.* Saqi Books, 1996.
Mëhilli, Elidor. *From Stalin to Mao: Albania and the Socialist World.* Cornell University Press, 2017.
Pojani, Dorina. "Urban Design, Ideology, and Power..." *Planning Perspectives* 30, no. 1 (2015): 67–94.
Vickers, Miranda. *The Albanians: A Modern History.* I. B. Tauris, 1995.

After 1945, Albania enters a new geopolitical alignment: communism. Here again, foreign influence is decisive – but in a different direction. First with the Soviet Union, then with China, Albania adopts and adapts external models of planning, industry and architecture.

As Elidor Mëhilli describes, Albania was not isolated till the early seventies. Till then it participated in a wider socialist world, importing expertise, technologies and ideas. From the Soviets come industrial planning systems, collective housing models and centralized urban structures. From China, especially after the break with the USSR, comes a different kind of influence – more focused on self-reliance, standardization and mass mobilization. Architectural education in Albania was institutionalized through the establishment of technical faculties in Tirana, marking the formation of a state-trained architectural class aligned with Soviet planning models and embedded within the broader project of socialist spatial production. This Faculty of Engineering later evolved into the Polytechnic University and today's Faculty of Architecture and Urbanism (FAU).

Architecture is asked to represent both ideology and identity, while operating within material scarcity and centralized control.

Buildings like the National History Museum of Albania and the Tirana International Hotel reflect this condition: large, symbolic and visible. The Pyramid of Tirana, designed by Pranvera Hoxha, Klement Kolaneci, Pirro Vaso and Vladimir Bregu, represents the peak of this system: a building that tries to embody a political figure – Enver Hoxha – while also signaling Albania's place within the socialist world.

1990–EARLY 2000S: COLLAPSE, INFORMALITY, RECONFIGURATION

Planning collapses; informality becomes the dominant spatial logic and the city evolves through bottom-up, self-organized processes rather than state control.

Abrahams, Fred C. *Modern Albania: From Dictatorship to Democracy in Europe.* New York University Press, 2015.
Aliaj, Besnik, et al. *Tirana: The Challenge of Urban Development.* Co-PLAN, Instituti për Zhvillimin e Habitatit, 2003.
Dhamo, Sotir. *Understanding Emergent Urbanism: The Case of Tirana, Albania.* Springer, 2021.
Pichler, Robert, and Edit Pula. *Albania's 90s: Photographs and Narratives.* Bahoe Books, 2020.
Pojani, Dorina. "Tirana: The City of the Future?." 2010.
Pojani, Dorina. "City Profile: Tirana." *Cities* 27, no. 6 (2010): 483–495.

The 1990s are marked by rapid and uneven urban growth. Without strong planning systems in place, construction expands quickly, especially at the edges of Tirana. Informal housing appears on a large scale. Near the center, informal businesses develop along the Lana River and in areas like Parku Rinia. The city becomes a mix of planned elements and spontaneous growth.

Public space becomes highly active and unpredictable. The central square – renamed Skanderbeg Square in 1991 – turns into a place for protests, markets, kiosks and everyday negotiation. The removal of the statue of Enver Hoxha during the student protests of 1991 marks a visible break, but also reveals how deeply space is tied to political change.

The Pyramid also continues to shift. Once a museum for the regime, it becomes a radio station, a nightclub, a conference center and even a NATO base during the Kosovo War in 1999. Its changing uses show how architecture can absorb and reflect political transitions without ever fully resolving its meaning.

In this period, Albania is influenced by a new set of external forces: Western development models, international funding institutions and global economic systems. These do not arrive as buildings, but as frameworks that shape how cities grow, how land is used and how space is valued.

EARLY 2000S-ONWARD: TRANSITION TO CONTEMPORARY FRAMEWORKS

Albania re-enters global systems; spatial development becomes tied to international expertise, sustainability discourse and EU-oriented planning frameworks.

51N4E, Falma Fshazi and Stefano Graziani. *How Things Meet*. Art Paper Editions, 2016.

Atelier Albania, iabr/UP and 51N4E. *The Metabolism of Albania: Activating the Potential of the Albanian Territory*. iabr/UP, 2015.

Fagu, Eled. *Tirana: Architectural Guide*, with an introduction by Alfred Diebold. DOM publishers, 2023.

Fischer, Bernd J., and Oliver Jens Schmitt. *A Concise History of Albania*. Cambridge University Press, 2022.

Forum A+P 14. *Visions for a New Tirana*. POLIS Press, 2014.

Musaj, Doriana. "The Unconventional Architectural Narrative of Albania." URBACT, 2023. https://urbact.eu/articles/unconventional-architectural-narrative-albania.

OMB (Observatory of the Mediterranean Basin). *When a River Flows: Strategies for Environmental, Touristic and Infrastructural Development of Albanian Rivers*. POLIS Press, 2018.

Pojani, Dorina. "Urban Design, Ideology, and Power..." *Planning Perspectives* 30, no. 1 (2015): 67–94.

Wilson, Peter. *Some Reasons for Traveling to Albania*. About Books, 2019.

Xhexhi, Klodjan. *Ecovillages and Ecocities: Bioclimatic Applications from Tirana*. Springer, 2024.

Yunitsyna, Anna, et al. *Current Challenges in Architecture and Urbanism in Albania*. Springer, 2021.

Building Architecture Culture. Biennale Architettura di Venezia 2025, podcast series in collaboration with Koozarch, Andi Arifaj, Adonel Myzyri and Anneke Abhelakh. https://albanianpavilion.al/podcast.

The projects in this book start here. From the early 2000s onward, the Albanian city is not simply updated; it is reclaimed. The painting of façades under Edi Rama reworks the surface of the city, turning color into a quiet act of re-seeing, as captured in the movie *Dammi i colori*. International competitions for places like Skanderbeg Square, with practices such as 51N4E, unfold alongside a renewed commitment to urban planning – gradually aligning with European frameworks while remaining shaped by everyday use, memory and local spatial logic.

LOCATIONS
OFFICES
PROJECTS

Z

Cover drawing: Skanderbeg Square, courtesy of 51N4E
pp. 4, 5, 10, 11: Collages by Linda van Deursen for *Building Architecture Culture*, Biennale Architettura di Venezia 2025, Albanian pavilion

51N4E
All images and documents © 51N4E except:
fig. 6: Collage by © Maks Velo
figs. 7, 13, 19, 31, 47: © Filip Dujardin
fig. 8: Painting by © Edi Hila
figs. 16, 22: © Blerta Kambo
figs. 20, 25, 29, 30, 33, 35, 39: © Maxime Delvaux
figs. 32, 34: © 51N4E & CENTRAL ofaau & iRI
figs. 49–52: © 51N4E & Plan Común

AIRES MATEUS E ASSOCIADOS
All drawings courtesy of Aires Mateus e Associados

ÁLVARO SIZA
All images courtesy of Álvaro Siza and Camilo Rebelo

ANDREA CAPUTO
All images © Marco Cappelletti

ANUPAMA KUNDOO ARCHITECTS
All images courtesy of Anupama Kundoo Architects

ARCHEA ASSOCIATI
pp. 85, 88, 89, 94: Photos © Pietro Savorelli e Associati

ARCHI-TECTONICS
pp. 97, 105 (t): "Old Bazaar" Photo by Sali Jonuzi, licensed under CC BY-SA 4.0
p. 99: "Abstract Art in the Hedgerow" Photo by Penny Mayes, licensed under CC BY-SA 2.0
pp. 100–106: Render/diagram/drawing/photo © by Archi-Tectonics
p. 103 (t/l): Vratsa – Kurpash Tower Photo by Nikolai Karaneschev licensed under CC BY-SA 3.0

ARQUITECTURA-G
All images courtesy of ARQUITECTURA-G

AVNER YASHAR ARCHITECTS
All images courtesy of Avner Yashar Architects

BAROZZI VEIGA
All drawings courtesy of Barozzi Veiga except:
p. 136: https://commons.wikimedia.org/wiki/File:Handdrawn_map_of_Albania_during_World_War_I.jpg
p. 138: source unknown

BIG
All images, renders, models courtesy of BIG – Bjarke Ingels Group except:
p. 170 (render t): © Yanis Amasri
p. 174 (render b): © Yanis Amasri

BOFILL TALLER DE ARQUITECTURA
p. 180, fig. 1: © Albanian Photographic and Graphic Art Collection
p. 181, figs. 2, 3: © Bofill Taller de Arquitectura
p. 182, figs. 4–6: © Maxime Delvaux
p. 183, fig. 7: Fragments from: 01. *The Garden of Eden*, Thomas Cole, 1828; 02. *The Shulamite*, John Roddam Spencer Stanhope, 1878; 03. *Gethsemane Prayer Garden*, Linda Curley, 2023; 04. *Garden of Golgotha*, James Tissot, 1886; 05. *Garden of Paradise*, Hieronymus Bosch, 1503–1515; 07. Drawing © Bofill Taller de Arquitectura
p. 184, figs. 8, 9: © Bofill Taller de Arquitectura; fig. 10: © Edi Hila, 1985
p. 186, fig. 11: Sketch by Camillo Praschniker, 1918

BOLLES+WILSON
All hand-drawn concepts: © Peter Wilson
pp. 192 (b/c, b/r), 193 (b/r), 196 (b/l), 198 (b/c), 201 (b/l), 203 (b/c), 204 (b/l, b/c): Photos © BOLLES+WILSON
pp. 192 (b/l), 196 (b/r), 197 (b/c), 199 (b/c), 200 (b/l, b/r), 201 (b/r), 206 (b/c): Photos © Roman Mensing
p. 202 (b/c): Rendering © BOLLES+WILSON – Juan González Blanco

CAMILO REBELO
All images courtesy of Camilo Rebelo

CASANOVA + HERNANDEZ ARCHITECTS
All images courtesy © Casanova + Hernandez except:
p. 223: Marubi museum: Three interior images in the middle: © Christian Richter; Image far right top © Blerta Kambo
p. 230: Shiroka: Aerial view © E. Zhabjaku

CEBRA
All models, renders and images courtesy of CEBRA except:
pp. 235, 236 (b/r), 237, 238 (t/l, b/r), 239, 240 (c/l, b/r), 241, 242: © Mikkel Frost

CHRISTIAN KEREZ
p. 245: Courtesy of Christian Kerez

CHYBIK + KRISTOF ARCHITECTS
All images © CHYBIK + KRISTOF Architects, produced by:
pp. 259, 264–266: CHYBIK + KRISTOF
p. 261: Alexey Klyuykov
p. 263: Filip Urban

CITYFÖRSTER ARCHITECTURE & URBANISM
figs. 1, 10, 12–14, 19–26, 30, 32–39, 42–53, 55, 56, 58–70: © CITYFÖRSTER
figs. 4–7, 9, 11, 15: © Martin Sabota
figs. 16, 18: © Jutta Benzenberg
figs. 17, 26, 29: © Blerta Kambo
fig. 27: Noizy feat. RAF Camora - Toto
fig. 28: Internet meme
fig. 31: © BOOM
figs. 34–36: © Alexander Wolf
figs. 37–39: © Armand Habazaj
fig. 40: © Eni Ajdini
fig. 41: © Loes Oudenaarde
fig. 46: © Andres Lopez
figs. 48, 58: © Will Boase
fig. 54: © Edi Hila
fig. 71: © Aida Lahi

COLDEFY
All images courtesy of Coldefy except:
p. 291 (b): © Fani Kurti
pp. 292, 294, 295, 296 (t/r), 297 (t/l), 298 (t/l): Drawings © Jacopo Foggini

DAVIDE MACULLO ARCHITECTS
p. 301: © Leonit Ibrahimi
All drawings by and courtesy of Davide Macullo

DILLER SCOFIDIO + RENFRO
All images courtesy of Diller Scofidio + Renfro except:
p. 320: Rendering, diagram © Gross. Max. Landscape Architects

EAA – EMRE AROLAT ARCHITECTURE
EAA – Emre Arolat Architecture Archives

ELEMENTAL
All images courtesy of Elemental

ENSAMBLE STUDIO
All images courtesy of Ensamble Studio

ESTUDI D'ARQUITECTURA TONI GIRONÈS
All drawings by and courtesy of Toni Gironès

GG-LOOP
All images courtesy of GG-loop

GROUPWORK
All images courtesy of GROUPWORK

HERZOG & DE MEURON
All images courtesy of Herzog & de Meuron except:
p. 399: Overview Tirana © Elton Xhafkollari; Skanderbeg Square © Filip Dujardin

IBUKU STUDIO
All images courtesy of IBUKU Studio

KENGO KUMA & ASSOCIATES
pp. 424, 426, 428, 430: Images/render © KKAA
p. 425: © Katsushika Hokusai, *Bridge in the Clouds* (from the series *Unusual Views of Famous Bridges in Various Provinces*), c. 1830–1834 Edo period, Japan; Mesi Bridge: © Diego Delso, *Mesi Bridge (Ura e Mesit), Shkodër, Albania*, 2014. CC BY-SA 4.0; Render: Brick Visuals
p. 427: © Katsushika Hokusai, *The Suspension Bridge on the Border of Hida and Etchū Provinces* (from the series *Unusual Views of Famous Bridges in Various Provinces*), c. 1830–1834; Ura e Kadiut (Ottoman bridge), Ura e Kadiut, Albania. Image from stock photography archive © Photononstop/Hemis; Render © Brick Visual
p. 429: Ryōan-ji Temple (rock garden), Kyoto, Japan; Old Bazaar scene, Albania; Illustration by © Hewdet Dada; Render © KKAA

KUEHN MALVEZZI
Drawings: © Kuehn Malvezzi
pp. 436, 438, 440: Renderings: © Kuehn Malvezzi; Visualization © OUT OF RAM
p. 442: Expo Albania Visualization: List Architecture-Urbanisme

LINA GHOTMEH—ARCHITECTURE
All images © Lina Ghotmeh—Architecture and © Lina Ghotmeh

LUCA DINI DESIGN & ARCHITECTURE
All images courtesy of Luca Dini Design & Architecture

MANUELLE GAUTRAND ARCHITECTURE
All images courtesy of Manuelle Gautrand Architecture

MASS STUDIES
All images courtesy of Mass Studies

MCA – MARIO CUCINELLA ARCHITECTS
p. 495: Image © Konpasu.de on Unsplash
pp. 496–502: Courtesy © MCA
p. 498: Black and white images © Eurind Caka
p. 499: Image by https://montenegro-for.me/wp-content/uploads/2016/06 South-Albanian-coast6.jpg
p. 501: Visual © Grafica Nomade

MIRALLES TAGLIABUE – EMBT ARCHITECTS
All images courtesy of Miralles Tagliabue – EMBT Architects

MVRDV
All images © MVRDV except:
pp. 522, 523: Photo Pyramid Kroll Markus used under a CC BY-SA 3.0 license https://commons.wikimedia.org/wiki/File:Tirana_Pyramid.JPG
p. 525: Photo Stairs Pyramid © Ossip van Duivenbode

NOA
pp. 539 (c/l, b/r), 540 (c/r), 546 (c/r): © Adobe Stock
pp. 539 (c/r, b/l), 540 (t/l, t/r, b/l, b/r), 541 (t/l, t/r, b/l), 545 (b), 546 (b/r): © NOA
pp. 541 (b/r), 542: © Aleksey Mokhov
pp. 543, 544 (t), 545 (t): © ATELIER 4, NOA
p. 546 (c/r): © Adobe Stock, © Unsplash

NUNO MELO SOUSA
All images © Atelier Nuno Melo Sousa except:
p. 549: © AIVA images

OFFICE KERSTEN GEERS DAVID VAN SEVEREN
All images © OFFICE Kersten Geers David Van Severen

OMA
pp. 576, 577, 580, 581: Image © Kontakt
pp. 578, 579: Image © Alex Retegan

OODA
All images courtesy OODA, two renders © PLOMP

OPPENHEIM ARCHITECTURE
p. 597: © MIR
p. 599: © Fat Tony Studio: Architecture in symbiosis, on-site concrete casting; © MIR: Crafting a Community, Pigment of Place, Excavation as Architecture, Living Working Artist Community, Earth mineral plasterwork at Folie Village; © Oppenheim Architecture: OA visit Berat, Skodra school, Team in Berat, Camouflaged Village Jala Beach
p. 600 (t/r): © MIR; p. 600 (c): Three small square images © Alamy; All other images © Oppenheim Architecture
p. 601 (t, b): © MIR; p. 601 (c): © Oppenheim Architecture
p. 602 (t/r, c/l): © MIR; p. 602 (c/c): Three small square images © Alamy; p. 602 (c/r, b): © Oppenheim Architecture
p. 603 (t/l): Black and white images © Alamy; p. 603 (c): Drawing © Oppenheim Architecture; All other images © MIR
p. 604 (t): © Fat Tony Studio; p. 604 (c/l): © MIR; All other images, voids and drawings © Oppenheim Architecture
p. 605 (t): © Fat Tony Studio; p. 605 (c): © Oppenheim Architecture; p. 605 (b): © MIR
p. 606: © MIR

RCR ARQUITECTES
All images © RCR Arquitectes

ROJKIND ARQUITECTOS
All images courtesy of Rojkind Arquitectos

SAM CHERMAYEFF OFFICE
All images © Oliver Helbig

SELGASCANO + FRPO
Image credits © selgascano + FRPO

SHIGERU BAN ARCHITECTS, JEAN DE GASTINES ARCHITECTES
All images courtesy of Shigeru Ban / Jean de Gastines

SOUTO MOURA - ARQUITECTOS
Drawings by Eduardo Souto Moura
Model photo © Arménio Teixeira
Renders © PLOMP + OODA

STEFANO BOERI ARCHITETTI
pp. 683, 685: Drawing © Stefano Boeri Architetti
p. 684: Image of fresco by Ambrogio Lorenzetti © Alamy
pp. 687, 689 (t, c): Image © Stefano Boeri Architetti
p. 688: Image © Lorenzo Masotto
p. 689 (b): Image © Paolo Rosselli

STEVEN HOLL ARCHITECTS
All images courtesy of © Steven Holl Architects except:
p. 698 (t/l insert image): Image courtesy of Agnieszka Kurant, *The End of Signature*, 2015, facade of the Solomon R. Guggenheim Museum, New York; Courtesy of the Solomon R. Guggenheim Museum, image © Kristopher McKay

STUDIO GANG
All images © Studio Gang except:
pp. 705, 710: Image © Eye of Science/Science Source
p. 707: Image Florida Museum © Court Whelan

STUDIO PRECHT
All images courtesy of Chris Precht Studio, made by MIR except:
p. 720: Image: that day in the park © Tian Fangfang

TALLER HECTOR BARROSO
All images courtesy of TALLER HECTOR BARROSO

TOYO ITO & ASSOCIATES, ARCHITECTS
All images courtesy of Toyo Ito & Associates, Architects except:
p. 743, fig. 4: alpventurer.com
p. 743, figs. 6, 7: balkanrivers.net
p. 744, figs. 4–6: Google Earth
p. 744, figs. 7–9: creativecommons.org
p. 745, fig. 1: Balfin Group
p. 745, figs. 2, 3: Google Earth
p. 746: Google Earth

VALERIO OLGIATI
pp. 755–758, 760, 761: Photo by Valerio Olgiati
pp. 756, 757, 761: Visualization by Valerio Olgiati
pp. 759–761: Plan by Valerio Olgiati

XDGA
All images courtesy of XDGA, except:
pp. 767, 774 (b), 779 (t, c): © unknown
pp. 768 (t), 769: © XDGA, Matthias van Rossen
pp. 770 (b), 771 (t/l): Drawing © Xaveer De Geyter
p. 773: Google Maps
p. 775 (t): © Maxime Delvaux
p. 781: © Frame

Like architectural projects, books often begin as ideas – sketched in fragments, shaped by many hands and only sometimes realized exactly as first imagined. Some remain conceptual; others take form through collective care, evolving into something more generous than any singular vision could contain.

This book gathers contributions from architectural voices across geographies, practices and lived experiences – voices that do not seek to converge into one, but to stand alongside one another. When one asks the same question of sixty architecture offices, one does not receive a unified answer, but a constellation of responses, each grounded in its own context. Editing, in this sense, becomes an act of listening: of holding space for differences, of preserving clarity while allowing each voice to retain its character and autonomy.

In honoring this plurality, we have chosen to preserve linguistic nuances, stylistic variations and cultural expressions. These are not inconsistencies, but traces of situated knowledge. Readers may encounter variations such as "façade" and "facade," or differing conventions in spatial references – where what is called the "first floor" in one context may be the "ground floor" in another. Such differences speak to the many ways of naming, knowing and inhabiting spaces.

The data and insights presented here are likewise open to multiple readings; they do not point to a single conclusion, but invite interpretation shaped by the reader's own context, experience and way of seeing.

While care has been taken to support clarity and coherence, this book does not claim universality or completeness. The perspectives shared here belong to their respective contributors and do not necessarily reflect those of the editors or publisher.

We acknowledge that knowledge production is entangled with questions of authorship, ownership and visibility. Every effort has been made to identify and obtain permission for all copyrighted material included in this publication. Images, illustrations and other third-party content are reproduced with permission, under applicable licenses or in accordance with relevant provisions. If any material has been included without proper acknowledgment or authorization, we warmly invite rights holders to contact the publisher so that this can be addressed with care in future editions.

We offer this book as a collective space – shaped by many voices, attentive to difference and open to being read in more than one way.

THE ALBANIAN FILES
Architecture and Freedom

EDITED BY
Anneke Abhelakh

FOREWORD
Edi Rama

CONTRIBUTORS
51N4E, Aires Mateus e Associados, Álvaro Siza, Andrea Caputo, Anupama Kundoo Architects, Archea Associati, Archi-Tectonics, ARQUITECTURA-G, Avner Yashar Architects, Barozzi Veiga, baukuh, BIG, Bofill Taller de Arquitectura, BOLLES+WILSON, Camilo Rebelo, Casanova + Hernandez Architects, CEBRA, Christian Kerez, CHYBIK + KRISTOF Architects, CITYFÖRSTER architecture & urbanism, Coldefy, Davide Macullo Architects, Diller Scofidio + Renfro, EAA – Emre Arolat Architecture, Elemental, Ensamble Studio, Estudi d'arquitectura Toni Gironès, GG-loop, GROUPWORK, Herzog & de Meuron, IBUKU Studio, Kengo Kuma & Associates, Kuehn Malvezzi, Lina Ghotmeh—Architecture, Luca Dini Design & Architecture, Manuelle Gautrand Architecture, Mass Studies, MCA – Mario Cucinella Architects, Miralles Tagliabue – EMBT Architects, MVRDV, NOA, Nuno Melo Sousa, OFFICE Kersten Geers David Van Severen, OMA, OODA, Oppenheim Architecture, RCR Arquitectes, Rojkind Arquitectos, Sam Chermayeff Office, selgascano + FRPO, Shigeru Ban Architects, Jean de Gastines Architectes, SOUTO MOURA – ARQUITECTOS, Stefano Boeri Architetti, Steven Holl Architects, Studio Gang, Studio Precht, TALLER HECTOR BARROSO, Toyo Ito & Associates, Architects, Valerio Olgiati, XDGA

COPYEDITING
Rita Forbes, Nutan Jaeger

PROOFREADING
Michael Pilewski

PUBLISHING COORDINATION
Hester van den Bold

DESIGN
Haller Brun, Amsterdam

LITHOGRAPHY, PRINTING AND BINDING
DZA Druckerei zu Altenburg, Germany

PAPER
Munken Lynx, 300 g/m²;
Forever Rose, 120 g/m²;
Lona Opak, 60 g/m²

© 2026 Lars Müller Publishers, the Editor and the Authors

No part of this book may be used or reproduced in any form or manner whatsoever without prior written permission, except in the case of brief quotations embedded in critical articles and reviews.

Lars Müller Publishers
Pfingstweidstrasse 6
8005 Zurich
Switzerland
+41 44 274 37 40
info@lars-mueller-publishers.com
www.lars-mueller-publishers.com

PRODUCT SAFETY
Producer:
Lars Müller Publishers GmbH
Responsible person in accordance with EU Regulation 2023/988 (GPSR):
Michael Klein, sales representative, Hub 1, 84149 Velden, Germany, +49 8742 964 552 2, gpsr@lars-mueller-publishers.com

ISBN 978-3-03778-800-4

Distributed in North America, Latin America and the Caribbean by ARTBOOK | D.A.P.
www.artbook.com

Sold and distributed in Albania, the Republic of Kosovo, North Macedonia and Montenegro by Dukagjini Sh.p.k., Shtëpia Botuese, ISBN 978-9951-33-025-1

Printed in Germany

ACKNOWLEDGMENTS
These pages present sixty contributions, made possible by the openness and support of the offices and their teams. My sincere thanks to all contributors, to the sponsors whose support brought this book into being and to the public institutions that accompanied the project.